**PAUL SELIGSON**
**DAMIAN WILLIAMS**
**EDUARDO TRINDADE**

2nd edition

English ID

Teacher's Book
3

Richmond

# Richmond

58 St Aldates
Oxford
OX1 1ST
United Kingdom

**ISBN:** 978-84-668-3057-7
**Second reprint:** 2022

**CP:** 944384
© Richmond / Santillana Global S.L. 2019

All rights reserved. No part of this book may be reproduced, stored in a retrieval system or transmitted in any form by any means, electronic, mechanical, photocopying, recording or otherwise, without the prior permission in writing of the Publisher.

---

**Publishing Director:** Deborah Tricker
**Publisher:** Luke Baxter
**Media Publisher:** Luke Baxter
**Managing Editor:** Laura Miranda
**Editor:** Glenys Davis
**Proofreaders:** Cathy Heritage, Diyan Leake
**Design Manager:** Lorna Heaslip
**Cover Design:** Lorna Heaslip
**Design & Layout:** Dave Kuzmicki
**Photo Researcher:** Magdalena Mayo
**Audio Production:** John Marshall Media Inc.

**Illustrators:** Bill Brown, Alexandre Matos, Beach-o-matic, Laurent Cardon, Guillaume Gennet, Phil Hackett, Alvaro Nuñez, Leonardo Teixeira, Rico

**Photos:**
123RF/mopic, Getty Images Sales Spain; A. G. E. FOTOSTOCK/Lubitz + Dorner; ALAMY/Everett Collection Inc, David Cattanach, Jim Newberry, Maciej Bledowski, Eddie Gerald, TP, Marmaduke St. John, PJF Military Collection, age fotostock, Marek Poplawski, Jemastock, Andrea Raffin, Jim O Donnell, Ian Allenden, WENN UK, runsilent, Jochen Tack, Elnur Amikishiyev, aberystwyth, B Christopher, ABC/Everett Collection Inc, Jess Kraft/Panther Media GmbH, Mim Friday, Astronaut Images, dbimages, dpa picture alliance, Cyberstock, Steve Sant, Terry Harris, ZUMA Press, Inc, Domiciano Pablo Romero Franco, Moviestore collection Ltd, Fernando Quevedo de Oliveira, Mpi04/Media Punch/Alamy Live News, Irina Fischer, Collection Christophel, Ink Drop, M4Os Photos, WENN Ltd, Panther Media GmbH; CARTOONSTOCK/Way, Roy Delgado, Ian Baker, Zuvela.O, Bucella, Mike Baldwin; GETTY IMAGES SALES SPAIN/Hero Images, Andriano_cz, Littlebloke, Soren Hald, Thinkstock, Kadmy, NikFromNis, BenLin, wwing, Bulgac, Gipi23, Jodiecoston, Champc, BartCo, Kike Calvo, Joe_Potato, Brosa, ASIFE, Vladimir Vladimirov, shootdiem, ZIG8, Fuse, ViewApart, BSIP, StockFood, Andreas Schlegel, Steve Hix, Tzogia Kappatou, Stephan Hoerold, Sirawit99, Purestock, Altrendo Images, Martin-dm, Dulezidar, comptine, Paul Zimmerman, Neustockimages, S-cphoto, RapidEye, Sally Anscombe, Jhorrocks, Daniel Schoenen, Moodboard, Lily Roadstones, ShutterOK, Kyle Lee/EyeEm, Catherine Ledner, TIMOTHY A. CLARY, Stockbyte, Monika Proc/EyeEm, Wavebreak, Weedezign, Westend61, Witthaya Pradongsin, Aiqingwang, Andy Sacks, Dave Reede, Portland Press Herald, Juanmonino, Alessandro De Carli/EyeEm, Fotog, NNehring, Peter Cade, Petrunjela, Tom Hoenig, Ktsimage, CaseyHillPhoto, Shironosov,
AndreyPopov, AntonioGuillem, Austinadams, Imagno, Karwai Tang, Kondor83, Leungchopan, Hanohiki, Elena Pueyo, Phaelnogueira, Filmwork, Nick Clements, Barcroft, Monty Rakusen, Lisa Stirling, marcduf, Wrangel, Johner Images, TVP Inc, RoNeDya, Jason LaVeris, JGI/Tom Grill, Rmnunes, MixMike, Alex Lapuerta, Llgorko, Tim Robberts, Steve Cicero, Jpa1999, South_agency, Alex Robinson, Ariel Skelley, Doug McKinlay, SergeyNivens, Humonia, Jeffrey Mayer, Joel Carillet, PeopleImages, Jupiterimages, Keith Brofsky, Klaus Vedfelt, Mike Coppola, Beinder, Marcelo Horm, Paul Bradbury, Luis Alvarez, Stuart Pearce, Studio-Annika, Wundervisuals, Andresr, KateSmirnova, Cecilie_Arcurs, GoodLifeStudio, Johnny Louis, Manuel ROMARIS, Martin Barraud, Mischa Keijser, da-kuk, Image Source, Paulprescott72, Philipp Nemenz, FreezingRain, Silverlining56, Zero Creatives, AleksandarNakic, Rayman, David Forman, Desiree Navarro, Igor Vershinsky, Alvis Upitis, Photos.com Plus, Priscilla Gragg, Simona Flamigni, Pumba1, Yuri_Arcurs, Yagi-Studio, PIKSEL, T3 Magazine, Alexander Spatari, Corbis Historical, Fancy/Veer/Corbis, Phil Walter, laszlo_szelenczey, Andrew Bret Wallis, Michael Heim/EyeEm, Hill Street Studios, Lee Whitehead/EyeEm, Pascal Le Segretain, Richard Theis/EyeEm, Mmac72, Nancy Honey, Andrey Vodilin/EyeEm, Ben Pipe Photography, GIUGLIO Gil/Hemis.Fr, Jose Luis Pelaez Inc, Monkeybusinessimages, Jean Baptiste Lacroix, Mint Images, Gareth Cattermole/TAS18, Narin Deniz Erkan/EyeEm, PhotoAlto/Odilon Dimier, Lowryn, Kittiyut Phomphibul/EyeEm, Mark Edward Atkinson/Tracey Lee, Manuel-F-O; ISTOCKPHOTO/Getty Images Sales Spain; SHUTTERSTOCK/Lucasfilm/Bad Robot/Walt Disney Studios/Kobal, 20th Century Fox/Paramount/Kobal, Red Umbrella and Donkey, Patrimonio designs Ltd, KA Photography/KEVM111, Ultimate Prods./Kobal, Lewis Tse Pui Lung, Gurgen Bakhshetyan, Moviestore Ltd, Netflix/Kobal, Moviestore collection Ltd, Intararit, Artazum, Ollyy; Tom Fishburne/Marketoonist.com; copyright Vixisystem; Penguin Random House; Arnos Design Ltd; www.govloop.com; copyright PLeIQ; www.italki.com; Faber & Faber; SPLASH NEWS; telfie.com; player.me; Starbucks; copyright Kengaru; geobeats; iTunes; IUCN; Gap; ARCHIVO SANTILLANA

**Videos:**
Andrew Thompson; Colin Beaven; IUCN; geobeats; Vicki Abeles; NIACE; Reason TV; watchwellcast

The Publisher has made every effort to trace the owner of copyright material; however, the Publisher will correct any involuntary omission at the earliest opportunity.

Impressão e acabamento: Forma Certa Gráfica Digital
Lote: 775040
Cód.: 290530577

# Contents

| | |
|---|---|
| ID SB Language Map | 4 |
| Introduction | 6 |
| **Features Presentation** | |
| Unit 1 | 24 |
| Unit 2 | 48 |
| Review 1 | 72 |
| Unit 3 | 76 |
| Unit 4 | 100 |
| Review 2 | 124 |
| Unit 5 | 128 |
| Mid-term Review | 152 |
| Unit 6 | 156 |
| Review 3 | 180 |
| Unit 7 | 184 |
| Unit 8 | 208 |
| Review 4 | 232 |
| Unit 9 | 236 |
| Unit 10 | 260 |
| Review 5 | 284 |
| SB3 Grammar | 288 |
| Sounds & Usual Spellings | 308 |
| Audioscript | 310 |
| Songs | 325 |

# ID SB Language map

| | Question syllabus | Vocabulary | Grammar | Speaking & Skills |
|---|---|---|---|---|
| **1** | 1.1 Do you know all your classmates? | | Review of present tenses | Ask questions to get to know someone |
| | 1.2 How do couples meet? | Relationships<br>Phrasal verbs | | Talk about relationships<br>Talk about how a couple met |
| | 1.3 How many Facebook friends do you have? | Types of friend | Review of question forms | Describe your relationships<br>Talk about your friends |
| | 1.4 Do you have many social media profiles? | Personality adjectives | Emphatic forms | Describe your personality<br>Express your opinions about social media |
| | 1.5 How much time do you spend online? | | | Read for main ideas and specific information |
| | Which do you do more: listen or speak? | Active listening phrases | | Practice listening actively |
| | **Writing 1:** A personal profile  p. 16 | **ID Café 1:** He said, she said  p. 17 | | |
| **2** | 2.1 How green are you? | Going green<br>Adjectives from verbs and nouns | | Discuss how you could be greener |
| | 2.2 How long have you been studying here? | Time / Frequency / Degree phrases | Present perfect continuous | Ask and answer about personal habits |
| | 2.3 How has the climate been changing? | The environment | Present perfect simple vs. Present perfect continuous | Talk about environmental problems in your city |
| | 2.4 What's the best ad you've seen recently? | | Simple past vs. Present perfect simple / continuous | Interview your partner |
| | 2.5 Do you support any charities? | Endangered species | | Expressing numerical information |
| | Have you made any lifestyle changes recently? | | | Encourage or discourage a friend |
| | **Writing 2:** A report  p. 28 | **ID Café 2:** Down to earth  p. 29 | **Review 1  p. 30** | |
| **3** | 3.1 Which city would you most like to visit? | Cities | | Describe a city |
| | 3.2 Was your last vacation as much fun as you'd hoped? | Social conventions | Past perfect | Talk about rules where you live<br>Talk about a place you've been to |
| | 3.3 Do you ever want to get away from it all? | Urban problems | | Conduct a survey and report on the findings about problems in your city |
| | 3.4 Have you ever missed any important dates? | Active listening phrases | Past perfect continuous | Share stories about missing an important event |
| | 3.5 Do you always follow the rules? | Common sign phrases | | Talk about rules and regulations |
| | When did you last break a rule? | Phrases for explaining and questioning rules | | Share stories about breaking a rule |
| | **Writing 3:** A narrative  p. 42 | **ID Café 3:** Global swarming  p. 43 | | |
| **4** | 4.1 Does your school system work well? | School life<br>do / get / make / take collocations | | Describe an ideal school |
| | 4.2 What's the ideal age to go to college? | College life | too / enough | Debate educational issues<br>Talk about choosing a career |
| | 4.3 What do you regret not having done? | | should have | Talk about regrets |
| | 4.4 What would you do if you won a million dollars? | | First and second conditional | Imagine what will / would happen<br>Talk about a goal or aspiration |
| | 4.5 What makes someone a genius? | | | Make predictions |
| | How do you deal with criticism? | | | Sympathize and criticize |
| | **Writing 4:** A blog  p. 54 | **ID Café 4:** AIQ: Artificial Intelligence Quotient!  p. 55 | **Review 2  p. 56** | |
| **5** | 5.1 Are you a shopaholic? | Shopping | | Make a "shopping haul" video |
| | 5.2 What shouldn't you have spent money on? | Money collocations | Third conditional | Talk about a mistake or something you wish you had done differently<br>Talk about ways to reduce personal debt |
| | 5.3 Have you ever borrowed money from a relative? | | Modals of possibility / probability | Present a crowdfunding project<br>Speculate about your partner's life |
| | 5.4 Have you ever bought a useless product? | Word formation | Adjective order | Share shopping experiences<br>Create an infomercial |
| | 5.5 Do you often buy things on impulse? | | | Read for confirmation<br>Talk about your experience with supermarkets |
| | When did you last complain in a store? | Shopping problems | | Make complaints and ask for a refund |
| | **Writing 5:** An advert  p. 68 | **ID Café 5:** Shop around  p. 69 | **Mid-term review:** Game  p. 70 | |

| | | Question syllabus | Vocabulary | Grammar | Speaking & Skills |
|---|---|---|---|---|---|
| 6 | 6.1 | What are you watching these days? | TV genres and expressions | | Talk about TV habits |
| | 6.2 | What's your favorite TV show ever? | | Restrictive relative clauses | Talk about first episodes of TV shows<br>Write a quiz about movies / music |
| | 6.3 | What was the last movie you saw? | | Non-restrictive relative clauses | Describe movies |
| | 6.4 | Where do you usually watch movies? | Movies | | Create a story for a movie |
| | 6.5 | Who are the wildest celebrities you know? | | | Understand details |
| | | When were you last surprised? | | | Express surprise |
| | Writing 6: A movie / book review  p. 82 | | ID Café 6: Best in show  p. 83 | | Review 3  p. 84 |
| 7 | 7.1 | Does technology rule your life? | Phrasal verbs | | Talk about your habits |
| | 7.2 | What was the last little lie you told? | | Reported speech (1) | Share stories about being deceived |
| | 7.3 | How much of your day is screen time? | Using touch screens | Indirect questions | Present an invention to make life easier |
| | 7.4 | Are machines with personality a good idea? | | Reported speech (2) | Talk about machines with personality<br>Write a questionnaire about tech habits |
| | 7.5 | How often do you use a pen? | | | Take notes while listening<br>Talk about a book |
| | | Do you enjoy a good argument? | Phrases for expressing your views | | Debate a topic |
| | Writing 7: A complaint email  p. 96 | | ID Café 7: The road NOT taken  p. 97 | | |
| 8 | 8.1 | How important are looks? | Photography and photos | | Talk about appearance and the effect of Photoshopping images |
| | 8.2 | Do you like watching illusions? | | Modal perfects – *must have, can't have, might have / may have* | Describe how an illusion is done |
| | 8.3 | Have you ever cut your own hair? | | Causative form | Talk about the things you do and the things you have / get done |
| | 8.4 | Do you have a lot of furniture in your room? | Furniture | Tag questions | Check information |
| | 8.5 | Is your listening improving? | | | Make predictions |
| | | What's the hardest part of language learning? | | | Express preferences |
| | Writing 8: An opinion essay  p. 108 | | ID Café 8: Small talk and smart phones  p. 109 | | Review 4  p. 110 |
| 9 | 9.1 | Does crime worry you? | Crime and violence | Review of verb families | Talk about crime |
| | 9.2 | How could your city be improved? | | Passive voice | Talk about a city's transformation |
| | 9.3 | Have you ever been to court? | Crime and punishment | | Decide on the right punishment for crimes |
| | 9.4 | Where will you be living ten years from now? | | Future perfect and continuous | Discuss ways to protect yourself from cyber crime |
| | 9.5 | Do you watch TV crime dramas? | | | Talk about stupid crimes<br>Identify sarcasm |
| | | Are you good at making excuses? | Phrases for giving excuses | | Give excuses |
| | Writing 9: A formal letter  p. 122 | | ID Café 9: A knight at the museum  p. 123 | | |
| 10 | 10.1 | What drives you crazy? | Moods<br>Binomials | | Talk about temperament |
| | 10.2 | What do you love to hate? | Common expressions with *for* and *of* | Gerunds and infinitives | Talk about pet peeves<br>Role-play an anger management session |
| | 10.3 | How assertive are you? | | Verb + gerund or infinitive | Test your assertiveness |
| | 10.4 | How similar are you to your friends? | Phrasal verbs | Separable and inseparable phrasal verbs | Talk about toxic people<br>Take a friendship test |
| | 10.5 | What do you find hardest about English? | | | Practice proofreading<br>Talk about your mistakes in English |
| | | Are you going to take an English exam? | Phrases for making recommendations | | Make recommendations |
| | Writing 10: A forum post  p. 134 | | ID Café 10: Mad men  p. 135 | | Review 5  p.136 |

Grammar p. 138      Verbs p.158      Sounds and usual spelling p. 160      Audioscript p. 162

# Introduction

This is the 2nd edition of Richmond's four-level American English course for monolingual adult and young adult learners whose mother tongue is Spanish or Portuguese. Together with iDentities 1 and 2, it forms the first six-level course purpose-built for Latin America, taking learners from Beginner to a strong C1 level.

With the right focus, embracing and celebrating familiar language while anticipating inevitable transfer errors, speakers of Spanish and Portuguese ought to learn to be both fluent and accurate in English more quickly than most.

This unique, highly original course, with a brand-new eye-catching design, motivating topics and constant opportunities for personalization, helps learners to express who they are—their personality, culture, their identity—in English. English iD helps you learn to be yourself in English.

## What do Romance-language speakers most expect and need from an English course?

You might want to note down your own answers before you read on.

Our research suggests that, above all, learners expect:

- to become fluent listeners and speakers as quickly as possible;
- confidence building—to know the L1 equivalent of new language items quickly so that they can overcome their fears and speak meaningfully in class;
- quick results, and a strong sense of progress;
- contemporary, locally pertinent, interesting content, tailored to their likely interests and linguistic needs. Real-life, adult, local relevance, with lots of personalization;
- overt teaching of grammar and vocabulary, a systematic approach to pronunciation, plenty of skills practice;
- specific help with writing and spelling;
- an appropriate, adult teaching style combined with strong self-study elements, including autonomous learning tools to speed up their learning: we provide keys to most of the material, audio for all longer texts, and all the listening and video activities are available on the Richmond Learning Platform for self-study;
- value—both for the time they invest and the money they spend.

## Methodology

English iD is in every sense a communicative course, teaching learners to speak in as short a time as possible and focusing on both fluency and accuracy.

**Fluency:** notice the multiple exchanges modeled throughout lessons in speech bubbles, or the number of Latinate cognates included in every text, with word stress marked in pink to give sts confidence to try to say them.

**Accuracy:** via the 110 **Common mistakes** (anticipating likely L1 transfer errors that should be avoided) presented in each lesson, or the 84 Notice tasks in the **Audioscript** to provide genuine contextualized help with pronunciation and spelling.

Learners need to be given opportunities to express their thoughts. English iD and, later, iDentities progressively adapt as the series evolves to reflect the best learning practices at each of the learner's advancing levels. Initially, English iD Starter relies on lots of short question-and-answer exchanges supported by lots of drilling in the *Student's Book*, to be done in class. Then, at subsequent levels, such drills become more discretionary, moving into both *Workbook* and *Teacher's Book*. At advanced levels, there is an increased focus on levels of formality, as a student's need to master various registers gradually increases.

The same goes for the lexis—where the initial simple task of matching vocabulary to pictures in the early levels of English iD becomes more abstract and contextualized—and grammar, where spoon-feeding is reduced and inductive learning increased, as learners' confidence and foreign language learning experience grow.

English iD provides the tools to allow you, the teacher, to incorporate your own pedagogical identity into the course, as well as to emphasize what you think will be more relevant for your learners.

## Advantaging Monolingual Classes

Globally, most classes are monolingual. English iD was conceived to facilitate monolingual classroom learning. The frequent lack of opportunity to speak English locally means teachers need to maximize fluency practice, getting the students to use the language as much as possible in class.

In monolingual classes, learners share the same L1 and most aspects of a culture, which a teacher can exploit. They share similar advantages / difficulties with English too, which should be a unifying "strength" for anticipating problems and errors. Accelerating through what is easier for learners, and spending more time on what is difficult, "sharpens" classes to maximize the learning potential.

Adults need a radically different approach from children, whose mother tongue is not yet established, and who learn like sponges, absorbing all the English you throw at them. Young adults' and adults' minds are different: they cannot help but translate—mentally at least—and immediately

# Introduction

resort to the mother tongue when they cannot find the words to express their thoughts in English. Rather than running against nature, English ID avoids this trap by gently embracing similar items when appropriate, but without ever forcing active use of L1, leaving that option up to you.

Paraphrasing Ur (2011), "teachers should choose procedures that lead to best learning by whichever students they're teaching" (extracted from *Vocabulary Activities*, Penny Ur, Cambridge University Press, 2011). We believe English ID's formula can really help native speakers of Spanish and Portuguese learn both more comfortably and more efficiently.

English ID embraces students' linguistic strengths. It helps students to use what they know and helps you, the teacher, to foresee these automatic transfers and focus appropriately on them. With English ID, students can easily enjoy what is easy and, at the same time, the more complex issues can be made clearer for them.

## Flexi-lessons

Each English ID lesson is linear, and can be taught directly from the page, with our interleaved *Teacher's Book* lesson plans reflecting and fully supporting this.

However, as we appreciate that all teachers and classes are different, English ID also provides multiple entry points for each lesson for you to choose from.

You can begin with:

- the suggested **warm-up** activity in every *Teacher's Book* lesson plan;
- the *Teacher's Book* books-closed presentation (either of main lexis or grammar);
- the **lesson title question**. Return to it at the end of class for sts to answer it better—a "test–teach–test" route through the lesson;
- a **Make it personal** from the page in the same test-teach-test way;
- the lesson's **song line**;
- the **Common mistakes**—board them corrected or focus on them on the page at the start of class to highlight what to avoid and thus maximize opportunities to get things right throughout the class;
- the **Grammar** pages for a more traditional, deductive presentation.

In addition, you can choose from these lesson routes for monolingual Spanish / Portuguese learners as monolingual classes allow you to be more proactive, and offer opportunities for more tailored, accelerated pedagogy:

- Divide lexical presentations into two phases: first, focus on cognates, then the other words. Have sts guess the pronunciation of the words they recognize.
- Read the lesson text (on-page reading or listening from the **Audioscript** section). In pairs, sts try to pronounce the pink-stressed words. Teach the class as usual, then come back to the words at the end of the class, and have sts pronounce them better.
- Underline the words which look the same (or similar) in Spanish or Portuguese, then check as the lesson evolves whether they are or are not true cognates, and how to pronounce them. This is especially good for weaker learners, as it helps them get familiar with texts in a non-threatening way.
- Do the same as above with suffixes.
- Speed up or avoid inductive presentations, by, e.g. the **Common mistakes** route above.
- Compare word stress, as in the presentation of the months in *Student's Book 1* on p. 35, ex. 3A.

## Key concepts

English ID promotes the three "friendlies": It is language-friendly, learner-friendly, and teacher-friendly.

### 1. Language-friendly

English ID is not just another international series. It is a language-friendly series, which embraces sts' existing language knowledge—a fundamental pillar of all foreign language learning through, e.g. exploiting cognates, familiar structures, famous song lines, and local cultural background—to help them better understand how English works.

### 2. Learner-friendly

English ID respects the learner's need to be spoken to as an adult, so sts explore a full range of topics requiring critical thinking. It also helps sts to negotiate and build their own new identity in English.

In addition, English ID:

- supports sts, helping them avoid obvious errors in form, word order, and pronunciation;
- motivates sts, as they discover they can recognize a lot of English, which they already have "inside themselves";
- offers a vast range of activities, resources and recycling in order to ensure sts have enough practice to finally learn to speak English.

# Introduction

## 3. Teacher-friendly

English ID respects each teacher's need to teach as he or she wants to. Some wish to teach off the page with minimal preparation, others dip in and out, while others largely follow the *Teacher's Book*. All these options have been built into English ID from the start.

The flexi-lesson structure helps teachers to individualize, personalize and vary classes, as well as focus on what is important for them.

## Key features

### 1. A 60-question syllabus

Every lesson begins with a question as the title, which serves as a natural warm-up activity to introduce and later review each lesson topic.

These questions offer:

- an introduction to the lesson topic, an essential component for a good lesson, as, in some cases, topics may be new to sts;
- a ready-made short lead-in to create interest, paving the way for the integration of skills, grammar, and content;
- an opportunity for sts to get to know and feel comfortable with each other before the lesson begins, facilitating pair and group work;
- an instant review or speaking activity, whenever you need one: sts in pairs can look back at the map of the book and ask and answer questions;
- a wonderful expression of syllabus;
- a useful placement test. Asking some of the 60 questions when sts are being level-tested is a good way to help place them appropriately.

### 2. A balanced approach to grammar

Our rich grammar syllabus offers an eclectic approach to meet the needs of all sts. It offers an innovative combination of:

- inductive grammar, with students discovering patterns and completing rules for themselves in and around the lesson-page grammar boxes;
- deductive grammar—the 20-page **Grammar** section, which regularly encourages sts to contrast English with their L1 and notice where English is easier, in order to motivate. This can be done in class for quick diagnostic work if sts are making lots of mistakes, or assigned as homework as a form of "flipping"—sts complete the grammar exercises before the forthcoming lesson, in order to speed up input and give more time for practice;
- implicit, contrastive grammar analysis, by showing what not to say via **Common mistakes**;
- a wide variety of extra grammar practice in Reviews, the *Workbook*, and on the Richmond Learning Platform, as well as suggestions for extra contextualized writing in the *Teacher's Book*.

### 3. It has to be personal

Not only the 60 lesson question titles, but each phase of every lesson (and most *Workbook* lessons) ends with **Make it personal** activities: real, extended personalization—the key stage in any language practice activity. Sts expand all topics and main language items into their own lives, opinions, contexts, and experiences. This is how sts continue to construct and consolidate their English identity. Successfully "making it personal" is what makes sts believe that they can be themselves in English.

### 4. Avoid common mistakes to speak better, more quickly

Most lessons include **Common mistakes**, a flexible resource to foster accuracy. We highlight what to avoid before, during, and / or after any lesson. **Common mistakes** helps maximize self- and peer-correction too. Sts are enabled to help and teach themselves, by anticipating and therefore more quickly avoiding, reviewing, and remembering typical learner errors.

If short of time, as teachers so often are, **Common mistakes** can help you cut through a longer, more inductive presentation and get to the practice activity more quickly. They are flexible, too: you can refer to them at any time in the lesson, usually the earlier the better.

### 5. Integrated skills

The fifth lesson in each unit is an integrated skills page, which gives sts the opportunity to immerse themselves in a highly engaging, contemporary topic and practice all four skills in real-world activities.

### 6. Classic song lines to "hook" language

English ID uses music in exercises, cultural references, images, and, most obviously, the authentic song lines in each lesson. In addition, music as a theme features prominently in several lessons.

Why music? Songs are often the most popular source of authentic listening practice in and out of class. Most sts have picked up a lot of English words through songs, ads, TV theme tunes, movie soundtracks, etc. But often they don't realize they know them or the exact meaning of what they're singing.

# Introduction

The song lines empower both teachers and sts by offering useful language references and pronunciation models; and an authentic source of student-friendly input to elicit, present, practice, personalize, extend, and "hook" almost anything.

Unique to English iD and iDentities, the song lines have a direct link to each lesson, whether to illustrate grammar, lexis, or the lesson topic, and are designed to provide an authentic hook to help sts remember the lesson and the language studied. Looking for the link provides an additional fun, puzzle-like element to every lesson.

English iD *Teacher's Book* offers a highly original useful **Songs** bank of cultural, background, and procedural notes for every song line, including the artist's name, suggestions on exactly where and how to exploit it, and optional activities. You can find this useful resource on pages 325–336.

**Tip** Of course, we don't suggest you use these songs in full, just the extract we've chosen. Besides, many aren't actually appropriate when you look at the complete lyrics, but the lines we've chosen are globally famous and should be easy to identify, find on the Internet, and be sung by at least some sts. Obviously, with your own classes you can exploit the song lines in a variety of ways.

Some ways to use song lines in English iD:

- play / show (part of) the song as sts come into class;
- sing / hum the song line and / or look for links to the song at an appropriate time during the class to help sts remember the lesson later;
- read and guess the artist's gender, message, etc.;
- analyze the song for pronunciation: rhyme, repeated sounds, alliteration;
- expand. *What comes before / after this line? What's the whole song about?*;
- change the tense or some words to make it more or less formal and see how it sounds. *Why did the artist choose this tense?*;
- provoke discussion around a theme / issue;
- ask *What do you associate the song with?*, e.g. a moment, vacation, dance, movie;
- search online for other songs that connect to the lesson in some way;
- use sections of the song as a class warm-up, review, listening for pleasure, an end of the lesson sing-along, etc.;
- board or dictate the line but add, subtract, or change some words for sts to correct it (similar to **Common mistakes**).

## Course structure and components

English coursebooks have often been too long, too repetitive, or inflexible, meaning teachers have either to rush to get through them—denying sts the practice they need to achieve an adequate degree of fluency—or start omitting sections, often leaving sts feeling frustrated. English iD was designed to be flexible, so you can tailor it to fit your schedule.

English iD has ...

- ten core units, each comprised of five approximately one-hour lessons, followed by an integrated **Writing** lesson and an iD **Café** video lesson;
- 20 pages of grammar reference with corresponding exercises;
- selected audioscripts that encourage sts to focus on specific listening points;
- *Workbook*: one page of review and extra practice material per lesson;
- Richmond Learning Platform for English iD, which can be accessed using the code on the inside front cover of the *Student's Book*;
- *Digital Book for Teachers*: IWB version of the *Student's Book*.

## Vocabulary

Vocabulary teaching is a particularly strong feature of English iD because of the variety of input and review options.

### 1. Picture Dictionary

The most popular way to teach / learn vocabulary is through some kind of "picture + key" approach, where students can work out the meaning from the visual, without the need to translate, and then cover and test themselves.

Every English iD unit begins with a contextualized, lesson-integrated picture dictionary. Core vocabulary is presented through various combinations of this basic four-step approach:

1. Match words / phrases to pictures.
2. Guess pronunciation (from the pink stress / sts' own linguistic experience, and growing knowledge of English).
3. Listen to the words in context and check / repeat as necessary.
4. Cover and test yourself / a partner, either immediately or any time later for review.

# Introduction

All **Reviews** begin by sending sts back to the picture dictionary elements in each unit to review and remember words. Almost all of the images in English ID are contextualized and used to present, review, and test vocabulary.

## 2. A cognate-friendly approach

Thousands of words with cognate relationships are common to English and most Latin languages. Over 1,500 of these are very common. There are also thousands of recognizable cognate-rooted words. By systematically building them into English ID, we feel we have created a unique opportunity for students to progress more quickly and more comfortably with English. Put simply, they can both understand and produce more language—and more interesting adult language—faster.

Throughout their learning process, students make cross-linguistic connections, so we have chosen to nurture this strategy systematically throughout English ID. It enhances both their language awareness and their English lexical knowledge, and makes learning more efficient.

English ID prides itself on helping students to expand their vocabulary quickly. Lexical presentations often separate what is "known / easy"—whether from "international" English, words already seen in the course, or near cognates—from "what is new / unfamiliar," to help students focus better.

Familiar words mainly require attention for pronunciation and spelling, whereas the unfamiliar require a lot more effort to learn meaning too. This provides a valuable additional "hook" into the student's memory.

Significant stress or word-formation patterns are regularly highlighted to enable "learning leaps."

English ID consciously works on developing the confidence the students need to begin to guess how words might be pronounced or spelled in English. Guessing—being willing to take a shot, bringing in words that you already know which might work well in English—is a key learning strategy, often ignored elsewhere.

Embracing cognates also allows much more interesting, more adult speaking, and listening tasks too, e.g., asking *Any coincidences / similarities / pronunciation surprises? What do you have in common? Who is more assertive?*, etc.

> **Tip** We do not suggest you drill all these words nor try to make them all into active vocabulary. In most cases, cognates are there just as passive vocabulary, actually helping sts understand more. We see no point in hiding words from sts when they can cope with them, and indeed usually enjoy doing so. The words which become active differ greatly from group to group and will always be your choice, not ours. We are simply trying to give sts access to more adult language more quickly.

# Skills

## Speaking

English ID teaches spoken English and prioritizes oral fluency. Fluency naturally precedes accuracy, and this is why English ID gives sts plenty of cognates to express themselves quickly, leading to accuracy sooner.

In order to learn both quickly and well, sts should be given every opportunity to try to express their ideas and opinions in comprehensible English at every stage of every lesson. After all, practice and personalization are the best way to improve and self-correct, and whatever method you use, accuracy will always be the last element of competence learners will acquire. In English ID, every lesson, be it a listening, vocabulary, grammar, reading, or writing focus, is full of controlled oral practice and personalized speaking opportunities, clearly marked and modeled by multiple speech bubbles on every page.

## Listening

English ID has a huge amount of recorded material, in both the *Student's Book* and the *Workbook*, which is all available on the Richmond Learning Platform.

Listening homework should be set as often as possible, as what sts most need is to spend the maximum time in the company of English in order to become truly confident when expressing themselves in English. These days this is relatively easy—they can listen while doing other things, at home, traveling, at the gym, etc.

In addition to the material included in the course itself, teachers may find some of the following suggestions helpful, either in or out of class:

- have sts create their own listening practice at this level—listening to music or podcasts, watching TV or movies, using bilingual websites to figure out what words mean, sending each other recordings in English via, e.g. WhatsApp;
- dictogloss short sections of any listening activity—listen and remember (or write down) all you can, then compare in pairs;
- pause at any time in any listening to check comprehension: *What do you think was said?* after any short section is a key question in trying to teach rather than keep testing listening.

If time permits ...

- sensitize sts to how words blur and have a variety of sound shapes in connected speech and elicit / explain how pronunciation changes;

# Introduction

- expose sts to "the difficult," e.g. phoneme variations in connected speech; dictate multiple examples of phrases containing the same weak forms;
- model processes used by L1 listeners: decoding sounds into words / clauses and building larger scale meaning;
- transcribe elision as they hear it: old people = *ole people*, a blind man = *a bly man*, etc;
- study and interpret, e.g. pairs: *He said he called* vs. *He said he'd call*.

The following are some ideas for listening homework that you could set your sts:

- listening to recordings of the class itself (flipped)—instructions, stories, pair work, role-play, etc.;
- web-based listening: songs, podcasts, searching online for the huge number of online lessons available now, YouTube, radio, audiobooks, TV (with subtitles in L1 & L2);
- homework partners—call / record messages, check answers with partner, dub favorite movie scene, etc.

## *Reading*

English ID provides substantial reading practice in terms of the amount available, and the complexity of cognate-rich texts, building on sts' existing language knowledge to gain fluency more quickly. We strongly suggest you break up longer texts, giving short tasks.

- Keep tasks to 2 or 3 minutes, then have sts share what they remember, and predict what comes next before reading on.
- Sts in pairs each read a different paragraph to create an information gap, then tell each other what they read.
- Give sts (via the digital board, cut up slips, or let them choose) random samples of the texts—a couple of lines from different paragraphs, or the first and last line of each paragraph, etc., to share what they understood and speculate about what else they will read.
- With any text, you can get sts to cover it with a sheet of paper, read one line at a time, guess what comes next in pairs, then unveil the next line to see if they were right. They then do the same with the next line, and so on.
- Make each st in a group responsible for finding the answer to one of the questions, then share with the group.
- Help sts experience different reading skills: skimming, scanning, etc., even within the same text, by setting different tasks, and perhaps giving them reading role-cards for different paragraphs or columns of text: A) Read and translate the text word by word.; B) Read the text in order to memorize as much of the information as you can.; C) Read the text for the general idea.; D) Read the text quietly to yourself at a comfortable speed.

These ideas and many more you will find expanded in the *Teacher's Book* notes.

## *Writing*

Our writing syllabus is primarily covered by the integrated **Writing** lesson at the end of each unit. Here sts are given a clear written model, a variety of tasks to analyze it, specific writing tips and a structured model to draft, check, then share with a classmate, before finally submitting it to you or posting on the class learning platform / wiki. The intention is to protect you, the busy teacher, from having to dedicate time to excessive marking of avoidable mistakes, as well as to help sts be more in control of their own writing.

## Pronunciation

The English ID **Audioscript** section is not just a script to be read or listened to with no clear focus. It's designed to provide real training with listening and pronunciation.

It aims to help sts learn to listen better as the course progresses by focusing on features of pronunciation:

- noticing sounds, stress, aspects of connected speech, intonation and spelling relationships;
- spoken language (e.g. noticing discourse signals such as fillers, pauses, repetition, self-correction, and interruptions);
- sub-skills of listening, like inferring, predicting, identifying main points in discourse, understanding attitudinal meaning and all aspects of listening.

Again, it is flexible and both teacher- and learner-friendly. All the tasks are "noticing" tasks. The tasks are always "highlighted," making them all free-standing, to avoid the need for teacher intervention, unless, of course, you wish to spend time here. So, you can choose to do them in class, or sts can do them on their own.

It is a good idea for sts to listen, read, and notice the audioscript tasks as extra preparation before a role-play. Rather than just listening (and reading) again and again, trying to memorize dialogues before role-playing them, these tasks give a clear focus for additional listening and pre-role-play pronunciation practice.

All new polysyllabic words are introduced in context, with the stress highlighted for students in pink. Regularly marking stress on new words (in the book and on the board) means you progress from just teaching form and spelling, on to really prioritizing teaching, modeling, and recording spoken language. Word stress is shown in pink only the first time a word appears. To include it each time would give no sense of syllabus or progress to sts.

The **Sounds and Usual Spellings** chart is another excellent resource. This gives two illustrated model words for each of the 40 sounds in U.S. English, and access to the phonetic symbol.

# Introduction

Knowing all the potential sounds in a language sets a ceiling on their guesses and builds confidence. If sts can learn those two words per sound, they should be able to have a reasonable guess at the pronunciation of words in a dictionary and begin to get comfortable with using phonetics. Remember, learning to guess pronunciation of new words is a key skill.

The table also provides model words to illustrate the usual spelling patterns for each sound. Sensitizing sts to sound–spelling combinations is a key part of learning to read, write, and pronounce with confidence.

To the extent that you choose to work on pronunciation, any of the following ideas may be helpful.

- Emphasize the relevance of the pronunciation tasks to improve listening comprehension and increasingly natural-sounding English.
- Make sure sts understand that their pronunciation does not need to be "perfect" or "near native," but it does need to be clear and facilitate communication. To that end, focus on features that most impinge on international communication with your particular learners.
- Explore what sts already know, e.g. from song lines, TV, their travels, etc., and have them record and listen to themselves imitating texts they like or wish to deliver better.
- Model new words in context rather than in isolation, e.g. in a phrase: *the environment* not just *environment*, so they get used to stressing and reducing. In this way, the focus on intonation, phrase or sentence stress, word boundaries, etc. increases.
- Respond naturally to incorrect models or effects of "wrong" intonation and encourage repetition to say it better, e.g. say *Excuse me?* in response to incorrect pronunciation or flat intonation.
- Highlight linking (a line between words: *an_orange*), pauses (/ = short pause, // = longer pause) and sentence stress shift (eliciting different meanings according to which words are stressed).
- Work on transcripts, e.g. shadow read text and sub-vocalize to self; notice and underline most stressed words / pauses / links. Turn any audioscript into a proper listening / pronunciation teaching vehicle.
- Spot the "music", e.g. help them hear changes of pitch.
- Have sts track, shadow, rehearse, imitate, repeat, and record themselves.

## Reviews

There is ample opportunity for review and recycling throughout the book via the six review lessons. These include many additional activities focusing on speaking, grammar, listening, reading, writing, self-test (error-correction), and point of view (debate). Some skills alternate across the review units, but all are thoroughly covered. Don't forget, you can always look back at the song lines and re-use the lesson question titles, too!

## Learner autonomy

English ID offers a clear layout, lessons that progress transparently, and many language explanations. While these features greatly facilitate classroom teaching, they also allow for easy review and autonomous learning. Depending on the classroom hours available, many activities in the course (e.g. selected vocabulary, grammar, reading, and writing tasks) could be assigned for homework. The student-friendly grammar boxes, with additional explanation in the **Grammar** section, also allow for easy review. The Reviews themselves can be assigned for homework also.

If it seems feasible, you may wish to consider "flipping" more of your classes, too. Before any major presentation or review activity, have sts search online for material to support the next lesson. This is especially useful for weaker sts, who might be struggling to keep up, but also works for stronger sts, who might even be able to lead the next class themselves.

Sts who regularly have to miss classes should be trained to use these routes to catch up. For example, how to:

- use the picture dictionary pages to cover the words and test themselves;
- listen again to texts which they have read in class via the audio on the Richmond Learning Platform;
- work on their own pronunciation using the pink word stress for all new polysyllabic words;
- do the audioscript tasks and use the **Sounds and Usual Spellings** chart;
- use the word list and phrase bank from the Richmond Learning Platform for constant review, e.g. by recording, listening to, and repeating the phrase bank on their phones, in their cars, etc.;
- ask and answer the question titles, plus follow-up questions;
- look at and avoid the **Common mistakes**;
- investigate and sing the song lines via the Internet, etc.;
- enjoy all the features of the Richmond Learning Platform. We suggest you spend some class time taking them through each of these features, and regularly reminding them how much they can do on their own.

# Introduction

## Richmond Learning Platform for English ID

This extremely useful and user-friendly blended learning tool has been developed in parallel with the series and combines the best of formal and informal learning to extend, review and test core lesson content. The full range of resources is available to teachers and sts who adopt any of the levels of English ID.

The Richmond Learning Platform content for English ID includes:

- Extra Practice Activities that cover all language points in the *Student's Books*. New activities have been added to accompany the 2nd edition. Sts can now record themselves interacting with the characters from ID **Café**, practice their pronunciation using the **Sounds and Usual Spellings** chart, and identify **Common mistakes**;
- Richmond Test Manager contains tests specifically created to review the content of English ID. Teachers can choose what to include in their tests and can choose between digital versions of the tests or printable versions;
- Skills Boost: extra reading and listening practice available in both interactive and PDF format;
- Resources for teachers, including sets of photocopiables for practice and reference;
- Complete downloadable audio and video.

The Richmond Learning Platform's key features and tools include:

- Class Materials, where teachers and sts can find all content related to the level of English ID they are using in class;
- Assignments—a tool that allows teachers to assign digital and non digital content for sts to complete by a specified date;
- Test Manager, where teachers can find all the test content for English ID, and build their own tests to be delivered in the format that suits their teaching. Once generated, tests can be assigned to the whole class or specific sts, to be completed by a specific date and time;
- Markbook allows sts to access their own scores, while teachers can view the scores of the whole class and have a number of options to view the details of their sts' progress;
- Forum is a tool for communication between members of the class and can be used to bring writing activities to life.

## Workbook

In the *Workbook*, a single page corresponds to each *Student's Book* lesson, designed to consolidate and reinforce all the main language. Exercises can be used in class, e.g. for fast finishers, or extra practice of specific areas.

The *Workbook* includes:

- a variety of exercises, texts, and puzzles to scaffold, continue practicing, and extend the main grammar and vocabulary of each lesson;
- Skills Practice: several listening activities per unit to continue practicing the most important skills outside class, plus plenty of short, enjoyable reading texts.

## Interleaved Teacher's Book

English ID offers a rich, complete, teacher-friendly, lesson plan for every left- and right-hand page of each lesson. It provides a complete step-by-step lesson plan from beginning to end, offering:

- lesson overviews and aims;
- an optional books-closed warm-up for every lesson;
- an alternative books-open warm-up based around the question title;
- step-by-step notes and suggestions for each on-page activity, including background information and language notes where appropriate;
- help with identifying the focus of each activity and any new language being presented, including additional help (where relevant) on presenting increasingly complicated grammar;
- language tips specifically highlighting areas that may be problematic for Spanish / Portuguese speakers;
- teaching tips to vary and hone your teaching skills;
- suggestions for multi-level classes (ideas for both stronger and weaker sts);
- a complete answer key and audioscript;
- a bank of original ideas for exploiting each song line in a different way, as well as background information and step-by-step teaching notes for the song lines.

## Digital Book for Teachers / IWB

The *Digital Book for Teachers* is a separate medium containing all the pages of the *Student's Book*. Teachers can use this resource to promote variety in their classes, at all stages of any lesson, so that sts can see the images on the IWB instead of looking at the book. It's particularly useful for operating the audio, zooming images, and adding zest and color to your classes!

On the next pages, you will find detailed information about all the features of English ID.

# English ID

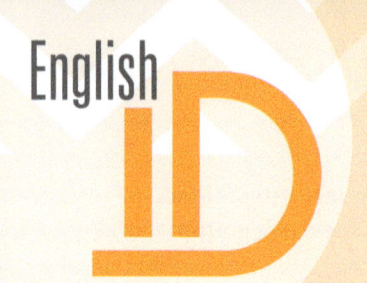

# Welcome to English ID!

*Finally, an English course you can understand!*

**Lesson titles** are questions to help you engage with the content.

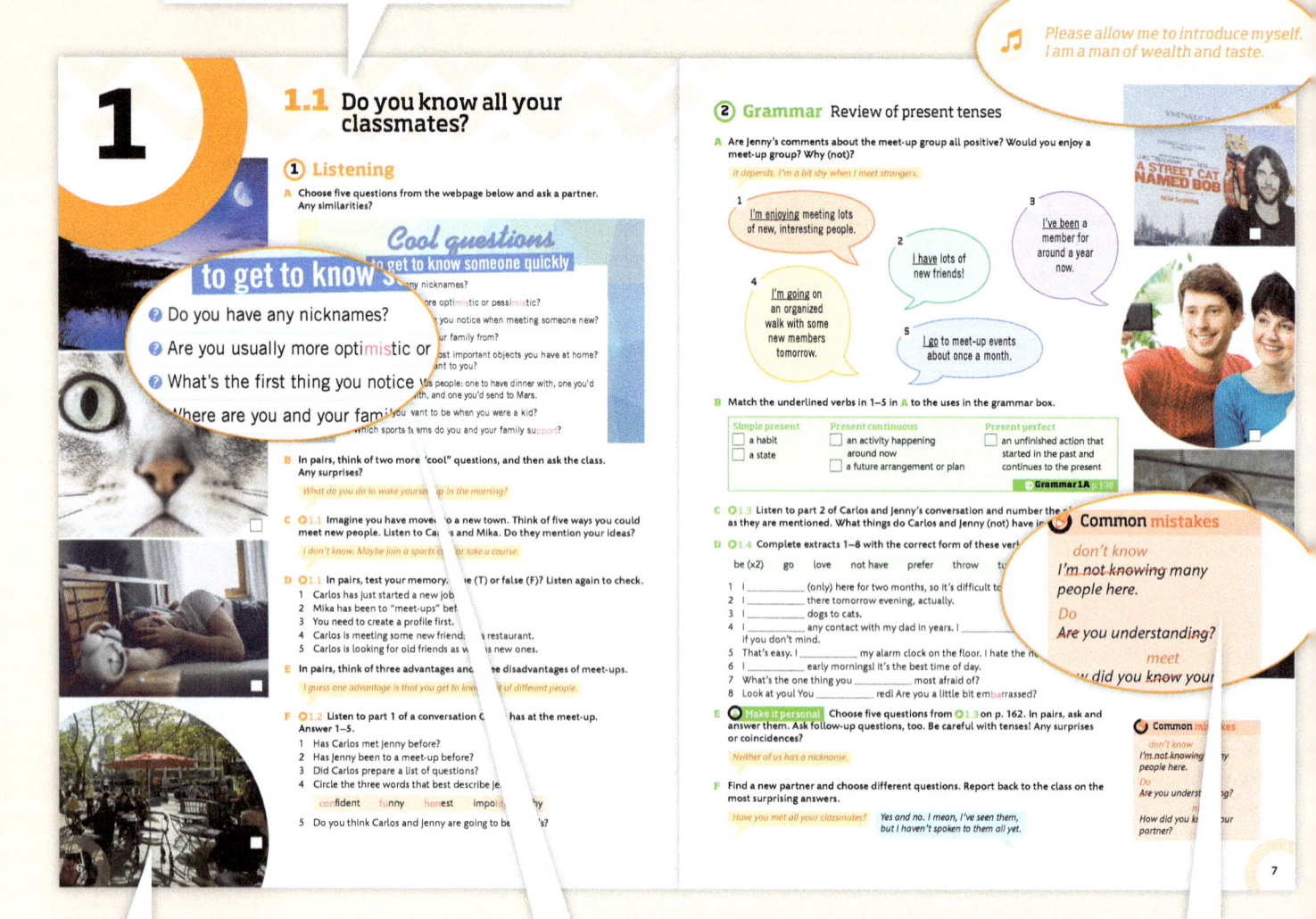

Famous **song lines** illustrate language from lessons.

♪ *Please allow me to introduce myself. I am a man of wealth and taste.*

## 1

### 1.1 Do you know all your classmates?

**① Listening**

**A** Choose five questions from the webpage below and ask a partner. Any similarities?

*Cool questions to get to know someone quickly*
- Do you have any nicknames?
- Are you usually more optimistic or pessimistic?
- What's the first thing you notice when meeting someone new?
- Where are you and your family from?
- What are the most important objects you have at home?
- ...which you'd want to send to Mars.
- ...two people: one to have dinner with, one you'd go out with, and one you'd send to Mars.
- ...want to be when you were a kid?
- Which sports teams do you and your family support?

**B** In pairs, think of two more "cool" questions, and then ask the class. Any surprises?

*What do you do to wake yourself up in the morning?*

**C** ◯1.1 Imagine you have moved to a new town. Think of five ways you could meet new people. Listen to Carlos and Mika. Do they mention your ideas?

*I don't know. Maybe join a sports club or take a course.*

**D** ◯1.1 In pairs, test your memory. True (T) or false (F)? Listen again to check.
1. Carlos has just started a new job.
2. Mika has been to "meet-ups" before.
3. You need to create a profile first.
4. Carlos is meeting some new friends in a restaurant.
5. Carlos is looking for old friends as well as new ones.

**E** In pairs, think of three advantages and three disadvantages of meet-ups.

*I guess one advantage is that you get to know lots of different people.*

**F** ◯1.2 Listen to part 1 of a conversation Carlos has at the meet-up. Answer 1–5.
1. Has Carlos met Jenny before?
2. Has Jenny been to a meet-up before?
3. Did Carlos prepare a list of questions?
4. Circle the three words that best describe Jenny.
   confident   funny   honest   impolite   shy
5. Do you think Carlos and Jenny are going to be friends?

**② Grammar** Review of present tenses

**A** Are Jenny's comments about the meet-up group all positive? Would you enjoy a meet-up group? Why (not)?

*It depends. I'm a bit shy when I meet strangers.*

1. I'm enjoying meeting lots of new, interesting people.
2. I have lots of new friends!
3. I've been a member for around a year now.
4. I'm going on an organized walk with some new members tomorrow.
5. I go to meet-up events about once a month.

**B** Match the underlined verbs in 1–5 in **A** to the uses in the grammar box.

| Simple present | Present continuous | Present perfect |
|---|---|---|
| ☐ a habit | ☐ an activity happening around now | ☐ an unfinished action that started in the past and continues to the present |
| ☐ a state | ☐ a future arrangement or plan | |

➤ Grammar 1A

**C** ◯1.3 Listen to part 2 of Carlos and Jenny's conversation and number the things as they are mentioned. What things do Carlos and Jenny (not) have in common?

**D** ◯1.4 Complete extracts 1–8 with the correct form of these verbs.

be (x2)   go   love   not have   prefer   throw   tu...

1. I _____ (only) here for two months, so it's difficult to...
2. I _____ there tomorrow evening, actually.
3. I _____ dogs to cats.
4. I _____ any contact with my dad in years. I _____ if you don't mind.
5. That's easy. I _____ my alarm clock on the floor. I hate the n...
6. I _____ early mornings! It's the best time of day.
7. What's the one thing you _____ most afraid of?
8. Look at you! You _____ red! Are you a little bit embarrassed?

**E** **Make it personal** Choose five questions from ◯1.3 on p. 162. In pairs, ask and answer them. Ask follow-up questions, too. Be careful with tenses! Any surprises or coincidences?

*Neither of us has a nickname.*

**F** Find a new partner and choose different questions. Report back to the class on the most surprising answers.

*Have you met all your classmates?* — *Yes and no. I mean, I've seen them, but I haven't spoken to them all yet.*

**Common mistakes**

~~don't know~~
~~I'm not knowing~~ many people here.

~~Do~~
~~Are you understanding?~~

~~meet~~
~~How did you know your~~ partner?

**Contextualized picture dictionary** to present and review vocabulary.

**Word stress** in pink on new words.

Focus on **Common mistakes** accelerates accuracy.

14

# Introduction

Stimulating **grammar** practice.

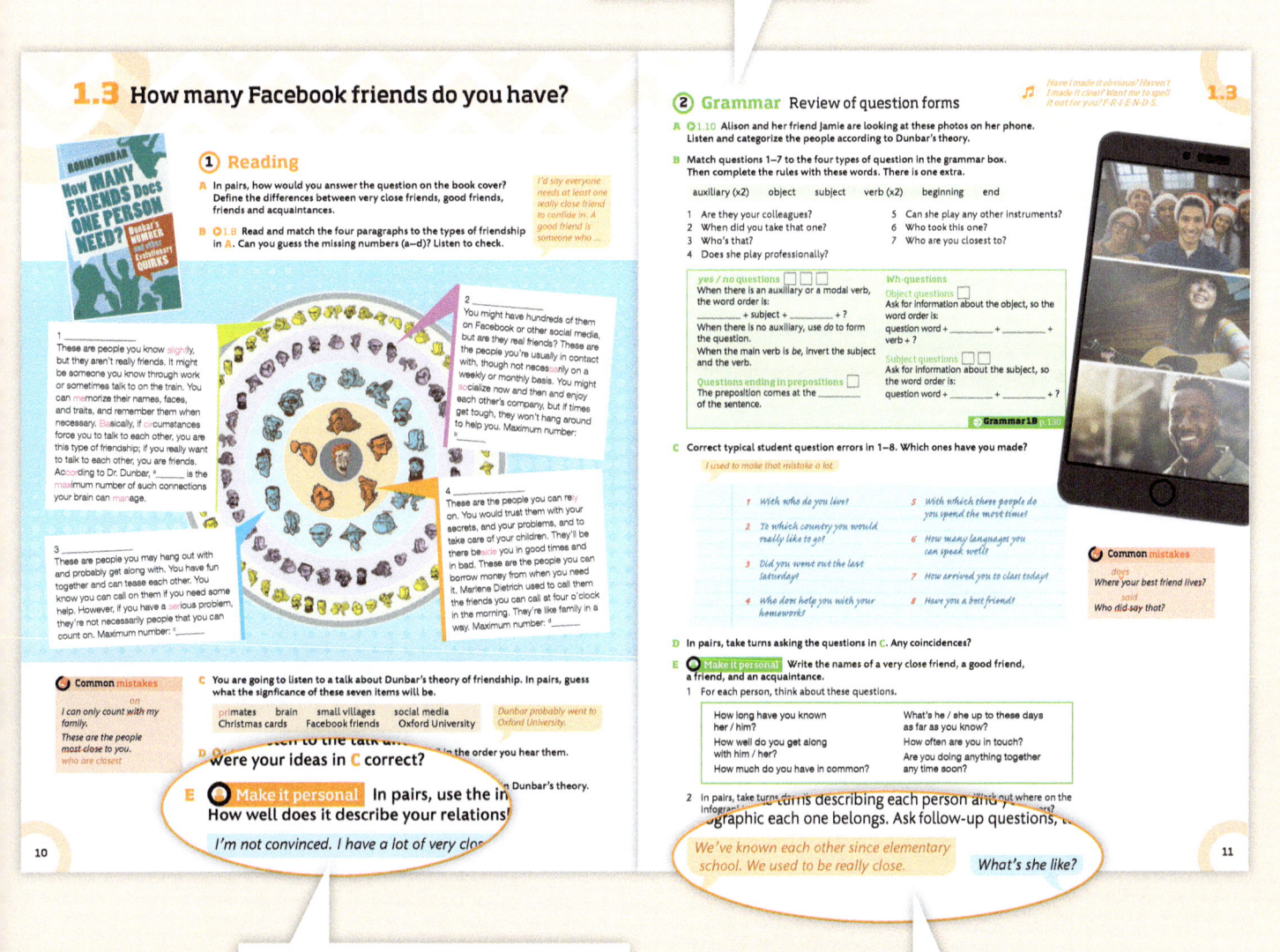

**Make it personal:** personalized speaking tasks to help you express your identity in English.

**Speech bubbles:** models for speaking.

**ID Skills:** extra reading and listening practice.

**ID in Action:** communication in common situations.

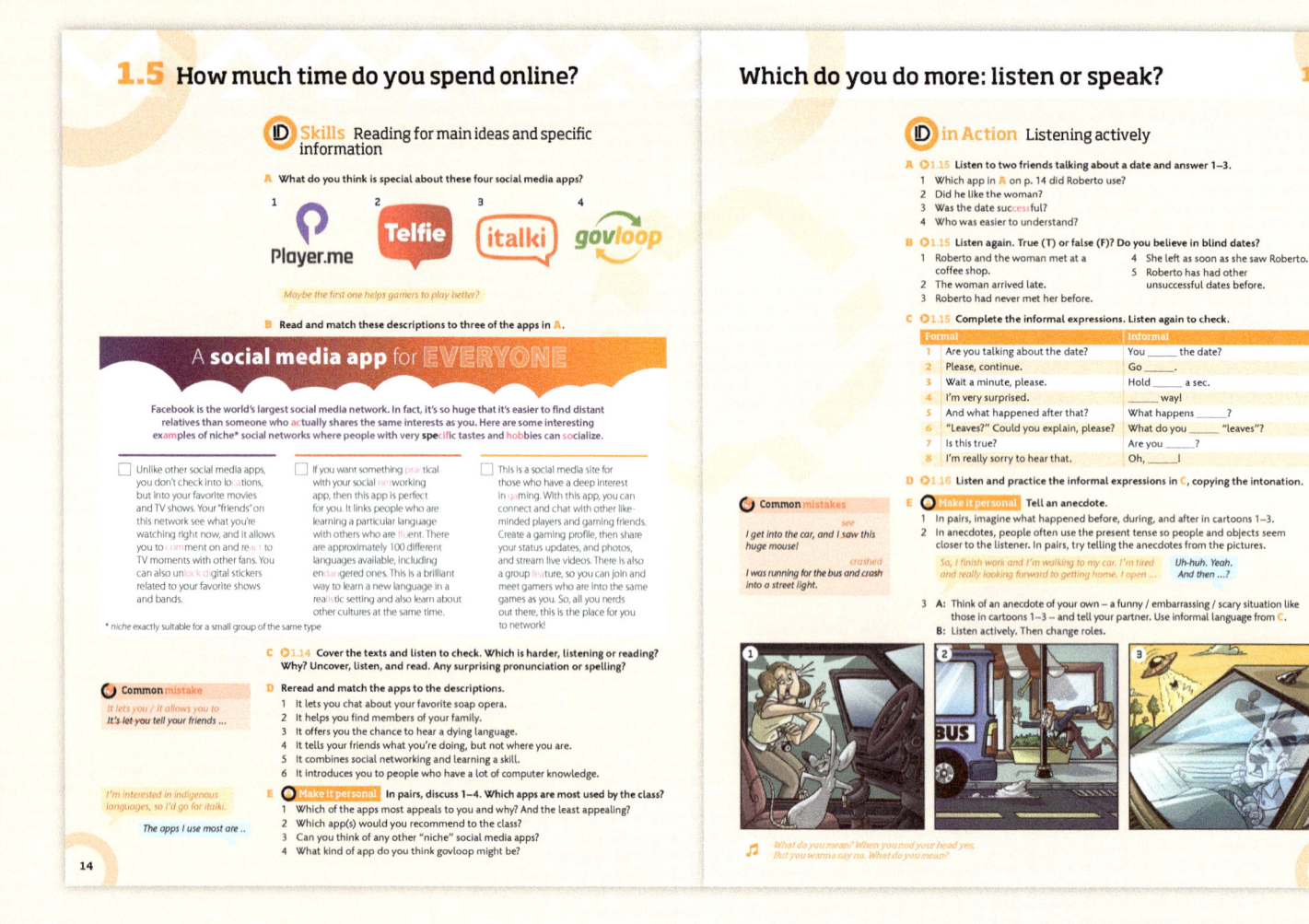

## 1.5 How much time do you spend online?

**ID Skills** Reading for main ideas and specific information

**A** What do you think is special about these four social media apps?

1. Player.me  2. Telfie  3. italki  4. govloop

*Maybe the first one helps gamers to play better?*

**B** Read and match these descriptions to three of the apps in **A**.

### A social media app for EVERYONE

Facebook is the world's largest social media network. In fact, it's so huge that it's easier to find distant relatives than someone who actually shares the same interests as you. Here are some interesting examples of niche* social networks where people with very specific tastes and hobbies can socialize.

- Unlike other social media apps, you don't check into locations, but into your favorite movies and TV shows. Your "friends" on this network see what you're watching right now, and it allows you to comment on and react to TV moments with other fans. You can also unlock digital stickers related to your favorite shows and bands.

- If you want something practical with your social networking app, then this app is perfect for you. It links people who are learning a particular language with others who are fluent. There are approximately 100 different languages available, including endangered ones. This is a brilliant way to learn a new language in a realistic setting and also learn about other cultures at the same time.

- This is a social media site for those who have a deep interest in gaming. With this app, you can connect and chat with other like-minded players and gaming friends. Create a gaming profile, then share your status updates, and photos, and stream live videos. There is also a group feature, so you can join and meet gamers who are into the same games as you. So, all you nerds out there, this is the place for you to network!

* niche exactly suitable for a small group of the same type

**C** 1.14 Cover the texts and listen to check. Which is harder, listening or reading? Why? Uncover, listen, and read. Any surprising pronunciation or spelling?

**D** Reread and match the apps to the descriptions.
1. It lets you chat about your favorite soap opera.
2. It helps you find members of your family.
3. It offers you the chance to hear a dying language.
4. It tells your friends what you're doing, but not where you are.
5. It combines social networking and learning a skill.
6. It introduces you to people who have a lot of computer knowledge.

**Common mistake**
*It lets you / It allows you to*
*It's let you tell your friends ...*

*I'm interested in indigenous languages, so I'd go for italki.*

*The apps I use most are ..*

**E** Make it personal In pairs, discuss 1–4. Which apps are most used by the class?
1. Which of the apps most appeals to you and why? And the least appealing?
2. Which app(s) would you recommend to the class?
3. Can you think of any other "niche" social media apps?
4. What kind of app do you think govloop might be?

## 1.5 Which do you do more: listen or speak?

**ID in Action** Listening actively

**A** 1.15 Listen to two friends talking about a date and answer 1–3.
1. Which app in **A** on p. 14 did Roberto use?
2. Did he like the woman?
3. Was the date successful?
4. Who was easier to understand?

**B** 1.15 Listen again. True (T) or false (F)? Do you believe in blind dates?
1. Roberto and the woman met at a coffee shop.
2. The woman arrived late.
3. Roberto had never met her before.
4. She left as soon as she saw Roberto.
5. Roberto has had other unsuccessful dates before.

**C** 1.15 Complete the informal expressions. Listen again to check.

| Formal | Informal |
|---|---|
| 1 Are you talking about the date? | You _____ the date? |
| 2 Please, continue. | Go _____. |
| 3 Wait a minute, please. | Hold _____ a sec. |
| 4 I'm very surprised. | _____ way! |
| 5 And what happened after that? | What happens _____? |
| 6 "Leaves?" Could you explain, please? | What do you _____ "leaves"? |
| 7 Is this true? | Are you _____? |
| 8 I'm really sorry to hear that. | Oh, _____! |

**D** 1.16 Listen and practice the informal expressions in **C**, copying the intonation.

**Common mistakes**
*see*
*I get into the car, and I saw this huge mouse!*
*crashed*
*I was running for the bus and crash into a street light.*

**E** Make it personal Tell an anecdote.
1. In pairs, imagine what happened before, during, and after in cartoons 1–3.
2. In anecdotes, people often use the present tense so people and objects seem closer to the listener. In pairs, try telling the anecdotes from the pictures.

*So, I finish work and I'm walking to my car. I'm tired and really looking forward to getting home. I open ...*
*Uh-huh. Yeah. And then ...?*

3. **A:** Think of an anecdote of your own – a funny / embarrassing / scary situation like those in cartoons 1–3 – and tell your partner. Use informal language from **C**.
   **B:** Listen actively. Then change roles.

*What do you mean? When you nod your head yes, But you wanna say no. What do you mean?*

# Introduction

**Writing** lessons integrated into each unit, with clear models and careful scaffolding to increase writing confidence.

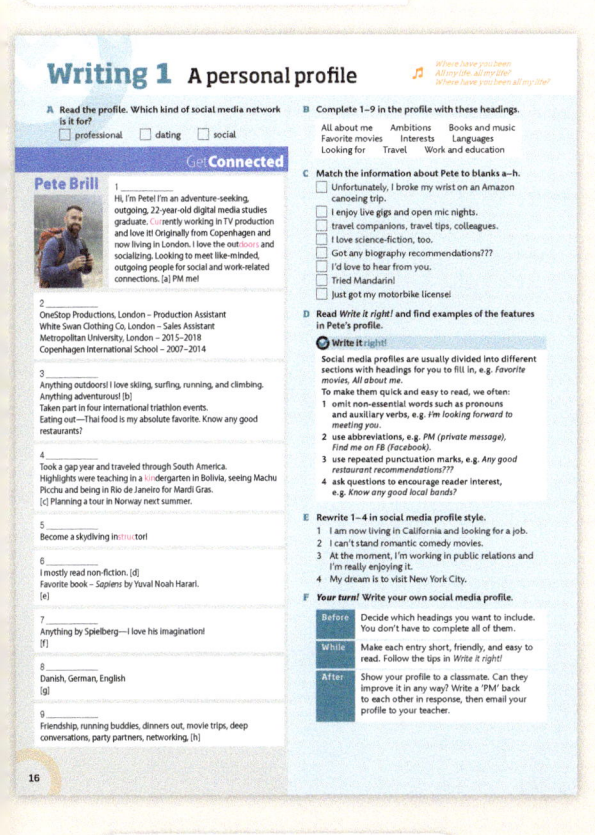

**ID Café:** sitcom videos to consolidate language.

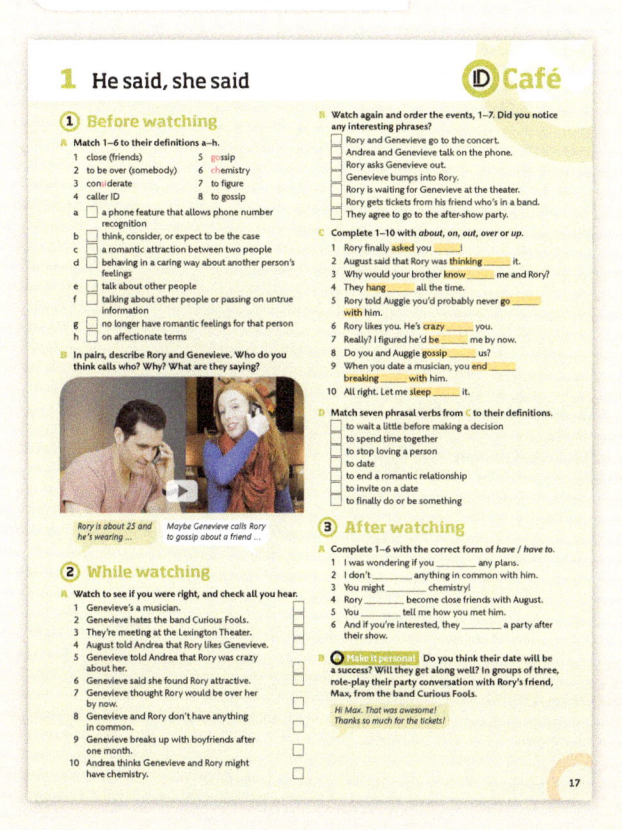

**Reviews** systematically recycle language.

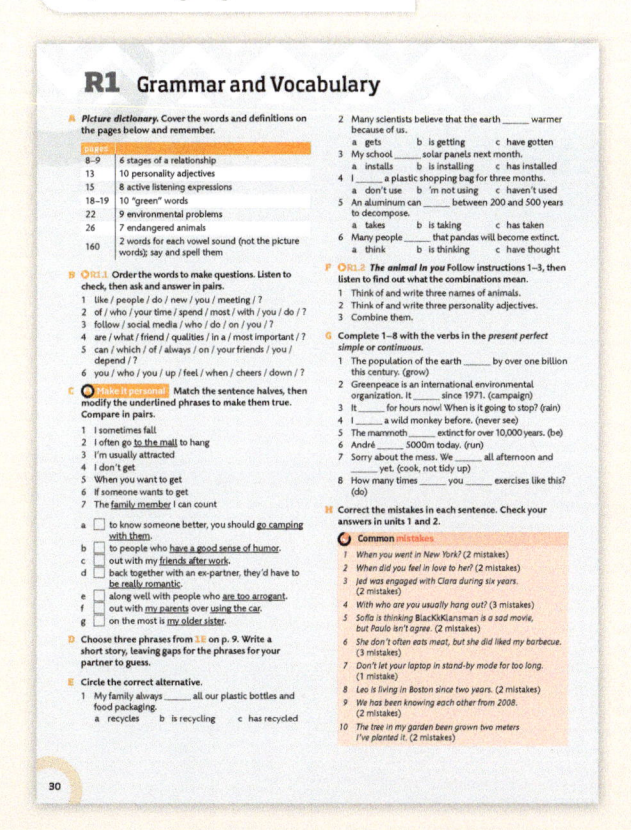

**Authentic videos** present topics in real contexts.

A complete **Grammar** reference with exercises. A full answer key can be found on the Richmond Learning Platform.

# Grammar Unit 1

## 1A Review of present tenses

**Simple present**

| Subject | Verb | Time phrase |
|---|---|---|
| I / You / We / They | hang out | on weekends. |
| He / She / It | meets up | twice a week. |

Use the **Simple present** for habits and states:
- *Johann and Melina usually **meet** for dinner once a month.*
- *She often **texts** during dinner. It annoys her boyfriend.*
- *I **hate** going to parties by myself. I always **take** a friend.*

Note: adverbs of frequency come before the verb.

**Present continuous**

| Question | Auxiliary | Subject | Verb phrase |
|---|---|---|---|
| What | are | you | doing here? |
| Where | is | he | going? |

Use the **Present continuous** for:
1 actions in progress.
- *I'm chatting to my mom.*
2 future arrangements.
- *She isn't coming tonight.*

Note: do not use stative verbs in the Present continuous.
*Do you understand me?* NOT *Are you understanding me?*

**Present perfect**

| Subject | Auxiliary | Past participle |
|---|---|---|
| I / You / We / They | have / 've have not / haven't | hung out there before. gone there before. |
| He / She / It | has / 's has not / hasn't | spent time with him. been too hot today. |

Form: have / has + past participle (for irregular participles list, see p. 158–159).

Use the **Present perfect** for:
1 past experiences without a specific time.
- *I've never been here before.*
2 completed actions from a past point in time to now.
- *We've just eaten.*
3 unfinished past: actions / states that began in the past and continue until now.
- *She's had three dates since she started speed dating.*

| Yes / No questions | Short answers |
|---|---|
| Have you (ever) been on a meet-up? | Yes, I have. No, I haven't. |
| Have they (ever) broken up before? | Yes, they have. No, they haven't. |
| Has she (ever) lost her cell phone? | Yes, she has. No, she hasn't. |

For short answers, do not contract the subject with the auxiliary.
*Yes, I have* NOT *Yes, I've.*

## 1B Review of question forms

**Yes / No questions**

| Auxiliary | Subject | Verb + object |
|---|---|---|
| Are | they | your workmates? |
| Do | you | know Natalie? |
| Have | you | been to London? |
| Can | you | play the piano? |

**Questions ending in prepositions**

| Question | Auxiliary | Subject | Verb phrase | Preposition |
|---|---|---|---|---|
| Who | do | you | want to speak | to? |
| Who | did | they | go to the party | with? |

**Object questions**

| Question | Auxiliary | Subject | Verb + object |
|---|---|---|---|
| What | do | you | want to eat? |
| Where | did | he | park the car? |

**Subject questions**

| Question (+ subject) | Verb + object |
|---|---|
| Which boy | won the prize? |
| Who | likes lemonade? |

## 1C Emphatic forms

| Subject | Auxiliary | Verb | Object |
|---|---|---|---|
| I | do | love | the sound of her voice. |

Use auxiliary + verb to emphasize agreement / disagreement.
- *"You don't seem to like him."*
- *"That's not true. I **do** like him."*

Use adverbs before the verb to emphasize an opinion or agreement / disagreement.
- *I **really** don't think he's going to show up!*
- *I **definitely** want to meet him sometime.*

Note: emphatic auxiliaries and adverbs are more common in speech than in writing.

# Unit 1

## 1A

1 Complete 1–6 with the *Simple present* or *Present continuous* of the verbs in parentheses.
1 He _____ with his friends this weekend. (travel)
2 Mara always _____ impatient when she _____ in long lines. (get / stand)
3 They _____ every night because they _____ classes. (not go out / have)
4 Ben and Amy _____ right now—I think they often _____. (not get along / argue)
5 You really _____ bored by this TV show. (seem)
6 So, how _____ him? (you know)

2 Use the phrases to describe each picture a–c. Try to use the *Simple present*, *Present continuous*, or *Present perfect*.

a Museum
guide works is explaining has never seen

b Eating competition
participating in an eating competition has to already eaten

c Skateboard park
hang out every Saturday has started is waiting

3 **Make it personal** Describe where you've been lately, what you do every weekend, and what you're planning to do next weekend.
*I always go to the same restaurants every weekend, so I have decided to try new places.*
*I've been to that new restaurant that's just opened. The Japanese place. And next weekend my friends and I are visiting a Turkish restaurant.*

## 1B

1 Write *yes / no* questions for these answers.
1 He likes this city.
2 They are good at soccer.
3 She can drive a truck.
4 The baby is awake.

2 Circle the correct preposition.
1 What were you waiting to / for?
2 Who are you so angry with / of?
3 What is she spending all her money in / on?
4 Which line are you standing in / at?

3 Write one subject and one object question for each sentence.
1 Joanna loves taking photographs.
2 The kids went into the yard.
3 Chris has lost his keys.
4 Marie likes George.

4 Order the words in 1–5 to make questions.
1 time / in / which / city / some / would / spend / like / you / to / ?
2 talking / what / been / about / the / gossip magazines / have / ?
3 learning / a / you / find / language / do / easy / ?
4 starred / who / watched / last / film / you / in / the / ?
5 you / talk / last / best / friend / to / when / did / your?

## 1C

1 Complete 1–6 with an emphatic auxiliary.
1 You know, she _____ look a little bit like Emma Stone.
2 Come to think of it, I _____ feel a bit tired.
3 Well, they couldn't make it to our party, but they _____ send us a card.
4 If I _____ seem stressed, it's only because of the thunderstorm.
5 It _____ sound too good to be true, doesn't it?
6 We _____ have to pay something to use this site—it's not free, you know.

2 Complete 1–5 with the best adverb below.

absolutely   certainly   definitely   really   sure

1 Are you _____ going to wear that orange shirt with those pants?
2 Well, she _____ told me she was getting the afternoon flight.
3 They _____ look as if they're having fun.
4 He _____ is a quiet sort of guy, isn't he?
5 I'm telling you, I'm _____, 100 percent certain I've seen him before!

# Introduction

Pictures to present and practice **pronunciation** with audio to accompany it on the Richmond Learning Platform.

## Sounds and usual spellings

- Difficult sounds for Spanish speakers
- Difficult sounds for Portuguese speakers

▷ To listen to these words and sounds, and to practice them, go to the pronunciation section on the Richmond Learning Platform.

### Vowels

- /iː/ i:
- /ɪ/ ɪ
- /ʊ/ ʊ
- /uː/ u:
- /ɛ/ ɛ
- /ə/ ə
- /ɜr/ ɜr
- /ɔ(r)/ ɔ(r)
- /æ/ æ
- /ʌ/ ʌ
- /ɑ(r)/ ɑ(r)

/iː/ three, tree, eat, receive, believe, key, E, C, D, E, G, P, T, V, Z
/ɪ/ six, mix, it, fifty, fish, trip, lip, fix
/ʊ/ book, cook, put, could, woman
/uː/ two, shoe, food, new, soup, true, suit, Q, U, W
/ɛ/ pen, ten, heavy, then, again, men, F, L, M, N, S, X
/ə/ bananas, pajamas, salad, minute
/ɜr/ shirt, skirt, work, turn, learn, verb
/ɔr/ four, door, north, fourth
/ɔ/ walk, saw, water, talk, author, law
/æ/ man, fan, bad, apple
/ʌ/ sun, run, cut, umbrella, country, love
/ɑ/ hot, not, on, clock, fall, tall
/ɑr/ car, star, far, start, party, artist, R

### Diphthongs

- /eɪ/ eɪ
- /aɪ/ aɪ
- /aʊ/ aʊ
- /ɔɪ/ ɔɪ
- /oʊ/ oʊ

/eɪ/ plane, train, made, stay, they, A, H, J, K
/aɪ/ nine, wine, night, my, pie, buy, eyes, I, Y
/aʊ/ house, mouse, town, cloud
/ɔɪ/ toys, boys, oil, coin
/oʊ/ nose, rose, home, know, toe, road, O

### Consonants

- Voiced
- Unvoiced

**TO MAKE THESE SOUNDS WE USE**

- our lips: p, b, m, w
- our teeth + another articulator: f, v, θ, ð
- the tip of the tongue: t, d, n, l
- the front of the tongue: s, z, ʃ, ʒ
- the back of the mouth: k, g, ŋ, h
- the tooth ridge: tʃ, dʒ, r, j

/p/ pig, pie, open, top, apple
/b/ bike, bird, describe, able, club, rabbit
/m/ medal, monster, name, summer
/w/ web, watch, where, square, one
/f/ fish, feet, off, phone, enough
/v/ vet, van, five, have, video
/θ/ teeth, thief, thank, nothing, mouth
/ð/ mother, father, the, other
/t/ truck, taxi, hot, stop, attractive
/d/ dog, dress, made, adore, sad, middle
/n/ net, nurse, tennis, one, sign, know
/l/ lion, lips, long, all, old
/s/ snake, skate, kiss, city, science
/z/ zoo, zebra, size, jazz, lose
/ʃ/ shark, shorts, action, special, session, chef
/ʒ/ television, treasure, usual
/k/ cat, cake, back, quick
/g/ goal, girl, leg, guess, exist
/ŋ/ king, ring, single, bank
/h/ hand, hat, unhappy, who
/tʃ/ chair, cheese, kitchen, future, question
/dʒ/ jeans, jump, generous, bridge
/r/ red, rock, ride, married, write
/j/ yellow, yacht, university

19

**Audioscript** activities to consolidate pronunciation.

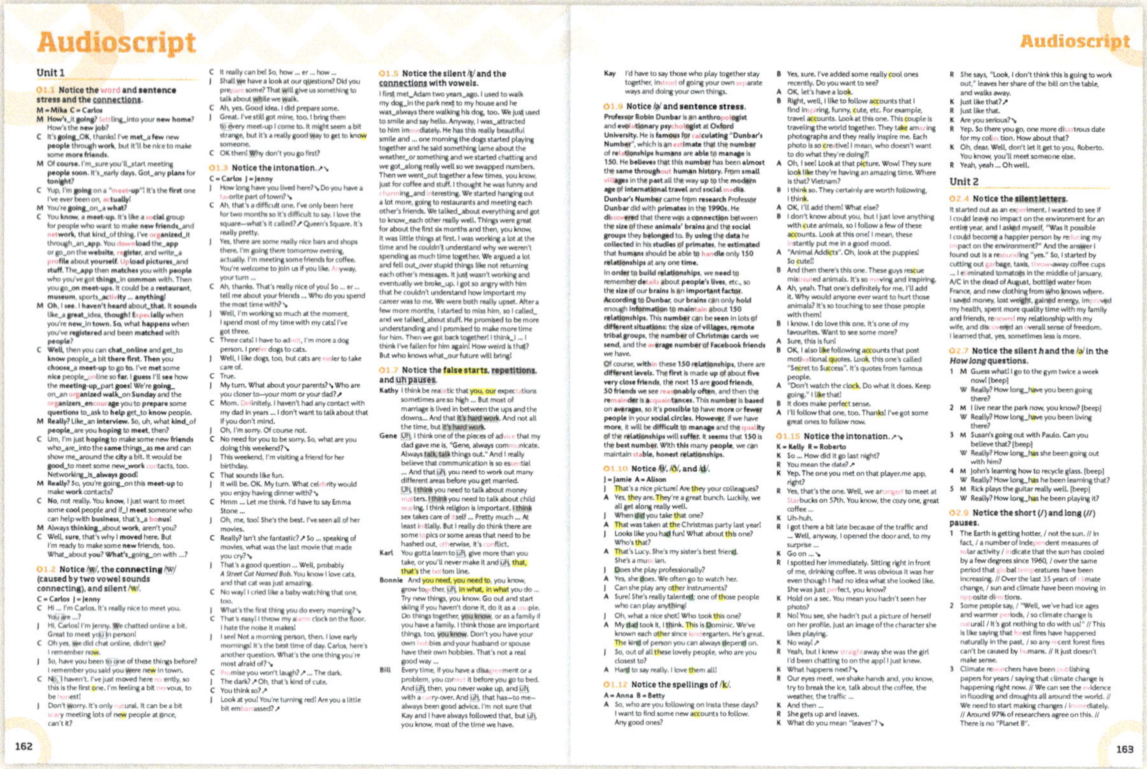

**Workbook** to practice and consolidate lessons with complete audio on the Richmond Learning Platform.

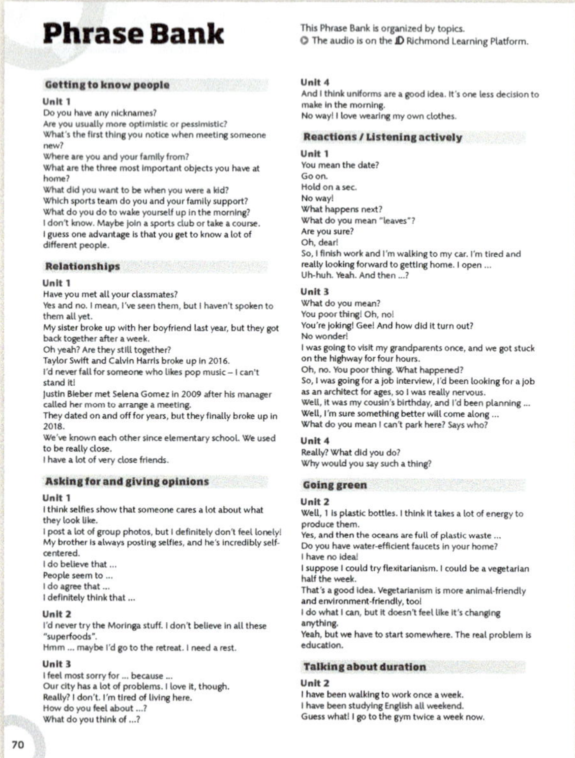

**Phrase Bank** to practice common expressions.

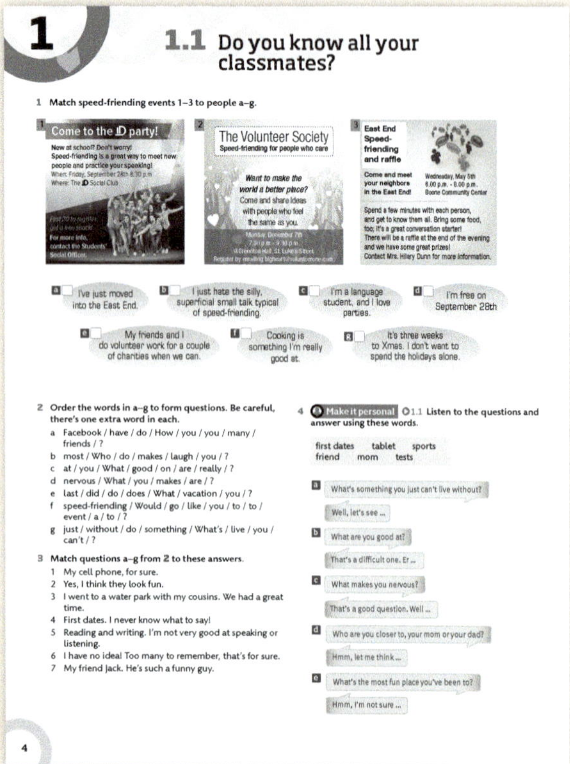

# English ID 2nd Edition Digital

## Richmond *Learning* Platform

- Teachers and students can find all their resources in one place.
- **Richmond Test Manager** with interactive and printable tests.
- Activity types including pronunciation, common mistakes, and speaking.

## New look

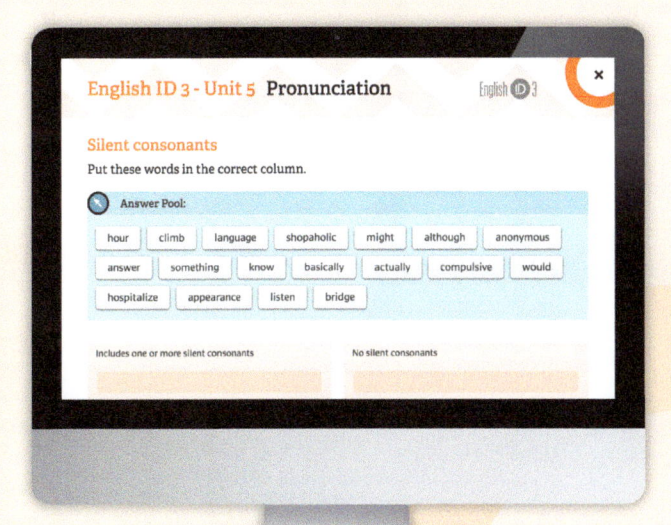

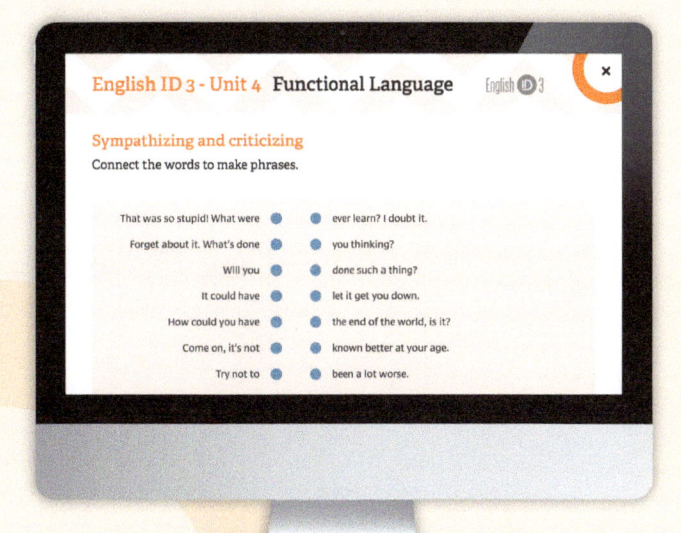

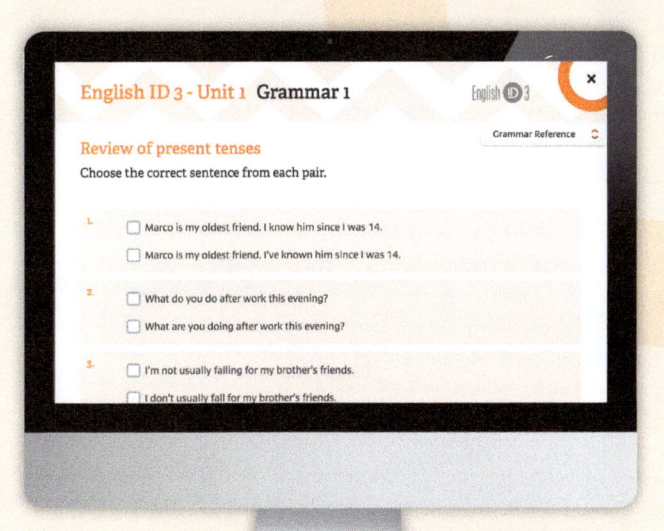

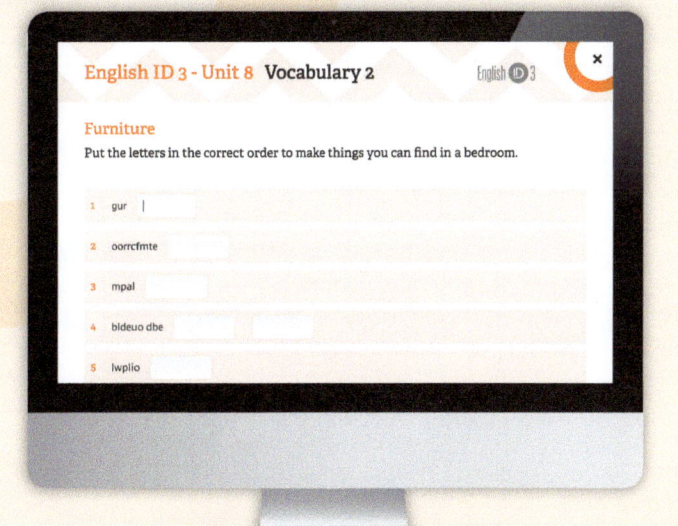

### English ID 3 - Unit 5 Pronunciation

**Silent consonants**
Put these words in the correct column.

Answer Pool:
hour | climb | language | shopaholic | might | although | anonymous
answer | something | know | basically | actually | compulsive | would
hospitalize | appearance | listen | bridge

Includes one or more silent consonants | No silent consonants

### English ID 3 - Unit 4 Functional Language

**Sympathizing and criticizing**
Connect the words to make phrases.

That was so stupid! What were — ever learn? I doubt it.
Forget about it. What's done — you thinking?
Will you — done such a thing?
It could have — let it get you down.
How could you have — the end of the world, is it?
Come on, it's not — known better at your age.
Try not to — been a lot worse.

### English ID 3 - Unit 1 Grammar 1

**Review of present tenses**
Grammar Reference
Choose the correct sentence from each pair.

1. ☐ Marco is my oldest friend. I know him since I was 14.
   ☐ Marco is my oldest friend. I've known him since I was 14.
2. ☐ What do you do after work this evening?
   ☐ What are you doing after work this evening?
3. ☐ I'm not usually falling for my brother's friends.
   ☐ I don't usually fall for my brother's friends.

### English ID 3 - Unit 8 Vocabulary 2

**Furniture**
Put the letters in the correct order to make things you can find in a bedroom.

1. gur
2. oorrcfmte
3. mpal
4. bldeuo dbe
5. lwplio

21

## New activities

**ⓘD Café:** Students watch the videos, do a language activity, and then record themselves taking part in a conversation with one of the characters from the video. Students can then download their conversation and share it with their teacher.

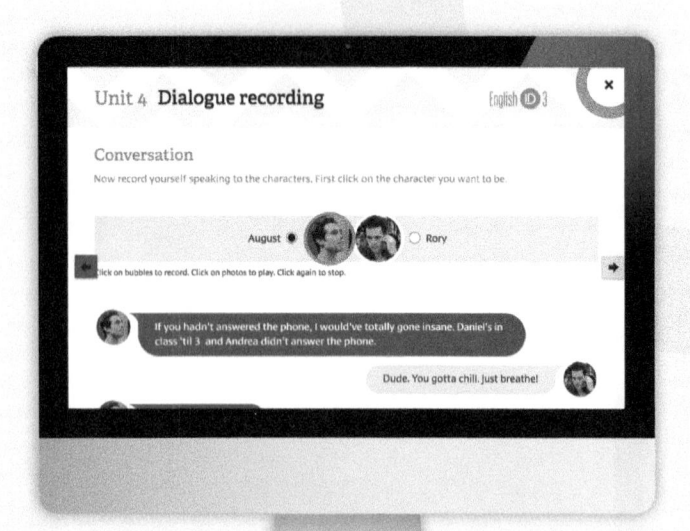

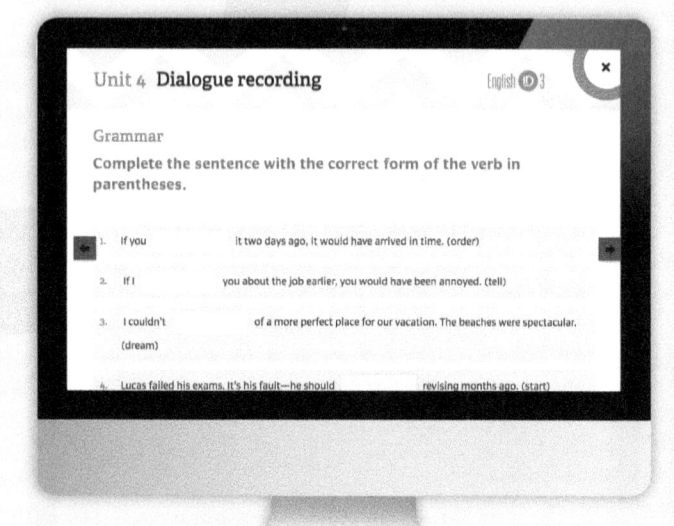

### Watch
Watch the video carefully. Questions will follow...

---

### Unit 4 Dialogue recording
English ⓘD 3

**Conversation**
Now record yourself speaking to the characters. First click on the character you want to be.

○ August   ○ Rory

Click on bubbles to record. Click on photos to play. Click again to stop.

> If you hadn't answered the phone, I would've totally gone insane. Daniel's in class 'til 3 and Andrea didn't answer the phone.

> Dude. You gotta chill. Just breathe!

---

### Unit 4 Dialogue recording
English ⓘD 3

**Grammar**
Complete the sentence with the correct form of the verb in parentheses.

1. If you _____ it two days ago, it would have arrived in time. (order)
2. If I _____ you about the job earlier, you would have been annoyed. (tell)
3. I couldn't _____ of a more perfect place for our vacation. The beaches were spectacular. (dream)
4. Lucas failed his exams. It's his fault—he should _____ revising months ago. (start)

# Introduction

**Common mistakes:** In order to revise this key feature of English ID, we have added a correct-the-mistakes activity for each unit.

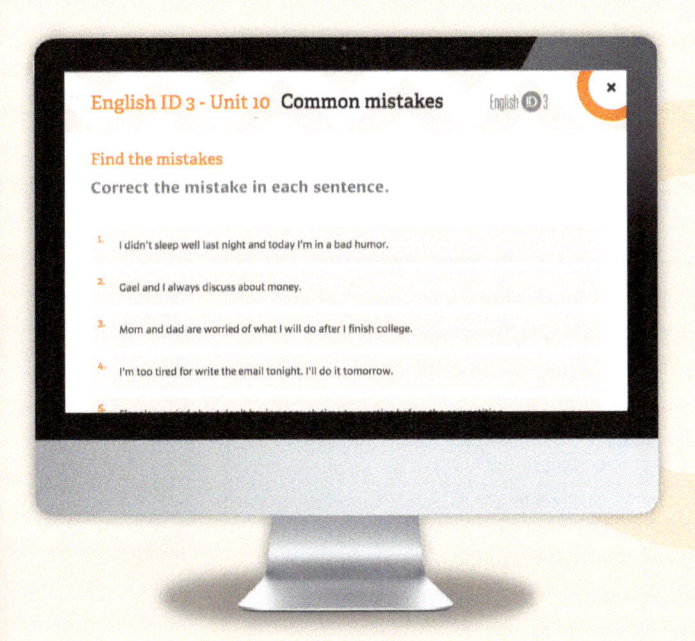

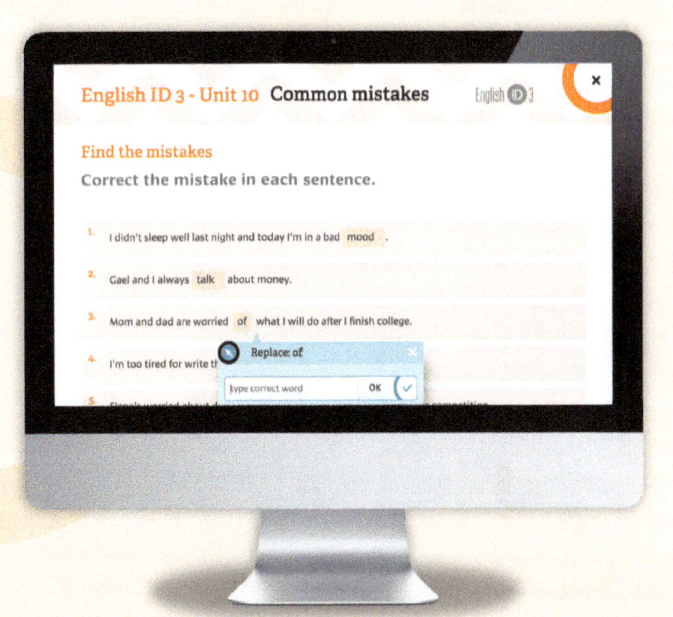

**Sounds and Usual Spellings:** For the 2nd edition, we have brought the famous ID chart to life with a new activity for each sound in the chart. Students can listen to the sounds and the example words and then record themselves and compare their recordings to the examples. These recordings can then be downloaded and shared with their teacher.

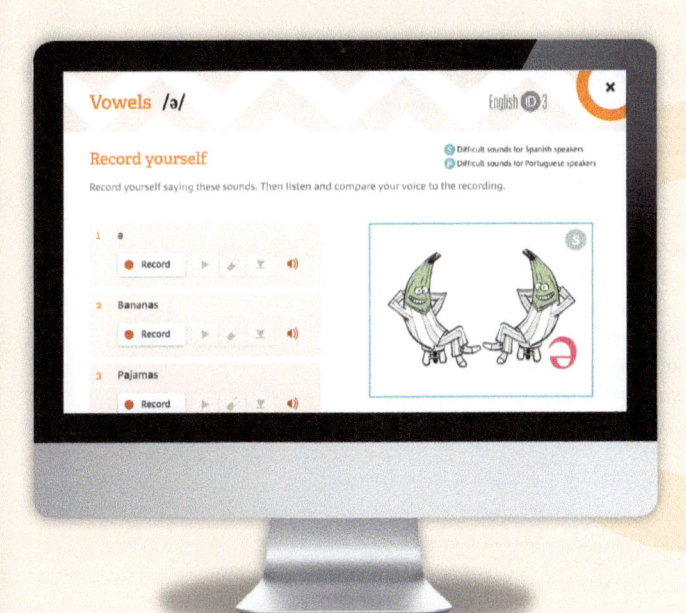

# 1

## 1.1 Do you know all your classmates?

### 1 Listening

**A** Choose five questions from the webpage below and ask a partner. Any similarities?

**Cool questions to get to know someone quickly**

- Do you have any nicknames?
- Are you usually more optimistic or pessimistic?
- What's the first thing you notice when meeting someone new?
- Where are you and your family from?
- What are the three most important objects you have at home? Why are they important to you?
- Choose three famous people: one to have dinner with, one you'd go on vacation with, and one you'd send to Mars.
- What did you want to be when you were a kid?
- Which sports teams do you and your family support?

**B** In pairs, think of two more "cool" questions, and then ask the class. Any surprises?

*What do you do to wake yourself up in the morning?*

**C** ▶1.1 Imagine you have moved to a new town. Think of five ways you could meet new people. Listen to Carlos and Mika. Do they mention your ideas?

*I don't know. Maybe join a sports club or take a course.*

**D** ▶1.1 In pairs, test your memory. True (T) or false (F)? Listen again to check.
1 Carlos has just started a new job.
2 Mika has been to "meet-ups" before.
3 You need to create a profile first.
4 Carlos is meeting some new friends at a restaurant.
5 Carlos is looking for old friends as well as new ones.

**E** In pairs, think of three advantages and three disadvantages of meet-ups.

*I guess one advantage is that you get to know a lot of different people.*

**F** ▶1.2 Listen to part 1 of a conversation Carlos has at the meet-up. Answer 1–5.
1 Has Carlos met Jenny before?
2 Has Jenny been to a meet-up before?
3 Did Carlos prepare a list of questions?
4 Circle the three words that best describe Jenny.

    confident   funny   honest   impolite   shy

5 Do you think Carlos and Jenny are going to be friends?

**Unit overview:** Through the contexts of meeting new people and social media, sts review and learn present tenses and question formation. They also study and use emphatic forms of auxiliaries and adverbs.

# 1.1 Do you know all your classmates?

**Lesson Aims:** Sts review present tenses in the context of meeting new people. They also ask questions to get to know their classmates.

### Function
Asking and answering questions to get to know people quickly.
Listening to people at a meet-up group.

### Language
I go to meet-up events about once a month.
I have lots of new friends!
I'm enjoying meeting lots of new, interesting people.
I'm going on an organized walk with some new members tomorrow.
I've been a member of this group for about a year now.

**Vocabulary:** Adjectives to describe personality (confident, funny, honest, impolite, shy, etc.).
**Grammar:** Simple present for habits and states; present continuous for an activity happening around now and a future arrangement; present perfect for the duration of a present state.

♪ Turn to p. 325 for notes about this song and an accompanying task.

**Warm-up** Welcome sts and introduce yourself briefly. Get to know sts' names.

Ask the whole class: *When you meet someone new, what questions do you usually ask?* Elicit a few questions from sts. Then, pair sts up and say: *Think of five cool questions to get to know someone quickly. Write them down.* Have pairs work together to brainstorm five questions. Circulate and monitor their work.

Have pairs exchange their sets of questions. Ask sts to interview their partners with the new set of questions. Classcheck by having sts tell the class what they've learned about their partners.

**Tip** Write the following phrases on the board while sts are working together:

*Well, let's see …*
*Hmm, let me think …*
*Hmm, I'm not sure. I'd have to think about that …*
*That's a difficult one. Uh …*
*That's a good question. Well …*

After you have classchecked, draw sts' attention to the phrases. Say: *When you need extra time before answering a question, these are useful expressions.* Go through the expressions with sts. Have them listen and repeat after you.

## 1 Listening

**A Books open.** Although sts are likely to look at the photos on the page, do not explore them now, as they will be covered later in the lesson (**2C**). Instead, have sts look at their sets of questions from the Warm-up activity. Then, point to the webpage on p. 6 and ask: *Did you ask similar questions?* Allow time for sts to read and compare questions briefly.

Have sts in each pair use five questions from the webpage to interview each other. Classcheck by having sts report their partners' answers to the whole class.

**B** In pairs, give sts a time limit to complete their questions. Classcheck by having each pair ask the class their questions.

**C** Pair sts up and have them think of five ways or places to meet new people. Classcheck. Tell sts they are going to hear two friends talking about ways to meet new people. Play ▶1.1 Paircheck. Replay the track if necessary. Classcheck.

> Ways and places mentioned: meet-up, an app, a website, a restaurant, a museum, a sports activity, an organized walk, networking

▶1.1 Turn to page 310 for the complete audioscript.

> **Tip** Have sts turn to the AS on p. 162. Sts listen again and notice the word and sentence stress and the connections.

**D** Say: *Carlos has just started a new job. True or false?* Have sts write T or F next to number 1. Have sts work in pairs to decide whether sentences 2–5 are true or false. Play ▶1.1 again so sts can check their answers. Classcheck.

> 1 T   2 F   3 T   4 F   5 F

**E** Ask the class: *What do you think of meet-ups? Would you ever try one?* Assign new pairs and have sts think of three advantages and disadvantages of meet-ups. Classcheck.

**F** Tell sts they are going to listen to Carlos speaking to someone at the meet-up. Have sts look at 1–5 and play ▶1.2 so they can answer the questions. Paircheck. Play the recording again if necessary. Classcheck.

> 1 Only online, not in person   2 yes   3 yes   4 honest, confident, funny   5 yes

▶1.2 Turn to page 310 for the complete audioscript.

## 2 Grammar  Review of present tenses

*Please allow me to introduce myself. I am a man of wealth and taste.*

**A** Are Jenny's comments about the meet-up group all positive? Would you enjoy a meet-up group? Why (not)?

*It depends. I'm a bit shy when I meet strangers.*

1. I'm enjoying meeting lots of new, interesting people.
2. I have lots of new friends!
3. I've been a member for around a year now.
4. I'm going on an organized walk with some new members tomorrow.
5. I go to meet-up events about once a month.

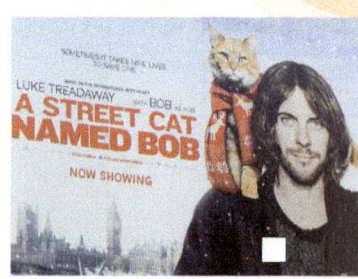

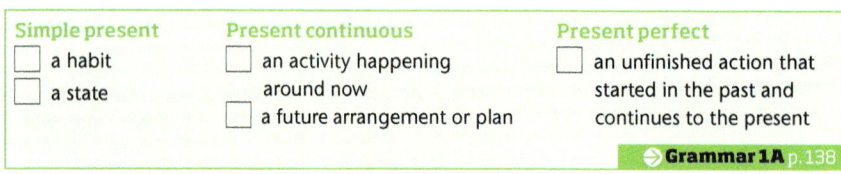

**B** Match the underlined verbs in 1–5 in **A** to the uses in the grammar box.

| Simple present | Present continuous | Present perfect |
|---|---|---|
| ☐ a habit | ☐ an activity happening around now | ☐ an unfinished action that started in the past and continues to the present |
| ☐ a state | ☐ a future arrangement or plan | |

➤ **Grammar 1A** p.138

**C** ▶1.3 Listen to part 2 of Carlos and Jenny's conversation and number the photos 1–7 as they are mentioned. What things do Carlos and Jenny (not) have in common?

**D** ▶1.4 Complete extracts 1–8 with the correct form of these verbs. Listen to check.

be (x2)   go   love   not have   prefer   throw   turn   not want

1. I _____ (only) here for two months, so it's difficult to say.
2. I _____ there tomorrow evening, actually.
3. I _____ dogs to cats.
4. I _____ any contact with my dad in years. I _____ to talk about that if you don't mind.
5. That's easy. I _____ my alarm clock on the floor. I hate the noise it makes.
6. I _____ early mornings! It's the best time of day.
7. What's the one thing you _____ most afraid of?
8. Look at you! You _____ red! Are you a little bit embarrassed?

**E** 🔘 **Make it personal**  Choose five questions from ▶1.3 on p. 162. In pairs, ask and answer them. Ask follow-up questions, too. Be careful with tenses! Any surprises or coincidences?

*Neither of us has a nickname.*

**F** Find a new partner and choose different questions. Report back to the class on the most surprising answers.

*Have you met all your classmates?*   *Yes and no. I mean, I've seen them, but I haven't spoken to them all yet.*

🔘 **Common mistakes**

don't know
I'm not knowing many people here.

Do
Are you understanding?

meet
How did you know your partner?

## 2 Grammar  Review of present tenses

**Language tip** Portuguese L1 speakers often have trouble understanding the present perfect for indefinite time in the past, because they do not use this structure in L1 for this purpose. Before section 2 (Grammar), make sure sts fully understand the difference between the use in L1 and English.

**A** Point to the comments on the page and say: *This is what Jenny said about the meet-up group.* Have sts read the comments then ask: *Were all Jenny's comments positive? Would you like to join a meet-up group? Why (not)?* Have sts discuss the question in pairs. Classcheck.

**B** Write sentence 1 from **A** on the board and underline the present continuous verb: *I'm enjoying meeting lots of new, interesting people.* Ask the class: *What verb tense is this?* Point to *Present continuous* in the grammar box and ask: *Is it something happening around now or is this a future arrangement?* Sts should write 1 in the correct box. Have sts work in pairs to match the remaining items, 2–5, from **A** to their correct uses in the grammar box.

> Simple present:  Present continuous:  Present perfect:
> (5) a habit  (1) an activity happening around now  (3) the duration of present state
> (2) a state  (4) a future arrangement

**Language tip** Draw sts' attention to the use of *around* in *I've been a member for around a year now*. Most sts will come up with *more or less*—a direct L1 translation, but push them towards *around* as that is what a fluent speaker would say.

**Common mistakes** In all lessons, it can be useful to write the common mistakes on the board before the start of the lesson. You can then use this as a reference point when dealing with the common mistakes feature in the book. Draw sts' attention to this throughout the lessons when the mistakes occur and encourage sts to self- or peer-correct. Read with the whole class and help sts relate their first language to English, asking the class if the sentence *I'm not knowing* is possible in their first language. Explain that state verbs, such as *like, know, seem, want,* and *understand* are not usually used in the present continuous.

**Stronger classes** Point out to sts that although the rule says state verbs are not normally used in the present continuous, media have used sentences such as "I'm lovin' it" (e.g. McDonald's).

➔ **Grammar 1A** page 138

**C** Direct sts' attention to the photos across pages 6 and 7 and ask: *What can you see in each one?* Tell sts they are going to listen to the rest of Carlos and Jenny's conversation and number the photos as they are mentioned. Play ▶ 1.3, then paircheck. Classcheck and ask: *What things do Carlos and Jenny have in common? What don't they have in common?*

▶ **1.3** Turn to page 310 for the complete audioscript.

> Things they have in common: they both like dogs, they both cried watching *A Street Cat Named Bob*.
>
> Things they don't have in common: Jenny's more of a cat person, Carlos is more of a dog person. Carlos isn't a morning person but Jenny loves early mornings.

**D** Write sentence 1 on the board with the gap and elicit which verb Carlos used and which form. Write the answer on the board. Have sts fill in the blanks in 2–8 with verbs from the box in the correct tense. Paircheck. Play ▶ 1.4 to classcheck. Write the answers on the board and elicit who said each one.

> 1 've only been  2 'm going  3 prefer  4 haven't had / don't want  5 throw  6 love  7 are  8 're turning

**E** **Make it personal** Direct sts to AS 1.3 on page 162, and direct their attention to the questions. Assign new pairs and have sts choose, ask and answer five of the questions. If time allows, you could turn this into a "speed-friending" game by having sts move and change partners every time you clap your hands. Allow 2–3 minutes for each new pair of sts to work together. Go around and listen to check they're using the tenses correctly, and make a note of any common errors for later class feedback. When they have finished, ask: *Were there any surprising answers? Any coincidences?*

**F** Assign new pairs and ask sts to choose different questions to ask and answer. At the end, invite volunteers to report back to the class on the most interesting answers they heard. Give sts feedback on their language, writing any common errors on the board to correct as a class.

➔ **Workbook** Page 4

## 1.2 How do couples meet?

### 1 Vocabulary  Relationships

**A** ▶1.5 Match the phrases to pictures 1–6. Listen to the story to check.

- [ ] be attracted to (someone)
- [ ] fall out (with someone)
- [ ] get along (well)
- [ ] get (back) together
- [ ] get to know someone
- [ ] break up

**Common mistakes**
~~fell~~ ~~with~~
I instantly felt in love ~~to~~ him!
~~to~~
Jack isn't married ~~with~~ Tina.

**B** In pairs, retell the story in **A**. Do you know anyone who broke up and then got back together?

*My sister broke up with her boyfriend last year, but they got back together after a week.*

*Oh yeah? Are they still together?*

**C** ▶1.6 Read the celebrity gossip article. Can you identify couples 1–3? Match the photos to the texts. Do you enjoy celebrity gossip?

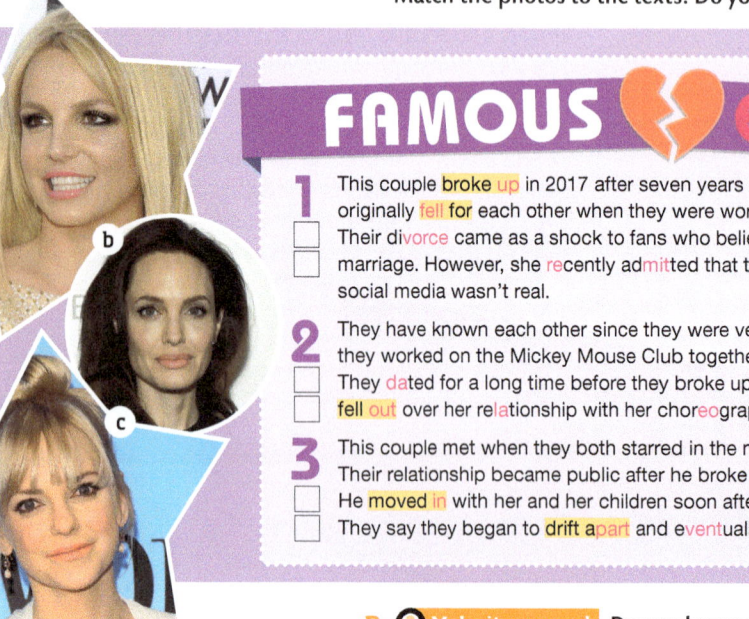

## FAMOUS EXES!

**1** This couple **broke up** in 2017 after seven years of **marriage**. They originally **fell for** each other when they were working on the same movie. Their **divorce** came as a shock to fans who believed they had the perfect marriage. However, she **recently** admitted that the **image** they showed on social media wasn't real.

**2** They have known each other since they were very young. They met when they worked on the Mickey Mouse Club together and used to **hang out**. They **dated** for a long time before they broke up. Some people say they **fell out** over her **relationship** with her **choreographer**.

**3** This couple met when they both starred in the movie *Mr. & Mrs. Smith*. Their relationship became public after he broke up with his first wife. He **moved in** with her and her children soon after. They have six children. They say they began to **drift apart** and **eventually** got divorced in 2016.

**D** 🔴 **Make it personal**  Do you know of any other famous break-ups? Or anyone who has fallen out with a boss, a friend, a family member, etc.?

*Taylor Swift and Calvin Harris broke up in 2016.*

8

## 1.2 How do couples meet?

**Lesson Aims:** Sts learn / practice phrasal verbs in the context of stories about love and relationships.

### Function
Listening to / Retelling a love story.
Reading / Listening to a celebrity gossip article.
Using phrasal verbs to talk about relationships.
Telling a love story.

### Language
I first met Adam two years ago.
This couple broke up in 2002 …
If you fall out of love with someone, you should …
My father met my mother when he crashed into her car one day.

**Vocabulary:** Relationships (to be attracted to, to fall out, to fall for, to get along well, to get back together, to get to know (someone) better, to split up).
**Grammar:** Phrasal verbs, review of the simple past.
**Before the lesson:** If possible, arrange seats in a horseshoe (semicircle) shape or in a line.

♪ Turn to p. 325 for notes about this song and an accompanying task.

**Warm-up** Tell sts that they are going to play a memory game. Have them sit in a semicircle and explain the rules of the game: The first student in line says his / her name and a (true) piece of personal information, e.g. *I'm Francisco and I'm an engineer*. The next student has to repeat that information and add some info about himself / herself, e.g. *He's Francisco and he's an engineer. I'm Joana and I live in São Paulo.*

Give prompts to guide the first sts and model the activity. Note that sts might tend to repeat a pattern—for example, saying their occupation again (e.g. *I'm a doctor* after the previous student says *I'm an engineer*). In order to avoid a simple substitution drill, ask sts to change topics each time or at least not to use the same type of information as the previous classmate.

Encourage classmates to help sts who have difficulty remembering the sentences. Be the last student in line, so you memorize sts' names and more info about them—sts like to see their teacher challenged!

### 1 Vocabulary Relationships

**A** Point to pictures 1–6 and allow sts some seconds to understand the story. Then ask: *Is this a typical love story? Is it familiar to anyone?* Have sts work in pairs and match pictures 1–6 to the correct phrases.

Play ▶1.5 and ask sts to point to the picture being talked about. Pause the track after each scene to check answers.

▶1.5 Turn to page 310 for the complete audioscript.

🔑
1 be attracted to (someone)   2 get along (well)
3 get to know someone (well)   4 fall out (with someone)
5 break up   6 get (back) together

**Tip** Ask sts to turn to AS 1.5 on p.162 and do the AS task with them. Play ▶1.5 again and have sts notice connected speech. Ask sts to chorally repeat sentences with underlined connected sounds, e.g. *I first me<u>t A</u>dam two year<u>s a</u>go* or *Then we wen<u>t o</u>ut together <u>a</u> few times.*

**B** Have sts work with different partners. Elicit the simple past forms of all the verbs in **A**. Then, have pairs work together to retell the story from the pictures in **A**. Monitor closely for accuracy. At the end, have six sts collaboratively retell the story to the whole class.

Have sts work in pairs to answer the question *Do you know anyone who broke up and then got back together?* Classcheck.

**Common mistakes**  Read with the whole class. Make sure sts use the correct past form of the verb *fall* and the correct preposition for the verbs *fall in love* and *marry*.

**Language tip**  Portuguese and Spanish L1 speakers tend to use the preposition *with* when using the verb *marry*. Before activity **1C**, make sure sts understand that, in English, we use the preposition *to* when we say, for example, *Michael is married to Pamela*, or we use no preposition at all when we say, for example, *Michael will marry Pamela*. Explain that we only use the preposition when we're using the structure *to be married + to*, e.g. *Julie **is married to** Albert. Carol will **be married to** Paul in about one year*. When we use the verb *marry* in any tense, it is used without a preposition. For example, *She's **marrying** John. Susan **married** Pete last year.*

**C** Point to the celebrities in the photos and ask if sts know their names. Have sts read the article and match the couples 1–3 to the celebrities' pictures. Paircheck. Play ▶1.6 to classcheck. Ask sts to discuss the final question in pairs. Classcheck by asking one or two individual sts the same question.

1  Ana Faris (c) and Ben Indra (d)
2  Britney Spears (a) and Justin Timberlake (f)
3  Angelina Jolie (b) and Brad Pitt (e)

**D** **Make it personal**  Discuss this question as a class, and write on the board any names sts give you. Read the speech bubble with the class. Encourage sts to ask each other questions to find out more about each situation.

# 1.2

*But ooh, this time I'm telling you, I'm telling you, We are never ever ever getting back together.*

**E** Reread the article and match the highlighted phrasal verbs from **C** to definitions 1–6.

1. _fall out_ (with so / over sth) — have an argument / fight
2. _____ (with so) — spend time together
3. _____ (together / with so) — start living in the same place
4. _____ (from so) — become emotionally distant
5. _____ (so) — fall in love with someone
6. _____ (with so) — end a relationship

**F** Complete the sentences with phrasal verbs from **E**.
1. My best friend and I started to _____ when we went to different colleges.
2. Do you want to _____ this weekend? We could go to the movies.
3. After two years of dating, my parents decided to _____ together. That was 20 years ago!
4. My brother and I _____ with each other over a stupid argument about money.
5. I _____ with my boyfriend because he hated my dog. Love me, love my dog!

**G** 🔴 **Make it personal** Complete 1–5 however you like. Compare with a partner. How many similar ideas?
1. If you fall out with someone you love, you should …
2. I like to hang out with people who …
3. I'd never fall for someone who …
4. In my opinion, couples drift apart if they …
5. Before you move in with someone, I think it's really important to …

*I'd never fall for someone who likes pop music – I can't stand it!*

### ⚠️ Common mistakes

~~split up~~
My son ~~terminated~~ with his first girlfriend.

~~drifted apart~~
They ~~distanced themselves~~ after ~~a discussion.~~
an argument

## 2 Listening

**A** ▶ 1.7 Listen to / Watch three couples who have been together for over 40 years. Check the items they consider most important.

| What's most important for a **lasting relationship**? | | |
|---|---|---|
| ☐ facing life's ups and downs | ☐ communication | ☐ shared interests |
| ☐ being flexible | ☐ physical attraction | ☐ solving problems quickly |

**B** Do you agree with their choices? Why (not)? What other advice can you think of?

**C** 🔴 **Make it personal** Think about a couple you know. How did they meet? How long were they / have they been together? In groups, share stories.

*Justin Bieber met Selena Gomez in 2009 after his manager called her mom to arrange a meeting. They dated on and off for years, but they finally broke up in 2018.*

**E** Ask: *What does **fall out** mean?* Refer sts to the definition chart and have them write the present form of the highlighted verbs from **C** beside their correct definitions. Paircheck. Classcheck.

🔑
2  hang out
3  move in
4  drift apart
5  fall for
6  break up

**F** Direct sts' attention to the first sentence and elicit the correct phrasal verb to complete the sentence. Sts then continue to complete 2–5. Peercheck then classcheck.

🔑
1  drift apart
2  hang out
3  move in
4  fell out
5  broke up

**Common mistakes**  Read with the whole class. Elicit the difference between the words which they might think have similar meanings, e.g. *split up / terminated*. Ask why the phrasal verbs are more suitable in each case. (They are less formal.)

**Language tip**  Approximately 50% of the 3000 most common words in English are cognates in Romance languages. But in some contexts, Latin origin words can be too formal. For example, *I think you should terminate your relationship with him.* Fluent speakers use a lot of phrasal verbs, which sound more natural.

**G**  **Make it personal**  Direct sts' attention to the first prompt and ask: *How can you finish this sentence?* Elicit their ideas (e.g. *hang out with them* and *talk about it*). Read the speech bubble with sts and ask if they agree with the comment. Then ask sts to work in pairs to complete sentences 1–5 with their own ideas, using phrasal verbs whenever possible. Circulate and monitor their writing. Change partners. Have sts compare their sentences in their new pairs. Classcheck by having sts say what ideas they had in common and what they disagreed about.

## 2  Listening

**A**  Ask the whole class: *What makes a relationship last?* Point to the items and ask: *Which four items do you think are most important?* Tell sts they are going to watch and listen to couples who have been together for more than 40 years.

Play ▶1.7 and ask sts to check the items that are mentioned. Replay ▶1.7. Paircheck. Classcheck.

▶1.7  Turn to page 310 for the complete audioscript.

🔑
facing life's ups and downs
being flexible
communication
shared interests
solving problems quickly

**Tip**  Have sts turn to the AS on p. 162. Sts listen again and notice the false starts, repetitions, and *uh* pauses.

**B**  Assign pairs and have sts discuss the questions. Encourage them to think of reasons for their answers. Classcheck by asking volunteers to report their ideas back to the class.

**C**  **Make it personal**  Divide the class into groups of three or four and ask sts in each group to share their stories about a couple they know. You may wish to model the activity and tell your own story to sts first. For example, say: *My father met my mother when he crashed into her car ...* . Encourage sts to respond and ask questions to find out more to make a dialogue, e.g. *Wow! What a way to get her attention! What happened after that?*

Draw sts' attention to the model in the speech bubble, but remind them that their story should be about a couple they know (rather than a celebrity couple). Closely monitor sts' stories for language accuracy and remind sts to use phrasal verbs from the lesson. When they have finished telling their stories, have each group choose the most interesting story to tell the whole class.

➜ **Workbook**  Page 5

# 1.3 How many Facebook friends do you have?

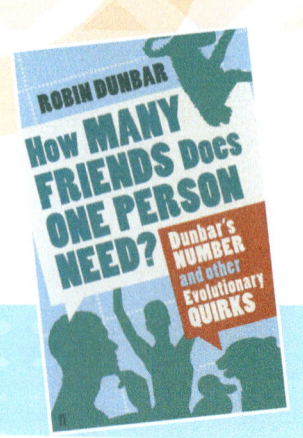

## 1 Reading

**A** In pairs, how would you answer the question on the book cover? Define the differences between very close friends, good friends, friends and acquaintances.

> I'd say everyone needs at least one really close friend to confide in. A good friend is someone who …

**B** ▶1.8 Read and match the four paragraphs to the types of friendship in **A**. Can you guess the missing numbers (a–d)? Listen to check.

**1** _____
These are people you know slightly, but they aren't really friends. It might be someone you know through work or sometimes talk to on the train. You can memorize their names, faces, and traits, and remember them when necessary. Basically, if circumstances force you to talk to each other, you are this type of friendship; if you really want to talk to each other, you are friends. According to Dr. Dunbar, a_____ is the maximum number of such connections your brain can manage.

**2** _____
You might have hundreds of them on Facebook or other social media, but are they real friends? These are the people you're usually in contact with, though not necessarily on a weekly or monthly basis. You might socialize now and then and enjoy each other's company, but if times get tough, they won't hang around to help you. Maximum number: b_____

**3** _____
These are people you may hang out with and probably get along with. You have fun together and can tease each other. You know you can call on them if you need some help. However, if you have a serious problem, they're not necessarily people that you can count on. Maximum number: c_____

**4** _____
These are the people you can rely on. You would trust them with your secrets, and your problems, and to take care of your children. They'll be there beside you in good times and in bad. These are the people you can borrow money from when you need it. Marlene Dietrich used to call them the friends you can call at four o'clock in the morning. They're like family in a way. Maximum number: d_____

### ⚠ Common mistakes

~~on~~
I can only count ~~with~~ my family.

These are the people ~~most close~~ to you.
who are closest

**C** You are going to listen to a talk about Dunbar's theory of friendship. In pairs, guess what the signficance of these seven items will be.

| primates | brain | small villages | social media |
| Christmas cards | Facebook friends | Oxford University | |

> Dunbar probably went to Oxford University.

**D** ▶1.9 Listen to the talk and number the items 1–7 in the order you hear them. Were your ideas in **C** correct?

**E** 🔴 **Make it personal** In pairs, use the infographic in **B** to explain Dunbar's theory. How well does it describe your relationships?

> I'm not convinced. I have a lot of very close friends.

10

# 1.3 How many Facebook friends do you have?

**Lesson Aims:** Sts review question forms through the contexts of listening to a book author's talk on friendship, and talking about their own friendships, Facebook friends, acquaintances, and so on.

## Function
Talking and reading about different types of friends.
Listening to a book author talk about friendship.
Listening to a woman talking about photos of her friends.
Talking about a friend, an acquaintance, and a very close friend.

## Language
Very close friends. These are the people you can rely on.
Good friends. These are the people you may hang out with and probably get along with.
We've known each other since kindergarten.
The kind of person you can always depend on.

**Vocabulary:** Types of friend (acquaintance, (very) close friend, good friend).
**Grammar:** Review of question forms.

♪ Turn to p. 325 for notes about this song and an accompanying task.

**Warm-up** Bring or download some photos of your (Facebook) friends, and show them to the class. Include a good friend, an acquaintance, a close friend, and a very close friend. Ask: *These are some of my (Facebook) friends. Can you guess what their relationship is to me?* Have sts work in pairs to discuss how they think you know them. When they are ready, get sts to ask you questions about them before you tell them who they are, and elicit/teach: *good friend, acquaintance* /əˈkweɪntəns/, *friend*, and *very close friend*, using the photos.

## 1 Reading

**A Books open.** Point to the book cover and ask the whole class: *How would you answer this question? Tell each other in pairs.* Classcheck by having sts report their partners' answers.

Explain that Dunbar's book describes four types of friends. Sts discuss the differences between the four types of friends in pairs. Classcheck, but don't give any answers yet.

**B** ▶1.8 Allow sts five minutes to read the text and match the paragraphs to the four types of friends, and guess the missing numbers. Then, play ▶1.8 for sts to check.

Peercheck, then classcheck sts' overall reading comprehension of the four definitions. Ask sts: *Do you agree with all four definitions? Do you have friends that fit all these categories?*

**Stronger classes** Sts who finish reading before their classmates can use the Internet to look up the words. After you classcheck the reading comprehension, ask these sts to share their findings with the class.

🗝
1  Acquaintances; 80
2  Good friends; 15
3  Friends; 50
4  Very close friends; 5

**Tip** The text offers opportunities to revise the zero conditional if time allows. There are many examples in the text:
*Basically, if circumstances force you to talk to each other, you are this type of friendship; if you really want to talk to each other, you are friends.*

Draw sts' attention to the first example and ask them to name the structure, then work in pairs and find the other examples.

**C** Tell sts they are going to listen to Dr. Dunbar talking about friendship. Focus on the words in the box and ask: *What do you think these things mean in the talk?* Read the example with the class. Assign new pairs to discuss the remaining items. Don't classcheck yet.

**D** Play ▶1.9 for sts to number the items in the order they hear them. Peercheck, then class check. Ask sts if their ideas from **C** were correct. Peercheck, then classcheck.

▶1.9 Turn to page 311 for the complete audioscript.

🗝
1  Oxford University (Professor Robin Dunbar is an anthropologist and evolutionary psychologist at Oxford University.)
2  small villages (The number of relationships humans can manage (150) has been the same through human history—from small villages to the modern age of social media.)
3  social media (see above)
4  primates (Dunbar did research with primates.)
5  brain (There's a connection between the size of the brain and the social group the animal belongs to.)
6  Christmas cards (This number can be seen in ... the number of Christmas cards we send, and the average number of Facebook friends we have.)
7  Facebook friends (see above)

**⚠ Common mistakes** Go through with the whole class. Tell sts to observe the correct use of the preposition *on* in the sentence *I can only count on my family*.

**E 👤 Make it personal** In pairs, sts use the infographic to explain Dunbar's theory. When they have finished, read the example with the class and have sts discuss in pairs how well it describes their own relationships. Classcheck.

## 2 Grammar  Review of question forms

*Have I made it obvious? Haven't I made it clear? Want me to spell it out for you? F-R-I-E-N-D-S.*

**A** ▶ 1.10 Alison and her friend Jamie are looking at these photos on her phone. Listen and categorize the people according to Dunbar's theory.

**B** Match questions 1–7 to the four types of question in the grammar box. Then complete the rules with these words. There is one extra.

auxiliary (x2)   object   subject   verb (x2)   beginning   end

1  Are they your colleagues?
2  When did you take that one?
3  Who's that?
4  Does she play professionally?
5  Can she play any other instruments?
6  Who took this one?
7  Who are you closest to?

---

**yes / no questions** ☐ ☐ ☐
When there is an auxiliary or a modal verb, the word order is:
_____ + subject + _____ + ?
When there is no auxiliary, use *do* to form the question.
When the main verb is *be*, invert the subject and the verb.

**Questions ending in prepositions** ☐
The preposition comes at the _____ of the sentence.

**Wh-questions**
**Object questions** ☐
Ask for information about the object, so the word order is:
question word + _____ + _____ + verb + ?

**Subject questions** ☐ ☐
Ask for information about the subject, so the word order is:
question word + _____ + _____ + ?

→ **Grammar 1B** p.138

---

**C** Correct typical student question errors in 1–8. Which ones have you made?

*I used to make that mistake a lot.*

1  With who do you live?
2  To which country you would really like to go?
3  Did you went out the last Saturday?
4  Who does help you with your homework?
5  With which three people do you spend the most time?
6  How many languages you can speak well?
7  How arrived you to class today?
8  Have you a best friend?

**Common mistakes**
          does
Where ˅ your best friend lives?
          said
Who did say that?

**D** In pairs, take turns asking the questions in **C**. Any coincidences?

**E** ⬤ Make it personal  Write the names of a very close friend, a good friend, a friend, and an acquaintance.

1  For each person, think about these questions.

| How long have you known her / him? | What's he / she up to these days as far as you know? |
| How well do you get along with him / her? | How often are you in touch? |
| How much do you have in common? | Are you doing anything together any time soon? |

2  In pairs, take turns describing each person and your relationship. Work out where on the infographic each one belongs. Ask follow-up questions, too. Any surprising answers?

*We've known each other since elementary school. We used to be really close.*

*What's she like?*

## 2 Grammar  Review of question forms

**A** Focus attention on the photos and ask: *Which of these people are Alison's friends, good friends, and very close friends, do you think?* and remind them of Dunbar's theory from p. 10. Play ▶ 1.10 for sts to check. Peercheck, then classcheck.

🔑
Suggested answers:
colleagues = friends, Lucy = friend/good friend, Dominic = very close friend

**B** Write the first two questions on the board and ask: *Which is a yes / no question? Which is a wh- question?* Then write: *Alison likes Lucy.*

Ask: *Which is the subject?* (Alison) and *Which is the object?* (Lucy). Cover *Alison* on the board and ask: *How do we ask a question to find out the subject?* (Who likes Lucy?). Then cover *Lucy* and ask: *How do we ask a question to find out the object?* (Who does Alison like?) and write the answers on the board.

Sts then match the questions in **B** to the types of question in the grammar box. Point out that the number of boxes shows how many questions there are of that type. Peercheck, then classcheck. Then, sts complete the grammar box with the words. Peercheck, then classcheck.

🔑
yes / no questions: 1, 4, 5 [auxiliary + subject + verb + ?]

Questions ending in prepositions: 7 [… the preposition comes at the end of the question]

Object questions: 2 [question word + auxiliary + subject + verb + ?]

Subject questions: 3, 6 [question word + verb + object + ?]

**Language tip** Portuguese and Spanish L1 speakers can have trouble with questions that end in prepositions as this doesn't occur in their L1. After sts do activity **2B**, focus on question 7 and give them some more examples of questions ending with prepositions, and compare these with their L1 structures so they understand the difference. Some possible examples are: *Who are you traveling **with**? Where are you going **to**? What are you buying this **for**?*

➡ **Grammar 1B** page 138

⚠ **Common mistakes** Read with the sts and elicit which is a subject question and which is an object question.

**C** Elicit the first answer from the class as an example. Sts correct the mistakes. Peercheck, then classcheck.

🔑
1  Who do you live with?
2  Which country would you really like to go to?
3  Did you go out last Saturday?
4  Who helps you with your homework?
5  Which three people do you spend the most time with?
6  How many languages can you speak well?
7  How did you come to class today?
8  Do you have a best friend?

**D** Sts ask the questions in pairs. When they have finished, assign new pairs and have sts repeat the task. Classcheck, asking sts if there were any coincidences.

**E** 🟢 **Make it personal** Ask sts to think of four different people: a very close friend, a good friend, a friend, and an acquaintance. Have sts write down the four names.

1  Tell sts to answer the questions about each person. Ask them to jot down notes in a chart, as in the example below:

| Alicia | José | Paulo | Luisa |
|---|---|---|---|
| four years | ten years | ten years | eight years |
| well | best friends | well | barely see her |
| … | | | |

2  Model the activity yourself. Tell sts that you are going to describe a person and they will guess whether this person is a very close friend, a good friend, a friend, or an acquaintance. If you did the warm-up, remind sts of your friends at the start of the lesson and go through the questions, answering them about your friends. Ask sts to guess which circle on the infographic they belong to.

**Weaker classes** Elicit and write sentences on the board for sts to use as a model when answering the questions. Then, allow sts time to prepare their descriptions.

a) I've known (José) for …
b) We get along really well …
c) We support the same soccer team … We are crazy about (Taylor Swift) … We work together …
d) He works with me … He's doing an MBA … I think she's living abroad …
e) We speak to each other on Skype every day … I never call him on the phone …
f) We're going to a dinner party next week … We're planning to go to the U.S.A. together …

Have sts work with new partners. Sts in each pair should tell each other about the people in their charts. The student who listens should guess the level of friendship being described: very close friend, good friend, friend, or acquaintance. Sts can also describe their age, appearance etc. Read the speech bubbles with sts and remind them to ask follow-up questions. Monitor closely for accuracy and offer help as needed.

At the end, invite volunteers to tell the class about one of their friends. Ask the group to guess what the level of friendship is.

➡ **Workbook** Page 6

# 1.4 Do you have many social media profiles?

*Selfies*

*Nature photos*

*Couple photos*

*Work photos*

*Group photos*

*Travel photos*

## 1 Reading

**A** Read the introduction to the article and the paragraph headings on the photos. What do you think each photo type says about the person?

*I think selfies show that someone cares a lot about what they look like.*

**B** ▶ 1.11 Read the article and match the paragraph headings in **A** to 1–6. Listen to check.

### Your INSTA PERSONALITY

Whether your social media posts are carefully planned or completely spontaneous, what you post reveals a lot more than you imagine. Psychological studies have found connections between personality, emotions, and the photos we post, showing Instagram can be a "window to your soul".

**1 _____**
Do you post a lot of these? If they are extreme images, e.g. taken while you are skydiving, it shows you have an adventure-seeking personality. If you enjoy posting funny ones, your followers can see that you are fun-loving and easygoing. But be aware that the need for "likes" reveals a desire for recognition and is often a sign that you are self-centered.

**2 _____**
If you often post images of yourself and your partner, it demonstrates a strong and stable relationship. We see two like-minded individuals who want to be together. Be careful about uploading too many of these. Ask yourself why you feel the need to prove yourself and your relationship to other people.

**3 _____**
If your profile has plenty of images of you with lots of people at parties, etc., sure, it sends the message that you're outgoing and sociable. However, it can also point to loneliness. Are you trying too hard to show everyone that you have plenty of friends?

**4 _____**
If you post photos of landscapes, it shows a thoughtful person who has the time to admire the beauty of his or her environment. On the other hand, it may also point to someone who is tired of the pace of life and needs some time off.

**5 _____**
Posting vacation images is a way of storing memories and emotions you felt while on your trip. A love of exploring the planet shows that you are open-minded and enjoy experiencing new places. Be aware that posting photos from a vacation is like posting an ad that you're not at home. Perhaps wait and post them when you're back home.

**6 _____**
If you post a lot of photos of your office, it shows your professional life is a priority for you. It can also mean that you want to portray yourself as a knowledgeable person with a high-status position. Or maybe you're just looking for promotion!

**C** True (T) or false (F)? Reread to check. Are you into Instagram?
1 Selfies show an adventurous, but sometimes fragile, personality.
2 Constantly posting couple photos is a sign of an insecure relationship.
3 Group photos can send both positive and negative messages.
4 Photos in a natural environment show someone who doesn't have much free time.
5 Posting travel photos can pose a security risk.
6 Workplace photos might mean you want to show people how important you are.

**D** ◯ **Make it personal** The article gives some advice about social media security. What other advice can you think of?

*Your friends may not always want you to tag them or show their locations.*

12

## 1.4 Do you have many social media profiles?

**Lesson Aims:** Sts learn personality adjectives and emphatic forms in the context of social media profiles.

### Function
Reading and listening to an article about what your social media profile says about you.
Giving advice about social media security.
Describing your personality.
Using emphatic forms to express opinions about social media.

### Language
Be aware that the need for "likes" reveals a desire for recognition.
This shows a thoughtful person who has the time to admire the beauty of their environment.
Wow! They certainly look like they're having an amazing time.
It does make perfect sense.

**Vocabulary:** Personality adjectives (adventure-seeking, easygoing, fun-loving, knowledgeable, open-minded, outgoing, self-centered, sociable, thoughtful).

**Grammar:** Emphatic forms: auxiliary verbs *do* and *does*; adverbs: *sure, certainly, definitely*.

♪ Turn to p. 325 for notes about this song and an accompanying task.

**Warm-up** As a class, brainstorm all the different types of social media they know (e.g. Facebook, Instagram, Snapchat, etc.) and write them on the board. Ask (and write on the board): *Which of these social media do you use? Do you like posting photos on social media? What do you post photos of?* Assign pairs for sts to discuss the questions. Classcheck.

## 1 Reading

**A Books open**. Direct sts' attention to the photos and elicit what they can see. Give sts one minute to read the introduction and the headings and ask: *What do you think each photo says about the person?* Sts discuss in pairs. Classcheck by asking different sts to give their opinions.

**B** Give sts three minutes to read the article and match the headings to the paragraphs. Tell sts not to worry if they don't understand every word, as they'll have a further chance to read it again more carefully. Play ▶1.11 for sts to check their answers. If time allows, pause after each paragraph and give sts time to:
– tell each other what they remember, or
– say the words in pink, or
– say somebody they know like this, if this is them, etc.

Ideally, use a different task after each pause.

Peercheck, then classcheck. Ask: *Do any of these types describe you?*

| | | | |
|---|---|---|---|
| 1 | Selfies | 4 | Nature photos |
| 2 | Couple photos | 5 | Travel photos |
| 3 | Group photos | 6 | Work photos |

**C** Sts read the article again more carefully and decide if the statements are true or false. Peercheck, then classcheck, and ask sts to explain why the false statements are false. Check sts understand the meaning of phrases such as *be aware* and *pace of life*.

1 T
2 F (It **can** be a sign of an insecure relationship.)
3 T
4 F (It shows someone who **may** need more free time)
5 T
6 T

**D** ● **Make it personal** Read the example with the class and ask: *What other advice can you think of?* Put sts into small groups to discuss. Monitor and help with ideas and vocabulary where necessary. When they have finished, ask a person from each group to share their advice with the class, then hold a class vote for the best piece of advice.

Suggested answers:

Discussing your job on social media can be a bad idea. You might accidentally leak important information about your employers to competitors.

Be aware that a lot of companies check potential employees' social media so you should make a good impression.

Make sure you know the people who request to follow you.

Make sure your photos are not geotagged (giving information about your location).

**Tip** Write on the board: *She gave me some good advices.* and ask: *What's wrong?* Check sts know that *advice* is uncountable. Ask: *What word can we use to make it countable?* (a piece of).

## 2 Vocabulary  Personality adjectives

♪ *Near, far, wherever you are,*
*I believe that the heart does go on.*

**A** Match the highlighted adjectives to definitions 1–10. Notice the hyphens.

| | | | | |
|---|---|---|---|---|
| 1 | _____ prepared to listen to new ideas | | 6 | _____ likes doing dangerous or unusual activities |
| 2 | _____ considering things very carefully and thinking about others | | 7 | _____ friendly; extroverted |
| 3 | _____ intelligent; knows a lot about something | | 8 | _____ relaxed |
| 4 | _____ with similar ideas and interests | | 9 | _____ thinking only about yourself and not other people |
| 5 | _____ enjoys having a good time | | 10 | _____ enjoying being with other people |

**B** 😊 Make it personal  In pairs, discuss the questions. Any discoveries?
1 Which of the adjectives in **A** best describe you?
2 Which kinds of images do you post?
3 Are the descriptions in the article true for you and your posts?
4 What about the images posted by your friends / people you follow? Are the opinions in the text true about them?

*I post a lot of group photos, but I definitely don't feel lonely!*

*My brother is always posting selfies, and he's incredibly self-centered.*

## 3 Grammar  Emphatic forms

**A** ▶ 1.12 Anna wants to find new Instagram accounts to follow. Listen to her talking to her friend Betty. What different types of accounts does she mention?

**B** ▶ 1.13 Listen and repeat sentences a–e in the grammar box. Notice the stress and cross out the wrong option in the rule.

> **Emphatic forms with adverbs**
> a Wow! They sure look like they're having an amazing time.
> b They certainly are worth following, I think.
> c That one's definitely for me.
>
> **With auxiliary *do***
> d I do love this one.
> e It does make perfect sense.
>
> With emphatic forms, auxiliaries and adverbs are usually **stressed** / **unstressed**.
>
> ➡ **Grammar 1C** p. 138

⏰ **Common mistakes**
*It does sounds interesting.*
      *say*
*They did ~~said~~ they were going to Japan next.*

**C** Complete Betty's comments with the words in parentheses and an appropriate verb.

1  **ANNA** Look at this one. What a view! Imagine being on that beach!
    **BETTY** Yes, it _____ like an amazing place. (does)

2  **ANNA** "Life's a journey, not a race."
    **BETTY** Yes, that _____ a good one to remember! (definitely)

3  **ANNA** I love this one of the man and the tiger together.
    **BETTY** They _____ to have a strong bond. (sure)

4  **ANNA** Oh, goodness. What a cute little ball of fluff! I want one.
    **BETTY** You _____ to get a kitten, don't you?! (do)

5  **ANNA** Look at them! Skydiving together.
    **BETTY** Hmm … They _____ braver than me. (certainly)

**D** 😊 Make it personal  Which of these views on social media do you agree with? Compare with a partner. Any interesting conclusions?
"Social media apps make us less sociable."
"Instagram is the best social media app there is."
"How many friends or followers I have matters to me."
"You should be over 16 to have a social media account."
"Running a social media account is a special skill."
"You can have too many social media accounts."

*I do believe that …*   *I do agree that …*
*People seem to …*
*I definitely think that …*

## 2 Vocabulary  Personality adjectives

**A** Direct sts' attention back to the text on p. 12 and the highlighted words. Have sts match them to definitions 1–10. Paircheck, then classcheck.

| | | | |
|---|---|---|---|
| 1 | open-minded | 6 | adventure-seeking |
| 2 | thoughtful | 7 | outgoing |
| 3 | knowledgeable | 8 | easygoing |
| 4 | like-minded | 9 | self-centred |
| 5 | fun-loving | 10 | sociable |

**Stronger classes** Extend the task further by asking one student in each pair to cover the columns with the meanings. They then test their partner to see if they can think of opposites for each word, e.g. *open minded / narrow-minded; thoughtful / thoughtless* etc.

**B** **Make it personal**  Assign new pairs. Ask a few sts: *Which of the adjectives best describes you? Why?* Draw sts' attention to the speech bubbles. Sts then discuss this and the other questions. Classcheck by asking sts if they discovered anything new about themselves from the article.

## 3 Grammar  Emphatic forms

**A** Tell sts they are going to listen to Anna talk to a friend about which new Instagram accounts she might follow. Remind sts of the different types of social media accounts in the article on p. 12 and ask: *What different types of accounts does she mention?* Play ▶ 1.12. Paircheck. Classcheck.

▶ 1.12 Turn to page 311 for the complete audioscript.

inspiring and funny accounts
travel accounts
ones with cute animals ("Animal Addicts", rescue animals)
motivational quotes ("Secrets to Success")

**Tip** Have sts turn to the AS on p. 163. Sts listen again and the notice the spellings of /k/.

**B** ▶ 1.13 Write two sentences on the board: *That one looks interesting.* and *Wow! That one sure looks interesting!* Ask sts to compare both sentences and raise the topic of emphasis. Point to the sentences in the grammar box and ask: *Which words are being used for emphasis?* Play ▶ 1.13 and pause after each sentence so sts can repeat. Replay the audio track and ask sts to underline stressed words and, in the rule at the bottom of the box, cross out the incorrect word. Paircheck. Classcheck by writing the answers on the board.

With emphatic forms, auxiliaries and adverbs are usually **stressed**.

**Tip** After sts read the grammar box in this activity, remind them that, up until now, they have learned that we only use the auxiliary verb *do* in negative and interrogative sentences, and that in these sentences it is usually unstressed. Make sure sts understand that in emphatic forms, the auxiliary verb *do* is also used in affirmative sentences and, because it is meant to emphasize the action that comes after it, it is usually stressed. Give them a few more examples and have them practice saying the sentences out loud: *I **did** tell you this was going to happen! She **does** work here every day! We **do** like her!*

➔ **Grammar 1C** page 138

**Common mistakes**  Read with the whole class. Explain that after emphatic auxiliaries we must use infinitive forms.

**C** Point to 1–5 and explain that Betty and Anna are now talking about other Instagram profiles. Have sts fill in the blanks with the emphatic forms provided and a suitable verb. Paircheck. Classcheck by eliciting each answer from a different student.

Suggested answers:
1 does look
2 's definitely
3 sure seem
4 do need
5 're certainly

**D** **Make it personal**  Ask: *What are your views on social media? How important is it to you?* Have pairs of sts read the six different opinions on online dating and decide which ones they agree with. Sts in each pair should compare and justify their views. Refer sts to the model language in the speech bubbles and remind them to use emphatic forms. Monitor pairs' discussions closely and take notes of any mistakes. Classcheck and provide sts with correction and feedback on their performance.

➔ **Workbook** Page 7

# 1.5 How much time do you spend online?

**Skills** Reading for main ideas and specific information

**A** What do you think is special about these four social media apps?

1. Player.me
2. Telfie
3. italki
4. govloop

*Maybe the first one helps gamers to play better?*

**B** Read and match these descriptions to three of the apps in **A**.

## A social media app for EVERYONE

Facebook is the world's largest social media network. In fact, it's so huge that it's easier to find distant relatives than someone who actually shares the same interests as you. Here are some interesting examples of niche* social networks where people with very specific tastes and hobbies can socialize.

☐ Unlike other social media apps, you don't check into locations, but into your favorite movies and TV shows. Your "friends" on this network see what you're watching right now, and it allows you to comment on and react to TV moments with other fans. You can also unlock digital stickers related to your favorite shows and bands.

☐ If you want something practical with your social networking app, then this app is perfect for you. It links people who are learning a particular language with others who are fluent. There are approximately 100 different languages available, including endangered ones. This is a brilliant way to learn a new language in a realistic setting and also learn about other cultures at the same time.

☐ This is a social media site for those who have a deep interest in gaming. With this app, you can connect and chat with other like-minded players and gaming friends. Create a gaming profile, then share your status updates, and photos, and stream live videos. There is also a group feature, so you can join and meet gamers who are into the same games as you. So, all you nerds out there, this is the place for you to network!

\* *niche* exactly suitable for a small group of the same type

**C** ▶ 1.14 Cover the texts and listen to check. Which is harder, listening or reading? Why? Uncover, listen, and read. Any surprising pronunciation or spelling?

**D** Reread and match the apps to the descriptions.
1. It lets you chat about your favorite soap opera.
2. It helps you find members of your family.
3. It offers you the chance to hear a dying language.
4. It tells your friends what you're doing, but not where you are.
5. It combines social networking and learning a skill.
6. It introduces you to people who have a lot of computer knowledge.

**Common mistake**
It lets you / It allows you to
It's let you tell your friends ...

**E** **Make it personal** In pairs, discuss 1–4. Which apps are most used by the class?
1. Which of the apps most appeals to you and why? And the least appealing?
2. Which app(s) would you recommend to the class?
3. Can you think of any other "niche" social media apps?
4. What kind of app do you think govloop might be?

*I'm interested in indigenous languages, so I'd go for italki.*

*The apps I use most are ..*

## 1.5 How much time do you spend online?

**Lesson Aims:** Sts practice reading for main ideas and specific information, and discuss their opinion in the context of social media apps.

### Function
Reading about social media apps.
Discussing different social media apps.

### Language
If you want something practical with your social networking app, then Italki is perfect for you.
It tells your friends what you're doing, but not where you are.

**Skills:** Reading for main ideas and specific information.

♪ Turn to p. 325 for notes about this song and an accompanying task.

**Warm-up** For a high-energy start, begin the class with rousing drills. Follow the model below. Alternate from individual to choral repetition.

| | |
|---|---|
| T | *She looks beautiful – Sure. She sure looks beautiful. Repeat.* |
| Sts | She sure looks beautiful. |
| T | *He seems like a nerd – Does. He does seem like a nerd. Repeat.* |
| Sts | He does seem like a nerd. |
| T | *Now you. You are difficult to please – Certainly.* |
| Sts | You're certainly difficult to please. |
| T | *She is not intelligent – Definitely.* |
| Sts | She's definitely not intelligent. |
| T | *I appreciate his honesty – Do.* |
| Sts | I do appreciate his honesty. |
| T | *She loves him – Does.* |
| Sts | She does love him. |
| T | *They're from Mexico – Certainly.* |
| Sts | They're certainly from Mexico. |
| T | *I'm an easygoing and thoughtful person – Sure.* |
| Sts | I sure am an easygoing and thoughtful person. |

### ID Skills Reading for main ideas and specific information

**A Books closed.** Ask: *Can you remember what we talked about last class?* Elicit the topic of social media. Then ask: *Can you tell me three common views or opinions people usually have about social media?*

**Books open.** Briefly introduce the names of the social media apps, have sts look at the names and logos for each and elicit guesses about the types of services each app is likely to offer.

**Language tip** In both Portuguese and Spanish, the preposition used for digital media is equivalent in English to the preposition *in*. So sts who speak these languages tend to use the preposition *in* when referring to digital or social media. At any time during **ID Skills**, make sure sts understand that, in English, the correct preposition used for digital or social media is *on*. Explain that we post something *on*, not *in*, Facebook, Twitter, Instagram, a blog; we read an article or piece of news *on*, not *in*, a news portal, etc.

**B** Have sts read the descriptions and match them to the apps' logos in **A**. Tell sts that there is one extra logo that will not be used. Paircheck. Classcheck. Ask: *In your opinion, which apps are the most useful?*

🔑
1 Telfie
2 italki
3 Player.me

**C** Ask sts to cover the texts in **B** and listen to check their answers. Play ▶1.14. Ask: *Which is harder, listening or speaking? Why?* Play the recording again and have sts read the texts at the same time. Ask: *Any surprising pronunciation or spelling?* Drill any words they tell you.

**D** **Common mistakes** Read through with the class. Assign new pairs and have them reread the text and match the apps to the descriptions, referring back to the texts. Classcheck.

🔑
| | | | |
|---|---|---|---|
| 1 | Telfie | 4 | Telfie |
| 2 | Facebook | 5 | italki |
| 3 | italki | 6 | Player.me |

**E** Ask sts to remain in the same pairs and discuss the questions. Draw sts' attention to the model language in the speech bubble. Classcheck by asking the questions to individual sts / the whole class.

# Which do you do more: listen or speak?

## ID in Action   Listening actively

**A** ▶1.15 **Listen to two friends talking about a date and answer 1–3.**
1. Which app in **A** on p. 14 did Roberto use?
2. Did he like the woman?
3. Was the date suc*cess*ful?
4. Who was easier to understand?

**B** ▶1.15 **Listen again. True (T) or false (F)? Do you believe in blind dates?**
1. Roberto and the woman met at a coffee shop.
2. The woman arrived late.
3. Roberto had never met her before.
4. She left as soon as she saw Roberto.
5. Roberto has had other unsuccessful dates before.

**C** ▶1.15 **Complete the informal expressions. Listen again to check.**

| | Formal | Informal |
|---|---|---|
| 1 | Are you talking about the date? | You _____ the date? |
| 2 | Please, continue. | Go _____. |
| 3 | Wait a minute, please. | Hold _____ a sec. |
| 4 | I'm very surprised. | _____ way! |
| 5 | And what happened after that? | What happens _____? |
| 6 | "Leaves?" Could you explain, please? | What do you _____ "leaves"? |
| 7 | Is this true? | Are you _____? |
| 8 | I'm really sorry to hear that. | Oh, _____! |

**D** ▶1.16 **Listen and practice the informal expressions in C, copying the intonation.**

**E** **Make it personal**   Tell an anecdote.
1. In pairs, imagine what happened before, during, and after in cartoons 1–3.
2. In anecdotes, people often use the present tense so people and objects seem closer to the listener. In pairs, try telling the anecdotes from the pictures.

> So, I finish work and I'm walking to my car. I'm tired and really looking forward to getting home. I open …
>
> Uh-huh. Yeah. And then …?

3. **A:** Think of an anecdote of your own – a funny / embarrassing / scary situation like those in cartoons 1–3 – and tell your partner. Use informal language from **C**.
   **B:** Listen actively. Then change roles.

### Common mistakes

*see*
I get into the car, and I ~~saw~~ this huge mouse!

*crashed*
I was running for the bus and ~~crash~~ into a street light.

♪ *What do you mean? When you nod your head yes, But you wanna say no. What do you mean?*

# 1.5 Which do you do more: listen or speak?

**Lesson Aims:** Sts learn informal expressions to respond as an active listener.

**Function**
Listening to friends talk about a blind date.
Telling an anecdote and responding actively.

**Language**
So ... how did it go last night? You mean the date?
Hang on a sec. You mean you hadn't seen her photo?

**Vocabulary:** Informal expressions for listening actively (Oh dear!, Hang on a sec., No way!, What happens next?, Go on ..., You mean ..., What do you mean ...?, Are you serious?).
**Skill:** Listening actively.

**Warm-up** Write the following questions on the board: *What makes a good first date? Who do you think should do most of the talking?* Put sts into groups of three and have them discuss the questions. Classcheck by asking the questions to the whole class.

## ID in Action  Listening actively

**A** Tell sts that they are going to hear two friends talking about a date. Say: *Roberto went on a first date with a woman he met through an app.* Explain that Roberto used one of the apps listed in **A** on p. 14. Invite volunteers to read questions 1–4 to the whole class. Play ▶1.15 and have sts listen for the answers to these questions. Paircheck. Classcheck.

▶1.15 Turn to page 311 for the complete audioscript.

> 1 Player.me   2 Yes, he did.   3 No, it wasn't.
> 4 Sts' own answers.

**B** Read statements 1–5 with the whole class and elicit some answers sts remember from the listening activity in **A**. Replay ▶1.15 so sts can mark true (T) or false (F) for items 1–5. Paircheck. Classcheck then give sts time to discuss their answers to the second question in pairs. Ask the same question to the whole class.

> 1 T   2 F   3 T   4 F   5 T

**C** Point to the Formal vs. Informal chart and have sts try to predict the answers. Play ▶1.15 again so sts can check their predictions. Replay as necessary. Classcheck.

Explain that informal language in English is usually shorter than its formal equivalent. Ask: *Do you do the same in your language? Do you use shorter language when speaking informally?*

> 1 mean   2 on   3 on   4 No   5 next   6 mean   7 serious
> 8 dear

**D** ▶1.16 Pair sts and ask them to take turns saying the informal expressions in **C**. Play ▶1.16 first for sts to listen to the intonation as a guide. Monitor sts' pronunciation closely. Encourage peer correction. Classcheck by having different sts say each of the informal phrases in 1–8.

**E** **Make it personal** 1 Point at the pictures and ask: *What's happening in each one?* Then ask what they think happened before, and after each cartoon.

2 Ask: *Do you ever use the present tense to tell a story in (sts' mother tongue)?* Help them reflect on the question with some examples.

**Common mistakes** Read with the whole class. Explain that present tenses can make anecdotes more vivid. Tell sts a brief story about something you've experienced or seen. Use present tenses to model the activity. For example, *I'm walking to work, sleepy as I can be, when I see an old friend from college sitting in a café just before me ...* .

3 Pair sts up and invite them to take turns telling an anecdote. Allow pairs some time to think of their stories and write down some notes. Explain that sts can also use one of the pictures as a basis for inventing and telling a story. Refer sts to the informal expressions in **C** and ensure that they listen actively and respond to their partners' stories. Monitor pairs closely for accuracy and offer help whenever necessary. At the end, invite volunteers to tell their stories to the whole class.

**Tip** Refer back to the title of the lesson ("Which do you do more: listen or speak?"). Ask sts to guess the correct answer. Then say: *On average we spend about 45% of our communicating time listening, 30% speaking, 16% reading and 9% writing.* Remind sts to try to listen to English as often as they can, ideally a little every day.

➡ **Workbook** Page 8

➡ **ID Richmond Learning Platform**

➡ **Writing** p. 16

➡ **ID Café** p. 17

# Writing 1  A personal profile

*Where have you been
All my life, all my life?
Where have you been all my life?*

**A** Read the profile. Which kind of social media network is it for?

☐ professional   ☐ dating   ☐ social

## GetConnected

**Pete Brill**

**1** _____
Hi, I'm Pete! I'm an adventure-seeking, outgoing, 22-year-old digital media studies graduate. Currently working in TV production and love it! Originally from Copenhagen and now living in London. I love the outdoors and socializing. Looking to meet like-minded, outgoing people for social and work-related connections. [a] PM me!

**2** _____
OneStop Productions, London – Production Assistant
White Swan Clothing Co, London – Sales Assistant
Metropolitan University, London – 2015–2018
Copenhagen International School – 2007–2014

**3** _____
Anything outdoors! I love skiing, surfing, running, and climbing. Anything adventurous! [b]
Taken part in four international triathlon events.
Eating out—Thai food is my absolute favorite. Know any good restaurants?

**4** _____
Took a gap year and traveled through South America.
Highlights were teaching in a kindergarten in Bolivia, seeing Machu Picchu and being in Rio de Janeiro for Mardi Gras.
[c] Planning a tour in Norway next summer.

**5** _____
Become a skydiving instructor!

**6** _____
I mostly read non-fiction. [d]
Favorite book – *Sapiens* by Yuval Noah Harari.
[e]

**7** _____
Anything by Spielberg—I love his imagination!
[f]

**8** _____
Danish, German, English
[g]

**9** _____
Friendship, running buddies, dinners out, movie trips, deep conversations, party partners, networking, [h]

**B** Complete 1–9 in the profile with these headings.

All about me   Ambitions   Books and music
Favorite movies   Interests   Languages
Looking for   Travel   Work and education

**C** Match the information about Pete to blanks a–h.

☐ Unfortunately, I broke my wrist on an Amazon canoeing trip.
☐ I enjoy live gigs and open mic nights.
☐ travel companions, travel tips, colleagues.
☐ I love science-fiction, too.
☐ Got any biography recommendations???
☐ I'd love to hear from you.
☐ Tried Mandarin!
☐ Just got my motorbike license!

**D** Read *Write it right!* and find examples of the features in Pete's profile.

### ✓ Write it right!

Social media profiles are usually divided into different sections with headings for you to fill in, e.g. *Favorite movies, All about me*.
To make them quick and easy to read, we often:
1 omit non-essential words such as pronouns and auxiliary verbs, e.g. *I'm looking forward to meeting you.*
2 use abbreviations, e.g. *PM (private message), Find me on FB (Facebook).*
3 use repeated punctuation marks, e.g. *Any good restaurant recommendations???*
4 ask questions to encourage reader interest, e.g. *Know any good local bands?*

**E** Rewrite 1–4 in social media profile style.
1 I am now living in California and looking for a job.
2 I can't stand romantic comedy movies.
3 At the moment, I'm working in public relations and I'm really enjoying it.
4 My dream is to visit New York City.

**F** *Your turn!* Write your own social media profile.

| Before | Decide which headings you want to include. You don't have to complete all of them. |
| --- | --- |
| While | Make each entry short, friendly, and easy to read. Follow the tips in *Write it right!* |
| After | Show your profile to a classmate. Can they improve it in any way? Write a 'PM' back to each other in response, then email your profile to your teacher. |

16

# Writing 1  A personal profile

🎵 Turn to p. 325 for notes about this song and an accompanying task.

**A** **Books closed**. Ask: *What's a personal profile? Where might you see one? Have you ever written one? What was it for?*

**Books open**. Focus attention on Pete's personal profile and ask: *What's his personal profile for?* Read the three options with the class, then give them a time limit of three minutes to read his profile and choose the correct answer. Paircheck, then classcheck.

🔑 social

Point to the last sentence in the first section and ask: *What does **PM** mean?* (private message). Explain that it can be both a verb and a noun.

**B** Say: *Pete's report is divided into 9 sections. What are they?* Elicit sts' ideas for the first section, but don't give the answer yet. Point to the headings in the box and check sts understand what they mean. Assign pairs and have sts match the headings to each section. Classcheck.

🔑
1  All about me    2  Work and education
3  Interests    4  Travel    5  Ambitions
6  Books and music    7  Favorite movies
8  Languages    9  Looking for

**C** Point to the sentences and say: *These are missing from the profile.* Give sts a minute to read them and check they understand them. Point to blank [a] in the personal profile and ask: *Which sentence goes here?* (I'd love to hear from you). Have sts complete the rest of the blanks. Paircheck, Classcheck.

🔑
a  I'd love to hear from you.    b  Just got my motorbike license!
c  Unfortunately, I broke my wrist on an Amazon canoeing trip.    d  Got any biography recommendations???    e  I enjoy live gigs and open mic nights.    f  I love science-fiction, too.
g  Tried Mandarin!    h  travel companions, travel tips, colleagues.

**D** Read the **Write it right!** box with the class, then have sts find examples of features 1–4 in the profile in pairs. Classcheck, and elicit what the full forms/missing words are.

🔑
1  Currently working in TV production ...; Originally from Copenhagen ...; living in London; Looking to meet ...; Just got my motorbike license!; Taken part in four ...; Know any good restaurants?; Took a gap year ...; Highlights were ...; Planning a tour ...; Got any biography recommendations???; Tried Mandarin!
2  PM me!
3  Got any biography recommendations???
4  Know any good restaurants?

**E** Write sentence 1 on the board. Elicit how it can be changed to sound more suitable for a social media profile, referring back to the features in the *Write it right!* box. e.g. ~~I am now~~ living in California and looking for a job. Have sts do the same for 2–3. Paircheck. Classcheck.

**F** *Your turn!*

**Before** Ask sts to choose at least five of the headings to include in their personal profile. They should include the first one, *All about me*. Give them time to think about what to include and make notes if they want to. Go around and help with vocabulary where necessary.

**While** Sts write their profiles individually, on separate pieces of paper. Go around and correct sts' writing where necessary. When they have finished, ask them to go back to the *Write it right!* box and see if they can include any more of the features in their profiles to improve them.

**After** Have sts work in pairs and ask partners to exchange profiles and read each other's work to paircheck and spot any mistakes in style, punctuation, grammar, or spelling. Ask them to write a PM back on the other side of the piece of paper with their recommendations. Then, ask sts to revise their writing at home and send it to you via email.

45

# 1 He said, she said

### ID Café

## 1 Before watching

**A** Match 1–6 to their definitions a–h.

1 close (friends)      5 gossip
2 to be over (somebody) 6 chemistry
3 considerate          7 to figure
4 caller ID            8 to gossip

a ☐ a phone feature that allows phone number recognition
b ☐ think, consider, or expect to be the case
c ☐ a romantic attraction between two people
d ☐ behaving in a caring way about another person's feelings
e ☐ talk about other people
f ☐ talking about other people or passing on untrue information
g ☐ no longer have romantic feelings for that person
h ☐ on affectionate terms

**B** In pairs, describe Rory and Genevieve. Who do you think calls who? Why? What are they saying?

*Rory is about 25 and he's wearing …*

*Maybe Genevieve calls Rory to gossip about a friend …*

## 2 While watching

**A** Watch to see if you were right, and check all you hear.

1 Genevieve's a musician. ☐
2 Genevieve hates the band Curious Fools. ☐
3 They're meeting at the Lexington Theater. ☐
4 August told Andrea that Rory likes Genevieve. ☐
5 Genevieve told Andrea that Rory was crazy about her. ☐
6 Genevieve said she found Rory attractive. ☐
7 Genevieve thought Rory would be over her by now. ☐
8 Genevieve and Rory don't have anything in common. ☐
9 Genevieve breaks up with boyfriends after one month. ☐
10 Andrea thinks Genevieve and Rory might have chemistry. ☐

**B** Watch again and order the events, 1–7. Did you notice any interesting phrases?

☐ Rory and Genevieve go to the concert.
☐ Andrea and Genevieve talk on the phone.
☐ Rory asks Genevieve out.
☐ Genevieve bumps into Rory.
☐ Rory is waiting for Genevieve at the theater.
☐ Rory gets tickets from his friend who's in a band.
☐ They agree to go to the after-show party.

**C** Complete 1–10 with *about, on, out, over* or *up*.

1 Rory finally asked you _____!
2 August said that Rory was thinking _____ it.
3 Why would your brother know _____ me and Rory?
4 They hang _____ all the time.
5 Rory told Auggie you'd probably never go _____ with him.
6 Rory likes you. He's crazy _____ you.
7 Really? I figured he'd be _____ me by now.
8 Do you and Auggie gossip _____ us?
9 When you date a musician, you end _____ breaking _____ with him.
10 All right. Let me sleep _____ it.

**D** Match seven phrasal verbs from C to their definitions.

☐ to wait a little before making a decision
☐ to spend time together
☐ to stop loving a person
☐ to date
☐ to end a romantic relationship
☐ to invite on a date
☐ to finally do or be something

## 3 After watching

**A** Complete 1–6 with the correct form of *have / have to*.

1 I was wondering if you _____ any plans.
2 I don't _____ anything in common with him.
3 You might _____ chemistry!
4 Rory _____ become close friends with August.
5 You _____ tell me how you met him.
6 And if you're interested, they _____ a party after their show.

**B** 🔘 **Make it personal** Do you think their date will be a success? Will they get along well? In groups of three, role-play their party conversation with Rory's friend, Max, from the band Curious Fools.

*Hi Max. That was awesome! Thanks so much for the tickets!*

17

# ID Café 1   He said, she said

## 1 Before watching

**A** Start off by eliciting the pronunciation of words with pink letters (words 3, 5, and 6). Then, drill pronunciation for words 1–8.

Read the first definition with the whole class and elicit the correct word. Have sts match words 1–8 to the correct definitions. Paircheck. Classcheck.

> 1 h   2 g   3 d   4 a   5 e   6 c   7 b   8 f

**B** Focus sts' attention on the characters in the picture. If sts have already studied with a previous level of **English ID**, find out whether they remember the characters' names. Ask: *Who are they? What are they doing?*

Then ask: *Why do you think Rory is calling Genevieve?* Have two sts read the model dialogue in the speech bubbles. Ask sts to work in pairs to predict the story. Classcheck.

## 2 While watching

**A** Tell sts that they are going to watch and listen to Rory calling and asking Genevieve out. Ask: *Where do you think he'll take her? A party? A romantic dinner?*

Have sts quickly read all nine statements. Explain that they should check the statements they hear in the video. Play ▶1. Paircheck. Classcheck.

> 1 T   2 F   3 T   4 F   5 F   6 T   7 T   8 T   9 T   10 T

**B** Tell sts that they are going to watch the video again as they order events, 1–7. Replay ▶1. Paircheck. Classcheck by writing the answers on the board. Ask sts if they heard any interesting phrases.

> 6, 3, 2, 5, 4, 7, 1

**C** Read sentence 1 with the whole class and elicit the correct preposition. Have sts fill in the blanks in sentences 2–10 with *about, on, out, over,* or *up*. Paircheck. Classcheck by writing the answers on the board.

> **Tip** If time allows, classcheck sts' answers by playing ▶1 with subtitles.

> 1 out   2 about   3 about   4 out   5 out   6 about
> 7 over   8 about   9 up; up   10 on

**D** Draw sts' attention to the sentences in **C** and say: *There are seven phrasal verbs here. What are they?* Have sts match the phrasal verbs in **C** to the seven definitions in **D**. Paircheck. Classcheck.

> think about it
> hang out
> be over (someone)
> go out with (someone)
> break up
> ask (someone) out
> end up

## 3 After watching

**A** Read sentence 1 and elicit the correct form of *have* to fill in the blank. Have sts complete sentences 2–6 with the appropriate forms of *have* or *have to*. Paircheck. Classcheck by writing the answers on the board.

> 1 have   2 have   3 have   4 has   5 have to
> 6 are / 're having

**B** ◯ **Make it personal**   Ask sts: *Do you think their date will be a success? Will they get along well?* Have two sts read the model dialogue in the speech bubbles to the whole class. Then, have sts work in groups of three to role-play their party conversation with Rory's friend Max. Classcheck by asking a group to perform their role-play for the class.

# 2.1 How green are you?

### 1 Vocabulary  Going green

**A** How are photos 1–10 each connected with being "green"?

> Well, 1 is plastic bottles. I think it takes a lot of energy to produce them.

> Yes, and the oceans are full of plastic waste …

**B** Match the highlighted words in the quiz to photos 1–10.

## The "going green" Quiz

We all know what we should be doing. But how green have you really gone?

**1** Leaving appliances on stand-by mode isn't environment-friendly because it wastes energy. Do you always unplug your computer or cell charger when not in use?  Y / S / N

**2** Disposable plastic bags can take up to 1,000 years to decompose. Do you reuse plastic bags or take a reusable cloth bag when you go shopping?  Y / S / N

**3** Leaving the faucet running when you brush your teeth twice a day can waste almost 8 gallons of water. Do you turn the faucet off while brushing your teeth?  Y / S / N

**4** Energy-efficient light bulbs last from 6,000 to 15,000 hours. Do you use energy-efficient light bulbs in your house or office?  Y / S / N

**5** Solar heating is a renewable energy source, and it can help you save as much as one-third off your monthly power bill. Does your house or apartment building have a solar heating system?  Y / S / N

**6** It takes more than 30 million barrels of oil a year to make the plastic for the world's bottled water. Do you use refillable bottles for water at home?  Y / S / N

**7** A Styrofoam cup takes 500 years to decompose. Do you use Styrofoam cups at work or home?  Y / S / N

**8** A typical American family produces 30% more household waste than a typical Mexican family. Do you separate organic and non-organic household waste?  Y / S / N

**9** More than 1.5 million Americans over the age of 17 are now vegan. "Flexitarianism"* is now on the increase, with a 60% global rise in new vegetarian branded products between 2011 and 2015. Do you ever eat vegetarian meals?  Y / S / N

**10** A carbon footprint calculates all the greenhouse gases we produce in our activities as individuals and measures them in units of carbon dioxide. The world average is about 4½ tons of carbon dioxide per person. Do you ever feel concerned about your carbon footprint?  Y / S / N

*flexitarianism *n* following a vegetarian diet with the occasional inclusion of meat

**Y** = Yes   **S** = Sometimes   **N** = No

**C** ▶2.1 Listen, read, and answer the quiz. In pairs, compare answers. Who's greener?

> We're both similar, but …

### Common mistakes

*left*
I ~~let~~ the lights on.

*wastes*
This fridge ~~spends~~ a lot of energy.

**Unit overview:** Through the contexts of the environment, natural disasters, advertisements, and threatened species, sts review and learn the present perfect simple / continuous vs. simple past. They also study and use expressing numerical information and phrases for encouraging and discouraging.

# 2.1 How green are you?

**Lesson Aims:** Sts learn and practice words related to going green and adjectives with the suffixes *-able*, *-friendly*, and *-efficient* in the context of greener, more sustainable lifestyles.

### Function
Reading / Taking a quiz on green actions.
Talking about how green people are.
Talking about how to be more green.

### Language
Leaving appliances on stand-by mode isn't environmentally friendly because it wastes energy.
Do you turn the faucet off when brushing your teeth?
I suppose I could try vegetarianism.

**Vocabulary:** Going green (appliances, bottled water, carbon footprint, energy-efficient light bulbs, faucet, household waste, reusable cloth bag, solar heating, styrofoam cups, vegan). Adjectives from verbs and nouns: *-able*, *-friendly*, *-efficient*
**Pronunciation:** /ɑ/ and /oʊ/
**Before the lesson:** If possible, bring some realia to class to pre-teach some of the words from p. 18–19, such as bottled water, a reusable cloth bag, an energy-efficient light bulb, and a styrofoam cup.

♪ Turn to p. 326 for notes about this song and an accompanying task.

**Warm-up** Take out the realia you have brought to class, or objects already in the classroom, related to the words on p. 18–19. Walk around the classroom, displaying or pointing to objects one by one, and drill pronunciation without writing any words on the board. Have sts repeat after you, test their memory and ask questions such as: *Is bottled water expensive in our city / country? What types of light bulbs do you use in your house? Do you carry your groceries in a reusable cloth bag? How often do you drink your coffee in styrofoam cups?*

## 1 Vocabulary Going Green

**A Books open.** Point to the photos on p. 19 and elicit any vocabulary sts already know. Draw sts' attention to photo 1 and elicit how it's connected with being "green". Read the example conversation with the class. Sts then discuss the other photos in pairs. Classcheck.

> Suggested answers:
> 1 Plastic bottles pollute the ocean.
> 2 Appliances use a lot of electricity.
> 3 It takes a lot of energy to produce styrofoam cups.
> 4 These types of light bulbs save energy.
> 5 This is renewable energy.
> 6 Lots of waste isn't recycled.
> 7 Your carbon footprint measures how much carbon your actions cause in the world.
> 8 This can avoid using polluting plastic bags.
> 9 Eating meat has a big impact on the environment.
> 10 It's important not to waste water.

**B** Point to the first highlighted word in the quiz (appliances) and elicit the correct picture (2). Have sts work in pairs to match the remaining highlighted words in the quiz to photos 1–10. Classcheck.

Point to photo 1 and write on the board: *a bottle of water* and *bottled water*. Raise sts' awareness of the fact that *bottled water* is an uncountable noun and that *a bottle of water* is a countable noun.

> 1 bottled water
> 2 appliance
> 3 styrofoam cup
> 4 energy-efficient light bulb
> 5 solar heating
> 6 household waste
> 7 carbon footprint
> 8 reusable cloth bag
> 9 vegan
> 10 faucet

**C** Point to the quiz in **B** and ask the whole class: *What's this quiz about?* Point to the Y, S, and N symbols and say: *Listen to the quiz and answer Yes, Sometimes, or No.* Play ▶ 2.1 and allow sts to take the quiz themselves.

> **Language tip** As a result of direct translation, Romance language speakers tend to use the equivalent to the verb *spend* in their L1 in relation to energy.

> **Common mistakes** Draw sts' attention to the Common mistakes and remind them that in English we use "waste" instead of "spend" when referring to energy. Read through the rubric with sts. Then pair sts up to compare their answers. Ask: *Who's the greenest person in our class?*

## 2 Pronunciation /ɑ/ and /oʊ/

▶ 2.2 Put these words in the correct column according to the underlined sounds. Listen to check.

| bottle | cloth | clothes | disposable | eco |
| product | program | solar | Styrofoam | |

| ɑ | oʊ |
|---|---|
| bottle | clothes |

*Heal the world. Make it a better place for you and for me and the entire human race.*

## 3 Vocabulary Adjectives from verbs and nouns

**A** We often form "green" adjectives by adding *-able*, *-efficient*, and *-friendly* to verbs and nouns. Match the endings to their meanings.

1 re*us*able cloth bag
2 energy-*efficient* light bulb
3 environment-*friendly* appliances

☐ that are safe for
☐ that use less
☐ that you can + verb

**B** ▶ 2.3 Make seven "green" phrases using the suffixes in **A**. Listen to check. Then ask about a partner's home.

1 water / *fau*cets
2 environment / de*ter*gents
3 fuel / *ve*hicles
4 recharge / batteries
5 energy / ap*pli*ances
6 re*use* / plastic containers
7 pet / in*sec*ticides

*Do you have water-efficient faucets in your home?*  *I have no idea!*

➔ **Grammar 2A** p. 140

**C** 🔴 Make it personal  What could you do to be greener?

1 Look back at the quiz on p. 18. How could you be greener for each question? Make notes.
2 Compare your notes with a partner. Do you agree with each other?

*I suppose I could try flexitarianism. I could be a vegetarian half the week.*

*That's a good idea. Vegetarianism is more animal-friendly and environment-friendly, too!*

3 Then discuss how your school / class could be greener. Report back. Choose the top five ideas.

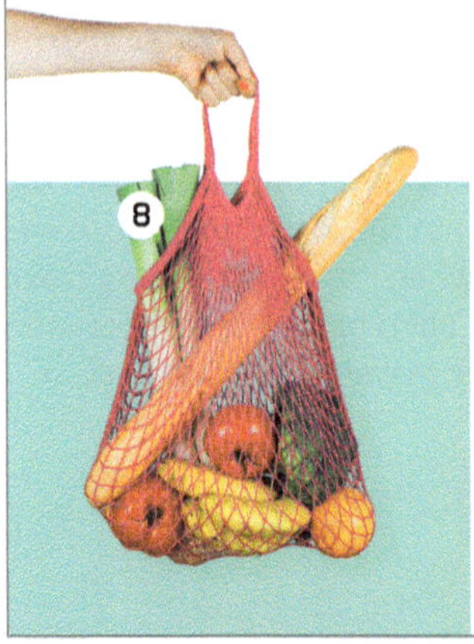

## 2.1

### 2  Pronunciation /ɑ/ and /oʊ/

**A** Pair sts up and have the pairs write the words next to the correct phonetic symbol. Play ▶ 2.2 so sts can check their answers. Classcheck and drill pronunciation for all words.

> /ɑ/ sock, clock: bottle, cloth, product
> /oʊ/ nose, rose: clothes, disposable, eco, program, solar, styrofoam

> **Stronger classes** Direct sts to the "Sounds and usual spellings" chart on p. 160 and have them practice saying word lists for sounds /ɑ/ and /oʊ/. After completing the classcheck, ask sts to recite for the whole class some of the extra words they remember from the pronunciation chart. Test sts by reading out extra words, e.g. *global, mode, office* etc., for them to add to the chart.

### 3  Vocabulary  Adjectives from verbs and nouns

**A** Drill the pronunciation of 1–3. Engage sts in choral and individual repetition. Write the highlighted endings *-able*, *-efficient,* and *-friendly* on the board and elicit or present more examples of adjectives with these suffixes, such as *a sustainable project, an adorable creature, a memorable moment, a cost-efficient trip, fuel-efficient airplanes, user-friendly software, a dog-friendly hotel*, or *a child-friendly restaurant*.

Have sts match 1–3 to their definitions. Paircheck. Classcheck and remind sts that in English, adjectives only have one form, i.e. they don't change for gender or plural and they always come before the noun.

> 1 that you can + verb
> 2 that use less
> 3 that are safe for

**B** Elicit the answer for item 1 as an example. Invite sts to create green phrases for items 2–7, adding *-able*, *-efficient*, or *-friendly* to the words provided. Ensure that sts notice singular / plural prompts and use the indefinite article when appropriate.

When they are ready, play ▶ 2.3 for sts to check their answers. Paircheck. Classcheck, drilling the phrases chorally and individually.

> 1 water-efficient faucets
> 2 environment-friendly detergents (also possible environmentally friendly)
> 3 fuel-efficient vehicles
> 4 rechargeable batteries
> 5 energy-efficient appliances
> 6 reusable plastic containers
> 7 pet-friendly insecticides

Have sts change partners. Refer them to the model dialogue in the speech bubbles. Ask them to take turns asking and answering questions about their homes, using phrases 1–7. Monitor sts' work closely for accuracy and offer help as necessary. Classcheck by having sts talk about their partners' homes.

→ **Grammar 2A** page 140

**C** **Make it personal** 1 Direct sts back to the quiz on p. 18. Look at the first question and elicit other ways they could be greener (e.g. only plug appliances in when you need them; don't keep charging a device when it's full etc.). Have them work alone to make notes on how to be greener in each situation.

2 Put sts into pairs to discuss their ideas. Read the example dialogue with them first. Classcheck and ask if sts agreed.

3 Allow time for sts to discuss the question together. Discuss the question as a class, making a list on the board of things you could do. Have the class vote on the ideas to choose their top five.

> Suggested answers:
> Recycle used paper.
> Stop using styrofoam cups.
> Reuse water bottles.
> Use solar energy for the building.
> Make sure you unplug all appliances at the end of the lesson.

→ **Workbook** Page 9

# 2.2 How long have you been studying here?

## 1 Listening

**A** ▶ 2.4 In pairs, interpret the poster. Is it for a comedy or a documentary? What do you think "No Impact Man" is about? Listen to / Watch the video to check your guesses.

*Do you think he's some kind of superhero?*

**B** ▶ 2.4 Remember what Colin said about these items. Then listen / watch again to check.

waste    travel and transportation
food and drink    shopping    money
health    relationships    happiness

*I think he said he didn't buy tomatoes in January. Did you hear that?*

**C** 🔘 **Make it personal** In pairs, answer 1–3. Any big differences?
1 Why do you think he made these changes? What impact will they have on the environment?
2 What three things could you change to have less impact on the environment?
3 Would you consider going "no impact" for a year? A month? A week? Why (not)?

## 2 Reading

**A** ▶ 2.5 Quickly read Al's blog. How green is his lifestyle these days? Circle 1, 2, or 3.

This morning I ran into an old friend on my way to work. He could hardly recognize me. "You look so … different," he said. "Have you been working out or something?" Well, yes, I've been working out like crazy every day, but I guess it's the "something" that has made the difference.

You see, I've been trying to copy the idea I saw in a documentary called *No Impact Man*. It's about a guy called Colin Beaven, who tries to have zero impact on the environment for a year. So instead of simply switching to energy-efficient light bulbs, buying eco-friendly cleaning products, avoiding disposable cups, and stuff like that, he takes the whole thing to the next level: no TV, no elevators, no public transportation, no household waste … The list goes on and on.

*No Impact Man* has had such an impact (!) on me that my family and I are trying to green up our lifestyles, too. For example, I've been walking to work at least twice a week, taking the stairs, using recycled paper, and so on. At home, we're beginning to recycle, trying to unplug all appliances, installing water-efficient faucets—you name it. And you know what? We've all been feeling great lately. But I think that's really as far as I can go. I'd never be able to give up TV, sell my precious car (which I've only been driving since Monday!), or buy used clothes.

So my question is: Can I make a difference, or am I wasting my time?

**B** Reread and find key points to justify your answer in **A**. Compare in pairs. Do you disagree at all? Is he wasting his time?

**C** What do the highlighted expressions mean?
1 ☐ eventually    2 ☐ more and more    3 ☐ etc.

**D** 🔘 **Make it personal** In pairs, share your own answers to Al's final question. Any conclusions?

*I do what I can, but it doesn't feel like it's changing anything.*

*Yeah, but we have to start somewhere. The real problem is education.*

# 2.2 How long have you been studying here?

**Lesson Aims:** Sts study and use the present perfect continuous to talk about recent habits and changes in their lives.

**Function**
Watching / Listening to *No Impact Man*.
Talking about going green or "no impact" for a year.
Reading a blog post about one man's green lifestyle.
Interviewing a friend about recent habits or changes.

**Language**
I started by cutting out garbage, taxis …
I couldn't possibly survive without my car.
I've been walking to work at least twice a week.
How long have you been reading this book? How long have you been going there?

**Vocabulary:** Time / Frequency / Degree phrases ( and so on … , and stuff like that … , the list goes on and on … )
**Grammar:** Present perfect continuous.
**Pronunciation:** The reduced form of *have* and *has*.
**Before the lesson:** If possible, arrange seats in a horseshoe / semicircle shape or in a line.

♪ Turn to p. 326 for notes about this song and an accompanying task.

**Warm-up** Tell sts to predict what a *no impact man* means. As sts say what comes to their minds, write their ideas on the board.

## 1 Listening

**A** Point to the poster and have sts read the DVD's title. Ask the whole class: *Is it a comedy or a documentary? Why is it called No Impact Man?* Read the example with the class and allow sts some time to guess and interpret the title in pairs. Play ▶2.4 ▶ for sts to check their guesses.

▶2.4 Turn to page 311 for the complete audioscript.

> It's a documentary about a man who performed an experiment: to have no impact on the environment for a year.

**Tip** Have sts turn to the AS on p. 163. Sts listen again and notice the silent letters.

**B** Direct sts' attention to the items in the box, and read the example with the class. Ask: *What did Colin say about these things? Can you remember?* Put sts in pairs to discuss. Then play ▶2.4 ▶ again for sts to check their answers.

> waste – cut out garbage and throw-away coffee cups
> travel and transportation – cut out taxis
> food and drink – stopped buying tomatoes in January and bottled water from France
> shopping – stopped buying new clothing
> money – saved money
> health – lost weight, gained energy, became healthier
> relationships – spent more time with friends, family, and wife
> happiness – he became happier

**C** ● **Make it personal** Pair sts up and have them ask and answer the questions. Classcheck by having sts report their partners' answers.

## 2 Reading

**A** Focus on the website and ask: *What kind of website is this? What's Al talking about?* Allow sts some time to skim through the text and answer. Say: *Al has watched Colin Beaven's video No Impact Man, and it has inspired him.* Point to men 1, 2, and 3, just above the top right section of the blog, and ask the class: *How green is Al's lifestye now?* Say: *Listen and read to find out.* Play ▶2.5. Classcheck.

> 2

**B** Ask sts to go back to the text in **A** and identify key points that justify their choice of answer. Paircheck. Classcheck.

> Al has "been walking to work at least twice a week, taking the stairs, using recycled paper, and so on." At home, Al and his family are "beginning to recycle, trying to unplug all appliances, installing water-efficient faucets." But he believes "that's really as far as [he] can go." He says, "I'd never be able to give up TV, sell my precious car (which I've only been driving since Monday!), or buy used clothes."

**C** Point to the text in **A** again and ask: *What do these highlighted expressions mean?* Have sts change partners and work in pairs to guess or infer meaning from the text. Classcheck.

> All the highlighted expressions mean *etc*.

**D** Point to Al's question at the end of the text in **A**. Have sts read the model sentences in the speech bubbles. Then ask sts to share their opinions in pairs, then open the discussion to the whole class.

> Suggested answers:
> He could walk to work more often, he could buy an electric car, he could cut down on the amount of TV he watches and cut down on other appliances. He could buy products that are made locally, he could try buying a few used clothes.

## 3 Grammar  Present perfect continuous

♪ *Lately I've been, I've been losing sleep, Dreaming about the things that we could be.*

**A** Sentences 1–3 are true. Find evidence in Al's blog in **2A**.
1  Al probably has a gym membership.   2  Al probably lives near his work.   3  Al has a new car.

**B** Follow the instructions in the grammar box.

> 1  Match examples a–c to the rules.
>   a  **Have you been working out** or something?
>   b  **I've been walking** to work at least twice a week.
>   c  **He's been driving** a brand new car since Monday.
>
>   Sentences _____ and _____ emphasize the duration of an action or state.
>   Sentence _____ has a general meaning of *lately*.
>
> 2  Cross out the group of words that CANNOT complete this sentence.
>   I've been working out _____.
>
>   a  How often?   *regularly, every day, on and off, twice a week*
>   b  How much?   *a little, a lot, like crazy, more and more*
>   c  Since when?   *since April, for (five) years, lately, recently*
>   d  When?   *three weeks ago, in 2015, yesterday, last year*
>
> 3  Use *since* + a point in time (moment) and *for* + a period of time (duration). Complete with *for* or *since*.
>
>   _____ 90 minutes   _____ yesterday   _____ four years   _____ 6:30 p.m.
>   _____ my whole life   _____ the rest of the day   _____ 2012   _____ June 4th

→ **Grammar 2B** p.140

**Common mistakes**

*have been*
I ~~am~~ walking to work once a week.

*have been studying*
I ~~study~~ English all weekend.

**C** Suzana has also watched *No Impact Man*. Use her notes to make sentences in the present perfect continuous. Which ones have you been doing recently?

|   | PAST | NEW HABITS | SINCE WHEN? |
|---|---|---|---|
| 1  TV | watch a lot | watch far less | she saw the documentary |
| 2  appliances | buy conventional | buy energy-efficient | lately |
| 3  disposable products | use lots | try to avoid | past few months |
| 4  car | use every day | walk to work | April |
| 5  household waste | throw away | kids recycle | last two weeks |
| 6  eco-friendly products | buy a few | husband buy lots | some time now |

1  She used to watch a lot of TV, but she's been watching far less TV since she saw the documentary.

## 4 Pronunciation

**A** ▶2.6 Listen and copy the reduced form of *have / has*, the weak form of *been*, the stress, and the intonation.

           /əv/      /bɪn/                              /əz/     /bɪn/
1  How long have you been living in this city?   2  How long has she been trying to go green?

**B** ▶2.7 Listen to a friend giving you news. Pause after the "beep" and ask a *how long* question using the reduced form of *have* and *has*. Then listen to check.

*Guess what! I go to the gym twice a week now.*

**C** **Make it personal**  In pairs, use these verbs to interview each other. Ask at least two questions for each verb. Any surprising answers?

*Really? How long have you been going there?*

| collect | drive | go | live | play | read | study | swim | watch | work |

*Are you reading anything now?*   *Yeah, I'm reading a graded reader.*   *How long have you been reading it?*

## 3 Grammar  Present perfect continuous

**A** **Books closed**. Read sentence 1, *Al probably has a gym membership*, and ask sts whether it is true or false. Do the same for sentences 2–3. Then, reveal that all the sentences are true.

**Books open**. Point to sentences 1–3 and ask sts to find and underline evidence for each statement in the text in **2A**. Paircheck. Classcheck by writing the answers on the board.

1 I've been working out like crazy every day (lines 2–3)
2 I've been walking to work at least twice a week (line 10)
3 which I've only been driving since Monday! (lines 13–14)

**B** Invite sts to work collaboratively to find out rules for themselves. Have sts complete item 1 in pairs. Classcheck. Point to the sentences on the board (see the answer key to **A**) and ask sts: *How would you classify these sentences?*

**Common mistakes**  Read with the whole class. Have sts go over item 2 and cross out option a, b, c, or d. Classcheck.

1 Sentences b and c emphasize the duration of an action or state. Sentence a has a general meaning of lately.
2 group d
3 for: 90 minutes, four years, my whole life, the rest of the day
   since: yesterday, 6:30 p.m., 2012, June 4th

**Language tip**  Romance language speakers can have trouble mastering the present perfect continuous, because they do not use the same structure as commonly in their L1. In Portuguese and Spanish, it's much more common to use the simple present, or present continuous. For example, the equivalent to *I've been studying here for three years* would be *I study English for three years* or *I am studying English for three years*. After activity **3B**, make sure sts understand that the present perfect continuous is much more commonly used in English than it is in their L1.

➡ **Grammar 2B** page 140

**C** Point to the woman in the photo and say: *Suzana's also seen the video No Impact Man and is now trying to go green*. Draw sts' attention to the prompts, and read example 1 with the whole class. Help sts write sentence 2 with the prompts given. Remind sts that they should use *used to* with an infinitive (without *to*) to talk about habits in the past, but that they should use the present perfect continuous to talk about Suzana's new habits. Paircheck. Classcheck.

1 She used to watch a lot of TV, but she's been watching far less TV since she saw the documentary.
2 She used to buy conventional appliances, but she's been buying energy-efficient ones / appliances lately.
3 She used to use lots of disposable products, but she's been trying to avoid them for the past few months.
4 She used to use her car every day, but she's been walking to work since April.
5 She used to throw away household waste, but her kids have been recycling it for the last two weeks.
6 She used to buy a few eco-friendly products, but her husband has been buying lots of them for some time now.

## 4 Pronunciation

**A** Point to sentence 1 and say: *Listen to this question and notice how the verb **have** is pronounced*. Play ▶ 2.6 and pause after the first question. Replay the track if necessary. Say: *Now listen to sentence 2. How do we pronounce **has** in this case?* Play the rest of ▶ 2.6. Classcheck.

Replay ▶ 2.6 for choral and individual repetitions. Monitor closely to ensure that sts produce weak forms of *have / has*.

**B** Point to the speech bubbles and say: *Listen and read*. Play ▶ 2.7 and pause after the first question. Play the prompt, *I live near the park now*, and pause the track. Say or elicit the question starter *Really? How long ...* and allow sts time to come up with the full question themselves. Correct any mistakes on the spot and encourage good pronunciation—reduced forms of *have / has*, connected speech, and falling intonation, as practiced in **A**. Follow the same procedure for the remaining items.

▶ 2.7  Turn to page 311 for the complete audioscript.

1 Really? How long have you been going there?
2 Really? How long have you been living there?
3 Really? How long has she been going out with him?
4 Really? How long has he been learning that?
5 Really? How long has he been playing it?

**C** **Make it personal**  Have two volunteers read the model dialogue in the speech bubbles. Then model the activity yourself by asking a student: *Do you drive?* If yes, ask: *How long have you been driving?* Ask another student: *How long have you been living in (city)?*

Invite a volunteer to ask you a question with one of the verbs from the box, e.g. *How long have you been working as a teacher?*

Have pairs of sts take turns asking and answering *How long have you been ...?* questions with the verbs provided. Monitor closely for accuracy and pronunciation. At the end, progress to an open pair activity; that is, have two sts at a time (preferably not two sitting together) ask and answer a question while the rest of the group listens.

➡ **Workbook**  Page 10

## 2.3 How has the climate been changing?

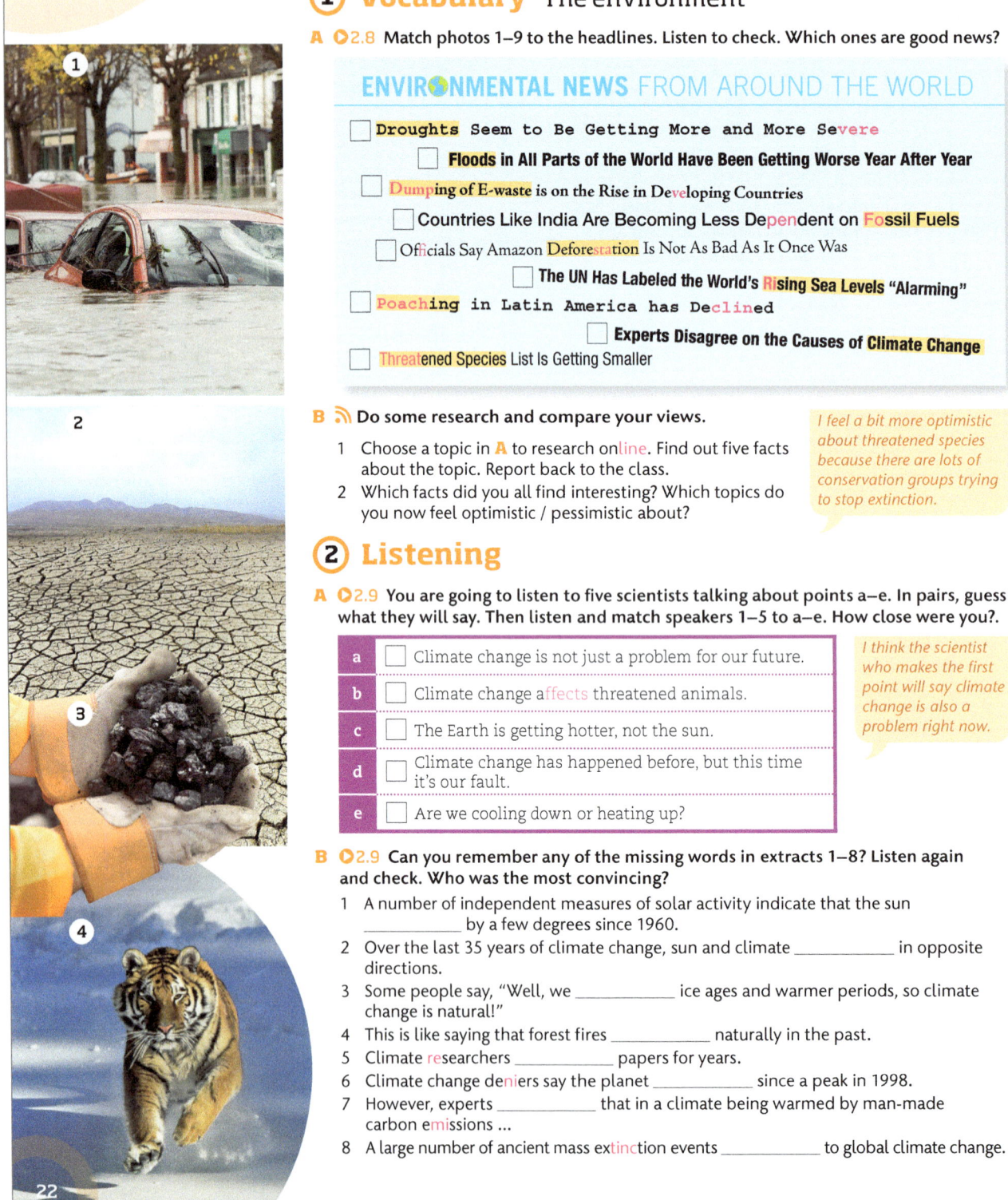

### 1 Vocabulary  The environment

**A** ▶2.8 Match photos 1–9 to the headlines. Listen to check. Which ones are good news?

**ENVIRONMENTAL NEWS FROM AROUND THE WORLD**

- ☐ Droughts Seem to Be Getting More and More Severe
- ☐ Floods in All Parts of the World Have Been Getting Worse Year After Year
- ☐ Dumping of E-waste is on the Rise in Developing Countries
- ☐ Countries Like India Are Becoming Less Dependent on Fossil Fuels
- ☐ Officials Say Amazon Deforestation Is Not As Bad As It Once Was
- ☐ The UN Has Labeled the World's Rising Sea Levels "Alarming"
- ☐ Poaching in Latin America has Declined
- ☐ Experts Disagree on the Causes of Climate Change
- ☐ Threatened Species List Is Getting Smaller

**B** 🔊 Do some research and compare your views.

1. Choose a topic in **A** to research online. Find out five facts about the topic. Report back to the class.
2. Which facts did you all find interesting? Which topics do you now feel optimistic / pessimistic about?

> *I feel a bit more optimistic about threatened species because there are lots of conservation groups trying to stop extinction.*

### 2 Listening

**A** ▶2.9 You are going to listen to five scientists talking about points a–e. In pairs, guess what they will say. Then listen and match speakers 1–5 to a–e. How close were you?.

| a | ☐ Climate change is not just a problem for our future. |
|---|---|
| b | ☐ Climate change affects threatened animals. |
| c | ☐ The Earth is getting hotter, not the sun. |
| d | ☐ Climate change has happened before, but this time it's our fault. |
| e | ☐ Are we cooling down or heating up? |

> *I think the scientist who makes the first point will say climate change is also a problem right now.*

**B** ▶2.9 Can you remember any of the missing words in extracts 1–8? Listen again and check. Who was the most convincing?

1. A number of independent measures of solar activity indicate that the sun _____ by a few degrees since 1960.
2. Over the last 35 years of climate change, sun and climate _____ in opposite directions.
3. Some people say, "Well, we _____ ice ages and warmer periods, so climate change is natural!"
4. This is like saying that forest fires _____ naturally in the past.
5. Climate researchers _____ papers for years.
6. Climate change deniers say the planet _____ since a peak in 1998.
7. However, experts _____ that in a climate being warmed by man-made carbon emissions …
8. A large number of ancient mass extinction events _____ to global climate change.

## 2.3 How has the climate been changing?

**Lesson Aims:** Sts study and practice present perfect vs. present perfect continuous through the context of climate change and natural disasters.

### Function
Reading / Listening to newspaper headlines.
Talking about climate change and natural disasters.
Listening to five people talking about climate change.
Talking about local natural disasters and problems.

### Language
Floods in all parts of the world have been getting worse year after year.
Climate change deniers say the planet has been cooling down since a peak in 1998.
The earth has been getting warmer since 1998.
Although the world has lost 8% of the Amazon Rain Forest, the rate of deforestation seems to be slowing.

**Vocabulary:** The environment (climate change, deforestation, droughts, dumping, floods, fossil fuels, poaching, rising sea levels, threatened).
**Grammar:** Present perfect simple vs. present perfect continuous
**Before the lesson:** Write these verbs / expressions on the board: *live, work, drive, study English, eat fast food, do exercises, read.*

♪ Turn to p. 326 for notes about this song and an accompanying task.

**Warm-up Books closed.** Have sts review and practice the present perfect continuous with an activity similar to **4C** on p. 21, but with books closed this time. Point out the words on the board (see *Before the lesson*) and tell sts they will be asking questions with these words.

Model the activity by asking a student: *Where do you live?* Then ask: *How long have you been living in (neighborhood / city)?* Have another student ask you a question. Explain that sts first need to ask about present habits, e.g. *Do you drive?* or *Are you reading anything at the moment?*, before they ask *How long have you been …?* Monitor closely and take notes for delayed correction.

### 1 Vocabulary  The Environment

**A** Draw sts' attention to the title of the lesson and say: *How has our weather been changing? What do your parents / grandparents say? Have you heard any good news about the weather recently?* Point to photo 1 (floods) and ask: *Do you think floods are caused by climate change?* Have sts repeat the word *floods* after you. Point to photo 9 (poaching) and ask: *Is poaching a problem in (your country)?*

**Books open.** Have sts look at the headlines and match them to photos 1–9. Paircheck. Play ▶ 2.8 so sts can check their answers. Classcheck.

> 2 (droughts), 1 (flood), 7 (dumping of e-waste), 3 (fossil fuels), 6 (deforestation), 8 (rising sea levels), 9 (poaching), 5 (climate change), 4 (threatened species)

Drill pronunciation of the highlighted words. Then ask: *Are there periods of droughts in our country? How severe are they? How long do they last? Where's our e-waste being dumped? Can it be recycled?*

**B 1** Tell sts to choose one of the headlines and use it as a search term on their mobile devices or class computer to find out more information. When they are ready, ask sts to report back what they found out to the class.

> Possible facts for drought:
> Drought is often caused by weather patterns. However, human activity can also be a cause. Deforestation, excessive irrigation, erosion, farming, and climate change are all human causes.

**2** Read the example opinion with the class and ask: *Do you agree? Why (not)?* Sts then discuss the questions in pairs. If time allows, open up the discussion to the whole class.

### 2 Listening

**A** Tell sts they are going to hear five scientists talking about climate change. In pairs, ask sts to predict what the scientists will say. Classcheck but don't confirm answers at this stage. Ask sts to listen and match the speakers to the sentences. Play ▶ 2.9. Paircheck. Classcheck.

▶ 2.9 Turn to page 311 for the complete audioscript.

> a 3  b 5  c 1  d 2  e 4

**B** Direct sts' attention to the first sentence and say: *Can you remember the missing words?* Elicit sts' ideas then give sts time to look at the rest of the sentences and try to remember the missing words. Play ▶ 2.9. Peercheck, then classcheck.

> | 1 | has cooled | 5 | have been publishing |
> |---|---|---|---|
> | 2 | have been moving | 6 | has been cooling down |
> | 3 | 've had | 7 | have shown |
> | 4 | have happened | 8 | have been linked |

**Weaker classes** You may need to give sts the infinitive form of the verbs for them to choose from.

## 2.3

*Everything is changing, And I've been here for too long. Going through the same things, I've been hurting too long.*

### 3 Grammar  Present perfect simple vs. Present perfect continuous

**A** Read sentence pairs a–c and match them to uses 1–3 in the grammar box.
  a  The earth has gotten warmer before.
     The earth has been getting warmer since 1998.
  b  Tigers have lived in India for two million years.
     Tigers have been living in India for two million years.
  c  In the last century, sea levels have risen by 10–20 cm.
     Sea levels have been rising over the last century.

> You can often use the *present perfect simple* or *present perfect continuous* interchangeably.
> Generally use the *present perfect continuous* to emphasize duration.
> Don't use the *present perfect continuous* with stative verbs.
> The *present perfect simple* emphasizes completion.

|   | Present perfect | Present perfect continuous |
|---|---|---|
| 1 | No difference | No difference |
| 2 | Completed action | Process happening now |
| 3 | How much / many? | Emphasis on how long |

➔ **Grammar 2C** p.140

**⚠ Common mistakes**

~~The problem *is getting* worse since 2010.~~ has been
~~We've been knowing about climate change for ages.~~ known

**B** Read the environmental news below and circle the correct verb tenses. Sometimes both options are possible.

New York's ¹**announced / been announcing** a plan to use human waste for renewable energy.

Scientists from Ohio University have ² **found / been finding** a way to produce hydrogen from urine.

In the past few years, the auto industry has ³ **looked / been looking** into several different ways to produce vehicles that are less dependent on fossil fuels.

The European Union has ⁴ **tried / been trying** hard to meet the goal of at least a 27% improvement in energy efficiency by 2030.

Despite poaching and a recent drought, Kenya's elephant population has ⁵ **increased / been increasing** year after year. It has ⁶ **increased / been increasing** by nearly 10% in the past three years.

Although the world has ⁷ **lost / been losing** 18% of the Amazon Rainforest, the rate of deforestation seems to be slowing.

**C** 🔵 **Make it personal**  In pairs, look back at **1A**. For each photo, answer 1–3. Compare your ideas with other pairs. Do they agree / disagree with you?
  1  Is this a major problem in your country / city?
  2  Has this problem recently gotten better or worse? How?
  3  Who's to blame for this, and why? What have they (not) done or (not) been doing?

> *Floods are a real problem in São Paulo.*
> *And it's gotten worse recently.*

**D** ▶ 2.10  🔵 **Make it personal**  **Dictation**. Write the five questions you hear. In pairs, answer them. Any similarities?

> *I've known my best friend for 15 years. We met in kindergarten!*

58

## 3 Grammar Present perfect simple vs. Present perfect continuous

**A** Have sts read the first pair of sentences. Write them on the board and ask: *Which one is in the present perfect continuous? What about the other one?*

**Common mistakes** Read the three rules in the grammar box with the whole group and refer sts to the examples showing that the present perfect and the present perfect continuous cannot always be used interchangeably. Highlight the use of *since* and emphasize that state verbs (e.g. *know*) are not used in continuous tenses.

Have sts match pairs of sentences a–c to grammar uses 1–3. Paircheck. Classcheck.

a 2   b 1   c 3

**Language tip** Portuguese and Spanish L1 speakers tend to have difficulty understanding that state verbs are not used in continuous tenses in English as they are used in their own languages. In order to reinforce this, after activity **3A**, write a few sentences on the board using the present perfect continuous wrongly with state verbs and have sts correct them to the present perfect simple. For example: ~~We've been liking~~ this TV series since it started years ago. ~~She's been knowing~~ about this issue for months. ~~I've been~~ better ~~understanding~~ the topic recently.

→ **Grammar 2C** page 140

**B** Point to the newspaper clippings and say: *Look at all this news about the environment. What are the main topics?* Allow sts to read briefly and then list the key points (renewable energy, poaching, deforestation). Point to the first story and elicit the correct answer. Have sts read each clipping and circle the correct verb tenses. Classcheck.

1 announced
2 found
3 looked / been looking
4 been trying
5 been increasing / increased
6 increased
7 lost

**C** **Make it personal** Direct sts back to the photos from **1A** and ask: *Can you remember what each photo shows?* Classcheck. Point to the questions and read the example with the class. Put sts in pairs to discuss the questions. Then join pairs together to find out if other sts agree. Classcheck.

**D** **Make it personal** Tell sts they are going to hear five questions. Say: *We are going to do a dictation. Write down the five questions you hear.* Play ▶ 2.10. Replay the recording if necessary. Classcheck by writing the answers on the board.

Have sts change partners and take turns asking and answering the questions. Monitor sts' work closely and take notes for delayed correction. Classcheck.

1 How long have you been living here?
2 Have you been studying English for long?
3 How long have you known your best friend?
4 Have you had a lot of work to do recently?
5 Have you been watching any good TV series recently?

→ **Workbook** Page 11

# 2.4 What's the best ad you've seen recently?

## 1 Reading

**A** Do you believe most ads you see? Why (not)? Read the pop-ups quickly. Which promise(s) do you find hard to believe?

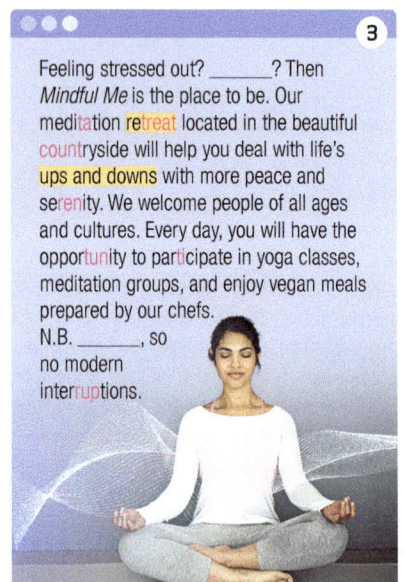

**1**

Thinking of upgrading your phone? _____? With the new, gorgeous green Sun 360, you get all the features you love: an ultrafast processor, powerful 12 MP camera, and an internal solar panel that allows up to eight hours of heavy, uninterrupted usage. Sun 360 produces the greenest cell phone on the market by using recycled materials. All of this, and it will still fit into your pocket! Introductory price—$259. _____

**2**

_____? Try Moringa Miracle Powder—the Moringa plant is a superfood believed to be one of the most nutritious foods on our planet. The leaves are packed with at least 92 different nutrients, vitamins, and minerals for good health. Just add our Miracle Powder to tea, soups, and smoothies, and start experiencing the benefits immediately.

**3**

Feeling stressed out? _____? Then *Mindful Me* is the place to be. Our meditation retreat located in the beautiful countryside will help you deal with life's ups and downs with more peace and serenity. We welcome people of all ages and cultures. Every day, you will have the opportunity to participate in yoga classes, meditation groups, and enjoy vegan meals prepared by our chefs. N.B. _____, so no modern interruptions.

**B** ▶ 2.11 Reread and complete the ads with 1–5. Listen to check. Practice the pink-stressed words.
1. Need some time out
2. Tired of batteries that won't last
3. Not looking your best
4. No cell phones or tablets allowed
5. Offer limited to one unit per customer

> **Common mistake**
> least like
> The one I'd ~~like least~~ to try is X.

**C** Read the information in the box and find eight examples of grammatical omission in the completed ads in **A**.

> To be shorter, friendlier, and sound more exciting, ads often omit articles, auxiliary verbs, or subjects.
> • (The) offer (is) only available in (the) U.S.
> • (Our Hybrid car is) greener than you thought.

*I'd never try the Moringa stuff. I don't believe in all these "superfoods"!*

*Hmm ... I'd most like to try the retreat. I need a rest.*

**D** Order ads 1–3 from *I'd most* to *I'd least* like to try.

## 2 Listening

**A** ▶ 2.12 Listen to the beginning of three conversations at a party. Which product in **1A** did each person buy?

**B** ▶ 2.13 Listen to the rest of the conversations. How many are satisfied customers?

*I went to a retreat in India where you couldn't speak for 10 days!*

**C** ▶ 2.14 True (T) or false (F)? Listen to check. Know any similar stories?
1. Beth has been on vacation.
2. Lorna doesn't believe in "superfoods".
3. Pedro's new cell phone battery dies after 90 minutes.
4. Pedro liked his old phone better.
5. Bruce left his old job because of the pay.
6. Bruce spent about a month away from New York City.

24

# 2.4 What's the best ad you've seen recently?

**Lesson Aims:** Sts continue to practice the present perfect continuous in the context of advertisements. They also use and compare simple past vs. present perfect and present perfect continuous.

### Function
Reading ads and inferring the meaning of new expressions.
Listening to (dis)satisfied customers.
Retelling stories.
Role-playing interviews with dissatisfied customers.
Interviewing a friend on different topics.

### Language
I worked there for over ten years, but ... I just couldn't handle the stress.
How long have you been learning Chinese online?
How has it affected your health?

**Vocabulary:** Retreat, up to, at least, life's ups and downs.
**Grammar:** Simple past vs. present perfect simple / continuous.
**Before the lesson:** Write the following prompts on the board:
A ... ever ... travel by plane?   Where ... fly to?   When ... go there?
B ... ever ... watch (name of a movie)?   Who ... watch it with?   When ... you watch it?

♪ Turn to p. 326 for notes about this song and an accompanying task.

**Warm-up** Review *Have you ever ...?* and simple past questions using the prompts on the board. Elicit questions from the prompts. Drill pronunciation. Sts then take turns interviewing their group members using the questions.

## 1 Reading

**A** Ask the whole class: *Do you believe things that adverts say? Why (not)?* Explore what sts can see in the photos (you may find it useful to have a photo of a moringa plant to check the meaning of leaf / leaves) and then have sts read the ads quickly to answer the question. Ask the whole group: *Which promise(s) do you find hard to believe? Why?*

> **Language tip** Before doing activity **1A**, remind Romance-speaking sts of the power of identifying cognates in texts. Explain that in the ads that they are about to read, there are a lot of cognates that can help them better understand the texts.

**B** Sts look at 1–5 and fill in the blanks. Then, play ▶2.11 to check. Paircheck. Classcheck.

> 1 Tired of batteries that won't last; Offer limited to one unit per customer
> 2 Not looking your best
> 3 Need some time out; No cell phones or tablets allowed

**C** Read the information in the box with sts. Elicit the first answer *(Are you) Thinking of upgrading your phone?*, then ask sts to find the remaining examples of grammatical omission. Paircheck. Classcheck.

> The five items from **B** & Thinking of upgrading your phone? Try Moringa Miracle powder ... Feeling stressed out?

**D** 🔥 **Common mistake**   Read through with sts and draw their attention to the correct word order and the model language in the speech bubbles. Sts order the products according to which they would most / least like to try. Classcheck and then tell sts which one you'd most and least like to try yourself.

## 2 Listening

**A** Play conversation 1 in ▶2.12 and then pause the track. Ask: *Which ad are they talking about?* (2) Say: *Now let's listen to conversations 2 and 3 and match them to the correct ads in* **A**. Resume ▶2.12. Paircheck. Classcheck.

▶2.12 Turn to page 312 for the complete audioscript.

> 1 Moringa miracle power   2 phone   3 meditation retreat

**B** Ask the whole group: *How many customers were satisfied?* Listen to the second half of the conversations and check. Play ▶2.13. Classcheck.

▶2.13 Turn to page 312 for the complete audioscript.

> 1 satisfied   2 dissatisfied   2 dissatisfied

> **Tip** Have sts turn to the AS on p. 162. Sts listen again and do the noticing tasks.

**C** Tell pairs to guess or decide from memory whether sentences 1–6 are true (T) or false (F). Play ▶2.14 for the full conversations. Classcheck.

> 1 F (She's been taking a superfood.)   2 T
> 3 F (It dies after an hour.)   4 T
> 5 F (He left because of the stress.)
> 6 F (He spent a month away from Chicago.)

## 3 Grammar  Simple past vs. Present perfect simple / continuous

*How long has this been going on?
You've been acting so shady,
I've been feeling it lately.*

**A** ▶ 2.15 Complete 1–6, and then listen to check. In pairs, remember all you can about each story.

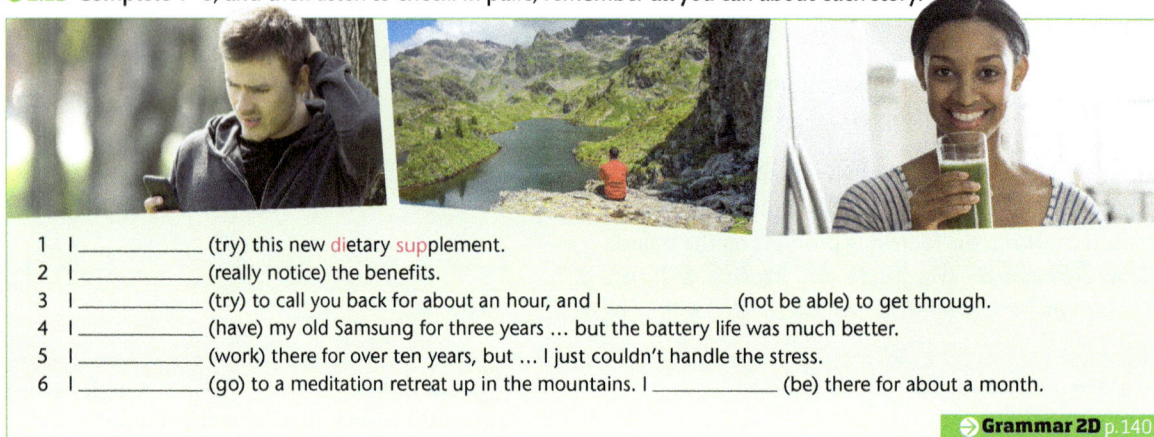

1  I _____ (try) this new dietary supplement.
2  I _____ (really notice) the benefits.
3  I _____ (try) to call you back for about an hour, and I _____ (not be able) to get through.
4  I _____ (have) my old Samsung for three years … but the battery life was much better.
5  I _____ (work) there for over ten years, but … I just couldn't handle the stress.
6  I _____ (go) to a meditation retreat up in the mountains. I _____ (be) there for about a month.

→ **Grammar 2D** p.140

*She's been trying a new superfood. It's made her feel much better.*

**B** ▶ 2.16 Form questions to ask the people in **A**. Listen to check.
How do you think they would reply?
1  you / got / a new phone / yet?
2  you / look for / a new job?
3  try / yoga / at the retreat?
4  how long / you / take / this supplement?
5  how / it / affect / your health?

**C** Read the pop-ups. Imagine you were tempted. In pairs, role-play a conversation about each one. Record the best one.

**Common mistakes**

                       lasted
James Dean's career has ~~lasted~~ less than a decade.

           had
I've ~~been having~~ this new tablet since March. I love it!

How            have you had
~~For how long do you have~~ that smart watch?

**LEARN CHINESE IN 6 MONTHS!**
Two hours a week, very little homework.
Learn in your sleep! First month free of charge.

Tired of dogs, cats, birds, and goldfish?
Maybe what you need is a **pet alligator!**
3000 happy owners can't be wrong. Come and choose yours today!
24-hour helpline: (555) 013-2689.

*How much Chinese have you learned? When did you start?*

*Have you bought a baby alligator?*

**D** **Make it personal** In pairs, choose a topic and interview each other. Report back with anything interesting you found out.

a collection    an artist, band, or TV show you love
follow your favorite sport    a get-rich-quick plan
something you're trying to learn    a recent change in your life

*I collect old vinyl pop records.*

*No way! How long have you been collecting them?*

*Well, it all started when …*

## 2.4

### 3 Grammar Simple past vs. Present perfect simple / continuous

**A** Focus on the photos of Pedro, Bruce, and Beth and ask the class: *Do you remember what problem each of these people has?* Draw sts' attention to blanks 1–6. Explain that sts will need to fill in the blanks using simple past, present perfect, or present perfect continuous. Sts should fill in blanks 1–6 with the correct verb tense. Paircheck. Play ▶ 2.15 so sts can check their answers.

> 1 've been trying   2 've really noticed
> 3 've been trying, haven't been able
> 4 had   5 worked   6 went, was

Pair sts up and have partners take turns retelling what happened to each customer, adding all details they remember from the stories. Closely monitor sts' stories and offer help as necessary. Classcheck by having three different sts retell one story each.

→ **Grammar 2D** page 140

**Common mistakes** Read through with the whole class. Elicit why the tense is wrong in each case. Encourage sts to refer back to previous grammar boxes in this unit where necessary.

**B** Elicit question 1 from sts. Sts write questions 1–5 using the correct verb tenses. Play ▶ 2.16 to classcheck. Have sts take turns asking and answering questions 1–5 in pairs. Monitor closely for accuracy. Classcheck by having sts report their partners' answers to the whole class.

> 1 Have you got a new phone yet?
> 2 Have you been looking for a new job?
> 3 Did you try yoga at the retreat?
> 4 How long have you been taking this supplement?
> 5 How has it affected your health?

**Stronger classes** Extend the task by asking sts to think of any more questions they would like to ask.

**C** Focus sts' attention on the pop-ups. Say: *Do either of these interest you? Why (not)?* Assign new pairs and explain that sts are going to role play two interviews, with student **A** playing someone interested in the Chinese course and student **B** playing someone interested in a pet alligator. Refer them to the prompts in the box and elicit some of the questions sts will need to interview each other.

Monitor closely and offer help whenever necessary. Then, ask sts to record one of the interviews on their cell phones or other recording device, if available. Allow sts time to listen to themselves. Then, invite volunteers to play their recorded interviews for the class.

**D** **Make it personal** Explain that sts are going to interview each other on one of the topics from the box. Sts may choose the topic about which they would like to be interviewed. Allow sts some thinking time to plan their questions and even jot down some notes before they actually start the activity.

Have sts work in pairs to interview each other using questions from this lesson, especially questions with present perfect continuous, present perfect, and simple past. Take notes while you monitor their work. At the end, provide sts with language feedback and have them report some of their partners' answers.

→ **Workbook** Page 12

## 2.5 Do you support any charities?

**ID Skills** Expressing numerical information

**A** 🔘 **Make it personal** In groups, answer 1–3. Share your answers with the class.
1 Find the animals' names in the chart. Which of them have you seen, either in the wild, in a zoo, or stuffed in a museum? What do you know about them?
2 Give three reasons why some species are more vulnerable to extinction than others.
3 Suggest two ways to help people care more about threatened species.

**B** ▶ 2.17 How many of these animals do you think might be left in the wild? Listen and fill in the middle column in the report. Anything shocking or surprising?

> I can't believe there are only about 800 gorillas left!

### Species we may never see again

| | Origin / Habitat | Number left in the wild | Other info |
|---|---|---|---|
| Giant panda | | fewer than ____ | |
| Monk seal | Islands of Hawaii | fewer than ____ | |
| Golden lion tamarin | | around ____ | |
| Mountain gorilla | | about 800 | discovered 120 years ago |
| North Atlantic right whale | | fewer than ____ | |
| Javanese rhino | | approximately ____ | |
| Ivory-billed woodpecker | | maybe ____ | |

**C** ▶ 2.17 Can you remember any other information to complete the report? Listen again and fill in the other columns where possible.

**D** You are going to watch a video about threatened species. Before you watch, in pairs, circle the alternatives you think are correct.

> We are living in the age of the ¹ **fifth / sixth** mass global extinction. Experts warn that within the next ² **30 / 50** years, we'll lose ³ **20% / 10%** of the entire species on the planet. And if trends continue, we'll lose ⁴ **a third / half** of our species in the next ⁵ **100 / 200** years. ⁶ **15% / 25%** of our mammal species are at risk of dying out in the wild.

**E** ▶ 2.18 ▶ Listen / Watch to check. How does this extract make you feel? Why?

> It makes me want to do something.

> Me, too. I think it's actually worse. I heard recently we've lost more than half the world's wildlife since 1970!

## 2.5 Do you support any charities?

**Lesson Aims:** Sts learn to express numerical information in the context of threatened species.

**Function**
Listening to a report on threatened species.
Watching / Listening to a video about animal extinction.

**Language**
How many giant pandas are left in the wild? Fewer than 2,000.
Twenty-five percent of our mammal species are at risk.

**Vocabulary:** Endangered species (extinction, golden lion tamarin, rhino, seal, vulnerable, whale, woodpecker). Expressing numerical information (a third, about … , approximately, around … , fewer than, half (of), maybe).
**Skill:** Expressing numerical information.

♪ Turn to p. 326 for notes about this song and an accompanying task.

**Warm-up** For a high-energy start, and more pronunciation and grammar practice, begin the class with rousing drills. Follow the model below. Alternate from individual to choral repetition.

T *Eat less recently. I've been eating less recently. Repeat.*
Sts *I've been eating less recently.*
T *Work out more for the past two weeks. I've been working out more for the past two weeks. Repeat.*
Sts *I've been working out more for the past two weeks.*
T *Now you. Avoid sugar—for the past few months.*
Sts *I've been avoiding sugar for the past few months.*

## ID Skills  Expressing numerical information

**A** Make it personal  Books open. Explore the photos with sts and ask which animals they can name. Refer sts to the names in the chart to help them and ask questions such as: *Where in the world can we see giant pandas?* Put sts into small groups and ask them to discuss the questions. Peercheck. Classcheck.

> 2 Suggested answers: Because of hunting, habitat destruction, and pollution
> 3 Suggested answers: Education, campaigns on TV, and in social media

**B** Ask: *How many of these animals do you think might be left in the wild?* Say that they're going to listen to a report on these animals. Point to the middle column and say: *Listen and complete this column with the numbers you hear.* Play ▶ 2.17. Peercheck, then classcheck and ask if there's anything shocking or surprising.

▶ 2.17 Turn to page 312 for the complete audioscript.

> Giant panda: fewer than 2,000
> The Hawaiian monk seal: fewer than 1,000
> Golden lion tamarin: around 3,000
> Mountain gorilla: about 800
> North Atlantic right whale: fewer than 400
> Javanese rhino: approximately 60
> Ivory-billed woodpecker: possibly none

**Tip** Drill and write the model question on the board: *How many giant pandas are left in the wild?* Elicit the answer (fewer than 2,000). Say the prompt: *Mountain gorillas.* Elicit the question: *How many mountain gorillas are left in the wild?* and the answer (about 800).

**C** Ask: *What other information can you remember from the report?* Give sts a minute or two in pairs to discuss what they can remember. Play ▶ 2.17 again for sts to complete the rest of the chart. Peercheck. Classcheck.

**Tip** Have sts turn to the AS on p. 164. Sts listen again and notice the silent /r/.

> Giant panda – Habitat: bamboo forests of China
> Other info: only 300 pandas in zoos
> Monk seal – Habitat: ocean around the islands of Hawaii
> Golden lion tamarin – Habitat: Atlantic forests of Brazil
> Other info: used to be only 200 in 1980
> Mountain gorilla – Habitat: African mountains
> Other info: under threat from poaching, war and deforestation
> North Atlantic right whale – Habitat: the Atlantic coast of North America
> Other info: have been protected from hunting for 70 years
> Javanese rhino – Habitat: Ujung Kulon National Park, Indonesia
> Other info: killed to make medicine
> Ivory-billed woodpeckers – Habitat: forests of the southeastern United States
> Other info: died out due to loss of habitat

**D** Tell sts they're going to listen to / watch a video about threatened species. Have sts work in pairs to guess the answers, circling the best options. Don't check answers yet.

**E** Play ▶ 2.18 ▶ so sts can check their answers. Classcheck.

> 1 sixth   2 30   3 20% (i.e. one fifth)
> 4 half (i.e. 50%)   5 100   6 25% (i.e. one quarter)

Ask the class: *How does this information make you feel? Can we do anything about it?*

# Have you made any lifestyle changes recently?

## ID in Action  Encouraging and discouraging

**A** Before watching the rest of the video, in pairs, brainstorm five ways to raise awareness of threatened species and change people's behavior.

*We should all be taught more about it at school.*

**B** ▶ 2.19  Read five extracts from the video. Then listen / watch and number them 1–5 in the order you hear them.
- ☐ Showing the loss of animals in faraway places may pull a few heartstrings …
- ☐ … the single most important factor behind taking action is our childhood experience.
- ☐ It's not the depressing accounts of the wildlife we are losing that moves us. It's awe and wonder …
- ☐ Have we forgotten what first inspired our love of nature?
- ☐ In all parts of the world, we're beginning to see that public awareness does lead to change.

**Common mistakes**
*There are almost no / There are hardly any*
~~Almost no~~ have pandas.
*I love ~~the~~ nature, ~~the~~ animals, and ~~all the~~ wildlife.*

*I disagree. Remembering what we've lost makes us more determined to …*

**C** Choose the best summary of the video, 1–3. Do you agree with them all? Why (not)?
1. Developing a love of nature is more important than thinking about what we have already lost.
2. Children need to be encouraged to spend more time in nature.
3. Showing images of species we have lost increases donations to animal charities.

**D** ▶ 2.20  Listen to five people explaining how they're going to help threatened species. Match each speaker 1–5 to these actions. There's one extra.
- ☐ Collect for charity
- ☐ Raise awareness online
- ☐ Reduce waste
- ☐ Sponsor an animal
- ☐ Use an environment-friendly product
- ☐ Volunteer at an animal shelter

**E** ▶ 2.20  Listen again. Are the speakers' friends encouraging 😊 or discouraging 😞?
1 ____  2 ____  3 ____  4 ____  5 ____

**F** ▶ 2.20  Listen again and complete the expressions for expressing encouragement and discouragement. Write three words in each blank.

| 😞 Why ¹_____ to (adopt a whale)? | 😊 Wow, you are determined! ⁴_____. |
| 😞 What is ²_____ (spending money on) …? | 😞 What's ⁵_____ (buying that)? |
| 😊 Keep up ³_____. | 😊 Every time? ⁶_____! |

**G** ⬤ **Make it personal**  Are you improving your lifestyle?
1. List three things (real or imaginary) that you have or haven't been doing, to improve your lifestyle.
2. In groups, take turns telling each other what you have or haven't been doing. Ask extra questions and use the expressions in **F** to encourage or discourage.
3. Share the most imaginative changes from your groups with the class. Which group is / has been making the most changes?

*I haven't been studying much outside class recently.*

*Don't give up. What's the point of paying for classes if you don't do homework?*

♪ *I got the eye of the tiger, a fighter*
*Dancing through the fire, 'Cause I am a champion*

# 2.5 Have you made any lifestyle changes recently?

**Lesson Aims:** Sts continue to practice the present perfect simple / continuous in the context of raising awareness of threatened species and making lifestyle changes. They also learn expressions to encourage or discourage new ideas.

### Function
Talking about recent changes in your lifestyle.

### Language
Way to go, Janet. What's the use of buying an electric car?
I've been trying not to eat too much.

**Vocabulary:** Endangered species (extinction, golden lion tamarin, rhino, seal, vulnerable, whale, woodpecker). Expressing numerical information (a third, about … , approximately, around …, fewer than, half (of), maybe).

**Skills:** Encouraging and discouraging.

## ID in Action  Encouraging and discouraging

**A** Tell sts that they are going to listen to / watch the rest of the video. Ask: *What do you think are the best ways to change people's behavior?*

🔥 **Common mistakes**  Read through with sts. Read the model language in the speech bubble, then assign pairs for sts to discuss. Classcheck.

**B** Have sts read the five extracts, then say: *Listen to / watch the rest of the video and number the sentences in the order you hear them.* Play ▶ 2.19 ▶. Paircheck. Classcheck.

🔑
3, 2, 5, 1, 4

▶ **2.19** Turn to page 312 for the complete audioscript.

**C** Give sts a minute to read the summaries then assign pairs to discuss which is the best summary. Classcheck.

🔑
1

**D** Tell sts they are going to listen to five people who have decided to take action to help threatened species. Ask sts to listen and match the speakers, 1–5 to the actions. There is one extra action. Play ▶ 2.20. Paircheck. Replay the track if necessary and classcheck.

▶ **2.20** Turn to page 312 for the complete audioscript.

🔑
1  Sponsor an animal   2  Raise awareness online
3  Collect for charity   4  Use an environment-friendly product
5  Reduce waste

**E** Tell sts they are going to listen to the conversations again. Say: *You heard people talking to friends about their ideas and actions to help the environment. How did those friends react? Were they positive?* Draw smiley and sad faces on the board and ask sts to draw either one or the other next to conversations 1–5. Replay ▶ 2.20. Paircheck. Classcheck.

🔑
1  discouraging   2  encouraging   3  encouraging
4  discouraging   5  encouraging

**F** Have sts read the discouragement and encouragement phrases in the chart. Play ▶ 2.20 again so sts can listen and complete the chart. Pause after each conversation, to focus sts' attention on the intonation of each sentence. Classcheck. If time allows, have sts turn to the AS on p. 164. Sts listen again and complete the noticing activities.

🔑
1  would you want to   2  the point of   3  the good work
4  Good for you.   5  the use of   6  Way to go!

**Tip** At any time during **ID in Action**, ask sts which animals are endangered in their own country. Have sts look up data about these animals on the Internet and ask: *What can we do to help and avoid extinction of these local endangered animals?* Encourage sts to share ideas of simple things they can put into practice in their cities in order to raise people's awareness about these issues.

**G** 😀 **Make it personal**  1  Divide the class into groups of three. Ask sts to write down three things (real or imaginary) that they have or haven't been doing to change their lifestyles recently. Monitor and offer help if necessary.

2  Within their groups, sts describe what they have or haven't been doing to improve, and partners respond encouragingly or discouragingly, using phrases from **F**.

3  Classcheck by having volunteers tell the class what they have been trying to improve. Encourage sts to respond with encouraging / discouraging phrases.

➡ **Workbook** Page 13

➡ Ⓓ **ID Richmond Learning Platform**

➡ **Writing** p. 28

➡ **ID Café** p. 29

# Writing 2  A report

*Why do I find it hard to write the next line?
Oh, I want the truth to be said,
I know this much is true.*

**A** Read Nina's report and mark ⊕ for the most popular and ⊖ for the least popular practices.
- [ ] using solar energy
- [ ] reusing plastic bags
- [ ] separating waste
- [ ] recycling containers

**To:** Ms. Lang, Geography Teacher
**From:** Nina Diaz
**Subject:** Going Green in the Neighborhood

**Going Green**

1 **Introduction:** The aim of this report is to describe the most and the least popular practices in this neighborhood to help save the environment. It also makes recommendations about what we can do to become greener. The findings are reported below.
2 **The survey:** This survey involved interviewing 30 people from the ages of 18 to 35 by asking them ten questions about popular practices to save the planet. Respondents had to say how often they did these things: always, sometimes, rarely, or never.
3 **Most popular practices:** The survey showed that the two most popular practices to protect the environment in our neighborhood are to recycle bottles, cans, and plastic containers, in addition to separating organic and non-organic household waste.
4 **Least popular practices:** The two least popular practices, according to the questionnaire, were reusing plastic bags, or using cloth bags for shopping, and installing solar heating systems in houses.
5 **Conclusion:** As we can see from this report, people in this neighborhood try to adopt some environmentally friendly practices. However, some simple things could also be done to make a difference to the planet. Therefore, I recommend we organize a campaign to stimulate the use of cloth bags and cardboard boxes for shopping.

**B** The report is divided into five headings. Which heading, 1–5:
- [ ] describes the survey?
- [ ] summarizes and makes suggestions?
- [ ] says why the report is being written?
- [ ] discusses the first point?
- [ ] discusses the second point?

**C** Read *Write it right!* Then mark 1–6 appropriate (A) or inappropriate (I) to include in a report.
1 I think this is a very important topic.
2 This report will present the results of a survey about protecting the environment.
3 In my opinion, respondents enjoyed the survey.
4 That's just great for the environment!
5 To summarize, the main ideas are easy to implement.
6 I also have some bad news!

**Write it right!**
- Begin reports with the names of the recipient and the author, and then the subject.
- Keep to the facts. Use personal opinions only in the conclusion.
- Use paragraphs with headings for each subtopic.
- Use formal language and fixed phrases to organize ideas and add clarity.
- Don't contract and be careful with punctuation.

**D** Mark 1–6 introduction (I), reporting an observation (R), generalizing (G), making a recommendation (M), or summarizing (S).
1 The objective of this report is to present / review …
2 The most / least common answer was …
3 It was found that …
4 In general …
5 This report describes …
6 In conclusion …

**E** Identify and correct four spelling, one punctuation, and two style mistakes in this draft.

This report's based on recent interviews about tourists' expectations in our city. Acording to the people interviewed, our main problem is adequate accomodation. Tourists complained they can't find enough family rooms or rooms with air-conditioning! They also reccomended establishing more tourist information points to provide better information and sugestions for tourists.

**F** **Make it personal** In pairs, choose one of the topics and prepare a five-question survey. Conduct it in class and record the results.

Use of technology for learning English.
Most popular free time activities.

**G** *Your turn!* Write a report in 100–180 words.

| Before | Look at the results from **F**. What are your conclusions? |
|---|---|
| While | Follow the five tips in *Write it right!* |
| After | Ask a classmate to read it and check formality, spelling, and punctuation, then email it to your teacher. |

# Writing 2 A report

♪ Turn to p. 326 for notes about this song and an accompanying task.

**A** **Books closed**. Ask: *What's a report? Why do people usually write reports? In what situations? Have you ever written one at work or school? What was it about?*

**Books open**. Focus sts' attention on Nina's report and ask: *What's her report about? What's the aim of it?* Go over the report's introduction with the whole class. Then, point out the topics above the report. Tell sts to read the topics and mark each one ⊕ (most popular practices) or ⊖ (least popular practices). Paircheck. Classcheck.

> – using solar energy
> – reusing plastic bags
> + separating waste
> + recycling containers

**B** Say: *Nina's report is divided into five parts. What are they?* Have sts identify and name each of the headings in **A**. Point at the five questions and ask: *Which heading describes the survey?* Have sts match each question to the correct heading from 1 to 5. Paircheck. Classcheck.

> 2, 5, 1, 3, 4

**C** Point to sentences 1–6 and say: *These sentences were written by students. Are they appropriate to include in a report?* Draw sts' attention to the tips for writing a report in **Write it right!** on the top right corner of p. 28. Have sts read the tips and mark sentences 1–6 as A (appropriate) or I (inappropriate). Paircheck. Classcheck.

> 1 I   2 A   3 I   4 I   5 A   6 I

**D** Read item 1 with the class and ask: *Which part of the report is this?* Ask sts to read items 1–6 and mark them as I (introduction), R (reporting an observation), G (generalizing), M (making a recommendation), or S (summarizing). Paircheck. Classcheck.

> 1 I   2 S   3 R   4 G   5 I   6 S

**E** Show sts the draft and ask: *What's this report about?* Tell them that there are seven mistakes: four spelling mistakes, two style, and one in punctuation. Instruct sts to find and correct all seven mistakes. Classcheck.

> This report is based on recent interviews about tourists' expectations in our city. According to the people interviewed, our main problem is adequate accommodation. Tourists complained they cannot find enough family rooms or rooms with air-conditioning. They also recommended establishing more tourist information points to provide better information and suggestions for tourists.

**F** 🎧 **Make it personal** Ask sts to work in pairs to prepare five questions for a class survey. Tell pairs to choose one of the topics provided. Monitor sts' work and offer help if necessary. Then, invite sts to stand up and mingle as they use their questions to interview their classmates about the topic they chose. Remind sts to take notes of their classmates' answers, as they will use these to write their reports in **G**.

**G** *Your turn!*

**Before** Working with the same partners as in **F**, sts should gather information and draw a conclusion from their class survey.

**While**
1 Have sts individually write the recipient's name, their own name, and the subject of the report, following the model in **A**.
2 Ask sts to write a first draft and give shape to their reports using the headings from **A** and expressions from **D**. Monitor and offer help at this stage. Then, have sts write their full reports in 100–180 words.

**After** Have sts work in pairs and ask partners to exchange reports and read each other's work to paircheck and spot any mistakes in style, punctuation, grammar, or spelling. Then, ask sts to revise their writing at home and send it to you via email.

# 2 Down to earth

## ID Café

### 1 Before watching

**A** Match the words to the photos. Which have you seen in real life?

- ☐ ja**guar**
- ☐ tamarin **mon**key
- ☐ **lo**gging
- ☐ **tou**can
- ☐ forest **ca**nopy

*None of them except logging, sadly!*

**B** 🟢 **Make it personal** In pairs, think of three ways we can help endangered species.

*I guess we could build more zoos.*

**C** In pairs, describe Daniel. What do you think he might be doing / saying?

*He might be doing an interview about endangered species.*

### 2 While watching

**A** Watch up to 1:30 to check your guesses, and then circle the correct alternative.
1. Daniel's in a **zoo** / **studio**.
2. He's been researching **wildlife** / **global warming**.
3. Daniel **has** / **hasn't** had a lot of pets.
4. He's been taking classes in **environmental science** / **climate change**.
5. He plans to be a **weatherman** / **reporter**.
6. Polar bears have been **dying of hunger** / **drowning in the sea**.
7. Lucy knows little about **endangered species** / **Antarctica**.
8. Daniel's talking about very **contemporary** / **controversial** issues.

**B** Watch from 1:30 to 2:40 and number these items as you hear them, 1–10. What else can you remember him saying?

- ☐ cover
- ☐ difference
- ☐ impact
- ☐ lights
- ☐ logging
- ☐ man**kind**
- ☐ recycling
- ☐ species
- ☐ walk
- ☐ victims

**C** Watch the second part again to check. Then, in pairs, answer 1–4.
1. Where has logging been going on?
2. Who have been **vic**tims of logging?
3. Which actions / things impact negatively on the earth?
4. Which actions make a difference?

**D** Watch from 2:40 to the end. Who said these words: Daniel, Lucy, or August? Can you remember the complete phrase?
1. coming
2. impressive
3. knowledgeable
4. heartbreaking
5. lunch place
6. dying to try
7. on me

### 3 After watching

**A** Complete 1–6 with the present perfect or present perfect continuous of the verbs.
1. He _____ always _____ a fanatic about weather and the environment. (be)
2. I _____ never _____ such an animal lover. (know)
3. _____ he _____ to be a weatherman? (study)
4. Daniel _____ environmental science classes. (take)
5. The effects of global warming _____ serious harm to wildlife. (cause)
6. This _____ for the past several years and the results _____ **de**vastating. (go on / be)

**B** 🟢 **Make it personal** Which items that Daniel talks about concern you most? In your opinion, what changes do we need to make to have the biggest positive impact on planet Earth?

*I think using hybrid cars will make a big difference.*

# ID Café 2 Down to earth

## 1 Before watching

**A** Point to the photos and ask: *Do you know what any of these animals are called?* Help sts to match the words to photos 1–5.

> 1 forest canopy   2 toucan   3 tamarin monkey
> 4 logging   5 jaguar

Have sts work in pairs to guess the pronunciation of the words with pink letters. Then, classcheck and drill pronunciation for all the words. At the end, ask: *Which of these have you actually seen in real life?* Have sts answer in pairs. Classcheck.

**B** **Make it personal** Point to the pictures in **A** and ask the whole class: *Which of these are endangered species?* Say: *Work in pairs and think of three ways we can help endangered species.* Invite a volunteer to read the model text in the speech bubble before sts begin. Encourage sts to take notes on their ideas. Classcheck.

**C** Show sts the picture and say: *Do you remember Daniel? What do you think he has been doing?* Have sts answer the question in pairs. Refer them to the model text in the speech bubbles. Classcheck sts' guesses.

## 2 While watching

**A** Say: *Now we're going to watch Daniel and find out what he's been doing. Watch the video and circle the correct alternatives.* Read through the sentences with the class so they know what to watch / listen for, then play ▶ 2 up to 1:30. Paircheck. Classcheck and ask: *Were your guesses correct?*

> 1 studio   2 global warming   3 has
> 4 environmental science   5 reporter   6 drowning in the sea   7 endangered species   8 controversial

**B** Read through the items with the class, then play ▶ 2 from 1:30 to 2:40. Have sts number the items 1–10 while they watch. Paircheck. Classcheck and elicit what sts can remember him saying about each one.

> 1 logging   2 cover   3 species   4 victims   5 mankind
> 6 impact   7 lights   8 walk   9 recycling   10 difference

**C** Read the questions with the class and elicit what sts can remember, but don't give any answers yet. Then play the second part of ▶ 2 again for sts to check their answers. Paircheck. Classcheck.

> (Suggested answers)
> 1 jungles / rainforests
> 2 different species (toucans, tamarind monkeys, jaguars)
> 3 leaving the lights on, using the car instead of walking, throwing garbage away which could be recycled
> 4 saving electricity, walking for short journeys, recycling

**D** Say: *Now we're going to watch the last part of the video. You'll see three people talking about the issues in the video: Daniel, Lucy, and August.* Read items 1–7 with the class and ask them to write D (Daniel), L (Lucy), or A (August) next to each one. Play ▶ 2 from 2:40 to the end. Paircheck. Classcheck, and elicit the whole phrases and write them on the board.

> 1 coming (Daniel) *Thanks for coming.*
> 2 impressive (August) *It was really impressive.*
> 3 knowledgeable (August) *You're really knowledgeable …*
> 4 heartbreaking (Lucy) *… it was heartbreaking.*
> 5 lunch place (August) *… there's a great lunch place nearby …*
> 6 dying to try (August) *… I've been dying to try.*
> 7 on me (August) *Lunch is on me!*

## 3 After watching

**A** Have sts fill in the blanks in sentences 1–6 with the present perfect or present perfect continuous forms of the verbs provided. Paircheck. Classcheck.

> 1 has / been
> 2 have / known
> 3 Has / been studying
> 4 has taken OR has been taking
> 5 have been causing
> 6 has been going on / have been

**B** **Make it personal** Ask all sts to change partners. Have sts work in their new pairs to answer the questions. Monitor sts' dialogues closely and take notes for delayed correction. Classcheck and provide sts with language feedback.

# R1 Grammar and Vocabulary

**A** ***Picture dictionary.*** Cover the words and definitions on the pages below and remember.

| pages | |
|---|---|
| 8–9 | 6 stages of a relationship |
| 13 | 10 personality adjectives |
| 15 | 8 active listening expressions |
| 18–19 | 10 "green" words |
| 22 | 9 environmental problems |
| 26 | 7 endangered animals |
| 160 | 2 words for each vowel sound (not the picture words); say and spell them |

**B** ▶R1.1 Order the words to make questions. Listen to check, then ask and answer in pairs.
1. like / people / do / new / you / meeting / ?
2. of / who / your time / spend / most / with / you do / ?
3. follow / social media / who / do / on / you / ?
4. are / what / friend / qualities / in a / most important / ?
5. can / which / of / always / on / your friends / you / depend / ?
6. you / who / you / up / feel / when / cheers / down / ?

**C** 🔵 **Make it personal** Match the sentence halves, then modify the underlined phrases to make them true. Compare in pairs.

1. I sometimes fall
2. I often go <u>to the mall</u> to hang
3. I'm usually attracted
4. I don't get
5. When you want to get
6. If someone wants to get
7. The <u>family member</u> I can count

a ☐ to know someone better, you should <u>go camping with them</u>.
b ☐ to people who <u>have a good sense of humor</u>.
c ☐ out with my <u>friends after work</u>.
d ☐ back together with an ex-partner, they'd have to <u>be really romantic</u>.
e ☐ along well with people who <u>are too arrogant</u>.
f ☐ out with <u>my parents</u> over <u>using the car</u>.
g ☐ on the most is <u>my older sister</u>.

**D** Choose three phrases from **1E** on p. 9. Write a short story, leaving gaps for the phrases for your partner to guess.

**E** Circle the correct alternative.
1. My family always _____ all our plastic bottles and food packaging.
   a recycles   b is recycling   c has recycled
2. Many scientists believe that the earth _____ warmer because of us.
   a gets   b is getting   c have gotten
3. My school _____ solar panels next month.
   a installs   b is installing   c has installed
4. I _____ a plastic shopping bag for three months.
   a don't use   b 'm not using   c haven't used
5. An aluminum can _____ between 200 and 500 years to decompose.
   a takes   b is taking   c has taken
6. Many people _____ that pandas will become extinct.
   a think   b is thinking   c have thought

**F** ▶R1.2 ***The animal in you*** Follow instructions 1–3, then listen to find out what the combinations mean.
1. Think of and write three names of animals.
2. Think of and write three personality adjectives.
3. Combine them.

**G** Complete 1–8 with the verbs in the *present perfect simple* or *continuous*.
1. The population of the earth _____ by over one billion this century. (grow)
2. Greenpeace is an international environmental organization. It _____ since 1971. (campaign)
3. It _____ for hours now! When is it going to stop? (rain)
4. I _____ a wild monkey before. (never see)
5. The mammoth _____ extinct for over 10,000 years. (be)
6. André _____ 5000m today. (run)
7. Sorry about the mess. We _____ all afternoon and _____ yet. (cook, not tidy up)
8. How many times _____ you _____ exercises like this? (do)

**H** Correct the mistakes in each sentence. Check your answers in units 1 and 2.

🔶 **Common mistakes**

1. When you went in New York? (2 mistakes)
2. When did you feel in love to her? (2 mistakes)
3. Jed was engaged with Clara during six years. (2 mistakes)
4. With who are you usually hang out? (3 mistakes)
5. Sofía is thinking BlacKkKlansman is a sad movie, but Paulo isn't agree. (2 mistakes)
6. She don't often eats meat, but she did liked my barbecue. (3 mistakes)
7. Don't let your laptop in stand-by mode for too long. (1 mistake)
8. Leo is living in Boston since two years. (2 mistakes)
9. We has been knowing each other from 2008. (2 mistakes)
10. The tree in my garden been grown two meters I've planted it. (2 mistakes)

# Review 1 Units 1-2

## Grammar and vocabulary

♪ Turn to p. 327 for notes about this song and an accompanying task.

**A** *Picture dictionary.* Pair sts up and have partners test each other and review the main vocabulary items in units **1** and **2**. Monitor throughout and correct vocabulary and pronunciation.

**Tip** In order to provide sts with as much fluency practice as possible, expand the activity into the mini-dialogues suggested below.

| Picture Dictionary | Procedures | Mini-dialogues / Suggested language |
|---|---|---|
| 6 stages of a relationship, p. 8–9 | Have sts hide the words in **1A** with a sheet of paper. Ask pairs to take turns pointing to pictures 1–6 and saying the six stages of a relationship. **Stronger classes:** Have sts hide the words in **1A** and retell the story by using pictures 1–6. | St A: (points to picture 1) <br> St B: *Be attracted to someone.* (points to picture 2) <br> St A: *Get along well with someone.* (points to picture …) <br> St A: *First, she was attracted to the guy.* <br> St B: *In this picture, they are getting along well.* |
| 10 "green" words, p. 18–19 | Have sts hide the quiz in **1A** with a notebook or a sheet of paper. Pair sts up and have them take turns pointing to pictures 1–10 and testing their partner. | St A: (points to picture 1) *What's this?* <br> St B: *It's bottled water.* (points to picture 2) *What's this?* |
| 9 environmental problems, p. 22 | Ask sts to hide the headlines in **1A** with a notebook or a sheet of paper and work in pairs to test each other on pictures 1–9. | St A: *What's picture 1?* <br> St B: *Floods. What's picture 5?* |

**B** Write item 1 on the board. Elicit the question and write it on the board. Sts order the rest of the questions in pairs. Play ▶R1.1 so sts can check their answers. Classcheck, then have sts ask and answer in pairs. Monitor and provide language feedback.

> 1 Do you like meeting new people?   2 Who do you spend most of your time with?   3 Who do you follow on social media?   4 What qualities are most important in a friend?   5 Which of your friends can you always depend on?   6 Who cheers you up when you feel down?

**C** **Make it personal** Have sts match items 1–6 to the correct endings in the column on the right. Classcheck.

> 1 f   2 c   3 b   4 e   5 a   6 d   7 g

Ask sts to change the underlined phrases to make true sentences about themselves. Pair sts up and have partners tell each other their modified statements. Classcheck.

**D** Refer sts to the phrases in **1E** on p. 9. Ask sts to choose three of them, and write a short story. When they have finished, ask them to cross out three phrases. Assign new pairs and ask students to read their stories to their partner, leaving gaps where the phrases are for their partner to guess.

**E** Ask sts to choose best options from a–c to complete items 1–6. Paircheck. Classcheck by writing the answers on the board.

> 1 a   2 b   3 b   4 c   5 a   6 a

**F** *The animal in you* Read instructions 1–3 with the whole class and ask sts to write down their answers.

Tell sts that the combinations are meant to reveal their personality. Play ▶R1.2 and have sts check the meaning of each combination. Ask: *Do you agree with the results?* If time allows, have sts turn to the AS on p. 165. Sts listen again and notice the intonation on the short questions.

▶R1.2 Turn to page 313 for the complete audioscript.

**G** Have sts fill in the blanks in sentences 1–8 with the present perfect simple or present perfect continuous forms of the verbs provided. Paircheck. Classcheck.

> 1 has grown   2 has been campaigning   3 has been raining   4 have never seen   5 has been   6 has run   7 have been cooking, haven't tidied up   8 have (you) been doing

**H** **Common mistakes** Copy item 1 on the board and elicit corrections from the whole class. Have sts work in pairs to correct sentences 2–10. Encourage sts to flip back through p. 6–27 and check their answers in units **1** and **2**. Classcheck.

> 1 When did you go to New York?
> 2 When did you fall in love with her?
> 3 Jed was engaged to Clara for six years.
> 4 Who do you usually hang out with?
> 5 Sofia thinks that *BlacKkKlansman* is a sad movie, but Paulo doesn't agree.
> 6 She doesn't often eat meat, but she did like my barbecue.
> 7 Don't leave your laptop in stand-by mode for too long.
> 8 Leo has lived in Boston for two years.
> 9 We have known each other since 2008.
> 10 The tree in my garden has grown two meters since I've planted it.

# Skills practice

♪ *I've been running through the jungle,*
*I've been running with the wolves, To get to you, to get to you,*
*I've been down the darkest alleys, Saw the dark side of the moon to get to you*

**R1**

**A** Listen to Al's blog ▶2.3 on p. 20 and pause after each paragraph. In pairs, summarize, then continue. Finally, read to check. Did you miss anything because:
 a  it was too fast to understand?
 b  you didn't think it was important?
 c  you didn't remember the words?
 d  of another reason?

**B** ▶R1.3 **Dictation.** Listen and write the numbers. In pairs, try to retell each fact. Listen again to check.

**C** ▶R1.4 Use the prompts to make questions 1–4. Listen to check and add the emphatic words.

1 nicknames?  *Do you have any nicknames?*

   *Not really, no. Although my brother calls me "big ears." Oh, it _____ annoy me!*

   *Aw! That's mean! They used to call me "potato" at school, but I've _____ no idea why.*

2 first / notice / meeting / new?

   *Oh, I'm _____ a shoe person. I always notice if people have dirty shoes.*

   *Me, I don't notice clothes, but I _____ notice teeth. If they have something in their teeth ... yuk!*

3 more often optimistic / pessimistic?

   *Oh, I don't know. I guess I'm about fifty-fifty.*

   *No, you always seem _____ laid-back and happy. I think you're a _____ positive person.*

4 only three electrical appliances?

   *Hmm, difficult. Only three? Well, the first is my laptop. I _____ use it almost every day.*

   *Lights? Do they count as an appliance? They _____ are important.*

**D** ▶R1.4 In pairs, imitate dialogues 1–4 in **C**. Listen again to compare with the audio.

**E** Read the title of the magazine article and first paragraph only. Guess what *Boston500* involves.

*Maybe it's a plan to make 500 companies do more to be greener.*

**F** Read the rest of the article and find:
1 two economic benefits of the scheme.
2 a reason for thicker walls.
3 a problem with current solar panels.
4 a use for windows.
5 a problem with using biodegradable waste.

## Save the world, save your money!

The city of Boston, capital of Massachusetts, and the most populous city in New England, is already one of the greenest cities in the U.S. Public transportation is eco-friendly, all the taxis are hybrids, and, with Grow Boston Greener, the city is trying to plant 100,000 trees by 2020. Now, with Boston 500, it has set its citizens a challenge: to go even greener. City officials claim that if just 500 families join the *Boston500* scheme they can each save $100 a year on their energy bills, cut 25% of dangerous gases, and create lots of new "green" jobs for the community.

So what is the *Boston500* scheme?
The idea is to encourage people to live in more efficient homes. Construction workers have already started building houses with thicker walls to protect against both high and low temperatures. Many homeowners have installed more energy-efficient appliances and use solar panels to power them, but they still need to buy some electricity, as solar panels don't usually generate enough. The ultimate goal, say developers, is to create houses that generate enough electricity to provide power for others as well.

Scientists and engineers have been working hard on this problem and there are some very innovative ideas out there. One plan is to turn windows into solar panels to increase the total area of panels—and they already have a prototype that works. Another is to use biodegradable waste—a smelly but efficient solution.

If the *Boston500* scheme is a success, we could all be paying less for electricity in the near future!

**G** In pairs, brainstorm ways to save energy at home. How many can you think of in two minutes?

*Some people put aluminum foil on the roof to reflect the sun.*

**H** ▶R1.5  **Make it personal**  **Question time!**
1 Listen to and answer the 12 lesson titles in units 1 and 2.
2 In pairs, practice asking and answering. Use the map on p. 2–3. Ask at least two follow-up questions, too. Which was the most interesting conversation?

*So, do you know all your classmates?*

   *No, there are a few new students I don't know.*

## Skills practice

**A** Briefly elicit what sts remember about the blog written by a man named Al who decided to try a greener lifestyle after watching the documentary *No Impact Man*. Pair sts up and play ▶ 2.3 from unit 2. Pause after each paragraph to allow partners to tell each other the paragraph's main ideas from memory. Classcheck and play the next paragraph. Repeat the process for the remaining paragraphs on the track.

> 1  Al met a friend, and his friend said he looked very different.
> 2  Al told his friend that he had been trying to copy the attitudes of a man named Colin Beaven, from the documentary *No Impact Man*, who tries to have zero impact on the environment.
> 3  The documentary has had so much impact on Al's life that he and his family have been trying to "green up" their lifestyles. The changes include going to work on foot at least twice a week, taking the stairs, and using recycled paper.
> 4  He wonders if he can make a difference or if he is wasting his time.

Have sts answer questions a–d in pairs. Classcheck sts' answers and find out if others agree.

**B** *Dictation.* Draw sts' attention to the pictures and tell them that they are going to listen to some facts about them. Explain that sts should listen and write the numbers they hear below each photo. Play ▶ R1.3. Paircheck. Replay ▶ R1.3 and classcheck by writing the answers on the board.

> 1  8, 12, 100 million
> 2  1990, 43(%), 2010, 21(%), ($)1.25, 2030
> 3  1, 33, 69, 2010, 6, 1, 42, 5, 40

▶ R1.3 Turn to page 313 for the complete audioscript.

> **Tip** Have sts turn to the AS on p. 165. Sts listen again and notice /θ/ and /ð/.

**C** Tell sts not to focus on the dialogues for now. Draw their attention to the prompt for item 1 and model forming the question. Have sts use the remaining prompts provided to form questions 2–4. Paircheck. Play ▶ R1.4 so sts can check their questions and fill in the blanks with the emphatic words they hear. Classcheck.

> 1  Do you have any nicknames?  does, absolutely
> 2  What's the first thing you notice when meeting someone new?  definitely, do
> 3  Are you more often optimistic or pessimistic?  so, really
> 4  If you could have only three electrical appliances at home, what would they be?  do, sure

**D** Have sts change partners and work in their new pairs to act out dialogues from **C**. Remind sts to stress the emphatic words. When all sts have finished, tell them to listen again and compare their sentence stress to the stress used in the audio. Play ▶ R1.4 again. Classcheck.

**E** Read the title of the article in **F** with the whole class and the first paragraph only and have sts guess or predict what the text will be about and what *Boston500* involves.

**F** Go over questions 1–5 with the class and ask sts to read the text to find the answers. Paircheck. Classcheck.

> 1  Boston500 could help people save $100 a year on their energy bills and create lots of new "green" jobs for the community.
> 2  Thicker walls protect against high and low temperatures.
> 3  Solar panels do not usually generate enough energy for a house.
> 4  Windows could be turned into solar panels to increase the area of panels on a house.
> 5  Biodegradable waste is smelly.

**G** Have sts change partners and ask: *In what ways can we save energy at home?* Refer sts to the model text in the speech bubble and then give sts two minutes to discuss the question in pairs. Classcheck ideas.

**H** **Make it personal**  *Question time!* Tell sts that they are going to hear twelve questions, which are the lesson titles from units **1** and **2**. Ask them to listen and briefly write down their personal answer to each question. Emphasize that sts do not need to write the questions down—only their answers.

Play ▶ R1.5. If necessary, pause after each question, but only long enough for sts to jot down very brief notes, e.g. *yes, no*, etc.

Have partners look at the **ID Book Map** on p. 2–3 and take turns asking and answering the lesson title questions from units **1** and **2**. Monitor sts' work closely for accuracy and encourage them to ask follow-up questions when appropriate. At the end, ask sts how they felt performing the task: *Do you feel comfortable with all the questions? Which ones are easy? Which ones are difficult?*

# 3.1 Which city would you most like to visit?

## 1 Vocabulary Cities

**A** Look at photos a–g. Do you recognize any of the cities? Find the highlighted words in texts 1–4 in the photos. What else can you see?

*These two look like fashionable neighborhoods …*   *There's a bridge in this one.*

**B** Read the texts. Can you guess which cities the people are describing?

**1**
OK, my turn now. "You're at the heart of the city, in the middle of the world's largest city square and the country's most important landmark. This square separates the country's capital from the "Forbidden City". Which Asian city is it?"

Hmm, I don't know. Is it _____?

Yeah, well done. At last you got one right!

**2**
Marta: Hey! I thought you'd be busy sightseeing. What are you doing online?
Ed: It's raining. Just having coffee and waiting for the rain to stop.
Marta: So … how do you like _____?
Ed: Well, if you like avenues full of skyscrapers, chaotic traffic, dangerous neighborhoods, and the ugliest harbor I've ever seen, it's the place to go.
Marta: Well, OK … Anything you do like, Mr. Grumpy?
Ed: Hmm … Well, streets and avenues are numbered, so it's easy to find my way around … I guess. And the city is mostly flat, so it's very easy to walk. It's very lively, I suppose. Lots going on, some good shopping. Oh, and then there's the huge park. And the statue. Yep, I think that's about it.

**3**
Second day in _____, this marvelous city. I'm at a beautiful beach right now, people exercising and sunbathing everywhere. Some of them even sunbathe standing up so they can be seen! Looking up to my right, I can see a magnificent statue, but to my left, up on the hill, is one of the most rundown areas of the city. It's really strange that only a few blocks away there's an upscale, fashionable neighborhood. You gotta love this place—so many great tourist spots, such a lot to do.

**4**
… such fabulous colonial architecture. If you have time, be sure to go all the way up to the 44th floor. There's an observation deck where you'll get an exceptional view of _____'s skyline. On a clear day, you can see the soccer stadium, lots of beautiful old churches, volcanoes, and even the pyramids. Problem is, this city is sometimes smoggy so we don't get too many really clear days, I'm afraid.

**Unit overview:** In unit 3, sts learn past perfect and past perfect continuous in the contexts of getting to know new places and cultures, discussing urban problems, and understanding, explaining, and questioning rules.

## 3.1 Which city would you most like to visit?

**Lesson Aims:** Sts learn and practice adjectives and expressions to describe places.

### Function
Reading about famous cities.
Identifying different text types.
Describing cities you'd like to visit.
Using alliteration to memorize words.

### Language
You're at the heart of the city.
And the city is mostly flat, so it's very easy to walk.
Well, I'd really like to visit Sydney.

**Vocabulary:** Cities (harbor, landmark, neighborhood, rundown, slums, skyline, skyscraper, smog, square, tourist spots, upscale). Expressions (at the heart of … , find my way around, it's the place to go).
**Grammar:** Review *such*, *so*, prepositions of place, *some* and *any*.
**Pronunciation:** /eɪ/

♪ Turn to p. 327 for notes about this song and an accompanying task.

**Warm-up** Have sts look back through p. 18–27 and, in pairs, take turns asking and answering the lesson question titles ("How green are you?" on p. 18, "How long have you been studying here?" on p. 20, and so on). Monitor sts' performance and take notes of any mistakes for delayed correction. Classcheck.

### 1 Vocabulary Cities

**A Books closed.** Ask: *Which city would you most like to visit?* Elicit as many answers as possible and write the city names on the board.

**Books open.** Point to photos a–g on p. 32–33 and the city names on the board. Ask: *Do you recognize any of your favorite cities in the photos? Can you guess where these photos were taken?*
Draw sts' attention to texts 1–4 on p. 32. Have sts focus on just the highlighted words in texts 1–4. Ask them to find what these words describe in photos a–g. Paircheck. Classcheck. Then ask: *What else can you see in the photos?*

> Cities are: a non-specified slum area  b Mexico City
> c Beijing  d Rio de Janeiro  e Dubai  f Sydney
> g New York
> square – photo c   skyscraper – photos e and g
> harbor – photos d and f   neighborhood – photos d and e
> skyline – photo g

**Stronger classes** Put sts into small groups and ask them to list five additional nouns / adjectives for each photo. This could be a competitive game where groups get a point for each word or phrase they can generate that no other group lists:

a old, cheap, dirty, unpainted buildings, sky, antennae
b smog, tall buildings, houses, trees, polluted, crowded
c palace, square, streetlights, people, grass, flags, umbrellas
d sea, beach, hills, waves, surf
e skyscraper, new buildings/architecture, modern, streetlights, fence, a bench, palm trees

**B** Say: *You can read about four different cities here. Read the texts and try to guess which cities these people are describing.* Pair sts up and allow them a few minutes to read the texts and discuss their guesses with their partners. Don't give any answers yet.

> 1 Beijing
> 2 New York
> 3 Rio de Janeiro
> 4 Mexico City

*Concrete jungle where dreams are made of,
There's nothing you can't do,
Now you're in New York.*

**C** ▶ 3.1 Match each text to its type. There is one extra type. Listen to check.
- ☐ Friends talking on WhatsApp.
- ☐ A guide talking to tourists.
- ☐ A vacation blog post.
- ☐ Friends playing a guessing game.
- ☐ Introduction to a guidebook.

**D** Write the underlined words and phrases in the texts next to their definitions. Describe examples of these features in your area.

| 1 | _____ noun [C] | a well-known building or site |
| 2 | _____ noun [C] | places / attractions popular with visitors |
| 3 | _____ phrase | know where you're going |
| 4 | _____ phrase | I recommend it |
| 5 | _____ phrase | in the most important place |

*We have a beautiful square in the heart of our town. It's a real tourist spot because it has such great cafés and restaurants.*

**E** Match the **bold** adjectives in the texts to their synonyms. Which adjectives would you use to describe your town, city, or another place you know? Why?

confused and disorganized    energetic and active    expensive and chic
neglected and poor    polluted    popular

*I'd say our city is chaotic. There's lots of traffic and millions of people.*

**Common mistakes**

~~such~~
It has a so beautiful architecture.

are so
The people is ~~such~~ friendly.

## ② Pronunciation /eɪ/

**A** ▶ 3.2 Cross out the words that do *not* have /eɪ/. Listen to check. Make a tongue twister with three or four of the words.

| eɪ | ancient | Asian | chaotic | dangerous | ~~fashionable~~ |
| | flat | skyscraper | stadium | statue | sunbathe |
| | traffic | upscale | volcanoes | | |

*A dangerous, ancient, Asian skyscraper!*

**B** **Make it personal** Think of a city you'd love to visit.
1. Spend a few minutes thinking about why you'd like to visit it and make some notes.
2. Describe the city, without naming it, for your partner to guess.

*The city I'd like to visit has beautiful beaches, great music, and some of the best colonial architecture in South America. It's well-known for its mix of European, African, and indigenous cultures. Famous landmarks include …*

3. Share your ideas with the class. Is there one place everybody would like to visit?

## 3.1

**C** Point to text 2 in **A** and ask: *What type of conversation is this? Is it an e-mail?* (Friends talking on WhatsApp). Have sts match the rest of the texts in **A** to the correct text types. Point out that there is one extra option. Play ▶ 3.1 for sts to listen and check. Paircheck. Classcheck. If time allows, play the track again, pausing for sts to repeat the words in pink.

> 1 Friends playing a guessing game.
> 2 Friends talking on Whatsapp.
> 3 A vacation blog post.
> 4 A guide talking to tourists.

**D** Have sts look at the underlined words and phrases in the texts in **A**. Model the activity. Ask: *Which phrase means "in the most important place"?* Instruct sts to copy the phrases next to the correct definitions in the box. Paircheck. Classcheck.

**Common mistakes** Read with sts and help them compare singular and countable forms of the same structure, e.g. *It has such a beautiful view.* and *He's such a friendly person.*

Assign pairs and ask: *Which adjectives would you use to describe your town, city, or another place you know? Why?* Have sts discuss in pairs. Classcheck.

> 1 landmark
> 2 tourist spots
> 3 find my way around
> 4 it's the place to go
> 5 at the heart of

**E** Point to the word *chaotic* in bold in text 2 and elicit the synonyms (*confused* and *disorganized*). Sts match the rest of the words in bold to their synonyms. Classcheck.

> confused and disorganized – chaotic
> energetic and active – lively
> expensive and chic – upscale
> neglected and poor – rundown
> polluted – smoggy
> popular – fashionable
> Question: Personal answers.

**Tip** As an extension task, ask sts to work in pairs and take turns describing a photo, a–g, until their partner guesses which photo they are describing. You could extend the task further by bringing in additional photos for sts to describe.

## 2 Pronunciation /eɪ/

**A** Focus on the pronunciation symbol and elicit the words *plane* and *train*. Explain that these words both have the sound /eɪ/. Ask: *What sound is this?* Next, elicit the pronunciation for *Asian* and ask: Does it have the /eɪ/ sound? Then, point to the word fashionable and ask: *How about **fashionable**? Does it have the sound /eɪ/?*

Explain that sts should cross out words in the box which do not have the sound /eɪ/. Paircheck. Play ▶ 3.2 so sts can check their answers. Pause after each word if necessary.

> fashionable, flat, statue, traffic

Drill pronunciation for all the words in the box, chorally and individually. Brainstorm a few more /eɪ/ words, e.g. *plane, train* etc. from the "Sounds and usual spellings" chart on p. 160.

> **Language tip** In Portuguese and Spanish, the phoneme /eɪ/ can only be produced by the combination of letters *ei* or *ey*. In English, the phoneme /eɪ/ can be formed by the combination of letters *ay*, or the single letter *a*. After sts do activity **2A**, have them sit in pairs and encourage them to write down as many examples of words they can think of with the phoneme /eɪ/ in both spellings (*ay* and *a*). When they are ready, have them share their lists with the whole class.

**B** **Make it personal** 1 Say: *You're going to talk about a city you'd like to visit.* Give sts a few minutes to work alone and think about what they're going to say and make notes. Go round and help with ideas and vocabulary where necessary. Encourage them to note as many details as possible, including tourist spots, weather, nightlife, the people, the food and everything else they know about the city.

2 Put sts in pairs to discuss their city, but make sure they don't say where it is. Read out the speech bubble examples first. Monitor closely through the activity and offer help as needed.

3 Invite volunteers to tell the whole class the reasons why they'd like to visit the city they chose. Ask sts if there is one place that everybody would like to visit.

➡ **Workbook** Page 14

# 3.2 Was your last vacation as much fun as you'd hoped?

## 1 Reading

**A** ▶3.3 Match the underlined words to photos a–h, and then circle the correct alternative in 1–9. Listen to / watch the video to check.

### VISITING HONG KONG FOR THE FIRST TIME?

Here's what you need to know:

1. It's **usual** / **rare** for people to <u>shake hands and bow</u> slightly.
2. When you greet people, you **should** / **shouldn't** <u>hug</u> them and <u>kiss them on the cheek</u>.
3. When you're walking through a crowd, you should gently <u>push your way through</u> and **say nothing** / **apologize**.
4. When you receive a gift, it's good manners to open it **later** / **immediately**.
5. Clocks make **good** / **bad** gifts.
6. When drinking tea, you should <u>pour</u> your **own** / **friends'** cup first.
7. In Hong Kong, it's OK to <u>blow on your soup</u> / **chew loudly**.
8. Leaving your <u>chopsticks</u> straight up means **good** / **bad** luck.
9. After eating, you **should** / **shouldn't** <u>leave a tip</u> on the table.

**B** If you were going to Hong Kong, which social conventions would be hard to adapt to?

> It would be difficult not to open a gift right away.

**C** 🗨 **Make it personal** What are the rules where you live? In small groups, write six tips for a foreign visitor and share them with the class.

> You shouldn't really talk on your phone on the train. People get annoyed and don't like it.

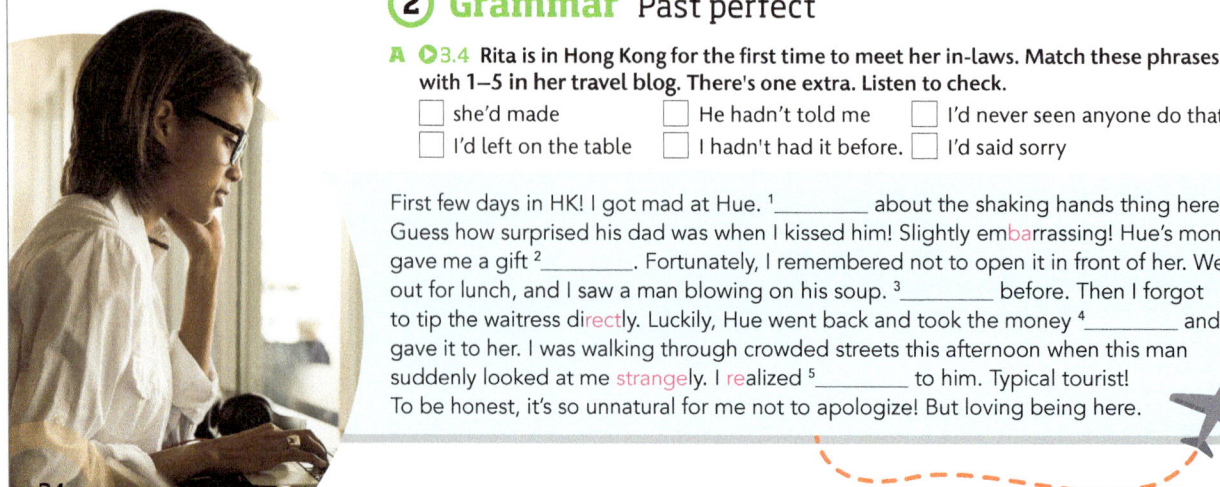

## 2 Grammar  Past perfect

**A** ▶3.4 Rita is in Hong Kong for the first time to meet her in-laws. Match these phrases with 1–5 in her travel blog. There's one extra. Listen to check.

- [ ] she'd made
- [ ] He hadn't told me
- [ ] I'd never seen anyone do that
- [ ] I'd left on the table
- [ ] I hadn't had it before.
- [ ] I'd said sorry

First few days in HK! I got mad at Hue. ¹_____ about the shaking hands thing here! Guess how surprised his dad was when I kissed him! Slightly embarrassing! Hue's mom gave me a gift ²_____. Fortunately, I remembered not to open it in front of her. Went out for lunch, and I saw a man blowing on his soup. ³_____ before. Then I forgot to tip the waitress di<u>rect</u>ly. Luckily, Hue went back and took the money ⁴_____ and gave it to her. I was walking through crowded streets this afternoon when this man suddenly looked at me stra<u>nge</u>ly. I <u>re</u>alized ⁵_____ to him. Typical tourist! To be honest, it's so unnatural for me not to apologize! But loving being here.

34

# 3.2 Was your last vacation as much fun as you'd hoped?

**Lesson Aims:** Sts learn and practice the past perfect via the contexts of visiting a place for the first time, experiencing different social conventions, and tweeting.

## Function
Taking a quiz and watching a video about a different culture.
Reading tweets about a visit to Hong Kong.
Reading about an exchange student in London.
Delivering a one-minute monologue about a place you visited.

## Language
It's usual for people to shake hands and bow slightly.
He hadn't told me about bowing!
By the time my stay was over, I'd learned my way around the city.
Last year, I went to this amazing place, you know? I'd never been there before and …

**Vocabulary:** Social conventions (blow on your soup, bow slightly, hug, leave a tip, kiss (on the cheek), pour, push your way through, shake hands).
**Grammar:** Past perfect; *by* + past expression + past perfect.
**Before the lesson:** Prepare sets of cards with vocabulary from lesson 3.1, using the words and phrases below.
harbor   landmark   slums   smog   skyline   square   upscale
at the heart of (the city)   find your / my way around   It's the place to go …   tourist spots

♪ Turn to p. 327 for notes about this song and an accompanying task.

**Warm-up** Divide the class into groups of three. Give each group a set of cards (see **Before the lesson**). Have sts take turns selecting a card and explaining its meaning in their own words for the rest of the group to guess. Instruct sts to begin by telling the group whether their card has a word or an expression. Monitor closely and offer help when necessary. At the end, ask: *Which word or phrase was the most difficult to guess? Which was the hardest to describe?*

## 1 Reading

**A** Explore photos a–h and elicit as many details from them as sts can supply. Use the pictures and descriptions to pre-teach vocabulary sts will see in the quiz: *hug, pour, blow on your soup, leave a tip, chopsticks, bow,* and *shake hands*. Have sts match photos a–h to the underlined words in the quiz. Classcheck. Read the quiz title with the whole class and ask: *Has anyone ever been to Hong Kong?*

Elicit the correct option for sentence 1, but don't give sts the answer yet. Sts work in pairs to guess what the customs in Hong Kong are and circle the best options for 1–9. Then, play ▶3.3 so sts can check their answers. Classcheck. If time allows, have sts turn to the AS on p. 165. Sts listen again and notice the short (/) and long (//) pauses.

▶3.3 Turn to page 313 for the complete audioscript.

🔑
a pour   b blow on your soup   c hug   d leave a tip
e kiss them on the cheek   f shake hands and bow
g chopsticks   h push your way through

1 usual   2 shouldn't   3 say nothing   4 later   5 bad
6 friends'   7 blow on your soup   8 bad   9 shouldn't

**B** Point to the quiz in **A** and ask: *If you were going to Hong Kong, which of these social conventions would be hard for you to adapt to?* Have sts read the model in the speech bubble. If necessary, write a model on the board: *I think I'd find it hard (not) to …*

Pair sts up to discuss the question. Classcheck by having sts tell the class which social conventions would be difficult for their partners to adapt to.

**Tip** Remind sts that, even in continents like Latin America, some customs might be different from one country to another. After activity **1B**, ask sts: *Have you ever met any tourists who have had trouble with social rules in your country, or region? Have you ever been in a difficult situation because of social rules in another country?* Allow sts some time to share their answers and experiences and remind them that learning a language also involves learning about the culture and habits of the countries where people speak that language as their L1.

**C** 🟠 **Make it personal** Say: *What about social conventions here in (your city)?* Split the class into groups of three and ask sts to write six rules for tourists visiting their city. Monitor and offer help as needed. Classcheck.

## 2 Grammar Past perfect

**A** Ask: *Do you read travel blogs? Which ones?* Tell sts that they are going to read Rita's travel blog. Ask them to read the rubrics and find out why she's in Hong Kong (to meet her in-laws). Have sts complete the text with options 1–5; there is one extra option. Paircheck. Play ▶3.4 so sts can check their answers. Classcheck, eliciting some of the false cognates in the text, e.g. *embarrassing, strangely* etc.

🔑
1 He hadn't told me   2 she'd made   3 I'd never seen anyone do that   4 I'd left on the table   5 I'd said sorry

**B** Reread the blog in **A** and complete the grammar box.

> 1 What happened first?
> Hue's mom <u>gave</u> me a gift that <u>she'd made</u>.
> ☐ She gave the gift.  ☐ She made the gift.
>
> The past perfect has only one form for all persons: *had / hadn't* + past participle. The past perfect shows a relationship with another past event. Use the past perfect for the earlier event and the simple past for the later event.
>
> 2 Match pictures a and b to the phrases below.
> ☐ When I arrived, everybody started leaving.
> ☐ When I arrived, everybody had left.
>
> ➔ **Grammar 3A** p.142

*For some reason I can't explain,
Once you'd gone there was never,
Never an honest word,
And that was when I ruled the world.*

**C** Complete Rita's tweets with the *past perfect* of these verbs. There's one extra verb.

be   commit   finish   make   read   not told   visit

In HK to meet the in-laws! I [1]_____ (never) on a long-haul flight before, so I was exhausted when we landed! #jetlag #experiencechina #exploreHK

I [2]_____ once that some of Hong Kong's skyscrapers had no 13th floor. Guess what? It's true! #superstitions

Made the mistake of wearing white yesterday. @Hue2008 [3]_____ me that it's the color of death. #embarrassing

When Hue's parents began their meal, I [4]_____ (nearly) mine! I didn't know I was supposed to wait for the hosts! #HongKong #dinnerout

Blew my nose in public yesterday, and everybody looked at me as if I [5]_____ a crime. What did I do? #cultureshock #HongKongculture

On way to HK airport. Hue said I [6]_____ a good first impression. His parents actually liked me. #relieved

**D** Bruno was an exchange student in London last year. Choose the correct alternative.
1 I loved most of the landmarks. I **thought / 'd thought** Big Ben was amazing.
2 At first I hated the food, but by the time I left, I **got / 'd gotten** used to it.
3 I was shocked to find out how fast Londoners **spoke / 'd spoken**.
4 It was nice to hear all the words I **learned / 'd learned** in class over the years.
5 By the time my stay was over, I **visited / 'd visited** most of the tourist spots.
6 My first car ride wasn't too bad. I **never drove / 'd never driven** on the left side of the road.

⏱ **Common mistakes**

been
I'd never ~~gone~~ to L.A. before.

gone
He'd already ~~went~~ when I arrived.

**E** 🗣 **Make it personal**  **Mystery Monologue!** **A**: Use questions 1–7 to plan a one-minute monologue about a place you've been to. Don't name the place. **B**: Wait until A finishes, and then guess the place or ask more questions. Then change roles. How many of you have been to the same place?
1 When did you go? How long did you stay?
2 Had you been there before? If so, how many times?
3 Had you heard a lot about this place / seen it on TV?
4 What were you surprised to discover?
5 Did you do / see / eat anything you'd never done / seen / eaten before?
6 What were the people like? Any different from what you'd imagined?
7 Was anything else special? Would you recommend it?

*Last year I went to this amazing place. I'd never been there before, and to my surprise, it was completely empty. I'd expected it to be full!*

**B** Do task 1 with the whole class. Point to and read the sentence *Hue's mom gave me a gift that she'd made* and ask: *What happened first?* Have sts check the right answer. Classcheck.

Draw a timeline on the board and pinpoint the two actions happening in the past, as below:
She made the gift. → She gave me the gift. → Now

Read the rule for the past perfect with the whole class. Focus on form, then elicit and write more example sentences from **A** on the board (*I had never seen …, He hadn't told me …,* and so on).

Draw sts' attention to the contracted form of *had* and help them compare contractions with *had* and *would*, as in *I'd never visited Hong Kong before* vs. *I'd like to visit Hong Kong*.

Have sts do task 2 individually and match pictures a–b to the correct answers. Classcheck.

1  She made the gift.
a  When I arrived, everybody started leaving.
b  When I arrived, everybody had left.

→ **Grammar 3A** page 142

**C** **Common mistake** Read with sts and explain the difference between the sentences. Have sts complete Rita's tweets with the verbs from the box, using the past perfect. Peercheck, then classcheck.

1  'd never been
2  'd read
3  hadn't told
4  'd nearly finished
5  'd committed
6  'd made

**D** Find out if any sts have been to or would like to visit London. If possible show some photos or images of tourist attractions in London and ask if the sts recognize any of the places. Tell them they are going to read about Bruno's experience as an exchange student in London. Have sts read 1–6 and underline the correct verb tenses. Remind sts to look for phrases which commonly signal the past perfect, e.g. *by the time / already*. Paircheck. Classcheck by writing the answers on the board.

1  thought          4  'd learned
2  'd gotten        5  'd visited
3  spoke            6  'd never driven

**E** **Make it personal** Tell sts that they are going to play a game called **Mystery Monologue!** Ask sts to prepare a one-minute monologue. Have a student read the model in the speech bubble. Read questions 1–7 with sts and explain that they should use the answers to these questions in their monologue. Allow sts time to work individually to answer the questions and plan what they are going to say.

Pair sts up. Have student **A** deliver his / her one-minute monologue, ask student **B** to wait until the end of the monologue to guess the place or ask more questions. Then, sts should change roles. Monitor sts closely and offer help, especially during individual planning. At the end, have a few volunteers recite their monologues and ask the whole group to guess the mystery places. Ask the class how many of them have been to the same place.

→ **Workbook** Page 15

# 3.3 Do you ever want to get away from it all?

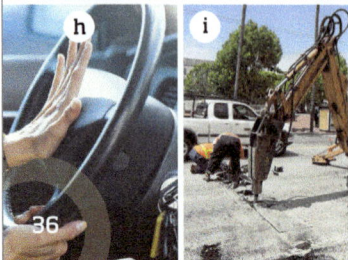

## 1 Vocabulary  Urban problems

**A** Read the magazine and match the highlighted words to the photos.

### The stresses of CITY LIVING

"The traffic is a nightmare. There's construction everywhere, and you get stuck in traffic jams every day. Drivers sometimes go through red lights and it's impossible to find a parking spot."

"There is so much pollution! The air is smoggy, there's trash everywhere, and there's noise pollution from the cars. People are always honking!"

"The crime rate is high. There is a lot of vandalism, car theft, and pickpocketing. I don't feel safe in my neighborhood."

"It's difficult to find a work-life balance, and there just isn't enough "me-time," We are all in debt and constantly connected to the Internet, but not to each other, so a lot of people suffer from loneliness and anxiety."

*That sounds just like where I live!*

**B** ▶ 3.5 Reread and listen to check the pronunciation of the highlighted words. Do you agree with all four opinions of city living?

**C** **Make it personal** In pairs, from the photos, choose the five most serious problems in your city. Can you agree on the order?

*I think the worst problem by far is the traffic.*

*No way! I'd say vandalism is a much more serious issue.*

**Common mistake**

*In my neighborhood, there is trash in every place.*
*everywhere*

## 2 Reading

**A** In pairs, list five ways you could escape the problems mentioned in 1B.

**B** ▶ 3.6 Read the article on p. 37. Are any of your ideas mentioned? Complete the article with a–f. Then listen to check echoing the pink-stressed words.

a  Overcome this by volunteering at an animal shelter.
b  Finding a quiet place to switch off and enjoy peace is so important.
c  Use lavender for relaxation and peppermint to invigorate.
d  Try by your window or on your balcony.
e  Try going to events to inspire your creative self.
f  It's not easy to find these things in the city, though.

# 3.3 Do you ever want to get away from it all?

**Lesson Aims:** Sts learn and practice phrases related to urban problems in the context of city living.

### Function
Reading and talking about urban problems.
Talking about your home town / city.
Reading about how to get away from it all.
Listening to people talk about changes in their lifestyle.
Conducting a survey about urban problems.

### Language
The crime rate is high.
People are always honking!
Even though you might not have a garden, you can grow food anywhere.
My nonstop lifestyle was driving me crazy.

**Vocabulary:** Urban problems (car theft, crime rate, constantly connected, find a parking spot, get stuck in traffic jams, go through red lights, honking, in debt, noise pollution, pickpocketing, roadworks, suffer from loneliness and anxiety, theft, trash, vandalism, work–life balance)

**Grammar:** verb + noun agreement

**Before the lesson:** Write the following sentence starters on the board:
*I did not have any money because …*
*We couldn't get a cheap hotel room because…*
*She'd already _____ by the time I _____ .*

♪ Turn to p. 327 for notes about this song and an accompanying task.

**Warm-up** Divide the class into pairs or small groups and have sts brainstorm endings for the sentence starters you wrote on the board (see **Before the lesson**). Give groups a point for each ending. Remind sts to use the past perfect for an event that happened before something else in the past.

## 1 Vocabulary   Urban problems

**A** **Books closed**. Write on the board: *Urban problems*. Ask: *What are the biggest problems for you in your town or city?*

Explore the photos with sts and use as a visual aid to elicit the vocabulary in them.

After covering all the photos and introducing as many new words as possible, draw sts' attention to the highlighted words in the text. Say: *You're going to read about four people describing problems in their city.* Have sts read the text then match the highlighted words to the photos. Paircheck. Classcheck and drill.

> a  get stuck in traffic jams   b  trash   c  car theft
> d  pickpocketing   e  constantly connected
> f  suffer from loneliness and anxiety
> g  work-life balance   h  honking   i  construction   j  vandalism

**B** Play ▶3.5 and have sts read the text again as they listen, paying particular attention to the pronunciation of the highlighted words. Ask: *Do you agree with them?* and have sts discuss the question in pairs. Classcheck by discussing as a class.

**C** **Common mistake** Read with the whole class. Then point to the photos and ask: *Does your city have these problems?* Have sts read the model sentences in the speech bubbles.

Have sts work in pairs, looking at the photos in **A** and listing the five most serious problems in their city. Instruct pairs to discuss and decide on the order of importance of the five problems. Monitor and correct any mistakes on the spot. Classcheck.

## 2 Reading

**A** Ask: *Do you ever want to get away from it all?* Put sts in pairs and ask them to list five ways to escape from some of the problems in **1A**. Classcheck by writing a list of sts' ideas on the board.

> Suggested answers:
> weekend trips, meditation/yoga, joining meet-up groups, spending less time online, taking public transportation

> **Language tip** Before sts read the article in **2B**, remind them that cognates are words that are similar to words in their own L1. For this reason, these words can, most of the time, help them to better understand texts. Give sts a few minutes to scan the article for cognates and ask: *How many cognates did you find? Did they help you to understand the article?*

**B** Give sts three minutes to read the article on p. 37 quickly and check if any of their ideas are mentioned. Classcheck by checking any of the ideas mentioned that you wrote on the board in **A**.

Direct sts's attention to sentences a–f and have them complete the article with the sentences. Peercheck. Play ▶3.6 for sts to check their answers, paying attention to the pink-stressed words. Classcheck.

> 1 f   2 c   3 a   4 d   5 b   6 e

♪ *It's like a jungle, sometimes it makes me wonder how I keep from going under. A-huh-huh huh-huh.*

## How to **get away** from it all

Living in a lively city is amazing, but the stresses and strains of urban life can affect our mental and physical health. Read the following tips to help you find a more balanced, peaceful city life.

### Nature
Natural light and fresh air will instantly make you feel better. ¹____ Try to find a park and go for a walk there, or just sit and read a book. You'll be amazed how these simple activities can improve your mood.

### Indulge your sense of smell
Clearly, the city does not smell pleasant. You can really transform your home environment and mental health with smell. ²____

### Get some pet therapy
If you've lived in the countryside, you'll notice how disconnected city dwellers are from nature and animals. ³____ Bonding with an animal naturally reduces anxiety, and loneliness can never be a problem while walking a dog!

### Grow something
Nowadays we're disconnected from where our food comes from. Even though you might not have a garden, you can grow food anywhere. ⁴____ Producing your own vegetables makes you appreciate food more, waste less, and feel closer to nature.

### Find some silence
We live among permanent noise—roadworks, traffic jams, phone calls, advertising, even our own minds are noisy. ⁵____ Just a few minutes every day will make you feel more positive.

### Do what you love
Everyone has a talent: painting, playing an instrument, or gardening, but we rarely spend time nurturing these gifts. When we take the time to do what we love, we feel more grounded. ⁶____ Life isn't all about work, money, and success!

**C** 🗣 **Make it personal** In groups, discuss these questions.
1 Which of the activities in the article have you tried to "get away from it all"? Which would you like to do?
2 What other things do you / people you know do to reduce the stress of modern life?

> *My brother turns off his phone for an hour every day. He says he enjoys the peace and quiet.*

> *I do the opposite. I listen to music or play video games.*

## 3 Listening

**A** ▶ 3.7 **Listen to three city dwellers describe changes they made in their lives. Complete the chart.**

|        | Problem | Change |
|--------|---------|--------|
| Raul   |         |        |
| Tomiko |         |        |
| André  |         |        |

**B** ▶ 3.8 **Complete 1–6 with these words. There is one extra. Then listen to check.**

| bother | driving | find | 'm | mind | stand | takes |

1 ... and my nonstop lifestyle was _____ me crazy.
2 I'm still just as busy, but it doesn't really _____ me as much.
3 Now, I _____ it annoying if I don't have time to eat properly.
4 It takes more time, but I don't _____ that.
5 I couldn't _____ coming home to an empty apartment every day.
6 I still find the city a bit lonely sometimes, but I _____ OK with it.

**C** Read *Common mistakes*. Then circle the correct alternatives in 1–4.
1 The noise **drive / drives** me crazy! Absolutely insane!
2 I love my city, but the huge lines really **annoy / annoys** me.
3 I can't stand people who **go / goes** through red lights.
4 There are massive traffic jams in my city, but that **don't / doesn't** bother me at all. I'm a cyclist!

> ⚠ **Common mistakes**
>
> drive
> All the traffic jams ~~drives~~ me crazy.
> (traffic jams = they)
>
> bothers
> Littering ~~bother~~ me a lot.
> (littering = it)
>
> doesn't
> The traffic ~~don't~~ bother me.
> (traffic = it)

**D** 🗣 **Make it personal** *City Stress Survey.* Choose a topic from the article. Write three questions and interview your classmates. Report your findings.

> *How often do you go for a walk in a park or the countryside?*

**C** 🗣 **Make it personal** Ask: *Which of the things have you tried to get away from it all?* Read the speech bubbles with the class. Have sts discuss the two questions in pairs. Classcheck by discussing the questions with the whole class.

## 3 Listening

**A** Tell sts that they are going to listen to three city dwellers describe changes they made to their lifestyles. Point to the chart and ask sts to pay attention to what the problem was and what they did to change their lifestyles. Play ▶ 3.7. Paircheck. Replay ▶ 3.7 if necessary. Classcheck by writing the answers on the board.

▶ 3.7 Turn to page 313 for the complete audioscript.

> 🔑
> Raul
> Problem: in debt, nonstop lifestyle, no work–life balance
> Change: started to play the piano again
>
> Tomiko
> Problem: poor diet, coffee, energy drinks snacks, takeouts
> Change: plans what to eat, takes time to shop and cook, going to grow her own food and do a gardening course
>
> Andre
> Problem: loneliness
> Change: got a cat
>
> **Tip** Have sts turn to the AS on p. 165. Sts listen again and notice the silent final letters.

**B** Point to the words in the box and have sts complete sentences 1–6 with suitable options. Peercheck. Play ▶ 3.8 to classcheck sts' answers.

> 🔑
> 1 driving
> 2 bother
> 3 find
> 4 mind
> 5 stand
> 6 'm

**C** ⚠ **Common mistakes** Read with the whole class. Then, ask sts to circle the correct alternatives in sentences 1–4. Classcheck by writing the answers on the board.

> 🔑
> 1 drives
> 2 annoy
> 3 go
> 4 doesn't

**D** 🗣 **Make it personal** Create a class survey. Have sts individually prepare three questions about city stress. Ask them to use vocabulary from this lesson and expressions from **C**. Draw their attention to the prompts in the speech bubble, which they can use as a model.

Walk around the classroom, monitoring sts' work and offering help as needed. Then, ask sts to stand up and mingle, interviewing as many classmates as possible with the questions they prepared. Monitor and take notes for delayed correction.

Classcheck by asking sts what kinds of answers were most common for each of the questions they asked. Provide sts with feedback on their performance and language use.

➔ **Workbook** Page 16

# 3.4 Have you ever missed any important dates?

## 1 Listening

**A** ▶3.9 From the pictures, imagine Juan and Sandra's stories. Listen to check. Were you close?

*OK, so it looks like Juan's going to work.*

Juan Alvarez from Bogotá

Sandra Machado from São Paulo

**B** ▶3.9 Listen again. True (T) or false (F)? How much more did you understand the second time? Who do you feel most sorry for? Why?

1. Juan had high hopes for the job interview.
2. Juan gave himself one hour to get there.
3. Sandra bought the tickets two weeks before the show.
4. Sandra and her friend managed to watch 30 minutes of the show.

*I feel most sorry for … because …*

> **Common mistake**
>
> missed
> I lost my flight.
>
> You **lose** objects, but you **miss** transportation, events, and opportunities.
> *I missed the chance to see U2 because I was sick.*

**C** Read ▶3.9 on p. 165 and write the underlined expressions in the chart.

| Listening actively | | |
|---|---|---|
| 1 | I'm not sure I understand. | *What do you mean?* |
| 2 | I'm sorry this happened to you. | |
| 3 | I'm not surprised to hear that. | |
| 4 | What happened in the end? | |
| 5 | I'm very surprised. | |

## 3.4 Have you ever missed any important dates?

**Lesson Aims:** Sts learn and practice the past perfect continuous through the context of narratives, especially stories of missing important events due to traffic jams.

### Function
Listening to sad stories about traffic jams.
Listening actively.
Retelling stories.
Telling a story about missing or forgetting something important.

### Language
A bus had gone through a red light and crashed into three cars.
What do you mean? No wonder!
When we finally got to the stadium, she'd been performing for well over an hour.
... I was going to the airport. We'd been away for two weeks ...

**Vocabulary:** Active listening phrases (No wonder! Oh no! What do you mean? You're joking!)
**Grammar:** Past perfect continuous.
**Before the lesson:** Write the following prompts on the board:
1 _____ in this city drives me crazy.
2 I can't stand people who _____.
3 _____ doesn't really bother me.
4 What annoys me most is _____.
5 I find _____ a bit annoying.
6 I believe the best solution for _____ is _____.

♪ Turn to p. 327 for notes about this song and an accompanying task.

**Warm-up** Review urban problems. Direct sts' attention to the sentence starters on the board (see **Before the lesson**) and invite volunteers to complete the sentences with their own opinion about urban problems in their city. Monitor closely for accuracy and offer help if needed.

Then, have sts work in pairs and tell each other their sentences. Ensure that sts pair up with classmates they don't usually work with. At the end, classcheck similarities by asking pairs: *What did you two find in common?*

### 1 Listening

**A** Point to the pictures and ask: *What's his name? What's her name? Where are they from?* Read the speech bubble with the whole class. Tell sts to work collaboratively in small groups and make up one story for Juan and another for Sandra, using what they can see in the pictures. Classcheck their stories. Then play ▶ 3.9. Ask: *Were your guesses close to the real stories?*

▶ 3.9 Turn to page 313 for the complete audioscript.

Juan had been trying to find a job as an architect for months and he was going to his third job interview that week. On the day of the interview there was a massive traffic jam. Juan arrived late and missed the interview.

Sandra had bought two tickets to see Taylor Swift and had been waiting for two months to see her live. On the day of the concert, she left work two hours early and went to São Paulo with a friend. The car broke down on the way to the concert because they hadn't checked the oil. When they finally arrived, Taylor Swift had already been singing for an hour.

**B** Have sts work in pairs to decide whether sentences 1–4 are true (T) or false (F). Play ▶ 3.9 again so sts can check their answers then discuss the final questions with the whole class.

1 T  2 F  3 F  4 T

**C** Ask sts to go to AS ▶ 3.9 on p. 165 and copy the underlined expressions next to their meanings in the chart. If time allows, play the audio track again for sts to listen and read the AS while noticing how the similar sounds link. Peercheck. Classcheck.

1 What do you mean?
2 You poor thing!
3 No wonder.
4 ... how did it turn out?
5 You're joking!

♪ *You only get one shot, do not miss your chance to blow. This opportunity comes once in a lifetime, yo.*

**D** 🗨 **Make it personal** Have you ever been stuck in traffic for a long time? In pairs, take turns sharing your stories. Remember to listen actively. Who has the funniest story?

*I was going to visit my grandparents once, and we got stuck on the highway for four hours.*

*Oh, no. You poor thing. What happened?*

## 2 Grammar  Past perfect continuous

**A** Read the example sentence and answer 1–3 in the grammar box.

> When we finally **got** to the stadium, **she had been singing** for well over an hour.
> 1. When they arrived:
>    a) was Taylor Swift already singing?   b) did the music stop?
> 2. Do we use the past perfect continuous for an action that:
>    a) had finished?              b) was in progress before another past action?
> 3. Is the form had(n't) +   a)  being?   b)  been + verb + -ing?
>
> ➡ **Grammar 3B** p. 142

**B** Complete 1–8 with the *past perfect* or *past perfect continuous* of these verbs. Use contractions.

arrange   dream of   drive   get up   go through   try   rain   wait for

1. Juan _____ to find a job as an architect for months.
2. He wasn't worried about the traffic as he _____ at 6.
3. He heard on the radio that a bus _____ a red light.
4. He didn't get the job he _____ since he graduated.
5. Sandra bought tickets for the show she _____ since she was 16.
6. Sandra's friend _____ to pick her up in her car.
7. They _____ for a little while when the car broke down.
8. They were stuck in traffic because it _____ nonstop.

**C** Complete the grammar box with the tenses below. Then, in pairs, role-play Juan and Sandra telling their stories. Retell the stories in your own words.

Past perfect   Past perfect continuous   Past continuous

> **Narrative tenses**
> The simple past is the most common past tense. In general, use the others like this:
> ¹_____: an action in progress at a point in the past.
> *I was chatting online when you called. Sorry!*
>
> ²_____: one action that happened before another in the past.
> *By 8 p.m. Jo had done all her work, so she went home.*
>
> ³_____: action in progress or repeated before a point in the past.
> *But she'd been working so hard she fell asleep in the car.*
>
> ➡ **Grammar 3C** p. 142

🔄 **Common mistakes**

had been   for
They ~~were~~ driving ~~during~~ 48 hours so they'd ~~been~~ very tired.
                              were

*So, I was going for a job interview. I'd been looking for a job as an architect for ages, so I was really nervous.*

**D** 🗨 **Make it personal** Have you ever missed or forgotten anything important? In groups, share stories and choose the saddest and funniest ones. Use these questions to plan what to say first.
1. What was the important date or event?
2. Had you been looking forward to it?
3. Why did you miss or forget it?
4. What happened?
5. How do you feel about it now?

*Well, it was my cousin's birthday, and I'd been planning ...*

*Had you spent many birthdays together in the past?*

**D** 🔴 **Make it personal** Ask: *Have you ever been stuck in traffic for a long time?* Ask two volunteers to read out the speech bubbles. Remind sts of the phrases for listening actively in **C**. Sts tell each other in pairs.

Nominate pairs to share their stories with the class. Ask: *Which story is the funniest?*

## 2 Grammar Past perfect continuous

**A** Go over the grammar box with sts and have them answer questions 1–3 on their own. Paircheck. Classcheck.

1  a
2  b
3  b

➔ **Grammar 3B** page 142

**B** Ask sts to fill in the blanks in items 1–8 with the verbs from the box. Ask them to use the past perfect or the past perfect continuous where appropriate. Remind them to use contracted forms. Paircheck. Classcheck by writing the answers on the board.

1  'd been trying
2  'd got up
3  'd gone through
4  'd been dreaming of
5  'd been waiting for
6  had arranged
7  'd been driving
8  'd been raining

**C** Point to the grammar box and ask sts to complete it with the words in the box. Paircheck, then classcheck.

Read the example with the class. Put sts in pairs and ask them to role play Juan and Sandra telling their stories in their own words. Classcheck by asking two volunteers to retell their stories to the class.

1  Past continuous
2  Past perfect
3  Past perfect continuous

**Language tip** As an effect of direct translation, Portuguese and Spanish L1 speakers tend to use the verb *lose* instead of *miss* in any situation where their L1 uses the verb *perder*. So, before having sts answer the question title of this lesson, remind them that, in English, we say that we *lost* a match, our keys, money, personal objects, etc. But we say that we *missed* important dates or appointments, the train, the bus, the flight, the ship, etc. Make sure sts understand the difference.

**D** 🟢 **Make it personal** Ask: *Have you ever missed or forgotten anything important?* Ask each student to write notes about their story with the aid of questions 1–5.

Read the model dialogue in the speech bubbles with sts. Divide the class into small groups and have them share stories and respond / listen actively to other group members' stories using expressions from **C** on p. 38. Classcheck. Ask: *Which was the saddest story? Which story was the funniest?*

Finish the lesson by referring sts back to the song line on the top of p. 39. Ask: *Do you agree with these words?*

➔ **Workbook** Page 17

# 3.5 Do you always follow the rules?

## ID Skills  Understanding rules and regulations

**A** ▶ 3.10 Match the signs to photos a–i. Listen to check. In pairs, think of two places where you might find each one. Which four are intended to be funny?

*That one could be at a public beach.*

Signs:
- DOGS MUST BE ON LEASH.
- TRESPASSERS WILL BE PROSECUTED (IF THE DOGS DON'T GET YOU FIRST.)
- SPEED LIMIT 10 MPH
- ATTENTION, DOG GUARDIANS! PLEASE PICK UP AFTER YOUR DOG. THANK YOU. ATTENTION, DOGS! GRRRR, WOOF. GOOD DOG.
- DON'T EVEN THINK OF PARKING HERE! UNAUTHORIZED VEHICLES WILL BE TOWED AWAY AT OWNER'S EXPENSE.
- PLEASE FASTEN SEAT BELT WHILE SEATED. LIFE VEST UNDER YOUR SEAT.
- SMILE! This building is under 24 hr surveillance.
- SWIM AT YOUR OWN RISK – THE SHARKS WILL BE DELIGHTED! BY THE WAY, NO LIFEGUARDS ON DUTY HERE.
- IN ORDER TO MAINTAIN A RELAXING ENVIRONMENT, PLEASE REFRAIN FROM CELL PHONE USE.

**B** ▶ 3.11 Match 1–10 to their meanings. Listen to a teacher to check.

| | Verbs | Meanings |
|---|---|---|
| 1 | refrain from | ☐ remove someone's car using another vehicle |
| 2 | pick up after | ☐ avoid |
| 3 | tow away | ☐ close securely |
| 4 | fasten | ☐ clean up someone's mess |
| | **People** | |
| 5 | a lifeguard | ☐ someone who enters private property without permission |
| 6 | a trespasser | ☐ someone who helps swimmers in difficulty |
| | **Expressions** | |
| 7 | under surveillance | ☐ whoever owns it will pay all costs |
| 8 | on duty | ☐ although you know it's dangerous |
| 9 | at owner's expense | ☐ working |
| 10 | at your own risk | ☐ monitored |

**C** In groups, create and share signs for places 1–6. Any funny ones?
1. an airport
2. a hospital
3. your favorite beach
4. your English school
5. a theater
6. a zoo

**D** 😊 **Make it personal**  Have you, or people you know, ever broken any of these (or similar) rules? Would you ever break any of them?

*My parents never used to pick up after their dog, but now they always do.*

## 3.5 Do you always follow the rules?

**Lesson Aims:** Sts learn language to talk about rules and regulations and talk about rules they, or people they know, have broken.

### Function
Understanding rules and regulations.
Talking about rules people have broken.

### Language
Please fasten seat belt while seated.
I'm afraid you can't park here.
My wife used to get into trouble all the time at school for not wearing the right uniform.

**Vocabulary:** Common sign phrases (at owner's expense, at your own risk, fasten, lifeguard, on duty, pick up after, refrain from, tow away, under surveillance).

**Before the lesson:** Write the following questions on the board: *What rules are there: -at your school? -at home? Which rules do you disagree with? Why?*

♪ Turn to p. 328 for notes about this song and an accompanying task.

**Warm-up** Show sts the questions on the board and have pairs of sts discuss them. Classcheck by having sts report their partner's answers.

### ID Skills Understanding rules and regulations

**A Books open.** Focus on the lesson title question, *Do you always follow the rules?* Have sts take turns asking and answering the question in pairs. Classcheck.

Point to and read the sign *Speed limit 10 mph* with the whole class. Point to photos a–i and elicit the corresponding photo for this sign. Ask sts to read the rest of the signs and match the remaining photos to these signs. Paircheck. Play ▶ 3.10 to classcheck.

Have sts work in pairs to think of at least two possible places where they might see each of the signs. Classcheck. At the end, ask the class: *Which signs are intended to be funny? Do you find them funny?*

▶ **3.10** Turn to page 313 for the complete audioscript.

- a Don't even think of parking here! Unauthorized vehicles will be towed away at owner's expense
- b Trespassers will be prosecuted (if the dogs don't get you first).
- c Smile! This building is under 24hr surveillance.
- d Attention, dog guardians! Please pick up after your dog. Thank you. Attention, dogs! Grrrr, woof. Good dog.
- e Swim at your own risk—the sharks will be delighted! By the way, no lifeguards on duty here.
- f In order to maintain a relaxing environment, please refrain from cell phone use.
- g Please fasten your seat belt while seated. Life vest under your seat.
- h Speed limit 10 mph.
- i Dogs must be on leash.

Suggested answers:
Signs intended to be funny are b, c, d, and e

**B** Ask sts to match the verbs, people, and expressions in the first column to their meanings in the second column. Paircheck. Play ▶ 3.11 to classcheck.

1. refrain from = avoid
2. pick up after = clean up someone's mess
3. tow away = remove someone's car using another vehicle
4. fasten = close securely
5. a lifeguard = someone who helps swimmers in trouble
6. a trespasser = someone who enters private property without permission
7. under surveillance = monitored
8. on duty = working
9. at owner's expense = whoever owns it will pay the costs
10. at your own risk = although you know it's dangerous

**C** Put sts into small groups. Ask them to look at the places and create a sign they'd expect to see in each place. Ask each group to show their signs to the rest of the class.

Suggested answers
1. a café – Only food bought at the café may be consumed here.
2. a hospital – Do not park. Ambulances only.
3. your favorite beach – No dogs allowed.
4. your English school – Please turn off your cell phone.
5. a theater – Please remain quiet during the performance.
6. a zoo – Do not feed the animals.

**D** **Make it personal** Pair sts up and have them discuss important rules by taking turns asking and answering these questions: *Have you ever broken any of these rules?* and *Would you ever break any of these rules?* You could start sts off by telling them about a rule you have broken in the past. Nominate several sts to tell the class about their discussion.

93

# When did you last break a rule?

## ID in Action  Explaining and questioning rules

**A** ▶ 3.12 Listen to three dialogues and circle the correct signs on p. 40. Which speakers 1–3 don't accept the regulations easily?

**B** ▶ 3.13 Complete 1–7. Listen, check, and copy the stress and intonation.

| Stating a rule | 1 | I'm a_____ you c_____ park here. |
| --- | --- | --- |
| Apologizing | 2 | I'm sorry. I didn't r_____ that. |
| Questioning a rule | 3 | What do you m_____ I can't park here? S_____ who? |
| | 4 | Oh, c_____ on! Be reasonable! |
| Reinforcing | 5 | I'm afraid s_____. |
| | 6 | I'm afraid n_____. |

### Common mistakes

| so | not | don't so |
| --- | --- | --- |
| I'm afraid yes. | I'm afraid no. | I think no. |

**C** ▶ 3.14 Match these confessions to photos 1–4. What rule(s) had they broken?

☐ Well, a few years ago I was on a work trip to Poland. I was crossing the street when these police officers suddenly stopped me and tried to give me a fine for crossing in the wrong place! I had no idea it was illegal! I didn't speak any Polish and pretended not to understand. In the end, they let me go with just a warning. Weird!

☐ Once, my brother was taking photos in the countryside in Egypt. Suddenly, two soldiers appeared and confiscated his camera. Apparently, without knowing it, he'd taken photos of a military installation. And he'd thought it was just a nice bridge over a river!

☐ My wife and I were visiting Rome and the Vatican. I'd been wearing shorts all day, around the museums and stuff, no problem, but then they wouldn't let me in to St. Peter's. I had to wait outside while my wife got to see it all. Anyway, lucky for me, it's a beautiful square.

☐ My wife used to get into trouble all the time at school for not wearing the right uniform. The wrong shoes, the wrong shirt, she never wore a tie, dyed her hair purple … She was a real punk and it all seemed so stupid to her. Actually, she's still a bit of a rebel today. That's why I love her!

**D** In pairs, role-play a sign from p. 40. Act it out for the class to guess which sign you chose.

*Excuse me, ma'am. Haven't you read the sign?*

*No, I'm sorry, I haven't. Is there a problem?*

*Well …*

**E** 🟠 **Make it personal**  **Confessions!** Have you / your friends ever gotten in trouble for breaking a rule? Share stories in groups. Who has been the most disobedient?

*Hmm … well, the police stopped my uncle for using his phone in the car.*

*Did he get a fine, or did they let him go with a warning?*

♪ *I don't want to go to school, I just wanna to break the rules.*

## 3.5 When did you last break a rule?

**Lesson Aims:** Sts learn expressions for explaining and questioning rules and practice narrative tenses in the context of talking about rules and regulations.

### Function
Listening to people explain and question rules.
Reading confessions.
Confessing rules you've broken.

### Language
I was crossing the road when these police officers suddenly stopped me and tried to give me a fine for crossing in the wrong place!

**Vocabulary:** Phrases for explaining and questioning rules (I'm afraid you can't … , I'm sorry I didn't realize that. What do you mean I can't … , Says who? Oh, come one! Be reasonable! I'm afraid so. I'm afraid not.).
**Grammar:** Review narrative tenses.
**Skills:** Explaining and questioning rules.

### ID in Action  Explaining and questioning rules

**A** Tell sts that they are going to hear three conversations about the signs in Skills **A**. Instruct sts to listen and circle the correct signs as you play ▶3.12. Paircheck. Classcheck. Ask sts: *Which speakers don't accept the regulations easily?*

▶3.12  Turn to page 314 for the complete audioscript.

> 1 cell phone   2 no parking   3 trespassers
> Speakers 2 and 3 don't accept the regulations easily.

**Tip**  Have sts turn to the AS on p. 165. Sts listen again and notice the intonation in questions.

**B** Elicit answers for sentence 1. Then, have sts fill in the blanks for sentences 2-6. Play ▶3.13 so sts can check their answers. Replay ▶3.13 and have sts listen and repeat, copying the intonation.

> 1 afraid / can't   2 realize   3 mean / Says
> 4 come   5 so   6 not

**Language tip**  Romance language speakers frequently make the mistakes in the common mistakes box, because that's similar to how they say these sentences in their L1. Sts might include the word *that* before *yes* or *no* in their answers, as a result of direct translation. When tackling the common mistakes box examples, make sure sts understand that in English we don't use *that yes* or *that no* with opinion expressions like *I'm afraid …, I believe …, I think …* . Instead we just use *so* or *not*. Ask sts a few questions for them to express their opinions, affirmative or negative, using *I'm afraid …, I believe …, I think …* .

**Common mistakes**  Read the examples with the whole class. Elicit examples of situations when you could use each phrase.

**C** Introduce photos 1-4 and have sts briefly describe details they can see in each of them. Tell sts to read the confessions and match them to photos 1-4. Play ▶3.14 so sts can check their answers. At the end, ask: *What rules had these people broken?*

> 3, 1, 4, 2
> crossing in the wrong place
> taking photos of a military installation
> wearing shorts at St. Peter's
> not wearing the right uniform

**D** Have pairs of sts role-play a situation about one of the signs in **A** on p. 40. Instruct sts to read the model dialogue in the speech bubbles first. Allow pairs some time to plan what they will say, if necessary. Encourage sts to act out as many situations and signs as they can. Monitor pairs closely and offer help whenever needed.

At the end, invite volunteer pairs to role-play situations for the whole class. Ask the class to guess which sign is being acted out.

**E**  **Make it personal**  Divide the class into small groups of three or four and have sts in each group share stories about breaking rules and getting in trouble for it (or not). Monitor sts' stories closely and take notes for delayed correction. Classcheck by asking the groups to report the funniest stories to the whole class. Provide sts with language feedback at the end.

➔ **Workbook** Page 18

➔ **ID Richmond Learning Platform**

➔ **Writing** p. 42

➔ **ID Café** p. 43

# Writing 3  A narrative

*Little did I know…*
*That you were Romeo, you were throwing pebbles,*
*And my daddy said, "Stay away from Juliet",*
*And I was crying on the staircase*
*Begging you, please, don't go.*

**A** *Innovation* magazine has held a "best vacation narrative" competition. Read the winning entry and circle the correct photo for the story.

## A vacation to remember
### By Stef Stiller

1. ☐ My best friend Karen hadn't had a vacation for a long, long time. ☐ She was desperate to go somewhere new and do something she had never done before. ☐ So, last winter, after looking into many options, she decided to go skiing in Courchevel, a resort in the French Alps.

2. When Karen arrived, she was so excited about the comfortable hotel, delicious food, and such incredible views. ☐ The following day, she joined a ski-school. The other skiers seemed like fun-loving, sociable people, so she knew she'd have a great time. Karen had never skied before, but the instructor Alain, was great and reassured her.

3. However, she found skiing so hard she almost gave up. She kept trying, but then a horrible thing happened. While she was going down a hill, she fell badly and broke her leg. Her special trip had turned into a nightmare. Unable to move, she was stuck in a hospital in Courchevel.

4. But she had a wonderful surprise. ☐ They visited every day and brought gifts. Karen began to fall in love with the French Alps and decided to stay and get a job. She worked in a ski-chalet, learned to ski, and guess what? Now she's an instructor herself!

**B** Which paragraph, 1–4, answers these questions?
- ☐ What was the hotel like?
- ☐ Why did she go there?
- ☐ Where did she decide to go?
- ☐ Who is the main character?
- ☐ What happened while she was there?
- ☐ What happened in the end?
- ☐ Who did she meet?
- ☐ When did she go?

**C** Reread and underline examples of *simple past* (SP), *past continuous* (PC) and *past perfect* (PP).

**D** Read *Write it right!* and notice the nine time expressions in the story. Can you think of any others?

### ✓ Write it right!
- To enrich a narrative, use a variety of past tenses.
- Sequence it with a mix of time expressions to start, end, and connect sentences.
- Use plenty of adjectives and adverbs to add color to your story and *so* and *such* to emphasize them.

**E** Complete 1–5 with a time expression and the correct form of the verbs in parentheses.

after    ago    finally    occasionally    while

1. _____ leaving all her bags in the hotel, she _____ for a walk. (go)
2. _____ Karen _____ on her own. (travel)
3. This story _____ a few months _____. (happen)
4. _____, she _____ to go skiing. (decide)
5. Her new ski-friends and Alain _____ her the whole time _____ she _____ in bed. (help / recover)

**F** Match 1–5 from **E** to the boxes in Stef's story.

**G** Circle the correct word in each pair.
1. Courchevel was **so / such** beautiful **/ beautifully** that she didn't want to leave.
2. The days passed **so / such** slow **/ slowly**.
3. It was **so / such** a special **/ specially** trip that she'll always remember it.
4. That trip complete **/ completely** changed her life!
5. Alain was **so / such** a friend **/ friendly** guy.

**H** *Your turn!* Choose one of this year's topics for *Innovation* magazine's competition and write an entry in 100–180 words.

*That was really embarrassing!*

*What a frightening experience!*

| Before | Note down the main events in your story. Use the questions in **B** to help. Number the events in the order you want to tell them. |
|---|---|
| While | Write four paragraphs. Follow the tips in *Write it right!* |
| After | Ask your partner to check spelling and punctuation and give suggestions before emailing it to your teacher. |

# Writing 3 A narrative

♪ Turn to p. 328 for notes about this song and an accompanying task.

**A** Point out the model narrative and ask: *What type of text is this?* (a narrative). *Who wrote it?* (Stef Stiller). *Have you ever taken part in a magazine or website's competition?* Ask sts to quickly read the story and choose the photo that corresponds to the story. Paircheck. Classcheck.

🔑 photo 1

**B** Refer sts to the narrative in **A** and ask: *How many paragraphs are there?* (four). Point out the list of questions and ask: *Which paragraph, 1–4, answers each question?* Paircheck. Classcheck.

🔑 2, 1, 1, 1, 3 / 4, 4, 2, 1

**C** Have sts re-read the narrative in **A** and mark each verb as SP (simple past), PC (past continuous), or PP (past perfect). Classcheck by writing the answers on the board.

🔑 hadn't had (PP) / was (SP) / had never done (PP) / decided (SP) / arrived (SP) / was (SP) / met (SP) / was (SP) / had never skied (PP) / reassured (SP) / looked (SP) / found (SP) / gave (SP) / kept (SP) / happened (SP) / was going (PC) / fell (SP) / broke (SP) / had turned (PP) / stuck (SP) / visited (SP) / brought (SP) / fell (SP) / decided (SP) / was (SP)

**D** Go over **Write it right!** with the whole class. Then, have sts look for nine time phrases in the model narrative in **A**. Classcheck and ask: *Can you find any others?*

🔑 **Time phrases:** for a long, long time; before; last; after; when; the following day; never; then; while

**E** Have sts fill in the blanks in sentences 1–5 with the time expressions from the box and the correct past form of the verbs provided. Paircheck. Classcheck by writing the answers on the board.

🔑
1 After, went
2 Occasionally, travels / traveled
3 happened, ago
4 Finally, decided
5 helped, while, recovered / was recovering

**F** Tell sts that sentences 1–5 in **E** are sentences that are missing from Stef Stiller's story in **A**. Show sts the five boxes in the story. Have sts match sentences 1–5 from **E** to their positions in the narrative in **A**. Paircheck. Classcheck.

🔑 3, 2, 4, 1, 5

**G** Read item 1 with the whole class and elicit the correct options. Have sts circle the correct options in each bold pair in items 2–5. Paircheck. Classcheck.

🔑
1 so, beautiful
2 so, slowly
3 such, special
4 completely
5 such, friendly

**H** *Your turn!* Tell sts that they are also going to submit a vacation narrative for *Innovation* magazine's competition. Go over both title options with sts and ask them to choose one for their composition of 100–180 words.

**Before** Have sts write a first draft with the main events in their story. Tell them that their composition should be three paragraphs long. Advise them to plan their writing by answering the questions in **B** and planning the information they want to include in each paragraph.

**While** Remind sts to apply the tips from **Write it right!** and to write their narrative in three paragraphs.

**After** Have sts exchange compositions for peer checking and help. Then, collect their work for more detailed marking.

# 3 Global swarming                                    ID Café

## 1 Before watching

**A** Are the photos city (C), coast (Co), landmark (L), or scenery (S)? In pairs, describe them in detail and include these adjectives.

| amazing | awesome | beautiful | buzzing |
|---------|---------|-----------|---------|
| chaotic | congested | crowded | historic |

*Photo 4 looks like somewhere in Asia.*

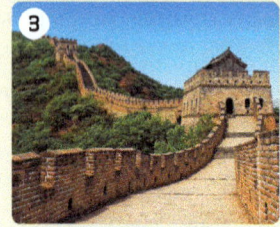

**B** ⬤ **Make it personal** In pairs, describe your favorite place or historical landmark.

*I saw the pyramids in Egypt five years ago. I'd never seen anything so old before!*

## 2 While watching

**A** Do you think 1–9 will be true or false? Watch and check (✓) your guesses. How many right?

1. ☐ August and Andrea had lived in many places before they moved back to the U.S.
2. ☐ Rory wants to go somewhere he has been before.
3. ☐ Silicon Valley is home of the computer nerds.
4. ☐ Rory has never been to Quebec City before.
5. ☐ August doesn't think New York is so chaotic.
6. ☐ Andrea and August lived in Buenos Aires.
7. ☐ Mexico City and New York are very crowded.
8. ☐ Rush hour in Mexico City is similar to New York.
9. ☐ Quebec City has lots of little cafés.

**B** Watch again and check the features of each place.

|  | Buenos Aires | Mexico City | New York | Quebec City |
|---|---|---|---|---|
| architecture |  |  |  |  |
| cafés |  |  |  |  |
| chaotic |  |  |  |  |
| good public transportation |  |  |  |  |
| historic landmarks |  |  |  |  |
| scenery |  |  |  |  |
| traffic |  |  |  |  |
| unpredictable weather |  |  |  |  |

## 3 After watching

**A** Circle the correct alternative(s).

1. The siblings had a lot of passport stamps because their **father / mother** was a photojournalist.
2. Rory goes to Dublin every year to **play soccer / visit his grandparents**.
3. August said they'd lived in **more than ten cities / more cities than he could name**.
4. Andrea and August mention "swarming like bees" to describe cities buzzing with **people / the noise of the traffic**.
5. Genevieve's gigs at the café draw **big / small** crowds.

**B** Complete 1–5 with the simple past or past perfect.

1. Rory _____ about visiting the West Coast. (think)
2. Rory didn't know they _____ in Argentina. (live)
3. Before Genevieve arrived for her gig, she _____ the others several times. (text)
4. August and Andrea _____ Rory pictures of Buenos Aires. (show)
5. Rory _____ in Dublin before he moved to the U.S. (live)

**C** ⬤ **Make it personal** Compare cities you know with those mentioned in the video. What would be your dream vacation destination?

*I've never been abroad, so I don't know any of these places.*

*Me neither. My home town, Trujillo, is a much smaller city, but it has some great colonial architecture.*

# ID Café 3  Global swarming

## 1 Before watching

**A** Write the following list of words on the board: *capital, coast, landmark, scenery*. Underline the first letter of each (and the first two letters of *coast*). Point to the top right picture and ask: *What's this?* (a coast). Instruct sts to write *Co* in the box provided. Have sts identify the rest of the pictures and mark them accordingly. Paircheck. Classcheck.

> 1 S  2 Co  3 L  4 C  5 L  6 S

Draw sts' attention to the adjectives in the box. To model the activity, point to the first picture and say: *This is amazing scenery.* Have sts work in pairs to make combinations of adjectives and places to express their opinions. Classcheck.

**B** 🔵 **Make it personal** Have sts work in pairs. Ask them to use the vocabulary from **A** to describe their favorite place or landmark to their partner. Refer them to the model text in the speech bubble. Classcheck by inviting volunteers to report their partners' answers to the whole class.

## 2 While watching

**A** Tell sts that Rory is planning his vacation, and August and Andrea are trying to help him decide where to go. Have sts quickly read the statements and ask them to watch the video and check the statements that are mentioned. Play ▶ 3. Paircheck. Classcheck.

> 1 T
> 2 T
> 3 T
> 4 T
> 5 F
> 6 T
> 7 F
> 8 T
> 9 T

**B** Go over the topics and cities in the chart with the class and replay ▶ 3 as sts check the features mentioned for each place. Paircheck. Classcheck.

|  | Buenos Aires | Mexico City | New York | Quebec City |
|---|---|---|---|---|
| architecture | ✓ |  |  | ✓ |
| cafés |  |  |  | ✓ |
| chaotic |  |  | ✓ |  |
| good public transportation |  |  | ✓ |  |
| historic landmarks | ✓ |  |  |  |
| scenery |  |  |  | ✓ |
| traffic | ✓ | ✓ | ✓ |  |
| unpredictable weather |  |  | ✓ |  |

## 3 After watching

**A** Have sts choose the correct alternatives for items 1–5 from memory. Paircheck. Classcheck.

> 1 mother  2 visit his grandparents  3 more cities than he could name  4 people  5 big

**B** Have sts fill in the blanks in sentences 1–5 with the simple past or the past perfect form of the verbs provided. Paircheck. Classcheck by writing the answers on the board or, if time allows, replay ▶ 3 with subtitles.

> 1 hadn't thought
> 2 had lived
> 3 had texted
> 4 showed
> 5 lived

**C** 🔵 **Make it personal** Have sts change partners. Ask: *What's your city like? What would be your dream destination?* Have sts work in their new pairs to ask and answer the questions. Refer them to the model text in the speech bubble. Classcheck by inviting volunteers to report their partners' answers to the whole class.

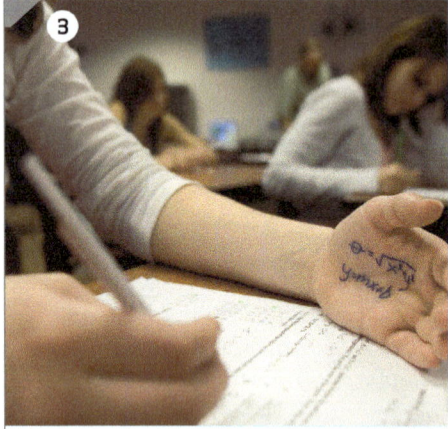

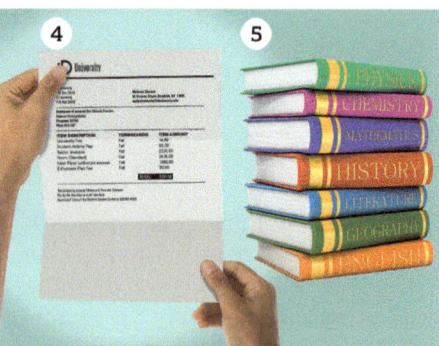

## 4.1 Does your school system work well?

### 1 Reading

**A** In groups, compare your thoughts when looking at photos 1–8.

*All the books remind me of my school bag. It was really heavy!*

**B** Say the subjects on the school schedule together. Pay attention to the pink-stressed syllables. In pairs, compare how you feel / felt about each one. Any good stories?

|       | Monday | Tuesday | Wednesday | Thursday | Friday |
|-------|--------|---------|-----------|----------|--------|
| 7:10  | Literature | Geography | Biology | Math | Chemistry |
| 8:05  | Math | Art | Information and Communication Technology | Math | Physics |
| 9:00  | Biology | Chemistry | History | Languages | Math |
| 9:50  | Break | – | – | – | – |
| 10:05 | Music | Math | Geography | Chemistry | Art |
| 11:00 | Physical education | Math | Languages | Physical education | Music |
| 11:55 | Lunch | – | – | – | – |
| 12:30 | History | Physics | Art | Literature | Literature |
| 1:25  | Languages | Philosophy | Music | Economics | Geography |
| 2:20  | Physics | Literature | Politics | Biology | Physical education |

*I used to hate math because the teacher couldn't explain it to us.*

**C** ▶ 4.1 Guess which countries have the world's best education systems, and why. Listen, read, and complete the first part of an article to check.

**Common mistake**
subject
My worst ~~material~~ was math.

### HEY, TEACHER, THOSE KIDS ARE DOING GREAT!

A certain education minister once joked that his country's education goal was a modest one: to be one of the best in the world. Well, looks like he's been successful. His country—which also has one of the largest per capita cell phone use on the planet—has the world's best school system, and 66% of its five and a half million population are university graduates. Here are some reasons why _____'s school system works so incredibly well and is considered the best in the world.

**Unit overview:** In unit 4, sts learn *should* + *have* + past participle construction and first and second conditionals in the contexts of education systems, school and college life, and ambitions. Sts also learn and practice *too* and *enough*.

# 4.1 Does your school system work well?

**Lesson Aims:** Sts use language related to school subjects and discuss topics related to education systems.

## Function
Talking about school subjects.
Reading about Finland's school system.
Comparing an education system to your own.
Talking about your ideal school.

## Language
I used to hate math because the teacher couldn't explain it to us.
... and 66% of its five and a half million population are university graduates.
They have one-on-one tutoring sometimes. We don't get that if we fail a test.
It'd be a nice modern building.

**Vocabulary:** School subjects. School life *verb* + *noun* collocations.

♪ Turn to p. 328 for notes about this song and an accompanying task.

**Warm-up** Have sts review p. 32–41 and, in pairs, take turns asking and answering the questions that form the lesson titles in unit 3. Monitor closely for accuracy. Take notes not only of sts' mistakes, but also of their best answers, to provide them with positive feedback as well. Classcheck.

## 1 Reading

**A** Read the example in the speech bubble with sts and ask which photo it relates to (5). Put sts into groups of three and ask them to look at the photos and compare their thoughts. Classcheck by asking a different volunteer to talk about each photo in turn.

**B** Point to the school schedule and read the school subjects with the class. Say each subject for sts to repeat, paying attention to which syllable is stressed. Then, write each subject on the board after sts have repeated it, underlining the stressed syllable. As you go along, ask questions to check understanding of the school subjects, e.g. *In which subject might you paint pictures?* (Art). *In which subject might you read and discuss books?* (Literature).

Art
Bi<u>o</u>logy
<u>Chem</u>istry
Ge<u>o</u>graphy
<u>His</u>tory
Infor<u>ma</u>tion and com<u>mu</u>nications tech<u>no</u>logy
<u>Lan</u>guages
<u>Lit</u>erature
Math
<u>Mu</u>sic
<u>Phys</u>ical Edu<u>ca</u>tion
<u>Phys</u>ics
<u>Pol</u>itics

Invite a volunteer to read the model in the speech bubble. Have pairs of sts take turns saying how they feel about each school subject in the schedule. Classcheck by having sts report some of their partners' opinions.

Read the song line on the top of p. 45 with sts and ask: *Do you know this song? Who recorded it? What's the song about?* If time allows, find the full lyrics online and explore more parts of the song on education.

**C** Ask: *Which countries do you think have the world's best education systems? Why?* Point to the title of the article and compare to the song line. Play ▶ 4.1 and have sts listen, read and complete the blank in the first part of the article. Paircheck. Classcheck.

Finland

**D** Why might this country's system be so good? Make a prediction about 1–8.
1. class size
2. discipline
3. homework
4. number of tests
5. public vs. private education
6. teachers' qualifications
7. popularity of arts subjects
8. uniforms

♪ *Hey, Teacher, leave them kids alone! All in all you're just another brick in the wall.*

*Maybe they have lots of expensive private schools.*

*Yes, I guess the teachers are well qualified, too.*

**E** ▶ 4.2 Read the rest of the article to check your predictions. How many were correct? Match the highlighted phrases to photos 1–8.

▶ Tuition fees? Forget it. Education is free and there are very few private schools.

▶ Classes are small, with rarely more than twenty students. The atmosphere is relaxed (lots of students don't wear uniforms or even shoes, only socks!), but students rarely behave badly. They hardly ever get kicked out of class or cheat on exams.

▶ Students in grades one through nine spend a lot of time each week taking classes in subjects such as art, music, and cooking. This helps to generate interest and motivate students.

▶ In Finland, kids have a lighter schedule than American students and do less homework, too—half an hour per day, tops. Having too much homework, they believe, can interfere with a child's passion for learning.

▶ During the first few years of school, students don't take tests. Instead, they get continuous feedback and a report card twice a year so their parents know if they're doing well. Students are actively encouraged to make mistakes and learn by doing.

▶ If students get low grades and fail* a test, they have extra support and one-on-one tutoring, if necessary. And it works really well. Every classroom has a teaching assistant to help students who are experiencing difficulties and everyone makes progress.

▶ What really makes the difference, though, is the status teaching enjoys in Finland. Education is the most competitive professional field in Finland—more so than medicine and law—and you must have a master's degree if you want to become a teacher.

\* the opposite of *pass*

## 2 Vocabulary School life

**A** Check the correct *verb + noun* collocations. Then scan the article in **1E** and *Common mistakes* to check.

| | do | get | make | take | |
|---|---|---|---|---|---|
| 1 | | | | | a class / tests |
| 2 | | | | | a low / high grade |
| 3 | | | | | homework |
| 4 | | | | | kicked out of class |
| 5 | | | | | mistakes |
| 6 | | | | | well (in school) |

**Common mistakes**

*doing*
My wife is ~~making~~ an MBA.

*take*
She'll have to ~~make~~ an exam at the end.

*passes*
If she ~~gets~~ the exam, she'll get a promotion at work.

*make*
She hopes she doesn't ~~do~~ too many mistakes.

**B** 🟠 **Make it personal** Follow the instructions.
1. In pairs, use the highlighted phrases and collocations in the article to compare the Finnish system with yours. How many differences can you find? Which would you introduce in your country?

   *They have one-on-one tutoring sometimes. We don't get that if we fail a test.*

2. Describe your ideal school, its policies, and schedule. Who came up with the best ideas? Any disagreements?

   *It'd be a nice modern building. We would only do a little homework every day and not take a lot of tests. And I think uniforms are a good idea.*

   *No way! I love wearing my own clothes.*

**D** Ask: *Why might Finland's education system be so good?* Have two sts read the model dialogue in the speech bubbles. Point to topics 1–8 and have sts discuss the topics and make their predictions in pairs. Classcheck sts' ideas.

**E** Play ▶ 4.2 as sts listen and read along to check the predictions they made in **D**. Classcheck.

Point to the first highlighted word and then direct sts' attention to photos 1–8 on p. 44. Ask: *In which photo can you see tuition fees?* (photo 4). Have sts continue matching the words in bold to photos 1–8. Classcheck.

1 class size: small, rarely more than 20 students
2 discipline: relaxed atmosphere, students rarely behave badly or get kicked out of class
3 homework: half an hour of homework per day, they believe homework interferes with passion for learning.
4 number of tests: students don't take tests for first few years. They get continuous feedback
5 public vs. private education: education is free, very few private schools
6 teachers' qualifications: teaching enjoys a high status, you must have a master's degree
7 popularity of art subjects: students spend a lot of time in art, music, and cooking classes
8 uniforms: no uniforms

Photos:
1 report card
2 schedule
3 cheat on exams
4 tuition fees
5 subjects
6 behave badly
7 fail a test
8 one-on-one tutoring

## 2 Vocabulary School life

**A** Model the activity. Ask: *Do you **do**, **get**, **make** or **take** a class or tests?* (take). Have sts check the corresponding verb in the chart. Tell them to work individually to check one verb for each school life item on the right. Paircheck. Then, ask sts to look for the correct answers in the text in **1E**. Classcheck.

1 take a class / tests
2 get a low / high grade
3 do/get homework
4 get kicked out of class
5 make mistakes
6 do well (in school)

**Language tip** Portuguese and Spanish L1 speakers can find the use of *do* and *make* confusing. When tackling the common mistakes box, make sure sts understand that, in English, we *do* an MBA, and we *do*, or *take*, a course, but we never say ~~make a course/an MBA~~. A good practical tip to make this clearer for Portuguese and Spanish speakers is to establish the difference between the verbs *do* and *make*, by comparing *do* with *hacer / fazer* (do the homework), and *make* with *preparar* (make a cake), or *cometer* (make a mistake).

**Common mistakes** Read the examples with the whole class and elicit why the crossed out verbs are incorrect.

**B** **Make it personal** 1 Ask sts to change partners. Instruct pairs to use the photos and highlighted phrases and collocations in the article to compare school life in Finland to their own country's schools. Refer sts to the model in the speech bubble. Monitor pairs' work closely and correct pronunciation mistakes on the spot, but leave other mistakes for delayed correction. Classcheck ideas and give sts language feedback on their performance.

2 Ask the class: *What's your idea of an ideal school? What policies and schedule would it have?* Divide the class into groups of three and have sts in each group share their views. Encourage them to use ideas from **1D**. Classcheck by having sts report their group members' opinions to the whole class.

➔ **Workbook** Page 19

## 4.2 What's the ideal age to go to college?

### 1 Listening

**A** ▶ 4.3 Listen to / Watch the trailer of a documentary about the education system in the U.S. Is it mostly positive or negative?

**B** ▶ 4.3 Listen / Watch again and check the three problems mentioned. Ignore the second column for now. Does it make you want to study there?

|  | The U.S. | My school |
|---|---|---|
| Too much homework. | | |
| Too much pressure to get into a good university. | | |
| Overcrowded classrooms. | | |
| Badly paid and demotivated teachers. | | |
| Too much emphasis on tests and grades. | | |
| Poor use of technology. | | |
| Discipline problems. | | |
| Not enough career counseling. | | |

### 2 Grammar *too / enough*

**A** Read the phrases in **1B** and the rules in the grammar box. Then correct the mistakes in the typical student errors 1–9 below.

| | | |
|---|---|---|
| 1 | **too** = more than necessary | Our classes start too early.<br>The classrooms get much too hot. |
| 2 | **enough** = the necessary amount | There was enough time to check my work.<br>Do you work hard enough? |
| 3 | **not enough** = less than necessary | There aren't enough chairs for everyone.<br>I wasn't sitting close enough to see. |

*too* goes before an adjective or adverb
*(not) enough* goes after an adjective but before a noun

➔ **Grammar 4A** p.144

              *a lot of*
1. My school was ~~too~~ fun. I really enjoyed it.
2. Are there windows enough in your classroom?
3. It was a too hard class. I didn't understand anything.
4. There was not money enough to buy new projectors.
5. I have too many friends at school. I feel lucky!
6. My teacher is too helpful. She's really friendly as well.
7. This is too difficult homework. I can't do it.
8. This exercise was very easy. It wasn't enough challenging for me.
9. I gave up Chinese because it was a too difficult language.

**B** 🟢 **Make it personal** Complete the *My school* column in **1B**. In pairs, share your experiences. Overall, are your feelings positive or negative? Any big differences?

> At my school, students have too much homework. It takes me four or five hours a day.

> Well, when I was in high school, I had a lot of homework, too.

## 4.2 What's the ideal age to go to college?

**Lesson Aims:** Sts practice *too* and *enough* in the context of school systems. They also learn vocabulary related to higher education.

**Function**
Watching / Listening to the trailer of a documentary.
Debating school systems.
Reading a website about choosing a career.
Talking about career choices.

**Language**
In America, if you don't earn a lot of money, something went wrong.
At my school, students have too much homework.
All my friends will major in business, so that's what I'll do.
If you could start over at high school, what would you change?

**Vocabulary:** Expressions related to college life (drop out of (college), get into (medical school) major, scholarship).
**Grammar:** *Too* and *enough*.
**Before the lesson:** Write the following questions on the board:
*Did you go to a public or private school? Where was (or is) it?*
*Did you have to wear a school uniform? What was it like?*
*Have you ever gotten into trouble because of a low grade?*
*Have you ever been kicked out of a class?*
*Are your kids doing well at school?*
*Who was your favorite teacher? Which subject did he / she teach?*

♪ Turn to p. 328 for notes about this song and an accompanying task.

**Warm-up** Point out the questions you wrote on the board (see **Before the lesson**). Pair sts up and have them ask and answer the questions. Ask sts to find three things they have in common with their partners. Classcheck.

### 1 Listening

**A Books closed.** Ask: *What do you remember about the Finnish education system?* Have as many sts as possible participate, saying what they remember from the previous lesson. Ask: *What about education in the U.S.? Is it good? Would you consider studying at an American university?*

**Books open.** Point to the photo of the video and tell sts that they are going to watch the trailer of a documentary about the U.S. education system. Set the video task by saying: *Watch and decide if what you see and hear is mostly positive or negative.* Play ▶4.3 ▶. Classcheck.

▶4.3 Turn to page 314 for the complete audioscript.

🔑 mostly negative

**B** Replay ▶4.3 ▶ and ask sts to notice and check the three problems mentioned. Paircheck. Classcheck.

Ask sts if they would like to study in the U.S. Encourage them to give reasons for their answers. If time allows, have sts turn to the AS on p. 166. Sts listen again and notice the sentence stress and weak forms.

🔑
too much homework
too much pressure to get into a good university
too much emphasis on tests and grades

### 2 Grammar  too / enough

**A** Reread the phrases in the chart in **1B** and go over the grammar box with sts. Then, ask sts to correct sentences 1–9. Paircheck. Classcheck.

**Tip** Fast finishers could write two more incorrect sentences for their partner to correct.

🔑
1. My school was a lot of fun. I really enjoyed it.
2. Are there enough windows in your classroom?
3. It was a hard class / The class was too hard. I didn't understand anything.
4. There was not enough money to buy new projectors.
5. I have a lot of / many friends at school. I feel lucky!
6. My teacher is very helpful. She's really friendly as well.
7. This is difficult homework. / This homework is too difficult. I can't do it.
8. This exercise was very easy. It wasn't challenging enough for me.
9. I gave up Chinese because it was too difficult / it was a difficult language.

➡ **Grammar 4A** page 144

**B** 🔵 **Make it personal** Point to the second column in the chart in **1B**. Ask sts to work individually to check phrases that are true according to their school experiences. Have sts read the model comments in the speech bubbles before they begin. After they have finished, pair sts and have them share facts about their schools. Classcheck. At the end, ask: *Do you feel mostly positive or negative? Did you find any big differences?*

**C** 🔘 **Make it personal** Read the Education Debate statements.
1 How much do you agree with them? (1 = strongly agree, 5 = completely disagree)
2 🔗 Research online to support your ideas.
3 In pairs, share your opinions and evidence. Do you have similar ideas?
4 Share your thoughts with the class. Any disagreements?

♪ *Baby, we don't stand a chance,
It's sad but it's true,
I'm way too good at goodbyes.*

### Education Debate
1. Pressure and competitiveness are positive for students.
2. Technology helps students learn better.
3. Training good teachers is the best investment a country can make.
4. There are too many problems with my country's education system.

*I think too much pressure can be very stressful for students.*

*You're absolutely right, but without enough competition, students can get lazy.*

## 3 Vocabulary College life

**A** Match the highlighted words in the website article below to their definitions.

| 1 | _____ | to specialize in a subject in college | 4 | _____ | to enter |
| 2 | _____ | to begin again | 5 | _____ | your main subject of study |
| 3 | _____ | money to pay for your education | 6 | _____ | to stop going to |

**B** ▶ 4.4 Reread and match classic mistakes 1–6 to the typical examples. Listen to check. Have you, or anyone you know, made these mistakes?

## 6 WAYS TO PICK THE WRONG CAREER

Are you going to be a graduate soon? Choosing a career is one of the most important decisions you'll ever make, so you'd better do it right. Here are six mistakes to avoid.

BY GABI WATSON

*A backup plan might be a good idea, in case 'being a celebrity' doesn't work out....*

### Classic mistakes
1. Living someone else's dream.
2. Doing what everybody else is doing.
3. Following your head, not your heart.
4. Being afraid to make big changes.
5. Being afraid of failing.
6. Not planning for the future.

### Typical examples

☐ "I can't throw away $40,000, drop out of college, forget about my business major, and start over."

☐ "I'd love to get a scholarship to go to Harvard, but it's so hard I won't even try."

☐ "All my friends will major in business, so that's what I'll do."

☐ "My parents have always wanted me to get into medical school. I can't disappoint them, and they are desperate for me to succeed."

☐ "I'd love to get a degree in music. I've already got my intermediate piano certificate, but what will I do when I graduate? How will I get a decent job?"

☐ "I have all the education I need. I'm not illiterate! It's time for fun, fun, fun!"

**C** 🔘 **Make it personal** Complete 1–5 with words from **A**. In pairs, ask and answer. Any disagreements?
1 If you could get a _scholarship_ to study anywhere in the world, where would you go?
2 How difficult is it to _____ a good college in your country?
3 What did you / would you like to _____ at college? Why?
4 Do you know anyone who _____ college? How did things go for him / her?
5 If you could _____ at high school, what would you change?

*I'd study gastronomy at the Sorbonne in Paris!*

⚠️ **Common mistake**
*I am graduated from law school.* =
*I majored in law.* /
*I have a law degree.*

C **Make it personal** 1 Have sts read the Education Debate statements then number the statements according to how far they agree with each one.

2 Ask sts to use their mobile devices or the class computer to research some of the ideas, using the statements as search terms.

3 Have sts change partners. Ask the new pairs to discuss statements 1-4 on the topic of education, sharing any information they found online. Monitor closely and offer help as necessary.

4 When they have finished, open the debate to the whole class and have sts share their ideas. Encourage them to agree or disagree and to justify their views.

Online research:
1 Competition can enhance performance when the competitive environment is healthy.
2 Technology helps make teaching and learning more meaningful and fun. However, it can change how the brain works, leading to problems with memory and attention.

### 3 Vocabulary   College life

A Focus on the highlighted words and phrases in the article in **3B**. Have sts match them to the correct definitions. Paircheck. Classcheck.

1 major in
2 start over
3 scholarship
4 get into
5 major
6 drop out of

B Ask: *Do you think it's easy to choose a career? What type of mistakes can people make?* Read the website's title and introduction with sts. Draw their attention to classic mistakes and typical examples listed on the website. Sts read the text and match the two columns. Paircheck. Play ▶ 4.4 to classcheck.

4, 5, 2, 1, 3, 6

Read the song line on the top of p. 47 with the whole class and find out if sts know the song or the singer who recorded it.

C **Make it personal**   Read question 1 with sts. Ask sts to use the words and phrases from **3A** to complete questions 2-5. Classcheck.

Ask sts to work in pairs to ask and answer the questions. Classcheck by asking individual sts to report their partner's answers.

1 scholarship
2 get into
3 major in
4 dropped out of
5 start over
Personal answers

**Language tip** As a result of direct translation, Portuguese or Spanish L1 speakers might use the verb *be* when talking about their graduation area. When dealing with the common mistake box on page 47, be sure to make it clear that, in English, we don't use the verb *be* to say we graduated in an area, or from a specific school. Explain that sts also have to be careful with the choice of the correct preposition: We graduate *from* an institution or school, but we graduate (or major) *in* a subject or an area of study.

**Common mistake**   Draw sts' attention to the Common mistake and elicit that *graduate* is a verb.

Use the example to draw sts' attention to the pronunciation of the suffix *–ate*. Tell sts this suffix is usually pronounced /eɪt/ in verbs and /ət/ in nouns and adjectives.
*Is Bill Gates a university graduate?*
*Mark Zuckerberg didn't graduate from Harvard.*
*Sue finally got her intermediate certificate.*
*Do you like chocolate?*

➔ **Workbook** Page 20

# 4.3 What do you regret not having done?

## 1 Listening

**A** In pairs, discuss the questions.
1. What kinds of regrets do people sometimes have about school?
2. Guess what these three people studied / are studying? What might they regret now?

**B** ▶ 4.5 Listen to three interviews about career choices and complete 1–3.

1. Justin says he should have studied _____ instead of _____.
2. Zoe studies _____, but she says she _____ writing.
3. George dropped out of _____ and became a _____.

**C** In pairs, do you know anybody who had trouble choosing a career? Are they happy now?

> Yes, me! I tried three completely different jobs until I found the right one for me.

> Really? What did you do?

## 2 Grammar *should have*

**A** ▶ 4.6 Match the sentence halves. Listen to check. Any resonate with you?

| | |
|---|---|
| 1 Dad wanted me to follow in his footsteps, but | ☐ I should have <u>chosen</u> another major. |
| 2 I'm way too old now. | ☐ I should have <u>gone</u> to music school years ago. |
| 3 Basically, journalism's not my thing. | ☐ I shouldn't have <u>listened</u> to him. |
| 4 I know it was a stupid decision, and | ☐ Should I have <u>persevered</u> a little more? |
| 5 Every day I wake up and ask myself: | ☐ I should have <u>thought</u> about it more carefully. |

**⚠ Common mistakes**

*have*
I should ~~studied~~ English when I was a kid.

*learning*
I regret ~~to not learn~~ English before.

**B** Reread 1–5 in **A** and the grammar box. Then answer 1–2.
1. What form are the underlined verbs in? Complete the form below.
   subject + should (not) + have + _____
2. How do you form questions?

> Use **should have** to express regret about something in the past.
> *I should have thought about it more carefully.* (= I didn't think about it carefully, and I'm sorry.)
> *I shouldn't have listened to him.* (= I did listen to him, and I regret that.)
>
> Also use **should have** to ask for or give advice about a past event.
>
> *What should I have studied instead?*
> *You should have been more open.*
> *You shouldn't have kept it secret.*

➡ **Grammar 4B** p.144

## 4.3 What do you regret not having done?

**Lesson Aims:** Sts learn and practice *should(n't)* + *have* + past participle to talk about regrets in the contexts of career choices and school life.

### Function
Listening to people talk about wrong career choices.
Talking about regrets.

### Language
He should've studied music instead of engineering.
I shouldn't have missed so many classes.
I shouldn't have told my boss she looked like a giraffe.

### Vocabulary:
**Grammar:** *Should(n't)* + *have* + past participle.
**Before the lesson:** Prepare a list of 20 to 25 irregular verbs of your choice from p. 158. Before sts arrive, write the infinitive form of the selected verbs on the board.

♪ Turn to p. 328 for notes about this song and an accompanying task.

**Warm-up** After you greet sts, tell them that they are going to play a game. Assign pairs. Point to the verbs on the board and say: *You have one minute to write down the past participle forms of all the verbs on the board.* When time is up, ask sts to check their answers against the list of irregular verbs on p. 158. Sts score one point for each correctly spelled participle.

## 1 Listening

**A** Read the questions with the class, then assign pairs for sts to discuss them. Classcheck.

1 Suggested answers: They didn't study hard enough. They didn't behave well. They chose the wrong subjects. They chose the wrong school. They made friends with the wrong people.

**B** Tell sts they're going to listen to Justin, Zoe, and George talk about their career choices. Read the sentences with the whole class and encourage sts to try to predict the missing words.

Say: *Listen to the interviews and fill in the blanks.* Play ▶ 4.5. Replay the track if necessary. Paircheck. Classcheck by writing the answers on the board.

▶ 4.5 Turn to page 314 for the complete audioscript.

1 Justin says he should've studied music instead of engineering.
2 Zoe studies journalism, but she says she can't stand writing.
3 George dropped out of university and became a dog walker

**Tip** Have sts turn to the AS on p. 166. Sts listen again and notice the weak form of /ə/.

**C** Ask: *Do you know anybody who had trouble choosing a career? Are they happy now?* Before sts answer, have them read the model in the speech bubbles. Pair sts up and ask them to share their stories with their partners. Classcheck.

## 2 Grammar *should have*

**A** Instruct sts to match the two halves of sentences 1–5. Play ▶ 4.6 so sts can check their answers. Read the question with sts and encourage them to share their answers with the class.

1 I shouldn't have listened to him.
2 I should've gone to music school years ago.
3 I should've chosen another major.
4 I should've thought about it more carefully.
5 Should I have persevered a little more?

**B** Allow the class more autonomy at this stage and encourage them to figure out the instructions by themselves. Ask sts to work in pairs, looking at sentences 1–5 in **2A** and answering questions 1–2. Monitor sts' work, offering help if requested.

**Common mistakes** Read with sts. Draw their attention to the position of *have* in the corrected sentence.

1 past participle
2 Should + subject + have + past participle?

→ **Grammar 4B** page 144

**C** ▶ 4.7 *Should've* is common in informal speech and writing. Listen and write down regrets 1–5. Notice the weak sound in the contractions /ʃʊdəv/ and /ʃʊdntəv/. In pairs, practice saying the sentences dramatically!

♪ *Too young, too dumb to realize that I should have bought you flowers and held your hand.*

1  *We should've gone by train.*

**D** Think of four regrets about your school days. Share them with your partner and then the class. What is the most common / unusual regret?

> *I shouldn't have missed so many classes.*   *Me, too. I should have participated more.*

**E** In pairs, write two *should have / shouldn't have* captions for each photo. Compare with other pairs. Choose the best caption for each photo.

> *I should have stayed home with Mom!*

**F** 🟢 **Make it personal**  **Oops, I did it again!** We've all done things we regretted later. What's your story?

1  Choose a topic below and prepare your story. Include a lie.
2  In groups, share your stories. Can you spot the lie?

| Your hair / looks | Disastrous vacations | Eating / drinking | Things you bought |
| Things you said | Relationships | Missed opportunities | Studies | Career |

> *I shouldn't have told my sister I didn't like her new dress.*

> *Why would you say such a thing? I think you're lying about that!*

**C** Point to the example sentence and say: **Should've** *is common in informal speech and writing.* Tell sts they'll hear five sentences about regrets and they need to write them down.

Play ▶ 4.7 for sts to write the sentences. Paircheck. Classcheck.

Replay ▶ 4.7 for sts to listen and notice the contracted form. Then have them practice saying the sentences in pairs. Monitor and check sts are producing the contracted forms correctly.

1 We should've gone by train.
2 You shouldn't have said that.
3 I should've helped you more.
4 He shouldn't have gone out last night.
5 You should've reminded me!

**Language tip** Portuguese and Spanish L1 speakers might have trouble forming the structure of the question title of this lesson (*What do you regret having done?*), because in their language they would use the equivalent to the prepositions *of* (*de*) or *for* (*por*), either before the chunk *not having done*, or at the beginning of the question. When tackling the question title of this lesson, make sure sts understand that, in English, we don't use a preposition with this structure. Ask sts to think of more examples of the same structure in their L1, and then in English, both negative and affirmative, to compare and make this clear.

**D** Ask two sts to each read one of the examples of regret in the speech bubbles. Have the class look at p. 48 and ask: *Do you regret having done anything at school? Do you regret not having done anything?* Ask sts to think of four regrets about their school days. Pair sts up and ask them to tell each other their regrets using the *should(n't) + have + past participle* construction. Refer sts to the list of irregular verbs on p. 158 for irregular participle forms.

**Weaker classes** Write the following sentence starter on the board: *I should've / shouldn't have + participle ...*

Monitor closely and correct any mistakes on the spot. Classcheck by inviting volunteers to report their partners' school regrets to the whole class. Remind sts that the *should + have + past participle* construction does not change for third person singular.

**E** Point to photo 2 and read the example caption in the speech bubble for sts. Have sts work in pairs to write captions for photos 1–4 using the *should(n't) + have + past participle* construction. Classcheck and have sts choose the funniest sentences in the class. Fast finishers can look for other photos in their book and write captions for those, too.

Suggested answers:
1 I should have got up earlier. / I shouldn't have stopped for coffee.
2 We should have worn raincoats. / We shouldn't have come out.
3 I should have been more careful. / I shouldn't have been going so fast.
4 I should have studied much harder. / I shouldn't have gone out the night before the exam.

**F** **Make it personal** Say: *We've all done things we regretted later, haven't we?* For item 1, point out the various topics. Have sts each choose one and write down a brief story about it. Remind them to include at least one regret sentence using the target language. Ask sts to include one lie in their story.

For item 2, split the class into groups of four or five. Within the groups, sts should take turns telling their stories. The other group members should try to spot the lie. Monitor sts' work and take notes for delayed correction.

Classcheck the lies sts have managed to spot and the most interesting stories. Provide sts with language feedback.

➔ **Workbook** Page 21

## 4.4 What would you do if you won a million dollars?

### 1 Listening

**A** Match the two halves of the quotes. Which ones do you like the most? Why?

| | |
|---|---|
| 1 If I had my life to live over, | ☐ you'll probably end up somewhere else. |
| 2 If you never try, | ☐ live as if you'll die today. |
| 3 If you don't know where you're going, | ☐ you'd never think a negative thought. |
| 4 If you realized how powerful your thoughts were, | ☐ you'll always get what you've always got. |
| 5 Dream as if you will live forever; | ☐ I'd dare to make more mistakes next time. |
| 6 If you always do what you've always done, | ☐ you'll never learn. |

*I like number 4. Positive thinking is very powerful.*

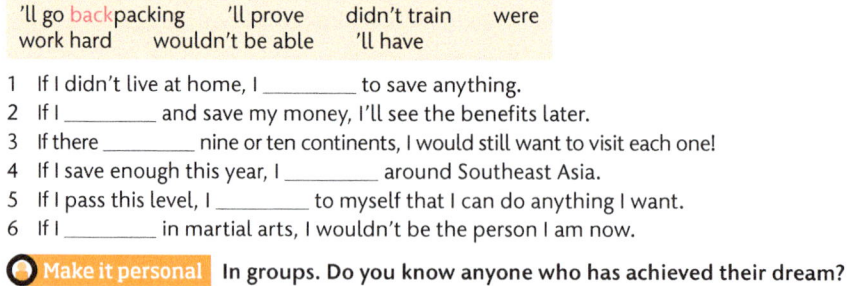

**B** Look at photos 1–6. What are the people's aspirations? Match them to these categories.

Career   Education / skills   Family life   Health and fitness   Travel

**C** How can these people achieve their goals? Do you have any similar goals?

*This couple want to own their own property.*   *They'll have to save a lot. Buying an apartment is so expensive. I'll never be able to get my own place.*

**D** ▶ 4.8 Listen to three people talking about their goals and aspirations. Match them to the photos in **B** and complete what they say.

Speaker 1: My big dream is …
Speaker 2: My main wish is …
Speaker 3: My ultimate aim is …

**E** ▶ 4.8 Listen again and complete 1–6 with the verb forms. There's one extra. Who do you think will achieve their goal?

'll go backpacking   'll prove   didn't train   were
work hard   wouldn't be able   'll have

1 If I didn't live at home, I _____ to save anything.
2 If I _____ and save my money, I'll see the benefits later.
3 If there _____ nine or ten continents, I would still want to visit each one!
4 If I save enough this year, I _____ around Southeast Asia.
5 If I pass this level, I _____ to myself that I can do anything I want.
6 If I _____ in martial arts, I wouldn't be the person I am now.

**F** 🔸 **Make it personal** In groups. Do you know anyone who has achieved their dream? What are your current aspirations? Share your best stories.

*My ultimate aim is to be a DJ.*

# 4.4 What would you do if you won a million dollars?

**Lesson Aims:** Sts learn and practice the first and second conditionals via the context of goals and aspirations.

### Function
Listening to people's goals and aspirations.
Talking about people who have achieved their goals.
Talking about your own goals and aspirations.

### Language
If I had my life to live over, I'd dare to make more mistakes next time.
They'll have to save a lot.
What kind of job would you like to get if you pass your test?

**Grammar:** First and second conditional.
**Before the lesson:** Write the following words and phrases on the board:
Travel to other countries
Get a good job
Study
Buy a house

♪ Turn to p. 329 for notes about this song and an accompanying task.

**Warm-up** Direct sts' attention to the phrases on the board. (see **Before the lesson**) Ask: *Which of these things are most important to you? Which have you already done?* Sts discuss the questions in pairs. Classcheck.

## 1 Listening

**A** Point to the quotes and say: *Here are some quotes about goals and aspirations.* Sts match the sentence halves. Paircheck, classcheck. Ask: *Which quotes do you like the most?*

1 If I had my life to live over, I'd dare to make more mistakes next time.
2 If you never try, you'll never learn.
3 If you don't know where you're going, you'll probably end up somewhere else.
4 If you realized how powerful your thoughts were, you'd never think a negative thought.
5 Dream as if you will live forever; live as if you'll die today.
6 If you always do what you've always done, you'll always get what you've always got.

**B** Point to photo 1 and ask: *What's her aspiration?* Have the class look at the remaining photos and identify what the people's goals and aspirations are and match them to the categories. Classcheck.

1 Travel  2 Career  3 Education / skills
4 Health and fitness  5 Family life

**C** Ask two students to read out the speech bubbles. Then, put sts into pairs to discuss what the other people need to do to achieve their goals. Classcheck.

Suggested answers:
1 Take time off work. Plan the trip.
2 Find out what qualifications and experience they need.
3 Study hard.
4 Take a course.
5 Save money.

**D** Tell sts they are going to listen to three of the people from the photos talking about their goals and aspirations. Play ▶ 4.8 and ask sts to complete what they say and match them to the photos in **1B**.

▶ 4.8 Turn to page 314 for the complete audioscript.

1 to own lots of different apartments – photo 5
2 to reach all seven continents – photos 1
3 to become an instructor and have my own training school – photo 4

**E** Have sts recall part 1 of the monologues from ▶ 4.8 in **D**. Then, read sentence 1 and elicit guesses by asking: *By living at home, what can he do?* Play the rest of conversation 1 in ▶ 4.8, and then pause the track. Classcheck. Have sts listen to the rest of ▶ 4.8 to complete the sentences. Classcheck.

1 wouldn't be able  2 work hard  3 were
4 'll go backpacking  5 'll prove  6 didn't train

**F** 🅜 **Make it personal**  Read the questions with the class, then assign groups to discuss them. Monitor and take notes for delayed correction. Classcheck by asking sts to share any interesting stories with the class, then give them feedback on their speaking.

## 2 Grammar  First and second conditional

🎵 *If I could turn back time, If I could find the way, I'd take back all those words that hurt you, And you'd stay.*

**A** Study the examples in the grammar box and complete the rules with these words.

"unreal" or impossible    real and possible    past    present (x2)    future

> **First conditional**
> *if* + simple present, *will* + infinitive
> *If I have time, I'll come and visit you.*
>
> Use the first conditional to talk about something that is ¹_____ .
> The *if* clause uses a ²_____ tense and talks about a ³_____ situation.
>
> **Second conditional**
> *if* + simple past, *would* + infinitive
> *If you had to spend a year with just one person, who would it be?*
>
> Use the second conditional to talk about something that is ⁴_____ .
> The *if* clause uses a ⁵_____ tense and talks about a ⁶_____ situation.
>
> *Remember: use the zero conditional (*if* + present simple, present simple) for facts or things that are generally true.
> *If you heat ice, it melts.*
> *Don't tell me you need me if you don't believe it.* (Ed Sheeran)
>
> ➔ Grammar 4C p.144

**B** Look back at the quotations in **1A**. Is each one in the first or second conditional?

**C** ▶4.9 Circle the correct alternative to make either first or second conditional sentences. Listen to check, and then repeat.
1. If I **have** / **did have** / **had** more time, I **'d practice** / **did practice** / **practice** the piano more.
2. If you **'ll save** / **would save** / **save** money now, you **'d have** / **'ll have** / **had** a good pension when you retire.
3. If we **knew** / **'d known** / **know** the answer, we **told** / **'d tell** / **tell** you.
4. You **are** / **'ll be** / **were** late if you **didn't take** / **won't take** / **don't take** the bus.
5. I **bought** / **'d buy** / **'ll buy** an apartment if I **have** / **'ll have** / **'d have** enough money.

**Common mistakes**
*If you ~~will~~ study hard, you will pass your test.*
*had*
*If I ~~would have~~ more space, I'd get a dog.*
*I'll be at school tomorrow unless I'd still feel ill.*
                           *I*

**D** In teams of two, race around the game. Write an ending for each segment before you go again. Which team can get to the end first?

**START** → If I don't go out this weekend … → I'll get up early tomorrow … → If I found a wallet … → If I don't pass my exams … → I'd be really excited …

Toss a coin … | Heads move 1 space | Tails move 2 spaces

**FINISH** ← If I knew the future … ← I won't complain … ← If I didn't have a smart phone … ← If my team wins … ← If I could learn something new …

**E** 👥 **Make it personal**  Think of a goal you have. Use the categories in **1B** to help you.
1. What is your goal and why? Prepare your answers to these questions.

   What is your goal?    What are you going to do to get there?
   Why do you want to achieve this?    What will the challenges / difficulties be?
   How will you feel if you achieve your dream? And if you don't?

2. In pairs, share your goals. Ask and answer follow-up questions. Any similar ones? Who has the most unusual goals?

*If I get my driver's license soon, I'll be able to get a better job.*

*What kind of job would you get if you passed your test?*

## 2 Grammar  First and second conditional

**A** Ask sts to read the grammar box and complete the rules with the words in the box. Paircheck. Classcheck. Remind sts that conditionals do not have to include *if*; they can also include *when, unless, even if, only if, in case*, etc. Draw their attention to the use of the comma in the example sentences.

> 1 real and possible   2 present   3 future
> 4 "unreal" or impossible   5 past   6 present

➔ **Grammar 4C** page 144

**B** Direct sts' attention back to the quotes in **1A** on p. 50. Ask: *Is each quote in the first or second conditional?* Sts discuss in pairs. Classcheck.

> 1 second   2 first   3 first   4 second   5 first   6 first

**Common mistakes**  Read with the whole class.

**Language tip**  When tackling the first mistake in the Common mistakes, make sure sts understand that, although the first conditional refers to a possible future situation, only one of the clauses actually goes into the future tense. You can use contrastive grammar to compare and show sts that, just like in Portuguese / Spanish, the *if* clause in a first conditional sentence stays in the present tense.

**C** Have sts read sentence 1 and choose the correct alternatives. Sts then complete the rest of the sentences. Paircheck. Play ▶ 4.9 to classcheck.

> 1 had, 'd practice   2 save, 'll have   3 knew, 'd tell
> 4 'll be, don't take   5 'll buy, have

**Stronger classes**  As an extension task, have sts speculate on the gender / age of speaker and context of each sentence before they listen. After listening, ask: *What would you have to change to make the other conditional form? How would the meaning change?*

**D** Tell sts that they are going to play a game. Divide the class into groups of four. In each group, assign two pairs: team 1 and team 2. If there is an odd number of sts in class, assign one group of three with two people on team 1 and one person on team 2.

Give each group two coins, one for team 1 and another for team 2. Ask sts to set their coins just in front of the first square – *If I don't go out this weekend ...* . Refer sts to the instructions on the page and demonstrate tossing a coin and getting heads (to move one space) and tails (to move two spaces).

Tell sts that team 1 will start the game. Ask them to toss their coin and move one (head) or two (tails) spaces. When team 1 stops at a space, each student in the pair must complete the sentence on it; that is, the team must come up with two different endings for the prompt. Remind sts to use first and second conditional sentences only. Explain that team 2 will check if the sentences are right or wrong. Then, it will be team 2's turn to play. If one (or both) ending for the sentence is not correct, sts have to wait one extra turn for the other team to play.

In each group, teams 1 and 2 should play against each other and alternate turns, moving across the board game and making first or second conditional sentence endings. The team to finish first is the winner.

Monitor groups closely and encourage peer correction. At the end, elicit some of the sentence endings sts remember from the game. If time allows, sts could make their own version of the game using their own ideas for sentence starters, e.g. *If I spoke English perfectly, ...* .

> Suggested answers:
> If I don't go out this weekend, I'll finish my assignment / I won't spend any money.
> I'll get up early tomorrow if I don't feel tired / if I set my alarm.
> If I found a wallet, I'd hand it in at the police station / I wouldn't keep it.
> If I don't pass my exams, I'll be very disappointed / I won't take them again.
> I'd be really excited if I won the lottery / if I met a famous person.
> If I could learn something new, I'd learn Mandarin / I'd learn to cook.
> If my team wins, I won't be surprised / I'll be really proud.
> If I didn't have a smart phone, I'd be very disorganized / I would talk to people more.
> I won't complain if they reduce the price.
> If I knew the future, I'd play the lottery.

**E** **Make it personal**  1 Ask sts to think of a goal they have. Direct their attention to the questions in the box and give them a few minutes to make notes on their answers. Go around and help with vocabulary where necessary. Remind them to use the categories in **1B** to help them.

2  Ask two students to read out the speech bubbles to the class. Assign pairs for sts to share their goals.

3  Nominate sts to share their goals with the class. Ask: *Any similar goals? Who has the most unusual ones?*

➔ **Workbook** Page 22

## 4.5 What makes someone a genius?

**ID Skills** Predicting and checking predictions

**A** Look at the photo and headline. Guess what the items below refer to.

5,000   IQ (intelligence quotient)   autism   trouble sleeping
learning disability   researcher   Stephen Hawking   huge equations

*Maybe he earns $5,000 a day?*

**B** Read in pairs to check. A: Read paragraph 1, B: Paragraph 2. Share what you remember. Then repeat. A: Read paragraph 3, B: Paragraphs 4 and 5.

# SMARTER THAN EINSTEIN?
Meet the 19-year-old who might change the way we see the world

¹ Jacob Barnett is what we might call a genius. He has an IQ of 170 and, in his free time, is developing an expanded version of the theory of relativity. Not bad for a 19-year-old, especially one who was diagnosed with Asperger's syndrome (a mild form of autism) and has trouble sleeping because he constantly sees numbers in his head! Not bad at all!

² At the age of two, Jacob—or Jake, as most people call him—still hadn't learned how to talk, so his parents suspected he might have a learning disability. As he grew up, however, they realized their son was actually incredibly gifted. By the age of three, Jacob could easily solve 5,000-piece jigsaw puzzles, calculate the volume of the cereal box while having breakfast, and learn by heart every single highway on the Indiana state road map. Just a few years later, while other kids were playing soccer or watching TV, Jake was having fun drawing complex geometrical shapes and writing huge equations on the living room windows.

³ By the time he had reached fifth grade, aged eight, it was clear that his mathematical ability was unusually high (at the level of a doctorate degree, actually!), so he dropped out of elementary school, taught himself all the math he needed to know in only one week, skipped high school, and enrolled at Purdue University, where he was allowed to attend advanced astrophysics classes. Five years later, Jake moved beyond the level of what his professors could teach him, so he eventually became a paid researcher—at only 13!

⁴ After college, Jake moved to Perimeter Institute, a place where the world's top thinkers, including Stephen Hawking, have taught. Jake was Perimeter's youngest ever student and submitted his master's thesis at 15. Today, he's still at Perimeter and the University of Waterloo.

⁵ For now, though, Jake's long-term plans are probably similar to the average teenager: to be happy doing something he finds challenging and rewarding. I wonder if he blames his autism for his early difficulties. If he wasn't autistic, however, he wouldn't be at the place he is right now. Autism is his way of viewing the world and it's because of that that he's able to do what he does so well.

**C** ▶ 4.10 True (T), false (F), or not mentioned (NM)? Listen and reread to check.
1. Jacob's speech developed when he was two.
2. Jacob enjoys playing soccer.
3. Jacob didn't attend high school.
4. Jacob has a "normal" social life.
5. Jake's very happy with his life.

**D** ▶ 4.11 In pairs, try to pronounce these words. Then listen to check. Any difficult ones?

| | | | | |
|---|---|---|---|---|
| **3 syllables** | theory | actually | constantly | easily |
| **4 syllables** | ability | incredibly | unusually | eventually |
| **5 syllables** | relativity | elementary | disability | |

**Guess the word!**
1 point = the right word
2 points = the right word and stress

**E** ▶ 4.12 Play **Guess the word!** Listen to the first part of the sentence, then say the missing word from **D** after the beep.

**F** ● **Make it personal** In pairs, answer 1–3. Any similar views?
1. Do you know anybody with a very high IQ?
2. Would you like to be like Jacob or have kids like him?

*Apparently, anyone with over 160 on an IQ test is 'profoundly gifted'. My dad scored 161!*

52

# 4.5 What makes someone a genius?

**Lesson Aims:** Sts continue to practice *should + have + past participle* and first and second conditionals through the contexts of predicting and checking predictions and expressing sympathy or criticism.

## Function
Predicting information from text titles and headlines.
Reading an article about a young genius.

## Language
He probably has a really high IQ.
Meet the 19-year-old who might change the way we see the world.

**Vocabulary:** Gifted, learn by heart, skip (high school), enroll (at university).
**Grammar:** Review first / second conditional.

♪ Turn to p. 329 for notes about this song and an accompanying task.

**Warm-up** Use the title question on the top of p. 52 to introduce the lesson topic to sts. Write the question *What makes someone a genius?* on the board and have sts discuss it in pairs. Classcheck and write their ideas on the board.

## ID Skills  Predicting and checking predictions

**A** **Books open.** Ask questions to introduce the text about Jacob Barnett. For example, point to the title and headline, and ask: *What might be special about this boy?* Point to the items in the box and have sts work in pairs to make predictions about the story using those ideas. Classcheck.

**B** Assign **A** and **B** roles within pairs and read the instructions with sts. Give them a time limit to read their first paragraph, then ask sts to share ideas with their partner before they read their second section. Classcheck.

> IQ (intelligence quotient): he has an IQ of 170 (very high – 140 is considered 'genius' level)
>
> Autism: he has Asperger's syndrome (a mild form of autism)
>
> trouble sleeping: he has trouble sleeping because he sees numbers in his head.
>
> learning disability: at age two his parents thought he had a learning disability
>
> jigsaw: by three he could solve 5000-piece jigsaws
>
> volume: he could calculate the volume of a cereal box during breakfast
>
> huge equations: he had fun drawing huge equations on the living room windows
>
> Stephen Hawking: after college, he moved to Perimeter Institute, where the world's top thinkers, including Stephen Hawking, have taught.

**C** Read items 1–5 with the whole group and elicit guesses from sts. Then play ▶ 4.10 for sts to listen and read to check their guesses.

> 1 F   2 NM   3 T   4 NM   5 T

**Extra task** Have sts choose a paragraph from the text and, in pairs, cover the paragraph, then uncover it line by line, guessing the first word of the next line as they work through the paragraph. Ask: *How many did you get right?*

**D** Point to the word *theory* in the chart and elicit the correct pronunciation from the whole class. Draw sts' attention to the number of syllables of the words in each column. Have sts work in pairs to practice pronunciation for all the words in the chart. Play ▶ 4.11 to classcheck and for sts to listen and repeat.

**E** Tell sts they're going to play **Guess the word!** Explain that they will guess the beeped words in sentences about Jacob Barnett, the genius from the article in **B**. Tell them that all the words are from the chart in **D**.

Play the first part of ▶ 4.12 and challenge sts to say the missing word before it is actually said on the recording. Sts must be fast; do not pause the audio track. Award one point for sts who say the right word and two for sts who say the right word with the correct pronunciation. Play the rest of ▶ 4.12 and continue the game.

> **Tip** If the number of sts is too large and it is difficult to hear which sts are pronouncing the word correctly, divide the class into two groups, team A and team B. Alternate turns, awarding sts' points to their teams.

▶ 4.12  Turn to page 315 for the complete audioscript.

> 1 disability        4 elementary
> 2 constantly        5 unusually
> 3 easily            6 eventually

> **Tip** Have sts turn to the AS on p. 166. Sts listen again and notice the connections and /t/, /d/, and /ɪd/.

**F** 🔴 **Make it personal** Read the questions with the whole class, then assign pairs for sts to discuss them. Classcheck by asking sts to share their ideas with the class.

# How do you deal with criticism?

**4.5**

## in Action  Sympathizing and criticizing

**A** ▶ 4.13 Listen to four dialogues and match them to the situations in the photos.

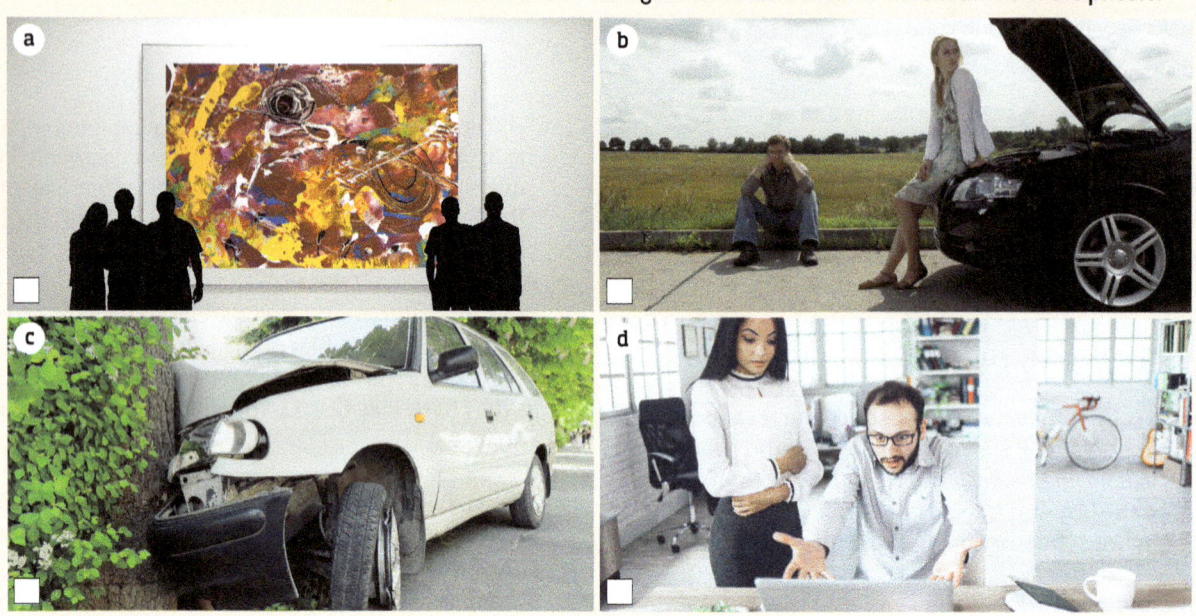

a  
b  
c  
d  

**B** ▶ 4.14 Listen again. After each beep, predict the next line from those in the chart. How many correct guesses?

| Dialogue | Sympathy | Criticism |
|---|---|---|
| 1 | It could have been worse. | Will you ever learn? |
| 2 | Don't let it get you down. | You should have known better. |
| 3 | What's done is done. | How could you do such a thing? |
| 4 | It's not the end of the world. | What were you thinking? |

**C** ▶ 4.15 Listen and repeat the expressions in **B**. Copy the intonation for each. In pairs, practice the expressions.

> **Common mistake**
> 
> *have*
> He shouldn't ~~had~~ bought that car.

**D** In pairs, answer questions 1–3 for each situation.
1. What should / shouldn't each person have done?  *The first person should have …*
2. Who do you feel most sorry for?
3. Have you or people you know ever had any problems like these?

**E** **Make it personal**  In pairs, tell a new story. Then change roles. Who was the most sympathetic listener? Whose story was funniest?
- A: Choose a context (a–f) and plan what to say.
- B: Ask follow-up questions and react to A's story using sentences from **B**.

| | | |
|---|---|---|
| **a** an accident that could have been a lot worse | **d** something important you forgot / missed |
| **b** an image or message you sent by mistake | **e** an unpleasant meeting |
| **c** something you bought on impulse | **f** a disastrous meal / vacation |

♪ *I should've known better than to cheat a friend, And waste a chance that I've been given. So I'm never gonna dance again, The way I danced with you.*

## 4.5 How do you deal with criticism?

**Lesson Aims:** Sts learn and practice expressions for expressing sympathy and criticism.

### Function
Listening to people sympathizing or criticizing others.
Telling a story and responding sympathetically or critically.

### Language
Don't let it get you down.
You should've known better.
It's not the end of the world.

**Grammar:** Review *should* + *have* + past participle
**Skills:** Sympathizing and criticizing
**Vocabulary:** Expressions of sympathy and criticism (It could've been worse, Will you ever learn? What's done is done.)

### ID in Action  Sympathizing and criticizing

**A** Have sts look at the photos and elicit as many details as possible by asking: *Where are these people? What might've happened? How do you think they feel?*

Tell sts that they are going to listen to four dialogues. Ask them to number photos 1–4 according to what they hear. Play ▶ 4.13. Paircheck. Classcheck.

▶ 4.13 Turn to page 315 for the complete audioscript.

> 1 c   2 d   3 b   4 a

**B** Tell sts that they are going to hear the four conversations again. Point to the chart and explain that, for dialogues 1–4, sts should guess whether the missing (beeped) sentences in the conversations will express sympathy or criticism.

Read both examples for dialogue 1 in the chart: *It could've been worse* vs. *Will you ever learn?* Point to both possibilities and say: *Listen to the first conversation again and, when you hear the beep, guess which sentence will be used.* Explain that sts will have four seconds to say it.

Play ▶ 4.14 and elicit, or prompt sts to guess, the sentence after the beep. Challenge them to do so within the pause in the audio track. Pauses are followed by correct answers.

> 1 It could've been worse.
> 2 You should've known better.
> 3 What's done is done.
> 4 What were you thinking?

**Tip** Have sts turn to the AS for ▶ 4.13/4.14 on p. 166. Sts listen again and notice the intonation of *What* and *Really*.

**C** Play ▶ 4.15 and ask sts to listen to all the sentences from the chart in **B** and copy the pronunciation and intonation they hear.

**D** **Common mistake**  Have sts change partners. Ask pairs to discuss questions 1–3 for the situations from **A**. Before sts start, go over the common mistake. Ensure that sts understand the structure used for criticizing, *should / could have* + past participle of the main verb. Monitor sts' work and take notes for delayed correction. Classcheck.

> Suggested answers:
> 1 She should have driven more slowly. / She shouldn't have driven into a tree.
> 2 He should have backed up his work. / He shouldn't have been so careless.
> 3 He shouldn't have bought the car. / He should have researched the car more carefully.
> 4 He should have realized who he was talking to. / He shouldn't have been so blunt.

**E** **Make it personal**  Assign roles **A** and **B** within pairs and have sts read the instructions for their roles. For a change, you may ask sts to explain (to you) what they have to do.

Have sts change roles. Monitor and offer help if necessary. At the end, ask: *Who was the most sympathetic listener in your pair?*

→ **Workbook** Page 23

→ **ID Richmond Learning Platform**

→ **Writing** p. 54

→ **ID Café** p. 55

# Writing 4  A blog

♪ *We could have had it all,*
*Rolling in the deep,*
*You had my heart inside of your hand,*
*And you played it, to the beat.*

**A** Use the title and photo to guess what the blog post will be about.

*It might be about contractions or funny expressions.*

**B** Read the post. Did you guess correctly? Do you think it is too late for the writer?

### "Shoulda, Coulda, Woulda"

"I shouldn't have done this." "I should've done that." (a) _____ Regret is something we all experience in life. I know, I have tons, but what's my biggest regret? My biggest regret is my choice of career. Yep, my career! Pretty big thing to get wrong, huh? Well, I did. (b) _____ Let's go back …

When I was eight years old, I started to learn to play the piano. I did it because my big bro was having lessons, too. Turns out I was way better at it than he was! (c) _____ Really, good, in fact. By the time I was 14, I had passed my grade 8 test. I loved it and played whenever and wherever I could. I started to compose my own stuff, and even had a gig playing in a local restaurant when I was 16. The tips were great! (d) _____

At 18, I had to make tough decisions. What did I want to do with the rest of my life? At that age, I was pretty focused on money. I wanted to do something I knew would give me a good income and stable future. (e) _____ playing piano in a restaurant wasn't that. So, I took a finance degree and I became a financial advisor, but I really regret that now. I had the dough, the stable future, but ten years down the line, what's missing?

I miss the music! I work long, hard hours and my piano is gathering dust. I hardly have time to play. (f) _____ I shouldn't have looked for the money. I should've stuck with something that gave me joy and fulfillment, but I guess it's too late now.

What do you think? Have you any shoulda, coulda, wouldas of your own? (g) _____

**C** Match 1–7 to a–g in the blog.
1 You guessed it,
2 Please share your regrets, and if you've managed to moved on from them!
3 Ever find yourself using these words?
4 How could I have let go of something so important to me?
5 Thank you to the generous patrons of Mama's Italian.
6 So, where did I take a wrong turn?
7 (Sorry, Mitch!)

**D** Read *Write it right!* Then match 1–7 in **C** to the different features commonly found in blogs.

✓ **Write it right!**

Common features of blogs are:
- rhetorical questions (a question asked to make a point rather than elicit an answer)
- humor
- informal / "chatty" language
- direct communication with the reader
- asking the reader for their ideas / opinions / experiences

**E** Find informal words and phrases in the blog to match the more formal ones below. Why are blogs written using this kind of informal language?

1 should have, could have, would have
2 many
3 That's correct
4 Isn't it?
5 brother
6 considerably
7 job
8 money

**F** Study the highlighted phrases in the blog. Then complete these sentences with the correct form of the verbs.

take    go out    not listen    send

1 I regret _____ to my heart.
2 I shouldn't have _____ last night
3 I would've _____ my dad's advice if I'd known.
4 I regret _____ that email.

**G** *Your turn!* Write a blog post in 120–180 words.

| Before | Choose a regret to write about. |
|---|---|
| While | Use informal language and the *Write it right!* tips. |
| After | Ask a partner to read your blog post, check spelling and punctuation, and leave a comment. Then send it to your teacher. |

# Writing 4  A blog

♪ Turn to p. 329 for notes about this song and an accompanying task.

**A** **Books closed**. Ask: *Do you ever read blogs? Which ones? Have you ever written a blog?* and discuss the questions as a class.

**Books open**. Point to the photo and read the title of the blog. Ask: *What do you think the blog post will be about?* Elicit ideas from the class and write them on the board, but don't give any answers yet.

> Suggested answers: regrets, learning new skills (e.g. how to play the piano)

**B** Give sts a few minutes to read the blog quickly and check their answer from **A**. Paircheck. Classcheck by checking any of the learners' guesses on the board which were mentioned in the text. Ask: *Do you think it's too late for the writer?*

**C** Point to blank (a) in the blog and ask: *Which phrase (1–7) is missing?* Elicit the answer, then ask sts to complete the rest of the blanks. Paircheck. Classcheck.

> a 3   b 6   c 7   d 5   e 1   f 4   g 2

**D** Ask: *What type of language do people use in blogs? Is it formal or informal? Can you think of any examples?* Then ask sts to read the **Write it right!** box to check their ideas. Point to *What's my biggest regret?* in the first paragraph and ask: *What's this?* (a rhetorical question). Have sts find examples of the other features. Paircheck. Classcheck.

> rhetorical questions: So, where did I take a wrong turn? How could I have let go of something so important to me?
>
> humor: (Sorry Mitch!); Thank you to the generous patrons of Mama's Italian.
>
> informal / "chatty" language: You guessed it, …
>
> direct communication with the reader: Ever find yourself using these words?
>
> asking the reader for their ideas / opinions / experiences: Please share your regrets …

**E** Read item 1 with the class and elicit the answer (the title of the blog post). Sts find the rest in the blog post. Paircheck. Classcheck and ask: *Why are blogs written in this kind of informal language?*

> 1 shoulda, coulda, woulda   2 tons   3 You guessed it
> 4 huh?   5 bro   6 way   7 gig   8 dough

**F** Focus sts' attention on the highlighted phrases in the blog post and ask: *What tense do we use after **I wish** and **If only** to talk about regrets?* (past perfect). Ask sts to complete the sentences. Paircheck. Classcheck and ask: *Are any of these sentences true for you? What happened?*

> 1 not listening   2 gone out
> 3 taken   4 sending

**G** *Your turn!* Tell sts they are going to write a blog post of their own in 120–180 words about a regret of their own.

**Before** Ask sts to choose a regret they have. Go round the class and help with ideas where necessary (e.g. skills, sports, things they said/didn't say, relationships, etc.)

**While** Give sts plenty of time to write their blog posts. Monitor and help with vocabulary/corrections where necessary. Remind sts to use informal language and refer them back to the **Write it right!** box.

**After** Assign pairs and ask sts to exchange their blog posts to check for spelling and punctuation, and make suggestions where they could use more of the informal language features from the **Write it right!** box. Ask sts to also add a comment at the bottom of the blog post. Ask sts to email you their final drafts for homework.

# 4 AIQ: Artificial Intelligence Quotient!

**iD Café**

## 1 Before watching

**A** Match 1–6 to their definitions a–f.

1 disciplinary action
2 calculated
3 input
4 outcome
5 procrastination
6 sophomore

a ☐ the result of something
b ☐ delaying things, not managing time
c ☐ punishment for breaking a rule
d ☐ planned
e ☐ a second year college student (U.S.)
f ☐ enter data into a computer

**B** ⊙ **Make it personal** Check the bills you pay monthly. Any paper bills or is it all online?

☐ cell phone    ☐ insurance    ☐ water
☐ electricity   ☐ Internet     ☐ other
☐ gas           ☐ mortgage

*The only mail I still get are fliers advertising services!*

**C** Guess which four bills August gets, and what's in the large envelope.

## 2 While watching

**A** Watch to 3:19 and check your ideas, and then check the three synonyms you hear for *intelligent / intelligence*.

☐ brilliant    ☐ crazy    ☐ Einstein
☐ genius       ☐ IQ       ☐ insane
☐ socially gifted

**B** Watch again and complete 1–5.

1 If you hadn't _____ the phone, I would've totally _____ insane.
2 Whatever happens, you _____ have done things any differently.
3 If only I hadn't been _____ of class … for _____.
4 Look, if I'd _____ more confidence, I would have _____ it immediately.
5 He _____ 've made me get up.

**C** How does his AIQ machine work? Order these steps, 1–5, then watch from 3:19 to the end to check. Do you think the letter will contain good news or bad?

☐ He inputs the presence or absence of people.
☐ The robot / machine calculates the outcome.
☐ It sends him a message.
☐ August types in his situation.
☐ He enters data about the scholarship.

## 3 After watching

**A** True (T) or false (F)? Correct the false statements.

1 August tried to contact several people.
2 Rory gives August good advice.
3 August was punished for a disciplinary action.
4 Daniel woke August up early.
5 August's program doesn't have a name yet.
6 August was in a higher physics class than Rory.
7 August lacks self-confidence.
8 His project results were great.
9 August won a scholarship for $25,000.

**B** Check all the correct answers. Do you ever procrastinate like this?

*Yes, quite often. It took me a long time to decide to …*

1 Why doesn't August want to open the letter?
  a ☐ He's not confident.
  b ☐ He's worried about the outcome.
  c ☐ He already knows the result.

2 Why is August the "king of procrastination"?
  a ☐ He keeps changing the subject.
  b ☐ His project is incomplete.
  c ☐ He won't open the letter.

**C** Why do we say it? Write C (change a subject), E (express regret), G (get a subject back on track), R (reassure) or S (speculate about the past).

1 ☐ If you hadn't …, I would've …
2 ☐ If only I hadn't …
3 ☐ You couldn't have done things any differently …
4 ☐ Hey, remember that time …
5 ☐ Stop changing the subject and get on with it.
6 ☐ If I'd had more confidence, I would've …

**D** ⊙ **Make it personal** In pairs, use the expressions in C to share past regrets or experiences. Any coincidences?

*If I'd had more confidence, I would have sung at the karaoke competition.*

*Do you think you'd have won?*

*You never know. The winner wasn't that good.*

55

# ID Café 1 AIQ: Artificial Intelligence Quotient!

## 1 Before watching

**A** Ask sts to match words 1–6 to the correct definitions. Help them with any words that are unfamiliar to them. Paircheck. Classcheck.

> 1 c  2 d  3 f  4 a  5 b  6 e

Then, ask sts to guess the pronunciation of the words that contain pink letters. Classcheck and drill pronunciation of all words.

**B** **Make it personal** Read the instructions with the whole class and have two sts read the model example in the speech bubble. Then, have sts discuss the questions in pairs. Classcheck by inviting volunteers to comment on their partners' answers.

**C** Point to the picture and ask: *Who's this? What's in the large envelope?* Have sts make predictions in pairs. Classcheck sts' predictions and tell them that they will find out the correct answer when they watch the video. Then ask: *What does August do? What are his interests?* Point to the robot on August's desk and ask: *What's this? Do you think it's August's creation?*

## 2 While watching

**A** Have sts quickly read the choices. Then play ▶ 4 up to 3:19 for sts to check the three synonyms they hear. Paircheck. Classcheck.

> brilliant, Einstein, genius

Ask: *So, what's in the large envelope?*

> In the envelope there is the letter informing that August is a finalist in the Artificial Intelligence design competition and a $25,000 scholarship.

**B** Go over sentences 1–5 with the class and have sts briefly predict the answers. Replay ▶ 4 and have sts fill in each blank with the correct verb in the correct form. Paircheck. Replay ▶ 4 with subtitles so sts can check their answers.

> 1 answered, gone  2 couldn't  3 kicked out, arguing
> 4 had, opened  5 should

**C** Ask: *What about August's invention? How does the program work?* Tell sts that they are going to watch the video again and put the steps in order. Play ▶ 4 from 3:19 to the end without subtitles. Paircheck. Classcheck.

> 4, 5, 1, 2, 3

## 3 After watching

**A** Have sts mark each statement 1–9 as true (T) or false (F). Paircheck. Classcheck by writing the answers on the board.

> 1 T
> 2 T
> 3 T
> 4 F
> 5 F
> 6 T
> 7 T
> 8 F
> 9 F

**B** Have sts work in pairs to check all the correct options to answer questions 1–2. Classcheck.

> 1 He's not confident. He's worried about the outcome.
> 2 He won't open the letter.

**C** Say: Look at the first sentence. *Why do we say it? To change the subject?* To speculate about the past? Have sts mark the purpose of each sentence as C (to change a subject), E (to express regret), G (to get a subject back on track), R (to reassure), or S (to speculate about the past).

> 1 S  2 E  3 R  4 C  5 G  6 S

**D** **Make it personal** Pair sts up and tell them that they are going to talk about past regrets and experiences. Encourage sts to use the expressions from **C**. Ask two sts to read the model dialogue in the speech bubbles for the whole class. Then, have partners share their regrets and past experiences. Monitor sts' discussions closely and take notes for delayed correction. Classcheck and provide sts with language feedback.

# R2 Grammar and Vocabulary

**A** *Picture dictionary.* Cover the words on the pages below and remember.

| pages | |
|---|---|
| 30–31 | 6 features of a city |
| 34 | 8 social rules in Hong Kong |
| 36 | 10 urban problems |
| 38 | 5 more active listening phrases |
| 40 | 10 verbs from regulations |
| 44 | 8 school words & 16 school subjects |
| 55 | 5 types of shopper |
| 160 | 2 words for each diphthong (not the picture words); say and spell them |

**B** ▶R2.1 Complete 1–6 with the correct form of the verbs in parentheses. Listen to check.

1. If you _____ as I tell you, you _____ into trouble. (do / get)
2. I can't understand what he's saying. If he _____ more slowly, I _____ more. (speak, understand)
3. When we _____ out of the restaurant, my car _____ there. Someone _____ it. (come / not be / take)
4. The authorities _____ that the athlete _____ drugs for months so they _____ him. (discover / use / disqualify)
5. I _____ to visit you if I _____ enough money, but I'm broke. (come / have)
6. I was really excited when I _____ in Barcelona. I _____ to it for ages. (arrive / look forward)

**C** ▶R2.2 In groups, imagine the rest of the story in pictures 1–3. Use a variety of tenses. Listen to compare stories and write the six past verb forms you hear. Have you had an experience like this?

*The three of them had spent the day packing all their camping stuff, and then they took the bus to the festival.*

**D** 🔴 **Make it personal** In pairs, circle *a*, *b* or *c* for 1–5 and explain your reasons.

1. Homework from this class:
   a too much   b the right amount   c not enough
2. Tuition fees in your country:
   a too low   b a fair price   c not low enough
3. Green spaces in your city:
   a too small   b perfect size   c not big enough
4. Buses or trains in your town / city:
   a too many   b a good number   c not enough
5. Tourists in your capital city:
   a too many   b the amount   c not enough

*I'm happy with the homework. And you?*   *Hmm. I don't think we do enough.*

**E** ▶R2.3 Match 1–5 to a–e to make short exchanges. Imagine who is speaking in each one. Listen to check.

1. Are we lost?
2. That was a dirty game.
3. I'm sorry. I shouldn't have said that.
4. I can't believe I crashed my car.
5. What! Vic's going out with Jill?

a ☐ You didn't know? Forget I said anything. I shouldn't have mentioned it.
b ☐ You really should have known better than to drive that fast.
c ☐ Yes! There should have been three red cards.
d ☐ Maybe. I think we should have turned left.
e ☐ I agree. But we all say stupid things sometimes.

**F** Correct the mistakes in each sentence. Check your answers in units 3 and 4.

🔴 **Common mistakes**

1. I'm graduated of math. (2 mistakes)
2. If you would got up earlier, you wouldn't lose the bus every morning! (2 mistakes)
3. "Did you do many mistakes?" "I think no." (2 mistakes)
4. He loves traveling. He's gone in every place in Europe. (2 mistakes)
5. L.A. is so big city and the people are such nice! (3 mistakes)
6. Studying hard don't mean you will get the test, but it helps. (2 mistakes)
7. I feel bad. I shouldn't to have ate all that pizza. (2 mistakes)
8. You should went at the party last night. (2 mistakes)
9. He was angry because he was waiting during 40 minutes before the police arrived. (2 mistakes)
10. People who goes to Miami are often surprised because they haven't expected Spanish speakers. (2 mistakes)

56

# Review 2 Units 3-4

## Grammar and vocabulary

♪ Turn to p. 329 for notes about this song and an accompanying task.

**A** ***Picture dictionary.*** Pairwork. Sts test each other and review vocabulary items learned in units 3-4. Throughout Picture dictionary tasks, monitor closely and correct vocabulary and pronunciation on the spot.

**Tip** In order to provide sts with as much fluency practice as possible, expand the activity into the mini-dialogues suggested below.

| Picture Dictionary | Procedures | Mini-dialogues / Suggested language |
|---|---|---|
| 6 features of a city, p. 32–33 | Sts cover texts in **1B**. In pairs, sts take turns pointing to pictures a–g and saying six features of a city. | St A: (points to picture d) *What's this?* <br> St B: *That's an upscale neighborhood near / by the beach.* (points to picture a) *What's letter a?* |
| 9 social rules in Hong Kong, p. 34 | Sts cover the text in **1A** and look at pictures a–h. In pairs, they name the customs in the pictures from what they remember to be usual or unusual in Hong Kong. | St A: *It's usual for people to shake hands and bow slightly.* <br> St B: *When you greet people, you shouldn't hug them or kiss them on the cheek.* |
| 10 urban problems, p. 36 | Sts cover the text in **1A** and take turns naming the urban problems (in New York or their own city) in pictures a–i. | St A: (points to picture i) *There's construction everywhere.* <br> St B: (points to picture a) *I always get stuck in traffic jams.* |
| 2 traffic stories, p. 38 | Ask sts to look at the pictures in **1A** and briefly retell / summarize Juan's and Sandra's stories. | St A: *The man was stuck in traffic and he missed the job interview.* <br> St B: *Sandra missed most of a Taylor Swift concert she had paid a lot of money to go to because her car broke down.* |

**B** Get sts to fill in the blanks in 1–6 with the correct form of the verbs given. Play ▶R2.1 to check. Classcheck.

> 1 had done / have gotten
> 2 spoke / would understand
> 3 came / wasn't / had taken
> 4 discovered / had been using / disqualified
> 5 would come / had
> 6 arrived / had been looking forward

**C** Divide the class into groups of three or four. Within their groups, sts collaboratively tell a story using pictures 1–3. Draw sts' attention to the model in the speech bubble and instruct them to use a variety of verb tenses to tell the story. Monitor and offer help. Then, play ▶R2.2 for sts to compare their narrative to the story in the audio.

> Possible answer: They arrived at the festival, but it had been canceled. Then, they decided to stay in a tent, but it started to rain. The weather was very bad, it was raining a lot and the wind was strong too. The wind destroyed their tent. They ended up cold and wet and without a shelter.

At the end, ask: *Have you ever had an experience like this?*

**Tip** Have sts turn to the AS on p. 167. Sts listen again and notice /w/ and /j/.

**D** **Make it personal** Ask sts to answer 1–5 according to their opinion. Have two sts read the model dialogue. In pairs, sts compare their views, 1–5. Classcheck.

**E** Read question 1 with the whole class and elicit the best answer from the options given. Sts match 1–5 to the answers. Paircheck. Play ▶2.3 to check answers.

> 1 d  2 c  3 e  4 b  5 a

**F** **Common mistakes** Sts correct Common mistakes sentences 1–10. Focus their attention on the number of mistakes between parentheses. Whenever sts are uncertain, encourage them to flick back through p. 26–45 and check their answers in units 3 and 4. Classcheck by writing the answers on the board.

> 1 I've graduated in math.
> 2 If you got up earlier, you wouldn't miss the bus every morning.
> 3 "Did you make many mistakes?" "No, I don't think so".
> 4 He loves traveling. He has been to every place in Europe.
> 5 L.A. is such a big city and the people are so nice!
> 6 Studying hard doesn't mean you will pass the test, but it helps.
> 7 I feel bad. I shouldn't have eaten all that pizza.
> 8 You should have gone to the party last night.
> 9 He was angry because he had been waiting for 40 minutes before the police arrived.
> 10 People who go to Miami are often surprised because they don't expect Spanish speakers.

# Skills practice

*I should have changed that stupid lock,*
*I should have made you leave your key.*

**R2**

**A** Read and listen to the four stories ▶3.14 on p. 41 and underline any words that are difficult to hear / understand. Listen again. Are they difficult because:
  a these words link to the following word?
  b they're unstressed and virtually disappear?
  c their pronunciation changes in context?

**B** ▶R2.4 Listen and complete extracts 1–6 from videos in units 3 and 4.
  1 Kissing _____ cheek _____ hugging _____ not practiced.
  2 Gifts _____ never opened _____ person _____ gave them.
  3 Fill _____ tea cups _____ others before pouring _____ own cup, _____ their cups _____ not empty.
  4 In America, _____ you don't earn _____ money, something _____ wrong.
  5 Everyone expects _____ superheroes.
  6 You have _____ smart and you have _____ involved _____ arts.

**C** ▶R2.5 Listen to and imitate each phrase.

**D** Look at the photo and title. Guess what these words refer to. Read the text to check your predictions.

  Netflix   12 years old   Spain   Calvin Klein
  Drake and Maroon 5   youngest person ever

  *Maybe she's the daughter of the owner of Netflix?*

**E** Reread. True (T) or false (F)?
  1 Millie Bobbie Brown had won nine awards before *Stranger Things*.
  2 She's half English, half Spanish.
  3 She has lived in at least three different countries.
  4 Her family moved to L.A. a week after she was spotted by a talent agent.
  5 She's also also worked as a pop singer and a model.
  6 She had appeared in two movies when this article was written.

**F** ▶R2.6 Cross out the word with the different underlined sound. Listen to check, then in pairs create a funny sentence with the remaining words. Say them slowly, then quickly.
  1 afr<u>ai</u>d <u>a</u>pples <u>A</u>sia th<u>ey</u> volc<u>a</u>no
    *In Asia they are afraid of an eruption from the volcano.*
  2 cr<u>a</u>zy f<u>a</u>shionable st<u>a</u>tue t<u>a</u>xi tr<u>a</u>ffic
  3 aw<u>ay</u> <u>eigh</u>t p<u>air</u> st<u>ay</u> str<u>aigh</u>t

**G** Role-play. Social rules
  1 In pairs, list three more "social etiquette" rules. Then exchange with another pair.
  2 A: You're a tourist. Mime breaking each rule.
    B: Explain the rules to A.

**H** ▶R2.7 ○ **Make it personal** **Question time!**
  1 Listen to and answer the 12 lesson titles in units 3 and 4.
  2 In pairs, practice asking and answering. Use the map on p. 2–3 and choose the two most interesting questions from units 3 and 4. Which one produces the most interesting conversation?

  *Which city would you most like to visit?*
  *There are lots of cities I'd love to see, but number one has to be …*

## Millie Bobby Brown

**Name:** Millie Bobby Brown
**Born:** 19 February 2004
**Occupation:** actor and model

### Next big thing?

Many people say that Millie Bobby Brown is the next big thing in Hollywood. What do they mean? She is already there!

Brown caught the attention of the world in 2016 with her role in the hit Netflix series *Stranger Things*, which she won approximately nine awards for! She achieved that when she was only twelve years old, but she had already acted in five different TV series. Pretty incredible, huh? Well, it's even more amazing when you realize that she was actually born in Spain to English parents, moved to England when she was four, and then to the U.S. when she was eight. In 2011, she was spotted by a talent agent at a drama class. Her family later moved to L.A. and after only a week, Millie was meeting talent agencies. After only three months in Hollywood, she was given her first TV role.

What a career so far! Millie is extremely hardworking. The adults she works with praise her for her maturity and talent. Although she is so young, she has already played some very challenging roles. Apart from film and TV, she has also starred in music videos with Maroon 5 and Drake and modeled for Calvin Klein. In 2018, she was the youngest person ever included on *Time* magazine's list of the "World's most influential people". In 2019, she'll be in her first movie, *Godzilla: King of the Monsters*. Watch out for this girl in the future!

## Skills practice

**A** Ask sts to go to p. 41 and look at stories in **ID in Action** C. Tell sts to listen to and read the text and underline any words that they find difficult to hear or understand. Play ▶3.14. Classcheck underlined words. Ask: *Why are these words difficult to understand?* Go back to p. 57 and have sts read options a, b and c. Replay ▶3.14 for sts to choose the best answer according to their perception. Classcheck.

**B** Tell sts they'll hear six extracts from videos in units 3 and 4. Play ▶R2.4 for sts to listen and complete 1–6. Paircheck. Replay if necessary. Classcheck by writing the answers on the board.

> 1 Kissing on the cheek and hugging are not practiced.
>
> 2 Gifts are never opened in front of the person that gave them.
>
> 3 Fill the tea cups of others before pouring your own cup, even if their cups are not empty.
>
> 4 In America, if you don't earn a lot of money, something went wrong.
>
> 5 Everyone expects us to be superheroes.
>
> 6 You have to be smart, you have to be involved in the arts.

**C** Say: *Let's practice pronunciation now.* Tell sts to listen and copy the exact intonation of each sentence they hear. Play ▶R2.5 for chorus repetition. If time allows, replay and get some individual repetitions.

**D** Point to the picture and ask: *Who's she? What does she do? Where was she born?* Then, ask sts to make two predictions in pairs about Millie Bobby Brown's career. Classcheck.

Point to the words and phrases and tell sts to discuss what they refer to in pairs. When they have finished, have sts read the text quickly to check their ideas. Paircheck. Classcheck.

> Netflix: caught the attention of the world with her role in the hit Netflix series *Stranger Things*
>
> 12 years old: she was 12 years old when she appeared in *Stranger Things*
>
> Spain: she was born in Spain
>
> Calvin Klein: she has modeled for Calvin Klein
>
> Drake and Maroon 5: she has appeared in their music videos
>
> youngest person ever: to be included in *Time* magazine's list of the "World's most influential people"

**E** Sts reread the text in **D** and mark statements 1–6 as true (T) or false (F). Paircheck. Classcheck.

> 1 F  2 F  3 T  4 F  5 F  6 F

**F** Sts compare the sounds of underlined letters in each of phrases 1–3 and cross out the odd ones. Paircheck. Play ▶R2.6 to check answers.

> 1 apples
>
> 2 crazy
>
> 3 pair

Then, ask sts to make sentences with the remaining words in 2–3, as the example in 1. Classcheck.

**G** *Role-play*. Change partners. In pairs, sts come up with three social etiquette rules and write them down. Monitor for accuracy and correct mistakes on the spot. Then, sts exchange rules with another pair.

In pairs, sts act out roles **A** and **B**. Student **A** role-plays a tourist breaking one of the social rules and student **B** explains the rule and gives student **A** tips on what's appropriate / usual according to the rule. Have sts change roles once. Classcheck by having a few pairs acting out the situations to the whole class.

**H** **Make it personal** *Question Time!* Tell sts they're going to hear twelve questions, the lesson titles from units 3 and 4. Ask them to listen and write their personal answers briefly onto their notebooks / a sheet of paper. Ensure sts understand they don't have to write the questions down, only their answers.

Play ▶R2.7. If necessary, pause briefly after each question, get sts to jot down very brief notes.

Sts look at the **ID Language Map** on p. 2–3 and take turns asking and answering the lesson title questions from units 3 and 4. Monitor closely for accuracy and encourage sts to ask follow-up questions when suitable. At the end, ask them how they felt performing the task: *Did you feel comfortable answering all the questions? Which ones were easy? Which ones were difficult?*

# 5

## 5.1 Are you a shopaholic?

### 1 Reading

**A** In pairs, list five things you expect from a store when shopping. Are your shopping habits and expectations similar to your parents'?

> *I expect good customer service.*
>
> *Yes, and I like it to be well organized, so I can find things easily.*

**B** Look at the cartoons. Who or what do you think Generation Z is? Read the introduction to the article to check.

## Gen Z TRANSFORMING THE SHOPPING EXPERIENCE

Generation Z, born between 1996 and 2012, came into a digital world with technology at the center of everything. This generation is expected to have a huge impact on the future of shopping. Let's examine how:

**TECHNOLOGY.** Members of Gen Z have a device they interact with constantly so, while shopping, they compare prices, read reviews, and even buy online. They still want to do in-store shopping, but they want an experience, and technology has to be at the center of this experience. Stores need smart phone self-checkouts, interactive screens, and virtual try-ons. A discount code and loyalty programs are an incentive and should be accessible online. Gen Z expects free Wi-Fi in stores. In fact, it is wise for stores to provide charging stations, so shoppers can keep their batteries full.

**HIGH EXPECTATIONS.** Gen Z is demanding. If the in-store experience doesn't meet their expectations, they move on. They want a store that embraces technology and makes products easy to test, but they still want human interaction. They have less patience and will instantly share a poor experience on social media. Attractive prices are still essential, or they'll just have Amazon deliver it to their door, again!

**INFLUENCERS.** Gen Z is influencing the decisions of the whole family. Apparently 70 percent of parents ask their kids for advice before they shop. Gen Z trusts friends rather than advertising and has a strong social media presence. Gen Zers post their thoughts and images of products on Snapchat, Instagram, and YouTube and want to connect directly with the brand. There is even a rising trend in videos, which are posted online, of shoppers displaying items they have recently bought and talking about them. Brands should use this user-generated content if they want to encourage brand loyalty with Generation Z.

**C** In groups, brainstorm how you think Generation Z is changing shopping. Then each read a different paragraph and report back. Were your ideas mentioned?

> *Well, they probably all shop online and don't go to real stores anymore.*

### Common mistakes

~~expect everything to be~~
My parents ~~wait that all is~~ really cheap.

~~most successful brand~~
Apple is the ~~mark of most success~~.

**D** ▶5.1 Listen, reread, and give the author's answers to 1–5. Do you agree with them all?
1. What should stores provide Gen Z shoppers with for in-store shopping?
2. What does Gen Z expect from a store in addition to technology?
3. What happens when Gen Z has a negative shopping experience?
4. How does Gen Z influence their parents?
5. How can stores encourage brand loyalty?

**E** ○ **Make it personal** How might shopping evolve in the next 30 years? Will there still be any small stores?

> *Maybe we'll have chip implants so we won't need cash or credit cards.*

58

**Unit overview:** In unit 5, sts learn and practice the third conditional and modal verbs to talk about possibilities and express uncertainty via the contexts of money and shopping. Sts also learn about adjective order and word formation.

## 5.1 Are you a shopaholic?

**Lesson Aims:** Sts learn and practice phrases related to modern shopping.

### Function
Talking about shopping preferences.
Reading about Generation Z and their shopping habits.
Listening to a radio program about "shopping haul" videos.
Making your own "shopping haul" or "anti-shopping haul" video.

### Language
I expect good customer service.
They still want to shop in-store, but they want an experience.
For shopaholics, these videos are entertaining.

**Vocabulary:** Expressions related to modern shopping (brand loyalty, charging station, discount code, free Wi-Fi, self-checkout, shop in-store, user-generated content, virtual try-on).

♪ Turn to p. 329 for notes about this song and an accompanying task.

**Warm-up** Ask sts to revisit p. 44–53 and, in pairs, take turns asking and answering the lesson title questions in unit 4. Monitor closely for accuracy and take notes of any mistakes for delayed correction. Ensure that sts ask follow-up questions when appropriate. Classcheck.

### 1 Reading

**A** Ask: *What things do you expect from a store when you're shopping?* and ask two volunteers to read out the examples in the speech bubbles. Put sts in pairs to list five things they expect and discuss the question. Classcheck.

> Possible answers: good customer service, store is well organized and tidy, good lighting and décor, free Wi-Fi, good website

**B** Write: *Generation Z* on the board and ask: *What's this?* Elicit sts' ideas but don't give any answers yet. Point to the cartoons and read them together. Give sts a minute to read just the introduction to the text to check. Classcheck.

> Generation Z is the generation born between 1996 and 2012.

**C** **Common mistakes** Ask: *How do you think Generation Z is changing the shopping experience?* Read the speech bubble with the class as an example, and go through the Common mistakes, then assign pairs to discuss the question. Classcheck by writing their ideas on the board.

Ask sts in their groups to each read a different paragraph, then report back to each other and check which of their ideas were mentioned. Classcheck and check off any of the ideas on the board that were mentioned.

**Language tip** In Portuguese and Spanish, the equivalent to the verb *wait* is also used to mean *expect* in most cases. For this reason, as a result of direct translation, sts who speak these languages commonly make the mistake in the Common mistakes box. Make sure to explain to sts that, in English, we use two different verbs (*wait* and *expect*) for different situations where they tend to use the same verb in their L1. Give sts a few more examples to make this distinction clear:
*I don't expect to get a discount—but I always ask!*
*I waited for the prices to fall—but they didn't.*

**D** Play ▶5.1 for sts to listen, read the article again, and give the author's answers to the questions. Paircheck. Classcheck.

> 1 smart phone self-checkout, interactive screens and virtual try-on. A discount code and loyalty programs should be accessible online, free Wi-Fi, charging stations
> 2 They expect human interaction.
> 3 They share it on social media.
> 4 They give them advice on what to buy.
> 5 By using user-generated content.

**E** **Make it personal** Give sts time to consider their answers individually, then assign groups for them to discuss their answers together. Classcheck by asking each group to report a prediction.

**Tip** Set up a role-play between a traditional shopper and Generation Z shopper. Encourage sts to think about their different roles and talk about their expectations when they go shopping and how they like to shop.

## 2 Vocabulary Shopping

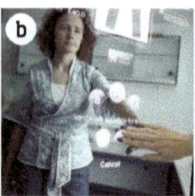

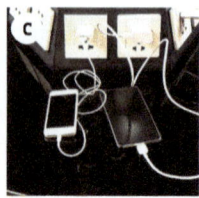

♪ *Baby, I don't need dollar bills to have fun tonight.*

**A** Match the highlighted words in the article to the photos.

**B** Complete 1–8 with the words in **A**. Which ones do you hear / say often?
1. There's no need to stand in that long line. They have _____ here.
2. My battery is running out. Are there _____ in here?
3. Smart brands use customers' _____, such as YouTube videos and blog posts, to advertise their products.
4. I would rather do _____ than shop online. At least you can try things on.
5. I've got a _____ for that store—you get 10% off everything today.
6. I can't get online to check the reviews. They don't even have _____ in here!
7. These glasses looked good on me with _____, but they don't look good in real life.
8. I don't have much _____ except for my cell phone—I'd never consider getting any other make.

**C** 🟠 Make it personal  In pairs, answer 1–3.
1. Are you a member of Generation Z?
2. Which points in the article do you agree / disagree with, and why?
3. How many of the people in the class shop like a Gen Z?

*I agree with a lot of it, but I still prefer to buy things online. It's so much easier!*

## 3 Listening

**A** Do you ever post images or videos of things you buy on social media? Why (not)? Have you seen (YouTube) vloggers describe things they have bought?

*No way, what for? Who would care about my shopping?*

**B** ▶ 5.2  You're going to listen to a radio program about "shopping haul" and "anti-shopping haul" videos on YouTube. Guess what these videos are.

**C** Listen again and complete 1–5.
1. A "shopping haul" video shows a vlogger _____ they've bought.
2. People watch these videos because it's satisfying to see how _____.
3. In an "anti-haul" video, vloggers talk about products they don't plan to buy because they think they are _____.
4. Kimberly Clark's first "anti-haul" video has had _____ views. Now there are over _____ "anti-haul" videos online.
5. Research shows that Millennials would much rather _____.

**D** 🟠 Make it personal  In pairs, make a "shopping haul" or "anti-shopping haul" video. Follow these instructions.
1. 📡 Decide which type of video to make. Search online for examples of these videos to give you ideas.
   - **Shopping haul:** Make notes about products you have bought recently (where, how much, why, how happy you are with them, etc.)
   - **Anti-shopping haul:** Make notes about products you don't think people should buy, explaining your reasons why.
2. Practice what you want to say. Then record yourselves using a cell phone or act out your video for the class. Who made the best one? Any future YouTube stars?

🟠 **Common mistake**

*Buying*
Buy things online is much more easy.
easier

*Today, we're gonna be showing you things that we're not actually gonna buy, then explain why.*

## 2 Vocabulary Shopping

**A** Point to the photos and elicit what sts can see. Remind sts of the highlighted words in the article in **1C** and ask: *Which photo shows **in-store shopping**?* (d). Sts match the rest of the highlighted words to the photos. Paircheck. Classcheck. Drill the phrases chorally and individually.

> a discount code
> b virtual try-on
> c charging stations
> d in-store shopping
> e self-checkout
> f user-generated content
> g brand loyalty
> h free Wi-Fi

**B** Elicit the first answer as an example. Sts complete the rest of the sentences. Paircheck. Classcheck.

> a self-checkouts
> b charging stations
> c user-generated content
> C in-store shopping
> d discount code
> e free Wi-Fi
> f virtual try-on
> g brand loyalty

**C** **Make it personal** Read the questions with the class, and ask a student to read out the speech bubble. Put sts in pairs to discuss the questions. When they have finished, invite a few sts to share their ideas with the class, and find out if other sts agree.

## 3 Listening

**A** If the technology is available, introduce the topic by showing a "shopping haul" video. Read the questions with the class, then put sts into pairs to discuss. Classcheck by asking a few sts to share their answers with the class.

**B** Ask: *What do you think "anti-shopping haul" videos are?* Play ▶5.2 for sts to listen and check.

▶5.2 Turn to page 315 for the complete audioscript.

> An anti-shopping haul is a video in which the vlogger encourages people to buy less by talking about products they think are useless or overpriced.

**C** Give sts a few minutes to try and complete the sentences from memory. Paircheck. Don't give any answers yet. Replay ▶5.2 for sts to check their answers. Paircheck. Classcheck by writing the answers on the board.

> 1 unpacking and describing items
> 2 people spend their money
> 3 useless or overpriced
> 4 100,000, 850,000
> 5 buy experiences than stuff

**Tip** Have sts turn to the AS on p. 167. Sts listen again and notice /m/, /n/, and /ŋ/ endings.

**Common mistake** Read with the class.

**D** **Make it personal** 1 Explain that sts are going to make a "shopping haul" or "anti-shopping haul" video. First, assign pairs and ask them to decide which type of video they're going to make, then have them read the relevant part of the box and make notes on their ideas. Go around and help with ideas and vocabulary where necessary.

2 When they are ready, ask sts to practice what they're going to say. Read the model language in the speech bubble with sts. When they feel confident enough, ask sts to record each other using their cell phones or perform their videos for the class. Ask: *Who made the best video?*

➔ **Workbook** Page 24

# 5.2 What shouldn't you have spent money on?

## 1 Listening

**A** How do people get into debt? List five things they can do to get out of debt.

**B** ▶5.3 Listen to a college graduate giving a talk to some freshmen about debt. Answer the question in **A** for her. Did she mention any of your ideas?

*She was 18 when she started getting into debt.*

**C** ▶5.3 Listen again. What is the significance of the following numbers?

| 18 | 25 | 30 | 50 | 2,000 | 12,000 | 20,000 |

**D** Match the verb and noun collocations. Check your answers in ▶5.3 on p. 167.

| Money collocations | |
|---|---|
| 1 take out / pay back / pay off | ☐ debt |
| 2 go on | ☐ money |
| 3 run out | ☐ of money |
| 4 waste | ☐ a shopping spree |
| 5 be in / get into / get out of | ☐ a loan / a credit card / an overdraft |

**E** 🗣 **Make it personal** Is there a lot of debt in your country?

*Absolutely, and not only students. Most of us spend our lives owing money to someone.*

## 2 Pronunciation Silent consonants

**A** ▶5.4 Pronounce these words. Listen to check. Know any others?

| debt | listen | castle | thumb | subtle | high | bought |

**⚠ Common mistake**

*had*
*If the word hadn't silent letters, I would have pronounced it correctly.*

**B** ▶5.5 Listen and cross out the two silent consonants in 1–5. In pairs, say the sentences simultaneously, as fast as you can.
1 I have no doubt you'll be able to pay off your debt.
2 The traffic cop whistled and told me to fasten my seatbelt.
3 It's difficult to understand signs in a foreign language.
4 My neighbors' daughter has moved out.
5 The police will climb the mountain to look for the bomb.

## 3 Grammar Third conditional

**A** Look at the example and answer 1–5 in the grammar box.

> If I'd **listened** to some advice, I wouldn't have **gotten** into financial mess.
> 1 Is she imagining changing the past or the present? Is that possible?
> 2 Did she take advice? Did she get into a financial mess? Can she change what happened?
> 3 What form are the bold verbs: simple past or past participle?
> 4 What is the full form of *I'd listened*: *I had listened* or *I would listened*?
> 5 Complete the form:
> If + subject + *had (not)* + _____, subject + _____ + past participle + phrase
> If you are not sure about the result, you can use *might / could have*:
> If I'd listened to advice, I might not have gotten into financial mess / could have avoided it.
>
> ➡ **Grammar 5A** p.146

# 5.2 What shouldn't you have spent money on?

**Lesson Aims:** Sts learn and practice the third conditional and the pronunciation of words with silent letters in the contexts of student debt and volunteering.

**Function**
Listening to a talk about student debt.
Talking about student debt in your country.
Talking about mistakes you've made.
Reading / Talking about volunteering.

**Language**
I started getting into debt when I was 18.
If I had started driving lessons when I was younger, it wouldn't have taken so long to get my license.
I'd volunteer to help with reading at my local primary school.

**Vocabulary:** Money collocations (be in / get into / get out of debt, go on a shopping spree, pay back / pay off a loan, run out of money, take out a loan / a credit card / an overdraft, waste money).
**Pronunciation:** Silent consonants.
**Grammar:** Third conditional.
**Before the lesson:** Write the following questions on the board: *When was the last time you used a discount code? What was it for? How big a discount did you get? What brands do you have brand loyalty for? Why? Do you prefer shopping online or in-store? Does it depend on the product?*

♪ Turn to p. 330 for notes about this song and an accompanying task.

**Warm-up** To review vocabulary from the last lesson, have sts work in pairs to ask and answer the questions you wrote on the board (see **Before the lesson**). Classcheck.

## 1 Listening

**A** **Books closed**. Write on the board: *in debt* and clarify what it means (to owe more money than you have). **Books open**. Put sts in pairs to discuss the question and make a list.

**B** Tell sts that they're going to listen to a graduate talking about debt. Ask them to listen and check if any of their ideas from **A** are mentioned. Play ▶5.3 for sts to check. Paircheck. Classcheck.

▶5.3 Turn to page 315 for the complete audioscript.

**C** Elicit what sts can remember but don't give any answers yet. Then, replay ▶5.3 for sts to check their answers. Paircheck. Classcheck.

> 18: She was 18 when she started getting into debt
> 25: There was 25% interest on her credit card debt
> 12,000: When she graduated she was $12,000 in debt
> 2,000: Her first salary was $2,000 a month
> 50: Her rent was more than 50% of her salary
> 20,000: When she was 25 she was $20,000 in debt
> 30: She set a goal to get out of debt by the time she was 30.

**D** Have sts match the verbs and nouns. Direct sts' attention to AS ▶5.3 on p. 167 to check answers.

> 1 take out / pay back / pay off a loan / credit card / an overdraft   2 go on a shopping spree   3 run out of money   4 waste money   5 be in / get into / get out of debt

**E** **Make it personal** Read the question with the whole class, then assign pairs for sts to discuss. Classcheck.

## 2 Pronunciation Silent consonants

**A** Have sts practice saying the words with silent letters. Play ▶5.4 to classcheck. As sts if they know any other words with silent consonants.

**B** Sts listen and cross out the silent letters. Paircheck. Play ▶5.5 so sts can listen and check their answers.

Model the activity with a student to demonstrate saying words together, simultaneously. Classcheck and drill.

> 1 dou~~b~~t / de~~b~~t   2 whis~~t~~led / fas~~t~~en   3 si~~g~~ns / forei~~g~~n
> 4 neighbors' dau~~gh~~ter   5 cli~~m~~b / bom~~b~~

**Language tip** Portuguese and Spanish L1 speakers tend to pronounce silent consonants in English as they don't have them in their own L1. Help them practice this aspect of English by giving them tongue twisters with words containing silent consonants, e.g., *I doubt your neighbor's debt can be paid.*

## 3 Grammar Third conditional

**A** Point to the example sentence in the grammar box. Ask sts to read the questions and answer in pairs. Classcheck.

> 1 the past, no   2 no, yes, no   3 past participle   4 I had listened   5 past participle, would have

**Language tip** Ask sts to translate the example sentences and compare the number of words in L1 and English. Ask: *Which uses more words?* (English). *Is the form similar?* (yes).

➔ **Grammar 5A** page 146

**5.2**

*It's a bittersweet symphony, this life.
Trying to make ends meet.
You're a slave to the money, then you die.*

**B** ▶5.6 Complete the third conditionals 1–5 with the verbs. Use contractions. Listen, check, and repeat.
1. If you _____ (tell) me you were in debt, I _____ (lend) you some money.
2. If he _____ (be) more sensible, he _____ (save) more money.
3. I _____ (not buy) a new car even if I _____ (earn) enough money last year.
4. If we _____ (pay) the bill on time, they _____ (not cut off) the electricity.
5. The bank _____ (might give) you a credit card if you _____ (ask) for one.

**Common mistake**

had
If I ~~would have~~ paid to park my car, I wouldn't ~~get~~ a parking fine.   have gotten

**C** Make sentences about the speaker in ▶5.3 using the third conditional.

*If she hadn't gone to college, she might not have gotten into debt.*

**D** 🟢 **Make it personal**  Think about a mistake you made or something you wish you'd done differently. In pairs, share your stories. Ask follow-up questions. Whose was the biggest mistake?

*If I hadn't played so many video games, I'd have been better at sport!*

*Which sports would you have played?*

## ④ Reading

**A** Look at the photos and read the first three lines of the website. What do you think Volunteer2Zero is?

**B** Read on to check. A: Read the main text, B: Read *How it works*. Then share. Were you right?

**C** ▶5.7 Cover the text and remember the five benefits of Volunteer2Zero. Listen and reread to check. Any surprises?

### Volunteer2Zero

Do you have a student loan?
Wondering how you're going to pay it back?
That's where Volunteer2Zero comes in …

**HOW IT WORKS**
→ You register with us as a volunteer or donor
→ You say where and how much time you can volunteer
→ Our donors decide what help they need and how much to sponsor you
→ You do work in your community and receive donations for every hour you volunteer
→ You pay off your debt and pay back your community. It's simple!
Volunteer2Zero

**Volunteer2Zero** is a crowdfunding idea with a difference. We all know that crowdfunding is getting lots of people to give small amounts of money in order to fund a project. But, with **Volunteer2Zero**, instead of just fund-raising to pay back your debts, you can give a little more in return and help make the world a better place.

With **Volunteer2Zero**, you can reduce your student debt by volunteering. In exchange for your time and skills, you will:
→ receive donations from your community
→ improve your professional skills
→ develop professional contacts
→ improve your community
→ increase your chance of graduating debt-free

**D** 🟢 **Make it personal**  Discuss.
1. Would Volunteer2Zero work in your country? Is crowdfunding common? Would you register with an organization like this?
2. List three things you could volunteer to do in your community.
3. In pairs, role-play a conversation with someone who got out of debt by joining Volunteer2Zero.

*I'd volunteer to help with reading at my local elementary school. I think some parents would donate to V2Z.*

*If I hadn't joined V2Z, I wouldn't have escaped from debt.*

## 5.2

**B** 🔑 **Common mistake** Read with the whole class. Then have sts look at sentence 1 and elicit the answer as an example, writing it on the board. Sts complete 2–5. Paircheck, then play ▶ 5.6 to classcheck.

> 1 had told, 'd have lent
> 2 'd been, 'd have saved
> 3 wouldn't have bought, 'd earned
> 4 'd paid, wouldn't have cut off
> 5 might have given, 'd asked

**C** Direct sts' attention back to the speaker in ▶ 5.3 and ask what they can remember about her. Write on the board: *She got into debt at 18. She took out credit cards.* Ask: *How can we make a third conditional sentence about this?* Elicit: *If she hadn't taken out credit cards, she wouldn't have gotten into debt.* Write the sentence on the board.

Sts make their own sentences. Monitor and check sts are forming the third conditional correctly. Paircheck, then classcheck by writing their sentences on the board, or invite sts to write their own sentences on the board.

> Suggested answers:
> 1 If she hadn't gone to college, she might not have gotten into debt.
> 2 If she hadn't got credit cards, her spending might not have got out of control.
> 3 If she hadn't taken some advice, she wouldn't have got into such a mess.
> 4 If she had told her parents, they would have gone crazy.
> 5 If she hadn't cut up her credit cards, she might have kept spending.

**D** **Make it personal** Ask two sts to read out the model dialogue in the speech bubbles. Give sts a few minutes to think of their stories and make notes if they want to.

When they are ready, assign new pairs for sts to share their stories. Classcheck by asking sts to share their stories with the class. Ask: *Whose was the biggest mistake?*

### 4 Reading

**A** Write: *Volunteer2Zero* on the board and tell sts that this is the name of a website. Ask them to look at the photos and read the first three lines of the website and guess what it is. Paircheck. Classcheck, but don't give any answers yet.

**B** Assign new pairs. Read the instructions with sts and allow time for them to read and share their answers. Ask: *How does Volunteer2Zero work? What does* **crowdfunding** *mean?* (collective financing).

> Volunteer2Zero is a crowdfunding idea, but instead of just fund-raising to pay back your debts, you can also do volunteer work.
>
> It works when you register with Volunteer2Zero, you say where and how much time you can volunteer. The donors sponsor you to do work in your community and you receive donations for every hour you volunteer. You pay off your debt and help your community.

**C** Ask sts to cover the text, then work in pairs to remember the five benefits of the website. Then tell them to uncover the text. Play ▶ 5.7 for sts to read, listen, and check. Classcheck.

> 1 receive donations from your community
> 2 improve your professional skills
> 3 develop professional contacts
> 4 improve your community
> 5 increase your chance of graduating debt free

**D** **Make it personal** Read the model in the speech bubble with the class, then assign new pairs to discuss the questions. Classcheck by asking sts to share their ideas and lists with the class.

➔ **Workbook** Page 25

# 5.3 Have you ever borrowed money from a relative?

## 1 Listening

the website Kickstarter  | the Statue of Liberty  | Mozart  | British rock group Marillion  | the Pebble smart watch

*Could Kickstarter be something to do with old motorbikes?*

**A** In pairs, share what the photos make you think of. Then guess what they have in common.

**B** ▶5.8 Listen to a lecture and check your ideas for **A**. Have you ever donated to a crowdfunding project?

*My cousin ran a marathon last year to raise money for cancer research. I donated to that.*

### Common mistake
~~The~~ crowdfunding is a great idea.

**C** ▶5.8 True (T) or false (F)? Listen again to check.
1 Crowdfunding has existed much longer than the Internet.
2 Only wealthy people funded the Statue of Liberty.
3 Crowdfunding has changed a lot over the years.
4 Marillion fans paid for the band's tour and albums.
5 Pebble Technology holds the record for the most money ever raised through crowdfunding.

*Let's raise money to clean our polluted river.*

**D** 🔸 **Make it personal** In groups, think of a project you could start with crowdfunding and why.

1 Make notes on your ideas. Use these questions to help you.

> How will you organize it?   Why should people donate to it?
> How much do you want to raise?   What will donors get in return?

2 Present your project to the class. How many people want to "donate" to it? Which one gets the most "donations" from the class?

## 2 Grammar  Modals of possibility / probability

### Common mistakes
We really must ~~to~~ go home.
          *be able to*
I'd love to ~~can~~ help in some way.

**A** ▶5.9 Try to complete excerpts 1–4. Listen to check.

1 Their fans _____ really love their music.

2 It _____ be bad for young **entre**pren**eurs**.

3 You _____ be surprised to learn.

4 It _____ work for you!

62

# 5.3 Have you ever borrowed money from a relative?

**Lesson Aims:** Sts learn about and use modal verbs in the context of speculating and expressing possibility and uncertainty.

### Function
Listening to a lecture on the history of crowdfunding.
Talking about possibilities and probabilities.
Speculating about classmates' lives.

### Language
Even before this, people used crowdfunding to raise money.
It could work for you!
You're in shape. I think you might work out a lot in your free time.

**Vocabulary:** Phrases to emphasize certainty / uncertainty ( I think ... , Hmmm ... not sure, No way! Surely ... ).
**Grammar:** Modals for possibility and probability: *must, can't, might, could*.
**Before the lesson:** Write the following sentences on the board:
1 I hate borrowing money. People never pay me back!
2 The bank loaned me three grand at 5% interest a month.
3 I loaned $2,000 from the bank, and now I owe them $5,000!
4 Never loan money to family or friends.
5 I forgot my pen at home. Can I lend yours?

🎵 Turn to p. 330 for notes about this song and an accompanying task.

**Warm-up** Review the differences in the meanings of the verbs *lend, loan*, and *borrow* with a short activity. Draw sts' attention to the sentences you wrote on the board (see **Before the lesson**) and ask them to find and correct three mistakes. Paircheck. Classcheck.

> 1 I hate lending / loaning money. People never pay me back!
> 3 I borrowed $2,000 from the bank, and now I owe them $5,000!
> 5 I forgot my pen at home. Can I borrow yours?

**Language tip** Portuguese and Spanish L1 speakers can have trouble distinguishing between the verbs *lend* and *borrow* as in their L1 they are represented by the same word. To review this issue with sts, remind them that, in English, when you temporarily *take* something from someone, you *borrow* it from that person; and when you temporarily *give* something to someone, you *lend* it to that person. To practice this with sts, write a few example sentences with *borrow* and *lend* on the board and, as you point at each example, ask them: *take or give?*

## 1 Listening

**A Books open.** Point to the photos and ask: *What do these photos make you think of? What do you think they all have in common?* Allocate pairs and have sts discuss the questions. Elicit sts' ideas, but don't confirm any answers yet.

**B** Tell sts that they are going to listen to a lecture on crowdfunding. Play ▶5.8 for sts to check their answers to **A**. Paircheck. Classcheck.

Read the model in the speech bubble with the class. Ask: *Have you or anyone you know ever donated to a crowdfunding project?* Have sts discuss in pairs. Classcheck by asking a few sts to share their experiences with the class.

▶5.8 Turn to page 315 for the complete audioscript.

> They were all crowdfunded in some way.

**C** Have sts briefly read sentences 1–5. Play ▶5.8 again and ask sts to mark true (T) or false (F). Paircheck. Replay ▶5.8 if necessary. Classcheck.

> 1 T   2 F   3 F   4 T   5 F

**Tip** Have sts turn to the AS on p. 167. Sts listen again and notice the connections and /t/, /d/, and /ɪd/ endings.

**D** 👤 **Make it personal**  1 Tell sts that they're going to think of their own crowdfunding project. Read the model language in the speech bubble with sts. Put sts into small groups to make notes, using the questions in the box to help. Monitor and help with ideas and vocabulary where necessary.

2 When they are ready, ask groups to present their projects to the class. After each presentation, ask other sts if they want to donate to it and why (not). Find out who gets the most donations at the end.

## 2 Grammar  Modals of possibility / probability

**A** Point to speech bubbles 1–4 and ask sts to fill in the blanks with one word. Paircheck. Play ▶5.9 so sts can check their answers.

> 1 must   2 can't   3 might   4 could

*I might be young, but I ain't stupid.
Talking around in circles with your tongue.*

**B** Study 1–4 in **A** and check the correct definitions in the grammar box. Then read the information. Do you find any of these difficult?

|  | must | can't | might | could |
|---|---|---|---|---|
| I'm 100% sure this is true. |  |  |  |  |
| I'm 100% sure this isn't true. |  |  |  |  |
| Maybe this is true. |  |  |  |  |

The opposite of *must* is *can't*. (NOT ~~mustn't~~)
You must be ready for the exam. You've studied a lot.
You can't be ready for the exam. You haven't studied at all.

You can use *may* instead of *might* or *could* in affirmative sentences.
The business may / might / could close because it isn't doing very well.
But *couldn't* does not mean the same as *may not* or *might not*.
The business is doing better so it may not / might not close. (NOT ~~couldn't close~~)

➔ **Grammar 5B** p. 146

**Common mistake**

was able to
I ran and ~~could~~ catch the last bus.

Use *was / were able to* to express success in the past.

**C** Complete these comments about crowdfunding projects with *must* or *can't*.

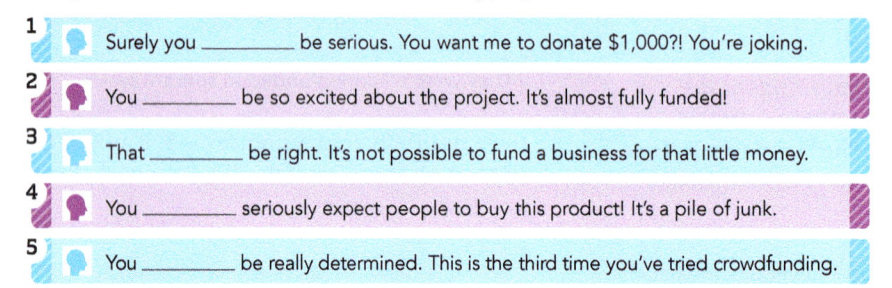

1. Surely you _____ be serious. You want me to donate $1,000?! You're joking.
2. You _____ be so excited about the project. It's almost fully funded!
3. That _____ be right. It's not possible to fund a business for that little money.
4. You _____ seriously expect people to buy this product! It's a pile of junk.
5. You _____ be really determined. This is the third time you've tried crowdfunding.

**D** ▶ 5.10 Listen to five different extracts. In pairs, guess and note your answers.
1. Who's Alberto talking to?
2. Where's Laura?
3. What's Ernie talking about?
4. Why's Tony breathing in and out like that?
5. What kind of problem does Susie have?

*I think he must be talking to his son.*

*Hmm ... Not sure. I think he might be talking to a friend.*

**E** ▶ 5.11 Listen to the complete conversations and check your guesses. Who's in the most difficult situation?

**F** *Fact or fiction?* In pairs, say whether 1–5 may be true.

1. Chewing gum is good for your teeth.
2. An ant can lift fifty times its own weight.
3. The brain is approximately 80% water.
4. Humans are the only living beings that can cry as the result of emotions.
5. You're more likely to have a heart attack on a Monday than on any other day.

*I think the first one might be true, but I'm not really sure.*

*Really? I actually think it could be bad for your teeth.*

**G** **Make it personal** In groups, speculate about each other's lives. Who's the best guesser?

Favorite free time activities?
Favorite stores / restaurants?
Musical taste?
Reasons for learning English?
Soccer fan? If so, what team?
Use of cell phone / the Internet?
How green they are?

*You must be quite green. You always bring a reusable bottle of water.*

*Yeah, and you never use plastic bags.*

*Yep—you're both right. I'm actually a member of Greenpeace!*

**B** Have sts study 1–4 in **A** and check the correct definitions in the grammar box. Paircheck. Classcheck.

> I'm almost sure this is true. – must
> I'm almost sure this isn't true. – can't
> Maybe this is true. – might / could

🔴 **Common mistake** Read with the whole class.

➡️ **Grammar 5B** page 146

**C** Point to 1–5 and say: *These are comments about a crowdfunding project. Look at what people are saying … Are they positive or negative?* Allow sts to quickly read the sentences.

Ask sts to fill in the blanks with *must* or *can't*. Classcheck.

> 1 can't   2 must   3 can't   4 can't   5 must

**D** Tell sts that they are going to play a guessing game. Explain that they are going to hear some short extracts of different conversations, and then they should guess the answers to questions 1–5.

Ask sts to read the model guesses in the speech bubbles and instruct them to use modals in their guesses for 1–5.

Read all the questions with sts and then play ▶5.10. After each extract, pause to allow sts to discuss possible answers in pairs. Monitor closely for the use of modal verbs and encourage sts to share and compare their guesses with the rest of the class. Classcheck in **2E**.

▶5.10 Turn to page 316 for the complete audioscript.

**E** Have sts listen to the conversations in full and check their guesses from **D**. Play ▶5.11 and classcheck.

▶5.11 Turn to page 316 for the complete audioscript.

> Suggested answers:
> 1 I think he might be talking to his cat.
> 2 She must be in an elevator.
> 3 He must be talking about his dog eating his homework.
> 4 I don't know. He could be doing yoga.
> 5 I think she might have a computer problem.

**Tip** Have sts turn to the AS on p. 167. Sts listen again and notice the intonation.

**F** Pair sts up. Ask them to look at statements 1–5 and decide whether they are *fact* or *fiction*. Have two sts role-play the model dialogue in the speech bubbles for the whole class and highlight the use of *might*, *could*, and the phrase *I'm not really sure*. Then, ask pairs to discuss 1–5. Monitor pairs' discussions closely and correct any mistakes on the spot. Classcheck sts' opinions first and then provide them with the answer key.

> 1 T (only sugar free gum)
> 2 F
> 3 F (It is 75% water.)
> 4 T (if crying refers to tears)
> 5 T

**G** **Make it personal** Assign groups of three or four sts randomly, or if you prefer, assign sts who usually sit away from one another to take part in the same groups.

Explain that sts should guess the answers to the questions for each of their group members. Allow sts two or three minutes to read the questions and jot down a few notes about their classmates.

When time is up, ask sts to read the model guesses in the speech bubbles. Then, sts have to do the same and make guesses about their classmates within the groups. Monitor sts' work and take notes for delayed correction.

At the end, ask: *Who's the best guesser in your group? Why?* Provide sts with feedback on their performance, as well as any necessary correction.

➡️ **Workbook** Page 26

# 5.4 Have you ever bought a useless product?

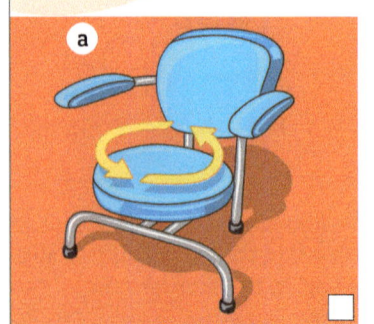

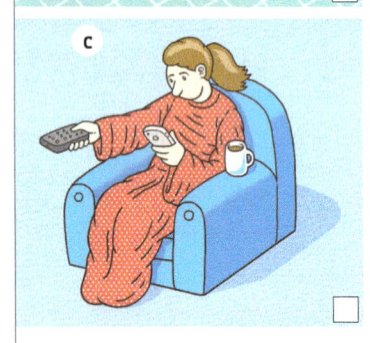

## 1 Reading

**A** Listen and read the introduction of an article about infomercials (= information + commercial). The writer:

☐ wants a refund on items she / he bought.
☐ is often disappointed with the products.
☐ is often entertained by infomercials.
☐ is angry about infomercials.

### TWO USELESS PRODUCTS I'VE BOUGHT

As far as I'm concerned, infomercials are an unappreciated art form. I mean, they are pure comedy, and who doesn't love to laugh? The truth is, though, that staying up and watching them can seriously interfere with my common sense. You see, I bought apparently useful products that promised to give me the physique of a good-looking fashion model, make me a math genius, and help me pass my exams. Yet, shockingly, guess what: I'm actually heavier now, I still have trouble understanding my credit card statement, and I'm currently taking all my exams again. Now, I don't want to generalize, but here, for your enjoyment, are two of the most useless gadgets I've ever bought.

#### 1 "READY TO SNUGGLE UP ON THE SOFA?"

But, you can't reach the remote or hold your cup of cocoa! Hug Rug, the blanket with sleeves, is the solution! Hug Rug is a blanket with sleeves, which means you can change channels, have a drink, or check your phone without getting cold. Hug Rug is super-soft to the touch and comes in eight gorgeous bright colors. Enjoy the convenience of free movement while also experiencing the comfort of a warm blanket. Read, watch TV, text your friends, even get takeout with Hug Rug, the blanket with sleeves."
OK, it is really cozy, but it looks ridiculous. And "free movement"?! Once I got into it, I couldn't figure out how to get out. Stick to a blanket.

#### 2 "FEELING THE EFFECTS OF SITTING AT YOUR DESK ALL DAY?"

It's time to tighten that tummy and get the flexibility you've been dreaming of with the Wonder Chair! Wonder Chair helps you flatten your abdominal muscles, massage your lower back, and improve your fitness. By doing our recommended exercises, you can fully train your upper, lower, and side abs. Help tone your lazy, aching muscles and get rid of your stiff appearance! This remarkable device also offers comfortable support for your spine, thighs, and arms. Don't waste another second! Sit at your desk with the Wonder Chair and wave good-bye to aches, pains and lethargy."
You'd better hope your office mates have a sense of humor. Sadly, mine didn't, so the chair stayed at home, and I got a gym membership.

**B** ▶5.12 In pairs, each read about one product and match it to a picture. Then tell your partner about it. Listen to check each other's answers.

**C** Match the underlined words to their definitions.

| 1 | _____ adj. | very beautiful or pleasant |
| 2 | _____ adj. | very special, amazing |
| 3 | _____ adv. | in fact |
| 4 | _____ verb | make flat / level |
| 5 | _____ verb | tone / make tighter |
| 6 | _____ adv. | now |
| 7 | _____ noun | cooked food from a restaurant that you buy to eat somewhere else |
| 8 | _____ noun [U] | pleasure |
| 9 | _____ adj. | good for nothing |

**D** ▶5.13 Listen to two friends talking about the product that isn't mentioned in the article. Why wasn't she happy with it? Which was the worst purchase?

**E** 🔘 **Make it personal** Think of an item you bought because of an infomercial / ad. Describe the product and ad to your partner. Why did you buy it? Did it work? Would you recommend it? Why (not)?

> I bought a hairdryer. It didn't work and I wasn't able to send it back.

# 5.4 Have you ever bought a useless product?

**Lesson Aims:** Sts look at and practice adjective order via the contexts of reading an article about infomercials and listening to and talking about frustrating shopping experiences.

## Function
Reading an article about infomercials.
Reading / Listening to unsuccessful shopping experiences.
Talking about a frustrating shopping experience.
Describing an infomercial.

## Language
As far as I'm concerned, infomercials are an unappreciated art form.
... here, for your enjoyment, are two of the most useless gadgets I've ever bought!
I bought some very expensive sunglasses and left them in a taxi.

**Vocabulary:** Word formation: suffix patterns for adjectives, nouns, verbs, and adverbs.
**Grammar:** Adjective order.

♪ Turn to p. 330 for notes about this song and an accompanying task.

**Warm-up** Ask sts to open their books to the "Sounds and usual spellings" chart for vowel sounds on p. 160. If you're teaching Spanish speakers, have sts focus on the symbol (S); or focus on (P) if your sts' home language is Portuguese. Tell sts that sounds have been marked with (S) or (P) when the phoneme is often mispronounced by speakers of that language. Have sts work in pairs to find the vowel sounds marked with (S) or (P) and take turns pronouncing the words in the drawings, as well as some of the words listed at the bottom of the page. Monitor their pronunciation closely and correct any mistakes on the spot. Ask: *Which sounds are difficult for you (personally)?*

## 1 Reading

**A** **Books closed**. Ask: *Do you ever watch infomercials? Do you have a favorite?*

Ask sts to listen and read the introduction of "Two useless Products I've Bought" and check the answer choice that best answers the question. Play ▶ 5.12. Pause the recording at the end of the introduction. Paircheck. Classcheck.

🔑 is often disappointed with the products.

**B** Assign pairs and read the instructions with sts. Allow time for sts to share their information when they have finished reading. Play ▶ 5.12 for sts to check each other's answers. Classcheck.

🔑 1 c   2 a

**C** Model the activity. Point to the first underlined word in the article, *actually*. Point to the box of definitions and synonyms and ask: *What does **actually** mean?*

🔑
1 gorgeous       6 currently
2 remarkable     7 takeout
3 actually       8 enjoyment
4 flatten        9 useless
5 tighten

**D** Point to the photos on the left side of the page and ask: *Which product was not mentioned in the article?* Check whether sts can name the product being advertised (self tan or fake tan).

Tell sts that they are going to hear two friends talking about this product. Say: *Listen to the dialogue and find out the answer to this question: Was the woman happy about it?* Play ▶ 5.13. Classcheck.

▶ 5.13 Turn to page 316 for the complete audioscript.

🔑 She wasn't happy with the fake tan because it was expensive, it smelled awful and it made her skin bright orange.

**Tip** Have sts turn to the AS on p. 168. Sts listen again and notice the intonation of the echo questions.

**E** 🔘 **Make it personal**  Demonstrate the activity by telling sts about a product you've bought after watching an infomercial, answering the questions as you go along. Give sts a few minutes to think of their own product and make notes if they want to. Assign new pairs and have sts discuss the questions. Classcheck by asking a few sts to share their experiences with the class.

## 2 Vocabulary  Word formation

♪ *I'm advertising love for free, so you can place your ad with me.*

**A** Complete the chart with the highlighted words from the article. Underline the suffixes.

| Nouns | Verbs | Adjectives | Adverbs |
|---|---|---|---|
| enjoyment | | | |

**Common mistakes**

My phone is full of useful~~l~~ features.

Please listen ~~carefuly~~ *carefully*.

**B** ▶5.14 Complete 1–8 with forms of the words in parentheses. Listen to check.
1  I bought it on impulse. It was pure __madness__ ! (mad)
2  It can't work the way they _____ it would. (advert)
3  I felt really _____ afterward. (guilt)
4  It seemed like a _____ product … (wonder)
5  … but it was such a _____. (disappoint)
6  This stuff is _____ quite _____. (actual / danger)
7  They go on and on in the infomercial about how _____ it is. (nature)
8  I guess it's just so _____ these days. (fashion)

**C** ● Make it personal  Think about 1–8 in **B**. When was the last time you felt like that? In pairs, each choose and share an experience. Whose was worse?

*I bought some very expensive sunglasses and left them in a taxi. I felt really guilty afterward—and stupid, too.*

## 3 Grammar  Adjective order

**A** Study the examples and circle the correct alternative in the grammar box. Then read the information below and underline the fact adjectives in **1A**.

> You'll get the physique of a [handsome] [fashion] model.   Help tone your [lazy], [aching] muscles.
> They can buy them in [gorgeous] [bright] colors.   Tom's a [nice] [little] kid.
>
> If we use two or more adjectives before a noun, [opinions] usually come **before** / **after** facts.
>
> I'm wearing the most expensive, round, contemporary, black, Korean, titanium, multi-function smart watch.
>
> If you have more than one fact adjective in a sentence, they tend to go in a particular order:
> number – size – shape – age – color – nationality – material – purpose + noun
> But don't worry, it isn't usual to use more than three adjectives together!
>
> ➔ Grammar 5C p.146

**B** Read infomercials 1–7 and correct five adjective order mistakes.

1  A spray that promises more attractive dark hair—instantly!

2  Glamorize your look with these star-shaped fashionable earrings.

3  A Japanese camping miraculous knife that can cut through anything!

4  A bizarre green plastic blanket with sleeves to keep you warm while watching TV.

5  Jeans that look fashionable, but feel like cotton comfortable pajamas.

6  A SMALL METAL INCREDIBLE ACCESSORY THAT CREATES GORGEOUS HAIRSTYLES INSTANTLY!

7  Throw out your leather brown ugly shoes and buy our fantastic waterproof boots today!

**C** ● Make it personal  📶 In small groups, search online for a funny or interesting infomercial. Act it out or describe the product to the class. Can your classmates guess what the product is? Who found the best / worst / funniest products?

# 5.4

## 2 Vocabulary Word formation

**A** 🔑 **Common mistakes** Direct sts' attention to the highlighted words in the article on p. 64. Instruct sts to copy these words into the correct column of the chart. Draw sts' attention to the common mistakes and read with the whole class. Ask sts to underline suffixes that helped them identify the word class. Paircheck. Classcheck by writing the answers on the board.

> **Weaker classes** For this activity, have sts work collaboratively in pairs.

| Nouns | Verbs | Adjectives | Adverbs |
|---|---|---|---|
| enjoy**ment** | tigh**ten** | use**less** | serious**ly** |
| solut**ion** | flat**ten** | gorg**eous** | apparent**ly** |
| conveni**ence** | | remark**able** | shocking**ly** |
| fit**ness** | | comfort**able** | actual**ly** |
| appear**ance** | | | current**ly** |

**B** Focus on the example sentence 1. Ensure that sts understand that they need to transform the root word given by adding a suffix. Complete number 2 with sts. Then, ask them to fill in the blanks with the given words and appropriate suffixes. Play ▶5.14 for sts to listen and check their answers. Classcheck.

> 1 madness
> 2 advertised
> 3 guilty
> 4 wonderful
> 5 disappointment
> 6 actually, dangerous
> 7 natural
> 8 fashionable

**C** 🔘 **Make it personal** Pair sts up. Ask pairs to look back at 1–8 in **2B** and share similar experiences or talk about the last time they felt like that. Classcheck sts' stories and ask partners: *Whose experience was worse?*

## 3 Grammar Adjective order

**A** Read the example sentences in the grammar box with sts and encourage them to notice the adjectives. Ask: *Which ones are opinion adjectives?* Then, have sts read and circle the correct rule for adjective order and underline the fact adjectives in **1A**. Classcheck. Ask: *Are these patterns similar in your language?*

> Opinion adjectives usually come before facts.

**Language tip** Adjective order is an area where Romance language speakers can have trouble. Before tackling the grammar box about adjective order in activity **3A**, remind sts that adjectives always come before nouns, and we also have to prioritize facts over opinions by putting the adjectives that describe facts closer to the noun (right before it) and the ones that state opinions further away (or before the ones that describe facts). To make this clearer to sts, you can make use of contrastive grammar and write a few examples with two adjectives (one fact and one opinion) in their own language on the board and have them say the equivalent in English.

➡ **Grammar 5C** page 146

**B** Direct sts to read infomercials 1–7 and find five mistakes in adjective order. Paircheck. Classcheck.

> 2 Glamorize your look with these fashionable star-shaped earrings.
> 3 A miraculous Japanese camping knife that can cut through anything!
> 5 Jeans that look fashionable but feel like comfortable cotton pajamas.
> 6 An incredible small metal accessory that creates gorgeous hairstyles instantly!
> 7 Throw out your ugly brown leather shoes and buy our fantastic waterproof boots today!

**C** 🔘 **Make it personal** Have sts go online and find a funny or interesting infomercial. Give them time to prepare to either act it out or describe it to the class. Make sure they don't say what the product is. Invite sts to act out / describe their infomercials to the class, then ask: *Can you guess what the product is? What was the best / worst / funniest product?*

> **Alternative task** Assign sts into groups of three. Write the following task on the board:
>
> | atomic broom   crash fix   miracle camera |
> | pigeon eliminator |
>
> 1 Choose one of the products from the box and decide what it does / why it's special.
> 2 Create a 30-second infomercial. Use some of the adjectives and fixed phrases from this lesson.
>
> You can also encourage sts to add their own ideas to the box.

➡ **Workbook** Page 27

## 5.5 Do you often buy things on impulse?

### Skills  Reading for confirmation

**A** In pairs, match the areas to photos a–c. Then list six more items in the photos. Which aspects of grocery store shopping do / don't you enjoy?

the bakery    a checkout    fresh fruit and vegetables

**B** Guess what "supermarket psychology" refers to? Read the introduction to the article to check. Who are "they"?

> I'd say it's probably about consumer behavior.

**C** In pairs, brainstorm how grocery stores "assault our five senses." Give an example for sight, hearing, touch, taste, and smell. Then quickly read and match each sense to a paragraph. Were your ideas mentioned?

**D** ▶ 5.15 Listen and reread carefully. A: read 1–4, B: read 5–8. How else do grocery stores make us spend more and how can we avoid it? Share your information.

## Supermarket PSYCHOLOGY

Ever noticed that whichever grocery store you go to, you'll inevitably find the same basic arrangement of products? It's a trick they play on us so we buy more and more things, even stuff we don't really need. Virtually all the products are carefully displayed to affect our shopping experience. Psychological tactics, you know. Clever devils! Read on to find out how grocery stores assault our five senses.

**1** You can rarely leave the grocery store through the same door you walked in. This means you'll have to go around the whole place and maybe buy more stuff on your way out. They even let you try tasty food and drink items to tempt you further, so you feel like you're eating for free while you explore this "wonderful world."

**2** Fresh fruits and vegetables are always right near the entrance. You think this is just by chance? No way. It's so you will feel fresh and happy at the start of your shopping adventure. They're nice to touch, too, and you feel you can choose the best ones for yourself. Plus, it's best to have these items near the entrance because of the sunlight. Smart, huh?

**3** Everyday items like dairy, meat, or rice are always at the back of the store. They know you want to get to the checkout as fast as possible, so they make you go all the way to the back, past the clothes, watches, and gadgets—the most lucrative items. You know, just in case.

**4** Ever feel hungry when you're doing your weekly shopping? Grocery stores know that food aromas make us hungry, so they have an in-store bakery and sometimes a restaurant, and the smell of food inspires us to buy more. They even use a manufactured bread-smell to catch customers on the street.

**5** Want to buy shampoo? Well, don't look straight ahead: the products at eye level are always the more expensive ones. The cheaper ones are either placed at the very bottom or really high up, on the top shelves. Yeah, right there.

**6** And why those long, endless aisles filled with unrelated products? Like cereals for breakfast next to a treat like candy. Well, parents usually buy boxes of cereal for their children, and when they make the mistake of taking them to the store, the magic happens: "I want to buy candy, Mommy. Pleeeaaaase."

**7** Ever find yourself singing as you shop? There's a reason you're more likely to hear The Eagles or Celine Dion than Foo Fighters or Iron Maiden. Slower music creates slower traffic, which means people shop for longer. Genius, huh?

**8** So, if this all sounds familiar, wise up! If you don't want to be a victim of these strategies, here's my advice: make a shopping list and stick to it!

**E** 🔵 **Make it personal**  In pairs, ask and answer 1–4. Do you regularly succumb to 'shopping psychology'? If so, what's your best example?

1. Which grocery stores do / don't you usually shop at? Why?
2. Do you visit every aisle? Do you stick to your list, or do you ever buy more?
3. Which tactics from the article have you noticed? Any others?
4. What psychology do you find in other stores? (travel agency, technology, clothes, cosmetics ...)

> Supermarket psychology doesn't work on me. I only buy what I need.

66

## 5.5 Do you often buy things on impulse?

**Lesson Aims:** Sts learn to name the five senses via reading an article about supermarket psychology.

**Function**
Reading an article about supermarket psychology.
Talking about how supermarket strategies influence you.

**Language**
... whichever supermarket you go to, you'll inevitably find the same basic arrangement of products.
It doesn't work on me 'cause I only buy the basics.

**Vocabulary:** The five main senses (hearing, sight, smell, taste, touch).
**Skills:** Reading for confirmation.

♪ Turn to p. 330 for notes about this song and an accompanying task.

**Warm-up Books closed.** Ask sts who does the grocery shopping in their house and where they usually shop. If necessary, explain the word *grocery*. Encourage sts to describe the places they mentioned, asking questions about the location / arrangement of products.

### ID Skills Reading for confirmation

**A Books open.** Point to the photos and ask: *Which parts of a grocery store are these?* Assign pairs and have sts match the photos to the places in the box. Elicit sts answers and discuss the questions as a class.

a Bakery   b Fruit and vegetable aisle   c Checkout

**Tip** Encourage sts to look very closely at the photos and, in pairs, list everything they can see. To classcheck, play a feedback game where pairs get a point for every word that only they have written down.

**B** Ask: *Have you ever heard about supermarket psychology?* Elicit possible definitions from sts and then instruct them to read the introduction to the article in **C**. Ask: *Were your guesses correct?* Refer to the introduction again and ask: *Who are they?* Classcheck.

Supermarket psychology is the tactics/tricks grocery stores use to encourage us to buy things. "They" are grocery store managers.

**C** Ask: *Can you name the five senses in English?* Elicit or teach the words *sight*, *hearing*, *touch*, *taste*, and *smell*.

Ask: *How do you think grocery store managers might assault our five senses?* Have sts discuss the question in pairs. Classcheck personal ideas. Have sts read and match each sense to a paragraph. Classcheck.

1 taste   2 touch   4 smell   5 sight   7 hearing

**D** Tell sts that they are now going to listen and reread the whole text again. Play ▶ 5.15. Pair sts and assign roles **A** and **B** within each pair. Explain that st **A** should look for answers in paragraphs 1–4, and st **B** should do the same for paragraphs 5–8. Allow time for partners to exchange their text findings. Classcheck. Elicit / check the meaning of: *by chance* (happen without being planned), *dairy* (milk, yogurt, cheese etc.), *stick to it* (don't make any changes).

You can rarely leave the grocery store through the same door you walked in. This means you'll have to go around the whole place and maybe buy more stuff on your way out.

Fresh fruits and vegetables are always right near the entrance, so you will feel fresh and happy.

Grocery stores use food aromas to make customers hungry.

Dairy, meat, or rice are at the back of the store, so they make you go all the way to the back, past the most lucrative items.

The products at your eye level are always the more expensive ones.

Cereals and candy are placed next to each other so that parents are forced to buy them for children

They play slow music to encourage customers to walk slower.

**E** 🎤 **Make it personal** Read out the model in the speech bubble. Assign new pairs and have sts answer the questions and discuss the types of supermarket psychology they've seen in the places. Classcheck by asking a few sts to share their ideas with the class.

Possible answers to 4:

cosmetics store: using black means that sight lines are easier to navigate. Black represents money and prestige. Shiny things often correspond with something clean and expensive.

technology store: trendy staff in trendy uniforms, minimalist décor, ability to try products.

clothing store: clothes are folded and stacked so you have to touch them and find out what the whole item looks like.

travel agency: posters with attractive images of beaches, cityscapes etc. Cheap flight/holiday prices in windows.

# When did you last complain in a store?

**ID in Action** Shopping problems

**A** ▶5.16 Listen to three dialogues. What are the three problems? Which were successful shopping experiences? Which one is most familiar to you?

**B** ▶5.16 Match the phrases and mark them C (customer) or SC (store clerk). Listen again to check. Have you ever worked in a store?

> **Common mistakes**
> My credit card was rejected / refused.
> declined
> What size (of shoe) do you use?
> take

| | Choosing | | |
|---|---|---|---|
| 1 | I like these shoes. Can I | ☐ | charge? |
| 2 | What size do you | ☐ | refund. |
| 3 | Do you have a size 10 | ☐ | take? |
| 4 | I'm sorry ma'am, | ☐ | card, please. |
| | **Paying** | | |
| 5 | Cash or | ☐ | declined. |
| 6 | Insert / Tap / Swipe your | ☐ | we're sold out. |
| 7 | I'm afraid your card has been | ☐ | in stock? |
| | **Complaining** | | receipt. |
| | | ☐ | try them on? |
| 8 | Unfortunately, we can't give you a | ☐ | exchange it for another one. |
| 9 | But we'd be happy to | | |
| 10 | I just need to see your | | |

**C** In pairs, cover the endings in **B** and test each other.

**D** ▶5.17 Can you remember the missing words? Listen to check.
1 It _____ impossible to _____ larger sizes. Can you _____ me when you _____ some in stock?
2 _____! I don't _____. It's a new card, and I _____ I'm not over my limit. There _____ be a problem with your card machine.
3 I'd _____ to _____ this phone. I _____ it here the other day, and it's _____.

> Hi. Are those shoes in the sale?
>
> I'm afraid I'm unhappy with this phone.

**E** In pairs, choose a situation from **B** and read ▶5.16 on p. 168 for one minute. Then role-play the situation. Who complained successfully?

**F** **Make it personal** In pairs, role-play a situation, 1–3, below. Use sentences from **B** and **D**. Who complained successfully?

**1** You bought a smart phone last week, but you don't like it anymore. You want to get a refund or exchange it for a new one. There's a slight scratch on the screen, though.

**2** You bought two pairs of jeans last month, but couldn't try them on because the store was too crowded. They don't fit. You want to exchange them or get a refund.

**3** You bought some strawberries at the grocery store, but when you got home, you noticed that some of the fruit was rotten. You want a refund.

♪ *There's a lady who's sure all that glitters is gold, And she's buying a stairway to heaven.*

# 5.5 When did you last complain in a store?

**Lesson Aims:** Sts listen to and role-play store clerk / customer dialogues about shopping problems.

**Function**
Listening to customer and store clerk's dialogues.
Acting out dialogues about shopping problems.

**Language**
Unfortunately, we can't give you a refund.
Why do you never have larger sizes? I'm not coming here again!

**Vocabulary:** Expressions related to shopping problems (I'm afraid your card has been declined. We'd be happy to exchange it for another one.)
**Skills:** Making complaints and asking for a refund.

## ID in Action  Shopping problems

**A** Write: *shopping problems* on the board and have the class brainstorm the types of problems people can have when purchasing goods. Tell sts that they are going to listen to three dialogues about shopping problems. Play ▶5.16 for sts to answer the questions. Peercheck. Classcheck.

> 5.16 Turn to page 316 for the complete audioscript.
>
> 1 The store didn't have her shoe size. (unsuccessful)
> 2 The credit card was declined. (unsuccessful)
> 3 The phone was scratched. (successful)

**Common mistakes**  Read with the whole class.

> **Language tip**  As an effect of direct translation, Romance language speakers commonly make these mistakes. To pre-empt this, remind sts that, although the words *rejected*, *refused*, and *use*, in these mistakes are cognates, these are not correct words in these contexts. Remind sts that, just because a word in English is a cognate in L1, it doesn't mean it can be used in the same context.

**B** Read sentence 1 and elicit the correct ending. Then ask: *Who says that: the customer or the store clerk?*

Instruct sts to match sentences 2–10 to the correct endings and then to write C for customer or SC for store clerk. Paircheck. Replay ▶5.16 to check answers.

> 1 I like these shoes. Can I try them on? (C)
> 2 What size do you take? (SC)
> 3 Do you have a size 10 in stock? (C)
> 4 I'm sorry, ma'am, we're sold out. (SC)
> 5 Cash or charge? (SC)
> 6 Insert / Tap / Swipe your card, please. (SC)
> 7 I'm afraid your card has been declined. (SC)
> 8 Unfortunately, we can't give you a refund. (SC)
> 9 But we'd be happy to exchange it for another one. (SC)
> 10 I just need to see your receipt. (SC)

**C** Have pairs of sts hide the right-hand column in **B** and test each other.

**D** Play ▶5.17 and ask sts to listen and fill in the blanks with the missing verbs. Classcheck and ask: *Which one sounds more polite?* Replay ▶5.17 and lead choral repetition of each sentence.

> 1 It <u>seems</u> impossible to <u>find</u> larger sizes. Can you <u>email</u> me when you <u>have</u> some in stock?
> 2 <u>Declined</u>! I don't <u>understand</u>. It's a new card, and I <u>know</u> I'm not over my limit. There <u>must</u> be a problem with your card machine.
> 3 I'd <u>like</u> to <u>return</u> this phone. I <u>bought</u> it here the other day and it's <u>damaged.</u>

**E** Have sts change partners. Ask pairs to choose one situation from **A** and study AS ▶5.16 on p. 168 for a minute. Then, have them close their books and act out their chosen dialogue. Monitor and encourage peer correction and collaboration. At the end, invite volunteer pairs to act out their dialogue from memory for the whole class.

**F** 🟠 **Make it personal**  Have sts change partners once again. In these new pairs, sts should choose one of situations 1–3 to act out. Ask sts to use sentences from **B** and **D**. Monitor and take notes for delayed correction. Round off the class with three different pairs role-playing one dialogue each for the whole group.

➡ **Workbook** Page 28

➡ Ⓓ **ID Richmond Learning Platform**

➡ **Writing** p. 68

➡ **ID Café** p. 69

# Writing 5  An advert

🎵 *Come on, vogue,
Let your body move to the music,
Hey, hey, hey
Come on, vogue,
Let your body go with the flow.*

**A** Read the ad and circle the correct alternative.
1. Shape U Shoe is mainly for people who **do / don't** go to the gym.
2. Shape U Shoe shoes come in **"one size fits all" / various sizes and colors**.
3. They are good for **your arms and legs / your legs and body position**.
4. To get the benefits you need to walk with Shape U Shoes 20 **times per week / minutes a day**.

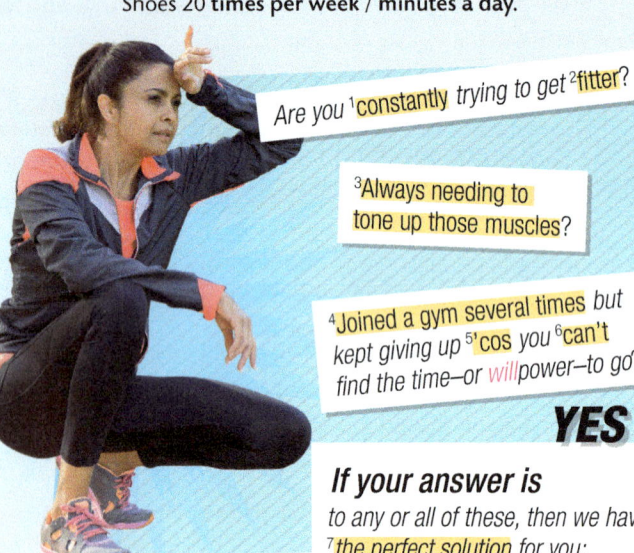

## Shape U Shoes

Are you ¹constantly trying to get ²fitter?

³Always needing to tone up those muscles?

⁴Joined a gym several times but kept giving up ⁵cos you ⁶can't find the time–or ⁷willpower–to go?

**YES**

If your answer is to any or all of these, then we have ⁷the perfect solution for you:

Shape U Shoes are a revolutionary, 100% effective product that help you get fit and tone up fast, in a safe, almost effortless way. They're ⁸the most modern and intelligent answer for those who, like you, are concerned about their health but are too busy to go to the gym. Walk in our shoes instead!

Shape U Shoes come in various gorgeous, stylish designs and colors. They strengthen legs and thighs, by boosting your muscle activity by up to 35% simply by walking. Imagine that! Shape U Shoes can also improve your posture. You will soon look and feel fitter, ⁹less tired, and get that shape you've been dreaming of. ¹⁰All these benefits without any risks!

Shape U Shoes are ¹¹the scientific solution that was missing in your life. Walking for just 20 minutes a day is ¹²the secret to ¹³a better and happier life! Remember, ¹⁴it's no miracle. It's Shape U Shoes!

Available online for next-day delivery. Satisfaction guaranteed!

**B** Read *Write it right!*, then match highlighted items 1–14 to rules a–d.

### ✓ Write it right!

To write a good ad,
a. use comparatives and superlatives. ☐☐☐☐
b. use emotive, exaggerated language to make opinions sound like facts. ☐☐☐☐☐
c. remove articles, auxiliaries, or subjects to make it short and exciting. ☐☐
 (Our new car is) faster than you thought.
 (The) offer (is) limited to the United States.
d. use informal language, such as contractions and abbreviations. ☐☐☐
 Don't wait any longer!
 You're gonna love this!

**C** Complete 1–6 with the adjective or adverb forms of the words in parentheses.
1. You'll be ___ ___ by the fast results. (total / surprise)
2. This product is 100% ___. (safety)
3. The most ___ solution to your problems. (efficiency)
4. Use it ___ to see ___ results. (regularity / wonder)
5. Achieve ___ results. (success)
6. Feel ___ ___ all the time. (complete / energy)

**D** Circle the correct alternative in 1–7.
1. Get **long beautiful / beautiful long** hair.
2. Looking for a **perfect new / new perfect** solution?
3. Feel like **an attractive young / a young attractive** model!
4. Take only one **gentle short / short gentle** walk a day.
5. A **strong new / new strong** body!
6. It's the **better / best** and **modernest / most modern** solution.
7. Learn English using the **faster / fastest** method with the **less / least** effort.

**E** *Your turn!* Write an ad in 130–150 words.

| Before | Choose a product (e.g. from **3C** in Lesson 5.4 on p. 65) and note down five adjectives to describe it. Think who it's for and how you can "sell" it. |
|---|---|
| While | 1 Begin your ad with a question or a catchy sentence.<br>2 Use tips a–d in *Write it right!*<br>3 End with a powerful statement. |
| After | Show your ad to three different classmates. Would they buy your product? Then email it to your teacher. |

68

# Writing 5 An advert

♪ Turn to p. 330 for notes about this song and an accompanying task.

**A** Have sts look at the Shape U Shoes ad and choose the correct alternatives for statements 1–4. Paircheck. Classcheck.

> 1 don't   2 various sizes and colors
> 3 legs and body position   4 20 minutes per day

**B** Read the tips in **Write it right!** with the whole class. Then, ask sts to match rules a–d to highlighted phrases 1–14 in the ad in **A**. Paircheck. Classcheck by writing the answers on the board.

> 1 b   2 a   3 c   4 c   5 d   6 d   7 b
> 8 a   9 a   10 b   11 b   12 b   13 a   14 d

**C** Have sts fill in the blanks in sentences 1–6 with the adverb or adjective forms of the words provided. Classcheck by writing the answers on the board.

> 1 totally surprised
> 2 safe
> 3 efficient
> 4 regularly, wonderful
> 5 successful
> 6 completely energetic

**D** Read item 1 with the class and elicit the correct answer. Then, have sts read 2–7 and circle the best adjective order in each bold pair. Paircheck. Classcheck.

> 1 beautiful long
> 2 perfect new
> 3 an attractive young
> 4 short gentle
> 5 strong new
> 6 best / most modern
> 7 fastest / least

**E** *Your turn!*

**Before** Tell sts that they are going to write an ad about a product of their choice. Suggest that sts look at lesson **5.4** for ideas. Have sts plan their writing by first listing five adjectives to describe the product. Then, have them answer these questions: *Who is it for? How can you "sell" it best?*

**While** Remind sts to come up with a catchy sentence to begin their ads. Remind them to follow the tips from **Write it right!** and to plan a good ending phrase. Tell sts' that their ads should be 130–150 words long. Monitor and offer help when requested.

**After** Divide the class into groups of four. Have the sts in each group exchange ads and decide which products they would buy. Classcheck sts' opinions and then collect their writing for marking or asks sts to email their ads to you.

# 5 Shop around

## ID Café

### 1 Before watching

**A** Match 1–7 to five of the definitions a–e.
1. A clothes hoarder
2. A discount shopper
3. A loyal shopper
4. An online shopper
5. A reluctant shopper
6. An upcycler
7. A shopaholic

a ☐ loves shopping sprees
b ☐ reuses materials (e.g. clothes, furniture) to create something new
c ☐ shops around to buy things when they're cheaper
d ☐ always buys clothes at the same store
e ☐ keeps all their clothes, never throwing any out

**B** ◉ Make it personal  Which of 1–7 in **A** best describes you and your friends?

> I guess I'm 4 for most things except clothes. I like to try things on before buying.

**C** Study Andrea's clothing rental website. In pairs, explain how it will work. Who might use it? What are the benefits? Would you use it?

*Shop Around*

Are you a:
- COMPULSIVE SHOPPER?
- CLOTHES HOARDER?
- TIME WASTER?

Don't Fret!
- CLOTHING RENTALS
- FAST PICK-UP
- ECONOMICAL RETURNS

> It could be good for clothes hoarders.

> Yeah, they could sell clothes they haven't worn.

**D** Watch the rest and number 1–9 the order these are mentioned.

| | | | |
|---|---|---|---|
| a performance | ☐ | Genevieve | ☐ |
| all the girls on campus | 1 | Lucy's actors | ☐ |
| dark clothing | ☐ | make curtains | ☐ |
| design clothing | ☐ | make money | ☐ |
| | | save money | ☐ |

### 2 While watching

**A** Watch the first two minutes and check: Andrea (A), Genevieve (G), or Lucy (L)?

| | A | G | L |
|---|---|---|---|
| 1 Has beautiful, sophisticated clothes. | | | |
| 2 Needs beautiful, new clothes. | | | |
| 3 Likes to wear dark clothes. | | | |
| 4 Works with demanding actors. | | | |
| 5 Used to be a mad shopper. | | | |

**B** Watch again and check all you hear.
1. What is Lucy doing?
   ☐ Demanding things.    ☐ Working with actors.
   ☐ Starring in a film.    ☐ Shooting a film.
2. How does Andrea describe her past behavior?
   ☐ Anxious.    ☐ Creative genius.
   ☐ Kidding.    ☐ Tired.
3. What does Andrea want to do?
   ☐ Make her own clothes.    ☐ Have better taste.
   ☐ Stop shopping.    ☐ Sew curtains.

### 3 After watching

**A** Match the noun and adjective used to describe it.
1. best            a ☐ clothes
2. crazy           b ☐ friend
3. creative        c ☐ genius
4. mad             d ☐ sizes
5. different       e ☐ shopper
6. shopping        f ☐ shopping
7. sophisticated   g ☐ spree

**B** Complete 1–4 with the correct adverb.

| actually | definitely | probably | seriously |

1. I _____ went a little crazy on spending.
2. No, _____ I believe it.
3. _____, I have an idea.
4. You are _____ the best friend anyone could ask for!

**C** ◉ Make it personal  In pairs, compare your usual taste in clothes and colors. Any surprises?

> I like to wear dark colors, especially at night.

> Not me. I'm into bright shirts or T-shirts.

# ID Café 5 Shop around

## 1 Before watching

**A** **Books closed.** Ask: *How often do you go shopping for clothes? Do you like shopping?* and have a brief class discussion.

**Books open.** Read the types of shoppers with the class, then ask sts to match them to five of the definitions. Paircheck. Classcheck. Ask sts if they can give you definitions for items 4 (an online shopper) and 5 (a reluctant shopper).

> 1 e  2 c  3 d  6 b  7 a

**B** **Make it personal** Ask a student to read the model in the speech bubble. Put sts into small groups to share their opinions. Classcheck and ask a student from each group to share any interesting information with the class.

## 2 While watching

**A** Tell sts that they are going to watch Andrea and Lucy talking about clothes. Ask: *Do these women like clothes?* If appropriate, ask the women in class: *How often do you buy clothes?* Then, ask the men the same question and compare.

Go over the chart with the class, and have sts check A (Andrea), G (Genevieve), or L (Lucy) for each description as they watch the video. Play the first two minutes of ▶ 5. Paircheck. Classcheck.

> 1 A  2 L  3 G  4 L  5 A

At the end, ask: *What's Andrea's business idea? What's her website about?*

**B** Have sts quickly read questions 1–3 and the options for each. Replay ▶ 5 as sts watch and check the correct answers. Paircheck. Classcheck.

> 1 Working with actors. / Shooting a film.
> 2 Anxious.
> 3 Make her own clothes. / Sew curtains.

**C** Write the following questions on the board for sts to discuss in pairs:
1 What kind of people might be interested in Andrea's website?
2 What are the benefits?
3 Would you use it?

Have partners take turns asking and answering the questions. Refer them to the model text in the speech bubbles and offer help if necessary. Classcheck.

**D** Tell sts they are going to put the words in the order in which they are mentioned in the conversation. Play the rest of ▶ 5. Paircheck. Classcheck.

> 1 all the girls on campus
> 2 Genevieve
> 3 dark clothes
> 4 a performance
> 5 Lucy's actors
> 6 make money
> 7 save money
> 8 design clothing
> 9 make curtains

## 3 After watching

**A** Have sts match adjectives 1–7 to the nouns in the right column, using the same combinations as the speakers in the video used. Paircheck. Classcheck or, if time allows, replay ▶ 5 with subtitles.

> 1 b  2 e  3 c  4 f  5 d  6 g  7 a

**B** Ask sts to fill in each blank with the correct adverb from the box. Paircheck. Classcheck by writing the answers on the board.

> 1 probably  2 actually  3 seriously  4 definitely

**D** **Make it personal** Invite two volunteers to role-play the model dialogue in the speech bubbles for the whole class. Then, have sts change partners. Ask the new pairs to talk together about their taste in clothes and colors. Ask partners to find at least one thing they have in common. Classcheck and ask: *Any surprises?*

# Mid-term review

## Game: 55 seconds

There are four games in each Unit square. ■ You have 55 seconds for each game. ■ The winner is the first team to get to 40 points.

### RULES
- 4 players: divide into Teams 1 and 2.
- Flip a coin to decide which team starts.
- Team 1 starts at Unit 1, Team 2 starts at Unit 5.
- Each team plays **TOPIC TALK**. Monitor the time (55 seconds) while the other team plays.
- Then take turns playing the other games in this order:
  **DESCRIBE ▶ DISCOVER   COUNT THE QUESTIONS   ROLE-PLAY   TOPIC TALK**
- Then move to the next unit. Read the instructions and scoring for each game before you start.

## UNIT 1
**TOPIC TALK**
- Relationships
- Friendship
- Personality

**DESCRIBE ▶ DISCOVER**

**COUNT THE QUESTIONS**

**ROLE-PLAY**

## UNIT 2
**TOPIC TALK**
- Going green
- The environment
- Endangered species

**DESCRIBE ▶ DISCOVER**

**COUNT THE QUESTIONS**

**ROLE-PLAY**

## UNIT 3
**TOPIC TALK**
- Cities
- Stress and relaxation
- Rules

**DESCRIBE ▶ DISCOVER**

**COUNT THE QUESTIONS**

**ROLE-PLAY**

# Mid-term review  Game: 55 seconds

The **55 Seconds** game is an extended collaborative speaking game. Pairs play against each other as two teams competing and scoring points.

**Tip** This is an opportunity for an oral evaluation of the class at the end or midpoint of the course, depending on whether you are using the split or the full edition. The aim is to generate enough speech to give an oral mark. Monitor sts closely, so you hear enough of each student's speech to be able to award a simple, impressionistic evaluation mark; for example:

**A = Excellent**
**B = Very good**
**C = Good**
**D = Needs improvement**

This can translate into a significant percentage – 20%, 30%, or even more – of your overall evaluation score for each student.

To play the game, divide the class into groups of four. Each group is divided into two teams of two. Within each pair, sts should decide who is student **A** and who is student **B**. Groups can toss a coin to decide which team starts the game.

Each of the five rectangles represents a unit, from unit **1** on the top left and continuing counterclockwise to unit **5** in the middle. There are four games in each unit square. Explain to sts that they will have 55 seconds for each game. One team monitors the time (55 seconds) while the other team plays. Once both teams have played all four games on a unit square, they should move on to the next one. The winner is the first team to reach a total of 40 points. They should shout out *40 finished!* when they get there.

To begin, team 1 should start at the square for unit **1** (top left), and team 2 should start at the square for unit **5** (bottom right). Teams should play the games in this order: first **Describe Discover**, next **Count the Questions**, then **Role-Play**, and finally **Topic Talk**.

Set up each game carefully the first time sts play it, so they know how to play it (see the examples below). Point out the instructions and scoring for each game above the unit 4 square. Have sts read the instructions before they start playing the game. To make sure they understand, ask them to give an example of what to do each time.

## Describe Discover

In this game, the opposing team chooses a noun, adjective, and verb from the unit, writes them on a piece of paper and gives it to student **A**. Then, student **A** must define and describe the word or phrase—without using the word itself—for student **B**, who listens, asks questions, and takes guesses until he / she identifies and says the word. The team scores 5 points for a correct discovery within the 55 seconds. Then sts change roles and repeat the process using a different word.

For example, if the word were *speed dating*, student **A** might say, *It's a noun. It's something you do with people you don't know. You go to a special place and meet lots of new people quickly. You ask questions and they ask you questions in a limited time, until you meet a person you like … .*

## Count the Questions

In this game, the opposing team chooses one of the small photos for the other team to speak about and counts the correct questions the sts are able to ask about it. Student **A** asks all the questions he / she can about the story behind the photo. Each question scores 1 point, so the more correct questions the student asks, the more his / her team scores. Student **B** answers student **A**'s questions however he / she likes, trying to be as imaginative as possible. They score 1 point per correct question. The sts on the other team make a note of any questions they think are wrong and can challenge them at the end. If any of the questions are found to be incorrect, the team loses the point scored. Then sts change roles and repeat the process using a different photo.

For example, questions for the first photo in the unit **1** square might be the following: *Who's the woman in the photo?* (The old lady on Facebook.) *Is she sleeping?* (No, she's using a computer.) *Is she alone? What's she wearing? Is she eating? What's she thinking? What's behind her?* Sts may make up any questions and answers they like; they do not need to match or remember the story from the book, as long as the question is accurate and the answer is reasonable for the question.

## Role-Play

In this game, teams act out the situations illustrated in the large cartoons. Encourage sts to be creative! Give them 30 seconds to prepare and 55 seconds for the role-play itself. First one team and then the other should act out the same role-play. If they land on the same role-play twice, they should change roles. Sts should be familiar with the idea of role-playing, as they have already done several role-plays during the course.

Teams should calculate their points at the end of each role-play. To score, teams begin with 10 points and lose:

- 1 point for each mistake the other team notices. (The opposing team should note mistakes and tell the other team at the end of the role-play.)
- 1 point each time they pause for 5 seconds or more. (The other team should time this accurately.)

# INSTRUCTIONS

## TOPIC TALK

The opposing team chooses a topic and counts the mistakes.
Talk about the topic together. Give opinions on the 🟢 and 🔴 points.
Score: Start with 10 points. Lose:
- 1 point for each mistake the opposing team notices.
- 1 point each time you pause for five seconds or more.

Calculate the points at the end. Use each topic only once.

## DESCRIBE ▶ DISCOVER

The opposing team chooses one noun, one adjective, and one verb from that unit, writes them on a piece of paper, and gives it to player A.
**A:** Define and describe three words without using the word itself.
**B:** Discover the word.
Score: 5 points for a correct discovery.

## COUNT THE QUESTIONS

The opposing team chooses a photo and counts the correct questions.
**A:** Ask your partner questions to find "the story behind the photo." The more questions you ask, the more points you score!
**B:** Answer A's questions however you like. Use your imagination!
Score: 1 point per correct question. Use each photo only once.

## ROLE-PLAY

Act out the situation in the cartoon. Be creative! You have 30 seconds to prepare.
Score: Start with 10 points. Lose:
- 1 point for each mistake the opposing team notices.
- 1 point each time you pause for five seconds or more.

Calculate the points at the end.

---

**UNIT 4** — TOPIC TALK
- Education
- Career choices
- Regrets

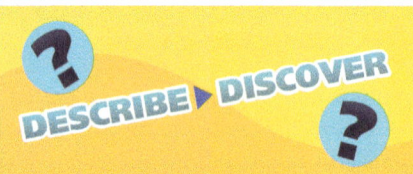

DESCRIBE ▶ DISCOVER

**UNIT 5** — TOPIC TALK
- Shopping
- Spending habits
- Useless products

DESCRIBE ▶ DISCOVER

**Tip** Before sts begin, you may wish to remind them of some useful fillers and hesitation devices, e.g. uh, er, erm, well, you know, I mean, right, you know what I mean, where was I, so, as I was saying, anyway, the thing is, actually, literally, basically.

## Topic talk

In this game, the opposing team chooses a topic from the three listed in the blue box and counts the mistakes as sts on the other team discuss the topic. In their discussions, sts should ask questions, give opinions on the pros and cons and generally say as much as they can that is relevant in 55 seconds. Then, sts should swap roles and the opposing team should choose a different topic for them to discuss. Remind sts to use each topic only once.

Teams should calculate their points at the end of each discussion. To score, teams begin with 10 points and lose:

- 1 point for each mistake the other team notices. (The opposing team should note mistakes and tell the other team at the end of the discussion.)
- 1 point each time they pause for 5 seconds or more. (The other team should time this accurately.)

Monitor closely as sts play, resolve any questions about what is or is not accurate and keep a running tally of teams' scores to keep the games competitive and add to the fun. If one group finishes very quickly, have them swap partners and play again.

# 6

## 6.1 What are you watching these days?

### 1 Vocabulary  TV genres and expressions

**A** ▶6.2 Match photos a–h to eight of the TV genres in question 1 of the survey. Listen to question 1 and repeat the genres. In your opinion, which are the best / worst shows on TV these days?

> ... isn't the worst show on TV, but it's not as good as it was.

# TV OR NOT TV?
### CHECK YOUR VIEWING HABITS!

**1** Which kinds of TV shows are you into?
- cartoons
- sports events
- stand-up comedy
- documentaries
- game shows
- music programs
- medical dramas
- talk shows (a)
- news programs
- reality TV
- sitcoms
- soap operas
- cooking programs
- wildlife programs

**2** Are / Were you addicted to any show or genre?
- yes
- no    If so, which? _____

**3** Is there any TV genre you can't stand?
- yes
- no    If so, which? _____

**4** How do you prefer TV shows in other languages?
- dubbed
- with subtitles

**5** Do you subscribe to any TV streaming services?
- yes
- no

**6** When did you last watch an entire season of a show?
- never
- ages ago
- recently (specify _____)

**7** What has the most influence on what you watch?
- favorable reviews
- friends' comments
- trailers
- other (specify _____)

**8** How many of each of these devices do you have at home?
- computer
- tablet
- smart phone
- TV

Which do you use most to watch TV?

> **Common mistake**
> watch
> I like to see TV at night.

**Unit overview:** In unit 6, sts study restrictive and nonrestrictive relative clauses in the contexts of TV, movies, and videos. Sts also watch a *How-to* video on how to make a movie and write their own tip on a different *How-to* topic using imperatives.

## 6.1 What are you watching these days?

**Lesson Aims:** Sts learn various TV genres, expressions, and TV-related vocabulary and use this vocabulary to talk about their personal viewing habits and programs in general.

### Function
Answering a survey on TV.
Listening to a father and daughter talk about their TV watching habits.
Talking about viewing habits.

### Language
Which kinds of TV shows are you into? How do you prefer foreign TV shows: dubbed or with subtitles?
The first TV I remember was in black and white, and it was massive.
Well, these days you can subscribe to lots of different services, so we have lots more options.

**Vocabulary:** TV genres (cartoons, soap operas, sports events, music programs, medical drama). TV-related vocabulary (trailers, talk shows, dubbed, subtitles, reviews, subscribe to, stream a show, trend on Twitter, cyber buddies, be into something, be addicted to something).
**Grammar:** Review simple present for habits and routines.

♪ Turn to p. 331 for notes about this song and an accompanying task.

**Warm-up** Have pairs of sts take turns asking and answering the lesson title questions from unit 5 on p. 58–67. Encourage sts to ask follow-up questions when appropriate. Monitor pairs closely and take notes of interesting answers, as well as the use of appropriate vocabulary and grammar, so you can provide sts with positive feedback at the end. Classcheck.

a talk show
b stand-up comedy
c game show
d sitcom
e medical drama
f music program
g cartoon
h cooking program

### 1 Vocabulary  TV Genres and expressions

**A Books closed.** Ask: *In your opinion, which are the best TV shows on your national channels these days? Which are the worst shows?* Have sts discuss the question in the lesson title in small groups. Encourage sts to ask follow-up questions when appropriate. Classcheck and find out which are the most/least popular TV shows at the moment.

Discuss the genres of the TV shows sts mentioned in the survey by asking: *What type of TV program is (name of show)? Is it a sitcom?* Ask the same question about more local shows to pre-teach some TV genres: *game shows, cartoons, reality TV, soap operas, documentaries,* and *news programs.*

**Books open.** Focus on the photos on p. 72–73 and find out whether sts recognize any of the programs, people, or characters. Point to photo a and ask: *What type of TV show is this?* (talk show). Get sts to look at question 1 in the survey and match photos a–h to eight of the TV genres. Paircheck. Classcheck.

## 6.1

**B** ▶6.1 Match the highlighted words in **A** to their meanings. Listen to a talking dictionary to check.

| 1 | _____ noun [C] | ads for a movie, showing extracts of it |
| 2 | _____ noun [C] | critics' opinions |
| 3 | _____ verb | pay regularly to receive something |
| 4 | _be into_ verb | really like something |
| 5 | _____ noun [C] | all the episodes in one year of a series |
| 6 | _____ noun [C] | on-screen translation of speech |
| 7 | _____ verb | spoken in the viewer's native language |
| 8 | _____ adj. | unable to stop doing something |

**C** Complete the comments with the items from **B**.

1 More than 100 million people worldwide _subscribe to_ Netflix.
2 The latest *Star Wars* movie received great _____ from all the critics.
3 Sometimes, I can't read the _____ fast enough, and I miss some of the dialogue.
4 I used to love *Downton Abbey*, but I got bored after the third _____ and stopped watching.
5 I saw a _____ for the new series of *Stranger Things* yesterday. Exciting!
6 I don't like _____ TV shows. It's better to hear the original language.
7 I used to be _____ *The Simpsons* when I was younger. I could watch episode after episode.
8 Everyone _____ *Game of Thrones* these days, but I don't like it.

**D** ▶6.2 🎧 **Make it personal** Listen and do the survey in **A**. In pairs, compare answers. Any big differences? Who's the class TV addict?

> *I was totally addicted to How I Met Your Mother a few years ago.*

## ② Listening

**A** ▶6.3 List five ways TV and viewing habits have changed since your parents' generation. Listen to a father and daughter and check any of your points that you hear. Are any other ideas mentioned?

> *People can watch TV anywhere and everywhere now.*

> *Yes, and my parents didn't use to have a remote control.*

**B** 🎧 **Make it personal** In groups, ask and answer 1–3. Any big differences?
1 Where do you watch TV? Who with? How much TV do you watch at home / somewhere else every week?
2 Would you prefer to watch TV the way the father did or the way the daughter does now? Why?
3 What's positive / negative about recent changes to TV programs and viewing habits? Is it similar for radio?
4 Does public TV have a future or will it all be private soon?

> *Well, these days you can subscribe to lots of different services, so we have a lot more options.*

> *True, but there are too many options sometimes.*

> *I sometimes watch English language programs with subtitles to practice my English.*

♪ *There's nothing on the TV, nothing on the radio that means that much to me.*

e

f

g

h

## 6.1

**B** Point to the highlighted words in question 1. Ask: *If you are into something, do you really like it or really hate it?* Have sts look at that part of speech and the definition in the box. Instruct sts to match the other highlighted words from **A** to the remaining definitions in the box. They should write the glossary or base form of the words. Paircheck. Play ▶ 6.1 so sts can check their answers. If time allows, refer sts to the AS on p. 168. Sts listen again and complete the noticing task.

▶ **6.1** Turn to page 316 for the complete audioscript.

1 trailers
2 reviews
3 subscribe to
4 be into
5 season
6 subtitles
7 dubbed
8 addicted to

**Language tip** Portuguese L1 speakers may use the word *legends* instead of *subtitles* as *legend* is a false cognate in Portuguese. In other words, it is a word that looks like the Portuguese equivalent to *subtitles*, but has a completely different meaning. Take the opportunity to remind sts that, although most of the words that are similar in L1 and English are real cognates, some are false cognates, or false friends. These are words that look like words in their L1, but have completely different meanings.

**C** Read the example with the class, then have sts insert the expressions from **B** into the phrases. Peercheck. Classcheck.

1 More than 100 million people *subscribe to* Netflix.
2 The new *Star Wars* movie received great *reviews* … .
3 Sometimes I can't read the *subtitles* fast enough … .
4 I used to love *Downton Abbey*, but I got bored after *season* 3 and stopped watching.
5 I saw a *trailer* for the new series of *Stranger Things* … .
6 I don't like *dubbed* TV shows.
7 I used to be *addicted to The Simpsons* when I was younger.
8 Everyone *is into* Game of Thrones these days, … .

**D** **Make it personal** Play ▶ 6.2 and have sts write their answers to the survey in **A** as they listen. Invite sts to work in pairs to compare their answers to the survey. At the end, ask pairs: *Did you find any big differences in your opinions? Who's the class TV addict?*

## 2 Listening

**A** Ask: *How do you think TV and TV watching habits have changed since your parents' generation? Think of five things.* Assign pairs and have sts make lists. Monitor carefully and help with ideas and vocabulary where necessary. Classcheck, and write any common ideas on the board as a list.

Play ▶ 6.3 for sts to check their ideas. Peercheck. Play the recording again if necessary, then classcheck and tick off any ideas from the list on the board that were mentioned.

▶ **6.3** Turn to page 316 for the complete audioscript.

Answers mentioned in the audio are:
nowadays color rather than black and white
TVs placed on wall taking up no space—used to be large (almost like an item of furniture)
Children would watch TV with their parents (parents chose what to watch)
Could only watch programs in real time—nowadays can stream and watch whenever and wherever you like
Don't discuss program with person watching in same room but post comments on social media

**Tip** Have sts turn to the AS on p. 168. Sts listen again and notice the sentence stress and weak forms.

**B** **Make it personal** Have sts change partners and ask and answer questions 1–4 in their new pairs. Refer the class to the model dialogue in the speech bubbles. Classcheck and ask: *Is anyone addicted to TV?*

**Tip** If time allows, have sts walk around the classroom and discuss questions 1–4 with as many classmates as possible, as if they were doing a class survey.

➡ **Workbook** Page 29

# 6.2 What's your favorite TV show ever?

## 1 Reading

**A** What do you know about *Stranger Things*? What genre is it?

*It looks like a sci-fi show.*

**B** ▶6.4 *Stranger Things* is a TV show that almost didn't make it past the pilot episode. Listen to two friends talking about it and answer 1–3.
1 How many times was *Stranger Things* rejected by TV companies?
2 Why was it rejected?
3 How many seasons have there been so far?

**C** List five reasons why a show might get canceled.

*Maybe it's had really bad reviews.*

**D** In groups of four, each read about a different show. Report back all you remember. Were any of your reasons in **C** there?

**E** ▶6.5 Listen, reread, and answer 1–6. Which show do you think sounds the best / worst? Why?
1 did the critics hate?
2 was a sci-fi program?
3 failed because the relationship between the actors wasn't realistic?
4 was a reality TV show?
5 involved three big Hollywood names?
6 managed to get one episode on TV?

*The Secret Talents show sounds awful! Who wants to know about celebrities' other talents?*

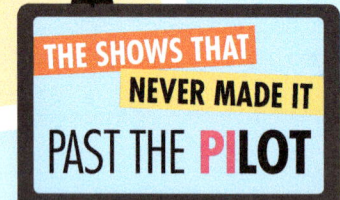

### THE SHOWS THAT NEVER MADE IT PAST THE PILOT

### Heat Vision and Jack

This pilot starred Jack Black and Owen Wilson and was directed by Ben Stiller. The plot centered around an astronaut who developed super powers. Black played the lead role and Owen Wilson was the voice of his talking motorbike! It sounds far-fetched and was not picked up by a TV station, but with such huge Hollywood actors, surely it deserved one series! Perhaps the superhero theme was ahead of its time.

### Secret Talents of the Stars

In this show, celebrities displayed talents we didn't know they had, and viewers would vote on the most talented celebrity. It sounds like a good idea, doesn't it? Unfortunately, in the pilot episode, the stars displayed talents that were similar to the ones they were already famous for. For example, ice skater Sasha Cohen showed off her acrobatic skills. Not entirely different from figure skating! The audience didn't see anything surprising or "secret," and the program was canceled after one episode because of low ratings.

### Mr. & Mrs. Smith

After the success of the movie with Brad Pitt and Angelina Jolie, ABC planned a spin-off television series. The story was set six months later and followed assassins John and Jane Smith's "normal" life in the suburbs with some spy action thrown in. Martin Henderson, who starred in *Grey's Anatomy*, and Jordana Brewster from *The Fast and The Furious* were chosen for the lead roles. However, critics said there was no chemistry between the two actors, and the series was never made. It's too bad, as it seems like a show that would appeal to fans of the movie!

### The Osbournes: Reloaded

The Osbournes were huge on MTV. Ozzy Osbourne's career was reborn, and the family became famous. When the MTV series ended, the Osbournes tried making a variety show for Fox. The show consisted of comedy, celebrity interviews, and live music. The network spent a lot of money on making and promoting the series. However, it cut the first episode from one hour to thirty-five minutes, and it was very heavily criticized by critics and viewers. Five episodes were filmed, but the show was canceled after just one.

# 6.2 What's your favorite TV show ever?

**Lesson Aims:** Sts practice relative pronouns and form restrictive relative clauses in the context of expressing opinions about TV shows and other well-known people or things.

## Function
Listening to people discussing a TV program.
Reading about TV shows that never made it past the pilot episode.
Talking about the pilot episode of your favorite TV show.
Writing a quiz about movies or music.

## Language
I'm really into *Stranger Things* at the moment. Have you seen it?
The plot centered around an astronaut who developed super powers.
I loved the first episode of *Mad Men*. It was so stylish!
Kiefer Sutherland is the actor who starred in *24* and whose father is also a famous actor.

**Vocabulary:** Phrases to describe TV shows: *far-fetched, ahead of its time, spin-off, thrown in, variety show.*
**Grammar:** Restrictive relative clauses

♪ Turn to p. 331 for notes about this song and an accompanying task.

**Warm-up** Pair sts up and make sure each pair has a pen and a sheet of paper. Explain that pairs will have one minute to write as many TV genres as they can think of. Time the activity and have all pairs start at the same time.

When time is up, ask pairs to count the number of TV genres they listed. Have the pair with the longest list call out their TV genres, as the rest of the pairs check similarities and add any differences to their lists. Write the words on the board to classcheck spelling. Drill pronunciation for all words.

At the end, have sts ask and answer the following questions in pairs: *What's your favorite TV show? Why do you like it? What channel is it on? What time is it on?*

## 1  Reading

**A  Books open.** Point to the photos on the top of p. 74 and ask: *Have you heard of / seen the show? What do you know about Stranger Things?* Elicit what sts know and if necessary, feed in information from the cultural notes below.

> **Cultural notes** *Stranger Things* is a science fiction horror show shown on Netflix, written and directed by the Duffer Brothers. Set in the 1980s, it tells the story of the disappearance of a young boy and shows supernatural events around the town where it's set. It stars Winona Ryder, David Harbour, and Finn Wolfhard, among others.

**B** Elicit or explain the meaning of *a pilot show* (the very first episode of a new series). Explain that if the pilot episode is not popular, or gets bad reviews, TV companies can cancel the rest of the series. Tell sts that they are going to listen to two friends talking about the show and why it almost didn't make it past the pilot episode. Go through the questions with the class and elicit their predictions, but don't give any answers yet. Play ▶6.4 for sts to listen and answer the questions. Peercheck. If time allows, have sts turn to the AS on p. 168 to check their answers. Classcheck and ask: *Did you guess correctly?*

> 1  between 15 and 20 times
> 2  TV executives didn't like the idea of a TV show that was about kids but wasn't for kids' TV
> 3  2 so far

▶6.4  Turn to page 317 for the complete audioscript.

**C** Assign pairs and have sts list possible reasons why a show might get canceled. Elicit suggestions from different pairs but don't confirm answers yet.

**D** Read the title of the article to the class and tell sts that they're going to listen to and read information about four TV shows that never made it past the pilot. Assign sts into groups of four. Each member of the group reads about a different show then reports back to their group and checks if their answers to **C** were correct. Classcheck.

**E** Play ▶6.5 for sts to listen and read the whole article and answer questions 1–6. Peercheck. Classcheck and ask: *Which show do you think sounds the best? Which sounds the worst? Why?*

> 1  The Osbournes
> 2  Heat Vision and Jack
> 3  Mr. & Mrs. Smith
> 4  Secret Talents of the Stars & The Osbournes
> 5  Heat Vision and Jack
> 6  Secret Talents of the Stars & The Osbournes

161

**F** Match the underlined words and phrases in the article to the definitions.
1 based on something that already exists
2 difficult to believe because it is very unlikely
3 much more advanced / modern than most other things
4 to include something extra
5 the estimated audience size of a TV or radio show.

♪ Want you to make me feel
Like I'm the only girl in the world
Like I'm the only one that you'll ever love

**G** 🔵 **Make it personal** In pairs, can you remember the pilot (or first) episode of your favorite TV show or movie series? What happened?

*I loved the first episode of* Mad Men. *It was so stylish!*

*I'm old enough to remember going to the first* Star Wars *movie! We were amazed by the special effects.*

## 2 Grammar  Restrictive relative clauses

**A** Match the sentence halves, then do the grammar box. Circle the right answer in 1 and 2 (ignore rule 3 for the moment).
1 *Heat Vision and Jack* is about <u>a man</u>
2 *Mr. & Mrs. Smith* was <u>a TV series</u>
3 *Secret Talents of the Stars* starred <u>celebrities</u>
4 *The Osbournes: Reloaded* was <u>a TV show</u>
5 Winona Ryder plays <u>a mother</u>

a ☐ that was based on a movie.
b ☐ whose talents the audience had not seen.
c ☐ who develops superpowers.
d ☐ whose son has gone missing.
e ☐ that got canceled after one episode.

🟠 **Common mistakes**
~~who~~
She's the actor that was in those awful comedies.
They sent us an app that we found ~~it~~ very useful.

|         | whose | that | who |
|---------|-------|------|-----|
| people  |       |      |     |
| things  |       |      |     |

1 Use restrictive relative clauses like those in a–e to give **essential** / **extra** information about someone or something.
2 The clause usually comes **before** / **after** the noun it describes.
3 When the pronoun is the object, you _____ a relative pronoun.

➡ **Grammar 6A** p.148

**B** Which sentence doesn't need a relative pronoun (*that, whose, who*)? Check in the article on p. 74. Then complete rule 3 in the grammar box.
1 It seems like a show that would appeal to fans of the movie!
2 In this show, celebrities displayed talents that we didn't know they had.

**C** Complete 1–5 with relative pronouns. Which two sentences don't need a relative pronoun?

1 *Glee* is a show _____ features high school students _____ can sing and dance.

2 Oprah Winfrey is a TV host _____ talent made her the most powerful woman on TV.

3 *Friends* is a sitcom _____ adults and kids still watch, even after 25 years.

4 Homer Simpson is a cartoon character _____ keeps saying "d'oh."

5 *The Tonight Show*, *The Late Show*, and *The Daily Show* are talk shows _____ millions of Americans watch.

**D** 🔵 **Make it personal** 🔊 In small teams, write a 5-question quiz about TV, movies, or music. Search online to find and check information. Play against another team. Who can get more answers right? Try to use restrictive relative clauses.

1 _____ is the actor who starred in "24" and whose father is also a famous actor.
2 _____ is the TV show that was canceled by Fox and renewed by NBC the following day!
3 _____ is the musician who's married to Jay-Z and was in Destiny's Child.

*I know the first one. It's Kiefer Sutherland, so that's one point to us.*

*And I have a feeling the answer to number two is "Brooklyn Nine-Nine."*

*And number 3 is definitely Beyoncé!*

**F** Point to the underlined phrase *far-fetched* in the article in **E** and ask: *If something is **far-fetched**, is it easy or difficult to believe?* (difficult). Ask sts to tell you which of the definitions it goes with. Sts match the rest of the underlined phrases to the definitions. Peercheck. Classcheck.

> 1 spin-off   2 far-fetched   3 ahead of its time
> 4 thrown in   5 ratings

**G** 🔵 **Make it personal**   Ask: *Can you remember the pilot (or first) episode of your favorite TV show? What happened?* Have a volunteer read the example in the speech bubbles, then assign pairs for sts to discuss. Classcheck, and find out what the most popular shows are.

## ② Grammar   Restrictive relative clauses

**A** Read item 1 and elicit the correct ending. Have sts match the sentence halves and paircheck. Classcheck by writing the answers on the board.

> 1 c   2 a   3 b   4 e   5 d

🟠 **Common mistakes**   Read with the whole class. Elicit why *who* is a better choice in the corrected sentence.

Instruct sts to study the sentences they matched and check the correct boxes in the grammar box chart, then circle the correct alternatives in rules 1 and 2. Make sure they ignore rule 3 for the moment. Classcheck.

> Grammar box:
> Use *whose* and *who* to describe people; use *that* to describe things
> 1 essential   2 after   3 don't need

➡ **Grammar 6A** page 148

**B** Point to the sentences and ask: *In which sentence can we omit the relative pronoun?* Have sts answer individually and paircheck. Then, tell sts to check their answers in the article on p. 74 in 1E and fill in the blank in rule 3.

> Sentence 2 doesn't need a relative pronoun.

**Language tip**   The omission of the relative pronoun in English can be tricky for Portuguese and Spanish L1 speakers as the relative pronoun is never omitted in L1. Give sts some more examples of the omission of the relative pronoun after they do activity **2B**. Remind sts that in English this omission is very common.

**C** Have sts fill in the blanks in 1–5 with the relative pronouns *whose*, *that*, or *who*. Tell sts that where more than one pronoun is possible, they should write both options. Paircheck. Classcheck. At the end, ask: *Which two sentences don't need a relative pronoun?*

> 1 that, who
> 2 whose
> 3 that
> 4 who
> 5 that
> Relative pronouns can be omitted in 3 and 5.

**Tip**   You could introduce a couple of jokes to illustrate restrictive clauses:

*What do you call a song which is sung in an automobile?* (A cartoon).

Have sts work in pairs to follow the model and make up their own jokes.

**D** 🔵 **Make it personal**   Tell sts that they're going to write a quiz about movies or music (or both, if they want). Arrange sts in small teams and read the example questions together. Ask sts to write at least five quiz items and tell them they can use their mobile devices to research the questions.

Monitor and help with vocabulary where necessary. Make sure sts are forming the restricted relative clauses correctly.

When they are ready, put teams together with another team to do their quizzes. Read the example dialogue with sts. If time allows, rotate the teams so they get to do all the quizzes. At the end, ask: *Who got most answers right?*

➡ **Workbook** Page 30

**6.2**

## 6.3 What was the last movie you saw?

### 1 Reading

**A** Which of the movies in the posters have you seen? Describe the plot for each in only four sentences, like this one for *Romeo and Juliet*.

"A boy and a girl fall in love and marry. They're forced to separate so she pretends to kill herself. Then he thinks she's dead so he kills himself. She finds him dead and really kills herself."

**B** ▶ 6.6 Insert phrases 1–4 in gaps a–d. Listen to check. Any pronunciation surprises? Do the gapped sentences in the article make sense without the phrases?

1 whose popularity was at its peak
2 who had been diagnosed with terminal cancer
3 who played Jake Sully
4 which became the fastest movie in history to reach a worldwide gross of $1 billion at the box office

## FOUR *curious* MOVIE FACTS

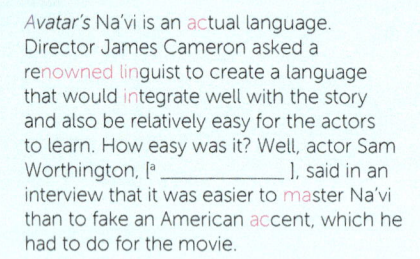

*Avatar's* Na'vi is an actual language. Director James Cameron asked a renowned linguist to create a language that would integrate well with the story and also be relatively easy for the actors to learn. How easy was it? Well, actor Sam Worthington, [a _____ ], said in an interview that it was easier to master Na'vi than to fake an American accent, which he had to do for the movie.

James Cameron, who also directed *Titanic*, initially didn't want the movie to have a theme song, even during the closing credits. Composer James Horner, however, secretly asked Celine Dion, [b _____ ], to record a demo of "My Heart Will Go On." Horner then played the song to James Cameron, who immediately changed his mind. The song won an Oscar and became one of the best-selling singles in history.

Actors Mark Hamill, who played the legendary Luke Skywalker, and John Boyega persuaded *Star Wars* director J.J. Abrams to allow *Star Wars* super-fan Daniel Fleetwood to see the movie before it was officially released. Fleetwood, [c _____ ], got to see the movie in a special screening at his home before he passed away.

*Avengers: Infinity War*, [d _____ ], was one of the best kept movie secrets ever! In order to keep the plot of the movie secret and avoid spoilers, Disney decided to give the cast* fake scripts**. The directors wanted to protect the movie, which eventually came out in 2018, because it had taken ten years to make. They wanted the audience to have the best experience possible when they went to see the movie.

*the group of actors in a movie or show
**the written story and instructions

### 2 Grammar Non-restrictive relative clauses

**A** Reread the movie facts article with the additions from **1B** and circle the correct alternatives in the grammar box.

1 Non-restrictive clauses give **essential** / **extra** information.
2 Non-restrictive relative clauses **use** / **don't use** commas.
3 You **can** / **can't** use *that* in a non-restrictive clause.
4 Non-restrictive clauses **always** / **don't always** need a relative pronoun.

➜ Grammar 6C p.148

**B** Find and underline five more examples of clauses like this in the article.

⚠ **Common mistake**
My favorite Batman movie is The Dark Knight, ~~that~~ won four Oscars.   which

# 6.3 What was the last movie you saw?

**Lesson Aims:** Sts study and practice inserting extra information with non-restrictive relative clauses through the context of listening to and reading about blockbuster movies.

**Function**
Reading about curious movie facts.
Adding extra information.
Listening to a radio quiz about a movie director.
Writing a short description of a movie.

**Language**
James Cameron initially didn't want *Titanic* to have a theme song.
*The Greatest Showman* was directed by Michael Gracey, who had never directed a movie before.
Which box office smash did Coogler direct in 2016?
*Jurassic Park*, which was written in 1990, inspired one of the most successful movie franchises of all time.

**Vocabulary:** Star (in a movie), sequel, plot.
**Grammar:** Non-restrictive relative clauses.
**Pronunciation:** Pauses in speech.
**Before the lesson:** Prepare a set of six paper cards for each group. On each card, write the name of a blockbuster movie or series: (1) *Titanic*, (2) *Star Wars*, (3) *Avatar*, (4) *The Lord of the Rings*, (5) *Harry Potter*, and (6) *The Avengers*.

♪ Turn to p. 331 for notes about this song and an accompanying task.

**Warm-up** Divide the class into groups of six. Give one set of cards (see **Before the lesson**) to each group. Explain that sts should take turns picking up a card and saying what the story is about. The other sts in the group should try to guess the movie title. The group that guesses all six movie titles fastest is the winner. Monitor and give suggestions, encouraging sts to describe the plot and setting, but not allowing them to say actors or characters' names. Classcheck. Ask: *Which movie was the most difficult to guess?*

## 1 Reading

**A Books open**. Point to the posters and ask: *Which of the movies have you seen? Can you describe the plot for each in four sentences?* Read the example with sts then have sts work in pairs to prepare their four-sentence plots. Classcheck.

**B** Point to the title of the article and ask: *Do you know any curious movie facts?* Point to phrases 1–4 and have sts choose the correct phrases to fill in blanks a–d in the article. Play ▶ 6.6 for sts to listen to and read the article and check their answers. Peercheck. Classcheck.

> a 3  b 1  c 2  d 4

Point to blank a in the first paragraph and ask: *If I read the sentence without phrase 3, will it still make sense?* Then, read the sentence without phrase 3. Do the same with the sentences containing blanks b–d. Lead sts to notice that phrases 1–4 could have been omitted.

## 2 Grammar  Non-restrictive relative clauses

**A** Have sts study the sentences in **1B** containing blanks a–d and circle the correct choices. Paircheck. Classcheck.

> 1 extra  2 use  3 can't  4 always

**Tip** Write the sentences below on the board and elicit the difference between them:

1. *Julia, whose mother is German, speaks four different languages.*
2. *The woman whose mother is German speaks four languages.*

Classcheck. Explain that, in sentence 1, *whose mother is German* is non-restrictive and only adds more detail.

Highlight the use of commas. Tell sts that, in sentence 2, the same phrase is restrictive and the clause restricts, i.e. specifies or defines, the woman who is being talked about.

Refer sts to **2A** in lesson 6.2 for examples of restrictive relative clauses. Reinforce the use of commas in nonrestrictive relative clauses (as in sentence 1 on the board) and the absence of commas in restrictive relative clauses (as in sentence 2).

**Common mistakes**  Read with the class to teach the concept of *that* vs. *which*.

→ **Grammar 6C** page 148

**B** Ask sts to find and underline five other non-restrictive relative clauses in the article in **B**. Paircheck. Classcheck.

> *Avatar:* … it was easier to master Na'vi than to fake an American accent, <u>which he had to do for the movie.</u>
> *Titanic:* James Cameron, <u>who also directed *Titanic*</u>, initially didn't want the movie to have a theme song.
> Horner then played the song to James Cameron, <u>who immediately changed his mind.</u>
> *Star Wars:* Actors Mark Hamill, <u>who played the legendary Luke Skywalker.</u>
> *Avengers:* The directors wanted to protect the movie, <u>which eventually came out in 2018,</u> because …

**C** Connect sentences 1–4 with relative pronouns. Have you seen this movie?

♪ *When the sharpest words wanna cut me down, I'm gonna send a flood, gonna drown them out. I am brave, I am bruised, I am who I'm meant to be, This is me.*

### Did you know …?

1  *The Greatest Showman* was directed by Michael Gracey. ~~He~~ , who had never directed a movie before.
2  This musical movie had a very popular soundtrack. It included hits like "This is Me" and "A Million Dreams".
3  The plot is based on the life of circus owner PT Barnum. He was born in 1810.
4  The main character is played by Hugh Jackman. His family is from Australia.

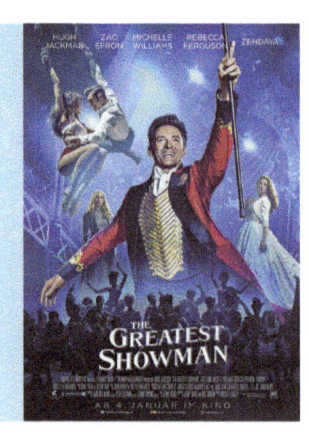

**D** Rewrite 1–4 using non-restrictive clauses. Write one more of your own.

1  Robert Downey Jr. was voted the best Marvel actor of all time by fans. He plays Iron Man.

2  The first *Iron Man* movie helped relaunch Downey Jnr.'s career. It was made in 2008.

3  Scarlett Johansson plays one of Marvel's first female superheroes in *Black Widow*. Her other movies include *Lost in Translation* and *Sing*.

4  *Avengers: Infinity War* is one of the highest grossing movies in history. It's the third *Avengers* film.

5  Stan Lee created many of the Marvel characters. He played cameo roles in many of the movies.

*Robert Downey Jr., who plays Iron Man, was voted the best Marvel actor of all time by fans.*

## 3 Pronunciation  Pauses in speech

**A** ▶ 6.7 Listen to part of a radio quiz about movie director Ryan Coogler. Circle the correct answer for each question in the quiz.

1  *Infinity Wars*    *Black Panther*    *Guardians of the Galaxy*
2  Soccer    Motor racing    Boxing
3  Barack Obama    Steven Spielberg    Morgan Freeman

**B** ▶ 6.7 Pausing when you speak gives you time to think and helps the listener to follow you. Insert speech pauses ( // ) in 1–5 where necessary. Listen again to check. In pairs, practice imitating the speaker.
1  This week we've been talking about moviemakers who have changed American cinema.
2  The first question is about Ryan Coogler, who many people consider to be one of the finest new moviemakers around.
3  *Creed*, which also starred Sylvester Stallone, was a spin-off from a classic series of movies, *Rocky*.
4  Well, it's a kind of sport that involves two people and a ring.
5  The movie, which won Stallone a Golden Globe, was highly acclaimed by critics.

**C** 🔘 **Make it personal**  Write a short description of a movie you know. Then in groups, read it for the others to guess the movie. Use non-restrictive relative clauses.

*_____, which was written in 1990, inspired one of the most successful movie franchises of all time. The stories are based on the science-fiction novels by Michael Crichton, who is an American author, screenwriter, movie director, and producer.*

*That's easy. I've seen all four of those movies. I do love dinosaurs. It's* Jurassic Park.

**C** Read sentence 1 with sts and make sure they notice the comma followed by a relative pronoun in the example. Have sts connect sentences 2–4 following the pattern from 1 and using an appropriate relative pronoun. Classcheck.

1 *The Greatest Showman* was directed by Michael Gracey, who had never directed a film before.
2 This musical movie, which had a very popular soundtrack, included hits like *This is Me* and *A Million Dreams*.
3 The plot is based on the life of circus owner P. T. Barnum, who was born in 1810.
4 The main character is played by Hugh Jackman, whose family is from Australia.

**Language tip** In Portuguese and Spanish, there's only one relative pronoun that's equivalent to *who, which,* and *that*. Sts who speak these languages as their L1 tend to use the relative pronoun *that* in all situations where they would use the equivalent *que* in their L1. Remind sts that, in English, they should use *who* for people and *which* for things.

**D** Read example 1 with the whole class and point out the placement of the nonrestrictive relative clause (in between commas). Have sts connect sentences 2–4 following the pattern from 1 and using an appropriate relative pronoun. Classcheck.

1 Robert Downey Jr., who plays Iron Man, was voted the best Marvel actor of all time by fans.
2 The first *Iron Man* movie, which was made in 2008, helped relaunch Downey Jr.'s career
3 Scarlett Johansson, whose other movies include *Sing* and *Lost in Translation*, plays one of Marvel's first female superheroes in *Black Widow*.
4 *Avengers: Infinity War*, which is the third *Avengers* film, is one of the highest grossing movies in history.
5 Stan Lee, who created many of the Marvel characters, played cameo roles in many of the movies.

## 3 Pronunciation  Pauses in speech

**A** Have sts look at items 1–3. Say: *You're going to listen to a radio quiz about a movie director. His name is Ryan Coogler. Have you seen any of his films?* Play ▶ 6.7 and have sts circle the correct answers. Paircheck. Classcheck.

1 *Black Panther*   2 Boxing   3 Barack Obama

▶ 6.7 Turn to page 317 for the complete audioscript.

**B** Say: *Pausing when you speak gives you time to think, express emotions, and breathe!* Explain that we sometimes fill pauses with phrases like *let me see …* or just *um …* and write these phrases on the board.

Then explain that pauses also help the listener follow and digest what we're saying. Point to numbers 1–5 and ask: *Where would you pause in these sentences?* Have sts insert slashes (//) to signal pauses. Paircheck. Play ▶ 6.7 again to classcheck. Then, write the answers on the board, or have sts turn to the AS on p. 168 to check their answers.

1 This week we've been talking about movie makers who have changed American cinema.
2 The first question is about Ryan Coogler, // who many people consider to be one of the finest new movie makers around.
3 *Creed*, // which also starred Sylvester Stallone, // was a spin-off from a classic series of movies, *Rocky*.
4 Well, // it's a kind of sport that involves two people and a ring.
5 The movie, // which won Stallone a Golden Globe, // was highly acclaimed by critics.

**C** **Make it personal**  Read the example with the class and elicit which film they think it describes (*Jurassic Park*). Have sts write their own short descriptions of a movie individually. Monitor carefully and encourage sts to use nonrestrictive relative clauses, and help with vocabulary where necessary.

When they have finished, assign groups and have sts read out their descriptions (ensuring they don't say the name of the movie) for other group members to guess. In feedback, nominate a student from each group to read out their description for the class to guess the movie.

➔ **Workbook** Page 31

## 6.4 Where do you usually watch movies?

### 1 Vocabulary  Movies

**A** ▶6.8  In pairs, take our quiz and find out who knows more. Listen and choose the answer from the options given. Then listen to the correct answer to check.

### Think you're an expert on movies and media? Try this quiz and prove it!

1. Which fantasy **prequel** to *The Lord of the Rings* did director Peter Jackson **shoot** in New Zealand between 2011 and 2013?

2. The video for which song by Luis Fonsi and Daddy Yankee became the most watched video in YouTube history, with over five billion views?

3. *Avengers: Infinity War* is an action movie about superheroes. The cast is like a "Who's Who" of Hollywood and includes many big names. Can you name three of them?

4. One of the biggest YouTube memes of 2013 was "Harlem Shake." There were over 33 hours of "Harlem Shake" **clips** up**load**ed every day. What did people do in the videos?

5. British actor Tom Holland **stars** as which wall-climbing superhero?

6. Andy Serkis, who was the gorilla in *King Kong*, had to learn to move like a chimpan**zee** in which famous **tri**logy?

7. What **role** does Liam Hemsworth play in the **block**buster *The Hunger Games*?

8. Which romance movie **set** in Indianapolis portrays two teenagers who are suffering from cancer?

9. Who wrote the script and directed the first *Star Wars* films?

**B** Match the highlighted words in the quiz to the definitions.

| 1 | _____ noun [C] | a movie that is released after another, but tells the story before it |
| 2 | _____ verb | to take photos for a movie / to film |
| 3 | _____ verb | to put a story in a certain time and place |
| 4 | _____ noun [C] | an extract from a video; a short video |
| 5 | _____ noun [C] | the part, or character, that an actor plays in a movie |
| 6 | _____ verb | to be the main character in a movie |

**C** ▶6.9  Listen to dialogues 1–3. Which three movies from **A** were they discussing?

**D** ▶6.9  Listen again. In which dialogues do they disagree? Who do you agree with?

**E** 🔶 **Make it personal**  Have you seen 1–9 in **A**? What did you think of them? Compare opinions in groups. Any similarities? Who has seen the most?

> I've seen lots of "Harlem Shake" videos. My class made one and uploaded it.

> Really? I didn't like them to be honest. I thought they were weird.

---

### ⚠ Common mistakes

"Despacito" is a catchy ~~music~~.
  song / tune
~~music~~       is
  The ~~musics~~ in that movie ~~are~~ great!
                                   like
  Adele sings ~~as~~ a bird.
                  as
  She stars ~~like~~ Jay's second wife.

# 6.4 Where do you usually watch movies?

**Lesson Aims:** Sts watch a "How to" video and use Imperative verbs to write their own tips on various topics.

### Function
Taking a media quiz.
Talking about videos and films you have seen.
Watching a How-to video on how to make a short video.
Writing tips and advice for a "How-to" video.

### Language
There were over 33 hours of Harlem Shake clips uploaded every day. What did people do in the videos?
I've seen lots of *Harlem Shake* videos. My class did one and uploaded it.
How to make a movie.
How to choose the right cast.

**Vocabulary:** Words related to movies and videos: *prequel, shoot, views, cast, portray.*
**Grammar:** Imperatives

♪ Turn to p. 331 for notes about this song and an accompanying task.

**Warm-up** Write *viral video* on the board and ask: *What's a viral video?* Have sts answer in pairs. Classcheck. Then, invite the pairs to discuss the following questions: *What is the best / funniest viral video you have ever watched? Have you ever uploaded a video on YouTube?* Classcheck by inviting volunteers to share their partners' answers with the class.

**Cultural note** A viral video is a video that becomes rapidly popular—worldwide or nationally—via Internet sharing, usually on websites such as YouTube or Facebook, or via email. Such videos often contain humorous or gossipy content.

## 1 Vocabulary  Movies

**A** **Books closed**. Ask: *How much do you know about movies? Do you watch a lot of movies?*

**Books open**. Point to the media quiz and say: *We're going to do a quiz to find out how much you know about movies.* Have sts take the quiz in pairs. Play ▶ 6.8 so pairs can check their answers. Classcheck and ask: *How many did you get right?*

▶ 6.8 Turn to page 317 for the complete audioscript.

| | |
|---|---|
| 1 *The Hobbit* | 4 dance |
| 2 *Despacito* | 5 Tom Holland is Spiderman. |
| 3 Possible answers: Robert Downey Junior, Chris Hemsworth, Chris Evans, Mark Ruffalo, Scarlett Johanson, Benedict Cumberbatch, and Chris Holland. | 6 *Planet of the Apes* |
| | 7 Gale Hawthorne |
| | 8 *The Fault in Our Stars* |
| | 9 George Lucas |

**B** Draw sts' attention to the highlighted words in **A**. Have sts match them to the correct definitions in the box. Paircheck. Classcheck.

1 prequel  2 shoot  3 set  4 clip  5 role  6 star

**C** Tell sts that they are going to hear three dialogues about the videos and movies from **A**. Say: *Listen and notice which movies or videos they are talking about.* Play ▶ 6.9 and have sts paircheck. Replay the track if necessary. Classcheck.

▶ 6.9 Turn to page 317 for the complete audioscript.

*Planet of the Apes*   *Despacito*   *Avengers: Infinity War*

**D** Say: *Listen again. In which dialogue do the speakers disagree?* Replay ▶ 6.9. Classcheck. Then ask: *Which person in dialogue 3 do you agree with?*

They disagree in dialogue 3.

**Common mistakes** Read with the whole class. and explain that *music* is uncountable, but *song* is countable.

**Language tip** Remind Portuguese L1 speakers that, despite being a cognate in Portuguese, the word *music* cannot be used interchangeably with the word *song*. Music is a more general term that we use to refer to the musical art itself, and it is never used in the plural. When we want to refer to a piece of music, or pieces of music, we use the word *song(s)*.

Write the following sentences from the quiz on the board:
*Tom Holland stars <u>as</u> which wall-climbing hero?*
*Andy Serkis ... had to learn to move <u>like</u> a chimpanzee.*

Elicit the meanings of the underlined words in the sentences (*like* = in a manner similar to; *as* = job). Say: **As** *and* **like** *are often confused. Both are used to compare actions, people or situations. Use* **like** *+ noun to express similarity.*

**E** **Make it personal** Invite two volunteers to read the model dialogue in the speech bubbles to the whole class. Divide the class into groups of three or four and have sts discuss the questions. Monitor sts' discussions and write down mistakes for delayed correction. Classcheck sts' ideas and provide language feedback.

## 6.4

### 2 Listening

*You still look like a movie.
You still sound like a song.
My God, this reminds me
Of when we were young.*

**A** In pairs, decide what is important to consider about the items below when making a video.

filming    light    permission    sound    story

*You need a quality camera with a good lens and plenty of memory space.*

**B** ▶ 6.10  Listen to / Watch the instructions on how to make a short video and see if your guesses are mentioned.

**C** ▶ 6.10  Read the summary notes on the video and try to remember the missing words. Then listen / watch again and fill in each blank with two words.

---

**Tips and tricks to making a SHORT VIDEO**

**PLAN YOUR SHOOT**
Think about: the topic. ¹_____ people? What do you want the video to ² _____ in the end?

**USE THE TECHNOLOGY AVAILABLE TO YOU**
You could use:
A ³ _____, a camcorder, a webcam, or a ⁴ _____.

**CAPTURE YOUR CLIPS**
Press the ⁵ _____ a few seconds before you start. Use a tripod to stop the camera from moving. Extra shoots and ⁶ _____ might be useful. Don't ⁷ _____ the top of the subject's head.

**BE CAREFUL WITH LIGHTING**
Shoot in a well-lit area.
⁸ _____ there is no bright light behind the subject.

**PLAN THE LENGTH OF SHOOT**
Plan ⁹ _____ in advance.
Don't talk about one thing for ¹⁰ _____.

---

**D** Read ▶ 6.10 on p. 169 to check. Compare the underlined items with those in **C**.

**E** Make five pieces of moviemaking advice and decide what elements in **A** they refer to.

| | | |
|---|---|---|
| 1 | Always | ☐ you are allowed to film in public places. |
| 2 | Think about | ☐ have a beginning, a middle, and an end. |
| 3 | Make sure | ☐ moving shots, try attaching the camera to a skateboard or office chair. |
| 4 | Never | ☐ continuity. If you have a shot from the middle of the day, the next scene shouldn't be at night. |
| 5 | If you want | ☐ underestimate the emotional power of silence. |

**F** 🔊 In groups, brainstorm and search online to find advice to include in a "how to" video on one of these topics. Use the underlined phrases from **E**.

How to get more views on YouTube    How to learn English faster    How to become a better dancer
How to live longer    How to study effectively    How to meet new people

**G** 😀 **Make it personal**  In groups of three, choose a title and decide your story. Tell the class and award an Oscar for the best idea. If you really like your idea, go out and film it—in English, of course!

One Wednesday evening    Rob and Rex    Thanks for everything

- *This retired couple fell in love a long time ago.*
- *But then they separated and married different people.*
- *Years later, they meet again and fall in love, and the movie is about how their children feel.*

## 2 Listening

**A** Say: *Imagine you're going to make a short video now.* Point to the items listed and ask: *How would these elements be important to you?* Pair sts up and have them read the model dialogue in the speech bubbles and discuss the elements in the box. Classcheck.

> Suggested answers:
>
> filming: be organized, plan everything in advance
>
> light: the scene should be well lit, the light should reflect the mood, should be "flattering" for the actors
>
> permission: need permission to film in certain places, might need permission if you are using a true story
>
> sound: sound should be clear, watch out for background noise such as cars, airplanes, people etc.
>
> story: it should be new, interesting, catch and keep attention

**B** Tell sts they're going to watch and listen to some tips on how to make a movie. Ask sts to see if any of their ideas from **A** are mentioned. Play ▶ 6.10 ▶. Replay the video if necessary. Classcheck.

▶ 6.10 Turn to page 317 for the complete videoscript.

**C** Tell sts that the notes in the text "Tips and Tricks to Making a Short Video" are from a student who watched the video. Have sts read the notes and predict the two missing words in each blank. Then, play ▶ 6.10 ▶ again, so sts can check their predictions. Classcheck.

> 1  How many
> 2  look like
> 3  digital camera
> 4  mobile phone
> 5  record button
> 6  still images
> 7  cut off
> 8  Make sure
> 9  your script
> 10 too long

**D** Point to the underlined words and phrases in **C**. Ask sts to find the equivalent words and phrases underlined in AS 6.10 on p. 169. Paircheck. Classcheck.

> in the end = when it is finished
>
> stop the camera from moving = keep it steady
>
> be useful = come in handy
>
> in advance = beforehand

**E** Say: *Let's look at more tips on how to make a movie.* Read item 1 with the whole class and match it to the correct ending. Then, have sts match the rest of the sentences. Paircheck. Classcheck.

> 1  Always have a beginning, a middle, and an end.
> 2  Think about continuity. If you have a shot from the middle of the day, the next scene shouldn't be at night.
> 3  Make sure you are allowed to film in public places.
> 4  Never underestimate the emotional power of silence.
> 5  If you want moving shots, try attaching the camera to a skateboard or office chair.

**F** Say: *Now you are going to write your own tips for a "how to" video.* Instruct sts to choose only one topic from the box and use their mobile devices to search online for tips. Have sts write at least five tips using the underlined words and expressions in **E**. If necessary, you could do an example with the class first, e.g. tips for "how to reduce stress". Have sts work in groups of four. Walk around the classroom and offer help as necessary. Classcheck by having groups read their tips to the whole class.

> **Tip** You may wish to have each group read their tips to the class without stating the topic, and then ask the class to guess which topic the tips are about.

**G** **Make it personal** Point to the pictures and read the titles with the whole class. Have sts read the model text and ask: *Which title is this text about?* (One Wednesday Evening).

Divide the class into groups of three and have each group choose a movie title and write a story for it. At the end, invite groups to read their stories to the whole class and award an Oscar to the best one.

> **Tip** If your sts are enthusiastic about the idea, encourage them to film their stories outside the classroom, in English, and assign a day to view their productions in class.

▶ **Workbook** Page 32

# 6.5 Who are the wildest celebrities you know?

**Skills** Understanding details

**A** Complete the text about Sia with these words.

| 2014 | Australia | broke | five |
|---|---|---|---|
| hits | musician | rising | single |

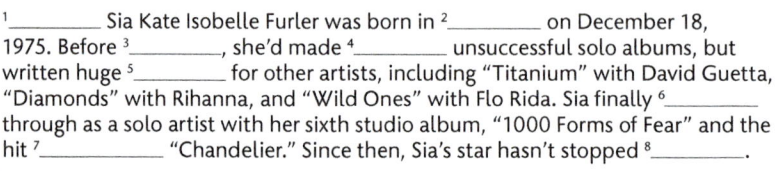

¹_____ Sia Kate Isobelle Furler was born in ²_____ on December 18, 1975. Before ³_____, she'd made ⁴_____ unsuccessful solo albums, but written huge ⁵_____ for other artists, including "Titanium" with David Guetta, "Diamonds" with Rihanna, and "Wild Ones" with Flo Rida. Sia finally ⁶_____ through as a solo artist with her sixth studio album, "1000 Forms of Fear" and the hit ⁷_____ "Chandelier." Since then, Sia's star hasn't stopped ⁸_____.

**B** In pairs, share what you know about Ellen DeGeneres and her TV show. Imagine three questions Ellen asked Sia. What would you like to ask Sia?

> Ellen's an American TV host who interviews famous people.

> I think she asked Sia why she wears a wig like that.

> She must have done. It's the most obvious question.

**C** ▶ 6.11 Listen to Sue telling Joe about Ellen's interview with Sia. Where did Sue watch the show?

☐ on TV  ☐ live in the studio  ☐ on YouTube

**D** ▶ 6.12 Listen to the second part of the dialogue and check the picture that best represents what happened.

**E** ▶ 6.13 Listen to the full dialogue. True (T) or false (F)? Correct the false ones. Did you understand most of it this time? Read ▶ 6.12 and ▶ 6.13 to check. Compare in pairs. If you missed anything, try to figure out why.
1. Both Sue and Joe like Ellen.
2. Joe knows more about Sia than Sue.
3. Ellen asked a surprising question.
4. Sia doesn't like going to the grocery store.
5. Joe didn't know Sue was in the audience.
6. Sia did not reveal her face.

**F** **Make it personal** In pairs, answer 1–2. Any similarities?
1. Do you often watch / listen to / read celebrity interviews? If so, which shows / magazines / sites are you into?
2. Describe a funny / interesting / embarrassing celebrity interview you've seen.

> I love James Corden's Carpool Karaoke, where he sings with musicians. Have you seen any of them? He actually did a great one with Sia!

**Common mistake**

It's not my thing.
It's ~~doesn't go with me.~~ /
It's ~~not the mine.~~

## 6.5 Who are the wildest celebrities you know?

**Lesson Aims:** Sts practice listening for details in the context of an interview with Sia on The Ellen DeGeneres show.

### Function
Talking about TV interviews.
Listening to two friends comment on a talk show.

### Language
I think she asked Sia why she wears a wig like that.
I can't get enough of Ellen. I think she's awesome.

**Skills:** Understanding details.
**Before the lesson:** Write the following words on the board in three columns, as shown:

| nice cool gorgeous ugly<br>intelligent delicious elegant<br>sophisticated interesting funny | young old new fast cheap<br>slow little American Italian<br>tall expensive | bus man book lady restaurant<br>product kid website president<br>watch food |
|---|---|---|

**Warm-up** Review adjective order using the list of words on the board (see **Before the lesson**). Tell sts that they should choose one word from each column and have pairs of sts say or write down as many meaningful combinations as they can think of in two minutes, e.g. "an intelligent young lady," "delicious Italian food," "an ugly little kid." (Note that sts should supply the articles *a* or *an* as necessary.) Classcheck.

### 1D Skills Understanding details

**A Books open.** Focus on the image on the photos and ask: *Who are these people?* (Sia and Ellen DeGeneres). *What kind of TV program is The Ellen DeGeneres Show?* (a talk show). Read the first sentence with sts and elicit the words to fill the first two blanks. Sts then complete the rest of the task. Classcheck.

> 1 musician  2 Australia  3 2014  4 five  5 hits  6 broke
> 7 single  8 rising

**B** Sts work in pairs to think of three questions they would like to ask Sia. Get class feedback on their questions, write the most interesting questions on the board.

**C** Tell sts that they are going to hear a woman named Sue talking to a friend about the interview with Sia on *The Ellen DeGeneres Show*. Play ▶6.11. Then, point to the answer choices in **B** and ask: *Where did Sue watch the interview?* Paircheck. Classcheck.

▶6.11 Turn to page 318 for the complete audioscript.

> live in the studio

**D** Point out the three illustrations and elicit what is happening in each of them. Then ask: *What do you think happened during the interview? Listen and choose the best picture.* Play ▶6.12 for the rest of the dialogue and have sts check the picture that best represents what took place. Classcheck.

▶6.12 Turn to page 318 for the complete audioscript.

> Picture 2

**Tip** Have sts turn to the AS on p. 169. Sts listen again and notice the intonation.

**E** Allow sts time to briefly read sentences 1-6. Then, explain that sts will listen to the full dialogue and mark the sentences true (T) or false (F). Play ▶6.13. Paircheck. Classcheck by asking sts to correct the false sentences. Then assign pairs and have sts discuss the questions and how much they understood.

> 1 T  2 F  3 F  4 F  5 T  6 T

**F** Read questions 1-2 with the whole class, and ask a volunteer to read the example in the speech bubble. Assign new pairs for sts to discuss the questions. Classcheck.

# When were you last surprised?

### ID in Action  Expressing surprise

**A** ▶6.14 Use your intuition to complete 1–5. Listen to check. Say them as emphatically as you can.

1. What? Get _____ of here!
2. Really? You're _____, right?
3. _____ way!
4. _____ you serious?
5. _____ goodness!

**B** ▶6.15 Listen to these extracts and underline the stressed syllables. Which are the most stressed?
1. She wrote those?
2. You were actually in the audience?
3. You mean they were just pretending?

## Pronunciation  Showing surprise

**C** ▶6.16 Read the information and listen to the mini-dialogue. In pairs, practice it, paying attention to stress and intonation. Who is the better mimic?

- To show surprise, echo information using a questioning intonation.
- Use word stress to highlight the really surprising information.
- Notice the use of *actually* to show something is really true.

A Did you know Lady Gaga's real name is actually Stefani Joanne Angelina Germanotta?
B Huh? Her name's Stefani? No way! She doesn't look like a Stefani!
A Well, you didn't think it was really Lady Gaga, did you?!

**D** ▶6.17 Listen to the mini-dialogues. What is each speaker's question implying?

1. ☐ Not your sister? ☐ Not buying? ☐ Not pizza?
2. ☐ Not your wife? ☐ Not rent? ☐ Not bigger?
3. ☐ Not Paula? ☐ Not a cat? ☐ Not for Christmas?
4. ☐ Not five? ☐ Not months? ☐ Not vegetables?

**E** In pairs. A: read aloud questions from ▶6.17 on p. 169, stressing one of the underlined words. B: Listen and choose the correct option from **D**.

**F** Make it personal  In pairs, play *Surprise me!*
A: Tell **B** three surprising facts about yourself. One should be imaginary.
B: Express surprise. Say if you think they're true. Change roles.

> Did I ever tell you that my sister once shared a cab with Emma Stone?

> No way! You mean your sister actually met Emma Stone?

> Yes, she offered to share her cab from the airport.

> That can't be true. I don't believe you.

♪ I'm gonna swing from the chandelier, from the chandelier
I'm gonna live like tomorrow doesn't exist, like it doesn't exist

# 6.5 When were you last surprised?

**Lesson Aims:** Sts listen to people expressing surprise and practice using echo questions to express surprise.

**Function**
Listening to people expressing surprise.
Practicing echo questions to express surprise.

**Language**
She wrote those?
Not your wife?

**Skills:** Expressing surprise.
**Pronunciation:** Showing surprise.

## ID in Action  Expressing surprise

**A** Read number 1 emphatically, as if you were angry or surprised, and prompt sts to fill in the blank. Encourage them to use their intuition to guess the missing words in items 2–5. Play ▶6.14 so sts can check their guesses. Replay ▶6.14 for choral repetition of these expressions.

> 1 out  2 kidding  3 No  4 Are  5 My

> **Language tip** In both Spanish and Portuguese, it is possible to express surprise to something a friend says by saying *Mentira!* which is the equivalent to the expression *That's a lie!* in English. At any time during **ID in Action**, remind Spanish and Portuguese L1 speakers that, although you can show surprise in English by showing disbelief, you would not use the equivalent to *Mentira!* to do so, as it could sound rude.

**B** Point to questions 1–3 and ask: *Do you remember Sue's friend's questions? Was he surprised by Sue's story?* Read question 1 with sts and ask volunteers to say the sentence aloud, copying the intonation they remember from the track.

Say: *Listen to these questions again and underline the most stressed word in each of them.* Play ▶6.15. Paircheck. Classcheck. Replay ▶6.15 for choral repetition.

> 1 She <u>wrote</u> those?
> 2 You were actually <u>in</u> the audience?
> 3 You mean they were <u>just</u> pretending?

## Pronunciation  Showing surprise

**C** Read the information in the box with sts, then play ▶6.16 for sts to listen and read the mini-dialogue, paying attention to the stress and intonation.

Assign pairs and ask them to practice the mini-dialogue. Monitor sts' intonation closely and correct any mistakes on the spot. Classcheck.

**D** Read the three answer choices for item 1 and tell sts that they are going to listen and check the question that correctly represents the surprise in the conversation.

Play dialogue 1 in ▶6.17. Paircheck. Classcheck. Play the rest of ▶6.17 and have sts check the correct questions in 2–4. Paircheck. Classcheck.

▶6.17 Turn to page 318 for the complete audioscript.

> 1 Not buying?  2 Not bigger?  3 Not a cat?
> 4 Not vegetables?

**E** Have sts turn to AS ▶6.17 on p. 169. Read the first question aloud, but with a different intonation than the one from the recording, e.g. *You're making <u>spaghetti</u>?* Have sts look at the answer choices for item 1 in **D** and elicit the correct surprise question for this new intonation (Not pizza?).

Explain that the meaning of the sentence changes according to the word that is stressed. In the same way, have pairs take turns shifting the word stress within the same questions in AS ▶6.17 and guessing which option in 1–4 in **D** best expresses the surprise. Sts should focus on the words that are underlined in the AS ▶6.17 on p. 169.

Classcheck by inviting volunteers to act out different surprises with the same questions from AS ▶6.17 and asking the whole class to say the correct surprise question from **D**.

**F** 🎧 **Make it personal**  Tell sts they are going to play a game called **Surprise Me!** Have two sts role-play the model dialogue in the speech bubbles for the whole class. Ask the class to read the instructions for roles **A** and **B**. Then, have pairs act out the roles.

Encourage sts to use surprise expressions from the lesson. At the end, provide language feedback and invite volunteers to act out their conversations for the whole class.

🎵 Turn to p. 331 for notes about this song and an accompanying task.

➡ **Workbook** Page 33

➡ Ⓘ **ID Richmond Learning Platform**

➡ **Writing** p. 82

➡ **ID Café** p. 83

# Writing 6  A movie / book review

*I think your love would be too much
Or you'll be left in the dust
Unless I stuck by ya
You're the sunflower.*

**A** Read the review and circle the correct alternative in 1–4.
1 The movie is based on a **book** / **true story** and the reviewer liked it **more** / **less** than she had expected.
2 The main characters are four **teenagers** / **robots** trying to **win** / **lose** a game.
3 **Some** / **All** of the characters are interesting and original and develop **well** / **badly**.
4 It's **boring** / **funny** and follows on **badly** / **well** from the original movie.
5 The reviewer **was** / **wasn't** impressed and would give it **two** / **four** stars out of five.

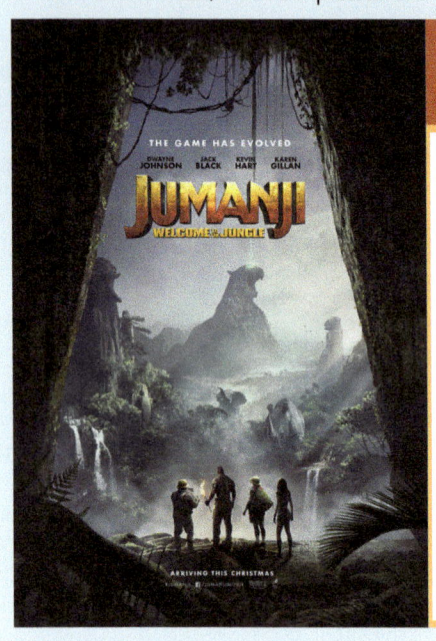

## REVIEW SECTION  Jumanji: Welcome to the Jungle

1 If you like action and adventure, try *Jumanji: Welcome to the Jungle*. Based on a children's novel, and sequel to the much-loved 1995 film of the same name, this terrific movie definitely exceeded my expectations.

2 The story is about four high school kids who discover an old video game console. They somehow end up in the game and become the avatars they chose. They have to beat the game or they will be stuck in Jumanji forever!

3 The movie captivates, not only because of the amazing special effects but also because of the intriguing new characters we meet. Unfortunately, the male and female characters are a bit stereotyped, but the story does focus on the way the characters change and think about themselves.

4 As well as the action-adventure element, this story has a lot of comedy and heart. Fans of the original movie will not be disappointed, as this version makes nostalgic references to the first. Because of that, those who loved the hilarious Robin Williams will be deeply touched by the tribute this film makes to the wonderful actor.

5 In my opinion, this is a great version as it will keep the original fans happy and combines action, special effects, comedy, and nostalgia. I'd say it's a must-see and I'd certainly suggest you watch it.

**B** In which paragraph, 1–5, does the reviewer:
- [ ] recommend it or not?
- [ ] mention the positive points?
- [ ] describe the plot?
- [ ] mention any negative points?
- [ ] describe what's being reviewed?

**C** Read *Write it right!* Then find extreme adjectives meaning:
1 very good (x3)
2 very interesting
3 very funny
4 very popular

### ✓ Write it right!

In reviews, use a variety of adjectives, including extreme adjectives with appropriate adverbs (*really, absolutely, completely, not very*).
- names as adjectives
  *Star Wars fans / X-Men movies / Twilight lovers*

To give extra information, use non-restrictive clauses between commas:
- *Spider-Man: Into the Spider-Verse*, which is the seventh Spider-Man movie, is the first computer-animated version of Stan Lee's story.
- Spielberg, who is famous for action movies, directs *Ready Player One*, a sci-fi fantasy where technology offers an escape from overpopulation and climate change.

**D** Reread *Write it Right!* and punctuate this short review with three commas, two periods, and one question mark. Capitalize where necessary.

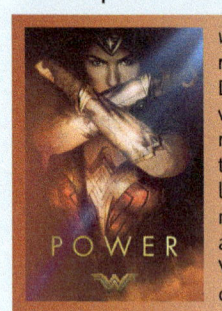

wonder woman which was released in 2017 tells the story of Diana, Princess of the Amazons when a pilot crashes on her remote island and tells her about the war in the world outside Diana leaves her home and sets off on a mission to save the world. israeli actor Gal Gadot plays Wonder Woman while stopping the war can Diana find out her true destiny

**E** *Your turn!* Choose a book / movie to review in 140–180 words.

| Before | Make notes for five paragraphs as in **B**. |
|---|---|
| While | Write your review. Follow the tips in *Write it right!* and use a friendly, informal style. |
| After | Ask a partner to read and check it. Then send it to your teacher. |

# Writing 6  A movie / book review

♪ Turn to p. 332 for notes about this song and an accompanying task.

**A** **Books closed.** Ask the class: *Have you seen any of the Jumanji movies? Did you like them? Why or why not? What about the critics? Were they positive about the movie?*

**Books open.** Have sts read the review and circle the correct alternatives in 1–5. Paircheck. Classcheck. Ask: *Do you often read movie reviews before going to the movie theater?*

🔑
1  book; more
2  teenagers; win
3  All; well
4  funny; well
5  was; four

**B** Point at the model review in **A** and ask: *How many paragraphs are there in this review?* (five). Then ask: *In which paragraph does the reviewer recommend / not recommend the movie?* Have sts match the questions to paragraphs 1–5. Paircheck. Classcheck.

🔑
5, 4, 2, 3, 1

**C** Read the first point in **Write it right!** (on extreme adjectives) with the whole class. Then, ask sts to find six extreme adjectives in the review in **A** that have the meanings listed in items 1–4. Paircheck. Classcheck and drill pronunciation for all six adjectives.

🔑
1  terrific, amazing, great, wonderful    2  intriguing
3  hilarious    4  much-loved

**D** Read the rest of **Write it right!** (on the punctuation of non-restrictive clauses) with the class. Have sts read the review of *Wonder Woman* and insert three commas, two periods, and one question mark. Sts should also capitalize where necessary. Paircheck. Classcheck.

🔑
*Wonder Woman*, which was released in 2017, tell the story of Diana, Princess of the Amazons. When a pilot crashes on her remote island and tells her about the war in the world outside, Diana leaves her home and sets off on a mission to save the world. Israeli actor Gal Gadot plays Wonder Woman. While stopping the war, can Diana find out her true destiny?

**E** *Your turn!*

**Before** Tell sts that they are going to write a five-paragraph movie review in 140–180 words. Ask them to choose a movie or a book they have seen / read and / or know reasonably well. Remind them that they can also search online for information about the movie / book. Have sts make notes for their five paragraphs. Each paragraph should answer one of the questions in **B**.

**While** Have sts write their reviews. Encourage them to follow the tips in **Write it right!** and to use an informal style.

**After** Pair sts up and have partners exchange reviews to paircheck and add information to each other's reviews if they have seen the movie too. Then, have sts hand in, or send you, their reviews for marking.

## 6 Best in show

### ID Café

### 1 Before watching

**A** Match the photos to descriptions 1–6.

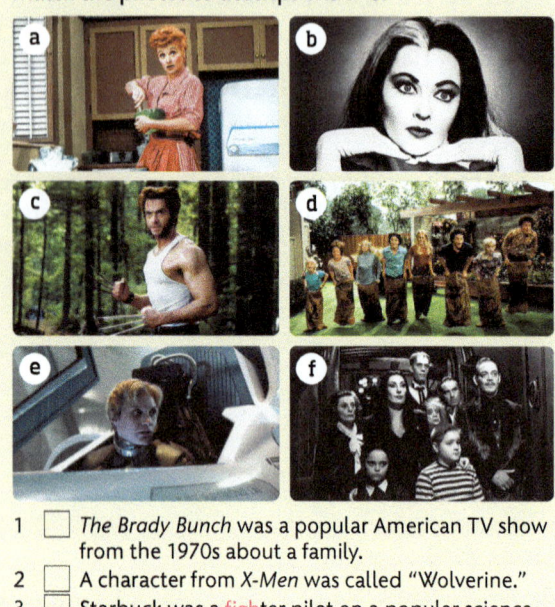

1. ☐ *The Brady Bunch* was a popular American TV show from the 1970s about a family.
2. ☐ A character from *X-Men* was called "Wolverine."
3. ☐ Starbuck was a fighter pilot on a popular science fiction TV show.
4. ☐ Lucille Ball was a famous redhead who had a show called *I Love Lucy*.
5. ☐ *The Addams Family* was a very creepy family that was on TV and on Broadway.
6. ☐ Lily Munster was a very nice "monster" who lived at 1313 Mockingbird Lane.

**B** 🔘 **Make it personal** Do you know any characters from **A**? Which are / were your favorite TV characters / sitcoms / series / theme tunes?

> *I think I've seen that Lucy show.*

> *As a kid, I used to love the Addams Family theme tune!*

### 2 While watching

**A** Watch to 3:12. Check all you hear.
1. ☐ Andrea looks like Lady Gaga and Morticia Addams.
2. ☐ Lucy doesn't know any 1960s TV shows.
3. ☐ The party will be full of nerds and geeks.
4. ☐ For the costume party, you dress as a character that you really like.
5. ☐ Andrea once won the "Best in Show" prize for her Superman costume.
6. ☐ Andrea thought dubbed TV shows were hilarious.
7. ☐ Diana Prince is Wonder Woman's alter ego.
8. ☐ Andrea says August is the family mutant.

**B** Order the story, 1–6. Then watch the rest to check.

☐ Andrea admires other costumes.
☐ Andrea confirms she isn't.
☐ August sees Paulo dressed as Superman.
☐ August thinks he'll win.
☐ Lucy says he did predict he'd lose to the perfect Superman.
☐ Lucy worries she's the only one from the 50s.

**C** Watch and check: August (A), Andrea (An), Lucy (L) or Paolo (P)?

|    |                                | A | An | L | P |
|----|--------------------------------|---|----|---|---|
| 1  | put on his wig first.          |   |    |   |   |
| 2  | tried on long and short wigs.  |   |    |   |   |
| 3  | repaired a costume.            |   |    |   |   |
| 4  | didn't really want to go.      |   |    |   |   |
| 5  | convinced her to go.           |   |    |   |   |
| 6  | forgot to check something.     |   |    |   |   |
| 7  | beat August last year.         |   |    |   |   |
| 8  | really expected to win.        |   |    |   |   |
| 9  | felt attracted to Paolo.       |   |    |   |   |
| 10 | felt defeated again.           |   |    |   |   |

### 3 After watching

**A** Complete the extracts with *who* or *that*.

August    She was the one [1]_____ kind of looked like a vampire.
August    And the people [2]_____ will be there are cool people, not just nerds.
Lucy    We watched so many American shows [3]_____ were dubbed in Spanish.
Lucy    Am I the only one here [4]_____'s dressed as a character from the 1950s?
Lucy    Well, didn't you say that the only person [5]_____ was going to beat you this year …

**B** *Play 20 questions!* **A**: Think of a famous person. **B**: Ask A *Yes / No* questions. How many questions did you have to ask before you guessed correctly?

> *Is this an actor who was on TV?*    *Yes, it is.*

# ID Café 6 Best in show

## 1 Before watching

**A** Have sts work in pairs. Point to the pictures as well as descriptions 1–6 and ask: *Do you know all these shows and characters?* Have sts work in pairs to match the pictures to the descriptions. Classcheck.

> 1 d   2 c   3 e   4 a   5 f   6 b

**B** 🔘 **Make it personal** Ask: *Which characters in A do you know? Have you actually seen them on TV or in movies?* What kind of movies and TV series do you like? Refer sts to the model text in the speech bubbles, then have them discuss these questions in pairs. Classcheck.

## 2 While watching

**A** Say: *August, Lucy, and Andrea are getting ready for a party. What kind of party is it?* Play the first 50 seconds of ▶ 6, as sts listen and answer the question. Classcheck.

> It's a costume party.

Have sts quickly read the statements and ask them to check the ones they hear and see in the video. Play ▶ 6 from beginning to end. Paircheck. Classcheck.

> 1, 3, 4, 6, 7, 8

**B** Instruct sts to order events 1–6 as they watch the video again. Play ▶ 6. Paircheck. Classcheck by writing the answers on the board.

> 4, 1, 6, 2, 3, 5

**C** Play ▶ 6 again. Have sts watch and check the statements to match each characters as they watch.

> 1  A
> 2  An
> 3  An
> 4  L
> 5  A
> 6  A
> 7  An
> 8  A
> 9  An / L
> 10 A

## 3 After watching

**A** Have sts fill in the blanks in August and Lucy's conversation with *who* or *that*. Paircheck. Classcheck.

> 1 who   2 who   3 that   4 who   5 who

**B** *Play 20 questions!* Tell sts that they are going to play a game. Have them change partners and play the game in pairs. Explain that student **A** should choose a famous person. Student **B** should ask student **A** up to 20 *Yes / No* questions to try to guess who the famous person is. Refer sts to the model text in the speech bubbles before they begin.

Monitor sts' questions for accuracy and take notes of any mistakes in question formation for delayed feedback. At the end, classcheck and ask: *How many questions did you have to ask before you guessed correctly?* Then, provide sts with language feedback.

# R3 Grammar and Vocabulary

**A** *Picture dictionary.* Cover the words or definitions on the pages below and remember.

| pages | |
|---|---|
| 60 | 5 money collocations |
| 64 | 9 "product" words |
| 67 | the endings of 10 shopping phrases |
| 72–73 | 8 TV genres |
| 78 | 10 words from the quiz |
| 161 | 2 words for each sound in lines 1 and 2 of the consonants chart (not the picture words) |

**B** Order the **bold** words in 1–4 to make adjective phrases and cross out the word that doesn't fit.

1  These **boots / hiking / comfortable / strange** are perfect for the mountains.

2  *Set in Love* is a **romantic / short / novel / well-written** of over 800 pages.

3  Lose yourself in this **new / video game / tasty / exciting**.

4  Make your own TV show with our **old / equipment / digital / easy-to-use**.

**C** In pairs, think of two endings for 1–8. Compare with another pair. Who has the funniest endings?

1  If you hadn't posted that photo, …
2  My parents wouldn't have got married if …
3  I'd have sent you a text if …
4  If I'd been born in the U.S., …
5  We'd have watched the show if …
6  If my father hadn't studied law, …
7  If I'd gone to bed earlier, …
8  We wouldn't have missed the bus if …

**D** ▶R3.1 Match 1–5 to the correct response a–e. Listen to check.

1  Have you seen my keys anywhere?
2  Uh … my … dog ate my homework.
3  So there was this documentary about the UFOs in Roswell and …
4  Allan isn't answering his phone.
5  Hey, what language are they speaking?

a ☐ Have you tried Skyping him? He might be online.
b ☐ Oh, come on! You can't believe that, surely.
c ☐ I don't know. It can't be English because I don't understand a word.
d ☐ Not again! They could be anywhere!
e ☐ Oh really? You must think I'm stupid.

**E** In pairs, write a mini-dialogue to extend one of a–e in **C** by at least four lines. Role-play it for the class.

*Well, I had them this morning. Can you help me look for them?*

**F** ▶R3.2 Add commas to these relative clause sentences if necessary. Listen, repeat, and copy the intonation.

1  I love my MP3 player which has over 2,000 songs.
2  I really like people who laugh easily.
3  Javier Bardem who starred in *No Country for Old Men* is one of my favorite actors.
4  My son just graduated which made me very proud.
5  It's difficult to find people who you can count on.
6  I'd like to get a phone that takes better photos.

**G** ◉ Make it personal  Change the underlined phrases in **F** to make 1–6 true for you.

**H** In pairs, add two more words with the same ending to each group. Mark the stress in the new words.

1  ac**tu**ally / **cur**rently
2  **use**less / **care**less
3  **ac**tion / **ques**tion
4  a**bi**lity / se**cu**rity
5  **com**fortable / re**cy**clable
6  **ce**lebrate / **grad**uate

**I** Correct the mistakes in each sentence. Check your answers in units 5 and 6.

◉ **Common mistakes**

1  If I knew you were here, I had have called. (2 mistakes)
2  Rob borrowed his phone for me. (2 mistakes)
3  That shirt look good. You should buy her. (2 mistakes)
4  It must to be difficult to be on debt. (2 mistakes)
5  When you pay with credit card online, you have to be carefull. (2 mistakes)
6  People which talk in theaters they annoy me. (2 mistakes)
7  That's the house in that they live. (2 mistakes)
8  Bruce Banner is a scientist who turn to the Hulk. (1 mistake)
9  Panama, that is famous for the canal, is a city amazing. (2 mistakes)
10  If I had eat less lunch, I wouldn't been so sleepy in the afternoon. (2 mistakes)

84

# Review 3 Units 5-6

## Grammar and vocabulary

♪ Turn to p. 332 for notes about this song and an accompanying task.

**A** *Picture dictionary.* Have sts work in pairs to test each other and review the main vocabulary items in units 5 and 6. Monitor sts throughout the picture dictionary activities and correct vocabulary and pronunciation on the spot.

**Tip** In order to provide sts with as much fluency practice as possible, expand the activity into the mini-dialogues suggested below.

| Picture Dictionary | Procedures | Mini-dialogues / Suggested language |
|---|---|---|
| 5 money collocations, p. 60 | Have sts hide the right-hand column with the nouns in **1D** with a notebook. Pair sts up and have partners take turns reading out the verbs in the left-hand column for their partner to respond with the correct noun. | St A: *take out ...*<br>St B: *a loan. Run out ...*<br>St A: *of money.* |
| 8 TV genres, p. 72–73 | Have pairs of sts hide the TV genres in **1B** with a notebook and take turns naming the types of TV shows in pictures a–h. | St A: (points to picture a) *This is a talk show.*<br>St B: (points to picture b) *This is a stand-up comedy.* |

**B** Have sts place the words in bold in the correct order to form adjective phrases. Tell them that one word is out of context and should be crossed out. Paircheck. Classcheck.

🔑
1 comfortable hiking boots, ~~strange~~
2 well-written romantic novel, ~~short~~
3 exciting new video game, ~~tasty~~
4 easy-to-use digital equipment, ~~old~~

**C** Assign pairs. Have sts work together to think of endings for 2–8. Join pairs into groups of four to listen to each other's endings and decide who has the funniest ending for each item. Classcheck.

**D** Have sts match items 1–5 to the correct responses. Paircheck. Play ▶R3.1 to classcheck.

🔑
1 d  2 e  3 b  4 a  5 c

**E** Have pairs of sts choose one of the scenarios in **C**, and write their own dialogue. Encourage them to use their imagination! Have different pairs act out a dialogue for the whole group.

**F** Have sts read sentences 1–6 and add commas to the underlined relative clauses where appropriate. Classcheck and then play ▶R3.2 for choral repetition.

1 I love my MP3 player, which has over 2,000 songs.
2 I really like people who laugh easily.
3 Javier Bardem, who starred in *No Country for Old Men*, is one of my favorite actors.
4 My son just graduated, which made me very proud.
5 It's difficult to find people who you can count on.
6 I'd like to get a phone that takes better photos.

**G** 🟠 **Make it personal** Ask sts to rewrite the underlined phrases in **F** to make true sentences about themselves. Then, have sts compare their sentences in pairs. Classcheck by having sts report their partners' sentences.

**H** Have sts add two more words with the same endings to groups 1–6. Then, ask sts to mark the stresses of the added words. Have sts compare their lists in pairs. Classcheck.

🔑
Possible answers:
1 fluently, quickly, lately
2 ambitionless, boneless, colorless, endless
3 abbreviation, education, abortion, acceleration, acclimatization
4 mobility, flexibility
5 vegetable, editable, achievable
6 abbreviate, accelerate, accumulate

**I** 🟠 **Common mistakes** Have sts correct sentences 1–10. Whenever sts are uncertain, encourage them to flip back through p. 58-81 and check their answers in units 5 and 6. Classcheck.

🔑
1 If I'**d known** you were here, I **would've** called.
2 Rob **lent me** his phone.
3 That shirt **looks** good on you, you should buy **it**.
4 It must **be** difficult to be **in** debt.
5 When you pay with **a** credit card online, you have to be **careful**.
6 People **who** talk in theaters annoy me.
7 That's the house they live **in**.
8 Bruce Banner is a scientist who **turns into** the Hulk.
9 Panama City, **which** is famous for the canal, is **an amazing city**.
10 If I **had eaten** less lunch, I wouldn't **have been** so sleepy in the afternoon.

181

# Skills practice

*Where did I go wrong?*
*I lost a friend somewhere along in the bitterness.*
*And I would have stayed up with you all night,*
*Had I known how to save a life.*

**R3**

**A** ▶R3.3 Listen to five sentences. What do they mean? Circle the correct alternative.
1. I'm **very sick / not joking**.
2. I think somebody **broke / will break** your machine.
3. He **likes / doesn't usually like** kids' movies.
4. They had **no money left / stolen money**.
5. They are **very popular / a waste of time**.

**B** Read the article and answer 1–6.
1. What do people receive from GoFundMe?
2. What does Peg want to do?
3. How did Peg learn about GoFundMe?
4. Who is Dan?
5. Do you pay to try GoFundMe?
6. Have you ever asked for sponsorship? If so, what happened?

> *I asked my friends and family. Only some of them gave me money though.*

### Help on the Internet

Why is everyone talking about GoFundMe? Because GoFundMe has helped thousands of people raise many millions of dollars online for amazing personal causes like school tuition, rock bands, medical bills, volunteer trips, business ideas, parties, travel expenses, even for animals and pets.

Let's take Peg, for example. Peg has a terrific opportunity to volunteer overseas but needs enough money for the flight and food. Luckily for Peg, her friends told her to check out GoFundMe, the easiest way to raise money online. Convinced by thousands of success stories, Peg decides to create her very own fundraising page on GoFundMe. Choosing a color, selecting a photo, and writing your information only takes a minute.

Now Peg's ready to tell the world about her cause. Inviting contacts and sharing with Facebook friends couldn't be easier. Peg's friend Dan notices her GoFundMe page on Facebook. Dan is happy to support his friend and gives her some money. He even helps tell other people for Peg. Peg gets an email each time a new donation is made. In just a few short days, she's nearly reached her goal. Once Peg's ready to get her money, she simply provides her banking information and receives the cash days later.

GoFundMe has helped Peg, and hundreds like her, raise lots of money online and can do the same for you. Click the "try it free" button and get started in less than a minute.

**C** ▶R3.4 Listen and underline ten differences between the text and the audio. Listen again to check. How many different expressions mean the same as what you read?

**D** *Feel 'n' Guess!* Play in groups.
A: Secretly put an object in a bag.
B, C, D: Feel it and speculate what it might be.

> *It's soft so it can't be a DVD.* — *Yes, it might be a …*

**E** *Keep, Kill, Ignore.* Talk about the options in 1–6 and choose one to keep, one to kill, and one to ignore.

| 1 | a news programs | 4 | a Horror |
|---|---|---|---|
|   | b soap operas |   | b Romance |
|   | c sitcoms |   | c Fantasy |
| 2 | a cartoons | 5 | a Dance music |
|   | b sports events |   | b Rock music |
|   | c documentaries |   | c Rap |
| 3 | a YouTube | 6 | a cell phones |
|   | b Facebook |   | b laptops |
|   | c Twitter |   | c vacations |

> *I guess we could kill news programs. I get most of my news online anyway.*

**F** *Shopping problems role-play.* In pairs, decide what kind of store you want to set your role-play in.
A: You're a customer. Buy something in the store, and then try to return it later.
B: You're the store assistant. Invent as many problems for the customer as you can.

> *Hi, do you have this in a bigger size?* — *I'm sorry, we're all on our break now.*
> *On your break? Are you serious?*

**G** ▶R3.5 🎧 **Make it personal** *Question time!*
Listen to the 12 lesson titles from units 5 and 6 in random order. Pause after each one to ask and answer in pairs. Ask follow-up questions, too. Any surprises?

> *Would you ever lend money to anyone?* — *Well, that would depend on who it was.*

# Skills practice

**A** Tell sts that they are going to hear five sentences from units 5 and 6. Instruct them to quickly read sentences 1–5. Focus on sentence 1 and say: *Listen to the first sentence and circle the correct choice*. Play sentence 1 in ▶R3.3 and pause the track. Classcheck. Resume the track and have sts circle the correct choices for sentences 2–5. Paircheck. Replay the track if necessary. If time allows, have sts turn to the AS on p. 169. Sts listen again and notice the disappearing consonants. Classcheck.

1. not joking
2. broke
3. doesn't usually like
4. no money left
5. very popular

▶R3.3 Turn to page 318 for the complete audioscript.

**B** Focus sts' attention on the title of the article and elicit predictions about the content. Have sts briefly read questions 1–5 and ask them to read the text to find the answers. Paircheck. Classcheck. Then, have sts ask and answer question 6 in pairs. Classcheck.

1. GoFundMe has helped thousands of people to raise many millions of dollars online for personal causes, like school tuition, rock bands, medical bills, volunteer trips, business ideas, parties, travel expenses, and even for animals and pets.
2. Peg wants to do a volunteer job. She wants to raise money to buy the ticket for the flight and pay for her food.
3. Her friends told her about GoFundMe.
4. Dan is Peg's friend.
5. No, you do not pay to try GoFundMe.
6. Personal answers.

**C** Point to the article in **B** and say: *Now listen to the text. While you listen, underline ten differences between the text and the audio.* Play ▶R3.4. Paircheck. Replay the track so sts can check their answers. Classcheck. Ask: *How many different expressions in this track mean the same thing?*

1. rock bands / sports teams
2. parties / special events
3. for example / for instance
4. for the flight and food / to cover her expenses
5. writing your information / typing a message
6. gives her some money / makes a secure online donation
7. tell other people / spread the word
8. get / withdraw
9. the cash / a deposit
10. lots of money / thousands of dollars

Expressions 2–10 mean the same.

**D** *Feel 'n' guess!* Sts work in small groups. They choose an object (a personal object or something from the classroom) and place it in a bag (or under a cloth, sweater, etc). The other sts take turns feeling the object and guessing what it is. Encourage sts to use modal of possibility / probability.

**E** *Keep, Kill, Ignore.* Tell sts that they are going to play a game. Have sts work in threes. Explain that in items 1–6, sts may choose to keep, kill or ignore topics a, b, and c, according to their personal views. Before sts begin, refer them to the model text in the speech bubble. Monitor groups closely and take notes for delayed correction. Classcheck sts' opinions and provide language feedback.

**F** *Shopping problems role-play.* Have sts change partners. Ask sts to begin by thinking about the type of store in which they want to set their role-play. Then, go over the instructions for sts **A** and **B** with the whole class and have two sts act out the model dialogue in the speech bubbles.

Then, assign a student **A** and student **B** within each pair and have pairs role-play the shopping problem. Monitor and take notes of sts' speech production for further comments. At the end, give the group language feedback and invite a volunteer pair to act out the dialogue for the whole class.

**G** **Make it personal** *Question time!* Tell sts that they are going to hear the twelve lesson title questions from units 5 and 6 in random order. Tell sts that you will pause after each question so they can ask and answer it in pairs.

Play ▶R3.5 and pause after the first question. Have sts ask and answer the question in pairs. Encourage them to ask follow-up questions when appropriate. Classcheck. Repeat the same procedure for all the questions on the track.

# 7

## 7.1 Does technology rule your life?

### 1 Reading

**A** In pairs, what's the message in the cartoon? Did it make you smile? What complaints about technology have you heard (recently)?

> I heard something about a virus that made private social media information become public.

> Yes, I heard about that, too.

**Common mistake**
~~Technology means communication without effort.~~
Technology means *effortless* communication.

**B** ▶ 7.1 In pairs, read only the introduction and first paragraph heading. Guess what the author will say. Then listen and read to check if you were right. Repeat with the other four paragraphs.

> I guess he or she will say we can check anything on our phones.

> And to be careful about fake news!

PROTESTING AGAINST NEW TECHNOLOGY – THE EARLY DAYS

---

## MODERN TECHNOLOGY —The Bright Side!

Every day, we hear so much negativity about modern technology and its impact on society: There are no jobs. We have no social skills. It's killing our creativity. Beware of Identity Theft! World destruction! The list goes on … But let's just calm down. We know technology has a down side, but, for a moment, can we focus on the many benefits it brings to us?

### Access to Information
Our parents used to have to go to a library and take out a book to find out the information they needed. Now, we access whatever we need to know instantly and anywhere. With the vast amount of data on the Internet, we can read the news, check the stock market, and buy tickets to a concert, all while we're on the train!

### Innovation and Creativity
The possibilities seem limitless. It was difficult to start a business years ago, but now with online selling platforms, anyone can set up a business at home. Creative people can easily sell their work online. Another example is crowdfunding. This leads to the creation of new businesses, further creativity, and more technology!

### Communication
Apparently, we are all zombies with our faces glued to our screens. Yes, we know we need to cut down on screen time and have more face-to-face time, but modern technology has made communication effortless! Before, it took weeks to get a letter to a relative in Australia. Now, we have email, cell phones, video conferencing, text messaging, and social media. You can reach anyone, anywhere, at any time.

### Entertainment
Where would the entertainment industry be without technology? We can store and enjoy endless music and movies with streaming apps. Like that new song you just heard on the radio? Download it instantly! We can play games with people on the other side of the planet. It also makes it easier for artists to break into the entertainment industry. Ed Sheeran and Justin Bieber were both discovered on YouTube.

### Education
Students can access courses remotely with distance learning. Of course, we also use technology in the classroom. Tablets and smartboards are commonplace, and lessons are much more engaging with visual information. But don't forget the countless educational apps you can download to help you pick up everything from French to ballroom dancing!

**Unit overview:** The main topics of unit 7 are phrasal verbs, reported speech, and indirect questions. Sts also learn and practice instructions for touch screens, and phrases for expressing opinions.

## 7.1 Does technology rule your life?

**Lesson Aims:** Sts learn and use phrasal verbs in the context of technology.

### Function
Talking about technology.
Listening to / Reading about modern technology.
Expressing opinions about technology.

### Language
I heard something about a virus that made private social media information go public.
Now, we access whatever we need to know instantly, and anywhere.
I think there's almost too much information.

**Vocabulary:** Phrasal verbs (break into, calm down, cut down on, find out, go on, pick up, set up, take out).

♪ Turn to p. 332 for notes about this song and an accompanying task.

**Warm-up** Have sts interview each other with the lesson title questions from unit 6 on p. 72–81. Encourage sts to ask follow-up questions whenever possible. Monitor their discussions closely and write down mistakes and very good or interesting answers for delayed feedback. To classcheck, say: *Tell me two things you have learned about your partner.*

### 1 Reading

**A** **Books open**. Point to the cartoon and ask: *What technology are the people complaining about?* Read the questions and ask two volunteers to read the mini-dialogue in the speech bubbles. Assign pairs for sts to discuss the questions. Classcheck and write the most common complaints about technology on the board.

**B** Point to the title and ask: *Do you think the article will be positive or negative about technology?* (positive—*the bright side* means good points about something). Have sts read the introduction and the first paragraph heading only. Assign pairs and have sts discuss what they think the author will say in the first paragraph. Play ▶ 7.1 up to the end of the first paragraph for sts to listen, read, and check their answers. Follow the same procedure for the remaining four paragraphs and headings.

♪ *They took the credit for your second symphony.*
*Rewritten by machine on new technology.*

**7.1**

**C** In pairs, reread and find …
1 two old-fashioned ways to access information.
2 three improvements to entertainment.
3 two ways technology increases innovation.
4 three improvements to education.
5 five ways dialogue has become easier.

**D** Complete 1–7 with the underlined items in the article. Which are true for you?
Modify the others to make them true.

1 I know how to protect myself against _____.
2 Some people say that Millennials don't have good _____ because they spend too much time on their smart phones.
3 I find it really annoying when I'm _____ a movie and the Internet goes down!
4 Children should be limited to one or two hours of _____ a day.
5 I'd like to take a _____ course one day.
6 I think face-to-face meetings are much better than _____.
7 I like buying secondhand items from _____.

**E** 🗣 **Make it personal** *Technology – the dark side!* Imagine you're a member of an "I hate everything about technology" group. In threes, list all the negative aspects imaginable. Then share with the class. Which, if any, do you think are, or will be, serious problems?

*There are too many choices now. It was easier to focus before.*

*Effortless? No way! It takes ages to learn to use technology well!*

*Yes, and people had better memories. You don't have to remember anything anymore. Your phone knows everything!*

## 2 Vocabulary  Phrasal verbs

**A** Match the **highlighted** phrasal verbs in the article to the definitions. Any you didn't know?

| 1 | _____ | learn a new skill |
| 2 | _____ | continue or persevere |
| 3 | _____ | begin to feel more relaxed and less emotional |
| 4 | _____ | start doing less of something |
| 5 | _____ | get something officially from somewhere |
| 6 | _____ | discover a fact or piece of information |
| 7 | _____ | start something such as a business |
| 8 | _____ | start to have success in your career |

🔶 **Common mistakes**

                  *cut down on*
My five-year-old needs to ~~reduce the~~ sugar.
*pick up*
I ~~take~~ a lot of English from subtitled movies.
*taken out*      *for*
We've ~~asked~~ a loan to pay ~~our~~ wedding.

**B** ▶ 7.2 The phrasal verbs are in the wrong sentences. Put them into the correct places. Listen to check. In pairs, imagine the context 1–8 were said in.
1 I don't want to work for someone else. I'd rather **cut down on** my own company.
2 You'll **break into** Spanish quickly if you spend time in a Spanish-speaking country.
3 When did you go on these loans on your credit card? Now you've got a huge debt!
4 I don't know what time the train is, but I can easily **calm down**.
5 Please **pick up** with what you're doing, and don't let us interrupt you.
6 I'm trying to **set up** the amount of caffeine I drink.
7 She was angry at first, but we managed to **take her out**.
8 It must be difficult for artists to **find out** the U.S. music industry.

*This sounds like a person who is fed up with their job.*

**C** 🗣 **Make it personal** *Three of each!* Write down …

- three things you should cut down on.
- three ways to pick up a new language.
- three things that help calm you down.
- three things you've found out so far during this course.

In groups, compare and ask questions. Any coincidences? Share one unusual response with the class.

*Do you know any good apps that can help you pick up a language?*

*Yes, there are lots! Duolingo is a good one.*

87

# 7.1

**C** Point to question 1 and elicit the answer as an example, but don't confirm yet. Have sts reread the article and answer questions 1–5 individually. Peercheck. Classcheck.

> **Possible answers**
> 1 In the past, people had to go to a library / take out a book to find out the information they needed.
> 2 watch movies or listen to music instantly, play games with people in other parts of the world, it's easier for artists to break into the entertainment industry
> 3 it's easy to start a business with online selling platforms, crowdfunding makes it easier to get finance
> 4 you can learn anywhere, lessons are more interesting, you can learn any subject
> 5 email, cell phones, video conferencing, text messaging, social networking

**D** Point to the first underlined phrase in the article (social skills) and ask: *Which statement does it complete?* (2). Sts complete the rest of the statements individually. Peercheck. Classcheck.

> **Tip** Ask sts, in pairs, to find examples of words with the suffix -*less* in the text (*limitless, countless, endless, effortless*). Elicit / explain what the suffix means (free from / without, e.g. *limitless* = without limit).

> 1 identity theft  2 social skills  3 streaming
> 4 screen time  5 distance learning
> 6 video conferencing  7 online selling platforms

Ask: *Which statements are true for you?* and ask sts to modify any which aren't true for them. You could give an example of your own to start them off, e.g. say: *I'm not sure how to protect myself against identity theft.* Give them time to prepare their answers then have a class discussion.

**E** **Make it personal** Read the questions with the whole class, and give sts a few mins to think about their ideas and make notes if they want to. Ask two volunteers to read the conversation in the speech bubbles, then assign pairs for sts to discuss the questions. Refer sts back to their notes for **C**, where they listed many positive aspects of technology, to help them compare / contrast their ideas. Classcheck, and ask: *Did you agree?*

## 2 Vocabulary  Phrasal verbs

**A** Read the definitions in the box with the class. Point to the highlighted phrasal verbs in the article and have sts match them to the correct meanings. Paircheck. Classcheck.

> 1 pick up          5 take out
> 2 go on            6 find out
> 3 calm down        7 set up
> 4 cut down on      8 break into

**B** **Common mistakes** Read through with the class. Remind Portuguese L1 speakers that *reduce* in this context is a false cognate. Read the first sentence with the class and ask them to identify the phrasal verb (cut down on). Ask: *Is this the correct phrasal verb? What should it be?* (set up). Sts put the phrasal verbs in the correct places individually.

Play ▶ 7.1 for sts to check their answers. Classcheck. Read the model language in the speech bubble with sts, then assign pairs for sts to imagine the context for each sentence.

> 1 I don't want to work for someone else. I'd rather <u>set up</u> my own company.
> 2 You'll <u>pick up</u> Spanish quickly if you spend time in a Spanish-speaking country.
> 3 When did you <u>take out</u> these loans on your credit card? Now you've got a huge debt.
> 4 I don't know what time the train is but I can easily <u>find out</u>.
> 5 Please <u>go on</u> with what you're doing and don't let us interrupt you.
> 6 I'm trying to <u>cut down on</u> the amount of caffeine I drink.
> 7 She was angry at first, but we managed to <u>calm her down</u>.
> 8 It must be difficult for artists to <u>break into</u> the U.S. music industry.

**C** **Make it personal** Point to the topics in the box and ask sts to work individually and write down three things for each item. Monitor and help with ideas and vocabulary where necessary.

When they are ready, assign groups and have sts compare their ideas. Classcheck and ask: *Any coincidences?*

> **Tip** When sts share their ideas, ask them not to say which of the topics in the box it's for. Sts listen and guess the topic.

➔ **Workbook** Page 34

## 7.2 What was the last little lie you told?

### 1 Reading

**A** In your experience, do salespeople always tell the truth? What kinds of promises might they make or lies might they tell?

> They might say a color looks great on you when it really doesn't!

**Common mistakes**
tell
I try to not say lies.
They sometimes exaggerate the true.
truth

**B** Read sales promises a–f and guess what device each one refers to.
a "Some of the keys are different, but it's basically the same thing."
b "Oh, yes, you can mount it on the wall yourself."
c "You'll be able to use it in any country, don't worry."
d "It works just as well as the famous brand, but at half the price."
e "There's lots of technical support online."
f "Look! It just arrived!"

> I think the first one could be a piano.

**C** Read the article and match promises a–f in **B** to tips 1–5. There's one extra promise.

### But How Was I to Know?

Christmas is just around the corner and chances are you'll be buying someone you love a new digital device of some sort. Today we bring you five hot tips to guide your holiday shopping and avoid trouble down the road.

**1** [f] Our first tip basically ap<u>plies</u> to any new <u>gadget</u> or household appliance. Companies race to <u>launch</u> new products before their com<u>petitors</u>. This means the early versions of the new technology may contain all sorts of horrendous <mark>bugs</mark> and <mark>break down</mark> in a matter of weeks. Allow brand new products time on the market so the most serious de<u>fects</u> can (hopefully!) be corrected.

**2** [ ] Well, theoretically, yes, but if you miss a <u>screw</u> or two, the TV may come crashing down on you after a week. These things weigh more than 100 lbs, so either put it on a table or get a professional to do the job because the <mark>warranty</mark> doesn't cover stupidity.

**3** [ ] The Rolex that your dad has been dreaming of is way too expensive, I know, but stay away from the cheap imitations you find on the streets. They might look good today, but what about next month? Not to mention that buying <u>fake goods</u> is illegal—Dad certainly won't thank you if the police catch him! Remember: If something looks too good to be true, it probably is.

**4** [ ] Buying a cell phone a<u>broad</u> can save you a few bucks, but first you've got to check whether you can even use it back home. Make sure it's un<u>locked</u> (that is, not tied to a particular <u>carrier</u>) and that the network is com<u>pat</u>ible. If you're scratching your head right now, get yourself a phone lo<u>cally</u>!

**5** [ ] If you buy an im<u>por</u>ted computer, keep in mind that the <u>keyboard</u> layout may be a little different from what you're ac<u>cus</u>tomed to. So what? Well, if you think you can learn to live without the "ç" or "ñ" <u>keys</u>, no big deal. Otherwise, think twice, or you may find yourself throwing the poor laptop out the window.

> I'd say tip 1 because it's the most general.

**D** ▶ 7.3 Listen, reread, and match photos a–e to the underlined words. Then match the <mark>highlighted</mark> words to definitions 1–5. What's the best tip, and which are irrelevant to you?

| 1 | _____ noun [C] | a company that provides phone or Internet services |
| 2 | _____ noun [C] | the written promise to fix something for free |
| 3 | _____ verb | to put something on the market |
| 4 | _____ noun [C] | electronic problems in a device |
| 5 | _____ verb | to stop working |

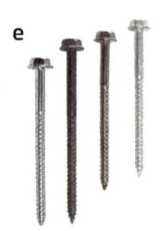

88

# 7.2 What was the last little lie you told?

**Lesson Aims:** Sts study and practice reported speech through the contexts of shopping and talking about the little lies people tell.

### Function
Talking about the little lies people tell.
Reading tips for holiday shopping.
Talking about shopping experiences.
Reporting what other people said.
Telling a story about a lie someone told

### Language
You'll be able to use it in any country, don't worry.
Buying a cell phone abroad can save you a few bucks, but …
No, I guess I'm just lucky when I buy things.
She told me that she would buy it.
The salesman said some of the keys were different.
The used-car salesman told me the car had only one careful owner. Well, …

**Vocabulary:** Gadget, launch, unlocked phone, warranty, keys (on a keyboard), carrier.
**Grammar:** Reported speech (1).

♪ Turn to p. 332 for notes about this song and an accompanying task.

**Warm-up** Put sts in A/B pairs. Ask student A to look at the phrasal verbs on p. 87 and test student B by choosing a verb (e.g. *set*). Student B must respond with the correct particle(s) (*up*). After they've been through the phrasal verbs, have them change roles so that student B tests student A.

## 1 Reading

**A** **Common mistakes** Read with the whole class. Elicit or explain the difference between *say* and *tell*.

Read the lesson title question, "What was the last little lie you told?" Have sts ask and answer the question in pairs. Encourage them to make follow-up questions to elicit details, e.g. *Who did you tell the lie to? Why? Did it work?* Classcheck by inviting volunteers to share their stories.

Read the questions with the whole class and ask: *When was the last time you spoke to a salesperson? Did they tell the truth?* Sts discuss the questions in pairs. Classcheck and find out if other sts agree.

> **Language tip** When reading the common mistakes with sts, remind them that when reporting what someone said, we can use either *say* or *tell* as the reporting verb, but each has a different structure. Make sure sts understand that when we report something using *tell*, we specify the audience/person to whom something has been told. For example, *She told me …* . When we report using the verb *say*, we report what was said immediately after the verb. For example, *He said he was late.*

**B** Tell sts that promises a–f are quotes from salespeople. Read the first one with the whole class and ask: *What product is the salesperson trying to sell?* Read the example in the speech bubble with sts and explain that keys might refer to a different keyboard on a laptop or a smart phone. Have sts work in pairs to read b–f and guess the product being sold. Classcheck sts' guesses.

**C** Tell sts to read the text before listening to the audio and explain that they should match promises a–f from **B** to tips 1–5 in the text. Remind sts that one promise in **B** will be left out.

🔑 1 f   2 b   3 d   4 c   5 a

> **Tip** Pair sts up and have them practice saying the words with pink letters in the text. Classcheck and drill pronunciation.

**D** Point out the underlined words in the article and photos a–e and ask sts to listen, reread, and match them. Play ▶ 7.3. Paircheck. Classcheck.

🔑 a fake goods   b keys   c unlocked   d gadget   e screw

> **Tip** Play ▶ 7.3 again. After each paragraph, pause the audio for sts to practice / drill / test each other on the pink words.

Point to the first highlighted word in tips 1–5 in **C** (launch) and elicit its meaning. Have sts find the correct definition in the box (3 verb, to put something on the market). Ask sts to match all the other highlighted words to the correct definitions in the box. Play ▶ 7.3. Paircheck. Classcheck.

🔑 1 carrier   2 warranty   3 launch   4 bugs   5 break down

At the end, ask pairs to discuss the question, *What's the best tip, in your opinion?* Have sts follow the model in the speech bubble, *I'd say tip 1, because …*

E **Make it personal** In pairs, complete 1–3 with the correct form of words from **D**, and then answer them. Any big differences?
1 Have you ever had to use the _____ for a product that doesn't work?
2 On a scale of 0 to 10, how happy are you with your cell phone _____? Why?
3 Have you ever bought a product a few days after it was _____? Did you have any problems or inital _____? Would you recommend it to a friend?
4 Have you ever been in a vehicle which suddenly _____ mid-journey?

*Well somebody told me you had a boyfriend
Who looked like a girlfriend
That I had in February of last year
It's not confidential, I've got potential.*

*No, I guess I've just been lucky when I buy things.*

## 2 Grammar  Reported speech (1)

A ▶7.4 Listen and match the five dialogues to paragraphs 1–5 in **1C**.

B ▶7.5 Complete extracts 1–5 in pencil. Use your intuition! Listen to check.
1 The salesman said some of the keys _____ different.
2 He said that it _____ just as well as the famous brand.
3 The delivery guy told me I _____ mount it on the wall myself.
4 On the site, it said I _____ be able to use it in any country.
5 The store manager said it _____ just _____.

C Compare a–f in **1B** with 1–5 in **B** and circle the correct alternatives in the grammar box.

> **Reported statements**
> 1 If the reporting verb is in the past (*said*, *told*), the main verb often **moves one tense back** / **remains the same**.
> 2 "That" is **necessary** / **optional**.
> 3 *Said* / *Told* requires an object (*me, her, John*).
>
> ➔ Grammar 7A p.150

**Common mistakes**
He said ~~me~~ he was sorry.
                                  *would*
She told ~~to~~ me that she ~~will~~ buy it.

D ▶7.6 Change the underlined words in 1–5 into reported speech. Listen to the end of the dialogues to check. All correct? Are any of the phrases or situations familiar to you?
1 "You will learn fast." He said …
2 "I'm here every week, and I can get you video games, too." He told me …
3 "It's easy, and it'll only take 10 minutes." He said …
4 "Lots of people have complained." They told …
5 "These tablets usually sell pretty quickly." She said that …

E ▶7.7 Report what each person said in cartoons 1–4. Listen to check. All correct? Are any of the phrases or situations familiar to you?

1 tell / do well
2 say / dog / be / friendly
3 tell / party / be / informal
4 say / you / not / arrive late

F **Make it personal** Think of a time you were told something untrue or wrong. Prepare your answers to 1–3. In groups, share your stories. Any similarities?
1 What was the situation?
2 What did the person say? How did you react?
3 What happened in the end?

*When I was a kid, my parents convinced me that the tooth fairy really did exist. Well, …*

*People often use the traffic as an excuse for being late. For example, …*

**E** 🔑 **Make it personal** Ask sts to fill in the blanks in sentences 1–4 using words from **D**. Paircheck. Classcheck. Then, have sts change partners and take turns asking and answering questions 1–4 in their new pairs.

🗝
1. warranty
2. carrier
3. launched, bugs
4. broke down

## 2 Grammar  Reported speech (1)

**A** Tell sts that they are going to hear five conversations about shopping problems. Play conversation 1 from ▶ 7.4 and then pause the track. Elicit the corresponding paragraph in **1C**. Play the rest of ▶ 7.4 and have sts match each conversation to the correct paragraph in **1C**. Paircheck. Replay the track if necessary. If time allows, have sts turn to the AS on p. 170 so they can do the noticing activities as they listen. Classcheck.

▶ **7.4** Turn to page 318 for the complete audioscript.

🗝
Speaker 1: paragraph 5
Speaker 2: paragraph 3
Speaker 3: paragraph 2
Speaker 4: paragraph 4
Speaker 5: paragraph 1

**B** Ask sts to use a pencil to fill in the blanks in sentences 1–5 with their predictions for what the correct words might be. Play ▶ 7.5 so sts can check their guesses.

🗝
1 were   2 worked   3 could   4 'd   5 had, arrived

⚠ **Common mistakes** Read the examples with the whole class. Remind sts of the different uses of *say* and *tell*.

**C** Point to sentence a in **1B** and have sts compare it with sentence 1 in **2B**. Emphasize that "some of the keys are different" become "were different" in reported speech. Have sts continue comparing sentences from **1B** to their reported-speech versions in **2B**. Classcheck their findings.

Ask sts to read the rules in the grammar box and choose the correct alternatives in items 1–3. Paircheck. Classcheck.

🗝
1. moves one tense back
2. optional
3. Told

➡ **Grammar 7A** page 150

**D** Read sentence 1 and ask a volunteer to change it into reported speech, beginning with *He said* … Have sts write sentences using reported speech for items 2–5. Play ▶ 7.6 to classcheck and write the answers on the board.

🗝
1. He said I would learn fast.
2. He told me he was there every week and he could get me video games too.
3. He said it was easy and it would only take 10 minutes.
4. They told me that lots of people had complained.
5. She said that these tablets usually sold pretty quickly.

**E** Point to the first picture and ask: *What do you think the mother told the boy?* Instruct sts to write or report what they think the people in the pictures said, using the verbs provided. Paircheck. Play ▶ 7.7 to classcheck and write the answers on the board (or have sts come and write them on the board). Ask sts if any of the situations are familiar to them.

▶ **7.7** Turn to page 318 for the complete audioscript.

🗝
1. You told me you'd done well this year.
2. You said your dog was friendly.
3. You told me the party was informal.
4. You said that you wouldn't arrive late.

**F** 🔑 **Make it personal** Tell sts to think of a time when they were told something that wasn't true or was wrong. Read questions 1–3 to sts and give them some time to prepare their stories and organize their ideas. Read the example in the speech bubbles. Draw sts' attention to the use of an emphatic auxiliary in the first speech bubble (**did** exist). Divide the class into small groups and have the sts in each group share their stories. Monitor sts' stories closely and write down any mistakes for delayed correction. Classcheck and provide language feedback.

➡ **Workbook** Page 35

# 7.3 How much of your day is screen time?

## 1 Vocabulary  Using touch screens

**A** Look at the photo. What do you think PleIQ might be? Who do you think it is designed for?

> PleIQ It looks like some type of …

**B** Read the description to check. Were you right? How does PleIQ work? What are the benefits?

⚠ **Common mistake**

This app was designed *by* for a teenager.

### Worried about your child's **screen time**?

Tired of seeing them aimlessly **swiping** left and right and **scrolling** through streams of pointless images? Look no further than PleIQ – a dynamic new app which transforms tablets and smart phones into educational tools.

PleIQ combines physical and digital aspects. The set contains eight cubes with letters, numbers, and other symbols, and an app. With augmented reality (AR), the symbols shown on the blocks are transformed into interactive, 3D cartoons. Children show a block to the screen, they **double-tap** on the icon they want to play with, and they can **zoom in** to see more details.

This invention, by Venezuelan innovator Edison Duran, attempts to improve screen time for children and reduce the educational divide by giving more children access to learning in their early years.

Parents have control. They can monitor their child's progress and add new items. Children can control how their app looks by **dragging and dropping** items into new locations.

With PleIQ, screen time is more constructive.

**C** ▶7.8 Cover **B** and match verbs 1–5 to the phrases. Listen and reread to check. Repeat the pink-stressed words. Then, in pairs, take turns miming 1–5 for the others to guess.

1 swipe  ☐ to see more details
2 scroll  ☐ through images
3 double-tap  ☐ left and right
4 zoom in  ☐ items into new locations
5 drag and drop  ☐ on an icon

**D** 🔵 **Make it personal**  In pairs, answer 1–3. Any good tips to share?
1 What are the best kids' apps you know? Why?
2 Each describe a favorite app, how it works, and why it's good.
3 How have apps improved your life? What's easier than it was before?

> I love Evernote Scannable! You just zoom into the document or card or whatever, and the app converts it into a scan. Then you can just scroll through all of your saved documents.

## 2 Listening

**A** ▶7.9 Neide Sellin is a young inventor from Brazil. What do you think her invention is? Listen to check.

> I'm not sure. It could be a vacuum cleaner.

**B** ▶7.9 Listen again. Number these 1–7 in the order you hear them. In pairs, explain their significance.

☐ dog  ☐ 6.5 million  ☐ 100  ☐ 3,000
☐ airports  ☐ 2020  ☐ 253 million

> That's the number of Brazilians who can't …

**C** 🔵 **Make it personal**  📡 In pairs, search online to find more inventions that have made the lives of people with disabilities easier.

> Stephen Hawking used a cheek-controlled communication system.

> And this meant he could speak through a computer.

# 7.3 How much of your day is screen time?

**Lesson Aims:** Sts study and practice indirect questions via the context of innovation. They also learn vocabulary related to using touch screens.

**Function**
Talking about apps.
Listening to a radio program about young inventors.
Discussing an invention.

**Language**
You just zoom into the document or card or whatever and the app converts it into a scan.
Neide has invented a robot guide dog called Lysa.
Could you tell me whether it could work in any type of car?

**Vocabulary:** Using touch screens (double tap, drag and drop, scroll, swipe, zoom in).
**Grammar:** Indirect questions.
**Before the lesson:** Write the following questions on the board: *What's your favorite gadget? How long have you had it? What do you use it for? What gadgets would you most like to have?*

♪ Turn to p. 332 for notes about this song and an accompanying task.

**Warm-up** Demonstrate the activity by describing your favorite gadget, answering the questions on the board (see **Before the lesson**). Encourage sts to ask you follow-up questions.

Put sts in pairs to discuss the questions for themselves. Classcheck, and find out if any sts have the same favorite gadgets.

## 1 Vocabulary Using touch screens

**A** **Books open**. Point to the photo and explain that PleIQ is an app. Ask: *What do you think PleIQ might be? Who do you think it is designed for?* Assign pairs for sts to discuss the questions. Classcheck, but don't give any answers yet.

🔴 **Common mistake** Read with the class and elicit the difference between *designed by* and *designed for*.

**B** Have sts read the description and check their ideas. Peercheck. Classcheck by asking one student to summarize how it works and another student to explain the benefits.

> PleIQ is a new app which transforms tablets and smart phones into educational tools. It is designed for children. It is made up of eight cubes with letters, numbers and other symbols, and an app. Children show a block to the screen, tap on the icon they want to play with, and zoom in to see more details.
>
> The benefits are that the app improves screen time and reduces the educational divide. Parents also have control over the app and can monitor their child's progress.

**C** Ask sts to use a piece of paper or notebook to cover the text in **B** and match the verbs to the phrases. Play ▶7.8 for sts to listen and re-read to check. Classcheck, and check understanding of the verbs by asking sts to mime them.

1 swipe left and right
2 scroll through images
3 double-tap on an icon
4 zoom in to see more details
5 drag and drop items into new locations

**D** 🔴 **Make it personal** Read the questions with the class, and ask a volunteer to read the example in the speech bubble. Sts discuss the questions in pairs. Classcheck by asking sts to share their favorite apps with the class and find out if other sts have the same favorite.

## 2 Listening

**A** Point to the photo and say: *This was invented by Neide Sellin, a young inventor from Brazil. What do you think her invention is?* Elicit sts' ideas then play ▶7.9 for sts to check their ideas. Peercheck, then classcheck.

▶7.9 Turn to page 319 for the complete audioscript.

> Her invention is a robot guide dog called Lysa.

**B** Play ▶7.9 for sts to listen and number the items in order as they hear them. Peercheck. Classcheck, then assign pairs for sts to explain the significance of each item. Read the example with sts before they start and elicit which item it refers to.

1 6.5 million (The number of Brazilian people who have vision problems.)
2 dog (guide dogs)
3 100 (There are 100 guide dogs in Brazil.)
4 2020 (By 2020 it is hoped that Lysa will be used outside.)
5 3,000 (Lysa costs $3,000.)
6 airports (Lysa is available at airports.)
7 253 million (Neide's ambition is to help the 253 million people around the world with vision problems.)

**C** 🔴 **Make it personal** Read the question with the class, then ask two volunteers to read out the mini-dialogue in the speech bubbles. Assign new pairs for sts to discuss the question. Classcheck.

## 3 Grammar  Indirect questions

🎵 *The world I love, The tears I drop*
*To be part of the wave, can't stop*
*Ever wonder if it's all for you?*

**A** Find how questions 1–4 are asked in ▶7.9 on p. 170. Complete the chart.

| Original question | Indirect question |
|---|---|
| 1  What is her latest development? | _____ |
| 2  How many guide dogs are there in Brazil? | _____ |
| 3  Is this really a more affordable option? | _____ |
| 4  How much does it cost? | _____ |

**B** Compare the two types of questions in **A**. Then answer 1–4 in the grammar box.

1 Which sounds more polite, the original question or the indirect question?
2 What is the word order for the subject and verb in indirect questions?
3 What happens to the auxiliary *do* in an indirect question?
4 If the answer to the question is *yes / no*, which word do you need to add?

➔ **Grammar 7B** p.150

> **Common mistakes**
>
> Excuse me, could you tell me where (is) the station?
>
> Do you know where did he go?
> went

**C** 📡 Correct the questions about innovations. Then search online to find the answers.

1 Can you tell me when was Bluetooth first invented?
2 Do you know who did invent the first cordless vacuum cleaner?
3 I'd like to know how many years did it take to produce the first wireless earphones?
4 I wonder when will driverless cars come onto the market?
5 Could you tell me if will e-readers ever replace books?
6 Do you know when is the next iPhone coming out?

**D** ▶7.10 Read the review and complete indirect questions 1–5. Listen to check.

**The Kenguru Car**

> Tired of having to collapse your wheelchair?
> Finally, a car designed with wheelchair users in mind!
> Simply maneuver your chair straight into your car and off you go!
> With a speed of 25 miles per hour and a range of 60 miles, you will be able to do your daily chores without any of the hassle.
> The Kenguru currently costs $25,000, but with the incentive of clean, green energy, it's worth it!

| | | |
|---|---|---|
| 1 | Who is it designed for? | Do you know _____? |
| 2 | How fast can it go? | I'd like to know _____. |
| 3 | How will it be helpful? | Can you tell me _____? |
| 4 | How much does it cost? | Could you tell me _____? |
| 5 | Can it travel very far? | I wonder _____. |

**E** 🔵 **Make it personal**  *Time to innovate!* In threes, choose a category and invent something to make life quicker, easier, and more efficient. Present it for the class to ask questions. Vote for the best idea.

| Driving and parking | Studying | Shopping | Communications | Housework | Food and cooking |

Use these questions to help you plan your presentation.
- What is your invention and how does it work?
- How will it be helpful in everyday life?
- How much do you think it will cost to make?
- How difficult / easy do you think it will be to produce?
- Is there anything else like it already? How is yours better or different?

*Could you tell us whether it could work in any type of car?*

*Do you know if people with disabilities would be able to use it?*

## 7.3

### 3 Grammar Indirect questions

**A** Read the questions with the class. Then, direct sts to AS ▶ 7.9 on p. 170 and ask them to find how the questions are asked there. Peercheck. Classcheck and write the indirect questions on the board, or invite sts to come and write them on the board.

1 Can you tell us what her latest development is?
2 Do you know how many guide dogs there are in Brazil?
3 I wonder if this is really a more affordable solution.
4 Do you have any idea how much it costs?

**B** Point to the two types of questions in **A** and ask sts to answer questions 1–4 in the grammar box. Peercheck. Classcheck.

1 indirect question
2 they are inverted
3 it gets dropped
4 if

→ **Grammar 7B** page 150

**Common mistakes** Read with the class and draw sts' attention to the position of the verb *be*, and the use of the simple past form of *go*.

**Language tip** In Portuguese and Spanish, the position of the verb in indirect questions does not change, so sts who speak these languages often make the errors in the common mistakes box. Pre-empt this kind of mistake by writing a few examples of indirect questions on the board and contrasting them with the equivalent in sts' L1.

**C** Point to questions 1–6 and explain that each one has a mistake. Have sts correct the indirect questions. Paircheck. Classcheck by writing the answers on the board, or inviting sts to write them on the board.

Put sts into three large groups and assign two of the questions to the sts in each group. Ask them to go online and research the answers to the questions and make notes. (Note: they don't have to work as a group, they can work individually to research the questions.) When they are ready, assign new groups of three with at least one of the sts from the three previous groups. Ask sts to share the information they found out. Classcheck and ask: *Any surprises?*

1 Can you tell me when Bluetooth was first invented? (In the 1990s)
2 Do you know who invented the first cordless vacuum cleaner? (Dyson)
3 I'd like to know how many years it took to produce the first wireless earphones.
4 I wonder when driverless cars will come onto the market. (by 2021)
5 Could you tell me if e-readers will ever replace books? (It is likely)
6 Do you know when the next iPhone is coming out? (This will depend)

**D** Have sts read the text, then ask: *Who is this invention for? Do you think it's a good idea? Why (not)?* Point to indirect questions 1–5 and have sts fill the gaps to complete them. Play ▶ 7.10 to check. Peercheck. Classcheck by writing them on the board. If time allows, play ▶ 7.10 again for sts to listen again / repeat to pay attention to the stress in indirect questions.

1 Do you know who it is designed for?
2 I'd like to know how fast it can go.
3 Can you tell me how it will be helpful?
4 Could you tell me how much it costs?
5 I wonder if/whether it can travel very far.

**E** **Make it personal** Focus attention on the categories and say: *You're going to come up with an invention for one of these categories*. Put sts in groups of three and give them a few minutes to decide on their invention.

When they are ready, explain that they're going to present their invention to the class. Point to the questions and have them plan their presentation, using the questions to help. If they want to, sts can also draw a picture of their invention.

When they are ready, have two volunteers read the indirect questions in the speech bubbles. Groups take turns to present their ideas to the class. While they are presenting, ask other sts to think of indirect questions they can ask about each one, and have a Q&A slot at the end of each one.

At the end, ask sts to vote for the best invention.

→ **Workbook** Page 36

# 7.4 Are machines with personality a good idea?

## 1 Listening

**A** In pairs, brainstorm how you (or people you know) use phone voice command features. Who uses it the most?

*I use it a lot. I can tell it who to call.*   *I only use it to choose songs to play.*

**Common mistake**
~~well~~
It doesn't work very ~~good~~.

**B** 🔴 **Make it personal** In pairs, answer 1–3. Which of you likes voice recognition better?
1 Do you have any voice-activated devices at home / in your car? How well do they work?
2 What other devices / appliances should / could be voice-activated?
3 How "intelligent" do you think voice recognition will become in the future?

*My GPS is voice-activated, but it's kind of stupid.*   *Oh yeah? How come?*

**C** ▶ 7.11 Listen to Bruce and Ann comparing their cell phones. Whose is better at voice recognition?

**D** ▶ 7.11 Listen again and answer 1–4 using one or two words. Are you more like Ann or Bruce?
1 Who gave Bruce his new phone?
2 What's his voice-recognition software called?
3 Did he expect the phone to be so smart?
4 What's Ann's voice-recognition software called?

*I'm definitely more like … because …*

**E** ▶ 7.11 Young people often use *like* in informal speech. Study examples 1–3. Then listen again. How many times do you hear the word *like*?
1 The party was, like, so cool. (filler speech)
2 I was like, "What are you doing?" and he was like, "Nothing." (quotative)
3 It took, like, forever to get here. (to signal exaggeration)

**F** ▶ 7.12 Listen to Ann asking Bruce's phone 1–5. Did it understand (U) or misunderstand (M)? Is it funny?
1 Where am I?
2 Will the weather get worse?
3 Do you love me?
4 Please call me an ambulance.
5 Make me a coffee.

**G** 🔴 **Make it personal** *Machines with personality!*
Complete 1–4 with your opinion, then compare in groups.
1 In my opinion, this cartoon …
2 My computer / tablet / phone thinks I'm …
3 I think machines with personality …
4 I'd like my … to have a personality so …

*I'd love to be able to talk to my fridge. It could suggest recipes, count calories, and help me stay healthy!*

*WHY ARE YOU SO STUPID?*

## 2 Pronunciation   -ed ending followed by /h/

**A** ▶ 7.13 Listen and repeat 1–3 from the dialogue in **1C**. Choose the correct alternatives in the box.
1 He asked if he bored me.
2 I asked him if he was hungry.
3 I asked her to text someone.

> When the final sound is /k/, -ed is pronounced: **/t/** / /d/
> The /k/ sound in *asked* is: **strong** / **weak**
> The /h/ sound in *him* and *her* is usually: **strong** / **weak**

**B** ▶ 7.14 **Dictation.** Listen and write Ann's five sentences. Then write them in direct speech.

# 7.4 Are machines with personality a good idea?

**Lesson Aims:** Sts learn and practice reporting questions, requests, and commands in the context of operating voice-activated devices.

**Function**
Listening to two friends giving voice commands to their phones.
Discussing machines with personalities.
Reporting questions, commands, and requests.

**Language**
Will the weather get worse?
Please call me an ambulance.
How intelligent do you think voice recognition will become in the future?
I asked my computer to read my new email.
The GPS told me to turn left.

**Vocabulary:** Voice-activated devices, voice commands, voice recognition. Review words related to using touch screens.
**Pronunciation:** -ed endings followed by /h/.
**Grammar:** Reported speech (2).

♪ Turn to p. 333 for notes about this song and an accompanying task.

**Warm-up** Pair sts up and ask each pair to write three indirect questions about their school, e.g. *Could you tell where the restroom is?* Then, join pairs to ask and answer their questions. Classcheck sts' questions and answers using open pairs.

## 1 Listening

**A Books closed.** Ask: *Can you operate your smart phone using voice commands? What can you do with it? How often do you use this feature?*

**Books open.** Refer sts to the model text in the speech bubbles on p. 92 and have them discuss the question in pairs. Classcheck.

**B** 🙂 **Make it personal** Read with the whole class. Have sts work in pairs, taking turns asking and answering questions 1–3. Classcheck by having sts report their partners' answers.

**C** Tell sts that they are going to hear Bruce and Ann comparing their cell phones. Have sts listen to answer the question as you play ▶ 7.11. Classcheck.

▶ 7.11 Turn to page 319 for the complete audioscript.

🔑 Bruce's phone is better.

**D** Play ▶ 7.11 again so sts can listen again and answer the questions. Paircheck. Classcheck.

🔑 1 his mom  2 Justin  3 no  4 Alice

**E** Read the examples with sts. Play ▶ 7.11 again and ask sts to count the examples of *like* in the conversation. Classcheck.

🔑 There are eight examples of *like* in the conversation.

**F** Say: *Now Ann's going to talk to Bruce's phone.* Point to questions 1–5 and ask: *How many of these questions do you think the phone will understand?* Have sts work in pairs to predict the answers. Then, play ▶ 7.12 and have sts check *understood* or *misunderstood* for 1–5. Paircheck. Classcheck.

▶ 7.12 Turn to page 319 for the complete audioscript.

🔑 1 M  2 U  3 U  4 U  5 U

**Tip** If time allows, there are lists of funny questions to ask Siri (or other device "personality") available via Internet search engines. Have sts find some questions and try them out.

**G** 🙂 **Make it personal** Point to the questions and read the example in the speech bubble with the class. Have sts discuss the questions in small groups. Classcheck by inviting volunteers to report their group's opinions to the class.

## 2 Pronunciation  -ed ending followed by /h/

**A** Elicit the past form of *ask* and the pronunciation of its -ed ending. Ensure that sts can pronounce /æskt/. Remind Portuguese L1 speakers that the *e* in *asked* is silent. Play ▶ 7.13 for sts to listen and repeat. Have sts circle the correct options to complete the rules. Paircheck. Classcheck.

🔑 1 /t/  2 weak  3 weak

**B** Prepare sts for dictation. Play ▶ 7.14 twice and challenge them to listen and write down Ann's five sentences. Paircheck. Classcheck.

▶ 7.14 Turn to page 319 for the complete audioscript.

🔑
1  I asked where I was.
2  I asked if the weather would get worse.
3  I asked him if he loved me.
4  I asked him to call me an ambulance.
5  I told him to make me a coffee.

## 3 Grammar  Reported Speech (2)

*Cause she knew what was she was doin'
When she told me how to walk this way!
She told me to walk this way, talk this way.*

**A** Look at the examples in **1F** and **2B**. Are rules 1–6 true (T) or false (F)?

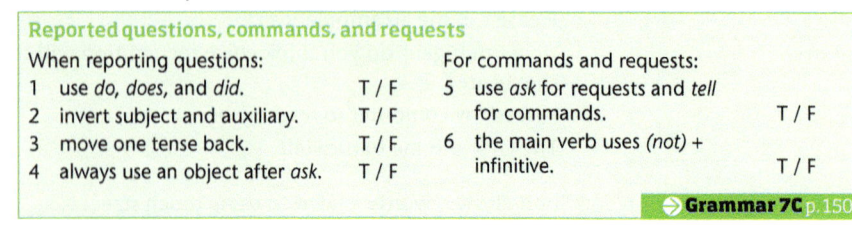

| Reported questions, commands, and requests | | | |
|---|---|---|---|
| When reporting questions: | | For commands and requests: | |
| 1 use *do*, *does*, and *did*. | T / F | 5 use *ask* for requests and *tell* for commands. | T / F |
| 2 invert subject and auxiliary. | T / F | | |
| 3 move one tense back. | T / F | 6 the main verb uses (*not*) + infinitive. | T / F |
| 4 always use an object after *ask*. | T / F | | |

➡ **Grammar 7C** p.150

**Common mistake**
She asked me ^for your contact details.

**B** Order the words to complete five "voice recognition disasters." Had any of your own?

Luke   I asked *my computer* / *read* / *to* my new email, and it started deleting messages instead!

Sue   I asked *it* / *rain* / *my phone* / *would* / *if* tonight and it said, "It's now 4 p.m."

Ron   The GPS told *to* / *turn* / *me* left, and I crashed into a tree.

Ian   The stereo asked *what* / *me* / *I* / *wanted* to listen to. I couldn't believe my ears!

Mitt   I asked *where* / *my GPS* / *I* / *was*, and he told *worry* / *me* / *to* / *not*. Can you believe that?

**C** Do you like autocorrect? Ever have problems with it? Last week it caused lots of problems for **Bruce** and **Ann**. Write their text conversations in reported speech.

*I love autocorrect. That is, when it guesses correctly!*

**1**
- Why are you late?
- I've just crashed my cat.
- What do you mean?
- No, no! Not my cat. The ___car___!
- Hate autocorrect.

**2**
- Are you hungry?
- Yeah, I want vegetarian blood.
- What?
- OMG. What I meant to say was vegetarian _____!

**3**
- Are you coming to the party?
- Can't. I broke my uncle.
- What?
- I mean _____, but it's still serious.

**D** ▶ 7.15  In pairs, say what you think Ann and Bruce meant for 1–3 in **C**. Then listen to check.

*You can crash into a cat, but you can't crash a cat, can you?*

**E**  ⬤ **Make it personal**   **Tech questionnaire** In pairs, follow the instructions.

1 Write six questions to find out about your classmates. For example:

*How many remote controls do you have and actually use?
Do you ever think your phone knows what you're thinking?
Do you think you need to cut down on your screen time?*

2 Ask as many of your classmates as you can. Make a note of their answers.
3 Report their answers back to your partner. Any unexpected answers?

*Angelika said she hadn't changed her phone for three years!*

*Really? Paul told me that he'd changed his yesterday.*

# 7.4

## 3 Grammar  Reported Speech (2)

**A** Tell sts to look at the sentences in **1F** and the five sentences they wrote down in **2B**, then have them choose true or false for the rules in the grammar box. Paircheck. Classcheck.

> 1 F  2 T  3 T  4 T  5 T  6 T

🟠 **Common mistake**  Read with the whole group.

➡️ **Grammar 7C** page 150

**B** Read the first sentence with sts and elicit the correct order of the words in bold. Instruct sts to continue reordering each sentence. Paircheck. Classcheck by writing the answers on the board.

> Luke: my computer to read
> Sue:  my phone if it would rain
> Ron:  told me to turn
> Ian:  asked me what I wanted
> Mitt: my GPS where I was, me not to worry

**C** Ask: *What about the autocorrect function on your phone? Do you use it? Does it cause you problems?* Have sts read Bruce and Ann's texts and restate them as reported speech. Clarify that Bruce's texts are in blue and Ann's are in green. To model the activity, point to the first question and say: *Ann asked Bruce … .* Elicit the completion of the sentence (why he was late). Ask sts to use the reported speech form with all the sentences in conversations 1–3.

> 1  Ann asked Bruce why he was late, and he said he'd just crashed his cat. Ann asked him what he meant, and he said that he meant his car, not his cat. He said that he hated autocorrect.
> 2  Bruce asked Ann if she was hungry and she said that she wanted vegetarian blood. Then she said that what she had meant to say was …
> 3  Bruce asked Ann if she was going to the party and she said she couldn't because she had broken her uncle. Then she said that she meant … But that it was still serious.

**D** Read the model in the speech bubble with the whole class and tell sts that they are going to make guesses about the blanks in Ann and Bruce's texts. Pair sts up and ask them to use their imagination to discuss and fill in the blanks in conversations 1–3. Then, play ▶ 7.15 so sts can check and correct their answers.

> 1  car
> 2  food
> 3  ankle

**E** 🟢 **Make it personal**  1 Read the examples with the class. Sts write six more questions individually. Monitor and help where necessary, and check sts are forming the questions correctly.

2  Have sts mingle and ask as many other sts as they can. Make sure they make a note of their answers.

3  Ask two volunteers to read out the examples in the speech bubbles. Assign new pairs and have sts report back their answers to each other. Monitor and check sts are using reported speech correctly. Classcheck by asking sts to report back anything surprising to the class.

➡️ **Workbook** Page 37

## 7.5 How often do you use a pen?

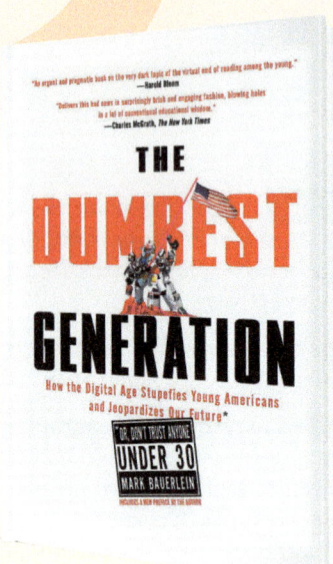

### Skills  Listening and note-taking

**A** Match words from the book cover to definitions 1–4. Who's the book about?

| 1 | _____ verb | have confidence in |
|---|---|---|
| 2 | _____ adj. | most stupid |
| 3 | _____ verb | makes stupid |
| 4 | _____ verb | puts at risk |

**Common mistakes**

It puts at risk the young people's futures.

People says this is true, but I disagree.

**B** 7.16 In pairs, answer 1–3. Listen to / Watch an interview to check. Would you consider reading a book like this?
1. How old do you think the author is? Why?
2. Which specific examples of digital culture do you think will be mentioned?
3. Which of these do you think American teens are becoming less interested in?

foreign affairs    leisure reading    partying    politics
social networking    studying for class    visits to museums

*Many are becoming less and less interested in foreign affairs.*

**C** 7.16 Read about note-taking. Then listen / watch again and complete the notes. Do any of 1–6 surprise or worry you?

> Note-taking is a useful learning skill to develop. When taking notes you should write as fast and economically as possible. Here are three ways to do that:
> - Focus on the most important information (facts, dates, numbers) + ignore less relevant details.
> - Omit articles, auxiliary verbs + prepositions—not usually important information.
> - Use figures for numbers (7 out of 10 = 70%), symbols ( > = more than) + abbreviations (sts = students).

1. Digital culture doesn't open teens to _____, artwork, _____, _____ + foreign affairs.
2. Most popular sites for teens: social networking = _____%
3. Time spent reading + studying: < _____ / week. (_____% of sts.)
4. Time spent social networking: _____ / week.
5. Dying habits: Leisure reading, visits to _____ + _____.
6. Technology in teenage bedroom: _____, _____, video game console, _____ → interesting than Antony, Cleopatra, and Caesar!

**D** **Make it personal**  Teens today. Are things changing? In groups, decide what's
1) similar and
2) different in your country. Cover these points:
- Do you mainly agree?
- Do any of the facts in **C** surprise or worry you? Why (not)?
- Are teenagers becoming less engaged? More isolated? More adventurous?
- What are the top three priorities among teens where you live?

*It seems to me that teenagers are a bit different.*

# 7.5 How often do you use a pen?

**Lesson Aims:** Sts practice taking notes while listening to / watching an interview with the author of a book called *The Dumbest Generation*.

### Function
Viewing / Listening to an interview with an author.
Listening and note-taking.

### Language
I'm here today with Mark Bauerlein, author of *The Dumbest Generation*, a provocative new book that says, "the digital age stupefies young Americans and jeopardizes our future."
… visits to libraries + museums. Technology in teenage bedroom: laptop, video game console, Blackberry.

**Vocabulary:** dumb(est), jeopardize, stupefy, trust.

♫ Turn to p. 333 for notes about this song and an accompanying task.

**Warm-up** Divide the class into groups of five. Ask each group to come up with five pieces of advice expressing "dos" and "don'ts" for learning English, e.g. always do your homework, don't miss classes, avoid texting or checking emails on your phone during class, watch movies in English, take notes about new vocabulary, don't be late for class, try to speak English outside class, etc.

When groups have finished, ask each student to pair up with a classmate from a different group. Have partners tell each other their group's "dos" and "don'ts." Classcheck by asking sts to report their partners' tips to the whole class. Encourage them to use reported speech by asking: *What did (partner's name) tell you to do?* (e.g. "Ana told me not to miss lessons and to avoid texting in class.")

## ID Skills  Listening and note-taking

**A** **Books open**. Direct sts' attention to the book title and have them read all they can on the book cover. Ask: *Would you like to read it?*

Read definition 1 and ask sts to find the matching word on the book cover. Then, instruct them to find the correct words for definitions 2–4. Paircheck. Classcheck. then ask *Who's the book about?*

🗝
1  trust
2  dumbest
3  stupefies
4  jeopardizes

**B** Have sts work in pairs to ask and answer questions 1–3 about the book. Play ▶ 7.16 ▶ so sts can check their answers. Classcheck.

▶ 7.16 Turn to page 319 for the complete audioscript.

🗝
1  Over 30, because the subtitle of the book is "Don't Trust Anyone Under 30".
2  Social networks, laptop, cell phone, video game console, iPod.
3  All topics except social networks.

**Tip** Have sts turn to the AS on p. 171. Sts listen again and notice Mark's hesitation / repetitions and Nick's listening sounds.

**C** Find out about sts' note-taking habits. Ask: *How often do you take notes in class? What about in work meetings or college lectures?*

Read the text on note-taking with the whole class. Then, have sts briefly read notes 1–6 and replay ▶ 7.16 ▶ as they listen and fill in the blanks. Paircheck. Replay the track if necessary. Classcheck and then discuss the final question with the whole class.

🗝
1  ideas, documents, politics
2  90
3  1 hr., 55
4  9 hrs
5  museums, libraries
6  laptop, cell phone, iPod

**D** 🔴 **Make it personal**  Assign groups and ask sts to refer to the information in **C** and answer the questions.

Monitor sts' work closely and take notes for delayed correction. Classcheck and ask: *Did you find any strong differences of opinion?*

# Do you enjoy a good argument?

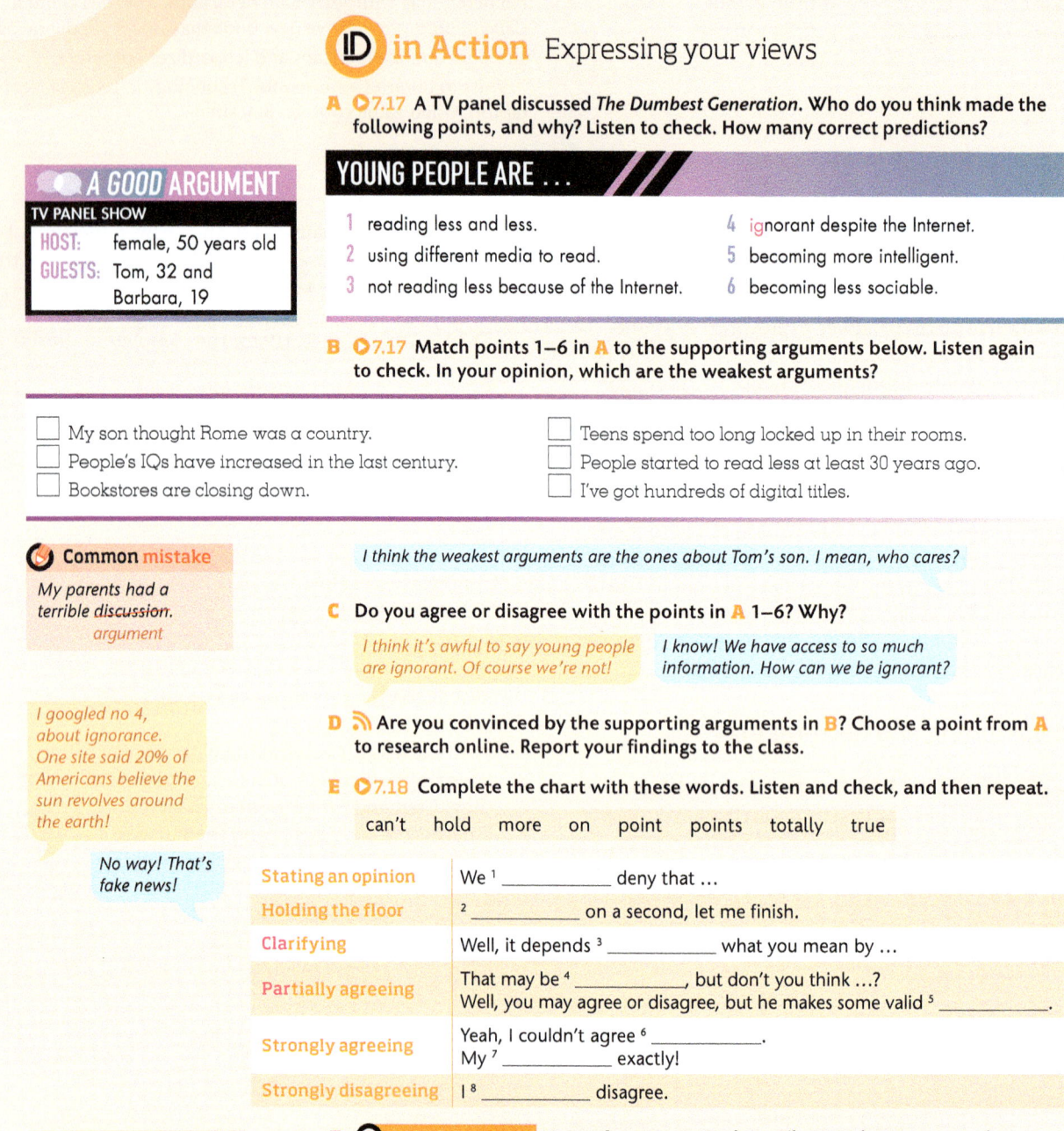

## ID in Action  Expressing your views

**A** ▶ 7.17 A TV panel discussed *The Dumbest Generation*. Who do you think made the following points, and why? Listen to check. How many correct predictions?

**A GOOD ARGUMENT**
TV PANEL SHOW
HOST: female, 50 years old
GUESTS: Tom, 32 and Barbara, 19

**YOUNG PEOPLE ARE …**

1 reading less and less.
2 using different media to read.
3 not reading less because of the Internet.
4 ignorant despite the Internet.
5 becoming more intelligent.
6 becoming less sociable.

**B** ▶ 7.17 Match points 1–6 in **A** to the supporting arguments below. Listen again to check. In your opinion, which are the weakest arguments?

- [ ] My son thought Rome was a country.
- [ ] People's IQs have increased in the last century.
- [ ] Bookstores are closing down.
- [ ] Teens spend too long locked up in their rooms.
- [ ] People started to read less at least 30 years ago.
- [ ] I've got hundreds of digital titles.

**Common mistake**
My parents had a terrible ~~discussion~~.
argument

*I think the weakest arguments are the ones about Tom's son. I mean, who cares?*

**C** Do you agree or disagree with the points in **A** 1–6? Why?

*I think it's awful to say young people are ignorant. Of course we're not!*
*I know! We have access to so much information. How can we be ignorant?*

*I googled no 4, about ignorance. One site said 20% of Americans believe the sun revolves around the earth!*

**D** 📶 Are you convinced by the supporting arguments in **B**? Choose a point from **A** to research online. Report your findings to the class.

*No way! That's fake news!*

**E** ▶ 7.18 Complete the chart with these words. Listen and check, and then repeat.

can't   hold   more   on   point   points   totally   true

| | |
|---|---|
| Stating an opinion | We ¹_____ deny that … |
| Holding the floor | ²_____ on a second, let me finish. |
| Clarifying | Well, it depends ³_____ what you mean by … |
| Partially agreeing | That may be ⁴_____, but don't you think …? Well, you may agree or disagree, but he makes some valid ⁵_____. |
| Strongly agreeing | Yeah, I couldn't agree ⁶_____. My ⁷_____ exactly! |
| Strongly disagreeing | I ⁸_____ disagree. |

*Welcome to "Hot Topic"! Our guests tonight are …*

**F** 🔴 **Make it personal**  *A good argument* In threes (host and two guests), choose a discussion topic and role-play a three-minute TV panel. First, think of your main points and supporting arguments. Take notes. What's your conclusion?

- Artificial intelligence will be used to replace teachers.
- We won't need to learn other languages because we will have translation technology.
- The Internet needs to be more strongly regulated.

♪ *Yeah, we're just young, dumb and broke, But we still got love to give*

# 7.5 Do you enjoy a good argument?

**Lesson Aims:** Sts practice expressing views after listening to / watching a TV debate about a book called *The Dumbest Generation*.

### Function
Viewing / Listening to a TV debate.
Expressing your views.

### Language
Well, you may agree or disagree, but he makes some valid points, don't you think?
That may be true, but don't you think there's something wrong here?

**Vocabulary:** Phrases for expressing views (Hold on a second , let me finish ... , I totally disagree ... , OK, point taken ... , Please, get to the point ... , We can't deny that ... , Yeah, I couldn't agree more).
**Skills:** Expressing your views.

## ID in Action  Expressing your views

**A** Tell sts that they are going to listen to a TV panel discussing the book from **ID Skills A**, *The Dumbest Generation*. Explain there are three people participating in the show, and draw sts' attention to the box with their names and ages.

Tell sts that they are going to listen and identify the person who made each point. Allow them a few seconds to read points 1–6. Then, play ▶ 7.17. Paircheck. Replay ▶ 7.17. Classcheck.

▶ 7.17  Turn to page 319 for the complete audioscript.

1 Tom   2 Barbara   3 Barbara   4 Host   5 Barbara   6 Tom

**B** Invite a volunteer to read the first supporting argument to the class. Draw sts' attention to points 1–6 in **A** and ask them: *Which point in A relates to this argument?* (4). In the same way, sts should match the rest of the supporting arguments to the other points in **A**. Paircheck. Play ▶ 7.17 again so sts can check their answers. Classcheck. Finally, ask the class: *In your opinion, which are the weakest arguments?*

4, 5, 1, 6, 3, 2

**Common mistake**  Read with the whole class.

**Language tip**  As a result of the similarity of the words *discussion* (English) and *discussão* (Portuguese) or *discusión* (Spanish), Portuguese or Spanish L1 speakers may use the word *discussion* when they actually mean *argument*. Make sure sts understand the difference.

**C** Ask: *Do you agree or disagree with points 1–6 in A?* Ask two volunteers to read out the mini-dialogue in the speech bubbles. Then, have sts discuss their opinions in pairs. Classcheck and find out by a show of hands how many people agree or disagree with each statement.

**D** Ask sts to choose one point from **A** then go online to check. Classcheck by asking sts to report their findings to the class.

**E** Ask sts to fill in the blanks with the words from the box. Play ▶ 7.18 so sts can check their answers. Then, replay the track for choral repetition, pausing after each sentence.

▶ 7.18  Turn to page 320 for the complete audioscript.

1 can't   2 Hold   3 on   4 true   5 points
6 more   7 point   8 totally

**Language tip**  As a result of direct translation, speakers of Romance languages could have trouble using the correct preposition in the expression *it depends on*. They may use the preposition *of* instead of *on*.

**F**  **Make it personal**  Divide the class into groups of three. Point to the sentences and ask groups to choose one of the topics. Within their groups, sts should role-play a three-minute TV debate.

Ask sts to prepare before the discussion starts. Assign roles **A**, **B**, and **C** within each group and then read the instructions with the whole class. Clarify that st **A** should agree with the statement chosen, student **B** should disagree, and student **C** should begin the debate, take notes, and decide whether student **A** or st **B** has the best arguments.

Encourage sts to come up with arguments to support their views and to use language from **C** and **D**. Allow groups two or three minutes for preparation before the debate. Monitor, taking notes for delayed correction. Classcheck by asking each group's student **C** to report the outcome of the debate.

➡ **Workbook** Page 38

➡ **ID Richmond Learning Platform**

➡ **Writing** p. 96

➡ **ID Café** p. 97

# Writing 7  A complaint email

*All I wanna do is (bang, bang, bang!)
And a (kkkaaa ching!)
And take your money.*

**A** Julio Cruz recently bought an LED TV. Read his email. True (T) or false (F)?
1. He bought it at a shopping mall.
2. He's had problems with the TV since he bought it.
3. There are two problems with the TV itself.
4. He had two problems with the service.
5. He lost the receipt but still wants his money back.
6. He expects a fast solution.

| To: | customerservice@ledtv10.com |
|---|---|
| From: | Julio Cruz |
| Subject: | Refund |

October 10th, 2013.

(a) _____ ,

1  I am writing to express total dissatisfaction with my purchase of a 42-inch-LED TV from your online store nearly a month ago. Unfortunately, your product has not performed at all well, and your service has been completely inadequate, to say the least.

2  Firstly, when I turned it on there were several spots on the screen, so I immediately called your service department, who told me the spots would soon go away. However, the problem has gradually been getting worse, and now it is almost impossible to watch any program comfortably.

3  Secondly, I am very disappointed because I've contacted your online support countless times, but they always seemed uninterested and unwilling to help. For instance, I was informed that they would send a technician to solve the problem, but this never happened.

4  Although you advertise top quality, both your product and your service are well below the standards I expected. As you can imagine, I am not satisfied. Therefore, to resolve the problem, (b) _____ . I attach a scanned copy of the receipt and must insist on receiving a full refund immediately or (c) _____ .

(d) _____ .

(e) _____ ,

Julio Cruz

**B** Match each paragraph to its purpose.
- [ ] action he wants to be taken
- [ ] reason for writing
- [ ] what happened when he used the product
- [ ] what happened when he complained

**C** Read *Write it right!* Then match 1–6 to gaps a–e in the email. There's one extra phrase.
1. Dear Sir / Madam
2. Yours sincerely
3. I would appreciate an immediate solution
4. Yours faithfully
5. I will be forced to take legal action
6. I look forward to hearing from you

### ✓ Write it right!

Start and end formal letters using:
- *Dear Mr. / Ms.* (+ last name) or *Dear Sir / Madam*, …
- a closing sentence:
  *I would appreciate a rapid response / I look forward to receiving your urgent reply.*
- *Yours sincerely,* (if you know the recipient's name) or *Yours faithfully,* (if you don't).

To express dissatisfaction and demand action use **firm but polite phrases**:
- *I am writing to complain about …*
- *I feel I am entitled to (compensation for all the inconvenience I have suffered).*

Avoid contractions or informal language.

**D** Underline the formal sentences in the email that correspond to 1–5.
1. Your service was horrible.
2. I've gotten in touch with you on the Internet.
3. Nobody wanted to help me.
4. You say your product's the best.
5. I want my money back.

**E** *Your turn!* Write a complaint email in 120–180 words.

| Before | Choose a problem below and make notes for paragraphs 1–4 in **B**. |
|---|---|
| While | Follow the tips in *Write it right!* Use formal language. |
| After | Email it to a classmate to check before sending it to your teacher. |

- You had a meal in a restaurant where the food and service was bad.
- You ordered an item of clothing online, but it is not as advertised on the website.
- You booked a holiday with a travel agency, but the hotel was not as advertised in the brochure.
- You took a long distance bus to a party. The bus left one hour late, arrived four hours late, and you missed the party.

# Writing 7  A complaint email

♪ Turn to p. 333 for notes about this song and an accompanying task.

**A** **Books closed**. Ask: *Have you ever written an email to complain about something? What was it? What happened?*

**Books open**. Allow sts some time to quickly read Julio's email and find out his reasons for complaining. Then, have sts reread the complaint email and mark statements 1–6 true (T) or false (F). Paircheck, then classcheck.

> 1 F   2 T   3 F   4 T   5 F   6 T

**B** Point to Julio's email and ask: *What's the aim, or purpose, of each paragraph?* Have sts match the purposes to paragraphs 1–4 in **A**.

> 4, 1, 2, 3

**C** Read **Write it right!** with the class. Then, have sts match phrases 1–6 to blanks a–e in **A**. Paircheck. Classcheck.

> 1 a   2 e   3 b   4 (not used)   5 c   6 d

**D** Read sentence 1 with the group and ask: *Is this appropriate in a formal email?* Ask sts to reread Julio's email in **A** and find the formal equivalent of each sentence, 1–5. Paircheck. Classcheck.

> 1 your service has been completely inadequate
> 2 I contacted your online support
> 3 they always seemed uninterested and unwilling to help
> 4 you advertise top quality
> 5 must insist on receiving a full refund

**E** *Your turn!*

**Before** Say: *Imagine you had problems with a product you bought.* Tell sts that they will be writing a four-paragraph email in 120–180 words. Have sts make notes for their four paragraphs, which should correspond to purposes 1–4 in **B**.

**While** Have sts write their complaint email. Remind them to follow the tips from **Write it right!** and to use formal language. Monitor and help with any queries sts might have while writing.

**After** Ask sts to change partners. Have partners exchange email addresses and send their complaint emails to each other for feedback. Then, ask sts to send you a final copy via email or to submit a paper copy.

# 7 The road NOT taken

## ID Café

### 1 Before watching

**A** Complete 1–5 with these words, and then match three of them to the photos.

| commuter | express | shocks | tow truck |
|---|---|---|---|
| transmission | | | |

1. ☐ A fast train that doesn't stop at every station is an _____.
2. ☐ A _____ moves a car that is broken down.
3. ☐ The _____ is the part of a vehicle that transmits the engine power to the wheels.
4. ☐ A _____ travels a long distance to work.
5. ☐ The _____ are the parts of a vehicle that absorb the energy from bumps in the road so the wheels run smoothly.

a   b    c

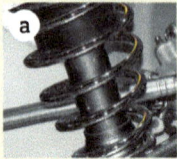

**B** 🔵 **Make it personal** Has your vehicle ever broken down? If so, what did you do? Was it easy to repair?

*Once I was on a bus that ran out of gas. The drivers behind us were furious.*

### 2 While watching

**A** Watch the video and check the correct answer in 1–3.
1. What did August ask Rory and Daniel?
   ☐ He asked if they needed help.
   ☐ He asked if they needed him to pick up anything else.
2. What did Rory tell Daniel that Genevieve said?
   ☐ Her car had broken down.
   ☐ She decided not to have dinner with them.
3. What did Paolo tell Andrea and Zoey about the trains?
   ☐ He said they'd have to cross back over and go back the other way.
   ☐ He warned them their train was going express.

**B** Watch again. Who said each line?
1. Her car broke down on the expressway.
2. Dinner's going to get cold.
3. It'll just be a party for five.
4. They were expecting us twenty minutes ago.
5. But don't expect me for dinner.
6. This isn't our stop. We've missed it.
7. It passes our stop so we had to get off here.
8. You'll have to cross over to the other side.
9. We're not gonna make dinner.
10. That's so nice of you.

### 3 After watching

**A** Complete 1–5 with these verbs. There's one extra.

| asked | offered | complained |
|---|---|---|
| called | told | wondered |

1. August _____ if Rory needed anything else.
2. Genevieve _____ Rory to tell him that she wouldn't make dinner.
3. August _____ where they were and why they were late.
4. Genevieve _____ Andrea and Zoey that her car needed repairs.
5. Paolo _____ to wait for the train with Andrea and Zoey.

**B** Complete 1–4 with these times.

| 20 mins | 45 mins | 2 hours | a bit |
|---|---|---|---|

1. Genevieve said the tow truck guy would take at least _____.
2. Rory told Daniel it would take _____ for her car to get fixed.
3. Andrea told August she would see them in _____.
4. Andrea and Zoey had to wait _____ for the next train.

**C** 🔵 **Make it personal** In threes, share your experiences of planning things that didn't work out. Tell the class the best story.

*Leo told us about a party he'd planned but no one came!*

# ID Café 7  The road NOT taken

## 1 Before watching

**A** Have sts look at the words in the box and ask: *Which words do you think are similar in (sts' mother tongue)?* (For example, sts may note that *express* and *transmission* may have cognates in their mother tongue.) Read sentence 1 and elicit the correct answer. Ask sts to fill in the blanks in sentences 2–5 with the correct words from the box. Encourage sts to focus on words they already know, either from their L1 or from their previous knowledge of English. Paircheck.

1. express
2. tow truck
3. transmission
4. commuter
5. shocks

Then, have sts match three of the sentences to the pictures a–c. Classcheck.

2 c  4 b  5 a

**B** *Make it personal*  Read the questions with the whole class and have sts take turns asking and answering them in pairs. Refer sts to the model text in the speech bubble. Classcheck by inviting volunteers to report their partners' stories to the whole group.

## 2 While watching

**A** Tell sts that August, Rory, and Daniel are preparing dinner for six people. Say: *They are expecting three female friends to come over for dinner.* Ask: *Who do you think they are?* Have sts guess the names of the three female characters (Andrea, Zoey, and Genevieve). Classcheck by playing ▶ 7 from the start to 00:01:30. Then, pause the video and ask for sts' predictions: *Who's coming for dinner? What are they having for dessert?*

Have sts read questions 1–3 and the answer choices for each. Play ▶ 7 from the start to 00:03:43 and have sts listen and answer the questions. Paircheck.

1. He asked if they needed him to pick up anything else.
2. Her car had broken down.
3. He said they'd have to cross back over and go back the other way.

**B** Read the first sentence with sts. Ask: *Who said this line?* Elicit answers but don't confirm at this stage. Play ▶ 7 again for sts to watch and note who said each line. Peercheck, then classcheck.

1 Rory  2 Rory  3 Daniel  4 Andrea  5 Genevieve
6 Zoey  7 Andrea  8 Paolo  9 Zoey  10 Andrea

## 3 After watching

**A** Have sts fill in the blanks in sentences 1–5 with the verbs provided. Paircheck. Classcheck.

1. asked
2. called
3. wondered
4. told
5. offered

**B** Have sts change partners and work in their new pairs to complete sentences 1–4. If time allows, replay ▶ 7 so sts can check their answers. Classcheck.

1. 45 minutes
2. 2 hours
3. a bit
4. 20 minutes

**C** *Make it personal*  Read the model text in the speech bubble with the whole class. Ask sts to think of a time they planned something, e.g. a party, a dinner, or a movie with friends, that didn't work out for some reason. Allow sts a couple of minutes to think of an experience and write down a few notes about it. Then, group sts in threes and have them share their stories in their groups. At the end, ask each group to choose a story to tell the class.

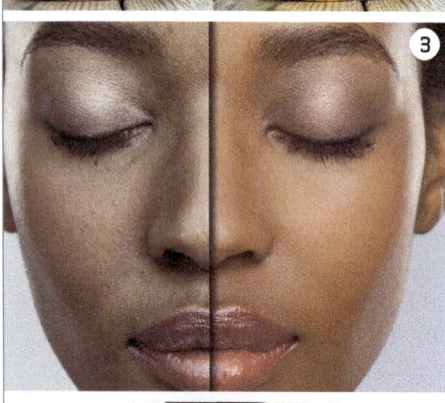

# 8.1 How important are looks?

## 1 Reading

**A** Is Photoshop a good thing? Have you used it? Would you use it?

> I use Photoshop to remove unnecessary objects from my photos – like trash cans!

> I've never used it. I like my photos to show reality.

**B** In pairs, take turns giving clues about the items in photos 1–5 until your partner guesses the item.

> It opens and closes.  Her eyes?  No, it's made of wood.  Is it red?

**C** ◯ 8.1 Listen and read the introduction to the article. In pairs, how do you think Photoshop has changed the world? Brainstorm five ideas. Then read and match photos 1–5 to a paragraph. Were all your ideas mentioned?

### How Photoshop HAS CHANGED THE WORLD

Adobe Photoshop is one of the most powerful image-editing tools in the world, and it has profoundly changed the art of photo retouching. What was once an expensive and time-consuming task is now a simple procedure with limitless possibilities. Here we take a look at how Photoshop has changed the way we view the world.

**HOW WE THINK ABOUT IMAGES**
"That must have been photoshopped!" [a _____ ] We even use "photoshop" as a verb to indicate that something doesn't look real.

**HOW WE VIEW THE HUMAN BODY**
A staggering 95 per cent of the human images we see are retouched. [b _____ ] The more camera-shy among us can photoshop away imperfections and it's great for simple things like removing red-eye. However, we are so used to photos being modified that seeing candid photos of celebrities, with all their imperfections, seems to shock us and many of these "un-photoshopped" images go viral.

**HOW IT'S USED IN ADVERTISING**
Look through any magazine and find an ad that hasn't been photoshopped. Good luck! Advertising has completely transformed since image manipulation. [c _____ ]

**HOW IT'S USED IN THE TRAVEL INDUSTRY**
Lots of vacationers wonder where the golden sand and blue skies are when they get to their destination. The sad fact is that travel companies doctor images. [d _____ ] This kind of manipulation only results in disappointed customers.

**HOW WE VIEW HISTORY**
Some of history's most iconic images were "photoshopped" before the software even existed! Photoshop has the power to alter the way we see history. [e _____ ] If not, they may be altered. With the recent craze of photobombing, politicians must be very grateful for Photoshop.

For better or worse, Photoshop is here to stay, and we are now so accustomed to seeing these images that often it doesn't even register that they've been photoshopped.

**D** ◯ 8.1 Complete the article with 1–5. Listen again to check. Has the article made you feel any differently about Photoshop?

1 Agencies can now just pay someone to make their ads for them without the need to take photographs!
2 As a result, Photoshop has changed our view of what is "normal."
3 For example, they might remove an ugly parking lot between your hotel and the beach.
4 Experts examine images in detail to make sure they give the right message.
5 These days, we are increasingly skeptical about the authenticity of images.

**Unit overview:** In unit 8, sts learn and practice modal perfects, tag questions, reflexive pronouns, and vocabulary related to furniture in the contexts of photography, visual illusions, and looks.

# 8.1 How important are looks?

**Lesson Aims:** Sts learn and use vocabulary related to photography and photographs in the context of Photoshop.

## Function
Reading about Photoshop.
Listening to an artist talk about their work.
Talking about images.

## Language
Yes, and the colors are brighter in this one.
Most of his images are silly and fun.
It looks like the giraffe is photobombing them!

**Vocabulary:** Photography and photos: camera-shy, candid, doctor (v), photobombing, photoshopped, red-eye, retouching.

♪ Turn to p. 333 for notes about this song and an accompanying task.

**Warm-up** Have sts interview each other with the lesson title questions from unit 7 on p. 86–95. Encourage sts to ask follow-up questions whenever possible. Monitor their discussions closely and write down mistakes and very good or interesting answers for delayed feedback. Classcheck and ask sts to tell you something interesting they found out about their partner.

## 1 Reading

**A Books closed**. Ask: *Do you like taking photos? What do you take photos of?* and have a brief class discussion.

**Books open**. Point to the photos and ask: *Do you think these photos have been changed in any way?* Elicit or explain what Photoshop is and assign pairs for sts to discuss the questions. It may be useful to give an example of your own first, e.g. *I always use Photoshop to remove red eye in my photos.* (Red-eye occurs when the camera flash is too close, making the pupil of the eye look red.) Classcheck by discussing the questions with the whole class.

**B** Assign pairs. Read the example in the speech bubbles with sts and then have them take turns giving clues about items in the photos until their partner names the item.

> **Language tip** After reading the text in **1C**, encourage sts to count the number of cognates with their L1 that they can find in the text. If necessary, remind them what cognates are. When they finish, have them discuss whether any / all these words helped them better understand the text. Were there any misunderstandings caused by false cognates? Remind Portuguese or Spanish L1 speakers that, when reading in English, it's a good idea to try and find as many cognates as they can and then use these words in order to help them understand the text.

**C** Play ▶ 8.1 for sts to listen and read the introduction to the article (stop the recording after the first paragraph). Assign pairs for sts to list five ways that Photoshop has changed the world. Classcheck by listing some of the sts' ideas on the board but don't confirm answers at this stage.

Have sts work individually to read the whole article and match the photos to the paragraphs in the article. Make sure they ignore the blanks in the text. Peercheck. Classcheck by asking sts to look at the list on the board and see if any of their ideas were mentioned.

⚷
1  how it's used in the travel industry
2  how it's used in advertising
3  how we view the human body
4  how we view history
5  how we think about images

**D** Read the sentences with the whole class. Have sts complete the article with sentences 1–5. Then, play ▶ 8.1 for sts to check their answers. Peercheck. Classcheck.

⚷
a 5  b 2  c 1  d 3  e 4

**D** 🗣 Make it personal  In groups, discuss 1–3.
1 Do you think Photoshop has had a positive or negative influence?
2 Do you think there should be more regulation of Photoshop in the media?
3 Has Photoshop affected your life in some way?

🎵 *So you can keep me
Inside the pocket of your ripped jeans,
Holding me closer 'til our eyes meet.
You won't ever be alone.*

Well, I guess it depends on how you use it. If you work in the advertising industry, then it has had a positive influence.

## 2 Vocabulary  Photography and photos

**A** Match the highlighted words in the article to the definitions.

| 1 | _____ | the red appearance of eyes in some photos |
| 2 | _____ | to change something in order to deceive people |
| 3 | _____ | describes someone who dislikes having his or her photo taken |
| 4 | _____ | making small changes to a photo in order to improve it |
| 5 | _____ | describes an image that has been manipulated by a computer program |
| 6 | _____ | the activity of ruining someone else's photo by moving into view just before it is taken |
| 7 | _____ | natural and informal |

**B** Complete 1–7 with the correct form of the words from **A**.
1 Greta Garbo disappeared whenever a photographer appeared. She was incredibly _____.
2 _____ your vacation photos to make the weather look better is really easy!
3 My camera has a special flash mode to reduce _____.
4 The court discovered that the prosecution had _____ the image.
5 The photographer managed to get a _____ photo of the princess laughing.
6 The photo on the front cover had been _____ to make him look muscular.
7 Did you see that great photo from the Oscars a few years ago? Even celebrities are into this _____ craze.

⚠ **Common mistake**

Do you like ~~that people take your photo~~?
having your photo taken

## 3 Listening

**A** ▶ 8.2 Look at James Fridman's Instagram account and answer 1–2. Listen to check. Were you right?
1 What is funny / unusual about the photos?
2 Who do you think James Fridman might be, and what does he do on social media?

**B** ▶ 8.2 Listen again and correct the errors in 1–5.
1 James Fridman is well-known for taking people's email requests for image alter*a*tions.
2 Most of his images are shocking and cruel.
3 Fridman encourages people to retouch their images to meet today's often unrealistic beauty standards.
4 One heart-warming example of James's work is a photo sent to him by a woman who was suffering from anxiety and low self-*e*steem.
5 She asked James to make her look younger.

**C** 📡 🗣 Make it personal  In small groups, go online and each find a good photoshopped image by James Fridman (or someone else). Show and explain your choice. Create a caption for it. Which are the funniest / cleverest?

Look at this one. It looks like the giraffe is photobombing them!

The caption could be, "I'm much better looking than him!"

# 8.1

**E** 🔑 **Make it personal** Read questions 1–3 with the whole class and have sts discuss them in pairs. Walk around the classroom to monitor pairs' discussions. Classcheck sts' opinions and provide feedback on their performance.

## 2 Vocabulary Photography and photos

**A** Draw sts' attention to the highlighted words in the text on p. 98. Ask the class to match them to definitions 1–7. Peercheck. Classcheck and drill the highlighted words.

🔑
1 red-eye
2 doctor
3 camera-shy
4 retouching
5 photoshopped
6 photobombing
7 candid

**B** Have sts use the words from **2A** to complete sentences 1–7. Paircheck. Classcheck.

🔑
1 camera-shy
2 Retouching
3 red-eye
4 doctored
5 candid
6 photoshopped
7 photobombing

## 3 Listening

**A** Point to the photo and say: *This is James Fridman's Instagram account. What's funny / unusual about his account?* Sts discuss the questions in pairs. When they are ready, play ▶ **8.2** for sts to check. Peercheck. Classcheck.

▶ **8.2** Turn to page 320 for the complete audioscript.

🔑
1 The photos are funny because the wrong person has been removed.
2 James Fridman might be a photographer or graphic designer. He might post unusual and funny images on social media.

**B** Read sentences 1–5 with the class and explain that there is a factual error in each sentence. Play ▶ **8.2** again for sts to listen and correct the errors. Peercheck. Classcheck.

**Tip** Have sts turn to the AS on p. 171. Sts listen again and notice /ɪ/ and /iː/.

🔑
1 James Fridman is well-known for taking people's Twitter requests for image alterations.
2 Most of his images are silly and fun.
3 Fridman does not encourage people to retouch their images to meet today's often unrealistic beauty standards.
4 One heart-warming example of James's work is a photograph sent to him by a woman who was suffering from an eating disorder and low self-esteem.
5 She asked James to make her look more beautiful.

**C** 🔑 **Make it personal** Divide the class into groups of three. Have sts go online to find an obviously photoshopped image. They can search for an image by James Fridman or use an image they have found elsewhere. Remind them to think of a caption for their image. Ask each group to present their image and caption to the whole class. You could have a class vote to decide which image is the funniest / cleverest.

➡ **Workbook** Page 39

## 8.2 Do you like watching illusions?

### 1 Listening

**A** In pairs, share what you know about Michael Jackson. Have you seen this video? Any idea how he did the illusion?

*I know he was in a group with his family before he went solo.*

*Maybe there was a metal pole in his jacket.*

**B** ▶8.3 Listen to two people guessing how they did the illusion. Did they mention your ideas? Do you think they are right?

**C** ▶8.4 Listen to someone explaining how the illusion was really done. Were the speakers in **B** correct? Did you guess correctly?

**D** ▶8.4 Listen again and complete 1–6. If there's time, watch the video!
1 The illusion appeared in the music video for _____.
2 The dancers were able to lean at an angle of _____ degrees.
3 The lean was performed by wearing a _____.
4 It had an _____ opening in the _____. This attached to a _____ on the floor.
5 During a concert in 1996, Michael Jackson _____.
6 Someone bought the item for $_____.

**E** 🔸 **Make it personal** Have you seen any spectacular performances by musicians?

*Did anyone see Pink's Grammy performance? She sang while hanging from the ceiling on a ribbon!*

### 2 Grammar Modal perfects

**A** Match the dialogue halves from **1B**. Then complete the grammar box.

1 How on earth did he do that?
2 Maybe it was something to do with his shoes.
3 Maybe he really could lean that far!
4 I guess his clothes were specially engineered.

a ☐ Yes, I suppose, he might have put magnets on them and on the floor.
b ☐ He was good, but not that good! He can't have been able to do that. It's impossible!
c ☐ Yeah, he may have had special pants made!
d ☐ He must have had wires attached to his jacket. It's the only explanation, surely!

🔸 **Common mistake**
*have gone*
He might went to a party.

1 Sentences a–d in **A** refer to the **present / past**.
2 The green verbs are the **simple past / past participle** form.
3 Check (✓) the modal verbs with the same meaning as the underlined words in a–c below.

|   | must have | can't have | might have may have |
|---|---|---|---|
| a I'm almost sure this happened. | | | |
| b Maybe this happened. | | | |
| c I'm almost sure this did not happen. | | | |

➡ **Grammar 8A** p.152

# 8.2 Do you like watching illusions?

**Lesson Aims:** Sts study and use modal perfects in the contexts of illusions.

**Function**
Listening to people talking about illusions.
Talking about illusions.
Guessing how magic tricks work.

**Language**
Well ... maybe it was something to do with his shoes.
She sang while hanging from the ceiling on a ribbon!
He might've been using mirrors or something.

**Grammar:** Modal perfects.
**Pronunciation:** Contractions.
**Before the lesson:** Write the following questions on the board:
1 *Have you ever been photobombed? What happened?*
2 *Do you retouch photos before you post them on social media?*
3 *Are you, or is anyone else you know, camera-shy?*

♪ Turn to p. 333 for notes about this song and an accompanying task.

**Warm-up** In order to review vocabulary from the last class, have sts work in pairs to discuss the questions you wrote on the board (see **Before the lesson**). Classcheck.

## 1 Listening

**A Books open.** Point to the photo and ask: *Do you know this video? Who is the artist?* Read the examples in the speech bubbles with the whole class, then have sts discuss the questions in pairs. Classcheck, and write sts' ideas on the board.

**B** Play ▶8.3 for sts to check their answers to **A**. Peercheck. Classcheck and ask: *Did you think the same? Do you think they're correct?*

▶8.3 Turn to page 320 for the complete audioscript.

> They think it could have been done with wires, magnets, real leaning, or specially engineered clothes.

**C** Tell sts that they're now going to listen to how it was actually done. Play ▶8.4 for sts to find out how the illusion was done. Peercheck. Classcheck.

▶8.4 Turn to page 320 for the complete audioscript.

> The dancers wore a special shoe, which had an opening in the heel. The opening connected to a hook on the floor of the stage. This stopped them falling down.

**D** Point to the sentences and ask if sts can remember any of the missing words. Play ▶8.4 again for sts to listen and fill the blanks. Peercheck. Classcheck. If time allows, have sts turn to the AS on p. 171 and complete the noticing activity as they listen again.

> 1 Smooth Criminal
> 2 45
> 3 special shoe
> 4 triangular, heel, hook
> 5 fell
> 6 $600,000

**E** 🟠 **Make it personal** Read the example with the class, then have sts discuss the question in pairs. Classcheck by asking sts to share any tricks they've seen.

## 2 Grammar Modal perfects

**A** ⚠️ **Common mistake** Ask sts to read the halves of dialogue from **1B** and match them, then complete the grammar box. Peercheck. Classcheck, then read the common mistake text with the class.

> a 2  b 3  c 4  d 1
> 1 past  2 past participle  3 a must have, b might have / may have, c can't have

➡️ **Grammar 8A** page 152

## 8.2

B ▶8.5 Rephrase 1–6 using past modals. Listen to check.
1 You saw David Blaine live?! I'm certain the tickets were very expensive!
   *The tickets must have been very expensive.*
2 It wasn't possible for him to know my date of birth.
3 I don't know how he did that trick. Maybe he had the ring in a secret pocket.
4 I'm 100% sure he didn't levitate.
5 The illusion didn't work properly. Perhaps he didn't practice it enough.
6 I'm certain it wasn't comfortable in that block of ice!

♪ *It must've been love, but it's over now. It must've been good, but I lost it somehow.*

### 3 Pronunciation contractions

A ▶8.6 Contractions are the norm in fast spoken English. Listen and repeat the answers in **2B** with contractions. Notice the links between *n't* and *'ve* /təv/.
   *The tickets must've been very expensive.*

B In pairs, go to ▶8.3 on p. 171 and practice reading the dialogue, changing the full forms to contractions using /mʌstəv/, /kæntəv/, and /maɪtəv/.

C In groups, speculate about events 1–6. Choose your best theory for each. Then compare with others. Who has the most interesting idea?

1 You find a wallet lying on the ground close to a gas station.
2 Your laptop is sitting open on your desk where you left it, but the screen is smashed.
3 You arrive home, and the floor is soaking wet.
4 Your classmate is wearing gloves on a hot day.
5 Your teacher has come to class wearing a dinner jacket / evening dress.
6 You arrive at work, and your boss is extremely angry.

*The driver might've put his wallet on the car roof when he was opening the door.*

*Yeah, I've done that with my phone!*

*And then he must've forgotten about it and started driving. What do you think?*

D ▶8.7 Read about two illusions. In small groups, how do you think they were done? Listen to someone describing the tricks. Did you guess correctly?

One of **David Blaine**'s first tricks to be shown on TV was levitation. Blaine positioned himself with his back to the audience, raised his arms, and to the crowd's amazement, appeared to lift off the ground at least 30 cm! He stayed there for a few seconds before returning to earth.

**David Copperfield**'s most famous trick was making the Statue of Liberty disappear. The trick was done in front of a live audience and on TV. Copperfield put a huge screen up in front of the statue. To prove it wasn't fake, the TV cameras were put in locked boxes, and a special radar screen showed the statue's position. When the screen was lowered, Lady Liberty had completely disappeared!

E ▶8.7 Listen again. T (true) or F (false)?
1 It doesn't really matter where David Blaine stands.
2 The trick is more effective in front of a large audience.
3 What Blaine wears will affect how well the trick works.
4 David Copperfield used distraction techniques.
5 The audience thought they were sitting still.
6 The trick was performed in partial darkness.

F **Make it personal** In small groups, find out how other well-known tricks or illusions are done. Describe / Mime it for the class to guess how it must have been done.

*I found a video where David Blaine pulls out a girl's teeth! Then her teeth reappear when he blows on them!*

# 8.2

**B** Read the example with the whole class, then ask sts to rephrase sentences 2–6 using modal perfects. Have sts paircheck and then listen to ▶8.5 to check their answers. Write the answers on the board as well.

> 2 He can't have known my date of birth.
> 3 He might have /may have had the ring in a secret pocket.
> 4 He can't have levitated.
> 5 He might not have practiced it enough.
> 6 It can't have been comfortable in that block of ice!

## 3 Pronunciation Contractions

**A** Say: *When we speak quickly in English, we often use contractions.* Read the example with the class, then tell sts they're going to listen to the answers in **2B** with contractions instead of full forms. Play ▶8.6 for sts to listen and repeat.

> **Language tip** To help Portuguese L1 speakers to better understand contractions in English, encourage them to think of a few examples of contractions they use in their L1 and have them identify the main differences. In Portuguese, there are quite a lot of contractions, and they're always with a preposition (+ pronouns, articles, or adverbs). By using contrastive analysis, help sts notice that in English, contractions happen with verbs, whereas in Portuguese they occur with prepositions.

**B** Refer sts to AS ▶8.3 on p. 171 and ask them to practice reading the dialogue, using contractions. Classcheck by asking a pair of sts to read it for the class.

**C** Read the example dialogue in speech bubbles with the whole class, then assign groups and have sts discuss how each situation happened. When they have finished, ask sts to compare ideas with another group. Classcheck and ask: *Who had the most interesting ideas?*

> Possible answers:
> 1 Someone might've dropped it.
> 2 Something could have fallen on it.
> 3 The washing machine might've leaked.
> 4 They might have burned their hands.
> 5 He/She might've gone to a party and stayed at a friend's house.
> 6 Someone must've made a terrible mistake.

**D** Write on the board: *David Blaine* and *David Copperfield*. Ask: *Have you heard of these people? What are they famous for? Have you seen any of their illusions?* Give sts a few minutes to read the texts, then assign groups for sts to discuss how they think they were performed. Then, play ▶8.7 for sts to check. Ask: *Did you guess correctly?*

▶8.7 Turn to page 320 for the complete audioscript.

**E** Play ▶8.7 again and have sts decide if the statements are true or false. Peercheck, then classcheck.

> 1 F  2 F  3 T  4 T  5 T  6 F

**F** 🔴 **Make it personal** Assign new groups, and have sts go online to find out about another illusion. When they are ready, ask each group to explain their illusion to the class. Ask: *How do you think it was done?* after each explanation. Then ask: *Which was the best one, do you think?*

➔ **Workbook** Page 40

## 8.3 Have you ever cut your own hair?

### 1 Listening

**A** In groups, answer 1–4. Do you all feel the same way about birthdays?
1. How do you like to celebrate your birthday?
2. What's your best birthday memory?
3. Which birthdays are significant in your country?
4. Have birthdays become too commercial?

*I like to have a special meal out, blow out my candles, then go dancing.*

**B** ▶8.8 Read the TV review. How do you think the critic rated the show? Listen and notice his tone of voice.

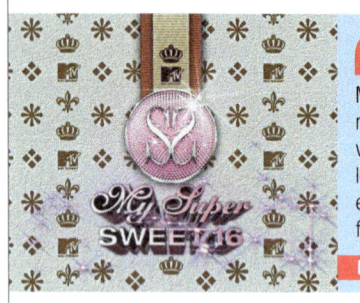

"*My Super Sweet 16* shows you all the fun, glamor, and excitement as kids prepare for their most important birthday celebration," says the MTV ad. OK. I get it. Your teenager is officially growing up. Fine. But there's nothing really sweet about *My Super Sweet 16* or *Quiero Mis Quinces*, its Latin version. Both shows are basically about a bunch of spoiled teens trying to look and act like adults as they prepare for their fifteenth or sixteenth birthday extravaganza. So don't waste your time. And be sure to keep your kids away from the TV—the show might give them some pretty expensive ideas.

BY JOEY MINOR

**C** ▶8.9 Listen to Brandon telling Courtney about his birthday party. True (T) or false (F)?
1. His party was inspired by the show.
2. His mom suggested a movie party.
3. It'll be an outdoor party.
4. He liked the suit his father bought.

*Wasn't Paris Hilton a little like that as a teen?*

**D** ▶8.10 Listen to the second part and the activities 1–6. Do you know any teens like Brandon?

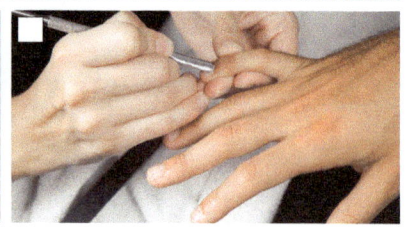

**E** ▶8.11 Match the two columns. Listen to extracts 1–6 to check.
1. Dad hired a fashion designer and
2. Your hair looks awesome! Tell me,
3. I spent four hours at the salon and
4. The pool's dirty and
5. Mom can't cook so
6. I'm exhausted!

☐ I **signed** all 200 invitations myself.
☐ we still need to have the cake **made**.
☐ we're going to have a new suit **made**.
☐ I got my nails **done**, too.
☐ Dad hasn't gotten it **cleaned** yet.
☐ did you have it **dyed**?

*Hey, Courtney, awesome news. So, I'm having a party ...*

**F** 🟠 **Make it personal** In pairs, role-play Brandon and Courtney's dialogue. Read ▶8.9 and ▶8.10 on p. 172 and use the photos in D to prepare. Do you like feeling spoiled?

# 8.3 Have you ever cut your own hair?

**Lesson Aims:** Sts learn and practice causative forms in the contexts of listening to a teenager's party preparations and talking about how self-sufficient one is at home.

**Function**
Talking about birthdays.
Reading a TV review.
Listening to a boy talk about his birthday preparations.
Talking about activities people hire others to do.

**Language**
What's the most significant birthday?
*My Super Sweet 16* shows you all the fun, glamour, and excitement …
Dad hired a fashion designer and we're going to have a new suit made.
I usually have my car washed by someone else.

**Vocabulary:** *Straighten (one's) hair, have (one's) nails done.*
**Grammar:** Causative form.

♪ Turn to p. 334 for notes about this song and an accompanying task.

**Warm-up** Ask sts to stand up and form a line according to the order of their birth month and day. Set the starting (January) and the ending point (December) of the line in the classroom. Encourage sts to mingle and ask classmates *When's your birthday?* so as to find out where they should stand in the line. Classcheck to make sure sts are in the correct order. After that, have each student pair up with the person standing next to him / her. Ask these pairs to sit together for the following activity.

## 1 Listening

**A** Books open. Ask: *Is your birthday an important date to you?* Point to questions 1–4 and have sts discuss them in pairs. Classcheck.

**B** Have sts briefly scan the text and say: *This is a TV review. What's the name of the show? How do you think the critic rated it?* Play ▶ 8.8 while sts read the text. Remind sts to pay attention to the speaker's tone of voice. Classcheck.

> The critic rated *My Super Sweet 16* in a critical way and does not recommend the TV program for teenagers.

**C** Tell sts that they are going to hear two teenagers talking to each other. Say: *Listen to Brandon telling Courtney about his birthday party.* Read sentences 1–4 with sts and ask them to write true (T) or false (F). Play ▶ 8.9. Paircheck. Classcheck.

▶ 8.9 Turn to page 320 for the complete audioscript.

> 1 T   2 F   3 T   4 F

**D** Point to the photos and say: *These activities were all in preparation for Brandon's party.* Ask: *Do you think he spent a long time planning his birthday party?* Have sts listen to the dialogue and number the photos in the order they are mentioned. Play ▶ 8.10. Replay the track if necessary. Classcheck.

▶ 8.10 Turn to page 320 for the complete audioscript.

> | 1 tailor | 4 pool |
> |---|---|
> | 2 hairdresser | 5 cake |
> | 3 manicure | 6 invitations |

**E** Read the first half of the sentence in 1 and elicit the correct ending from the second column. Instruct sts to match sentences 1–6. Play ▶ 8.11 so sts can check their answers.

> 1 Dad hired a fashion designer and we're going to have a new suit made.
> 2 Your hair looks awesome! Tell me, did you have it dyed?
> 3 I spent four hours at the salon and I got my nails done, too.
> 4 The pool's dirty and Dad hasn't gotten it cleaned yet.
> 5 Mom can't cook so we still need to have the cake made.
> 6 I'm exhausted! I signed all 200 invitations myself.

**F** 🎧 **Make it personal** Have sts change partners and prepare to role-play Brandon and Courtney's dialogue. Remind them to read AS 8.9 and 8.10 and look at the photos to help them. Monitor as they work and make notes to give feedback on their performance. Ask a confident pair of sts to perform their role play for the class then discuss the final question with the whole class. Classcheck by inviting volunteers to report their partners' answers.

217

## 2 Grammar  Causative form

**A** Read the grammar box. Then answer 1–3.

> Use **have** / **get** + object + past participle to talk about services or actions that other people do for you.
> In causatives, **have** and **get** mean the same, but **get** is more common in spoken English.
> To emphasize that you did something without help, use a *reflexive pronoun*.
> - "Where did you get your hair cut?"
> - "Oh, I cut it *myself*, actually."
> - "We couldn't get anyone to redecorate, so we did it *ourselves*."
>
> → Grammar 8B p.152

*Now he's getting a tattoo. yeah, he's getting ink done. He asked for a "13" but they drew a "31."*

1. Which preparations for the party did Brandon do himself?
2. Who did the other activities? Which do you think was the most expensive?
3. Match pictures a and b to the phrases.
   - ☐ I had my photo taken with Zac Efron.
   - ☐ I took a photo of Zac Efron.

**B** In pairs, remember the preparations for Brandon's party using the photos in **1D**. Then role-play **1D** again, switching roles. Be careful with causatives.

*I can't remember. Did he have his hair dyed, or cut, or just dried?*

**C** ▶ 8.12 Complete comments 1–5 from Brandon's very spoiled friends with the causative of these verbs. There's one extra. Listen to check. Do you know anyone like this?

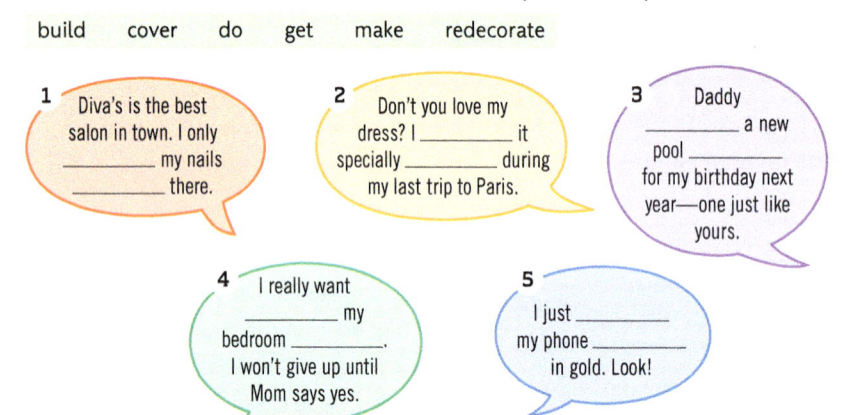

build   cover   do   get   make   redecorate

1. Diva's is the best salon in town. I only _____ my nails _____ there.
2. Don't you love my dress? I _____ it specially _____ during my last trip to Paris.
3. Daddy _____ a new pool _____ for my birthday next year—one just like yours.
4. I really want _____ my bedroom _____. I won't give up until Mom says yes.
5. I just _____ my phone _____ in gold. Look!

### Common mistakes

get my hair cut
I usually ~~cut my hair~~ at Hairway to Heaven.

have your eyes checked
Did you ~~check your eyes~~ last week?

had this tattoo done
I ~~did this tattoo~~ when I was 16.

*Could you fix a broken faucet?*

*I'd probably try to do it myself. And then get someone to do it for me!*

*Really? I don't know how to. I'd have to get it fixed.*

**D** 🟢 **Make it personal**  In groups, ask and answer to find out who's the most self-sufficent. What would be different if you had a lot more money? Who would survive best on a desert island?

### HOW SELF-SUFFICIENT ARE YOU?

Do / Could / Would you do these activities yourself?

Do / Would you get them done for you?

iron / clothes   fix / broken faucet   paint / house   build / home
change / flat tire   clean / bedroom   make / dinner   clean / windows
   wash / car   grow / food

## 2 Grammar Causative form

**A** Go over the rules in the grammar box with sts. Point to statements 1–6 in **1E** and ask: *Which activity did Brandon do (himself)?* (sign the 200 invitations). Ask: *Who did the other activities? Which do you think was the most expensive?* Then, have sts look at pictures a–b and mark the corresponding sentences in item 3. Classcheck.

> 1  Brandon signed the invitations himself.
> 2  A tailor made his suit, a hairdresser did his hair, a nail technician did his nails, a cleaner cleaned the pool, a baker made the cake.
> 3  I had my photo taken with Zac Efron: b
>    I took a photo of Zac Efron: a

Draw sts' attention to the lesson title question on the top of p. 102: *Have you ever cut your own hair?* Have sts answer in pairs. Then, write on the board: *I usually have my hair cut every two months.* Ask sts: *How often do you have your hair cut?*

→ **Grammar 8B** page 152

**Common mistakes**  Read with the whole class. For each example, ask: *Who did the action, you or someone else?*

> **Language tip**  Romance language speakers can have trouble understanding and using the causative form, because this structure doesn't exist in their L1. Before tackling the common mistakes box, ask individual sts *Who cuts your hair?* As they answer, encourage them to realize that they do not cut their own hair, so translating from their L1, where they say the equivalent to *I ~~cut my hair~~ yesterday* doesn't translate correctly into English. It should be *I had my hair cut yesterday.* Do the same with the other examples from the common mistakes box.

**B** Have sts look at the photos in **1D** and, in pairs, recall the preparations for Brandon's party, e.g. *He had his hair dyed*, *He got his nails done*, and so on.

> **Weaker classes**  Write the following prompts on the board and drill a few examples before sts begin working in pairs. Write:
> *have / hair / dye*
> *swimming pool / clean, cake / make*
> *nails / do, suit / make, sign / invitations*

Point to the first photo and ask: *What did he get done for the party?* Write on the board and drill the sentence, *He had his hair dyed.* Make sure sts understand that they need to use the past participle form of the verb and elicit more examples if necessary. Then, have sts in each pair take turns describing the preparations for Brandon's party. Classcheck.

Assign new pairs and have sts role-play **1D** again, paying attention to their use of causatives.

> He had a suit made.
> He had his hair dyed.
> He had his nails done.
> He had the pool cleaned.
> He had a cake made.

**C** Have sts complete Brandon's friends' comments with the causative form of the verbs provided. Paircheck. Classcheck with ▶ 8.12.

> 1  get / done
> 2  had / made
> 3  is going to get / built
> 4  to get / redecorated
> 5  had / covered

**D** **Make it personal**  Read the activities with sts and briefly ask if they enjoy doing them: *Do you enjoy ironing your clothes? What about washing your car?*

Divide the class into groups of three. Ask sts: *How self-sufficient are you?* Read and drill the three questions, and have two sts read the model dialogue in the speech bubbles to the whole class. Then, have sts in each group ask and answer questions and talk about the activities listed. Monitor closely for accuracy and offer help whenever necessary. Classcheck.

→ **Workbook** Page 41

## 8.4 Do you have a lot of furniture in your room?

### 1 Vocabulary Furniture

**A** ▶8.13 Listen. Which bedroom is the designer describing? Match items a–k to these words.

☐ bookcase  ☐ chair  ☐ closet  ☐ comforter  ☐ dresser
☐ double bed  ☐ lamp  ☐ mirror  ☐ nightstand  ☐ pillow  ☐ rug

**B** In pairs, use words in **A** to describe ten differences between rooms 1 and 2. If necessary, use a dictionary for the other items of furniture.

*You can see a closet in room 1, but not in room 2.*

**C** **Make it personal** Which bedroom do you prefer? Why? Is either similar to yours? What does each one tell you about its owner?

*I imagine the first one belongs to a woman because …*

### 2 Listening

**A** ▶8.14 Listen to two friends talking about the second bedroom. What has happened?

**B** ▶8.15 Listen to the second part of the dialogue. Why did they do it?

**C** ▶8.15 Listen again. Check what they have done in the room.
☐ changed the rug
☐ replaced the lamps
☐ bought a new mirror
☐ painted the walls
☐ painted some furniture
☐ bought new pillows and a new comforter
☐ had the bookcase made
☐ had the windows cleaned

> **Common mistake**
> much
> How ~~many~~ furnitures do you have?

**D** **Make it personal** In pairs, answer 1–4. Any surprises?
1. How would you feel if this were done to you?
2. Have you ever made a nice surprise for someone like this? Has anyone ever done it for you?
3. Which room in your house would you most like to change? How? Why?
4. What would your ideal bedroom look like?

*I can't stand my living room. The paint is a horrible color. I'm going to have it repainted one of these days.*

# 8.4 Do you have a lot of furniture in your room?

**Lesson Aims:** Sts look at tag questions and learn vocabulary related to furniture in the contexts of having a room redecorated and surprising a friend.

## Function
Listening to a description of a room.
Listening to friends talking about changes made in a room.
Asking and answering with tag questions.

## Language
The bureau, bedside table and wardrobe are all white.
I got some of the guys to come over and help me last weekend.
You haven't done anything crazy, have you?
He'll love it, won't he?

**Vocabulary:** Furniture (bedside table, bookcase, chair, closet, comforter, dresser, double bed, lamp, mirror, pillow, rug).
**Grammar:** Tag questions.
**Pronunciation:** Intonation in tag questions.

♪ Turn to p. 334 for notes about this song and an accompanying task.

**Warm-up** Review names for the parts of a house. Make a quick sketch on the board of a house floor plan. Alternatively, if technology is available, google images of house floor plans that show beds in the bedroom, an oven in the kitchen, and other items to elicit rooms and furniture names.

## 1 Vocabulary Furniture

**A Books closed.** Ask: *Do you have a lot of furniture in your bedroom?* Elicit or pre-teach vocabulary with simple line drawings on the board or photos from the web of bedrooms that contain pillows, a bedside table, a rug, and so on.

**Books open.** Tell sts that they are going to listen to a description of one of the bedrooms. Say: *Listen and decide which photo is being described: photo 1 or photo 2, and match the words to the photos.* Play ▶8.13. Paircheck. Classcheck.

▶8.13 Turn to page 320 for the complete audioscript.

> Bedroom 1
> a chair  b double bed  c lamp  d mirror  e closet  f dresser
> g bedside table  h pillow  i bookcase  j comforter  k rug

**Tip** Have sts turn to the AS on p. 172. Sts listen again and notice the three-syllable words.

**B** Have sts work in pairs to compare rooms 1 and 2. Encourage sts use the furniture words from **A** to describe the differences between the rooms, and to find out the vocabulary to describe other items of furniture in the rooms. Classcheck by asking each pair to contribute a sentence. Give one point for each original sentence that no other pair has come up with.

**C** 🔵 **Make it personal** In pairs, sts should discuss the questions. Refer them to the model text in the speech bubble. Classcheck sts' opinions.

## 2 Listening

**A** Tell sts that they are going to listen to two friends talking about the second bedroom. Read the question. Play ▶8.14 for sts to listen and answer the question. Classcheck

▶8.14 Turn to page 320 for the complete audioscript.

> A friend has redecorated his room mate's bedroom.

**B** Have sts listen to the rest of the dialogue. Ask: *Why did he change the room like that?* Play ▶8.15. Classcheck. Then ask: *Do you think his housemate will laugh? Will he like the changes?*

▶8.15 Turn to page 321 for the complete audioscript.

> Because Tom has been in hospital.

**C** Go over the items with the whole class. Tell sts that they are going to listen to the dialogue again and check what they've done. Play ▶8.15 again. Paircheck. Replay ▶8.15 if necessary. If time allows, have sts turn to the AS on p. 172. Sts listen again and notice the intonation. Classcheck.

> changed the rug
> painted the walls
> painted some furniture
> had the bookcase made

**D** 🔵 **Make it personal** Have sts change partners. Ask them to take turns asking and answering questions 1–4 in their new pairs. Classcheck by having each student report his / her partner's answers to the whole group.

## 3 Grammar  Tag questions

*Well, I've heard there was a secret chord
That David played and it pleased the Lord
But you don't really care for music, do you?*

**A** ▶8.16 Listen to the extracts and complete 1–6 with these phrases. There's one extra.

did you?   don't you?   hasn't it?   isn't it?   was it?   won't he?   have you?

1 You haven't done anything crazy, _____?
2 It's great, _____?
3 He'll love it, _____?
4 You didn't do it all yourself, _____?
5 That rug wasn't there before, _____?
6 You know he's going to be over the moon, _____?

**B** Look at **A** and complete rules 1–5 in the grammar box with these words.

negative   ask for agreement   positive
check information   do   statement   verb

1 Use a tag question to _____ or _____.
2 A tag question goes at the end of a _____.
3 Use the same auxiliary _____ and tense in the tag question as the statement.
4 In statements without an auxiliary verb, use _____ in the tag question.
5 With + statements, use a _____ tag. With − statements, use a _____.

➔ Grammar 8C p.152

**Common mistakes**

Your dad loves tennis, ~~no~~? *doesn't he*
You're not hungry again already, ~~do~~ you?
You were here yesterday, ~~was~~ you? *are* *weren't*

## 4 Pronunciation  Intonation in tag questions

**A** ▶8.16 Read the information, then listen again and mark ↗ or ↘ in **3A**.

Tag questions can have two different functions depending on your intonation.
Rising ↗ intonation is usually a real question. It means "I'm not sure, so I'm checking."
Falling ↘ intonation is more like a statement. It means "I'm not really asking. I just want you to agree."

**B** ▶8.17 Listen to Tom's reaction. How many tag questions do you hear? Did he get upset?

**C** ▶8.17 In pairs, try to complete 1–4. Listen again to check.
1 But _____ you'd be discharged tomorrow, _____?
2 You _____ about doing this, _____?
3 You _____ serious, _____?
4 That's the rug _____ in the department store, _____?

**D** Complete 1–4 with tag questions and select the best answer for you.

1 You really like **action movies**, _____?
  a Yeah, I love them.
  b They're OK, I guess.
  c Actually, I hate them.

2 You're **from the capital**, _____?
  a Uh-huh.
  b How could you tell?
  c Nope.

3 You've never **been to the U.S.**, _____?
  a No, never.
  b No, but I'd love to.
  c Yes, I have.

4 You didn't **go out last night**, _____?
  a No, I didn't.
  b I did, actually.
  c Why do you ask?

**E** 🎯 **Make it personal**  Replace the **bold** words in **D** with your own ideas. In pairs, ask and answer. Vary the verbs / tenses, and add follow-up questions. Share your best exchange with the class.

*You really like baseball, don't you?*   *It's OK, I guess, but I prefer basketball.*   *Why's that then?*

## 3 Grammar  Tag questions

**A** Have sts look at the tag questions and read the sentences briefly. Play ▶8.16 as sts listen and fill in the blanks with the tag questions provided. Classcheck.

| 1 have you? | 4 did you? |
|---|---|
| 2 isn't it? | 5 was it? |
| 3 won't he? | 6 don't you? |

**Language tip** Romance language speakers may have problems forming tag questions. For example, in Portuguese and Spanish there are no auxiliary verbs, so although these languages have their equivalent to tag questions, they are not formed with an auxiliary verb. In order to ask tag questions in Portuguese or Spanish, speakers of these languages use the main verb, or sometimes other words, like *né* in Portuguese, for example, or the equivalent to *yes* or *no*. After section 4 (Pronunciation), have sts go back to **3A** and, in pairs, take turns saying extracts 1–6 to their partner for them to say the equivalent in their L1. Encourage them to also notice the rising and falling intonation in their L1 and compare it to the English equivalent.

**B** Ask sts to study the sentences in **A** and complete the rules in the grammar box. Paircheck. Classcheck.

1. check information, ask for agreement
2. statement
3. verb
4. do
5. negative, positive

➔ **Grammar 8C** page 152

## 4 Pronunciation  Intonation in tag questions

**A** Go over the information in the text with the whole class. Explain that the same tag question can have different intonations depending on the speaker's intention.

Play ▶8.16 again and ask sts to mark each of the tags in **3A** with arrows. Peercheck. Classcheck and ask: *How sure is each person?*

**B** Tell sts that they are going to hear Tom's reaction when he returns home and sees his new bedroom. Read the questions with sts. Play ▶8.17. Paircheck. Replay ▶8.17 if necessary. Classcheck.

▶8.17 Turn to page 321 for the complete audioscript.

Four tag questions. No, he didn't.

**C** Ask sts to work in pairs and complete the tag questions from memory. Then, play ▶8.17 again so sts can check their answers. If time allows, have sts turn to the AS on p. 172 to notice the intonation as they listen. Classcheck.

1. But you said you'd be discharged tomorrow, didn't you?
2. You've been thinking about doing this, haven't you?
3. You aren't serious, are you?
4. That's the rug I saw in the department store, isn't it?

**D** Have sts fill in the blanks in questions 1–4 with the correct tag questions and then answer the questions about themselves. Classcheck.

| 1 don't you? | 3 have you? |
|---|---|
| 2 aren't you? | 4 did you? |

**E** ● **Make it personal**  Tell sts to transform 1–4 in **D** into original questions by replacing the words in bold with their own ideas, e.g., *You really like baseball, don't you?* Tell them they can also change positive sentences to negative, e.g. *You don't really like …, do you?*

Pair sts up and have them take turns asking and answering the questions they came up with. Encourage sts to use a variety of verbs / tenses and to ask follow-up questions, too. Classcheck by having each student report his / her partner's answers.

**Tip** If time allows, have all sts stand up and mingle, asking their questions to as many classmates as possible. Classcheck and ask if there were any similar answers.

➔ **Workbook** Page 42

# 8.5 Is your listening improving?

## Skills Predicting

**A** In pairs, compare the logo makeovers. Do you prefer the old or the new versions?

*I prefer the old iTunes logo.*  *I don't know. I kind of like the new one.*

Old / New

*My guess is they won't mention ...*

**Common mistakes**

~~they won't~~
~~I guess they're not going to~~ mention why.
Use *will* when it's just a guess / there's no evidence.

~~it's going to~~
Look at those clouds – ~~it'll rain.~~
Use *going to* when it's probable / there's clear evidence.

**B** ▶8.18 In pairs, guess what will not be discussed in a college lecture on logo makeover, and why. Listen to check. Were you right?

☐ why the logos changed    ☐ consumers' reactions    ☐ the cost involved

**C** ▶8.19 Read about predicting. Then look at 1–6, listen to the second part, and predict what the lecturer will say after each beep.

> Predicting what the speaker is about to say is a very useful listening strategy. Here are three clues to listen for:
> 1 Use of adverbs:
>   Dad was rushed to the hospital. <u>Fortunately</u> ... — You know it's good news.
> 2 Use of linking words:
>   The economy was good last year. <u>However</u> ... — You know it's a contrast.
>   Electric cars are greener. <u>In addition</u> ... — You know it's another point.
> 3 Intonation:
>   "Would I like to live abroad?" "Hmm ..." ↘ — You know the answer is probably no.

**Instagram**
1 She'll mention something **positive / negative**.
2 She'll talk about **original / new** users.
3 She **likes / doesn't like** the logo transformation.

**Starbucks**
4 Customers **liked / didn't like** the new logo.
5 She'll give **her opinion / a suggestion**.
6 She'll **explain what she said / make a new point**.

**D** ▶8.20 In pairs, predict what happened to the Gap logo transformation. Use these questions. Listen to check.
1 How old was the logo?
2 How did people react?
3 Why did Gap want to change it?
4 What happened to the company president?

**E** ▶8.21 Predict how many words you will hear in gaps 1–3. Contractions count as two words. Listen to check. Order the four logos from most to least successful.
1 To mark the occasion, _____ thought: "Hey, let's create a new logo and drop the words 'Starbucks Coffee'."
2 However, Instagram was trying to attract new users—you know, people _____ visited the site before.
3 They _____ create something modern and contemporary, but, boy, were they wrong.

# 8.5 Is your listening improving?

**Lesson Aims:** Sts predict information in listening activities via the context of talking about famous logos.

**Function**
Comparing old and new logos.
Listening to and predicting information.

**Language**
The new iTunes logo is weird, isn't it?
She'll mention something negative.
She'll talk about new users.

**Vocabulary:** College lecture, fortunately, however, in addition, logo, makeover.
**Skills:** Predicting.

**Warm-up** For a high-energy start, begin the class with rousing drills. Follow the model below. Alternate between choral and individual repetition.

T   *You haven't done anything crazy. – You haven't done anything crazy, have you? Repeat.*
Sts You haven't done anything crazy, have you?
T   *You really like going to the beach. – You really like going to the beach, don't you? Repeat.*
Sts You really like going to the beach, don't you?
T   *Now you. You're from San Francisco.*
Sts You're from San Francisco, aren't you?
T   *You didn't start learning English this year.*
Sts You didn't start learning English this year, did you?
T   *She's from London.*
Sts She's from London, isn't she?

**Stronger classes** Signal or prompt rising intonation (thumbs up) or falling intonation (thumbs down) for each tag question.

## 1D Skills Predicting

**A Books open**. Point to the old and new logos and have two sts read the model dialogue in the speech bubbles. Pair sts up and have them look at the changes made to the logos in the chart and discuss which ones they prefer. Classcheck, then ask sts if they can think of any other logos that have changed recently.

**B** Tell sts that they are going to hear the beginning of a college lecture about logo makeovers. Ask: *Which of these topics do you think will not be discussed?* Read topics with sts and play ▶8.18 as they listen and decide which topic is missing. Classcheck.

▶**8.18** Turn to page 321 for the complete audioscript.

> The cost involved

**C** Go over the information about predicting with the whole class. Then, tell sts that they are going to make predictions as they listen to someone lecturing about Instagram's and Starbucks' logos. Read sentence 1 with the class. Play ▶8.19 and pause when you hear the first beep. Then ask: *Will she mention something positive or negative?* Have sts underline their guesses. Resume ▶8.19 so sts can check their answers. Repeat the procedure for sentences 2–6, pausing the track at each beep. Sts can also check answers by turning to the AS on p. 172. Classcheck.

▶**8.19** Turn to page 321 for the complete audioscript.

| | | | |
|---|---|---|---|
| 1 | negative | 4 | didn't like |
| 2 | new | 5 | her opinion |
| 3 | doesn't like | 6 | explain what she said |

**Common mistakes** Read with the whole class. Draw sts' attention to the difference between a prediction with evidence and a prediction without evidence.

**D** Ask: *Do you know the clothes company called Gap?* Tell sts that this company's logo changed as well. Point to the phrases and have sts work in pairs to guess the story based on these phrases. Classcheck sts' guesses. Play ▶8.20 to check.

▶**8.20** Turn to page 321 for the complete audioscript.

> 1 It was about 20 years old.
> 2 They wanted to create something modern and contemporary.
> 3 They hated it.
> 4 The president of the company was fired.

**E** Read sentence 1 and elicit predictions by asking: *How many words are missing in this blank?* Have sts guess the number of words missing in the blanks in 1–3. Play ▶8.21 so sts can check their answers. Replay the track if necessary.

> 1 they must've
> 2 who might've never
> 3 must've tried to

# What's the hardest part of language learning?

## ID in Action  Expressing preferences

**A** *Logo Game!* Draw an authentic logo for 1–6. Compare in small groups. How many are the same? Score one point for each unique logo. Who's the class "Picasso"?

> Awesome! I didn't know you could draw so well.

| 1 a sports clothing company | 3 a car manufacturer | 5 a TV channel |
| 2 a fast food chain | 4 a tech company | 6 a fashion label |

**B** In pairs, think of two companies for categories 1–6 in **A** and answer 1–3.
1. Which has a simpler logo?
2. Which is more famous? Does the logo help?
3. Do you prefer one company over the other? Why (not)?

> I prefer Ray-Ban. Their designs are cooler.

**C** ▶ 8.22 Listen to two students leaving the lecture on logos on p. 106. Which logo(s) do they both like?

**D** ▶ 8.22 Try to remember the missing words. Listen again to check.

1. I love this class. It's really _interesting_.
2. Which one do you like _____?
3. _____ are OK, I guess.
4. I think I like the old one better _____ the new one.
5. I don't really like _____ of them.
6. I actually prefer the second one _____ the first.

### Common mistakes

~~more~~ better
I like ~~more~~ grammar than pronunciation.

~~than~~ to
I prefer English ~~than~~ French.

~~is~~ are
I think both channels ~~is~~ great. (both = they)

~~both~~ either
Pizza or pasta? I don't want ~~both~~ for lunch.

**E** Study *Common mistakes*, then correct 1–4. Do you agree with these opinions?
1. Both Facebook and Twitter has good logos, I think.
2. I like Chrome best than Safari.
3. Beyoncé or Shakira? Hmm … I don't like both of them.
4. I prefer cats than dogs. Actually, I can't stand dogs.

> Let's see … First one … Yeah, I think so. I mean, they're so recognizable.

**F** Make it personal  *English-learning preferences.* Interview three students and check (✓) their preferences. Use these words to help.

> Which one are you better at: grammar or vocabulary?

easy   fun   good at   helpful   irritating   useful

| Learner profile | 1 | 2 | 3 |
| --- | --- | --- | --- |
| grammar OR vocabulary | | | |
| listening OR reading | | | |

| Learner profile | 1 | 2 | 3 |
| --- | --- | --- | --- |
| pair work OR individual work | | | |
| speaking freely OR being corrected | | | |

**G** Make it personal  Report back to the class. Any major differences?

> Two people in my group prefer grammar to vocabulary.

> Well, here everybody likes vocabulary better.

♪ I know someday you'll have a beautiful life,
I know you'll be a star
In somebody else's sky,
But why can't it be mine?

## 8.5 What's the hardest part of language learning?

**Lesson Aims:** Sts learn and practice how to express preferences about English learning experiences.

**Function**
Comparing brands.
Talking about English learning preferences.

**Language**
I prefer Ray-Ban. Their designs are cooler.
Which one are you better at: grammar or vocabulary?

**Vocabulary:** Expressing preferences *(prefer (something) to, like (something) better, both, either).*
**Skills:** Expressing preferences.

### ID in Action  Expressing preferences

**A** Tell sts that they are going to play **Logo Game!** Have sts draw one logo in each of the categories 1–6.

Divide the class into groups of five and have sts within each group compare their logos to see if any are the same. Explain that sts score a point for each unique drawing. At the end, ask: *Who's the class Picasso?*

**B** Point to 1 in **A** and elicit the names of two actual sports clothing companies, e.g. Nike and Adidas. Have sts write these down and continue their list by adding two examples of real companies for each of the categories 2–6. Read the example with sts, then ask them to answer questions 1–3 about the companies they listed. Classcheck.

**C** Ask: *Do you remember the college lecture on page 106?* Say: *We're going to listen to two students who have just attended the lecture. Let's hear what they say about it.* Play ▶ 8.22 and have sts listen to find out which logo both speakers like. Paircheck. Replay the track if necessary. Classcheck.

▶ 8.22 Turn to page 321 for the complete audioscript.

🔑 The old Gap logo

**D** Have sts try to fill in the blanks for sentences 2–6 from memory. Replay ▶ 8.22 so they can check their answers. Classcheck.

🔑
1 interesting  2 better  3 Both  4 than  5 either  6 to

**E** **Common mistakes**  Go over with the whole class then have sts correct sentences 1–4. Paircheck. Classcheck. Then, have sts change partners. Ask: *Do you agree with these opinions?* Have the new pairs look at 1–4 again and discuss ideas with their partners. Classcheck.

🔑
1 Both Facebook and Twitter **have** good logos, I think.
2 I like Chrome **better** than Safari.
3 Beyoncé or Shakira? Hmm … I don't like **either** of them.
4 I prefer cats **to** dogs. Actually, I can't stand dogs.

**Language tip** Romance language speakers frequently make the first two mistakes in the common mistakes box as a result of direct translation. Make sure sts understand that we don't say ~~we like one thing more than the other~~, we say that *we like one thing better than the other*. Give them options to compare using this structure. For example: Italian / Japanese food; sports cars / SUVs; etc. When analyzing the second mistake, point out that, although we used *than* in the previous structure when expressing preferences, we don't use it when using the verb *prefer* to express preferences between two or more things, we use *to*. Give them some more examples of things for them to compare in pairs, using this second structure, with the verb *prefer*.

**F** **Make it personal**  Go over the chart and the model question with the whole class. Drill possible questions sts can use to elicit information for items 1–4, e.g., *Which one are you better at …? Which one do you prefer …?* Tell sts that their answers should include the words from the box.

Have sts work in groups of four, so they have three classmates to interview. Monitor and offer help if necessary.

**Tip** Alternatively, ask all sts to stand up and mingle with their classmates until they have interviewed three classmates.

**G** **Make it personal**  Divide the class into groups of four. Have sts work in their new groups to compare their findings from **F** using the notes they have written down on their charts. Classcheck.

🎵 Turn to p. 334 for notes about this song and an accompanying task.

➡ **Workbook** Page 43

➡ **ID Richmond Learning Platform**

➡ **Writing** p. 108

➡ **ID Café** p. 109

# Writing 8  An opinion essay

*♪ 'Cause all of me loves all of you.
Love your curves and all your edges,
all your perfect imperfections.*

**A** Read Damir's opinion essay and check the best title for it.
☐ Beauty in the media   ☐ Beauty: the good and bad sides   ☐ Five steps to being more attractive

<mark>It is usually said that</mark> beauty is hard to define. At the same time, being beautiful, or at least being worried about the way you look, has become increasingly important in our society. Is this positive or are people getting obsessed with appearance?

<mark>On the one hand</mark>, taking care of your appearance has many advantages. In general, this leads both men and women to become more interested in a healthier lifestyle. <mark>For instance</mark>, they try to exercise and adopt better eating habits. All this, of course, has a positive effect on looks. <mark>In addition</mark>, these days it is much easier and cheaper to have beauty treatments that can boost your self-esteem and therefore make you feel happier.

<mark>On the other hand</mark>, some people are fanatical about having wonderful hair, the thinnest body, and the most attractive face. Many end up wasting a small fortune trying to do so. This false concept of perfection is usually imposed by the media, which makes us want to look like actors, sports stars, or supermodels. This image, of course, is not realistic for most people. <mark>So</mark>, the desire to look absolutely gorgeous can lead to stress, eating disorders, and even serious illness.

<mark>To summarize</mark>, I strongly believe that emphasizing perfection and physical attractiveness at all costs has extremely negative effects. It would be much better if people were more concerned about feeling good and taking care of their health.

**B** Which of structures 1–3 does Damir use to organize his opinion essay?
1  introduction + argument(s) for or against only + conclusion
2  introduction + one argument for + several arguments against + conclusion
3  introduction + argument(s) for + argument(s) against + conclusion

**C** Read *Write it right!* and match 1–6 to the <mark>highlighted</mark> conjunctions in the text.
1  Introducing arguments   4  Exemplifying
2  Contrasting             5  Summarizing
3  Adding                  6  Expressing consequences

### ● Write it right!

In opinion essays, use a variety of conjunctions to organize and contrast your arguments.
- It's important to take care of your appearance. <mark>However</mark>, you should not become obsessed.
- <mark>Even though</mark> mass media, <mark>like</mark> TV, are important, they also have a negative influence, <mark>so</mark> be selective and don't just follow what others do.

Some conjunctions are followed by commas.
- However, / In addition to that, / Therefore,
Some mean the same.
- <mark>Although / Even though</mark> she looked great, she had plastic surgery.
- <mark>Despite</mark> his doctor's recommendations, he went on a radical diet.

**D** Match 1–5 to an equivalent expression.
1  It is usually said that     ☐ Moreover
2  So                          ☐ In short
3  For instance                ☐ Therefore
4  In addition                 ☐ For example
5  To summarize                ☐ People believe that

**E** Circle the correct option (a or b). Sometimes both options are correct (c).
1  _____ some models are dangerously thin, fashion magazines still use them.
   a Although      b However      c both
2  Fruit and vegetables are healthy. _____, they're sometimes cheaper than processed food.
   a In addition   b Moreover     c both
3  Doing aerobic exercises, _____ cycling and swimming, helps you stay in shape.
   a such as       b like         c both
4  Some people follow ridiculous diets. _____ they can get sick.
   a Therefore     b Although     c both
5  _____, feeling healthy is more important than being attractive.
   a To summarize  b In conclusion c both

**F** *Your turn!* Write an essay in 120–180 words entitled *You have to spend a lot of money to stay fit and healthy*.

| **Before** | Note some arguments for and against. Choose a structure from **B** and organize your notes. |
|---|---|
| **While** | Write four paragraphs following the tips in *Write it right!* Try not to repeat any conjunctions. If you're writing on a computer, turn spell check off. |
| **After** | Ask a colleague to check spelling and formality or turn spell check on and see how many words you got wrong. Check conjunctions and punctuation before sending it to your teacher. |

# Writing 8  An opinion essay

🎵 Turn to p. 334 for notes about this song and an accompanying task.

**A** Have sts look at Damir's essay. Ask: *How many paragraphs can you see? Is this essay written in a formal or an informal style?*

Point to the three title options. Ask: *What's the best title for Damir's essay?* Have sts read the titles and choose the best one. Paircheck. Classcheck.

🗝 Beauty: the good and bad sides

**B** Refer to Damir's essay in **A** and ask: *How did Damir organize his text?* Point to structures 1–3 and have sts choose the text organization Damir used. Paircheck. Classcheck.

🗝 structure 3

**C** Read **Write it right!** with the whole class. Then, draw sts' attention to the highlighted conjunctions in the model essay in **A** and ask sts to match the conjunctions to items 1–6. Paircheck. Classcheck.

🗝
1   It is usually said that; On the one hand
2   On the other hand
3   In addition
4   For instance
5   To sum up
6   Consequently

**D** Have sts match phrases 1–5 to the equivalent conjunctions in the right column. Paircheck. Classcheck by writing the answers on the board.

🗝
1   People believe that
2   Therefore
3   For example
4   Moreover
5   In short

**E** Ask sts to choose the correct option for each statement. Paircheck. Classcheck.

🗝
1 a   2 c   3 c   4 a   5 c

**F** *Your turn!*

**Before** Write the essay title on the board: *You have to spend a lot of money to stay fit and healthy.* Ask the whole class: *Do you agree?* Have sts discuss the statement in pairs for about two minutes. Then, classcheck sts' opinions. Ask sts to make their own notes of arguments for and against the statement in the essay title. Tell sts to use one of the structures in **B** to organize their text.

**While** Have sts write a four-paragraph essay of 120–180 words. Remind them to follow the tips from **Write it right!** and to avoid repeating conjunctions, varying them as much as possible.

Tip  If you are assigning the essay for homework, advise sts to turn off the spell check on their computers while they write.

**After** If sts are writing their essays in class, have them exchange essays for peer checking. If they are writing their essays at home on a computer, they should now turn on spell check to see how many words they misspelled. Have sts check the variety of conjunctions before handing in their essays.

# 8 Small talk and smart phones  ID Café

## 1 Before watching

**A** Match the get phrases to their meanings.

1. have a manicure
2. have a pedicure
3. permit someone a luxury
4. visit a barber / stylist
5. have your car serviced
6. complete a project
7. have a "2 for 1"

a. get two things (done) for the price of one
b. get something difficult done
c. get your fingernails done
d. get your hair done
e. get a tune up
f. get / be pampered (a spa day, a special dessert)

**B** ⚫ Make it personal  Which of 1–7 in **A** have you done recently? How is / was your experience?

> *I got a pedicure done once. Never again! It really hurts.*

> *I love being pampered. I get my nails done every week.*

**C** Look at the photo. Guess five phrases from **A** you think you will hear.

## 2 While watching

**A** Watch up to 2:06 to check. What else did you pick up?

**B** Watch the video and complete 1–6 with the correct form of *get* or *get* + past participle. Watch again to check. Who said 1–6? What else did you hear?

1. You had to _____ that video _____.
2. It wasn't easy _____ all those martial arts shots.
3. This is heaven. I love _____ my nails _____.
4. I'm going to _____ my hair _____.
5. I should have _____ a tune-up long ago.
6. We never _____ to talk the other night!

**C** Watch the rest. How many voicemail messages are there? What good news does each of them get?

**D** Order the events 1–6. Watch again from 2:06 to check.
- [ ] Dr Moreno calls Zoey about her job application.
- [ ] Genevieve submitted a song for Daniel's TV show.
- [ ] Lucy changes her mind.
- [ ] Lucy says she doesn't want to ruin her nails.
- [ ] They all find out they got the jobs they applied for.
- [ ] Zoey and Genevieve listen to their messages.

**E** ⚫ Make it personal  Do you still use voicemail? How often do you a) put off answering messages immediately? b) use flight mode? c) switch your phone off completely?

> *I sometimes put off difficult messages.*

## 3 After watching

**A** True (T) or false (F)? Correct the false statements.

1. Lucy took Genevieve to a spa to thank her for her help.
2. Andrea and Paolo obviously don't like each other.
3. Zoey comes to the spa for a "two-for-one."
4. Genevieve put off getting a tune-up and got stranded at the mechanic's.
5. Zoey got a call about a job in the History department.
6. Lucy didn't want to answer her phone because she'd just gotten her nails done.

**B** Match 1–8 to their meanings a–h.

1. I owe you one.
2. They had on-camera chemistry.
3. That's putting it mildly.
4. It was a total disaster.
5. I should've gotten a tune-up.
6. I kept putting it off.
7. I ended up paying an arm and a leg.
8. It went from bad to worse.

a. ☐ Everything went wrong.
b. ☐ I delayed doing it.
c. ☐ I spent too much money.
d. ☐ It needed to be checked and fixed.
e. ☐ It's not an exaggeration.
f. ☐ They seem compatible on screen.
g. ☐ It's my turn to help you.
h. ☐ It started bad then became horrible.

**C** *Role-play.* In threes, create a "salon dialogue". Include at least two phrases from **1A** and **3B**. Role-play it for the class to spot which phrases you use.

> *Hi, Ale. What are you doing here?*  *I'm getting my …*

109

# Café 8  Small talk and smart phones

## 1  Before watching

**A** Read item 1 with students (have a manicure) and elicit the correct meaning from phrases a–f. Have sts match the remaining items to their meanings. Peercheck. Classcheck.

**B** **Make it personal**  Ask: *Do you get these services done? Have you ever gotten them done?* Invite two volunteers to read the model dialogue in the speech bubbles. Have sts work in pairs to talk about activities 1–7 in **A**. Monitor sts' discussions closely and correct any mistakes on the spot. Classcheck.

**C** Have sts look at the photo from the video in **2A**. Say: *Where do you think these women are? What do you think they're going to do?* Ask which phrases from **1A** they think they will hear. Classcheck but don't confirm answers at this stage.

## 2  While watching

**A** Elicit the names of the characters in the picture (Genevieve, Lucy, Zoey). Tell sts that the characters are at a beauty salon. Play ▶ 8 up until 2:06 for sts to watch and check their answers to **1C**.

**B** Have sts quickly read statements 1–6, and ask them to fill in each blank with the correct form of either *get* or *get* + past participle. Play ▶ 8 so sts can check their answers. Paircheck. Classcheck.

> 1 get / done (Genevieve)
> 2 getting (Lucy)
> 3 getting / done (Lucy)
> 4 get / done (Zoey)
> 5 got (Genevieve)
> 6 got (Genevieve)

**C** Play the whole video and ask sts to listen to answer the questions. Peercheck. Classcheck.

> Three messages—they all find out they got the jobs they applied for.

**D** Replay ▶ 8 and ask sts to order events 1–6 in the order in which they appear in the video. Paircheck. Classcheck by writing the answers on the board.

> 2, 1, 4, 3, 6, 5

**E** **Make it personal**  Have sts change partners and work in their new pairs to answer the questions about cell phone useage. Classcheck.

## 3  After watching

**A** Tell sts to read statements 1–6 and mark each one true (T) or false (F) then have them correct the false statements. Paircheck. If time allows, replay ▶ 8 so sts can check their answers. Classcheck.

> 1 T
> 2 F
> 3 T
> 4 T
> 5 F
> 6 T

**B** Have sts match sentences 1–8 to the correct meanings a–h. Paircheck. Classcheck.

> 1 g  2 f  3 e  4 a  5 d  6 b  7 c  8 h

**C** **Role-play**. Tell sts to work collaboratively in threes to create a salon dialogue. Explain that sts' dialogues should include at least two of the phrases in **1A** and **3B**. Monitor pairs' work and offer help if necessary. Then, have partners role-play their dialogues. At the end, invite volunteer pairs to act out their dialogues for the whole class.

# R4 Grammar and Vocabulary

**A** *Picture dictionary.* Cover the words and definitions on the pages below and remember.

| pages | |
|---|---|
| 87 | 8 phrasal verbs |
| 88 | 5 common objects |
| 89 | 4 reported speech stories |
| 97 | 5 transportation words |
| 99 | 7 photography words |
| 102 | 6 party preparations |
| 104 | 11 bedroom items |
| 161 | 2 words for each sound in lines 3 and 4 of the consonants chart (not the picture words) |

**B** In pairs, describe Sam Soccer's pre-match ritual. Which action is different? Why?

*OK, so he has his uniform dry-cleaned before each match.*

uniform / dry-clean

cleats / check

hair / cut and dye

photo / take

**C** *Role-play.* A: Interview Sam about his game day ritual. B: You're Sam. Be creative!

*So, Sam. On game days, what time do you get up?*

*Well, for away games we normally sleep in a hotel. We get woken up at …*

**D** ▶R4.1 Listen to the three tongue twisters. Which underlined ending is different? Listen again and practice saying the twisters.

1 a ask<u>ed</u>  b park<u>ed</u>  c start<u>ed</u>
2 a a<u>cc</u>use  b a<u>cc</u>ident  c e<u>xc</u>uses
3 a a<u>cc</u>elerate  b a<u>cc</u>ommodate  c e<u>x</u>periment

**E** ▶R4.2 Order the words in 1–7 to make sentences. Add the correct punctuation.

1 you / this / works / show / Can / how / me / phone / ?
2 you / this / stops / know / Do / where / bus / ?
3 I / if / tomorrow / it / will / wonder / rain
4 take / sugar / you / don't / milk / You / and / do / ?
5 forget / email / won't / will / You / to / you / send / that / ?
6 this / for / you / tell / me / Could / what / cable / is / ?
7 you / off / know / turn / Do / to / this / how / machine / ?

**F** In pairs, imagine what five pieces of news the people in photos 1 and 2 could have just received.

*He might have gotten a message from an old girlfriend.*

**G** In pairs, plan a surprise birthday party for a friend. Discuss what you need to do / have done and who is doing what.

*Are we going to make a cake?*

*No, let's have one made.*

**H** Correct the mistakes in each sentence. Check your answers in units 7 and 8. What's your score, 1–10?

**Common mistakes**

1 I asked to you don't turn on it. (3 mistakes)
2 Why you didn't say me hello? (2 mistakes)
3 Could you tell to me what does it say? (2 mistakes)
4 Do you know where is mall? (2 mistakes)
5 It depend of many things. (2 mistakes)
6 I don't know where is he. He might went to work. (2 mistakes)
7 I painted my nails at the salon. Don't they look great? (2 mistakes)
8 You should to cut on down screen time. (2 mistakes)
9 He likes more the cars than the motorbikes. (2 mistakes)
10 "I prefer rock than pop." "Really? I don't like both." (2 mistakes)

# Review 8 Units 7-8

## Grammar and vocabulary

♪ Turn to p. 334 for notes about this song and an accompanying task.

**A** **Picture dictionary.** Pair sts up and have partners test each other and review the vocabulary in units 7 and 8. Monitor and correct vocabulary and pronunciation on the spot.

**Tip** In order to provide sts with as much fluency practice as possible, expand the activity into the mini-dialogues suggested below.

| Picture Dictionary | Procedures | Mini-dialogues / Suggested language |
|---|---|---|
| 5 common objects, p. 88 | Have sts hide the text in **1C** with a notebook or a sheet of paper and look only at pictures a–e. Ask sts to work in pairs to test each other on the five common objects shown in the pictures. | St A: (points to picture a) *What are these?*<br>St B: *They're fake watches or goods.* (points to picture b) *What's letter b?*<br>St A: *That's a computer keyboard.* (points to picture …) |
| 6 party preparations, p. 102 | Tell sts to cover the statements in **1E** with a notebook or a sheet of paper and, in pairs, try to recall the party preparations from pictures 1–6. | St A: (points to the first picture) *Have your hair straightened.*<br>St B: (points to the second picture) *Have the pool cleaned.* |

**B** Ask sts: *Are you superstitious?* Say: *Look at Sam Soccer. He's a soccer player and has a pre-match ritual.* Have a student read the model text in the speech bubble to the whole class.

Ask: *Which activity did he do by himself?* Have sts say each step of Sam Soccer's ritual using the prompts. Classcheck.

> He has his uniform dry-cleaned.
> He has his cleats checked.
> He has his photo taken.
> The different action is: He cuts and dyes his (own) hair.

**C** **Role-play.** Have sts change partners. Tell them that they are going to role-play an interview with Sam Soccer. Refer sts to the model dialogue in the speech bubbles. Monitor and take notes for further correction. At the end, invite a volunteer pair to act out the interview for the whole class. Then, provide language feedback.

**D** To convey the concept of a tongue twister, write a model on the board: *She sells seashells by the seashore.* Challenge sts to say it as fast as they can. Draw sts' attention to the underlined ending in item 1 and ask: *Which sound is different: a, b, or c?* Have sts listen and check as you play the first sentence of ▶R4.1. Classcheck. Play the rest of ▶R4.1 and have sts choose the different sound in sentences 2–3. Paircheck. Classcheck. Replay ▶R4.1 and have sts practice saying the tongue twisters in pairs.

▶R4.1 Turn to page 341 for the complete audioscript.

> 1 started   2 accuse   3 accommodate

**E** Have sts reorder the words to make sentences adding punctuation marks where appropriate. Paircheck. Classcheck.

> 1 Can you show me how this phone works?
> 2 Do you know where this bus stops?
> 3 I wonder if it will rain tomorrow.
> 4 You don't take sugar and milk, do you?
> 5 You won't remember to send that email, will you?
> 6 Could you tell me what this cable is for?
> 7 Do you know how to turn off this machine?

**F** Have sts work in pairs to guess what news the people in photos 1–2 have just received. Refer sts to the model in the speech bubble before they begin. Classcheck sts' guesses.

**G** Sts work in pairs to plan a surprise birthday party for a friend. Monitor and offer help if necessary. Classcheck by inviting volunteer pairs to perform their dialogues for the whole class.

**H** **Common mistakes** Ask sts to correct sentences 1–10. Encourage sts to flip back through p. 72–91 and check their answers in units 7 and 8. Classcheck.

> 1 I asked you not to turn it on.
> 2 Why didn't you say hello to me?
> 3 Could you tell me what it says?
> 4 Do you know where the mall is?
> 5 It depends on many things.
> 6 I don't know where he is. He might've gone to work.
> 7 I had my nails done at the salon. Don't they look great?
> 8 You should cut down on screen time.
> 9 He likes cars more than motorbikes.
> 10 "I prefer rock to pop." "Really? I don't like either."

# Skills practice

**R4**

♪ *I wonder, when I sing along with you, if everything could ever feel this real forever, if anything could ever be this good again.*

**A** Quickly reread the Photoshop text on p. 98. Then listen to ▶ 8.1, pausing every 12 seconds to write down the last five words you hear. Then reread to check.

**B** ▶ R4.3 Listen to five extracts from ⓘ 3 and count the words in each. Contractions count as one word.

**C** ▶ R4.3 Listen again and write the full extract. Check in pairs. Which words are hardest to understand?

**D** List eight electronic items you own. Order them from the most to the least important. In pairs, compare and explain.

> *I couldn't live without my refrigerator. It's too hot here not to have cold drinks.*

**E** In pairs, think of three things each person could be saying. Share the funniest with the class.

> *"I told you …"*

> *"I thought you said …"*

**F** Read the article opposite. True (T), false (F), or not mentioned (N)? Have you had a bad experience with builders?
1. Emreth installed the new items himself.
2. The bathroom cost more than he expected.
3. Emreth owns this small apartment.
4. Both the bath and the shower were dangerous.
5. When the bath fell it nearly killed Emreth.
6. Workers at WallsUp blame Emreth.
7. All the characters in the story are male.

**G** ● Make it personal  **Getting things done?**
Choose three verbs and write questions about the services people use. Ask four classmates and report the results.

| clean | check | cut | (re)decorate |
| deliver | do | dye | iron | repair |
| renovate | service | test |

> *When was the last time you had your eyes tested?*

> *She said she'd had them tested a month ago because she couldn't see the TV!*

**H** **Role-play.** Using smart phones
 A: Imagine you're a Martian and have no idea what a smart phone is.
 B: Explain three functions to the Martian. Then change roles.

> *Hello, human. What's that in your hand?*

**I** ▶ R4.4 ● Make it personal  **Question time!**
In pairs, listen to the 12 lesson titles in units 7 and 8. Pause after each one and guess what your partner's answer will be. Correct each other's wrong guesses. Any surprises?

> *Does technology rule your life?*

> *I think you'll answer, "No, I actually love technology."*

> *You're right! And your answer will be …*

## Expensive bath

An L.A. homeowner has learned the hard way that you have to be careful when you get home renovations done. Emreth Jones, 42, paid $15,000 for a new bathroom, and another $10,000 to fix the mistakes after a building inspection. "It's terrible," he said. "I wanted to get a new bath and shower put in upstairs. I thought it would be simple."

The building inspector noticed that the workers had seriously weakened the floor when they installed the bath and shower.

"The bath might have come through the floor at any moment," said Jones. "If it had hit me, that would have been it."

The manager of WallsUp declined to comment, although an employee claimed it was Jones' fault.

"He asked us if we could do it cheaply. And he didn't tell us he would get an inspection."

## Skills practice

**A** **Books open**. Ask sts to turn to p. 98. Allow them exactly one minute to reread the text about Photoshop.

**Books closed**. Tell sts that they are going to listen to the same text and practice taking notes. Explain that you will pause the audio every 12 seconds, and sts should then write down the last five words they heard. Play ▶8.1, pausing after every 12 seconds. At the end, replay ▶8.1 so sts can check the notes they have taken. Ask: *How much did you get right?*

**B** Tell sts that they are going to listen to five extracts from tracks they have heard in this level. Say: *Count the number of words you hear in each sentence.* Emphasize that sts should write down the number of words after they hear each sentence. Play ▶R4.3, pausing after each extract for students to write down the number of words. Paircheck. Classcheck.

1 nine words  2 nine words  3 eight words
4 eight words  5 seven words

**C** Say: *Now listen again and write the sentences*. Replay ▶R4.3 as sts listen and write down the sentences. Paircheck. Classcheck by writing the answers on the board. Then ask: *Which words are the hardest to understand?*

1 I started to miss him and I called him.
2 Hue's dad looked so surprised when I kissed him.
3 Can you tell me how the problem started?
4 The store manager said it'd just arrived.
5 I wonder if you can help me.

**D** Ask sts to list eight electronic devices they own, putting the items in order from the most to the least important. Have pairs compare and explain their choices. Refer sts to the model in the speech bubble. Classcheck.

**E** Have sts change partners. Ask the new pairs to imagine what each person is saying in the cartoons and role-play the complete dialogues. Monitor sts' sentences closely and correct any mistakes on the spot. Then, ask two or three pairs to join to form groups and have the sts in each group compare their stories and choose the funniest. Classcheck by inviting groups to share their funniest lines.

**F** Focus sts' attention on the article title and photograph. Elicit opinions about how expensive the bathroom is and if sts would enjoy having a similar one at home.

Have sts read the text and decide whether each sentence is true (T), false (F), or not mentioned (N). Paircheck. Classcheck by writing the answers on the board.

1 F  2 T  3 T  4 T  5 N  6 T  7 N

Ask: *Have you ever had a bad experience with builders?* Have sts discuss the question in pairs. Classcheck.

**G** **Make it personal**  Ask sts to choose three verbs and write questions about the services people have done. Monitor their work closely and correct as much as possible. Then, have sts stand up and mingle. Explain that they should interview four classmates using the questions they wrote. At the end, invite volunteers to tell the group the three most interesting answers they heard.

**H** **Role-play**. Read the instructions for student **A** and student **B** with the whole class. Assign new pairs and have sts act out dialogues about smart phones. Encourage them to change roles for each dialogue. Classcheck and have three different pairs role-play one dialogue each for the whole group.

**I** **Make it personal**  *Question time!* Tell sts that they are going to hear the twelve lesson title questions from units 7 and 8. Tell them that you will pause after each question so they can ask and answer it in pairs. Play ▶R4.4 and pause after the first question. Have sts work in pairs to ask and answer the question. Encourage sts to ask follow-up questions when appropriate. Classcheck. Repeat the procedure for the remaining questions on the track.

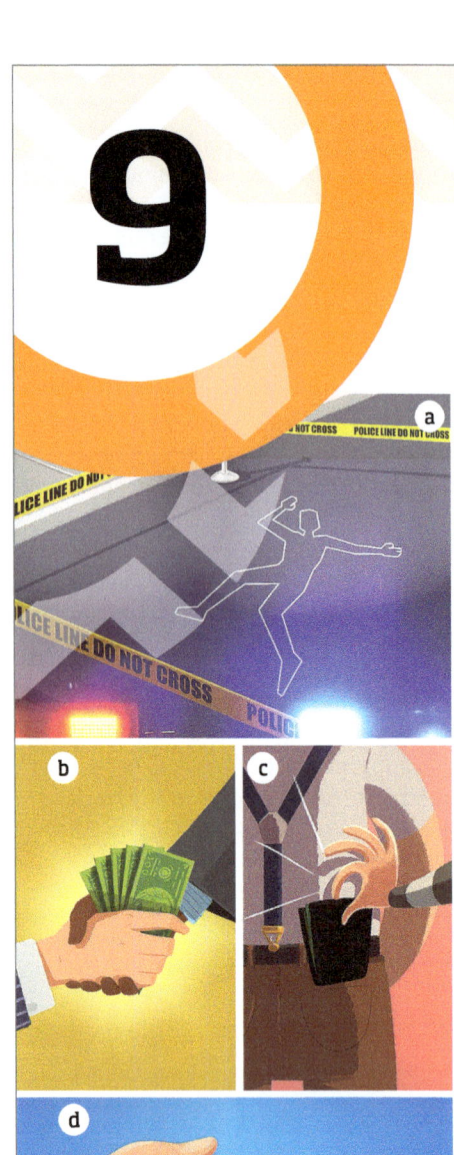

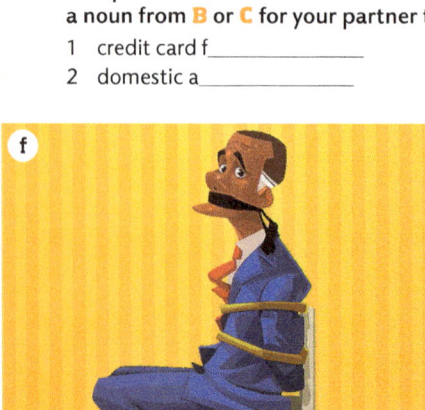

# 9.1 Does crime worry you?

## 1 Vocabulary  Crime and violence

**A** ▶9.1 Quickly match the text types to extracts 1–6. Then listen and read to check. Which type do you read the most?

*I'm always tweeting.*

☐ a tweet  ☐ a discussion forum for students of English
☐ a newspaper article  ☐ a discussion forum for travelers

**1** I spent four days in São Paulo. Lots of locals told me to be careful. I was, and it was cool. I heard a few crime stories, from credit card fraud to kidnapping. Maybe they're exaggerating. Anyway, enjoy your stay there. The food and nightlife are amazing!

**2** Organized crime in Chicago has seen a fall. Statistics released recently show a 20% decrease in burglaries between June 2017 and 2018.

**3** Murder of millionaire shocks Jacksonville. Ex-husband main suspect.

**4** Got stopped for speeding. Actually thought about offering the cop $100, but remembered bribery is also a crime. Must slow down in future. #stupid
← Reply  ⇄ Retweet  ★ Favorite

**5** 89-YEAR-OLD BOXING GRANDMA SENT TO PRISON FOR DOMESTIC ABUSE AND DRUG DEALING.

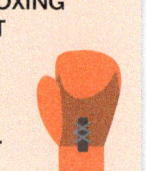

**6** OK, I think I can help you. Theft is a noun, and it is when someone takes something from you without you knowing. So, for example, if you were walking down the street and I ran by and stole your purse, that would be theft. So, in a way, tax evasion and music piracy are forms of theft, too. Robbery is a noun, too, but that's different: it usually involves violence or fear. Steal is a verb. Someone steals something from you. Hope that helps! 😊

☐ a newspaper headline  ☐ a headline from a satirical news website

**B** ▶9.2 Match the highlighted words to pictures a–g. Listen to check.

**C** Complete 1–4 with other crimes from the texts. Then, in pairs, mime a noun from **B** or **C** for your partner to say it.

1 credit card f_____  3 tax e_____
2 domestic a_____  4 music p_____

*Ha ha. That's brilliant! A burglary.*

112

**Unit overview:** The main topics of unit 9 are a review of verb families, passive voice, future perfect and future continuous, and vocabulary on crime and punishment.

# 9.1 Does crime worry you?

**Lesson Aims:** Sts learn to talk about different types of crime. They also review and practice verb tenses they have learned so far.

### Function
Reading and identifying different text types.
Deciding which crimes are the most and least serious.
Listening to people answer questions about crime.
Doing a class survey about crime.

### Language
Murder of millionaire shocks Jacksonville.
To me, credit card fraud is the least serious crime.
I've been living in this neighborhood for, what, two years and I've never seen a robber.
Most students, four out of five actually, think credit card fraud has increased.

**Vocabulary:** Crime and violence (bribery, burglaries, drug dealing, kidnapping, murder, robbery, theft).
**Grammar:** Review of verb families.

♪ Turn to p. 334 for notes about this song and an accompanying task.

**Warm-up** Have sts work in pairs, taking turns asking and answering the lesson title questions from unit 8, p. 98–107. Encourage sts to ask follow-up questions when appropriate. Classcheck by inviting volunteers to report their partners' answers to the whole class.

## 1 Vocabulary

**A Books open.** Draw sts' attention to the various types of text on the page. Ask: **Which one is a tweet?** (4). Play ▶ 9.1 as sts listen and read along. Have sts match extracts 1–6 to the correct text types as they listen. Paircheck. Classcheck then ask sts: *Which type do you read the most?*

1 a discussion forum for travellers
2 a newspaper article
3 a newspaper headline
4 a tweet
5 a headline from a satirical news website
6 a discussion forum for students of English

**B** Point to the highlighted words in the texts in **A**. Have sts match the words in bold to photos a–g. Play ▶ 9.2 for sts to check their answers. Classcheck and drill pronunciation of all the highlighted words.

▶ 9.2 Turn to page 321 for the complete audioscript.

a murder
b bribery
c theft
d drug dealing
e burglaries
f kidnapping
g robbery

**C** Ask sts to hide the texts on p. 112 with their notebooks or a sheet of paper and then try to complete the types of crimes mentioned in 1–4. Paircheck. Then, allow sts to look at the texts in **A** to check their answers. Classcheck and drill pronunciation of these terms.

Mime a crime noun for the sts to guess. In pairs, sts mime and guess other nouns from **B** or **C**.

1 fraud
2 abuse
3 evasion
4 piracy

**D** Complete 1–4 with the words below. There are two extra.

| burglary | robbery | robs | steal | stealing | thefts |

1 There was an armed _____ at the gas station last night. Three men threatened the staff with guns and stole $6,000 in cash.
2 Unfortunately, we have had several _____ of personal property in the building recently.
3 They were so poor, they had to _____ food in order to feed themselves.
4 Many people install alarms to protect their houses against _____.

**E** 🔴 **Make it personal** Choose the three most and least serious crimes in **B** and **C**. In groups, compare your lists. Can you reach a consensus?

*To me, credit-card fraud is the least serious crime.*

*Well, it depends on the amount of money you steal, doesn't it?*

🎵 *Everybody wanna steal my girl*
*Everybody wanna take her heart away.*
*Couple billion in the whole wide world,*
*Find another one 'cos she belongs to me.*

🔴 **Common mistakes**
*stealing*
I saw you robbing my wallet!
*stolen*
Help! My cell phone was robbed!
*robbed*
Have you ever been stolen?
*robbed*
What? Your grandmother stole a bank?

## ② Listening

**A** ▶9.3 Listen and match short interviews 1–5 to the questions. There's one extra question.

**Which of the crimes listed**
☐ do you worry about the most?
☐ do you worry about the least?
☐ have / has affected someone you know?
☐ will probably increase in the next 10 years?
☐ would you like to eradicate for ever?
☐ shouldn't be considered a crime?

**B** ▶9.3 Listen again. True (T) or false (F)? Correct the false ones. Who do you empathize with?
1 He doesn't think people should pay for digital content.
2 People saw a robber in his neighborhood last year.
3 A middle-aged man broke into her neighbor's house.
4 The government is introducing new laws next year.
5 She has taught her kids to yell if a stranger approaches them.

*Certainly not the first guy. I produce digital material myself!*

## ③ Grammar Review of verb families

**A** Match the examples in 1–4 to the forms below, and name the four tenses. Then add a past example to each category, 1–4.

English verbs fall into four categories:
1 Simple (states, habits, single actions): *I study* English.
2 Continuous (progress): *I am studying* English.
3 Perfect (links a point in time with a previous action): *I have studied* English.
4 Perfect continuous (progress before a point in time): *I have been studying* English.
Knowing how each one works can help you make different past, present, and future verb combinations more easily.

➡ **Grammar 9A** p.154

*Example 1 is in the ... tense.*

*A past example for aspect 1 could be "I didn't study English at school."*

☐ S + be + -ing   ☐ S + have + been + -ing   ☐ S + have + past participle   ☐ S + verb

**B** Name the tense in audio extracts 1–4. Order them from easiest to hardest for you.
1 I've lived in this neighborhood for, what, two years …
2 You're simply downloading a song!
3 What has the government been doing to change things?
4 I don't see any way out.

**C** 🔴 **Make it personal** Use the survey in **2A** to interview two classmates. What are the most common answers?

*Most students, four out of five actually, think credit-card fraud has increased.*

*The crime everybody I asked would eliminate forever is …*

**D** Have sts complete 1–4 with the words in the box. Peercheck. Classcheck.

🔑
1 robbery  2 thefts  3 steal  4 burglary

**Common mistakes** Read with the whole class. Explain that the verb *steal* is used when the criminal carries items or money away with him / her (or drives a stolen car away). Say: *When a bank is robbed, thieves steal money.* Ask: *When a person is robbed, what do thieves usually steal?* (money, phones, watches, jewelry, and so on).

**E** **Make it personal** Ask sts to list the three most and least serious crimes from **B**–**C**. Divide the class into groups of four and have sts in each group compare their lists. Refer sts to the model text in the speech bubbles. Classcheck.

## 2 Listening

**A** Read the questions in the chart with the class, but do not have sts answer them yet, as they will do so later in **3C**. Tell sts that they are going to listen to five people answering these questions. Say: *Listen to find out which question person 1 is answering.* Play the first part of ▶9.3 and pause the track after the first answer. Classcheck. Then, play the rest of ▶9.3, as sts listen and match speakers 2–5 to the correct questions. Classcheck.

▶9.3 Turn to page 321 for the complete audioscript.

🔑
1 … shouldn't be considered a crime?
2 … do you worry about the least?
3 … have / has affected someone you know?
4 … will probably increase in the next 10 years?
5 … do you worry about the most?

**B** Tell sts that they are going to listen to the five speakers again. Ask them to read sentences 1–5 briefly and play ▶9.3 again. Have sts mark sentences 1–5 true (T) or false (F) and then correct the false statements. Paircheck. If time allows, have sts turn to the AS on p. 172 and do the noticing activity as they listen. Classcheck.

🔑
1 T
2 F —The speaker has lived in the neighborhood for two years and never seen a robber.
3 F —A blonde woman in her 40s broke into the neighbor's house.
4 T
5 F —She has taught her kids to run if a stranger approaches them.

## 3 Grammar Review of verb families

**A** Ask sts to read the information in the grammar box and match the forms to the tenses. Peercheck. Classcheck.

🔑
1 continuous  2 perfect continuous  3 perfect  4 simple

**Language tip** Portuguese L1 speakers can have more problems with the present perfect than other tenses because although they have this structure in their L1, it is not as commonly used as in English. When reviewing verb families in section 3 (Grammar), remind Portuguese L1 speakers that the present perfect links the past to the present, in situations where they would use the simple present in their L1. For example: *I have studied English for 2 years; They have lived here since 2015;* etc. Write the example sentences on the board (with timelines showing the connection between the past and the present) to help sts understand the difference.

➜ **Grammar 9A** page 154

**B** Point to sentence 1 and ask: *What tense is this?* Have sts name the tenses in sentences 2–4 in pairs then order them according to which they find the most / least difficult. Classcheck.

🔑
1 present perfect simple       2 present continuous
3 present perfect continuous   4 simple present

**C** **Make it personal** Divide the class into groups of three. Point to the survey in **2A** and ask sts to interview the other people in their groups with those questions. Have sts take notes of their partners' answers.

Then, assign new groups so that sts are each working with a totally different set of sts. Have them work in their new groups to compare their notes on the survey, as exemplified in the speech bubble. Classcheck sts' survey results.

➜ **Workbook** Page 44

## 9.2 How could your city be improved?

### 1 Reading

*I believe it's the second biggest city in Colombia.*

**A** ▶9.4 In pairs, brainstorm what you know about Medellín. Listen and read the introduction. Then cover it. What can you remember?

## Medellín Reinvented

Twenty years ago, if someone had said they were going on vacation to Medellín, Colombia, you'd have called them crazy. *Time* magazine once called it "the most dangerous city on earth." Civilized society had been destroyed, drug cartels ruled, and violence was part of everyday life. Fast-forward to the present and things couldn't be more different. Medellín is a city with plenty to celebrate and is fast becoming a hot destination! But why? Well, here are five things that I believe have brought a dramatic change to this fascinating city.

*Maybe this cable car has made traveling much safer?*

**B** ▶9.4 In pairs, look only at the photos and captions in the rest of the article to guess how each feature has helped reinvent Medellín. Then listen, read, and check. Were your guesses correct?

### Public transportation

The public transportation network can take some credit for bringing peace to the city. MetroCable, the network of cable cars, connects poor and middle-class Medellín, both literally and symbolically, and this helped to reduce urban violence. Also, until 2011, the residents of Comuna 13, one of Medellín's poorest neighborhoods, had to climb 500 steps to get home. The commute has been reduced to five minutes thanks to outdoor escalators. These escalators gave people a sense of dignity and pride, which I think also had an impact on crime.

*MetroCable*

### Innovation

Another reason I was impressed by Medellín is its urban development. It won the prestigious Lee Kuan Yew World City Prize award in 2016. This award is known as a kind of "Nobel Prize" for urbanism. It recognizes Medellín's transformation into a model of sustainable urban innovation. As well as the famous escalators and cable cars, Medellín's art galleries and public spaces were praised.

*Art in Botero Square*

*Street art murals in Comuna 13*

### The arts

Medellín's art scene is also flourishing. Renowned artist Fernando Botero was born here and donated lots of his distinctive art to his home city. This also brings tourists to the area. Back in Comuna 13, previously the most notorious area, fantastic street art can be found. Local residents act as tour guides, giving them work and pride in their neighborhood. They explain with passion the personal stories told by the colorful murals. The tour really gave me an understanding of the history and transformation of Medellín.

### Nature

Colombia is second only to Brazil for its biodiversity. It is home to 10% of the world's species! Protected areas are being expanded all the time. Some of these areas are accessible by MetroCable, including Arvi Park, where you escape urban life by walking, biking, and horse-back riding.

*Arvi Park*

*Flower Festival*

### The "City of Eternal Spring"

Colombia is one of the world's biggest flower exporters, and billions of dollars' worth of flowers are exported every year. Medellín is in bloom all year round. The weather is a perfect 22–23 degrees Celsius whatever the season, and there are flowers everywhere you look all year round: on balconies, terraces, gardens, and parks. Thousands of tourists visit during "Feria de las Flores," and it was one of the most joyful and creative things I've ever seen. The festival will definitely be put on my list of favorite things to do in Latin America.

114

# 9.2 How could your city be improved?

**Lesson Aims:** Sts study and practice the passive voice in the context of talking about improvements made in the Colombian city of Medellín.

### Function
Listening to / Reading about how developments changed Medellín.
Talking about changes that could be made in one's own city.
Reading tweets and quotations.

### Language
Fast-forward to modern day and things couldn't be more different.
These cable cars connect poor and middle-class Medellín, both literally and symbolically …
Outdoor escalators! Wonderful idea. I really think they should be adopted as a model for lots of other cities!

**Vocabulary:** Cable cars, cartels, civic centers, escalators, homicides.
**Grammar:** Passive voice.
**Before the lesson:** Prepare index cards with crime-related vocabulary from the last lesson. Write one type of crime on each card, e.g. *bribery, burglary, credit card fraud, domestic abuse, drug dealing, kidnapping, murder, music piracy, robbery, tax evasion.* Bring in a map of South America or find one online to show the location of Medellín.

♪ Turn to p. 335 for notes about this song and an accompanying task.

**Warm-up** Have sts play a guessing game in groups of four. Give each group one set of cards (see **Before the lesson**) and have them turn the cards face down. Explain that sts should take turns drawing a card describing the crime for the rest of the group members to guess. Each correct guess scores one point for the student who guessed it right and one point for the student who described it.

Monitor sts' descriptions and guesses closely for accuracy and pronunciation. At the end, find out who scored more points in each group and provide sts with language feedback.

## 1 Reading

**A** **Books closed**. Ask: *What do you know about Medellín?* Display the map of South America—have sts find the location. Assign pairs for sts to discuss the question. Elicit any ideas sts have and write them on the board.

**Books open**. Point to the the text and explain that this is the introduction to a blog about Medellín. Play ▶9.4, pausing after the introduction. Have sts listen and read the introduction and see if any of their ideas from **A** are mentioned. Peercheck. Classcheck and check any ideas on the board that are mentioned.

**B** Point to the photos and captions and ask: *How have these features helped reinvent Medellín?* Give sts time to guess how each feature has helped. Play ▶9.4 for sts to listen and read the rest of the blog. Peercheck. Classcheck.

> **Tip** Break the text down into manageable portions. Have sts work in pairs and read section by section. Allocate a different section to each pair. When they have finished reading, put sts into small groups to share information about the section they have read.

## 9.2

**C** Reread and answer 1–5. Practice the pink-stressed words.
1. How has public transportation helped to reduce crime in Medellín?
2. How does the flower festival help the economy?
3. Why was Medellín awarded the Lee Kuan Yew World City Prize?
4. How do the street art tours help visitors learn about the city?
5. How is Medellín protecting its biodiversity?

🎵 *Sweet dreams are made of this, who am I to disagree? I travel the world and the seven seas…*

**D** 🔵 **Make it personal** In small groups, discuss 1–4. Any disagreements?
1. Which things do you think best explain Medellín's transformation?
2. Have any of the things in the article happened in your city?
3. Which other improvements could make your city better?
4. What would you put on your list list of favorite things to do in Latin America?

*For me, it was because the violence ended.*

### 2 Grammar  Passive voice

**A** Study the underlined phrases in **1C**. Then read the grammar box and circle the correct alternative in rules 1–3. Is the form similar in your language?

> Use the passive voice when the "doer" of a verb is unknown, unimportant, or obvious. It is often used to move important information to the front of a sentence.
> 1. The passive voice is formed with **have / be** + the **simple past / past participle**.
> 2. The verb *be* can go in **the present or past / any tense or form**.
> 3. **For / By** is used to show who did the action.
>
> ➡ Grammar 9B p. 154

🔴 **Common mistakes**

Roses, carnations, and orchids are ~~growing~~ in Colombia.
    grown

                        ignored by
This story has been ~~ignoring~~ for the press.

**B** Complete the tweets about the article with these forms. There's one extra. Which are relevant where you live? In pairs, add a tweet of your own.

| will be | are being | can't have been | has been | should be | to be |

**@PedroH:** Outdoor escalators! Wonderful idea. I really think they ¹_____ adopted as a model for lots of other cities!

**@grumpyoldman:** Places really can change! It's incredible how much crime ²_____ reduced because of things like this!

**@donnamaria:** It's amazing how the arts can help. Two new art galleries ³_____ built right now. Kids need art in their lives. #arttherapy

More natural areas need ⁴_____ protected. If Medellín keeps improving, the tourist industry will take over.

Honestly? I doubt these changes ⁵_____ sustained. These things take too much time and money.

**C** ▶9.5 Complete the quotes about cities with the verbs in parentheses. Listen to check. In groups, choose your favorite. Which is the most popular?
1. Buildings do not make a city. A city _____ (make) by the people who live there.
2. Cities are places where money _____ (make), but life _____ (lose).
3. By its nature, a city provides what otherwise _____ (could / give) only by traveling.
4. Villages and towns _____ (swallow up) by cities. Soon there will be no countryside at all.
5. The way you view the future _____ (change) by living in any big city.

*Our favorite quote is … because …*

**D** Look at **2B** on p. 113. Say 1–5 in the passive voice.

**E** 🔵 **Make it personal** *Passive Favorites!* In pairs, ask and answer full passive voice questions about your favorites in each square. Any coincidences?

*Who's your favorite device made by?*
*It's made by Samsung. It's my phone.*

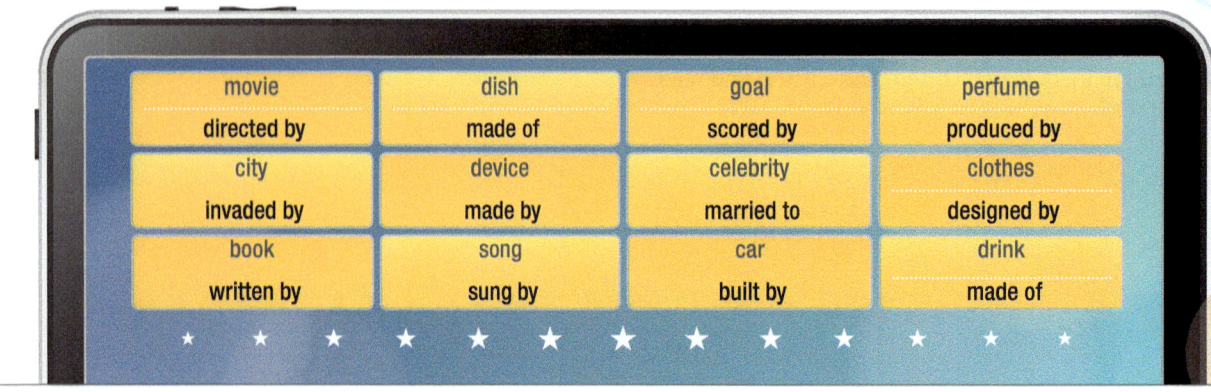

| movie | dish | goal | perfume |
| directed by | made of | scored by | produced by |
| city | device | celebrity | clothes |
| invaded by | made by | married to | designed by |
| book | song | car | drink |
| written by | sung by | built by | made of |

115

## 9.2

**C** Ask sts to reread the article in **B** and answer the questions. Peercheck. Classcheck.

🔑
1. Public transportation has connected poor and middle-class areas and given people a sense of dignity and pride in where they live.
2. The flower festival brings a lot of tourists to the city.
3. The prize recognized Medellín's transformation into a model of sustainable urban innovation.
4. Local residents act as tour guides. Visitors can learn about the personal stories of the area told by the colorful murals.
5. Biodiverse areas are being expanded all the time.

**D** 🔵 **Make it personal** Have sts change partners and ask: *Which things do you think best explain the city's transformation? Would these things make a difference to your city?* Have sts discuss questions 1–4 in pairs. Classcheck.

**Tip** If, coincidentally, you are teaching in the city of Medellín, adapt the last question: *Would these things make a difference to other cities?*

### 2 Grammar  Passive voice

**A** ⏺ **Common mistakes** Point to the underlined phrases in **1B**. Tell sts to study them and then choose the correct alternatives in the grammar box. Paircheck. Classcheck. Read the common mistakes with sts.

🔑
1 be, past participle   2 any tense or form   3 By

**Language tip** Sts who speak Portuguese or Spanish as their L1 may benefit from contrastive grammar when learning the passive voice, as the structure is the same in both English and their L1. Have sts analyze and compare passive voice structures in their L1 to the equivalent in English. Encourage them to notice that the structure for the passive voice in both their L1 and in English is the same.

➡ **Grammar 9B** page 154

**B** Have sts fill in the blanks in the tweets with the verbs in the box. Paircheck. Classcheck. Pair sts up and ask them to discuss the tweets and explain which points they agree or disagree on. Classcheck sts' opinions.

🔑
1 should be   2 has been   3 are being   4 to be   5 will be

**C** Read quote 1 with sts and elicit how to fill in the blank with the verb provided at the end of the sentence. Have sts form the passive voice of the verbs provided to complete quotes 1–5. Play ▶9.5 so sts can check their answers.

🔑
1 is made   2 is made, is lost   3 could be given
4 are being swallowed up
5 will be changed (also possible: is changed/can be changed)

**D** Ask sts to go to p. 113 and point to activity **2B**. Have pairs of sts take turns saying sentences 1–5 in the passive voice. Monitor pairs' sentences closely for accuracy, and correct any mistakes on the spot. Classcheck by writing the answers on the board.

🔑
1 Digital content shouldn't be paid for.
2 A robber was seen in his neighborhood last year.
3 Her neighbor's house was broken into by a middle-aged man.
4 New laws are being introduced next year.
5 Her kids have been taught to yell if a stranger approaches them.

**E** 🔵 **Make it personal**  1 Say: *You're going to play* **Passive Favorites!** Point to the prompts in the first box, then ask two sts to read the conversation in the speech bubbles as a model dialogue. Sts then play the game by asking and answering questions for each square. Go around and help with ideas and vocabulary where necessary.

When sts have finished, classcheck by asking: *Were there any coincidences? Did you have the same favorites?*

**Extra activity** Write the following instructions on the board:

*In groups, prepare a presentation about a city you know well.*

1 Use the following prompts to help you.
   … languages are spoken
   … was born there
   … district is packed / crowded with
   … is based / located in
   … was invented / discovered
   … was built by …
   … food is served in …

2 Present your city to a partner / group of classmates. Do they know this city?

3 Listen to your classmates' presentations. Would you like to visit this city?

➡ **Workbook** Page 45

# 9.3 Have you ever been to court?

## POP CRIME?

Back in July, 22-year-old Chicago student Michael Lewis was driving home very late from a friend's house. He was listening to loud music in his car. Oh, with his windows down, naturally. The neighbors weren't happy, of course, and they called the police. Michael was **sent to jail** for the night, but was **released** the next day—free as a bird to **ter**rorize the neighborhood again! A week later, more loud music at 2 a.m. This time, Michael was **charged with** diso**r**derly **con**duct and **taken to court**, but there was no **evi**dence against him, so Michael was **acqui**tted. Free as a bird, again. Third week, more loud music. Trouble is, there was a police car pa**trol**ling the neighborhood. So Michael had to face the judge again, but this time things got serious: Michael was **convic**ted. He was **sentenced to** three days in jail and had to pay a $1,000 **fine**. But, for some reason, the judge decided to give him an alternative. The judge asked Michael what his least favorite kind of music was. It turns out that Michael was not a fan of classical music. The judge's alternative was to listen to classical music for thirty hours. Easy choice, right? Not for Michael. After twenty minutes of Mozart and **Beet**hoven, he chose the original punishment.

### 1 Vocabulary  Crime and punishment

**A** In pairs, imagine the story in the pictures. Then read to check. Were you close?

> A guy was leaning on his car at night listening to loud music …

**B** ▶9.6 Match the **highlighted** words and phrases to the pictures. Listen to a dramatized version of the text to check. What kind of music would be a punishment for you?

> I'd hate to be forced to listen to …

**C** 🎤 Make it personal  In pairs, use only the pictures to remember Michael's story. Take turns describing each scene.

### 2 Listening

**A** ▶9.7 In pairs, look at the punishments and guess the crimes. Listen to check.

*ONLY AN IDIOT WOULD DRIVE ON THE SIDEWALK TO AVOID A SCHOOL BUS.*

*RIIIIIIIING!!!*

**B** ▶9.7 Listen again and match the phrases to 1 and 2. Fair punishments?

- ☐ charged with
- ☐ sentenced to
- ☐ taken to court
- ☐ ordered to pay
- ☐ sent to jail
- ☐ released

116

# 9.3 Have you ever been to court?

**Lesson Aims:** Sts learn and use vocabulary on crime and punishment in the contexts of reading, listening to, and talking about breaking the law and being taken to court.

### Function
Reading a story about a student who listened to loud music.
Listening to two unusual punishments for crimes.
Talking about celebrities' crimes.
Deciding what punishment is best.

### Language
The neighbors weren't too happy, of course, and they called the police.
Everyone will be arrested unless I get that phone now!
In 2006, Axl Rose was ordered to pay a huge fine after biting a man's leg.
I think the old lady should be sentenced to at least 10 years.

**Vocabulary:** Crime and punishment: be charged with, be ordered to, be sentenced to, be sent to jail, be released, be taken to court.
**Grammar:** Prepositions. Review of passive voice.
**Before the lesson:** Write the following questions on the board:
*Do you often play music at a loud volume at home? In your car? Why (not)?*
*Do you have any noisy neighbors? Have you ever complained to them about it?*
*Can people be punished for playing music too loudly in your city?*

♪ Turn to p. 334 for notes about this song and an accompanying task.

**Warm-up** Point out the questions on the board (see **Before the lesson**) and have sts discuss them in pairs. Classcheck by asking sts to report their partners' answers.

## 1 Vocabulary Crime and punishment

**A Books open**. Point to the pictures and ask sts to hide the text with a notebook or a sheet of paper. Say: *What happened? Look at the pictures and guess the story in pairs.* Then, have sts quickly read the text to check their guesses. Ask: *Were you close to the real story?*

**B** Focus on the highlighted words and phrases in the text and ask sts to match them to the pictures. Tell sts that not all pictures depict a word or phrase in bold and that some pictures may show more than one word or phrase. Play ▶9.6 to classcheck. Then ask: *What kind of music would be a punishment for you?*

1 picture not used
2 sent to jail
3 released
4 charged with
5 taken to court / acquitted
6 taken to court / convicted
7 sentenced to / fine
8 picture not used

**C 🔴 Make it personal** Have sts work in pairs to retell the story from the pictures only, without reading the text. Encourage sts to use new vocabulary (*be sent to jail, be released*, etc.). Monitor their stories closely and offer help as necessary. Classcheck by inviting volunteers to retell different parts of the story.

## 2 Listening

**A** Point to pictures 1 and 2 and have pairs of sts guess what crimes the people are being punished for. Play ▶9.7 so sts can check their answers.

▶9.7 Turn to page 322 for the complete audioscript.

a A woman drove dangerously—on the sidewalk to get around a bus that was dropping off children.
b A phone rang in San Francisco's District Court and, as nobody confessed to owning the phone, the judge sent all the people present to jail

**B** Briefly read the phrases with sts and ask them to listen again and identify which phrases are about story 1 and which are about story 2. Play ▶9.7 again. Paircheck. Classcheck.

Story 1: taken to court, sentenced to, was ordered to pay
Story 2: charged with, sent to jail, released

> *Breaking rocks in the hot sun.*
> *I fought the law and the law won.*

**C** Complete extracts 1–11 with these prepositions. Then check in ▶9.7 on p. 173. How do you try to learn prepositions?

| at | from | in (x2) | on | to (x4) | under | with |

1 Thirty-two-year-old Shena Hardin was caught _____ camera driving on a sidewalk.
2 The judge sentenced her _____ an embarrassing punishment.
3 She was told to stand _____ a busy intersection.
4 Just to add _____ her humiliation … she was ordered to pay $250 _____ court costs.
5 It was an ordinary morning _____ San Francisco's District Court.
6 Bring it _____ me now.
7 All 42 people present were charged _____ disturbing the peace.
8 All 42 people present were sent _____ jail.
9 The judge was permanently removed _____ office.
10 He said he had been _____ a lot of stress.

> *I memorize a personal example: I work **in** Quito, **in** Bellavista, **on** Av. 6 September **at** number 347.*

> **Common mistakes**
> of / about     in
> Think in me when I'm to jail.

**D** 🎙 **Make it personal** 📡 In pairs, search online for a crime story in the news. Figure out how to summarize it in simple English. Then tell the class.

> *A woman was caught on camera pushing someone else's car out of a parking space with her car so she could park there. She damaged the car and was charged with reckless driving!*

## ③ Pronunciation -ed

**A** ▶9.8 Listen how *-ed* links to **vowels** and **consonants**. Is the *-ed* sound clear or does it link? Listen again and repeat.

| -ed = /ɪd/ | clear | links |
|---|---|---|
| 1 … be arrested unless I get that phone now! | | |
| 2 … decided to give him an alternative. | | |
| **-ed = /t/** | | |
| 3 … were released, of course. | | |
| 4 … be sentenced to a week in jail. | | |
| **-ed = /d/** | | |
| 5 … no one confessed at all. | | |
| 6 … was permanently removed from office. | | |

> **Remember:** The pronunciation of *-ed* depends on the last sound (not spelling) in a regular verb.
> • /d/ after a voiced consonant – lived /lɪvd/
> • /d/ after a vowel sound – studied /stʌdiːd/
> • /t/ after an unvoiced consonant – liked /laɪkt/
> • /ɪd/ after /t/ or /d/ – wanted /wɑntɪd/

**B** ▶9.9 **Celebrity gossip!** Write full sentences for 1–5. Listen to check. Do you know any similar stories?

1 Justin Bieber / arrest and release / bail for $2,500 / driving dangerously
2 Axl Rose / order / pay a huge fine after biting a man's leg
3 Lindsay Lohan / sentence / 10 days' community service
4 Michelle Rodriguez / send / jail / 18 days
5 Lauren Hill / confess and serve / three months in jail / tax evasion

> *Wasn't Josh Brolin arrested for fighting back in 2013?*

**C** 🎙 **Make it personal** In groups, decide on the right punishment for each crime. Do you all agree?

> Man arrested for burglary after breaking into house to use bathroom

> Teen charged with kidnapping after taking girlfriend on surprise trip

> Elderly woman faces robbery charge after trying to rob a bank with a banana

> 20-year-old hacks into college computers and changes own grades

> **Common mistake**
> I think he should to do 100 hours' community service.

> *We've agreed the bank robber should be sentenced to at least five years.*

> *No, that's not fair. I mean, what if she dies in prison?*

## 9.3

**Common mistakes** Read with the whole class.

**Language tip** Romance language speakers tend to make the first mistake as a result of direct translation. Take the opportunity to remind sts that, in English, the verbs *think* and *dream* are used with the same two prepositions (*of* / *about*). This can cause confusion with another preposition which they use in their L1 and tend to translate. For example, saying *I dreamt with you last night*, instead of *I dreamt of / about you last night*.

**C** Ask sts to complete sentences 1–10 with the prepositions. When they are ready, have sts check their answers with AS ▶ 9.7 on p. 173. Classcheck.

| | | | |
|---|---|---|---|
| 1 | on | 6 | to |
| 2 | to | 7 | with |
| 3 | at | 8 | to |
| 4 | to, in | 9 | from |
| 5 | in | 10 | under |

**D** **Make it personal** Read the example in the speech bubble with the whole class. Give sts a few minutes to go online and find a local crime story. Remind them of the vocabulary in **A** and ask them to retell their stories in pairs.

### 3 Pronunciation -ed

**A** Review pronunciation of *-ed* endings with the information in the box. Show sts the chart and have them predict the sounds of *-ed* + vowels and *-ed* + consonants in connected speech. Play ▶ 9.8 and have sts listen for whether *-ed* is pronounced clearly or linked to the following sound. Sts should mark the chart accordingly. Replay ▶ 9.8. Paircheck. Classcheck.

| | | | |
|---|---|---|---|
| 1 | clear | 4 | links |
| 2 | links | 5 | clear |
| 3 | clear | 6 | links |

**Tip** Replay ▶ 9.8 for choral repetition.

**B** Tell sts to look at items 1–5 and write complete sentences using the simple past in the passive voice. Play ▶ 9.9 to classcheck. Then, pair sts up, read the example in the speech bubble, and have them try to recall similar stories about celebrities. Classcheck.

1 Justin Bieber was arrested and released on bail for $2,500 for driving dangerously.
2 Axl Rose was ordered to pay a huge fine after biting a man's leg.
3 Lindsay Lohan was sentenced to 10 days' community service.
4 Michelle Rodrigues was sent to jail for 18 days.
5 Lauren Hill was ordered to serve three months in jail after / when she confessed to tax evasion.

**C** **Make it personal** Divide the class into groups of four and ask groups to look at the crimes in the headlines and discuss possible punishments for each of them. Encourage sts to use vocabulary from p. 116.

**Common mistake** Read with the class. Remind sts to use the bare form of the verb (without *to*) after the modal *should*. Monitor closely and take notes for later correction, so that you do not interrupt sts' thoughts. Correct prepositions on the spot. Classcheck ideas.

➔ **Workbook** Page 46

# 9.4 Where will you be living ten years from now?

"You borrowed $27,000 over the years to study computer sciences. According to our files, you now owe us $1.83."

## 1 Listening

**A** ▶9.10 In pairs, look at the cartoon and answer 1–4. Then listen to part one of a radio show to check your answer to question 4. Were you right?
1. Who / Where are the cartoon characters?
2. Guess what happened to the man's debt.
3. What do you imagine will happen next?
4. Will cybercrime get better or worse in the future?

*Hmm ... I don't know. It might've been a mistake.*

**B** ▶9.10 Listen again and complete 1 and 2 with numbers.
1. The radio show host gives _____ examples of cybercrime.
2. He says it will be the world's biggest problem some time before _____.

**C** ▶9.11 Listen to part two. How worried is Deniz Kaya?

**D** ▶9.12 Using the photos, think of three reasons why cybercrime will get worse. Listen to part three to check. Any correct guesses?

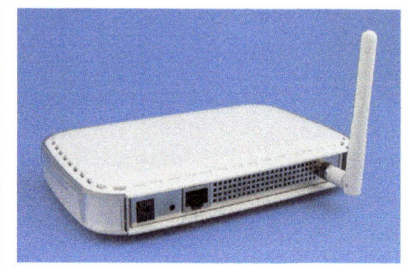

**Common mistake**
By
Until 2040 I'll be retired.

**E** ▶9.12 Listen again. True (T), false (F), or not mentioned (N)?
1. Deniz says some hackers are teenagers.
2. The Facebook Messenger virus starts when you watch a video.
3. It was created by Facebook.
4. Future e-devices won't need protection.
5. Cybercriminals often hack computers for fun.
6. Currently, 20 percent of all phones are under attack.

**F** Match the highlighted words to the definitions.
1. By 2025, cyber attacks will have become the world's top **threat**.
2. He'll be telling us if we should take these **warnings** seriously.
3. Cybercriminals will be **carrying out** attacks wirelessly, and we won't be protected.
4. They will have developed the ability to **spread** viruses across multiple devices very, very easily.
5. Cybercriminals will have **targeted** 20 percent of all the world's smart phones.

| | to perform, conduct |
| | to try to attack someone or something |
| | to affect more items / to increase / to develop fast |
| | a person or thing that could cause serious problems |
| | messages that tells us about a possible danger |

**G** **Make it personal** In pairs, have you ever had a major cyber problem? How do you protect yourself from cyber attacks? Any novel ideas? Who's more careful?

*A year ago, I lost all my data. The worst part was losing my photos.*

*I try to create really difficult passwords.*

**H** ▶9.13 Listen to part four and Deniz's advice on how to protect yourself. Did he mention any of your ideas?

118

# 9.4 Where will you be living ten years from now?

**Lesson Aims:** Sts look at and practice the future perfect and future continuous through the contexts of talking about cybercrime and life in ten years' time.

## Function

Listening to a radio show about cybercrime.
Talking about preventing cyber attacks on privacy.
Reading and making predictions about the future.

## Language

They can delete or change computer records, create fraudulent documents, and sell classified information.
I try to create really difficult passwords.
Soon, most people will be working from home.
A cure for the common cold will have been discovered by 2030.

**Vocabulary:** Carry out, cyber attacks, cybercrime, spread, target, threat, warning.
**Grammar:** Future perfect and future continuous.

♪ Turn to p. 335 for notes about this song and an accompanying task.

**Warm-up Books closed**. Put sts into small groups. Revise the passive voice by asking questions about the celebrities from p. 117 **3B**. Ask: *What happened to Justin Bieber / Axl Rose / Lindsay Lohan* etc. (He was arrested ... / He was ordered to pay ... / She was was sentenced to ... ). Give points for correct answers. Encourage sts to help each other to self-correct.

## 1 Listening

**A** **Books open**. Draw sts' attention to the cartoon and have them answer questions 1–4 in pairs. Classcheck. Tell sts that they are going to listen to a radio show about the case to check their answers. Play ▶9.10. Classcheck.

▶9.10 Turn to page 322 for the complete audioscript.

1 The cartoon characters are at the student loans office.
2 The man probably hacked the system to lower his debt.
3 The man will be punished.
4 worse

**B** Have sts quickly read sentences 1 and 2 and ask them to listen and fill in the blanks. Play ▶9.10 again and have sts write the two numbers. Paircheck. Classcheck.

1 three
2 2025

**C** Ask: *How worried do you think Deniz Kaya is? Listen to part two of the show and find out.* Play ▶9.11. Paircheck. Classcheck.

Deniz is very worried about this problem.

**D** Say: *Deniz thinks cybercrime will only get worse in the future. Look at these photos and think of three reasons why cybercrime will get worse.* Have sts work in pairs. Classcheck sts' opinions and guesses. Then, play ▶9.12 so sts can check their answers. Ask: *Any correct guesses?*

Pic 1 – Malware is becoming more intelligent.
Pic 2 – There is a new generation of hackers.
Pic 3 - Cyber criminals will be carrying out more and more attacks wirelessly.

**E** Go over statements 1–6 with the class. Replay ▶9.12 as sts listen and mark each statement true (T), false (F), or not mentioned (N). Paircheck. Replay the track if necessary.

1 T  2 T  3 F  4 F  5 N  6 F

**Common mistake** Read through with sts.

**Language tip** Romance language speakers can make this mistake as a result of direct translation. In both Portuguese and Spanish, the word sts use in this context is equivalent to *until*. Remind sts that, in English, we use *by* with a date or time reference when we mean that something might / will happen before that time. Point out that as always, the context is important when translating.

**F** Have sts read sentences 1–5 and find the correct definition for each of the highlighted words. Paircheck. Classcheck.

3 5 4 1 2

**G** **Make it personal** Ask: *How do you protect yourself from cyber attacks?* Have sts answer in pairs. Classcheck by inviting volunteers to report their partners' answers.

**H** Play ▶9.13 for sts to check their ideas from **G**. Classcheck and ask: *Were any of your ideas mentioned?*

Use a unique password for everything. Each one should have at least 8 characters and be a combination of letters, symbols and words.
Be very aware of what you click on. Just don't do it.
Make sure you regularly back up your files.
Another important point is to always install the latest updates.
Don't ignore the messages your computer sends you.

## 2 Grammar Future perfect and continuous

*We'll be raising our hands, shining up to the sky 'Cause we got the fire, fire, fire, yeah we got the fire, fire, fire.*

**A** Reread 1–5 in **1F** and complete the rules in the grammar box with these words.

be    have    continuous    perfect

| Use the future ¹_____ for an action completed before a point in the future. |
| Form: *will / won't* + ²_____ + past participle |
| Use the future ³_____ for an activity in progress at a point in the future. |
| Form: *will / won't* + ⁴_____ + -*ing* verb |

→ **Grammar 9C** p.154

**B** Complete 1–5 with the *future perfect* or *continuous*. What will you be doing in ten years?

*I won't be working in ten years. I'll have retired.*

### FIVE CAREERS FOR 2030

**PRIVACY MANAGER:** If you think you've lost some of your privacy, get ready. By 2030, you ¹_____ most of it. (lose)

**NANO MEDICS:** Good news! In the next few years, you ²_____ nanotechnology to treat most of your health problems. (use)

**BOOK-TO-APP CONVERTERS:** In five years, you ³_____ paper books. Everybody will use an e-device. Just wait and see. (not read)

**3D PRINTING ENGINEERS:** By the end of the decade, the demand for 3D printing ⁴_____. (double)

**TURBINE SPECIALIST:** We ⁵_____ using electricity, but we will be getting more from green sources such as wind turbines, which need a lot of maintenance. (not stop)

**Common mistakes**

~~I will graduate from college by 2022.~~ *in*

When we celebrate our next anniversary, we will ~~be~~ married for 50 years. *have been*

I'll be studying this weekend while everyone else ~~will be~~ relaxing. *is*

**C** Match 1–5 to photos a–e. Write full sentences in the *future perfect* or *continuous*.

**The Optimist's Guide to the Next 20 Years**
1. ☐ soon / most people / work from home
2. ☐ we / stop / global warming / by 2040
3. ☐ scientists / discover / a cure for the common cold / by 2040
4. ☐ in next few years / most people / drive / electric cars
5. ☐ by / end / decade / all public places / install / free Wi-Fi

**D** 🔘 **Make it personal** In pairs, use the photos in **C** and the phrases below to make predictions.

I'm pretty sure (that) …    It's possible (that) …    I doubt (that) …

*It's possible that we'll all be driving electric cars by 2030.*

*Really? I doubt that very much. I think lots of people will have stopped driving completely.*

## 2 Grammar  Future perfect and continuous

**A** Point to sentences 1–5 in **1F**. Have sts study the sentences and complete the grammar box. Read task 1 with sts and explain that they should identify the tense and voice of the sentence and then write the sentence number in the corresponding box in the chart. Paircheck. Classcheck.

1. perfect
2. have
3. continuous
4. be

➔ **Grammar 9C** page 154

**B** Point to the five careers for 2030 and briefly name them with sts (privacy manager, nanomedics, book-to-app converters, 3D printing engineers, and turbine specialist). Have sts fill in the blanks with the verbs provided, using the future perfect or the future continuous in the active voice. Classcheck, then drill the contracted forms.

1. will have lost
2. will be using
3. won't be reading
4. will have doubled
5. won't have stopped

**Common mistakes**  Read with the whole class. There is a difference in meaning in the sentences with *in* and the sentences with *by*. The sentence *I will graduate from college in 2018* is not wrong, but it has a different meaning from *I will have graduated from college by 2018*. The first sentence means that the person will finish college in 2018. The second sentence means that the person will have finished college by that year, which means he / she will finish college **before** that year. Ask: *What will you be doing in ten years' time?* Then, pair sts up and have partners tell each other their plans and predictions for their own future, following the model in the speech bubble. Classcheck.

**C** Tell sts that they are now going to look at optimistic predictions for the future. Have sts match 1–5 to photos a–e. Classcheck.

Read item 1 and elicit a complete sentence from the class. Have sts write sentences for 1–5 using the future perfect or the future continuous. Classcheck.

1. Soon most people will be working from home. – photo b
2. We will have stopped global warming by 2040. – photo e
3. Scientists will have discovered a cure for the common cold by 2040. – photo d
4. In the next few years most people will be driving electric cars. – photo c
5. By the end of the decade all public places will have installed free Wi-Fi. – photo a

**D** **Make it personal**  Ask sts to hide sentences 1–5 in **C** with a notebook or a piece of paper and look only at photos a–e. Go over the sentence starters provided and elicit or give examples for each, e.g. *I'm pretty sure that people will be working from home in the future.* Point out that *that* in parenthesis is optional.

Have sts change partners and work in their new pairs to make predictions using the language and photos on the page. Monitor pairs closely and take notes for delayed correction. Classcheck and provide sts with language feedback.

➔ **Workbook** Page 47

# 9.5 Do you watch TV crime dramas?

## ID Skills  Identifying sarcasm

**A** Quickly read the article and match 1–4 to the crimes in **1B** and **1C** on p. 112.

### CRIME DOESN'T PAY. ESPECIALLY IF YOU'RE A DUMB CRIMINAL.

**1** 24-year-old Harry Zimmerman walked into the local convenience store with a gun and told the cashier to put all the money in a bag. On his way out, Zimmerman saw a bottle of Scotch behind the <u>coun</u>ter and told the cashier to put it in the bag, too, which the woman re<u>fused</u> to do because she suspected he might be under 21. So, <u>to prove his age</u>, Zimmerman, <u>a man of prin</u>ciples, showed her his driver's license, took the bottle, and ran away. A few minutes later …

**2** Forget "the dog ate my homework." Today's kids have <u>infinitely better ideas</u>. Like 22-year-old Brazilian student Susan Correia, for example, who was charged with reporting a false crime. One day, Susan called her mother in tears and told her that she'd just managed to escape from an old de<u>ser</u>ted house, where three armed men had held her <u>cap</u>tive for a whole day. <u>In de</u>spair, her mother called the police, who soon discovered that Susan had actually spent the day at a friend's house. At the police station, Susan admitted that …

**3** Rashia Wilson of Tampa, Florida, was sentenced to 22 years in prison for buying a $70,000 sports car and giving her one-year-old son <u>a relatively inex</u>pensive $40,000 birthday party—you know, <u>just like the ones your parents used to throw</u>. Unfortunately, the self-pro<u>claim</u>ed queen of fraud (yes, that's what she called herself – <u>subtle, huh?</u>) took lots of photographs revealing how she'd been using <u>tax</u>payers' money and, believe it or not …

**4** Today's <u>ultra-smart criminals</u> come from Iowa. Police had an easy time finding wanted criminals Joey Miller and Matthew McNelly. Before breaking into an apartment, these <u>masters of dis</u><u>guise</u> decided to hide their real identities. How did they do this? Well, <u>they covered their faces in permanent marker pen</u>. The thing about permanent marker pen is that … <u>it's permanent</u>.

> *First one … Well, let's see. Maybe he left his driver's license at the store and went back to get it?*

**B** ▶9.14 In pairs, match the titles to stories 1–4 in **A**. Predict how they end. Listen to check. Did you guess them all?

☐ How to make your mark  ☐ Nope, it never happened
☐ Old enough to break the law  ☐ Social media mistake

**C** Read the information. Then mark the underlined items in **A** sarcastic (S) or not sarcastic (N). Is sarcasm common in your community?

> *Well, my friends and I are sarcastic with each other. A lot!*

> *Yeah, but when people don't understand you're joking, they can get upset.*

De<u>tec</u>ting <u>sar</u>casm in writing, without intonation or facial expressions, isn't easy. Here are four tips:
- If a sentence looks sar<u>cas</u>tic, read it out loud. You might "hear" the sarcasm.
- Ask yourself, "Does it make sense in this context?" "Thanks, American Air, for losing my bags again this year!" is a clear example of sarcasm.
- Look for examples of exaggeration: "Aren't you the greatest cook in the world?"
- Consider the style. Informal writing usually contains more sarcasm.

**D** 🔵 **Make it personal**  In pairs, answer 1–4. Any surprises?
1 In your opinion, who was the dumbest criminal?
2 What punishments should the people in **A** receive?
3 Have you ever committed a small crime?
4 What would you do if you were Susan's mom or dad?

> *I think all of them were pretty stupid, but the guy who showed his ID was the worst.*

# 9.5 Do you watch TV crime dramas?

**Lesson Aims:** Sts learn how to identify sarcasm in writing.

## Function
Reading and identifying sarcasm.

## Language
… giving her one-year-old son a relatively inexpensive $40,000 birthday party.

… these masters of disguise decided to hide their real identities

**Vocabulary:** Expressions describing people: a man of principles, self-proclaimed. Phrases for giving excuses.

**Before the lesson:** Write the following questions on the board:
*Will you have saved enough money to buy a new car by this time next year?*
*Will you have finished your English course five years from now?*
*By this time next week, what important thing will you have done?*
*What will you be doing tomorrow between 8 and 9 p.m.?*
*Will you be working in 20 years' time?*

♪ Turn to p. 335 for notes about this song and an accompanying task.

**Warm-up** Review the future perfect and the future continuous by pointing out the questions on the board (see **Before the lesson**) and having sts discuss them in pairs. Classcheck.

## ID Skills  Identifying sarcasm

**A** Focus on the text title, *Crime doesn't pay. Especially if you're a dumb criminal.* Elicit predictions about the text. Tell sts that they are going to read stories about four not very clever criminals. Have them read the stories. Refer sts to **1B–1C** on p. 112 and ask them to use the vocabulary on these pages to name the crimes described in paragraphs 1–4. Paircheck. Classcheck.

> 1 robbery  3 theft
> 2 kidnapping  4 burglary

**B** Read the four titles with the whole class and have sts match them to stories 1–4 in **A**. Classcheck.

> 1 Old enough to break the law.
> 2 Nope, it never happened.
> 3 Social media mistake
> 4 How to make your mark.

Ask: *How do you think stories 1–4 end? What will happen next?* Have sts work in pairs to make predictions. Then, classcheck sts' guesses and play ▶9.14 to check.

> 1 Harry was arrested.  2 Susan was charged with reporting a false crime.  3 Rashia was sentenced to 22 years in prison.
> 4 Joey and Matthew were arrested.

**C** Read the information in the box with the whole class. Draw sts' attention to the underlined phrases in the text in **A** and have them mark S (sarcasm) or N (no sarcasm) for each. Paircheck. Classcheck.

> to prove his age – N
> a man of principles – S
> infinitely better ideas – S
> In despair, her mother called the police – N
> a relatively inexpensive – S
> just like the ones your parents used to throw – S
> subtle, huh? – S
> ultra-smart criminals – S
> masters of disguise – S
> they covered their faces in permanent marker pen – N
> it's permanent – N

**D** **Make it personal**  Pair sts up and have them discuss 1–4 with regard to the stories in **A**. Refer sts to the model answer in the speech bubble. Classcheck by inviting volunteers to comment on their partners' answers.

# Are you good at making excuses?

## ID in Action  Giving excuses

**A** In pairs, imagine the story behind the five headlines. Then change partners. Were any of your ideas the same?

*Maybe they thought the mayor was corrupt and wanted to access his computer to prove it?*

- [ ] ARMED GANG BREAKS INTO MAYOR'S HOUSE
- [ ] 70-YEAR-OLD ARRESTED FOR FLYING WITH SNAKE
- [ ] BURGLAR FALLS ASLEEP IN VICTIMS' BED
- [ ] 14-YEAR-OLD DRIVER SCARES JACKSONVILLE
- [ ] TERROR THREAT ON FLIGHT 207

**B** ▶ 9.15 Listen and match the headlines to dialogues 1–3. There are two extra headlines.

**Common mistake**

say / tell them
He will ~~tell~~ he's sorry.

**C** ▶ 9.16 Guess each person's excuse. Listen to the dialogue endings to check. Were the excuses believed? Were any of the stories similar to yours in **A**?

*I think the burglar is going to say he entered the wrong house.*

**D** ▶ 9.17 Complete 1–5. Listen, check, and repeat, copying the stress and intonation.

1 This is not what it looks _____.
2 Just _____ me out, please!
3 It's not what you're _____.
4 It's not what it _____.
5 _____, I can explain.

**E** ○ Make it personal  **Not guilty!**

1 Brainstorm what's happening in each photo, and why. Which other people might be in each situation?
2 In pairs, choose and role-play a photo.

*Hey, what do you think you're doing?*

*Just a minute! This is not what it looks like. I was just ...*

♪ *I don't wanna close my eyes, I don't wanna fall asleep, Cause I'd miss you, baby, And I don't wanna miss a thing.*

# 9.5 Are you good at making excuses?

**Lesson Aims:** Sts look at and practice phrases for making excuses.

**Function**

Listening to people giving excuses.
Acting out excuses.

**Language**

Wait a minute. This is not what it looks like!
It's not what it seems! Just hear me out!

**Vocabulary:** Phrases for giving excuses.
**Skills:** Giving excuses.

## ID in Action  Giving excuses

**A** Read the headlines with sts and make sure that they understand each one. In pairs sts imagine the story behind the headlines. Then change to a new partner to see if they have the same ideas. Get class feedback on sts' ideas, but don't confirm answers at this stage.

**B** Tell the class to listen to dialogues 1–3 and match each dialogue to the correct headline. Tell sts that there are two extra headlines, which will not be used. Play ▶9.15. Paircheck. Classcheck.

1. Burglar falls asleep in victims' bed
2. 14-year-old driver scares Jacksonville
3. 70-year-old arrested for flying with snake

▶9.15 Turn to page 322 for the complete audioscript.

**C** Tell sts that, in the next track, each of the criminals in **A** will try to give an explanation for what they were doing. Read the model in the speech bubble to the whole class. Say: *Guess their excuses*. Have sts discuss in pairs. Play ▶9.16 so they can check their guesses. Classcheck.

▶9.16 Turn to page 322 for the complete audioscript.

**Tip** Have sts turn to the AS on p. 173. Sts listen again and notice the sentence stress and weak forms.

**Common mistake**  Read with the whole class. Remind sts of the difference between *say* and *tell*. We use *say* + what was said. (He will say he is sorry.) We do not need to know who received the message. We use *tell* followed by who received the message. (He will tell them he's sorry.)

**Language tip** Remind sts that they have already seen similar mistakes with verbs *say* and *tell* in lesson 7.2, when they dealt with reported speech. After you read the TB explanation note for this mistake, have sts give other examples, in reported speech using *say* and *tell*. Encourage Romance-language—speaking sts to make comparisons with their L1 structures, where they also use both verbs (*say* and *tell*) for reporting.

**D** Have sts complete excuses 1–5. Play ▶9.17 to classcheck. Replay ▶9.17 for choral repetition.

1 like   2 hear   3 thinking   4 seems   5 Hold on.

**E** **Make it personal**  1 Point to the photos of different situations, assign pairs and ask sts to answer the questions for each of the photos.

2 Ask sts to choose one of the photos to role-play. Have sts read the instructions for roles **A** and **B** and encourage them to use language from **D**. Monitor closely and offer help only if requested. Then, invite volunteer pairs to act out their dialogues for the whole class.

Have sts change roles and role-play a situation from a different photo. Repeat the same procedures for monitoring and classchecking.

→ **Workbook** Page 48

→ **ID Richmond Learning Platform**

→ **Writing** p. 122

→ **ID Café** p. 123

# Writing 9 A formal letter

*Don't it always seem to go,
That you don't know what you've got till it's gone;
They paved paradise,
And put up a parking lot.*

**A** Read the headline from a local newspaper article and the letter written in response to it. Answer 1–4.

**White Rose Park Set for Closure!
Town council seeking to sell land to construction company**

1 Who's Melissa writing to?
2 Why's she writing and how does she feel?
3 Find six reasons she thinks it's a bad idea.
4 What are her two suggestions?
5 Who does she want to make contact with?
6 How does her home and place of work connect to the project?

> Melissa Gil
> 23a White Rose Lane
> Grangetown
> melgil@electromail.com
> 202-555-0152
>
> The Editor
> The Evening Post
> Mill Lane
> Grangetown
>
> Dear Editor,
>
> Re: White Rose Park Set for Closure
>
> 1 I'm writing to you ¹_____ express my huge disappointment after reading your article.. The whole community must be saddened to hear about the possible closure of White Rose Park. What is the town council thinking? How can they close one of the few safe play spaces ²_____ the area simply in order to make quick, easy money by selling the land?
>
> 2 Closing the park would affect the entire community. White Rose Park has been used for sports and recreation by local children and families for generations. In the summer, it is used to host concerts and the very popular annual folk festival.
>
> 3 People are always complaining that children have far too much screen time. How are they supposed to spend time outdoors if there is nowhere to go? What will the younger members of our community be doing ³_____ five years' time with no safe space to play? My little nephew will be extremely sad when he hears about this.
>
> 4 Perhaps local residents could set up a charity organization to raise funds to maintain the park. We could also start a petition and get as many people as possible to sign it. We can then present this ⁴_____ the town council.
>
> 5 I'd be very interested to hear ⁵_____ other people who are interested in getting involved to help save the park.
>
> Yours faithfully,
>
> *Melissa Gil*
> Melissa Gil
> Second grade teacher, White Rose Elementary School

**B** Complete 1–5 in her letter with the prepositions.

| from | in (x2) | to | with |

**C** In which paragraph, 1–5, does Melissa:
- ☐ suggest possible solutions/ideas?
- ☐☐ describe her opinion on the news story and express her feelings with examples?
- ☐ request contact from other readers?
- ☐ refer to the news story and explain why she is writing?

**D** Read *Write it right!* Then find three style errors in the letter.

> ✓ **Write it right!**
>
> When writing a formal letter to a newspaper:
> - put your full name, address, phone number, and email address at the top of the letter.
> - refer to the article you are writing about with the headline and date of publication.
> - keep your letter short and to the point. Make sure it only contains relevant information.
> - use a formal style, no contractions, etc.
> - you can ask questions or make suggestions.
> - end the letter in an appropriate way.

**E** 🔵 **Make it personal** In pairs, read the headlines from a local newspaper. Brainstorm possible solutions and ideas for each story.

> Language center to close all evening and mid-week English classes. Now weekends only!

> Historical buildings to be demolished to construct downtown highway.

> Train and bus prices to double!

> No more nightlife! All venues must close at midnight, even on weekends!

**F** *Your turn!* Choose a headline from E (or one from a real local newspaper) and write a "letter to the editor". Write 120–180 words.

| Before | Note ideas for your letter. |
|---|---|
| While | Follow the tips in C and the tips in *Write it right!* |
| After | Share with a partner to check formality, spelling, and punctuation, then send it to your teacher. |

122

# Writing 9 A formal letter

🎵 Turn to p. 335 for notes about this song and an accompanying task.

**A** **Books open**. Point to the photo and read the headline with the class. Say: *You're going to read a letter written to the newspaper about this article. What do you think they'll say in the letter?*

Give sts a few minutes to read the letter (ignoring the blanks) and answer the questions. Paircheck. Classcheck.

🔑 Suggested answers
1  the editor of the newspaper
2  to express her concerns about possible plans to close White Rose Park
3  few safe places to play in the area; would affect the whole community; used by many for sports and recreation; used in the summer for concerts / folk festival; children will have nowhere to go; her nephew will be sad
4  residents could set up a charity / start a petition
5  other people who would like to get involved
6  she lives locally and is a teacher at the local school

**B** Point to the first blank in the letter and ask which preposition is missing (*to*). Have sts complete blanks 2–5 with the rest of the prepositions. Paircheck. Classcheck.

🔑 1 to   2 in   3 in   4 to   5 from

**C** Read through the questions with the class, then have sts match them to paragraphs 1–5 in the letter. Paircheck. Classcheck.

🔑
4
2, 3
5
1

**D** Read the **Write it right!** box with the class. Then ask sts to find three style errors in the letter in **A**. Paircheck. Classcheck and write the correct versions on the board.

🔑 2 x contractions (I'm writing … , I'd be very interested), date of publication missing in the reference to the newpaper article

**E** 👤 **Make it personal**   Read the first headline with the class. Ask: *What will happen in this situation?* Elicit one or two ideas and write them on the board. Assign pairs and ask sts to think of more ideas for each headline. Classcheck and write sts' ideas on the board.

**F** *Your turn!* Tell sts that they're going to write a formal letter for one of the headlines in **E**.

**Before** Ask sts to use their ideas from **E** and make their own notes of possible solutions. Tell sts to think about what other information they can include in each paragraph, using the questions in **C** to help.

**While** Have sts write a four- or five-paragraph formal letter of 120-180 words. Remind them to follow the tips from **Write it right!** and to keep it short and to the point.

**After** If sts are writing their letters in class, have them exchange essays for peerchecking. Either way, when they have finished, have them email it to you. If they chose a real headline, they can send it to the editor of the newspaper.

## 9 A knight at the museum

### ID Café

### 1 Before watching

**A** 🔴 **Make it personal** Which of these have you visited? List three items you'd expect to find in each. What's the most interesting exhibit you've ever seen?
1 an art gallery
2 a natural history museum
3 a planetarium

*I loved the recent Da Vinci exhibit. It was awesome!*

**B** In which of 1–3 in **A** would you expect to find an exhibit on the items below?
☐ armor
☐ black holes
☐ bones
☐ dinosaurs
☐ fossils
☐ gemstones
☐ mammals
☐ mummies
☐ sculptures

**C** Use the photo, lesson title and the information in **A** and **B** to guess where August and Rory are. What are they saying? Who do they meet? What might happen next?

*Maybe they're ... waiting to meet ...*

### 2 While watching

**A** Watch and check all you hear.
1 ☐ It's museum week and August was given two free tickets.
2 ☐ Rory has never been to the museum before.
3 ☐ Genevieve is not bringing anyone with her.
4 ☐ Rory has always been fascinated by dinosaurs.
5 ☐ Rory was given a tour of the museum.
6 ☐ Genevieve says mummies are "kind of creepy."
7 ☐ August's text to Zoey didn't reach her.
8 ☐ Zoey got lost and was rescued by Paolo.
9 ☐ Today is the last day the film on black holes will be shown.
10 ☐ Paolo works in the museum.

**B** Watch again and complete 1–6 with the *passive voice*. What else did you hear this time?
1 Rory      Well, I _____ always _____ by dinosaurs as a kid.
2 August    You know where all the different bears and mountain lion exhibits _____ _____.
3 August    Mummies! These mummies _____ recently _____ in ...
4 August    Since you're a biologist and your studies _____ _____ on animals.
5 August    Next thing I knew she _____ _____ in the crowd.
6 Genevieve She says when she came back, August _____ _____. And she _____ a tour of the museum by Paolo!

### 3 After watching

**A** Answer questions 1–7.
1 What had Genevieve done before she got to the museum?
2 Whose studies were focused on mammals and biology?
3 Who was Zoey with after she got lost?
4 Who is "kind of like a knight in shining armor"?
5 Where else has August seen Paolo, and how does he feel about him?
6 What did August do to try to find Zoey?
7 In which exhibit room did August get distracted?
8 Why does Rory think Paolo might be wearing armor?

**B** Match the phrases 1–6 to the functions. Can you remember how each phrase ends and who said it?

| Describing an experience | Making a suggestion |
|---|---|
| ☐ ☐ ☐ | ☐ ☐ ☐ |

1 It's my first time at ...
2 I was fascinated by ...
3 Let's go see ...
4 One minute I was ... and the next ...
5 Maybe we should ...
6 Do you want to go see an exhibit on ...?

**C** *Role-play.* In pairs, imagine you're art critics at a museum. Show each other photos from your phones or from this book and comment on them.

*This is an amazing photo. The light and colors are really impressive.*

*Yes, and the composition is perfect, too. A work of genius!*

123

ism # Café 9   A knight at the museum

## 1  Before watching

**A** **Make it personal** **Books closed**. Say: *There are many types of museum in the world. What types do you know?* Elicit sts' ideas.

**Books open**. Point to the three types of museum in **A** and ask: *Which of these have you visited?* Assign pairs for sts to share their ideas and make lists of which items they'd expect to see in each. Classcheck by asking sts to share their ideas with the class.

**B** Elicit the meaning of *armor* (coverings or hard "clothes" to protect soldiers in battle) and explain that soldiers used to wear armor made of metal. Ask: *Where do you think we could see armor? In an art museum, a natural history museum, or a planetarium?* Have sts write the correct number in the box. Sts continue numbering the items. Paircheck. Classcheck.

> 1  sculptures
> 2  armor, bones, dinosaurs, fossils, gemstones, mammals, mummies
> 3  black holes

**C** Point to the photo and ask: *Where are Rory and August? What do you think they're going to do?* Have sts discuss the questions in pairs. Classcheck sts' predictions and tell them that Rory and August are at a museum.

## 2  While watching

**A** Tell sts that they are going to watch a video of Rory and August at the museum. Add that Genevieve is coming too. Have sts quickly read all the sentences and explain that they should check the statements that are mentioned as they watch and listen to the video. Then, play ▶ 9 as sts watch, listen, and check the statements that are mentioned. Paircheck. Classcheck.

> 1, 2, 4, 6, 8, 9, 10

**B** Have sts read 1–6 and tell them to fill in the blanks with verbs in the passive voice as they watch and listen to the video once more. Play ▶ 9 again. Paircheck. Classcheck by writing the answers on the board.

> 1  was / fascinated
> 2  are displayed
> 3  were / discovered
> 4  were focused
> 5  was lost
> 6  was gone / was given

## 3  After watching

**A** Have sts answer each question from memory in pairs. If time allows, play ▶ 9 again for sts to check their answers. Classcheck.

> Suggested answers:
> 1  she got her hair done
> 2  Zoey
> 3  Paolo
> 4  Paolo
> 5  the gym—he's a little jealous / envious
> 6  send a text
> 7  the History of Earth room
> 8  Genevieve said "he's like a knight in shining armor"

**B** Point to the phrases and say: *Look at these phrases from the video and decide if they're describing an experience, or making a suggestion.* Classcheck.

> Describing an experience: 1, 2, 4
> Making a suggestion: 3, 5, 6

**C** **Role-play**. Have sts change partners. Tell the new pairs to imagine that they are art critics visiting a museum. Have them find photos on their phones or on any page of the book and work together to make comments about them. Before pairs begin, invite two volunteers to read the model dialogue in the speech bubbles to the whole class.

Monitor pairs' discussions and take notes for delayed correction. At the end, invite volunteer pairs to act out their dialogues for the whole group. Then, provide the class with language feedback.

259

# 10

## 10.1 What drives you crazy?

### 1 Vocabulary  Moods

**A** ▶10.1 Read and match the highlighted words to photos a–h. Listen to check.

**What is your temperament?**

Cool as a cucumber, occasionally moody, or chronically short-tempered?

| | | |
|---|---|---|
| 1 | Do you ever wake up feeling grumpy? | Y \| N |
| 2 | Do you have nervous habits, like biting your nails or scratching yourself? | Y \| N |
| 3 | Do you ever get fed up with activities and people you actually like? | Y \| N |
| 4 | Do you ever get annoyed by people who are constantly in a good mood? | Y \| N |
| 5 | Do you ever swear when other drivers do something stupid? | Y \| N |
| 6 | Do you sometimes go from smiling to crying to singing in a matter of hours? | Y \| N |
| 7 | Do you ever yell at people for no serious reason? | Y \| N |
| 8 | Do you ever have to count to ten and take a deep breath, or else you'll explode? | Y \| N |

**CALCULATE YOUR SCORE**

For each *Yes* answer, give yourself the same number of points as the question number, e.g., 1 point for a yes in question 1, 3 points for question 3, and so on.

**27–36:** Hey, calm down! Being this explosive can be bad for you!

**18–26:** You're temperamental, but not dangerous. Learn to recognize your anger and relax.

**9–17:** You have your moments of madness, but, in general, you're pretty easygoing. Well done!

**0–8:** You're the king / queen of cool. Nothing can upset you. Or … Are you simply hiding your true self?

**B** ▶10.2 Listen, read, and take the quiz. Calculate your score and read what it means. Do you agree?

> I'm not convinced it's all true. I don't think that "nothing can upset me"!

**Common mistakes**

*mood*
My boss was in a bad ~~humor~~ again.
She has no sense of humor.

*argue / fight*
We respect each other and never ~~discuss~~.

**C** Match 1–4 to a highlighted word from **A**. Then write another example for your partner to match to the word.
1 "Keep your voice down. Do you want the whole building to hear you?"
2 "I love that you are always so happy. Nothing ever gets you down!"
3 "She was very calm and relaxed before her interview."
4 "Be careful, the tiniest little thing can make the boss angry."

**Unit overview:** The main topics of unit 10 are moods, binomials, separable and inseparable phrasal verbs, and verbs followed by gerund or infinitive.

# 10.1 What drives you crazy?

**Lesson Aims:** Sts look at and practice binomials and vocabulary on moods in the context of talking about how they feel in various situations.

**Function** Taking a quiz about moods.
Talking about what one does in different moods.
Listening to people taking a quiz.
Talking about what affects one's mood.

**Language**
Do you ever wake up feeling grumpy?
Why do you think you're always so grumpy in the morning?
Hey, what's that supposed to mean? I have my ups and downs, but I'm pretty stable ... right?
I'm in a much better mood in summer than in winter.

**Vocabulary:** Moods: fed up, grumpy, in a good mood, swear, yell (at someone). Binomials: again and again, each and every, little by little, more or less, peace and quiet, sick and tired, sooner or later, step by step, ups and downs.

♪ Turn to p. 335 for notes about this song and an accompanying task.

**Warm-up** Ask sts to look at the lesson title questions from unit 9, p. 112–121, and take turns asking and answering them in pairs. Encourage sts to ask follow-up questions when appropriate. Classcheck by inviting volunteers to report their partners' answers to the whole class.

## 1 Vocabulary Moods

**A Books open.** Focus on photos a–h and elicit how some of the people might be feeling. Encourage sts to use words they already know, e.g. *happy, angry, sad*, etc.

Point to the highlighted words in the quiz. Have sts match the highlighted words to photos a–h. Paircheck. Play ▶10.1 to classcheck.

  a  grumpy
  b  yell
  c  in a good mood
  d  swear
  e  short-tempered
  f  moody
  g  fed up
  h  cool as a cucumber

**B** Ask: *And you? What type of person are you?* Tell sts that they are going to take a quiz to find out. Play ▶10.2 as sts listen to and read the quiz in **A**. Instruct them to answer yes (Y) or no (N) for each question.

At the end, have sts calculate their own score according to the instructions in the top right corner of the quiz and read what their results mean. Read the model comment in the speech bubble to the whole group. Pair sts up and have partners comment on their results. Classcheck.

**⊘ Common mistakes** Read with the whole class and find out if the example sentences could be true for them.

**Language tip** In Portuguese and Spanish, the equivalent to the word *mood* is *humor*, which turns the word *humor* into a false cognate in this case. Point out that in the second part of the first sentence, the word *humor* becomes a real cognate. Help sts notice that the same real/false cognate issue happens with the word *discuss* in the second sentence. *Discuss* can be both a real cognate in, for example, *Discuss with a classmate …* and a false cognate as in the second mistake in the box. Encourage sts to think of more words that can be both a real and a false cognate.

**C** Point to sentence 1 and ask: *Which of the highlighted words in the quiz does this go with?* (yell). Have sts match the other sentences to the words, then write their own sentences for the other words. Peercheck. Classcheck.

  1  yell
  2  in a good mood
  3  cool as a cucumber
  4  short-tempered

# 10.1

D **Make it personal** Go back to your quiz answers. In pairs, ask follow-up questions to find out who is moodier? Any surprises?

*You're hot then you're cold, you're yes then you're no, you're in and you're out, you're up and you're down.*

*You mean you're never grumpy? What's your secret?*

*Life is short, and I'm just happy to be alive!*

## 2 Listening

A ▶10.3 Listen to a couple talking about the quiz. Which three answers do they disagree on?

*Carlos reminds me of my brother. A bit grumpy!*

B ▶10.3 Listen again. True (T) or false (F)? Do they remind you of anybody?
1. Carlos thinks Gloria is short-tempered.
2. Gloria is thinking of taking yoga classes.
3. She used to like her job.
4. She finds her job repetitive.
5. She's looking for a new job.
6. Carlos has seen Gloria swear at other drivers.

## 3 Vocabulary  Binomials

A ▶10.4 Binomials are pairs of words connected by a conjunction or (e.g. *loud and clear*) a preposition (e.g. *step by step*). Try to complete 1–6, then listen to check. Are 1–6 true for you? Know any others?

1. I have my ups and _____, but I'm pretty stable.
2. Little by _____, I'm learning how to relax.
3. I'm sick and _____ of waking up early.
4. I need some peace and _____ in the morning.
5. I hate doing the same things again and _____.
6. Sooner or _____, I'll need to start looking for a new job.

*Not me. I'm much more emotional than that.*

B Work in pairs. Take turns to say part of a binomial for your partner to complete.

*Peace and ...*  *... quiet. Sooner or ...*  *... later. More or ...*  *... less. Again and ...*

C **Make it personal** Which of these items affect your mood the most? Choose your top three, and then share ideas in groups. What's the most influential factor?
- what you eat
- the weather
- exercise
- the time of day
- the day of the week
- the season
- other people's moods
- the news
- your workload

*I definitely have my ups and downs, but I'm usually in a better mood in winter, when it's cooler.*

## 10.1

**D** 🔵 **Make it personal** Read the example question and answer in the speech bubbles with the whole class. Assign new pairs and have sts ask and answer further questions. Classcheck by asking sts to tell you something interesting they found out about their partner.

## 2 Listening

**A** Tell sts that they are going to hear a couple talking about the quiz from **1A**. Say: *Listen and tell me which three answers they disagree on.* Play ▶10.3. Paircheck. Replay ▶10.3 if necessary. Classcheck.

▶10.3 Turn to page 322 for the complete audioscript.

> Do you ever get fed up with activities and people you actually like?
> Do you ever swear at other drivers?
> Do you ever yell at people?

**B** Quickly read statements 1–6 with sts. Play ▶10.3 again for sts to listen and mark true (T) or false (F) for each statement. Paircheck. Classcheck.

> 1 T  2 F  3 T  4 T  5 F  6 F

## 3 Vocabulary Binomials

**A** Write the following extract from the listening on the board: *I have my ups and downs,* and say: *Ups and downs is a binomial. Binomials are pairs of words connected by a conjunction or preposition. Their word order is fixed, so learn them as chunks.* Then, elicit item 1 as an example. Play ▶10.4 and pause after sentence 1 to check the answer. Instruct sts to fill in the remaining blanks in sentences 2–6. Paircheck. Play the rest of ▶10.4 so sts can check their answers.

> 1 downs
> 2 little
> 3 tired
> 4 quiet
> 5 again
> 6 later

**B** Assign new pairs, and ask one student to close their book, while their partner reads part of a binomial to test them. Read the examples in speech bubbles with the whole class. When they have finished, have sts change roles and repeat. Ask sts to test their partners with any other binomials they know, e.g. *bread and …* (butter), *fish and …* (chips) etc.

**C** 🔵 **Make it personal** Have sts recall the lesson title question at the top of p. 124. Then, point to the phrases listed and ask: *Which of these items affect your mood the most? Choose the top three.*

Divide the class into groups of four. Refer sts to the model dialogue in the speech bubbles. Have them work in groups to compare things that affect their moods and to choose the most influential factor for the group. Classcheck.

➡ **Workbook** Page 49

## 10.2 What do you love to hate?

### 1 Grammar  Gerunds and infinitives

**A** Read the definition. Does the example annoy you? Do you have a pet peeve?

> **Pet peeve** noun [C] — something that annoys you very much or makes you extremely angry.
> One of my pet peeves is people eating with their mouths open.

> Yes! When someone talks during a film and then asks, "Who's he?" "What happened?" etc.

**B** ▶10.5 Complete 1–10 with a–j. Listen to a radio show to check.

a  interrupting you
b  playing with
c  ringing the bell
d  to put their trash
e  being the first
f  to call you
g  to pick
h  knocking first
i  using the word
j  not returning

### PEOPLE'S TOP PET PEEVES
We asked and you voted! Here are the results:

1. People who are addicted to _____ their phone.
2. _____ to arrive at a party.
3. When someone uses a finger _____ their teeth.
4. People who are too lazy _____ in the trash can.
5. People who promise _____, and then they don't.
6. Friends who honk instead of _____ when they come to pick you up.
7. Bad phone habits, like _____ texts or phone calls.
8. People who keep _____ "like."
9. When people keep _____ when you talk.
10. People who suddenly open the door without _____ first.

**C** In pairs, match 1–10 in **B** to the rules in the grammar box.

| Use a gerund | Use an infinitive |
|---|---|
| • as the subject of the sentence: ☐ | • to express purpose: _____ |
| • after certain verbs: ☐☐☐ | • after adjectives: _____ |
| • after prepositions: ☐☐☐ | • after certain verbs: _____ |
| Form the negative by adding *not* before the gerund. | Form the negative by adding *not* before the *to*. |

→ Grammar 10A p.156

#### Common mistakes

       *of not*
Dad's afraid ~~of don't~~ finding a new job.

Students who are too lazy ~~for~~ do their homework.
     *to*

      *not to*
I asked you ~~to not~~ keep interrupting.

       *not to*
We told you ~~to not~~ chew gum.

**D** Complete 1–5 with the gerund or infinitive form of the verbs in parentheses.
1. _____ (not know) who a text message is from is really annoying.
2. I get really mad when I find it difficult _____ (sleep).
3. People who use social media _____ (show off).
4. I don't like people who avoid _____ (make) eye contact.
5. People telling you _____ (not use) your phone and then theirs rings!

**E** In pairs, compare your feelings about the pet peeves in **B** and **D**. Which are your top three?

I can't stand ...
I don't like ...
I don't mind ...
... doesn't bother me.

**F** 🟢 Make it personal  In groups, brainstorm more pet peeves. Use 1–5 to help. Choose your group's favorite.
1. People who _____ without / after / before _____.
2. People who try to _____ by _____.
3. _____ing in the middle of the night / early in the morning.
4. People who keep / enjoy / avoid / insist on _____.
5. People who are too _____ to _____.

> People who change the TV channel without asking.

> Yeah, and taxi drivers who keep talking about themselves!

126

# 10.2 What do you love to hate?

**Lesson Aims:** Sts study and use gerunds, infinitives, and prepositions in the contexts of pet peeves and anger management.

### Function
Reading and talking about top ten pet peeves.
Listening to an anger management session.
Role-playing an anger management session.

### Language
I can't stand being the first to arrive at a party.
They say I'm too impatient and ... they're probably right.
Mario, welcome to the group. What brings you here?

**Vocabulary:** Common expressions with *for* and *of* (accuse (someone) of, afraid of, apologize for, thank you for, tired of).
**Grammar:** Gerunds and infinitives.
**Before the lesson:** Write the following prompts on the board:

Sooner or later I'll have to ...          I hate ... again and again.
I'm sick and tired of ...                 I need some peace and quiet ...
Learning English is more or less ...      Little by little ...

♪ Turn to p. 335 for notes about this song and an accompanying task.

**Warm-up** Ask sts to use the prompts on the board (see **Before the lesson**) to make true sentences about themselves. Pair sts up and have partners tell each other their sentences and find two things in common. Classcheck.

## 1 Grammar  Gerunds and infinitives

**A** **Books open**. Have sts read the lesson title question and the dictionary entry for *pet peeve*. Ask: *Does it annoy you when people chew gum with their mouths open?* Then ask: *Do you have a pet peeve?* Read the model answer in the speech bubble and have sts ask and answer the question in pairs. Classcheck.

**B** Draw sts' attention to the survey. Read the website title with sts and have them fill in the blanks with phrases a–j. Paircheck. Play ▶10.5 so sts can check their answers.

▶10.5 Turn to page 323 for the complete audioscript.

| | | |
|---|---|---|
| 1 | playing with | 6 ringing the bell |
| 2 | Being the first | 7 not returning |
| 3 | to pick | 8 using the word |
| 4 | to put their trash | 9 interrupting you |
| 5 | to call you | 10 knocking first |

**C** Tell sts to study sentences 1–10 and match them to the rules in the grammar box. Paircheck. Classcheck.

| Use a gerund | Use an infinitive |
|---|---|
| - as the subject of the sentence: 2 | - to express purpose: 3 |
| - after certain verbs: 7 8 9 | - after adjectives: 4 |
| - after prepositions: 1 6 10 | - after certain verbs: 5 |

**Common mistakes** Read with the whole class.

**Language tip** Speakers of Romance languages can have trouble using gerunds because in their L1, gerunds aren't used in the same way. When teaching section 1 (Grammar), make sure sts understand that although in their L1 all of the uses in the grammar box in **1C** would use an infinitive, in English they must always analyze the context and, if they have any of the situations that are in the left column of the grammar box, they should use a gerund instead of an infinitive. In other words, in English, the gerund (*-ing* ending) does not always translate to the gerund (*-ndo* ending) in their L1.

→ **Grammar 10A** page 156

**D** Tell sts to complete sentences 1–5 with the verbs in the correct form. Peercheck. Classcheck.

1 Not knowing   2 to sleep   3 to show off   4 making
5 to not use

**E** Have a pair of sts model the dialogue in the speech bubbles. Pair sts up to discuss the pet peeves in **B** and **D** and decide on their top three.

**F** **Make it personal**  Have two sts read the model dialogue in the speech bubbles. Divide the class into groups of three. Sts use sentence frames 1–5 to write more pet peeves and then choose the group's favorite. Give examples of your own pet peeves to start them off, e.g. *People who never stop interrupting. People eating popcorn at the cinema.* etc. Classcheck.

## 10.2

### 2 Listening

**A** ▶10.6 Listen to an anger management group and match the four people (Jim, Mia, Julia, and Vince) to the pet peeves in **1B**.

**B** ▶10.6 Listen again and circle the correct alternative.
1. Julia **is** / **isn't** new to the group.
2. Mia **agrees** / **disagrees** with her employers' opinion of her.
3. Jim's girlfriend says he is too **sociable** / **aggressive**.
4. Jim responds to Vince's criticism **sincerely** / **sarcastically**.
5. The coach wants to **change the subject** / **use the argument as an example**.

*'Cause we were just kids when we fell in love*
*Not knowing what it was*
*I will not give you up this time*

*Take a deep breath and count to 10.*

### 3 Vocabulary Common expressions with *for* and *of*

**A** ▶10.7 Listen and repeat extracts 1 and 2. Notice the stress and the weak forms, then circle the correct alternative in the box.

> /əˈfreɪdəv/      /wɒnə/    /fər/
> 1 I'm afraid_of losing my job.    2 I want_to thank you for being so honest.
> The prepositions *of*, *for*, and *to* are usually **stressed** / **unstressed** and the *o* is pronounced /ə/.

**B** ▶10.8 Try to complete extracts 1–6. Listen to check. Then repeat.
1. She accuses me _____ _____ aggressive.
2. I'm sick and tired _____ _____ that kind of English.
3. I apologize _____ _____ your sensitive ears!
4. There's just no _____ _____ bad grammar.
5. Remember there are ways _____ _____ with this.
6. We are responsible _____ _____ our anger.

**C** Complete the mind maps with the examples from **B**.

ADJECTIVE — VERB (thank (you)) — NOUN → **FOR**

afraid — ADJECTIVE — VERB — NOUN → **OF**

*My Spanish teacher used to say that a lot.*

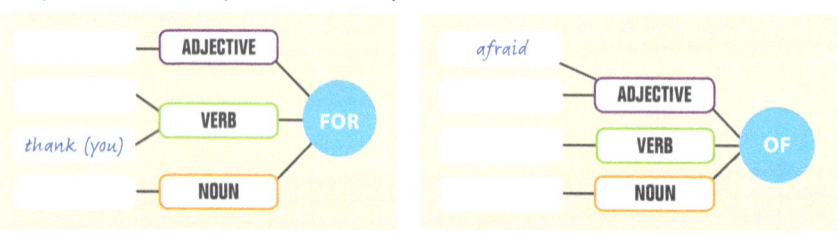

**D** ▶10.9 Guess what they are saying. Listen to compare. Were you right? What would you have said / done?

*You should apologize ... I'm sick and tired ...*

*I'm afraid ... There's an easy way ...*

*I'd have told him to forget the wedding!*

**Common mistakes**
of
I'm afraid ~~about~~ flying.
for helping
Thank you ~~to help~~ me with my project.

**E** 🔲 **Make it personal** In groups, role-play your own anger management session. Choose your pet peeves and elect the coach. Who's the angriest student?

*Mario, welcome to the group. What brings you here?*    *Well, I'm sick and tired of ...*

127

## 2 Listening

**A** Focus on the cartoon and ask: *What type of class is this? What might you learn in this type of class?* Explain the concept of anger management to sts.

> Possible answers:
> How to control impulsive behavior, i.e. counting to 10 before acting/responding
> Self-awareness and recognizing triggers that make you angry
> How to meditate
> Frustration management (e.g. writing in an anger diary)
> Breathing techniques and relaxation strategies

Tell sts that they are going to listen to part of this anger management class. Point to pet peeves 1–10 in **1B** and explain that each person will mention one pet peeve. Say: *Listen to find out who mentions what.* Play ▶10.6. Paircheck. Replay if necessary. Classcheck.

▶10.6 Turn to page 323 for the complete audioscript.

> Mia – bad phone habits (pet peeve 7)
> Jim – addicted to phone (pet peeve 1)
> Vince – people who keep saying *like* (pet peeve 8)
> Julia – people who keep interrupting you (pet peeve 9)

**B** Have sts quickly read statements 1–5. Play ▶10.6 again as sts listen and circle the correct alternatives. Paircheck. Classcheck.

> 1 isn't
> 2 agrees
> 3 aggressive
> 4 sarcastically
> 5 use the argument as an example

**Tip** Have sts turn to the AS on p. 174. Sts listen again and notice /juː/ and /uː/.

## 3 Vocabulary Common expressions with *for* and *of*

**A** Have sts look at extracts 1 and 2. Ask them to listen and pay attention to how the prepositions *of, to,* and *for* are pronounced in each of the sentences. Play ▶10.7. Have sts read the box and circle the correct alternative. Classcheck. Replay ▶10.7 for choral repetition.

> unstressed

**B** Ask sts to fill in the blanks in sentences 1–6. Play ▶10.8 so sts can check their answers as you write them on the board. Then, replay ▶10.8, pausing after each sentence for choral repetition. Monitor closely for pronunciation of weak forms of prepositions. Elicit / explain the meaning of any unfamiliar phrases, e.g. *to be sick and tired of something* (to be bored or annoyed to the point of not wanting to do something anymore).

> 1 of being  2 of hearing  3 for upsetting  4 excuse for
> 5 of dealing  6 for controlling

**C** Point to the mind maps and elicit the first possible answer. Have sts complete the rest of the mind maps with the examples from **B**. Encourage sts to think of their own examples for each phrase to help them remember it.

> *For* mind map: responsible (adjective), apologize (verb), excuse (noun)
> *Of* mind map: sick and tired (adjective), accuse (verb), ways (noun)

**Common mistakes** Read with the whole class. Refer sts back to the mind map for more examples.

**D** In pairs, sts use the prompts provided to guess what the people in the photos are saying. Classcheck sts' ideas. Play ▶10.9 so they can check their guesses. Ask: *Were you right? What would you have said / done?* If time allows, have sts turn to the AS on p. 174. Sts read as they listen and notice the pronunciation of /s/, /z/, and /ʃ/.

▶10.9 Turn to page 323 for the complete audioscript.

**E** **Make it personal** Divide the class into groups of five. Within their groups, sts should elect a coach for an anger management session. Other sts should play the roles of angry people, choosing pet peeves they need to learn how to deal with. Refer sts to the model text in the speech bubbles to get them started. Monitor and offer help if requested. Classcheck by asking: *Who's the angriest student?*

➔ **Workbook** Page 50

# 10.3 How assertive are you?

## 1 Listening

**A** In pairs, answer 1–3. Any disagreements?
1. What mistake has the teacher made?
2. Why does no one want to tell him?
3. Can we train people to be more as**ser**tive?

*Yeah, I think so. A friend of mine took a course like this once.*

**B** ▶10.10 Listen to the first part of a training course on assertiveness. Answer 1–2.
1. What is their definition of assertiveness?
2. What are the benefits of being assertive?

**C** ▶10.11 Listen to the whole course and complete the notes. Is it all good advice?

"Not ME. YOU go tell him it's misspelled."

> ### As**ser**tiveness
> - Assertiveness is a way of ¹_____
> - It's difficult to tell the difference between ²_____
> - As**ser**tive people are good at ³_____ because they can reach a com**pro**mise
> - You shouldn't expect other people to ⁴_____
> - You can control your own actions, but you can't ⁵_____
> - It's important to ⁶_____ when confronting people you disagree with
> - You have to learn to say ⁷_____
> - Try saying "I will" instead of ⁸_____

> **Common mistake**
> *tell*
> I can't ~~say~~ **tell** the difference between X and Y.

## 2 Grammar  Verb + gerund or infinitive

**A** Look at the highlighted items in ▶10.11 on p. 175. Underline the gerunds and circle the infinitives after *stop*, *try*, and *remember*. Then complete the grammar box with *-ing* or *to*. Does your language make this distinction?

> **Gerund and infinitive after *stop*, *try*, and *remember***
> If you use two verbs together, the second one can be either a gerund or an infinitive. Sometimes there's no difference in meaning:
> - I **began** to study / studying English when I was six.
> - I **like** to listen to / listening to classical music while I'm driving.
>
> But there are a few important exceptions.
> *Stop* + _____: Not do something anymore.
> *Stop* + _____: Interrupt what you're doing in order to do something else.
> *Try* + _____: Make an effort to do something.
> *Try* + _____: Do something and see if it works.
> *Remember* + _____: Remember that you did something in the past.
> *Remember* + _____: Remember that you should do something.
>
> ▶ **Grammar 10B** p.156

> **Common mistakes**
> *chatting*
> Please stop ~~to chat~~ on your phone at lunch. Turn ~~it~~ off **it**.

## 10.3 How assertive are you?

**Lesson Aims:** Sts study and practice verbs followed by gerunds and / or infinitives via the context of assertiveness.

### Function
Listening to a student from an assertiveness training school.
Reading / Taking an assertiveness test.
Responding to critical situations.

### Language
No! My counselor told me about this, I have to stand up for myself!
An uncle you meet regularly at family dinners is very critical of you and your career. You ...
I'd start telling the guy he's wrong. I'd try talking and see if it worked.

**Vocabulary:** *Assertive, assertiveness.*
**Grammar:** Verb + gerund or infinitive.
**Before the lesson:** Write the following questions on the board:
1  Are you afraid _____ flying?    2  Do you apologize _____ arriving late?
3  Have you ever been accused _____ doing something you didn't do?    4  Are you good _____ making new friends?

♪ Turn to p. 335 for notes about this song and an accompanying task.

**Warm-up** Show sts the questions on the board (see **Before the lesson**) and ask them to fill in the blanks with a suitable preposition. Classcheck. Then, have sts take turns asking and answering 1–4 in pairs. Classcheck.

1 of   2 for   3 of   4 at

## 1 Listening

**A** **Books open**. Have sts read the lesson title and ask what the lesson is about. Have them look up the word *assertive*. Classcheck sts' findings. Then ask: *How assertive do you think you are?* Draw sts' attention to the cartoon and have them discuss the answers to questions 1–3 in pairs. Classcheck. Ask sts about the cartoon: *Did you find it funny? Do you often see cartoons these days? Where?*

> The teacher has misspelled *assertiveness* and no one is telling him because the class is full of nonassertive people.

**B** Tell sts they are going to listen to the first part of a training course on assertiveness. Read the questions with the whole class, then play ▶10.10 for sts to answer the questions. Peercheck. Classcheck.

> 1  Assertiveness is a way of communicating your needs and wants, but without hurting other people.
> 2  Assertive people are better managers. They are good at negotiating because they can understand the opponent's argument and can reach a compromise more easily. They are also less stressed because they are more self-confident.

**C** Point to the first blank and elicit possible answers. Play ▶10.11 and have sts fill the blanks in the notes. Peercheck. Replay ▶10.11 if necessary. Classcheck.

▶10.11 Turn to page 323 for the complete audioscript.

> 1  communicating your needs and wants, but without hurting other people.   2  assertiveness and aggression.   3  negotiating   4  know what you want.   5  control other people.   6  stay in control and be positive   7  to say "no" more often   8  saying "I could", or "would"

**⊙ Common mistake** Read with the class. Speakers of Romance languages make this mistake as a result of direct translation. Explain that *tell the difference between* is a fixed expression in English and requires the verb *tell*, not *say* as in their L1.

## 2 Grammar Verb + gerund or infinitive

**A** **⊙ Common mistakes** Write: *stop, try,* and *remember* on the board. Refer sts to AS ▶10.11 on p. 174–175 and ask them to underline the gerunds and circle the infinitives after these verbs. Read through the common mistakes with sts. Then, ask sts to complete the grammar box. Peercheck. Classcheck, then ask sts if their own language makes the same distinction.

| Stop + -ing | Try + -ing |
| Stop + to | Remember + -ing |
| Try + to | Remember + to |

**Tip** Introduce the grammar by writing this quotation on the board:

*The moment you stop to make mistakes is the moment you stop to learn.*

Elicit the correction, or just show them the corrected version and elicit the difference in meaning.

*The minute you stop making mistakes is the minute you stop learning.* Miley Cyrus

➡ **Grammar 10B** page 156

# 10.3

B ♪10.12 Read a questionnaire from the training course. Match a–h to 1–8 and circle the correct alternative. Listen to check and practice the highlighted words.

🎵 *I am not afraid to keep on living*
*I am not afraid to walk this world alone*

a  stop **talking** / **to talk** to her
b  try **staring** / **to stare** at them
c  try **crying** / **to cry** or something
d  stop **standing** / **to stand** there politely
e  stop **showing** / **to show** up for these family dinners
f  he'll probably **trying** / **try** to find a way to get the money
g  instead, you write a "Remember **calling** / **to call** Jane" note
h  hey, I remember **lending** / **to lend** you some money a while ago

## TEST YOUR ASSERTIVENESS

**1** An uncle you meet regularly at family dinners is very critical of you and your career. You:
- ☐ say nothing and be friendly. Who wants conflict in the family?
- ☐ ¹_____. Forever. And tell everyone why.
- ☐ ask your uncle why he keeps criticizing you.
- ☐ ²_____. Maybe a little drama will work. Who knows?

**2** A close friend has just broken up with her boyfriend. She needs some emotional support. The phone rings, and you see her number. You're finishing an urgent report at work. You:
- ☐ don't pick the phone up. ³_____.
- ☐ ⁴_____. The report can wait.
- ☐ say you're busy and can only talk for five minutes.
- ☐ are tough. Tell her she should stop crying and forget about him. Then hang up.

**3** Your cousin borrowed $1,500 and promised to pay you back by April 30. It's October, and you still haven't heard from him. You:
- ☐ say nothing and accept the fact that you'll never see that money again.
- ☐ want to talk to him, but you keep putting it off. Give him a few more months. ⁵_____.
- ☐ explain why you need the money and negotiate a payback plan and a new deadline.
- ☐ call him and, in the middle of the conversation, say "⁶_____," as if you'd just remembered.

**4** You're standing in line at the bank, and someone cuts in front of you. You:
- ☐ smile and say, "Excuse me, perhaps you didn't realize there is a line."
- ☐ ⁷_____—perhaps they'll notice how annoyed you are.
- ☐ just stay where you are. A few more minutes won't make any difference.
- ☐ ⁸_____—push back in front of them.

C  In pairs, choose the most assertive reaction to 1–4 in B. What would your personal response be? Are your answers similar?

> *In the first one I'd probably stop going to those family meals.*

D  **Make it personal**  In groups, say what you would do in situations 1–5. Who's the most assertive? Is it possible to be too assertive?

**1** The passenger next to you is playing a loud video game. The flight attendant has already asked him to turn it off.

**2** You find out that someone at work / school has been spreading rumors about you.

**3** The waiter brings your food after a very long wait, and, when it finally arrives, it's cold.

**4** You have a friend who is consistently 15 to 20 minutes late when meeting you.

**5** A coworker / classmate you interact with for hours and hours has bad breath.

> I'd start _____ing / to _____.

> I'd stop _____ing / to _____.

> I'd try _____ing and see if it worked.

> I'd try to find a way of _____ing.

> I'd _____.

**B** Point to the questionnaire the candidates took when they joined the course and tell sts that there are phrases missing. Have sts place phrases a–h in the correct blanks. Paircheck. Play ▶ 10.12 to classcheck.

🔑
1 Stop showing up for these family dinners
2 Try crying or something
3 Instead, you write a "Remember to call Jane" note
4 Stop to talk to her
5 He'll probably try to find a way to get the money
6 Hey, I remember lending you some money a while ago
7 Try staring at them
8 Stop standing there politely

**C** Ask sts to look at the test in **B** once again and work in pairs to decide which response is the most assertive for situations 1–4. Classcheck.

Then ask: *What would your personal response be to each of these situations?* Have partners tell their answers. Then, classcheck by asking sts to report their partners' answers to the whole class. Ask: *Were your answers similar?* Elicit / explain the meaning of any unfamiliar phrases, e.g. *cuts in line* (to push in front of someone in a line).

🔑
1 ask your uncle why he keeps criticizing you
2 don't pick up the phone, write a reminder note to call your friend
3 negotiate a payback plan
4 smile and say, "Excuse me, perhaps you didn't realize there is a line."

**D** 🟢 **Make it personal** Assign sts into groups of three or four. Have sts tell each other what they would do in situations 1–5. Point out the model text in the speech bubbles and encourage sts to use the sentence frames in their answers. Monitor pairs' discussions closely for accuracy and encourage peer correction. Take notes for delayed correction. Classcheck and provide sts with language feedback.

➡ **Workbook** Page 51

# 10.4 How similar are you to your friends?

*I must admit a couple of my friends sometimes drive me crazy.*

*Me too. I have a friend who's a terrible gossip.*

## 1 Listening

**A** ▶10.13 Do all your friendships make you happy? Why (not)? Imagine what "a toxic friend" is. Listen to / Watch the start of a vodcast to check.

**B** ▶10.13 Listen / Watch again and check all the points you hear. Imagine what you will hear in the next part.
1. ☐ In a relationship, both people's needs have the same importance.
2. ☐ Friends and significant others should try to make you happy.
3. ☐ Toxic relationships take away our energy.
4. ☐ Sometimes even close friends can be toxic.
5. ☐ Toxic relationships can impact all aspects of our lives.
6. ☐ The program will suggest ways to escape from toxic relationships.

**C** ▶10.14 Listen to / Watch the rest of the vodcast and match the two columns.

| Antitoxic step | Main idea |
|---|---|
| 1 Diagnose the relationship. | ☐ Establish certain limits and be firm. |
| 2 Recognize your role. | ☐ Ask other people for advice. |
| 3 Build **boun**daries. | ☐ Stay away from people who treat you badly. |
| 4 You can't change other people. | ☐ Res**pect** yourself, and others will respect you. |
| 5 Get a second opinion. | ☐ Ask yourself how this person makes you feel. |
| 6 Look out for yourself. | ☐ Do you put other people before yourself? |

⚠ **Common mistakes**

relationship
I'm in a stable relation.

look out for / look after / take care of
You have to look for yourself.

**D** In pairs, summarize the video's advice from the pictures.

*Some relationships can take away our energy and …*

**E** 🟧 **Make it personal** What are the most important things in a friendship? Write your top five. Compare with a partner. Agree on three.

*Sharing the same sense of humor has to be one of them.*

130

# 10.4 How similar are you to your friends?

**Lesson Aims:** Sts study and practice separable and inseparable phrasal verbs through the context of *toxic friends* and how to deal with them.

### Function
Watching a video podcast about *toxic friends*.
Talking about what good friends are supposed to do.
Reading a friendship test.

### Language
And then we're going to help you extricate yourself from that unhealthy situation, pronto!
Friends and partners are supposed to give you energy and lift you up when you're down.
I never argue with my friends.

**Vocabulary:** Phrasal verbs (lift (somebody) up, bring (somebody) down, come down with (something), figure (something) out, boss (somebody) around, stick to (somebody / something)).
**Grammar:** Separable and inseparable phrasal verbs.
**Before the lesson:** Write the following questions on the board:
1. During class, how often do you stop _____ the phone or text somebody? (answer)
2. Have you tried _____ the online exercises on the ID Portal? (do)
3. Do you remember _____ a cartoon last class? What was it about? (read)
4. Will you remember _____ today's homework? (do)

♪ Turn to p. 336 for notes about this song and an accompanying task.

**Warm-up** Show sts the questions on the board (see **Before the lesson**) and ask them to complete the sentences with the gerund or infinitive form of the verbs provided. Classcheck. In pairs, sts take turns asking and answering 1–4. Classcheck.

| 1 to answer | 3 reading |
| 2 doing / to do | 4 to do |

## 1 Listening

**A Books closed.** Ask: *Do all of your friendships make you happy?* Write *toxic friend* on the board and ask sts to work in pairs to guess the meaning of the phrase. Don't confirm answers yet.

**Books open.** Play ▶10.13 so sts can check their answer. Then ask: *Who do you think suffers more from this problem: men or women?*

▶10.13 Turn to page 324 for the complete audioscript.

A friend that makes you feel bad

**B** Have sts quickly read statements 1–6. Replay ▶10.13 and ask sts to check the points they hear. Paircheck. Replay ▶10.13 if necessary. Classcheck. Then, elicit sts' predictions about what they are going to see / hear in part 2.

1, 2, 3, 5, 6

**C** Tell sts that part 2 gives viewers / listeners step-by-step tips on how to deal with toxic friends. Preteach the literal meaning of *doormat* (show an image of one) and tell sts that they are going to hear this word in the recording.

Play ▶10.14 and have sts match the two columns in the chart. Paircheck. Classcheck. Ask: *What does "doormat" mean in this context?*

▶10.14 Turn to page 324 for the complete audioscript.

3, 5, 4, 6, 1, 2

**D** Have pairs of sts summarize the advice given in ▶10.13 and ▶10.14 using the four pictures. Classcheck.

**Common mistakes** Read with students.

**Language tip** The first common mistake is caused by a false cognate for sts who speak either Spanish or Portuguese as their L1. Sts say *Estoy en una **relación** estable* / *Estou em uma **relação** estável* in Spanish and Portuguese respectively. This leads them to use the word *relation*, which in this case becomes a false cognate. Remind sts that in other situations, the word *relation* can be a real cognate. For example: *In relation to what we discussed yesterday*. Remind sts that the key to identifying a real / false cognate is to look at the context.

**E Make it personal** Ask: *What are the most important things in a friendship?* Ask sts to write their top five things. Help with vocabulary where necessary. When they're ready, assign new pairs for sts to compare their ideas. Fast finishers could search online for good quotes about friends / friendship. Classcheck by asking sts to share their best ideas with the class.

## 10.4

♪ *Oh, angel sent from up above*
*You know you make my world light up*
*When I was down, when I was hurt*
*You came to lift me up*

### 2 Vocabulary  Phrasal verbs

**A** Complete the definitions with the highlighted phrasal verbs. How many are literal meanings?

- Friends are supposed to give you energy and **lift you up** when you're down.
- How do you know if a friend is **bringing you down**? Well, in much the same way that you know you're **coming down with** a cold.
- If a friend or partner is stealing your **sunshine**, you need to **figure out** what you're doing to allow them to do this.
- Are they constantly **bossing you around**?
- Once you know the boundary that you want to set, **stick to** it! Draw your line in the sand.

1 _____ sb _____: tell somebody what to do
2 _____ sb _____: make somebody feel happier
3 _____ sb _____: make somebody feel sad
4 _____ sb / sth _____: find the answer, understand
5 _____ sth: continue, not change your mind
6 _____ sth: become sick with something

**B** 🟢 **Make it personal**  Complete 1–4 with verbs from **A**. In pairs, ask and answer. Any surprises?

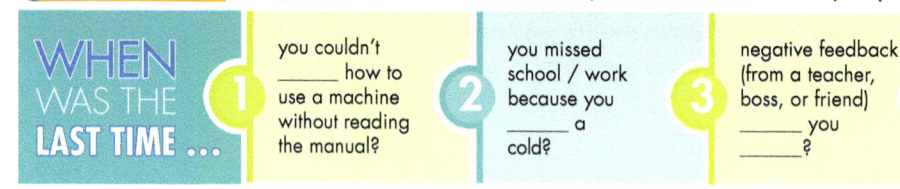

**WHEN WAS THE LAST TIME ...**

1 you couldn't _____ how to use a machine without reading the manual?
2 you missed school / work because you _____ a cold?
3 negative feedback (from a teacher, boss, or friend) _____ you _____?
4 you made a resolution? How long did you _____ it?

### 3 Grammar  Separable and inseparable phrasal verbs

**A** Read the grammar box, and then write separable (S) or inseparable (I) next to 1–6 in **2A**.

When a phrasal verb needs an **object**, sometimes you can separate the **verb** and **particle** (you can split **them** **up**), and sometimes you can't.
1 Most phrasal verbs with one particle are separable. If you use a pronoun, it always goes in the middle: *Turn* **on** *the TV*. / *Turn the TV on*. / *Turn it on*.
2 But some common phrasal verbs with one particle are inseparable: *I'm looking* **for** *a job*. If you're not sure, say it out loud, separating the verb and the particle. If the verb is inseparable, the sentence will sound really strange! *I'm looking a job for* (!)
3 Phrasal verbs with two particles are usually inseparable: *She cut* **down on** *sugar*.

➔ **Grammar 10C** p. 156

🟠 **Common mistake**
When you buy new shoes, try on ~~them~~ first.
                    ^them

**B** Reread the questionnaire in **2B** on p. 129. Underline six phrasal verbs and mark them S or I.

**C** Complete 1–6 using *it / them* and the particles below. Do you like tests like these?

with (x3)    to    up (x2)

**FRIENDSHIP TEST**
1 I never argue with my friends. I have never fallen out _____.
2 If one of my friends is feeling sad, I know how to pick _____.
3 I consider some of my friends to be like family. I get along so well _____.
4 If I make a promise to a friend, I will stick _____.
5 If the phone rings and it's a friend, even if I'm really busy, I'll always pick _____.
6 I don't see some of my friends often enough. I'd like to hang out _____ more often.

**D** 🟢 **Make it personal**  In groups of four, ask and answer the friendship test. Add follow-up questions, too. Any unusual stories or perspectives?

*Do you ever fall out with friends?*    *Hardly ever, but there was this one time ...*

131

# 10.4

## 2 Vocabulary  Phrasal verbs

**A** Read sentence 1 with the whole class and elicit the correct definition of the highlighted phrasal verb (2). Then, have sts match the rest of the highlighted phrasal verbs to definitions 1–6. Peercheck. Classcheck. Ask: *How many of these phrasal verbs are literal meanings?* (none of them).

1 boss sb around
2 lift sb up
3 bring sb down
4 figure out sb / sth
5 stick to sth
6 come down with sth

**B** **Make it personal**  Have sts fill in the blanks with phrasal verbs from **A**. Paircheck. Pair sts up and have them ask and answer questions 1–4. Classcheck by inviting a few volunteers to share their answers.

1 figure out
2 came down with
3 brought you down
4 stick to

## 3 Grammar  Separable and inseparable phrasal verbs

**A** Read the grammar box with the whole class. Then, instruct sts to write S (separable) or I (inseparable) next to sentences 1–6 in **2A**. Paircheck. Classcheck.

1 S   2 S   3 S   4 S   5 I   6 I

**Common mistake**  Go over with the whole class.

→ **Grammar 10C** page 156

**B** Tell sts to reread the quiz in **2B** on p. 129, then find and underline seven phrasal verbs. Instruct them to write S (separable) or I (inseparable) for each occurrence. Paircheck. Classcheck.

showing up – I
broken up with – I
don't pick the phone up – S
hang up – S
pay you back – S
keep putting it off – S

**C** Tell sts that they are going to read a friendship test. Ask them to fill in the blanks in sentences 1–6 with the correct particle(s) from the box and the object pronoun *it* or *them*. Classcheck by writing the answers on the board. At the end, ask the whole class: *Do you agree that these are all good tests of a friendship?*

1 with them
2 them up
3 with them
4 to it
5 it up
6 with them

**D** **Make it personal**  Have two sts read the model dialogue in the speech bubbles. Divide the class into groups of four and have sts work in their groups to ask and answer questions using the phrasal verbs from **3C**. Allow sts some time to prepare and make notes before they begin talking. Monitor groups' discussions closely and write down mistakes for delayed correction. Classcheck and provide language feedback.

→ **Workbook** Page 51

# 10.5 What do you find hardest about English?

*That's not me at all. I find writing hard, especially spelling.*

*For me, it's speaking. The most difficult thing is pronunciation.*

*I'm bad at listening. It's really hard to understand native speakers.*

**Common mistakes**

*pronouncing*
I have difficulty to pronounce new words.

*trouble / difficulty using*
I have a problem to use the present perfect.

*find it easy*
I have facility to remember new expressions.

## Skills Proofreading

**A** Mark 1–6 with S (same as / similar to me) or N (not like me). In groups of four, compare ideas. What's the most difficult skill?

| Easy | | Difficult | |
|---|---|---|---|
| 1 | I think I'm good at grammar | 4 | I find it hard to read fast |
| 2 | I have no trouble remembering new words | 5 | I have trouble expressing my ideas |
| 3 | I'm comfortable writing in English | 6 | I have a lot of difficulty understanding native speakers |

**B** ▶10.15 Now write 1–6 from **A** in the gaps in the messages. Then listen to check.

**C** In pairs, read each message, ignoring the blanks for now, and find …
1. two unnecessary words (cross them out).
2. two missing words (insert them).
3. a missing *s* in a word (add it).
4. a misuse of *-ing* (correct it).

Feeling frustrated with your English? Worried you might not be making enough progress? Wondering what the best way forward is? Send us your message, and we'll try to help you in next week's podcast.

**1** My name's Bruna, I'm have twenty-three years old, and I'm from Bucaramanga, in Colombia. I've studied English four years, and some things are easy, but others are very hard! For example _____ (I love rules!), but when I have to interact with other people, _____ and I hesitate a lot. My teacher says that I'll get better, she say it's only a matter of time. But sometimes I thinking I never to become fluent.

**2** I'm Byung-Sang, from Seoul. I have studied English since I was a little boy, but, to be honest with you, I don't like English. I can communicate well, _____ (especially emails), but listening is nightmare. _____. Once I spent two week in London, and I am felt really lost. Do you know about if there anything I can do to improving my listening?

**3** When I read, I try understand each and every word on the page, but people saying this is a bad habit. I have a friend who she is a teacher, and she told me do not worry about all the new word. But, honestly, _____, for general comprehension. What do you think? There's another problem: How can I use the new vocabulary? _____, but it's hard for me to use them. Any suggestions? Omar, from Istanbul.

**D** **Make it personal** Complete 1–4 with the phrasal verbs in the correct form. Then discuss them in pairs. Are you good proofreaders?

pick up    figure out    look up    put off

1. I _____ all of the mistakes in **B**.
2. I always _____ words in the dictionary if I'm not sure of the spelling.
3. I proofread my work immediately. I never _____ (it) until later.
4. I always check my grammar and _____ any mistakes myself.

# 10.5 What do you find hardest about English?

**Lesson Aims:** Sts study and practice how to proofread and correct pieces of writing in the context of reflecting on their own progress as language learners.

### Function
Proofreading and correcting mistakes.
Talking about your own mistakes in English.

### Language
What are your most common mistakes?

**Vocabulary:** be comfortable doing (something), find it hard / difficult to do (something), have (no) trouble doing (something), proofreading.
**Before the lesson:** Write the following questions on the board:
1  Are you pleased that you're about to finish one more level of the course?
2  Do you think you've made the most of the course so far? Why / (not)?
3  Do you think you should or could have studied more?
4  How much do you think your English has improved since the beginning of this course?

**Warm-up** Start off the lesson by chatting to sts about how they feel on (or about) the last day of class. Point out the questions on the board (see **Before the lesson**) and have sts discuss them in pairs. Classcheck.

## ID Skills  Proofreading

**A** Have sts read statements 1–6 and write S (similar to me) or N (not like me) for each one. Divide the class into groups of four. Have two sts read the model dialogue to the whole class. Ask sts to work within their groups to compare their marks for sentences 1–6 and find out which is the most difficult skill among the learners in their group. Classcheck.

**Common mistakes**  Go over with the whole class.

> **Language tip** When tackling the first common mistake, explain that when we want to say that something is difficult for us, we say *I have difficulty + verb (ing)*. For example: *I have difficulty understanding native speakers.*
>
> The third mistake occurs as a result of direct translation for Romance language speakers. This is because *facility* is a false cognate that actually means a building, or structure.

**B** Have sts add 1–6 from **A** to the gaps in the messages. Play ▶10.15 for sts to listen and check. Classcheck.

> 1, 5, 3, 6, 4, 2

**C** Read the webpage introduction with sts. Tell the class that there are several mistakes in the messages. Put sts in pairs and have them read and find the answers to 1–4. Classcheck.

> 1  My name's Bruna, I'm **have** twenty-three years old, and I'm from Bucaramanga, in Colombia. I've studied English **for** four years, and some things are easy, but others are very hard! … My teacher says that I'll get better, she say**s** it's only a matter of time. But sometimes I **think** I **will** never to become fluent.
>
> 2  … I can communicate well, I'm comfortable writing in English (especially emails), but listening is **a** nightmare. … Once I spent two week**s** in London, and I **am** felt really lost. Do you know **about** if there **is** anything I can do to **improve** my listening?
>
> 3  When I read, I try **to** understand each and every word on the page, but people **say** this is a bad habit. I have a friend who **she** is a teacher, and she told me **do** not **to** worry about all the new word**s**. …

**D** **Make it personal**  Have sts complete 1–4 with the phrasal verbs in the correct form. Paircheck. Classcheck.

> 1  figured out
> 2  look up
> 3  put it off
> 4  pick up

Divide the class into pairs. Have the sts in each group take turns asking and answering questions 1–4. Encourage them to take notes of their partners' views. Classcheck by inviting volunteers to report their partners' answers.

# 10.5 Are you going to take an English exam?

**ID in Action** Making recommendations

**A** In pairs, list two ways to improve your listening, speaking, reading, writing, grammar, vocabulary, and pronunciation. Share with the class.

*To practice listening, watch TV first without subtitles, then again with subtitles to check.*

**B** ▶10.16 Listen to the podcast. Check the two recommendations the teacher makes to each student. Do you agree?

**BRUNA**
1. ☐ Spend some time abroad.
2. ☐ Don't worry too much about mistakes.
3. ☐ Find someone you can practice with.
4. ☐ Think carefully about what you want to say.

**BYUNG-SANG**
1. ☐ Watch both easy and difficult videos.
2. ☐ Increase your vocabulary.
3. ☐ Don't use subtitles.
4. ☐ Improve your pronunciation.

**OMAR**
1. ☐ Vary your reading strategies.
2. ☐ Take a reading course.
3. ☐ Use a monolingual dictionary.
4. ☐ Learn expressions, not isolated words.

**C** ▶10.17 Match the two columns. Listen to check and repeat.

| Making recommendations | |
|---|---|
| 1 Try to focus … | ☐ learning "make an effort" instead of "effort"? |
| 2 Have you thought … | ☐ of practicing is watching Internet videos. |
| 3 A good way … | ☐ consider giving pronunciation a little more attention. |
| 4 You should … | ☐ reading slowly all the time. |
| 5 Try to avoid … | ☐ on expressing your ideas fluently. |
| 6 How about … | ☐ about asking a friend to practice with you? |

**D** Paircheck. **A:** Cover the first column and remember the full sentence. **B:** Check. Then change roles.

**E** Role-play the recommendations for the students as a dialogue.
**A:** You're a student. **B:** You're the teacher.
Change roles and suggest extra ideas.

*So, Bruna, are you pleased with your progress?*

*Well, yes and no. I still have difficulty speaking. What do you suggest?*

**F** **Make it personal** Think about your English, and note your strengths and weaknesses in two columns, plus any action ideas. Compare in groups, make more recommendations, and note down the best ideas.

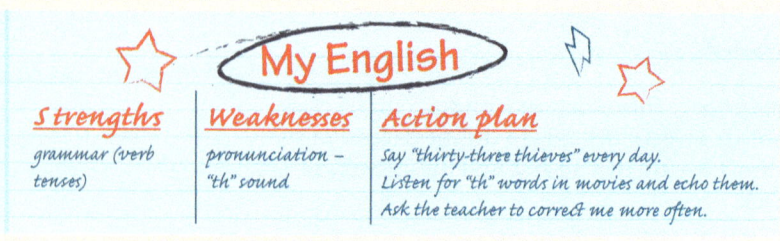

**My English**

| Strengths | Weaknesses | Action plan |
|---|---|---|
| grammar (verb tenses) | pronunciation – "th" sound | Say "thirty-three thieves" every day. Listen for "th" words in movies and echo them. Ask the teacher to correct me more often. |

♪ *I'm only human. I make mistakes. I'm only human. That's all it takes. Don't put your blame on me.*

*I'm OK with grammar—especially verb tenses. But I find pronunciation hard, like the "th" sound.*

*Have you thought about using a pronunciation book with audio to practice? Or finding some pronunciation videos on YouTube?*

# 10.5 Are you going to take an English exam?

**Lesson Aims:** Sts learn how to make recommendations in the context of talking about their own progress as language learners.

### Function
Listening to a teacher's recommendations.
Role-play teacher—student dialogues.
Talking about your own English and making recommendations.

### Language
How about learning *make an effort* instead of *effort*?
Try to avoid reading slowly all the time.
Have you thought about paying attention to the *th* sound in movies?

**Vocabulary:** Expressions for making recommendations (A good way is ... , How about ... , Try to focus on ...).
**Skills:** Making recommendations.

## ID in Action  Making recommendations

**A** Say: *List two ways to improve your listening, speaking, reading, writing, grammar, vocabulary, and pronunciation.* Have sts discuss their ideas in pairs. Classcheck by writing their ideas on the board.

**B** Tell sts that they are going to listen to the podcast as a teacher makes recommendations for Bruna, Byung-Sang, and Omar. Ask sts to listen and check the two recommendations given to each student. Play ▶10.16. Paircheck. Replay the track if necessary. Classcheck. Ask: *Were any of your ideas from A mentioned?*

▶10.16 Turn to page 324 for the complete audioscript.

> Bruna – 2, 3
> Byung-Sang – 1, 4
> Omar – 1, 4

**C** Point to the chart and say: *Try to remember more of the teacher's recommendations and match these two columns.* Play ▶10.17 so sts can check their answers. Classcheck. Replay the track and ask sts to repeat sentences 1–6. Correct intonation on the spot.

> 1 Try to focus on expressing your ideas fluently.
> 2 Have you thought about asking a friend to practice with you?
> 3 A good way of practicing is watching Internet videos.
> 4 You should consider giving pronunciation a little more attention.
> 5 Try to avoid reading slowly all the time.
> 6 How about learning "make an effort" instead of "effort"?

**D** Assign sts into A/B pairs. Ask them to hide the second column of the chart in **C** with a notebook or a sheet of paper. Have partners take turns saying 1–6 as full sentences from memory. Monitor for accuracy and intonation. Encourage peer collaboration and correction. At the end, ask: *Which sentence was the most difficult to remember?*

**E** Have sts role-play a student–teacher dialogue based on the students' messages and the teacher's podcast. Ask them to use language from **ID Skills B** and **ID in Action B** and **C**. Monitor them and offer help whenever necessary. Then, ask sts to change roles and role-play the dialogue one more time. Finally, invite volunteer pairs to act out their dialogues for the whole class.

**F** **Make it personal**  Focus on the headings *Strengths, Weaknesses, and Action Plan* on the chart. Review the examples provided for each section. Then, ask sts to think about their own English and write notes in each of the columns.

Divide the class into groups of four. Ask sts to tell their group members what their strengths and weaknesses are and what action plan they thought of. Explain that sts should listen to their classmates and make more recommendations to help, as in the model comments in the speech bubbles. Have two sts read this model to the whole class before sts begin their discussions. Then, have sts in each group share their ideas and try to help one another. Monitor and offer help if necessary. Classcheck.

Round off the lesson by congratulating sts on reaching the end of the course and encourage them to keep up the good work!

♪ Turn to p. 336 for notes about this song and an accompanying task.

➡ **Workbook** Page 52

➡ **ID Richmond Learning Platform**

➡ **Writing** p. 134

➡ **ID Café** p. 135

# Writing 10  A forum post

*Go, go, go*
*Figure it out, figure it out, but don't stop moving*
*Go, go, go*
*Figure it out, figure it out, you can do this*

**A** Read the forum post, ignoring any mistakes. What advice does Lara ask for? Does she get a good response?

---

**Good English school in the center of Edinburgh?**  Sep 5th, 19:02

Hi, I'm planning to come to the UK for ~~learning~~ *to learn* English during four weeks. I'm not sure which city would be a good place to stay. I'm thinking about Edinburgh. What do you suggest? Also, if you was me, what would you do about accommodations? Do you think it's better stay with a host family or in a hostel or an apartment?
Could you suggest a good school in Edinburgh? Is a good city for students? I'm 23 years old. What do you advise me doing?
Thanks in advance.

*LaraVenice*

**Re: Good English school in the center of Edinburgh**  Sep 6th, 07:31

Have you thought about to contact the British Council? They are the country's cultural ambassadors. They have offices all over the world and will help you figure out where to go. You should have a look at schools on ARELS (Association of Recognized English Language Services), too.
IMO Edinburgh is a great place for study! There's a university and lots of things to do and places to explore. You ought to contact the University. They probably have courses and plenty of informations for overseas students. As far as accommodation is concerned, how about stay with a host family? You'll learn much more about the culture and also get used to the Scottish accent faster! 😊 Good luck!

*CatCrazy21*

---

**B** Reread, find, and correct
1. five more mistakes with the use of gerunds and infinitives.
2. five more common mistakes.

**C** Underline five phrases used for asking for advice and circle four phrases for giving advice.

**D** Match the sentence halves.

1. You ought
2. You shouldn't
3. How about
4. Have you thought
5. Why don't you

- about speaking to your tutor?
- leave the door unlocked.
- go to bed early tonight?
- hiring a bicycle?
- to call your mother.

**E** Read *Write it right!* Then find examples of indirect questions in the forum posts.

### ✓ Write it right!

- Internet forums are useful places to share / get information.
- Forums have rules, so make sure you check and follow them.
- **A**cronyms such as OP (original poster) and TBH (to be honest) are often used to make communication faster. These are informal.
- Use indirect questions when asking for information to sound more polite.
- You can use more direct questions when you are familiar with the person you are chatting to online.

**F** What do you think the acronyms in 1–5 mean? Use these words to help you.

| as (x2) | at | by | in | laugh | loud |
| moment | my | opinion | out | possible |
| soon | the (x2) | way |

1. BTW, have you thought about asking your tutor?
2. I'm a bit busy ATM. I'll call you later.
3. IMO, the Scottish accent is difficult to understand.
4. I'll think about it and let you know ASAP.
5. That's the funniest photo ever! LOL.

**G** 🎤 **Make it personal**  In pairs, what advice would you give to someone coming to study language in your hometown?

**H** *Your turn!* Write a forum post asking for advice on one of the following topics.

- Help! I'm giving a class presentation.
- Nice places to walk my dog
- Best restaurant for a family celebration

| Before | Decide what advice you want to ask for. |
|---|---|
| While | Follow the tips in *Write it right!* |
| After | Use more direct questions when you are familiar with the person you are chatting to online. |

# Writing 10  A forum post

🎵 Turn to p. 336 for notes about this song and an accompanying task.

**A** **Books closed**. Ask: *Do you ever post on forums to ask for advice?* Elicit sts' answers and have a brief class discussion.

**Books open**. Point to the forum post and say: *Lara is asking for advice, and someone has responded.* Ask sts to read the post and answer the questions. Remind sts to ignore the mistakes as they read. Paircheck. Classcheck.

> 🔑 Lara asks for advice about where to study English in Edinburgh. She gets a very good response with lots of useful information.

**B** Focus attention on the error in the first sentence, then have sts find five more errors with the use of gerunds and infinitives. Paircheck. Classcheck.

> 🔑
> 1 Do you think it's ~~better stay~~ better to stay
> What do / would you advise me ~~doing~~ to do?
> Have you thought about ~~to contact~~ contacting …
> Edinburgh is a great place ~~for~~ to study!
> … how about ~~stay~~ staying
>
> … ~~during~~ for four weeks
> If you ~~was~~ were me
> accommodations
> Is a good city … = Is it a good city …
> informations

**C** Point to the question "What do you suggest?" in Lara's forum post and ask: *Is this a phrase for asking for advice or giving advice?* (asking). Sts underline and find four more phrases for asking for advice and circle four phrases for giving advice. Paircheck. Classcheck.

> 🔑
> **asking for advice:** What do you suggest? … what would you do about … Do you think … Could you suggest … What would / do you advise me to do?
>
> **giving advice:** Have you thought about … You should … You ought to … How about …

**D** Have sts match the sentence halves in pairs. Classcheck.

> 🔑
> 1 to call your mother.
> 2 leave the door unlocked.
> 3 hiring a bicycle?
> 4 about speaking to your tutor?
> 5 go to bed early tonight?

**E** Read the **Write it right!** box with the class. Then, ask sts to find examples of indirect questions in the forum posts.

> 🔑
> Could you suggest a good school in Edinburgh?
> Have you thought about contacting the British Council?
> As far as accommodation is concerned, how about staying with a host family?

**F** Read the sentences with the class, and elicit the first answer as an example. Sts decide what the rest of them mean. Paircheck. Classcheck and ask: *What other abbreviations do you know?*

> 🔑
> 1 by the way
> 2 at the moment
> 3 in my opinion
> 4 as soon as possible
> 5 laugh out loud

**G** 👤 **Make it personal** Read the question with the class, then elicit one or two ideas. Assign new pairs and have sts think of ideas. Classcheck and write their ideas on the board.

**H** *Your turn!* Tell sts that they're going to write their own forum post asking for advice. Read the three topics with the class.

**Before** Ask sts to choose one of the topics.

**While** Have sts write a short forum post asking for advice. Remind them of the advice in the **Write it right!** box and the phrases for asking for advice in **C** and **D**. Go around and help with vocabulary where necessary.

**After** When they have finished, assign pairs and have sts email their posts to each other in order to respond, then forward the exchange to you.

# 10 Mad men

## ID Café

### 1 Before watching

**A** Match 1–6 to their definitions a–f.
1. brood and mope around
2. knock some sense into people
3. watch chick flicks and cry your eyes out
4. work your fingers to the bone
5. yell like Tarzan
6. stereotyping

a ☐ to work incredibly hard
b ☐ to cry a lot watching a rom-com-type movie
c ☐ to make someone behave more logically
d ☐ to label something as "typical" in a negative way
e ☐ to express anger or emotion in a loud, primitive way
f ☐ to obsess about what makes you unhappy

**B** ◯ **Make it personal** In pairs, share your experiences of 1–7.

> When her boyfriend doesn't call, my sister broods and mopes.

### 2 While watching

**A** Watch to 2:00 and answer 1–4. Check all you hear.
1. According to the guys, on a girls' day out, they ...
   ☐ cry their eyes out.   ☐ shop.
   ☐ watch a "chick flick."   ☐ sit in a spa.
   ☐ complain about men.   ☐ gossip.
   ☐ get their nails done.   ☐ laugh at men.
   ☐ do their hair.
2. What really annoys August the most?
   ☐ that he's tired of competing
   ☐ that Paolo is always the "hero"
   ☐ that he's scared
   ☐ that he's not a knight in shining armor
3. Seeing a shrink means you have to
   ☐ sit in an office.   ☐ talk about your life.
   ☐ work out your problems.   ☐ pay unnecessarily.
4. What makes Rory angry?
   ☐ losing a game   ☐ cooking for other people
   ☐ sitting on the bench   ☐ having no confidence

**B** Watch the video again and order what happened, 1–10.
☐ The guys talk about how to solve their problems.
☐ Rory wonders what a "girls' day out" is all about.
☐ August complains about Paolo's heroic behavior.
☐ Daniel says he's pretty happy and confident.
☐ Daniel explains what he thinks women do when they are out together.
☐ August reminds Rory about how cooking was a disaster.
☐ Daniel recommends that August talk to a therapist.
☐ Rory realizes that Daniel is right.
☐ Rory thinks that stereotyping is a bad idea.
☐ They end up relaxing by playing video games.

**C** Complete the excerpts. Who says them? Watch again to check.

| beating | boxing | brooding | chasing |
| competing | complaining | experiencing |
| jumping | moping around | using |

1. What if the science foundation starts _____ my ideas without my permission?
2. Rory, you're mad because of the time you wasted _____ after Genevieve.
3. I've seen you both _____ the extremes of emotions. Some days practically _____ for joy, other days _____ and _____.
4. _____ stinks!
5. Stop _____.
6. Yep, nothing's ever so bad that a little _____ can't cure.
7. _____ you two at video games makes me feel the number one winner.

### 3 After watching

**A** True (T) or false (F)? Correct the false statements.
1. August needs to build up more muscles and more confidence.
2. Daniel tells Rory and August to stop complaining.
3. Daniel thinks video games are a bad solution.
4. August says that yelling like Tarzan is a great therapy.
5. Rory tried punching an avatar to deal with stress.

**B** ◯ **Make it personal** Do you use video games to relax? In groups, share suggestions for working out anger or stress. Which works best for you?

> Dancing is a great way to de-stress.

> Hmm ... For me, yelling and exercising is much better.

**C** ◯ **Make it personal** Which ID Café characters do you like the most and the least: Andrea, August, Daniel, Genevieve, Lucy, Paolo or Zoey?

> I really like Genevieve. I'd love to be a musician, and she seems really confident.

# ID Café 10 Mad men

## 1 Before watching

**A** Say: *We're going to watch a video of Daniel, Rory, and August. The girls won't show up – it's girls' night out.* Ask: *Do you think the guys are going to feel happy being alone?*

Have sts read expressions 1–6 and work in pairs to match them to the correct definitions. Classcheck.

> 1 f   2 c   3 b   4 a   5 e   6 d

**B** 🔑 Make it personal   Assign pairs, then read the example in the speech bubble with sts. Ask pairs to discuss their experiences of 1–6 from **A**.

## 2 While watching

**A** Go over questions 1–4 and the answer choices with sts. Ask them to check the correct answers as they watch and listen to the video. Play **Video 10**. Replay the video if necessary. Classcheck.

> 1 cry their eyes out; watch a "chick flick"; do their hair; shop; get their nails done; sit in a spa; complain about men; gossip; laugh at men
> 2 that Paolo is always the "hero."
> 3 sit in an office; talk about your life
> 4 sitting on the bench (during a soccer match)

**B** Tell sts to order events 1–10 as they watch the video once again. Allow sts some time to read the statements, then replay **Video 10**. Paircheck. Classcheck.

> 2, 5, 9, 3, 7, 1, 6, 4, 8, 10

**C** Ask: *Do you remember what Daniel said about his ideas and the science foundation?* Point to sentence 1 and elicit the correct answer. Classcheck. Have sts fill in the blanks in sentences 1–7 with the words and phrases from the box. Paircheck. If time allows, replay **Video 10** so sts can check their answers. Classcheck.

> 1 using (Daniel)
> 2 chasing after (Daniel)
> 3 experience, jumping, brooding, moping around (Daniel)
> 4 Competing (August)
> 5 complaining (Daniel)
> 6 boxing (August)
> 7 Beating (Daniel)

## 3 After watching

**A** Have sts read sentences 1–5 and mark each one true (T) or false (F), then have them correct the false statements. Paircheck. Classcheck by writing the answers on the board.

> 1 T
> 2 T
> 3 F (Daniel thinks video games are a good solution.)
> 4 T
> 5 T

**B** 🔑 Make it personal   Ask: *Do you use video games to relax?* Ask two volunteer sts to read out the model dialogue in the speech bubbles. Then, put sts in groups to share their suggestions. Classcheck by asking a student from each group to share their ideas with the class.

**C** 🔑 Make it personal   Pair sts up and ask: *Which of the characters do you like the most and the least? Why?* Have sts discuss the question with their partners. Classcheck.

# R5 Grammar and Vocabulary

**A** *Picture dictionary.* Cover the words on the pages below and remember.

| pages | |
|---|---|
| 112 | 7 crimes |
| 116 | Michael's story |
| 118 | 3 cybercrime risks |
| 119 | 5 optimistic predictions |
| 124–125 | 8 mood words and phrases |
| 127 | 6 expressions with *of* and 6 with *for* |
| 130 | 4 pieces of advice from the video |
| 131 | 6 phrasal verbs from the definitions |
| 161 | 2 words for each sound in lines 5 and 6 of the consonants chart (not the picture words) |

**B** Rewrite 1–6 using the *passive voice*. Do you remember which units of D 3 refer to them?
1. Millions of Americans watch late night talk shows.
2. Technology is killing our creativity.
3. Dyson invented the first cordless vacuum cleaner.
4. Disney gave the cast of *Avengers: Infinity War* fake scripts.
5. Do you think our voices will operate more technology in the future?
6. Brandon is holding his party outside.

**C** Complete signs 1–6 with *to, for,* or *of*. In pairs, think of two places where you might see each of them.

1. All thieves will be taken ____ court.
2. If you're afraid ____ change—give it to me.
3. Thank you ____ not smoking.
4. Tired ____ being single?
5. Ticket machine under maintenance. We apologize ____ any inconvenience.
6. Not responsible ____ personal items left in vehicles.

*The first one looks like it's in some kind of store.*

**D** 🔊 Make it personal  Circle the correct alternative. In pairs, ask and answer. Any surprises?
1. How many times do you stop **to have / having** a break at work / school?
2. Do you worry about **to be / being** robbed online?
3. Can you remember **to learn / learning** to ride a bike?
4. Have you ever tried **to camp / camping**?
5. Do you always remember **to wash / washing** your hands before **to eat / eating**?

*I stop maybe three or four times a day.* — *And what do you do on your break?*

**E** 🔊 R5.1 Listen to three dialogues and match verbs 1–7 to the particles. Listen again and find one more phrasal verb in each dialogue.

| 1 get | ☐ with |
| 2 figure | ☐ down |
| 3 stick | ☐ into |
| 4 lift | ☐ out |
| 5 come down | ☐ to |
| 6 bring | ☐ up |
| 7 boss | ☐ around |

**F** Make ➕ or ➖ predictions about these topics 20 years from now. Compare in pairs. Any different opinions?

climate change   colonize the moon
discover time travel   end poverty   over-population
pandas disappear   use house phones

*I guess we'll be starting to colonize the moon.* — *Really? I don't think we'll have started by then.*

**G** Correct the mistakes in each sentence. Check your answers in units 9 and 10. What's your score, 1–10?

**Common mistakes**
1. They tried to steal the shop but didn't rob anything. (2 mistakes)
2. This photo was took secretly and has been showing on the Internet. (2 mistakes)
3. Hurry up! By the time we get the theater, the movie will start. (2 mistakes)
4. People shouldn't to go in prison for theft. (2 mistakes)
5. Do you worry with not to pass the final exams? (2 mistakes)
6. Remember locking the doors after to leave. (2 mistakes)
7. I like the people who are smiling all the time. (2 mistakes)
8. Do you want to go with me out to a party this night? (2 mistakes)
9. I'm good with speaking but I have difficulty to understand. (2 mistakes)
10. Is it easy for to use correctly prepositions? (2 mistakes)

# Review 1 Units 8-9

## Grammar and vocabulary

♪ Turn to p. 336 for notes about this song and an accompanying task.

**A** ***Picture dictionary.*** Pair sts up and have partners test each other and review the vocabulary in units 9 and 10. Monitor sts closely throughout the picture dictionary tasks and correct vocabulary and pronunciation on the spot.

Replay ▶R5.1 and ask sts to listen for one additional phrasal verb in each dialogue. Paircheck. Classcheck by writing the answers on the board.

| Picture Dictionary | Procedures | Mini-dialogues / Suggested language |
|---|---|---|
| 7 crimes, p. 112 | Have sts hide the texts in **1A** with a notebook. Ask them to work in pairs, taking turns pointing to pictures a–g and naming seven types of crime. | St A: (points to picture a) *Murder.*<br>St B: (points to picture b) *That's bribery.* |
| Michael's story, p. 116 | Ask sts to hide the text about Michael with a notebook or a sheet of paper and, in pairs, retell the story based on the pictures. | St A: *Michael decided to listen to loud rap music in his car in the middle of the night.*<br>St B: *The neighbors called the police and he was sent to jail.* |
| 3 cybercrime risks, p. 118 | Have sts look at the pictures in **1D** and, in trios, make predictions about cybercrime in the future. | St A: *Attacks will be carried out wirelessly, and we won't be protected.*<br>St B: *Viruses will spread across multiple devices very easily.* |
| 8 mood words and phrases, p. 124–125 | Have sts hide the quiz in **1A** with a notebook or a sheet of paper and ask *How often …?* questions about the moods in pictures a–h. | St A: *How often do you wake up feeling grumpy?*<br>St B: *Every day. How about you?*<br>St A: *Only if I don't get enough sleep.* |

**B** Ask sts to rewrite 1–6 using the passive voice. Paircheck. As you classcheck each sentence, ask sts which unit it refers to.

> 1 Late night talk shows are watched by millions of Americans.
> 2 Our creativity is being killed by technology.
> 3 The first cordless vacuum cleaner was invented by Dyson.
> 4 The cast of *Avengers: Infinity War* was given fake scripts by Disney.
> 5 Do you think more technology will be operated by our voices in the future?
> 6 Brandon's party is being held outside.

**C** Read sign 1 with the class and elicit the correct preposition from sts. Tell them to complete signs 2–6 with *to*, *for*, or *of*. Paircheck. Classcheck. Then, have sts talk in pairs and discuss where they would most likely find each sign. Classcheck sts' guesses.

> 1 to  2 of  3 for  4 of  5 for  6 for

**D** **Make it personal** Have sts choose the correct verb form, infinitive or gerund. Classcheck. Pair sts up and have them take turns asking and answering 1–5. Classcheck.

> 1 to have  2 being  3 learning
> 4 camping  5 to wash, eating

**E** Allow sts a few seconds to look at the verbs and particles in the dialogues. Then, play ▶R5.1 for sts to match the verbs to the particles. Paircheck. Classcheck.

**Tip** In order to provide sts with as much fluency practice as possible, expand the activity into the mini-dialogues suggested below.

> 1 get into  2 figure out  3 stick to  4 lift up
> 5 come down with  6 bring down  7 boss around
> Extra phrasal verbs: 1 turn out, 2 give up, 3 look out for

▶R5.1 Turn to p. 324 for the complete audioscript.

**F** Have sts write down positive or negative predictions about what life will be like twenty years from now, using the ideas in the box.

Invite two volunteers to read the model dialogue in the speech bubbles to the whole class. Then, have sts compare their predictions in pairs. At the end, ask: *Any different opinions?*

**G** **Common mistakes** Have sts correct sentences 1–10. Encourage sts to flip back through p. 124–133 and check their answers in units **9** and **10**. Classcheck.

> 1 They tried to rob the shop, but didn't steal anything.
> 2 This photo was taken secretly and has been shown on the Internet.
> 3 Hurry up! By the time we get to the theater, the movie will have started.
> 4 People shouldn't go to prison for thefts.
> 5 Do you worry about not passing the final exams?
> 6 Remember to lock the doors after leaving.
> 7 I like people who smile all the time.
> 8 Do you want to go out with me to a party tonight?
> 9 I'm good at speaking, but I have difficulty understanding.
> 10 Is it easy to use prepositions correctly?

# Skills practice

♪ *Hey, Jude, don't make it bad*
*Take a sad song and make it better*
*Remember to let her into your heart*
*Then you can start to make it better*

**R5**

**A** Listen again to the four stories ▶9.12 on p.120 one at a time. After each one, reread and underline any words that were difficult to hear. Are they:
- a unfamiliar?
- b words with unexpected pronunciation?
- c words which "disappear"?
- d difficult for another reason?

**B** 🎧 **Make it personal** In groups, which do you think is the worst, and why?

1. a bribery    b tax evasion    c music piracy
2. a Mondays    b rainy days    c getting up early
3. a preparing food    b washing dishes    c ironing
4. a big hands    b big feet    c big head
5. a being tired    b being thirsty    c being hungry

**C** Read and order the paragraphs in this article.

### Cup of History

☐ In 1966, the Jules Rimet was on display in London, ahead of the World Cup there. On Sunday, March 20, the security guards noticed that the cabinet ¹_____ (open) and the trophy ²_____ (steal). The police ³_____ (start) an investigation, but the trophy ⁴_____ (find) a week later by a man walking his dog.

☐ In 2018, the World Cup ⁵_____ (hold) in Russia, a historic first for the "new" trophy! It ⁶_____ (win) by France for the second time, making them one of only six teams to ⁷_____ (win) it more than once.

☐ Italy won the competition in 1938 and so the trophy ⁸_____ (display) in Rome. When the country ⁹_____ (occupy) by the German army, an Italian FIFA official ¹⁰_____ (hide) the cup in a shoebox under his bed to keep it from the Nazis.

☐ Since the World Cup started in 1930, there ¹¹_____ (are) two trophies. The original, the Jules Rimet, ¹²_____ (give) permanently to Brazil in 1970, after they won their third tournament. This cup has many interesting stories around it.

☐ In 1983, the cup was stolen again, this time in Rio de Janeiro. It ¹³_____ (never / find) to this day.

**D** Complete **C** with the correct form of the verbs in parentheses. Past or present? Active or passive? Simple or perfect?

**E** Complete 1–5, then share in pairs. Any similarities?
1. I'm sick and tired of _____.
2. _____ is getting better, little by little.
3. Most _____ have its / their ups and downs.
4. I go to _____ when I need some peace and quiet.
5. It annoys me when I have to _____ again and again.

*I'm sick and tired of this weather. When will it change?*

**F** ▶R5.2 Order the story, 1–5. Listen to check.

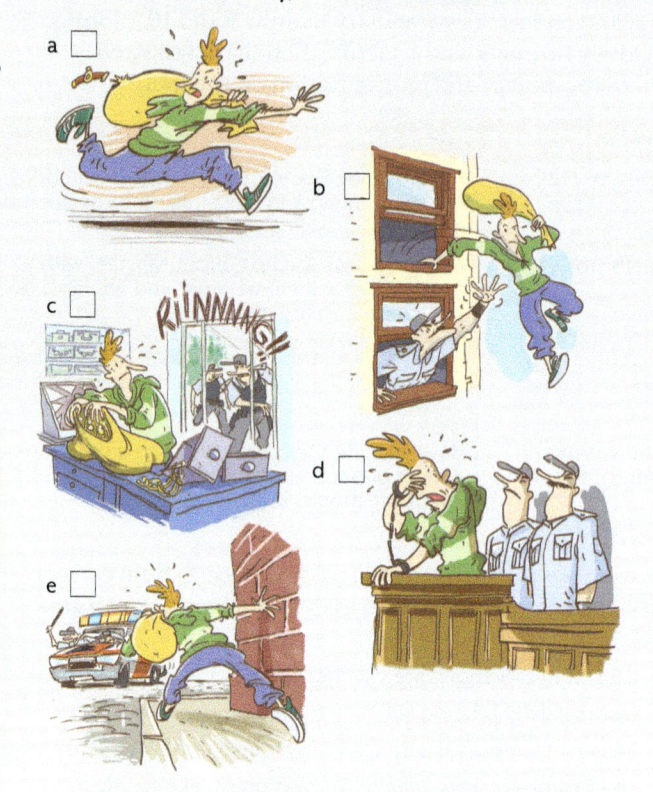

a ☐   b ☐   c ☐   d ☐   e ☐

**G** ▶R5.3 **Dictation.** Listen and write six extracts from **F**. Listen again, and repeat.

**H** ▶R5.4 🎧 **Make it personal** Listen to these pet peeves and react in pairs. How do they make you feel?

*Oh, I really hate it when people do that.*   *Really? It doesn't bother me much.*

**I** Role-play. In pairs, choose a pet peeve.
A: You are doing this action.
B: You are annoyed by it. Complain to **A**.

PLAYING LOUD MUSIC   ENTERING WITHOUT KNOCKING
CELL PHONES AT THE MOVIES   BITING NAILS   EXCESSIVE PESSIMISM
CHEWING WITH MOUTH OPEN   SINGING OFF THE BEAT

**J** ▶R5.5 **Question time!**
In pairs, listen to the 12 lesson titles in units 9 and 10. Pause after each one and tell each other the **opposite** of your normal answer. Ask follow-up questions, too, for fun.

*Does crime worry you?*   *No, not at all. I love it when people rob me.*

## Skills practice

**A** Ask sts to turn to p. 120. Inform them that the stories there are not complete. Tell sts that they are going to listen to and read the four stories in **ID Skills A**. Ask them to underline any words that are difficult to understand as they listen. Play ▶9.14. Classcheck.

Then, have sts look at p. 137 again and answer questions a–d about each underlined word. Classcheck.

**B** **Make it personal** Divide the class into groups of three. Have sts work within their groups to discuss items 1–5, deciding which option a–c is the worst and justifying their opinions. Monitor sts' discussions and take notes for delayed correction. Classcheck their opinions and provide language feedback.

**C** Point to the article and ask: *What's the text about?* Then, have sts order the paragraphs. Tell sts to ignore the blanks for the moment. Paircheck. Classcheck.

> 4, 3, 1, 5, 2

**D** Have sts complete the article in **C** with the correct tense of the verbs provided. Additionally, ask sts to write down the name of the verb tense and whether it is in the active or passive voice. Classcheck.

> 1  had been opened – past perfect, passive
> 2  had been stolen – past perfect, passive
> 3  started – past simple, active
> 4  was found – past simple, passive
> 5  was held – past simple, passive
> 6  was won – past simple, passive
> 7  have won – past perfect, active
> 8  was displayed – past simple, passive
> 9  was occupied – past simple, passive
> 10  hid – past simple, active
> 11  have been – present perfect, passive
> 12  was given – past simple, passive
> 13  has never been found – present perfect, passive

**E** Ask sts to complete sentences 1–5 about themselves. Walk around the classroom and monitor for accuracy. Have sts compare their sentences in pairs. Ask them to find at least two things in common. Classcheck similarities between pairs by asking: *What did you find in common?*

**F** Have sts order the pictures in the story 1–5. Play ▶R5.2 to classcheck. If time allows, have sts turn to the AS on p. 175 so they can read, listen, and complete the noticing activity.

> 1 c   2 b   3 a   4 e   5 d

▶R5.2 Turn to page 324 for the complete audioscript.

**G** *Dictation*. Tell sts that they are going to hear six extracts from **F**. Say: *Listen and write down the six sentences.* Play ▶R5.3. Paircheck and replay in case sts haven't caught all the words. Classcheck by writing the answers on the board.

> 1  The police arrived at the shop.
> 2  He jumped out of the window.
> 3  He turned the wrong way.
> 4  He stopped running.
> 5  He was convicted of burglary.
> 6  He started to cry.

Then say: *Now listen and repeat.* Replay ▶R5.3 for choral repetition.

**H** **Make it personal** Write *pet peeves* on the board and elicit a definition for this term. Tell sts that they are going to listen to five pet peeves and then discuss them in pairs. Ask: *How do these pet peeves make you feel?* Have two sts read the model dialogue in the speech bubbles. Then, play ▶R5.4 and pause after the first pet peeve. Allow sts time to discuss it in pairs. Classcheck. Follow the same procedure for the remaining pet peeves on the track.

**I** *Role-play.* Read the instructions for student **A** and student **B** with the whole class. Assign new pairs and have sts act out dialogues about the pet peeves. Encourage sts to change roles for each dialogue. Classcheck and invite four pairs to role-play one dialogue each for the whole class.

**J** *Question time!* Tell sts that they are going to hear the twelve lesson title questions from units 9 and 10. Pair sts up and say: *After each question, I'll pause, and then you should tell each other the opposite of your normal answer.* Have two sts read the model in the speech bubbles for the whole class. Then, play ▶R5.5 and pause after the first question. Have sts answer this question in pairs. Encourage then to ask follow-up questions for fun. At the end, classcheck by inviting volunteers to share the funniest answers.

# Grammar Unit 1

## 1A Review of present tenses

### Simple present

| Subject | Verb | Time phrase |
|---|---|---|
| I / You / We / They | hang out | on weekends. |
| He / She / It | meets up | twice a week. |

Use the **Simple present** for habits and states:
- Johann and Melina usually **meet** for dinner once a month.
- She often texts during dinner. It **annoys** her boyfriend.
- I **hate** going to parties by myself. I always **take** a friend.

Note: adverbs of frequency come before the verb.

### Present continuous

| Question | Auxiliary | Subject | Verb phrase |
|---|---|---|---|
| What | are | you | doing here? |
| Where | is | he | going? |

Use the **Present continuous** for:
1 actions in progress.
- I'**m chatting** to my mom.
2 future arrangements.
- She **isn't coming** tonight.

Note: do not use stative verbs in the Present continuous.
Do you understand me? NOT ~~Are you understanding me?~~

### Present perfect

| Subject | Auxiliary | Past participle |
|---|---|---|
| I / You / We / They | have / 've<br>have not / haven't | hung out there before.<br>gone there before. |
| He / She / It | has / 's<br>has not / hasn't | spent time with him.<br>been too hot today. |

Form: have / has + past participle (for irregular participles list, see p. 158–159).

Use the **Present perfect** for:
1 past experiences without a specific time.
- I've never **been** here before.
2 completed actions from a past point in time to now.
- We'**ve** just **eaten**.
3 unfinished past: actions / states that began in the past and continue until now.
- She'**s had** three dates **since** she started speed dating.

| Yes / No questions | Short answers |
|---|---|
| Have you (ever) been on a meet-up? | Yes, I have.<br>No, I haven't. |
| Have they (ever) broken up before? | Yes, they have.<br>No, they haven't. |
| Has she (ever) lost her cell phone? | Yes, she has.<br>No, she hasn't. |

For short answers, do not contract the subject with the auxiliary.
Yes, I have NOT ~~Yes, I've.~~

## 1B Review of question forms

### Yes / No questions

| Auxiliary | Subject | Verb + object |
|---|---|---|
| Are | they | your workmates? |
| Do | you | know Natalie? |
| Have | you | been to London? |
| Can | you | play the piano? |

### Questions ending in prepositions

| Question | Auxiliary | Subject | Verb phrase | Preposition |
|---|---|---|---|---|
| Who | do | you | want to speak | to? |
| Who | did | they | go to the party | with? |

### Object questions

| Question | Auxiliary | Subject | Verb + object |
|---|---|---|---|
| What | do | you | want to eat? |
| Where | did | he | park the car? |

### Subject questions

| Question (+ subject) | Verb + object |
|---|---|
| Which boy | won the prize? |
| Who | likes lemonade? |

## 1C Emphatic forms

| Subject | Auxiliary | Verb | Object |
|---|---|---|---|
| I | do | love | the sound of her voice. |

Use auxiliary + verb to emphasize agreement / disagreement.
- "You don't seem to like him."
- "That's not true. I **do** like him."

Use adverbs before the verb to emphasize an opinion or agreement / disagreement.
- I **really** don't think he's going to show up!
- I **definitely** want to meet him sometime.

Note: emphatic auxiliaries and adverbs are more common in speech than in writing.

# Unit 1

## 1A

**1** Complete 1–6 with the *Simple present* or *Present continuous* of the verbs in parentheses.
1. He _____ with his friends this weekend. (travel)
2. Mara always _____ impatient when she _____ in long lines. (get / stand)
3. They _____ every night because they _____ classes. (not go out / have)
4. Ben and Amy _____ right now—I think they often _____. (not get along / argue)
5. You really _____ bored by this TV show. (seem)
6. So, how _____ him? (you know)

**2** Use the phrases to describe each picture a–c. Try to use the *Simple present*, *Present continuous*, or *Present perfect*.

a **Museum**
guide works
is explaining
has never seen

b **Eating competition**
participating in an eating competition
has to
already eaten

c **Skateboard park**
hang out every Saturday
has started
is waiting

**3** 🟢 **Make it personal** Describe where you've been lately, what you do every weekend, and what you're planning to do next weekend.

*I always go to the same restaurants every weekend, so I have decided to try new places.*
*I've been to that new restaurant that's just opened. The Japanese place. And next weekend my friends and I are visiting a Turkish restaurant.*

## 1B

**1** Write *yes* / *no* questions for these answers.
1. He likes this city.
2. They are good at soccer.
3. She can drive a truck.
4. The baby is awake.

**2** Circle the correct preposition.
1. What were you waiting **to** / **for**?
2. Who are you so angry **with** / **of**?
3. What is she spending all her money **in** / **on**?
4. Which line are you standing **in** / **at**?

**3** Write one subject and one object question for each sentence.
1. Joanna loves taking photographs.
2. The kids went into the yard.
3. Chris has lost his keys.
4. Marie likes George.

**4** Order the words in 1–5 to make questions.
1. time / in / which / city / some / would / spend / like / you / to / ?
2. talking / what / been / about / the / gossip magazines / have / ?
3. learning / a / you / find / language / do / easy / ?
4. starred / who / watched / last / film / you / in / the / ?
5. you / talk / last / best / friend / to / when / did / your?

## 1C

**1** Complete 1–6 with an emphatic auxiliary.
1. You know, she _____ look a little bit like Emma Stone.
2. Come to think of it, I _____ feel a bit tired.
3. Well, they couldn't make it to our party, but they _____ send us a card.
4. If I _____ seem stressed, it's only because of the thunderstorm.
5. It _____ sound too good to be true, doesn't it?
6. We _____ have to pay something to use this site—it's not free, you know.

**2** Complete 1–5 with the best adverb below.

absolutely    certainly    definitely    really    sure

1. Are you _____ going to wear that orange shirt with those pants?
2. Well, she _____ told me she was getting the afternoon flight.
3. They _____ look as if they're having fun.
4. He _____ is a quiet sort of guy, isn't he?
5. I'm telling you, I'm _____, 100 percent certain I've seen him before!

289

# Grammar  Unit 2

## 2A Adjectives from verbs and nouns

- *I only use rechargeable batteries in my devices.*
- *She bought a very space-efficient apartment.*
- *This software is really user-friendly!*

Form adjectives by adding -able, -efficient, and -friendly to verbs and nouns.

-**able** means "can be done:" *drinkable, breakable, doable.*
Verbs ending in *-e* ➙ cut *-e* + *-able*.
- reuse ➙ reusable
- recycle ➙ recyclable
- love ➙ lovable

Exception: *rechargeable*

Use a hyphen between nouns and **-efficient** or **-friendly**.
- *She bought an energy-efficient washing machine.*
- *We took our nephews to a child-friendly restaurant.*

## 2B Present perfect continuous

| Subject | have / has | been + -ing |
|---|---|---|
| I / You / We / They | have / haven't | been sitting here for hours. |
| He / She | has / hasn't | been waiting for the bus since 8:30. |
| It | has / hasn't | been raining all afternoon. |

**Form:** *have / has* (not) + *been* + verb + *-ing*.
Use contractions: *have = 've / haven't, has = 's / hasn't*

| Question | have / has + subject | been + -ing |
|---|---|---|
| What | have I / you / we / they | been talking about? |
| How long | has she / he / it | been doing it? |

Use the **Present perfect continuous** with:
- **since** to indicate a point in time: *1989, eight o'clock, yesterday = a moment*
- **for** to indicate a period of time: *a few hours, six months, 20 years = a duration*

## 2C Present perfect vs. Present perfect continuous

You can often use **Present perfect** or **Present perfect continuous** interchangeably.
- *I've lived here since 2010.*
- *I've been living here since 2010.*

### Present perfect

Use the **Present perfect** to describe activities that have or haven't been completed from a past point in time until now.
- *Agatha's written ten books in ten years.*

### Present perfect continuous

Use the **Present perfect continuous** to emphasize the time a process or series of events took. It can also be used to describe an activity that is unfinished or temporary.
- *They've been hanging around with Mary lately.*
- *Agatha's been writing books since she was in her 20s.*

Don't use the Present perfect continuous with a stative verb (e.g. *be, have, know, understand*).

## 2D Simple past vs. Present perfect simple / continuous

### Simple past

| Subject | Past tense of verb | Object |
|---|---|---|
| I / You / He / She / It / You / We / They | traveled | to the North Pole. |

Use the **Simple past** for completed actions in the past.
- *Jordan Romero reached the top of the Everest when he was only 16.*

### Present perfect

Use the **Present perfect** to connect the past and present and to describe how much has been completed.
- *The explorer has climbed a lot of mountains in his life.*
- *The polar ice caps have melted over the past 30 years.*

### Present perfect continuous

Use the **Present perfect continuous** to describe how long something has been happening.
- *He's been exploring exotic environments since he graduated from school.*
- *The polar ice caps have been melting since the 1980s.*

"According to this, you haven't been waiting long enough for treatment."

# Unit 2

## 2A

**1** Cross out the incorrect adjective in 1–5.
1. She always brings **recycling** / **recyclable** bottles to the store.
2. He likes the **usable** / **user-friendly** features of his new dishwasher.
3. We have **energy-efficiency** / **energy-efficient** lights in our house.
4. I only use **natural-friendly** / **nature-friendly** detergents.
5. **Disposing** / **Disposable** batteries are bad for the environment.

**2** Describe photos a–d. Use adjectives from verbs and nouns.
*Well, I guess it's child-friendly but ...*

a   b   c   d

## 2B

**1** Complete 1–5 with the correct form of *have*.
1. _____ he been saving money for a new car?
2. What _____ you been doing all day?
3. Where _____ they been storing all those recyclable cans and boxes?
4. _____ you been listening to the news today?
5. _____ it been raining here?

**2** Complete 1–5 with the *Present perfect continuous* of these verbs.

buy   collect   live   swim   work out

1. How long _____ you _____ watches?
2. They _____ in their new heated pool.
3. I _____ every day for the past three weeks.
4. Mario _____ next door for six years.
5. My mom _____ eco-friendly products since I was a kid.

**3** ⬤ Make it personal   Describe what you've been doing lately at work / school / home.
*I've been working out at the gym twice a week, but I haven't been running since I hurt my knee.*

## 2C

**1** Circle the correct option in 1–5.
1. She has **walked** / **been walking** to and from school every day since she was ten.
2. We've **tried** / **been trying** three different products and we still can't get this shirt clean.
3. He's never **traveled** / **been traveling** on a luxury cruise ship before.
4. They have **used** / **been using** energy-efficient appliances in their house recently.
5. I haven't **done** / **been doing** my housework as often as I should.

**2** Complete the dialogues with the correct form of the verb in parentheses.
1. A: Where _____? There is mud all over your shoes. (walk)
   B: Oh, I _____ the garden and it _____ my shoes wet. (water / get)
2. A: I'm absolutely exhausted. I _____ since 8 a.m. (drive)
   B: Wow. You should let me drive for a while. I _____ at all. (not drive)
3. A: You _____ yourself enough time to get ready for work this morning. (not give)
   B: This old alarm clock _____ the right time for years! (keep)

## 2D

**1** Order the words in 1–5 to make questions.
1. have / how / you / long / been / the / phone / using / you / that / bought / new / ?
2. flooding / has / any / been / there / you / where / live / ?
3. government / doing / to solve / has / the / been / problems / environmental / our / what / ?
4. know / the North Pole / did / that / global / you / has / warming / caused / at / melting / ?
5. since / the laws / enforced / been / about / pollution / have / they / made / were / ?

**2** ⬤ Make it personal   Write your responses to the questions in **1**.

# Grammar Unit 3

## 3A Past perfect

| Subject | Auxiliary | Past participle |
|---|---|---|
| I / You He / She / It We / They | had / 'd | never been to Hong Kong before. |
| | | already left by the time the suitcases appeared. |
| | had not / hadn't | had anything to eat for nearly 24 hours. |
| | | ever been abroad until this trip. |

Form:
● and ● = Subject + *had* (*not*) + past participle.
Use *'d* contractions for ● and *hadn't* for ● sentences.
● = *Had*(*n't*) + subject + past participle?
▸ *Had* you *taken* medicine before you flew?
▸ *Hadn't* you ever *seen* that before?
▸ What *had* you *eaten* before you got sick?

Note: when the main verb is *have*, *had* will appear twice, either together or separated by an adverbial expression.
▸ We *had* already *had* lunch when they called.
▸ Before I met her, I *had had* serious problems in my relationships.

Use the **Past perfect**:
1 for actions that happened before another past action.
▸ I didn't start studying English until after I*'d finished* high school.
2 to express past wishes and expectations.
▸ My birthday party was better than anything I*'d expected*!
▸ The movie was more thrilling than they*'d hoped*!

Expressions like *already, before, by the time, never, until recently*, etc. indicate the duration of the event or when it happened.
▸ When the electricity went out, they'd *already* gone to bed.
▸ She'd never met a celebrity *before*.
▸ *Until recently*, I hadn't used that website.

## 3B Past perfect continuous

| Subject | Auxiliary | been | Verb + *-ing* |
|---|---|---|---|
| I / You He / She / It We / They | had / 'd | been | living there for a long time. |
| | had not / hadn't | | standing in line for several hours. |

Form:
● and ● = Subject + *had* (*not*) + *been* + verb *-ing*.
Use *'d* contractions for ● and *hadn't* for ● sentences.
● = *Had*(*n't*) + subject + *been* + verb *-ing*?

Use the **Past perfect continuous** to emphasize the duration of an action that was in progress before another past action.
▸ It *had been raining* for hours before the game started.
▸ We*'d been walking* in the park when we encountered our old friend.

Note: don't use the Past perfect continuous with stative verbs.

## 3C Narrative tenses

### Simple past
Use the **Simple past** to talk about past actions and states.
▸ I *graduated* from high school and then I *went* to college.

### Past continuous

| Subject | was / were | Verb + *-ing* |
|---|---|---|
| I / He / She / It | was / wasn't | getting ready to go out. |
| You / We / They | were / weren't | listening to me. |

Use the **Past continuous** to talk about actions in progress at a point in the past.
▸ I *was working* at a summer camp for three months.

Use the **Simple past** to talk about actions that interrupt actions in the **Past continuous**.
▸ I *was walking* home when I *saw* Julia.

### Past perfect
Use the **Past perfect** to emphasize that one action happened before another in the past.
▸ He made breakfast after he *had taken* a shower.

If the sequence is clear, use the **Simple past**.
▸ He made breakfast after he *took* a shower.

### Past perfect continuous
Use the **Past perfect continuous** to emphasize the duration of an action that was completed in the past.
▸ We*'d been studying* all afternoon before the examiner arrived.
▸ How long *had* you *been dating* before you got married?

# Unit 3

## 3A

1 **Complete the dialogues with the *Past perfect* or *Past simple* of the verbs in parentheses.**

1. A: How was your trip to Italy? _____ you ever _____ there before? (be)
   B: It was great. I _____ there before. It was my first time. (be)
2. A: _____ you _____ Italian before you went there? (study)
   B: Yes, but I _____ more than a few words. (not learn)
3. A: _____ you _____ in time to see the festival? (arrive)
   B: No. By the time I got there, it _____ just _____. (end)

2 **Describe the events in each of a–c in two or three sentences. Use the *Past perfect*.**

## 3B

1 **Complete 1–5 with the *Past perfect* or *Past perfect continuous* of the verbs in parentheses.**

1. We _____ video games for almost two hours before the outage. (play)
2. Imagine if dinosaurs _____ because of climate change. (not die out)
3. She _____ for long when the lightning suddenly woke her up. (not sleep)
4. They _____ on coming to the party with us, but they had a family emergency at the last moment. (plan)
5. The tigers were pacing their cage because they _____ yet. (not eat)

2 **Correct the mistakes in 1–5.**

1. The manager had been warning him twice to stop using his cell in the theater.
2. They were towing our car because we had been parking in a tow-away zone.
3. She was still feeling confused even after the officer had gave her directions.
4. The law that all dogs must be on a leash had be in effect for thirty years.
5. Her wedding wasn't as perfect as she's hoped.

3 **◯ Make it personal** Describe five "first times", or things you had never done before. Use the topics from the box, plus any others you can think of.

> (buy) your own computer, phone, or car   (drive) a car
> plan a party   (ride) a horse or a bicycle   travel by plane

*I had been living on the farm for one month but I hadn't ridden one of the horses …*

## 3C

1 **Circle the correct alternatives to complete the anecdote.**

Last Sunday, I ¹ **went / was going / had gone** to the cinema with my sisters. We ² **didn't drive / weren't driving / hadn't been driving** for very long when suddenly a small dog suddenly ³ **ran / was running / had run** out in front of us. It ⁴ **happened / was happening / had been happening** too fast, and I ⁵ **wasn't seeing / hadn't seen / hadn't been seeing** the dog before it ⁶ **ran / was running / had been running** out. We ⁷ **stopped / were stopping / had stopped** the car and ⁸ **got / were getting / had gotten** out. We ⁹ **were all feeling / had all felt / had all been feeling** very upset. We ¹⁰ **looked / was looking / had looked** under the car. Luckily, we ¹¹ **hadn't hit / weren't hitting / hadn't been hitting** the dog at all. It ¹² **hid / was hiding / had been hiding** under the car! We were very relieved!

2 **◯ Make it personal** Describe a time when you thought something bad had happened, but it ended happily.

# Grammar Unit 4

## 4A *too / enough*

**Use:**
- **too** before an adjective when something is more than necessary.
  - Some students are **too** proud to ask for help.
  - You're never **too** old to learn something new.
- **enough** after an adjective / adverb, but before nouns when something is the necessary amount.
  - I didn't get to class early **enough** to get a good seat.
  - There wasn't **enough** time to get everything done.

**Note:** don't use **too** with adjectives + noun to mean *very*. Her family are very nice people. NOT ~~Her family are too nice people.~~

**Use:**
- **too many** before plural C nouns.
  - They have **too many** problems to deal with.
- **too much** before U nouns.
  - There's **too much** pressure to get a high score on the exam.

**Note:** when U nouns have a plural meaning or with *types of / kinds of*, use **too many**.
  - There are **too many** types of fish in this aquarium!

## 4B *should have*

Use *should have* + Past participle:
1. to express a regret.
   - You **shouldn't have left** your drink near the computer.
2. to speculate about the past.
   - We **should have known** there would be a test today.
3. to give / ask advice about a past event.
   - What **should** I **have done** instead?

**Form:**
Subject + *should* (*not*) + *have* + past participle.

**Note:** we often use the contraction *'ve* in spoken English.
- She **should've** called to tell me she wasn't coming.
- I **should've** realized you would be late.
- You **shouldn't've** gone cycling without a helmet.

## 4C First and second conditional

**First conditional**

| If | Subject | Simple present | Subject | will / won't | Infinitive |
|---|---|---|---|---|---|
| If | I | have time, | I | will | buy some bread on the way home. |
| If | you | don't listen, | you | won't | know what to do. |

Use the **First conditional** to talk about real and possible future situations.

**Second conditional**

| If | Subject | Simple past | Subject | will / won't | Infinitive |
|---|---|---|---|---|---|
| If | I | could be anything I wanted, | I | would | be a lawyer. |
| If | they | didn't study so hard, | they | wouldn't | get such good grades. |

Use the **Second conditional** to talk about "unreal" or imaginary situations.

The *if* clause can come first or second. Use a comma separating the clauses when the *if* clause comes first.
- I'll buy some bread on the way home if I have time.
- They wouldn't get such good grades if they didn't study so hard.

We can also use **when** or **as soon as** with the same sentence structure as with *if*.
- **When** I get there, I'll call you.
- I'll call you **as soon as** I get there.

We can use **can / could / may / might** instead of *would*.
- If you studied a bit harder, you **might** get a higher score.

# Unit 4

## 4A

**1** Circle the correct alternative in 1–5.
1 The print was **too** / **enough** small for her to read.
2 They've canceled the class because there weren't **too few** / **enough** people signed up.
3 The school was criticized because it didn't have **enough** / **too many** teachers.
4 Students complained that they were under **too much** / **enough** pressure to get good grades.
5 The educators thought the exams were **too** / **enough** hard for most students.

**2** Complete 1–5 with *too much* or *enough*.
1 I don't have _____ time to read my notes before the test begins.
2 He has _____ time on his hands—he just plays video games all day.
3 Kindergarten children seem to get _____ homework.
4 I've got _____ money saved to buy a new tablet!
5 He hasn't done the dishes in days, so there aren't _____ cups for all of us.

**3** 🟢 **Make it personal** Describe these things. Use *too* and *enough* in your sentences.

apps on my phone     space in my room
free time     friends on Facebook     work
homework     hours in a day

*I don't have enough free time!*

"If you ask me, he's come too far too fast."

## 4B

**1** Correct the mistakes in 1–6.
1 He should had organized his time better.
2 We should to have taken the bus instead of the subway.
3 They should have not given out their phone number.
4 You should listened to your father's advice.
5 It should've be easy to find his house with your GPS.
6 You should haven't left your wallet at the restaurant.

**2** Order the words in 1–4 to make sentences. Then match 1–4 to a–d.
1 for / have / she / studied / should / more / exam / the / .
2 we / taken / road / that / should / have / not / .
3 pin / written / have / I / down / should / number / the / .
4 alarm / set / clock / have / should / they / their / .

a ☐ We got lost.
b ☐ I couldn't take out any money.
c ☐ They were late for class.
d ☐ She failed her test.

**3** 🟢 **Make it personal** Describe things you shouldn't have done or should've done differently.

*I should've started learning English earlier. I still find it difficult.*
*I shouldn't have gone out last night. I'm exhausted.*

## 4C

**1** Check the correct ending for the sentences.
1 If you saw your favourite movie star,
   ☐ what will you do?
   ☐ what would you do?
2 If you are in trouble,
   ☐ I'll always help you.
   ☐ I'd always help you.
3 I'll see you later
   ☐ if you go to the party.
   ☐ if you went to the party.
4 I'd lend you my phone
   ☐ if you take care of it.
   ☐ if you took care of it.
5 If I knew the answer,
   ☐ I'll tell you.
   ☐ I'd tell you.
6 What would you do
   ☐ if you fail your exams?
   ☐ if you failed your exams?

**2** 🟢 **Make it personal** Complete the sentences so that they are true for you.
1 If I had one week left to live …
2 If I go out this weekend …
3 If I have enough money …
4 If I could go anywhere in the world …

# Grammar Unit 5

## 5A Third conditional

| If Clause | | | Result Clause | | |
|---|---|---|---|---|---|
| If | I / you / he / she / we / they | had been on time, | I / you / he / she / we / they | would've | gotten a seat. |
| | | 'd read the book, | | might've | understood the lecture. |
| | | hadn't called, | | wouldn't have | come to the party. |

Use the **Third conditional** to express past wishes or possible past events and their probable results.
- If **you'd had** more time, **what** would you have done?
- **How** would the world be different today if **we'd had** computers 100 years ago?

**Form:**
If + subject + had (not) + past participle + subject + would have + past participle + phrase.
**Note:** use **might / could have** when the result is less sure.
- If I'd lost some weight, I could have won the race.

"Mom, would you have married Dad if you had seen him in high definition first?"

## 5B Modals of possibility / probability

Use **can / can't** or **could / couldn't** to show possibility.
- You **can't** be serious.
- I thought you **could** do it.
- He **can't** be hungry again!
- It's midnight! Who **could** it be at the door?
- It **can't** be the kids! They're all in bed!

Use **might** or **must** to show degrees of certainty or uncertainty.
- I **might** go to the party tonight, but I'm not sure.
- You **must** be tired after your long flight.
- Yeah, I **may** just call in for half an hour.

**Note:** you can use **may** instead of **might** or **could**.

## 5C Adjective order

- It's a very **effective herbal** remedy.
- That **talented Spanish** actress is their new spokesperson.

Fact adjectives follow this order:

| size | age | shape | color | material | purpose | + noun |
|---|---|---|---|---|---|---|
| little | old | square | red | brick | elementary | school |

- It was a **little, old, square, red, brick elementary** school.

**Note:** try not to use more than three adjectives together.
- He's a very **nice, smart, young** guy.

Opinion adjectives (*amazing, friendly, good, interesting, nice, pretty,* etc.) usually come before fact adjectives (*American, metal, tall, young,* etc.).
A nice young man NOT ~~A young nice man~~

**Note:** add a comma after each consecutive adjective.

| Opinion | Fact | Noun |
|---|---|---|
| a delicious | square chocolate | brownie |
| a funny | new stand-up | comedian |
| an ugly | old plastic | bag |

You can change the position of fact and opinion adjectives for emphasis. Put the most important adjective next to the noun.
- It's a **boring, old** story. → It's the same **old, boring** story.
- He had an **ugly, large** bag. → He had a **large, ugly** bag.

"Brilliant! A 3-D, holographic, pop-up annual report. Hopefully, no one will notice what a lousy year we had."

# Unit 5

## 5A

**1** Match *If* clauses 1–6 to result clauses a–f.
1. If the alarm hadn't gone off,
2. If the Internet had been working,
3. If it had been an easier test,
4. If the sign hadn't been hidden,
5. If my phone hadn't run out of battery,
6. If we'd planned better,

a ☐ she wouldn't have missed the turn.
b ☐ there would've been enough food.
c ☐ I would've called you.
d ☐ he would've checked the schedule.
e ☐ more students might have passed it.
f ☐ you would've been really late.

**2** Correct the mistakes in 1–5.
1. If you hadn't procrastinated, you'd had enough time to study.
2. I would've tell him if I would've seen him.
3. If you had bought a lottery ticket, you might win a lot of money.
4. We could been in the race if we'd sent our applications in on time.
5. If I hadn't found her when I did, she would lost.

**3** 🟢 **Make it personal** Describe what would have happened *if* …

… you'd learned another language.
… you'd found some buried treasure.
… you'd been born the opposite gender.
… you'd been a professional athlete.

*If I'd been a professional athlete, I would've been a soccer player.*

## 5B

**1** Match 1–5 to comments a–e.
1. I walked five miles to get here.
2. He hasn't eaten very much today.
3. Sorry, sir, you don't have enough money in your account.
4. There's no sound from the TV.
5. I heard thunder in the distance.

a ☐ He might be hungry. Offer him something.
b ☐ You can't be serious! How could that be?
c ☐ There may be a storm coming.
d ☐ You must be tired!
e ☐ It could be the speakers.

**2** Circle the correct alternative in 1–5.
1. Studies show that lack of exercise **can** / **might** not lead to obesity.
2. Sugar-free chewing gum **can't** / **might not** be so good for your teeth.
3. He didn't realize that his car **could** / **must** get such good mileage.
4. It **might not** / **could** be so easy to find a replacement for that device.
5. It **can** / **must** be a really long wait for a table at this restaurant.

**3** Complete 1–5 with *can't* or *must* and these verbs.

believe    imagine    keep    realize    think

1. I _____ _____ listened to her entire story again!
2. You _____ _____ that this is a controversial subject.
3. She _____ _____ how you got him to talk about it.
4. My friends _____ _____ I'm crazy to go out with him.
5. Don't tell her—she _____ _____ a secret.

## 5C

**1** Order the words in 1–5 to make sentences.
1. wearing / long-sleeved / he / blue / was / a / T-shirt / cotton / .
2. new / we / car / washed / shiny / red / our / sports / .
3. the road / put / a / big / cone / plastic / the / construction / on / crew / orange / .
4. for / you / look / should / small / gray / house / wooden / old / a / .
5. scary / dressed up / monster / green / huge / a / like / he / .

**2** Describe each photo using as many adjectives as you can.

a  b  c

**3** 🟢 **Make it personal** Describe what you are wearing. Use as many adjectives as you can.

*I'm wearing a beautiful, blue and white cotton skirt.*

# Grammar Unit 6

## 6A Restrictive relative clauses

**Restrictive relative clauses** identify the word(s) they refer to. They are essential for meaning and don't need commas.

| Sentence 1 | Sentence 2 | Subject of relative clause |
|---|---|---|
| A guest sang last night. | The guest was Rihanna. | The guest *who* sang last night was Rihanna. |
| The class is meeting now. | It's in room 3. | The class *that* is meeting now is in room 3. |
| The man's dog is so smart. | He lives next door. | The man *whose* dog is so smart lives next door. |

| Sentence 1 | Sentence 2 | Object of relative clause |
|---|---|---|
| We bought a new apartment. | It's in Dubai. | The new apartment *that* we bought is in Dubai. |
| She's in love with a movie star. | He's Will Smith. | Will Smith is the movie star *that* she's in love with. |
| I met a man. | His sister is in my class. | I met a man *whose* sister is in my class. |

Use relative clauses to connect two ideas with a relative pronoun.
- Shh! The game show *that* we're all addicted to is on now.
- The contestant *who's* winning is from Atlanta.

### Relative pronouns

|  | Subject | Object | Possessive |
|---|---|---|---|
| People | who, that | who, whom | whose |
| Things | that | that |  |

**Note:** *that* can only be used in restrictive relative clauses. It is optional when it refers to the object of the sentence.
- The soap opera she's addicted to is *Another World*.

## 6B Non-restrictive relative clauses

**Non-restrictive relative clauses** are not essential. They add extra information and need commas.

| Subject | Non-restrictive clause | Phrase |
|---|---|---|
| Calvin Harris, | who is from Scotland, | is my favorite DJ. |
| My favorite band, | (which is) One Direction, | is from the UK. |
| The party I went to, | which was last Saturday, | was really fun. |
| The girl in my class, | whom I had never met before, | was from Argentina. |
| Shakira, | whose voice is amazing, | is a world-famous singer. |

Use non-restrictive relative clauses to give additional information.
- *Lady Gaga, who sang at 9 p.m., was unable to leave the theater.*

Form non-restrictive relative clauses with **who / whom**, **whose**, and **which**.
The non-restrictive clause always comes between two commas or a comma and a period.

Note:
- do not use *that* in a non-restrictive clause.
- do not repeat the subject or object pronoun in the clause.

*Miami, which is one of the most exciting cities in the world, is an expensive place.*
NOT ~~Miami, that is one of the most exciting cities in the world, it is an expensive place.~~

*The movie that we want to see is playing at 9 p.m.*
NOT ~~The movie that we want to see it is playing at 9 p.m.~~

"The editor who turned down the first Harry Potter book, say hello to the publisher who took a pass on Stephen King."

# Unit 6

## 6A

**1** Complete the dialogue with *who*, *that*, or *whose* when necessary.

A: So tell me about the concert ¹_____ you went to yesterday.
B: It was great! There were two performances ²_____ were perfect.
A: Really? Wow! Who performed?
B: The first singer ³_____ I heard was Bruno Mars! He's awesome.
A: I love him! Isn't he touring with ... oh, what's the name of that band ⁴_____ lead singer is from New Jersey?
B: That's Bon Jovi. They're the band ⁵_____ Bruno sang with! There were lots of people in the audience ⁶_____ were amazed by their performance.

**2** Which gaps, 1–6 in **1**,
   a) could also be *which*?
   b) are correct with no relative pronoun?

**3** Combine the two sentences with *who*, *that*, *which*, or *whose*.
1 I'm sick of that talk show host. She complains too much.
2 We always watch the international news. It's on at 6 p.m.
3 Meghan's not interested in the guy. His ex-girlfriend just broke up with him.
4 *Star Trek* is a sci-fi show. It has been popular since the 1960s.
5 There are a lot of movies. They are based on superheroes.

## 6B

**1** Correct the mistakes in 1–5.
1 This movie, that is based on a novel by Virginia Woolf, won many awards.
2 My favorite author, which I've liked since grade school, is J.K. Rowling.
3 They speak a language, that is called Basque, we hadn't heard before.
4 I saw Emma Stone, who's latest movie was brilliant, in the mall this morning.
5 He loves dancing to "Gangnam Style," that is a popular music video from South Korea.
6 Tom Cruise who's one of world's richest actors, he has three children and three ex-wives.

**2** Match columns A, B, and C to make non-restrictive relative clauses.

**A**
1 The first book I read,
2 Cardi B,
3 That TV show,
4 My first teacher,
5 The time machine in *Back to the Future*,

**B**
☐ which was set in 1985,
☐ which was canceled after three episodes,
☐ who I remember well,
☐ which I really loved,
☐ whose real name is Belcalis Marlenis Almánzar,

**C**
☐ performed for a huge audience.
☐ was Mrs. Rodriguez.
☐ was called *Zero Hour*.
☐ was a Delorean.
☐ was *Harry Potter*.

**3** Order the words in 1–5 to make relative clauses. Remember to use commas in the non-restrictive clause.
1 the movie / saw / which / that / I / Academy Awards / two / favorite / won / my / is / .
2 known for / has / shows / which / Canada / great / is / its / locations / popular / TV / a lot of / .
3 one of / famous / Johnny Depp / is / who / actors / in his fifties / most / Hollywood's / .
4 is / J.K. Rowling / who / the / of / crime / author / the / novel / Robert Galbraith / really / is / .
5 last / superheroes / *The Avengers* / movie / which / about / is / was / summer / released / a / .

**4** 🟢 **Make it personal** Describe your favorites in these five categories. Use non-restrictive relative clauses to give additional information.

movie    movie star    movie character    novel    TV show

*My favorite TV show is Brooklyn Nine-Nine, which is set in New York, I think it is really funny.*

# Grammar Unit 7

## 7A Reported speech

| Direct speech | Subject | Reporting verb | Reported speech |
|---|---|---|---|
| I **go** there every day. | I | said (that) | he / she **went** there every day. |
| I **am working** here. | You | told (me, him, her, etc.) | he / she **was working** there. |
| We'll **travel** tomorrow. | He | | you / they **would travel** the next day. |
| I **would try** if I **could**. | She | | he / she **would have tried** if he / she **could have**. |
| They **went** to the U.S. | We | | they **had gone** to the U.S. |
| I **was talking** to her. | They | | he / she **had been talking** to her. |
| We **had done** this before. | | | you / they **had done** that before. |

Use **Reported speech** to report what someone said / told (you).
**Form:**
- a Simple past reporting verb (*said*, *told*, etc.).
- the main verb moves one tense back.

In reported speech, also remember to change:
- pronouns (*I* → *he* / *she*; *we* → *they*)
- place and time expressions (*this* → *that*; *here* → *there*, *tonight* → *that night*; *yesterday* → *the day before*, etc.)

The most common reporting verbs are: *describe, emphasize, explain, mention, observe, recommend, report, say, speculate, state, suggest, tell (someone)*.

**Note:** use an object (*you, me, her, John,* etc.) with **tell**.
*She told me she was traveling.* NOT ~~She told she was traveling.~~

## 7B Indirect questions

| Expression | *if* / *whether* / *wh* word | Statement |
|---|---|---|
| Do you have any idea | if | I could leave my luggage here? |
| | whether | there's free Wi-Fi in the lobby? |
| | what / which | payment methods I can use? |
| Do you know / remember | when | the restaurant opens? |
| Could you tell me | where | the restroom is? |
| | why | I can't get my keycard to work? |
| Can you tell me | how | to get to the nearest bank? |
| | who | is in charge here? |

Use indirect questions to sound more polite.
For *yes / no* questions, use *if* or *whether*. **Whether** is more formal.
**Form:**
Indirect question expression + *if* / *whether* / *wh* word + inversion of auxiliary and subject.
**Note:** don't use a question mark with the indirect question expressions *I wonder* or *I'd like to know*.

## 7C Reported questions, commands, and requests

### Reported questions

Use expressions like *He asked me* and *They wanted to know* to report questions.
- "Do you know the answer?" → I asked him if he knew the answer.
- "What time does the flight leave?" → They wanted to know what time the flight left.
- "Where did I leave my purse?" → She wondered where she had left her purse.

**Form:**
- as in reported speech, the main verb moves one tense back and there are changes to pronouns and place and time expressions.
- use the same word order as a statement.

*They asked us who the man was.* NOT ~~They asked us who was the man.~~

- reported questions end with a period, not a question mark.

**Note:** use an object with *ask*.

### Reported commands and requests

Use *ask* when reporting requests and *told* when reporting commands.
- "Can I see your passport, please?" → He asked to see my passport.
- "Place your bags on the X-ray machine." → She told me to place my bags on the X-ray machine.

**Form:**
- commands and requests are usually reported using **(not) + to + infinitive**.
- "Please remember! Don't forget the homework!" → He told us **not to forget** the homework.

- *ask* and *tell* are followed by an object.
- She **asked / told them** to help her.

# Unit 7

## 7A

**1** Correct the mistakes in 1–7.
1 He said he doesn't know where was the parking lot.
2 She mentioned that she won't be back in time for the party.
3 She said she not know where was David.
4 They never told us where is the party.
5 He explained why there will be an extra charge on the bill.
6 He said me that he wasn't going to Lima.
7 They told they would be late.

**2** Complete 1–5 with the correct form of these verbs.

be    learn    locate    mention    not know

1 The teacher promised that we _____ Spanish in three weeks!
2 He told us he _____ if he could fix the Internet connection.
3 We wondered where the restrooms were _____.
4 She _____ that the concierge would not be back until 1 p.m.
5 The manager said that the elevators _____ broken.

## 7B

**1** Complete 1–5 with the words below.

what    when    whether    where    who

1 Do you know _____ the changing rooms are?
2 I'd like to know _____ or not the flight will be on time.
3 Could you tell me _____ the Internet is going to be working again?
4 Do you have any idea _____ he was trying to say?
5 Could you tell me _____ I have to contact to solve this problem?

**2** Match 1–5 to a–e to form indirect questions.
1 I wonder if you can
2 Could you please
3 Do you happen to know
4 Could you tell me whether
5 Do you have any idea what

a ☐ what time the train leaves?
b ☐ this button on my phone is for?
c ☐ this bus is going downtown or not?
d ☐ tell me where I put my keys.
e ☐ remind us when the next flight leaves?

**3** You're a polite tourist in a hotel. Prepare indirect questions to ask about five of these things.

ATM    cheap stores    free parking    free Wi-Fi
good restaurant    gym    restroom    safe
swimming pool

*Could you tell me where the restroom is?*

## 7C

**1** Order the words in 1–6 to make sentences.
1 asked / knew / if / he / get / to / repair / how / shop / I / to / a / .
2 she / me / take / Main Street / left / a / to / told / on / .
3 not / for / late / the / told / they / us / to / be / lecture / .
4 actor / reporter / asked / what / was / favorite / the / his / movie / the / .
5 her / asked / instructor / what / in / time / hand / could / she / the / paper / the / .
6 soccer player / the / time / training / what / started / new / asked / the / coach / the / .

**2** Complete 1–4 with reported questions.
1 A: Excuse me, is there an ATM nearby?
  B: Sorry, what did you ask me?
  A: I asked _____.
2 A: What's your rate for a single room?
  B: Excuse me, I didn't understand what you said.
  A: I asked _____.
3 A: Do you know where the bus station is?
  B: Pardon me? I didn't catch what you said.
  A: I asked _____.
4 A: Did you talk to your girlfriend about it?
  B: What did you say?
  A: I asked _____.

**3** Report the instructions using *You told us (not) to.*
1 Don't blame me.
2 Keep calm and carry on.
3 Don't worry, be happy.
4 Enjoy yourselves but don't go crazy!

301

# Grammar Unit 8

## 8A Modal perfects – *must have, can't have, might / may have*

Use **Modal perfects**:
1. to speculate about the past.
   - You **must have** been really upset when that happened.
   - It **can't have** been easy to give up chocolate!
2. to express possibility or uncertainty.
   - They **might have** left the party early … I don't see them!
   - Do you think the area **may have** flooded?

Form:
Subject + modal + *have* + past participle.
Note:
*must have* = we're sure something **did** happen
*can't have* = we're sure it **didn't** happen

## 8B Causative form

Use the **Causative** form to talk about services / actions that other people do for you.
- Do you know where I can **have my car fixed**?
- She doesn't **get her hair styled** by a professional.
- You **got your teeth whitened**, didn't you?
- Are you **getting your computer fixed**?
- We're going to **have a class photo taken** at school tomorrow.

Form:
Subject + *get* / *have* + object + past participle.
Remember: *get* / *have* can be in any tense.
Note: when other people do bad things to you, it's more common to use *have* instead of *get*.
- He **had** his car stolen last night.
(He didn't ask / pay anyone to do it = not a service.)

## 8C Tag questions

| Tag question | |
|---|---|
| ⊕ Statement | ⊖ Question tag |
| We**'re** crazy to be doing this, | **aren't** we? |
| She **has** already **traveled** to Europe, | **hasn't** she? |
| I think Chris and Sue **went** to the beach, | **didn't** they? |
| He **had planned** on coming over, | **hadn't** he? |
| I'm sure you**'ll** be fine, | **won't** you? |
| ⊖ Statement | ⊕ Question tag |
| She **didn't** do this correctly, | **did** she? |
| You **have no** idea what I'm talking about, | **do** you? |
| They **weren't** married, I think, | **were** they? |
| I **haven't told** her anything, | **have** I? |
| He **would never** ask her out, | **would** he? |
| We**'ve got nothing** to lose, | **have** we? |

Form:
- Subject + ⊕ statement + comma + ⊖ auxiliary + subject?
- Subject + ⊖ statement + comma + ⊕ auxiliary + subject?
- Keep the tenses the same.

Use:
- rising intonation to check information that you are not sure about.
- falling intonation to state your opinion and invite the other person to comment.

Note:
- a **question tag** is the "mini-question" after the comma.
- a **tag question** is the whole sentence, plus the "mini-question."
- even when the verb in the statement is ⊕, if its meaning is ⊖ because of words like *never, no, nothing, nobody*, etc., the **question tag** should be ⊕.
  - You never enjoyed sports at school, **did you**?

"But in your business, being laughed at is *good*, isn't it?"

# Unit 8

## 8A

**1** Complete 1–5 with *can't have, may have, must have,* and the past participle of the verb in parentheses.

1. You drove from Chicago to L.A.! That _____ a long time! (take)
2. I don't know why the traffic is so slow. There _____ an accident. (be)
3. That loud sound _____ all the animals. (scare)
4. "What was that noise?" "I don't know, it _____ a cat or something." (be)
5. Well, she _____ too hard for her keys. They're on the table! (look)

**2** Prepare at least two sentences about each photo a–d, using *must have / might have / can't have* to apologize, criticize, or sympathize.

A: *Excuse me, but this bill can't have been calculated correctly. It's too expensive.*
B: *Sorry, but you might have forgotten this is a French gourmet restaurant.*

## 8B

**1** Complete 1–5 with the correct form of *have / get* of these verbs.

break   change   check   install   rebuild   steal

1. Do you go to Dr. Smith to _____ your teeth _____?
2. This neighborhood is getting dangerous. Joe _____ his car _____ last night.
3. Their kitchen looks really nice now, after they _____ it _____.
4. My car sounds a little strange. I think I need to _____ the oil _____.
5. Grandpa _____ his house _____ into, so he _____ an alarm _____ and now he feels more secure.

**2** Describe two things you can get done by these people.
a  a beauty technician
b  a mechanic
c  a doctor
d  a construction worker
e  an artist
*You could get your nails done by a beauty technician.*

## 8C

**1** Complete 1–6 with the correct tag.
1. This coat doesn't make me look overweight, _____?
2. You were going to say "yes," _____?
3. I'm not very good at managing these files, _____?
4. That's absolutely incredible, _____?
5. They haven't gone home yet, _____?
6. She got her car fixed before the trip, _____?

**2** Look at photos a–d and make tag questions using the words in parentheses.

a  He / can't
b  You / not like
c  You / not study
d  It / hot

**3** Correct the mistake in these tag questions.
a  That boy's too young to drive, isn't it.
b  Lots of kids don't eat enough vegetables, don't they?
c  You'll never speak English if you don't practice, won't you?
d  There are too many plastic bottles in the world, aren't they?

# Grammar Unit 9

## 9A Review of verb families

| Time \ Family | Simple | Continuous | Perfect | Perfect continuous |
|---|---|---|---|---|
| **Present** | ➕ He **studies** English.<br>➖ They **don't work** together.<br>❓ **Does** she **live** near here? | ➕ I'**m writing** an essay.<br>➖ She'**s not working** today.<br>❓ **Are** you **kidding** me? | ➕ I'**ve lived** here since 1998.<br>➖ You **haven't seen** her for a long time.<br>❓ **Has** she **bought** anything since then? | ➕ Global warming **has been getting** worse recently.<br>➖ We **haven't been waiting** for long.<br>❓ How long **has** she **been working** here? |
| **Past** | ➕ We **danced** all night long yesterday.<br>➖ I **didn't go** to Mary's party.<br>❓ **Did** you **hear** what she said? | ➕ They **were fighting** again.<br>➖ She **wasn't crying** because of you.<br>❓ **Were** they **talking** about her? | ➕ I'**d left** by the time they arrived.<br>➖ They **hadn't arrived**.<br>❓ **Had** they **called** you before you left? | ➕ We'**d been trying** that before she called.<br>➖ They **hadn't been talking** to each other.<br>❓ **Had** he **been living** with her before she moved to the U.S.? |

## 9B Passive voice

### Simple passive

| | | | |
|---|---|---|---|
| Present | am / is / are (not) | | The chefs here **are known** for their amazing dishes. |
| Past | was / were (not) | Past participle | These sweaters **were made** in Ireland. |
| Future | will / won't | | **Will** the construction **be completed** by 2030? |

### Perfect passive

| | | | | |
|---|---|---|---|---|
| Present | have / has (not) | | | **Has** the bank **been authorized** to send money? |
| Past | had / hadn't | been | Past participle | I wanted to buy that painting but it **had already been sold**. |
| Future | will / won't have | | | It **won't have been built** by next month. |

### Continuous passive

| | | | | |
|---|---|---|---|---|
| Present | am / is / are (not) | | | How cool! You'**re being followed** on Twitter. The website **is being watched** by the authorities. |
| | | being | Past participle | |
| Past | was / were (not) | | | In January 2019, Facebook **was being used** by over 2.25 billion people. |

In the active voice, the subject does the action and the object receives the action.

In the passive voice, the receiver is the subject and the "doer" is optionally included as the object.

**Active:** Tony washed the dishes.
**Passive:** The dishes were washed (by Tony).

Use the passive voice:
1. to emphasize that receiving the action is more important.
2. if you don't know (or don't want to mention) who does the action.

## 9C Future perfect and continuous

### Future perfect

Use the **Future perfect** to talk about a future action that will be finished before another future time or action.
▸ *By next week, we'**ll have been** together for six months!*
Form: **will (not) have** + **past participle** + phrases like *by the time, by the year (2030), in (hours)*.

### Future continuous

Use the **Future continuous** to talk about an action in progress at a certain future time.
▸ *By this time tomorrow, **we'll be lying** on a beautiful beach.*
Form: **will (not)** + **be** + verb + **-ing**.

# Unit 9

## 9A

**1** Complete 1–6 with *Present* or *Past*, *Simple* or *Continuous* form of the verbs in parentheses.

1 We _____ our time this morning. There's no need to rush. (take)
2 I _____ at the light when the bike ran into my car. (wait)
3 She _____ to download that file but her laptop froze halfway through. (try)
4 Students always _____ new words on that language website. (pick up)
5 We _____ in dangerous areas at night. (not walk)
6 _____ you _____ TV when I texted you? (watch)

**2** Complete the dialogues with the correct form of the verbs. Use contractions where possible.

1 A: What _____? (you / do)
   B: Well, I _____ this show about the history of crime. It's so interesting. (watch)
2 A: Really? I _____ you _____ into history. (not know) (be)
   B: Yeah, I guess I _____. _____ the story of Al Capone? (be) (you / hear)
3 A: Oh, yeah! _____ he the guy who _____ alcohol back in the 20s? (be) (sell)
   B: Yep, that _____ him. He _____ one of the most notorious criminals in history, until he _____ in 1947. (be) (be) (die)

**3** Describe pictures a and b. Use as many verb tenses as you can.

a

b

## 9B

**1** Complete 1–6 with *has / have / had + been*.

1 We're sorry. The phone number _____ changed.
2 I tried to download the song, but the site _____ shut down.
3 Lately it seems like books _____ replaced by digital texts.
4 The movie _____ nominated for three awards, but didn't win any.
5 They _____ (not) _____ notified of the flight's cancellation and are still waiting at the airport!
6 Excuse me, ma'am. _____ your passport _____ stamped?

**2** Correct the seven mistakes.

Welcome to the ALCATRAZ NATIONAL PARK. Our website is designing to help you understand the history of Alcatraz.
Our visitors' center has just being renovated and guided tours being given every hour. Alcatraz prison is built in 1933 and have been one of the most famous federal prisons in the U.S.
The National Park Service is being dedicated to keeping the park up to date, clean, and accessible for all visitors. The park will be not held responsible for cancellation due to weather.

## 9C

**1** Complete 1–5 with the *Future perfect* or *Future continuous* of the verbs in parentheses.

1 The new student center building _____ by the time school starts. (not finish)
2 I really don't know what I _____ next week. (do)
3 By next June, I _____ in this town for five years. (live)
4 I think the government _____ this problem for years to come. (debate)
5 Don't worry, they _____ the exhibit before you see it. (not take down)

**2** 🟢 **Make it personal** Describe what you think will be happening or have happened in the future to at least five of these.

extinction of animals    genetically-modified food
new forms of transportation    growing old
living in space    soccer players' salaries

*By 2050, I think people will be living on Mars.*

305

# Grammar Unit 10

## 10A Gerunds and infinitives

Use **gerunds**:
1 as the subject of a sentence
2 for an activity in progress
3 after prepositions or adjective + prepositions
4 after specific verbs

▸ *Listening to music always calms him down.*
▸ *I really don't like looking at your mess.*
▸ *She never asks before using my computer!*
▸ *We are sick of standing here and waiting for tickets.*
▸ *She got angry without knowing the whole story.*

| Verb + gerund | | | |
|---|---|---|---|
| admit | deny | imagine | regret |
| adore | dislike | keep | risk |
| advise | enjoy | mind | spend (time) |
| avoid | fed up with | miss | suggest |
| can't help | feel like | practice | understand |
| consider | finish | quit | waste (time) |

Use **infinitives**:
1 to express purpose
2 after adjectives
3 after specific verbs

▸ *I'm studying hard to get good grades.*
▸ *It will be impossible to finish this on time.*
▸ *I was stupid not to tell the truth.*

**Form:** must have = we're sure something **did** happen
can't have = we're sure it **didn't** happen

| Verb + infinitive | | | |
|---|---|---|---|
| afford | demand | offer | remember |
| agree | expect | plan | seem |
| appear | fail | prepare | stop |
| arrange | forget | pretend | wait |
| ask | hope | promise | want |
| decide | manage | refuse | wish |

## 10B Verb + gerund or infinitive

Using the gerund **G** or infinitive **I** after *forget, remember, stop,* and *try* changes the meaning.

| Forget | |
|---|---|
| **I** not do something that you should do / have done. | I forgot **to bring** my ID! |
| **G** a planned activity that is canceled. | Well, you can forget **coming** to my party! I'm uninviting you. |

| Remember | |
|---|---|
| **I** remember something you should do. | He never remembers **to lock** his car. |
| **G** remember an event or action in the past. | I remember **seeing** her at the party. |

| Stop | |
|---|---|
| **I** interrupt an activity to begin another. | She was lost so she stopped **to get** directions. |
| **G** interrupt or quit something. | She stopped **smoking** last year. |

| Try | |
|---|---|
| **I** make an effort to do something. | He'll try **to go** to your party, but he's very busy. |
| **G** do something and see if it works. | I'll try **talking** to her about it. She might change her mind. |

After certain verbs, there is little change in meaning.
▸ *She doesn't like talking / to talk about her problems.*
▸ *I prefer working / to work alone.*

| Verb + gerund or infinitive | | | |
|---|---|---|---|
| begin | continue | like | prefer |
| choose | hate | love | start |

## 10C Separable and inseparable phrasal verbs

### Separable phrasal verbs

Most phrasal verbs with one particle are **separable** and can take a direct object (*the book, your friend*) between the verb and the particle or after the particle. If the object is a pronoun, it **must** go between the verb and the particle.

▸ *Mike was afraid to ask Julie out, but he finally called her up.*
▸ *We tried to cheer the team up by taking them out.*

Mike finally called her up. NOT ~~Mike finally called up her.~~

### Inseparable phrasal verbs

With **inseparable phrasal verbs**, objects (and pronouns) cannot come between the verb and particle.
*She turned into a princess.* NOT ~~She turned a princess into.~~
Verbs with more than one particle are usually inseparable and the object follows the second particle.

▸ *I know what you're going through. It's a really hard time.*
▸ *Let's catch up when we're not so busy.*
▸ *You know he's not easy to get along with.*

| Separable | Inseparable |
|---|---|
| Don't **throw** the bottles **away**. | I'm **looking forward to** it. |
| Can I **try** your glasses **on**? | Will we ever **run out of** oil? |
| Can you **turn** the heat **up**? | If I make a plan, I **stick to** it. |
| **Switch** your phone **off**! | I'm sorry, we've **sold out**. |
| **Plug** it **into** the wall socket. | This sofa **turns into** a bed. |
| I **cut** salt **out** of my diet. | What's that statue **made of**? |
| I'm cooking. Please **keep** the cat **away**. | My car **broke down** on the highway. |
| Please **hear** me **out**! | The office was **broken into**. |
| Stop **putting** it **off**! | Nick hasn't **showed up** yet. |

# Unit 10

## 10A

**1** Complete 1–5 with the correct form of these verbs.

avoid   call   like   promise   wake up

1  I _____ last night to ask for your advice.
2  She _____ answering texts or calls when she's having dinner.
3  I've never _____ playing video games.
4  We often _____ feeling too tired to work.
5  She always _____ to help me tidy up, but she never does.

**2** Correct two mistakes in each of 1–6.

1  I don't mind to drive you for the train station.
2  She's not interested on listen to his problems.
3  It's a very interesting subject for talking about.
4  They got fed up with hear to neighbor's noisy party.
5  I hope you seeing again one day soon.
6  I usually prefer watch movies to read books.

## 10B

**1** Circle the correct alternative in 1–5.

1  Lee's so afraid of **making** / **to make** a mistake that he doesn't try.
2  You can try **change** / **changing** my mind if you want, but it won't work.
3  After joining www.stopthejunk.com we stopped **to get** / **getting** spam.
4  Alex hadn't thought about **to do** / **doing** anything special for her birthday.
5  I can't stand people who bump into me on the street without **to apologize** / **apologizing**.

**2** Match 1–5 to a–e to make sentences.

1  I'm looking forward to
2  They've planned on
3  We prefer not
4  She hopes
5  Don't forget

a ☐ to sit near the aisle.
b ☐ to turn on the security system when you leave.
c ☐ to graduate next year so she can get a job.
d ☐ seeing you next weekend! We'll have a great time.
e ☐ visiting the art museum this Saturday.

**3** Describe photos a–d using *forget*, *remember*, *stop*, and *try*.

*In the first photo, I hope she doesn't forget to pack her passport.*

## 10C

**1** Complete 1–6 with the correct separable or inseparable phrasal verb and an object.

cut down on   grow up   look at   pick up
run into   run out of

1  Jose _____ in a beautiful neighborhood of Buenos Aires.
2  Yumi needed bread but forgot to _____ after work.
3  They're mad at Jeff and hope they don't _____ at the party.
4  Lu eats too many sweets. She's trying to _____.
5  The pop star walked by and he couldn't stop _____.
6  My car's _____ so I can't drive you to the station.

**2** Order the words in 1–5 to make sentences.

1  with / wants / she / boyfriend / break / her / to / up / .
2  put / can't / up / noise / I / all / on / weekend / with / that / the / .
3  that / should've / tried / you / sweater / on / .
4  he / can / he / call / any / time / up / us / wants / .
5  away / best / when / seven / was / my / I / old / moved / years / friend / .

**3** 🟢 **Make it personal** Correct the mistakes in 1–5. Then prepare questions for 1–5.

1  When I learn a new word, I try it on with my friends.
2  Tom is going to ask out her on a date.
3  It's difficult to figure it out what new words mean.
4  He always forgets to turn the lights before he goes to bed.
5  She'd been making a cake when she ran out eggs of.

*How do you remember new words?*

307

# Sounds and usual spellings

**S** Difficult sounds for Spanish speake[rs]
**P** Difficult sounds for Portuguese spe[akers]

▶ To listen to these words and sounds, and to practice them, go to the pronunciation section on the Richmond Learning Platform

## Vowels

| /iː/ | three, tree, eat, receive, believe, key, B, C, D, E, G, P, T, V, Z |
|---|---|
| /ɪ/ | six, mix, it, fifty, fish, trip, lip, fix |
| /ʊ/ | book, cook, put, could, woman |
| /uː/ | two, shoe, food, new, soup, true, suit, Q, U, W |
| /ɛ/ | pen, ten, heavy, then, again, men, F, L, M, N, S, X |
| /ə/ | bananas, pajamas, salad, minute |

| /ɜr/ | shirt, skirt, work, turn, learn, verb |
|---|---|
| /ɔr/ | four, door, north, fourth |
| /ɔ/ | walk, saw, water, talk, author, law |
| /æ/ | man, fan, bad, apple |
| /ʌ/ | sun, run, cut, umbrella, country, love |
| /ɑ/ | hot, not, on, clock, fall, tall |
| /ɑr/ | car, star, far, start, party, artist, R |

## Diphthongs

| /eɪ/ | plane, train, made, stay, they, A, H, J, K |
|---|---|
| /aɪ/ | nine, wine, night, my, pie, buy, eyes, I, Y |
| /aʊ/ | house, mouse, town, cloud |

| /ɔɪ/ | toys, boys, oil, coin |
|---|---|
| /oʊ/ | nose, rose, home, know, toe, road, O |

308

☐ Voiced
☐ Unvoiced

# Sounds and usual spellings

## Consonants

|   | | | | |
|---|---|---|---|---|
| our lips | p | b | m | w |
| our teeth + another articulator | f | v | θ | ð |
| the tip of the tongue | t | d | n | l |
| the front of the tongue | s | z | ʃ | ʒ |
| the back of the mouth | k | g | ŋ | h |
| the tooth ridge | tʃ | dʒ | r | j |

TO MAKE THESE SOUNDS WE USE

/p/ pig, pie, open, top, apple
/b/ bike, bird, describe, able, club, rabbit
/m/ medal, monster, name, summer
/w/ web, watch, where, square, one
/f/ fish, feet, off, phone, enough
/v/ vet, van, five, have, video
/θ/ teeth, thief, thank, nothing, mouth
/ð/ mother, father, the, other
/t/ truck, taxi, hot, stop, attractive
/d/ dog, dress, made, adore, sad, middle
/n/ net, nurse, tennis, one, sign, know
/l/ lion, lips, long, all, old

/s/ snake, skate, kiss, city, science
/z/ zoo, zebra, size, jazz, lose
/ʃ/ shark, shorts, action, special, session, chef
/ʒ/ television, treasure, usual
/k/ cat, cake, back, quick
/g/ goal, girl, leg, guess, exist
/ŋ/ king, ring, single, bank
/h/ hand, hat, unhappy, who
/tʃ/ chair, cheese, kitchen, future, question
/dʒ/ jeans, jump, generous, bridge
/r/ red, rock, ride, married, write
/j/ yellow, yacht, university

# Audioscript

## Unit 1

**▶ 1.1 Notice the word and sentence stress and the connections.**

M = Mika  C = Carlos

M How's_it going? Settling_into your new home? How's the new job?
C It's going_OK, thanks! I've met_a few new people through work, but it'll be nice to make some more friends.
M Of course. I'm_sure you'll_start meeting people soon. It's_early days. Got_any plans for tonight?
C Yup, I'm going on a "meet-up"! It's the first one I've ever been on, actually!
M You're going_on_a what?
C You know, a meet-up. It's like a social group for people who want to make new friends_and network, that kind_of thing. I've organized_it through_an_app. You download the_app or go_on the website, register, and write_a profile about yourself. Upload pictures_and stuff. The_app then matches you with people who you've got things_in common with. Then you go_on meet-ups. It could be a restaurant, museum, sports_activity ... anything!
M Oh, I see. I haven't heard about_that. It sounds like_a great_idea, though! Especially when you're new_in town. So, what happens when you've registered and been matched with people?
C Well, then you can chat_online and get_to know people_a bit there first. Then you choose_a meet-up to go to. I've met some nice people_online so far. I guess I'll see how the meeting-up_part goes! We're going_on_an organized walk_on Sunday and the organizers_encourage you to prepare some questions to_ask to help get_to know people.
M Really? Like_an interview. So, uh, what kind_of people_are you hoping to meet, then?
C Um, I'm just hoping to make some new friends who_are_into the same things_as me and can show me_around the city a bit. It would be good_to meet some new_work contacts, too. Networking_is_always good!
M Really? So, you're going_on this meet-up to make work contacts?
C No, not really. You know, I just want to meet some cool people and if_I meet someone who can help with business, that's_a bonus!
M Always thinking_about work, aren't you?
C Well, sure, that's why I moved here. But I'm ready to make some new friends, too. What_about you? What's_going_on with ...?

**▶ 1.2 Notice /w/, the connecting /w/ (caused by two vowel sounds connecting), and silent /w/.**

C = Carlos  J = Jenny

C Hi ... I'm Carlos. It's really nice to meet you. You are ...?
J Hi, Carlos! I'm Jenny. We chatted online a bit. Great to meet you in person!
C Oh yes, we did chat online, didn't we? I remember now.
J So, have you been to one of these things before? I remember you said you were new in town.
C No, I haven't. I've just moved here recently, so this is the first one. I'm feeling a bit nervous, to be honest!
J Don't worry. It's only natural. It can be a bit scary meeting lots of new people at once, can't it?

C It really can be! So, how ... er ... how ...
J Shall we have a look at our questions? Did you prepare some? That will give us something to talk about while we walk.
C Ah, yes. Good idea. I did prepare some.
J Great. I've still got mine, too. I bring them to every meet-up I come to. It might seem a bit strange, but it's a really good way to get to know someone.
C OK then! Why don't you go first?

**▶ 1.3 Notice the intonation. ↗ ↘**

C = Carlos  J = Jenny

J How long have you lived here? ↘ Do you have a favorite part of town? ↘
C Ah, that's a difficult one. I've only been here for two months so it's difficult to say. I love the square—what's it called? ↗ Queen's Square. It's really pretty.
J Yes, there are some really nice bars and shops there. I'm going there tomorrow evening, actually. I'm meeting some friends for coffee. You're welcome to join us if you like. Anyway, your turn ...
C Ah, thanks. That's really nice of you! So ... er ... tell me about your friends ... Who do you spend the most time with? ↘
J Well, I'm working so much at the moment, I spend most of my time with my cats! I've got three.
C Three cats! I have to admit, I'm more a dog person. I prefer dogs to cats.
J Well, I like dogs, too, but cats are easier to take care of.
C True.
J My turn. What about your parents? ↘ Who are you closer to—your mom or your dad? ↗
C Mom. Definitely. I haven't had any contact with my dad in years ... I don't want to talk about that, if you don't mind.
J Oh, I'm sorry. Of course not.
C No need for you to be sorry. So, what are you doing this weekend? ↘
J This weekend, I'm visiting a friend for her birthday.
C That sounds like fun.
J It will be. OK. My turn. What celebrity would you enjoy having dinner with? ↘
C Hmm ... Let me think. I'd have to say Emma Stone ...
J Oh, me, too! She's the best. I've seen all of her movies.
C Really? Isn't she fantastic? ↗ So ... speaking of movies, what was the last movie that made you cry? ↘
J That's a good question ... Well, probably *A Street Cat Named Bob.* You know I love cats, and that cat was just amazing.
C No way! I cried like a baby watching that one, too.
J What's the first thing you do every morning? ↘
C That's easy! I throw my alarm clock on the floor. I hate the noise it makes!
J I see! Not a morning person, then. I love early mornings! It's the best time of day. Carlos, here's another question. What's the one thing you're most afraid of? ↘
C Promise you won't laugh? ↗ ... The dark.
J The dark? ↗ Oh, that's kind of cute.
C You think so? ↗
J Look at you! You're turning red! Are you a little bit embarrassed? ↗

**▶ 1.5 Notice the silent /t/ and the connections with vowels.**

I first met_Adam two years_ago. I used to walk my dog_in the park next to my house and he was_always there walking his dog, too. We just used to smile and say hello. Anyway, I was_attracted to him immediately. He has this really beautiful smile and ... one morning the dogs started playing together and he said something lame about the weather_or something and we started chatting and we got_along really well so we swapped numbers. Then we went_out together a few times, you know, just for coffee and stuff. I thought he was funny and charming_and interesting. We started hanging out a lot more, going to restaurants and meeting each other's friends. We talked_about everything and got to know_each other really well. Things were great for about the first six months and then, you know, it was little things at first. I was working a lot at the time and he couldn't understand why we weren't spending as much time together. We argued a lot and fell out_over stupid things like not returning each other's messages. It just wasn't working and eventually we broke_up. I got so angry with him that he couldn't understand how important my career was to me. We were both really upset. After a few more months, I started to miss him, so I called_ and we talked_about stuff. He promised to be more understanding and I promised to make more time for him. Then we got back together! I think_I ... I think I've fallen for him again! How weird is that? But who knows what_our future will bring!

**▶ 1.7 Notice the false starts, repetitions, and uh pauses.**

**Kathy** I think be realistic that you, our expectations sometimes are so high ... But most of marriage is lived in between the ups and the downs... And that it's hard work. And not all the time, but it's hard work.
**Gene** Uh, I think one of the pieces of advice that my dad gave me is, "Gene, always communicate. Always talk, talk things out." And I really believe that communication is so essential ... And that uh, you need to work out many different areas before you get married. Uh, I think you need to talk about money matters. I think you need to talk about child rearing. I think religion is important. I think sex takes care of itself ... Pretty much ... At least initially. But I really do think there are some topics or some areas that need to be hashed out, otherwise, it's conflict.
**Karl** You gotta learn to uh, give more than you take, or you'll never make it and uh, that, that's the bottom line.
**Bonnie** And you need, you need to, you know, grow together, uh, in what, in what you do ... Try new things, you know. Go out and start skiing if you haven't done it, do it as a couple. Do things together, you know, or as a family if you have a family. I think those are important things, too, you know. Don't you have your own hobbies and your husband or spouse have their own hobbies. That's not a real good way ...
**Bill** Every time, if you have a disagreement or a problem, you correct it before you go to bed. And uh, then, you never wake up, and uh, with a carry-over. And uh, that has—to me—always been good advice. I'm not sure that Kay and I have always followed that, but uh, you know, most of the time we have.

# Audioscript

Kay  I'd have to say those who play together stay together, instead of going your own separate ways and doing your own things.

## 1.9 Notice /ə/ and sentence stress.

Professor Robin Dunbar is an anthropologist and evolutionary psychologist at Oxford University. He is famous for calculating "Dunbar's Number", which is an estimate that the number of relationships humans are able to manage is 150. He believes that this number has been almost the same throughout human history. From small villages in the past all the way up to the modern age of international travel and social media. Dunbar's Number came from research Professor Dunbar did with primates in the 1990s. He discovered that there was a connection between the size of these animals' brains and the social groups they belonged to. By using the data he collected in his studies of primates, he estimated that humans should be able to handle only 150 relationships at any one time.

In order to build relationships, we need to remember details about people's lives, etc., so the size of our brains is an important factor. According to Dunbar, our brains can only hold enough information to maintain about 150 relationships. This number can be seen in lots of different situations: the size of villages, remote tribal groups, the number of Christmas cards we send, and the average number of Facebook friends we have.

Of course, within these 150 relationships, there are different levels. The first is made up of about five very close friends, the next 15 are good friends, 50 friends we see reasonably often, and then the remainder is acquaintances. This number is based on averages, so it's possible to have more or fewer people in your social circles. However, if we have more, it will be difficult to manage and the quality of the relationships will suffer. It seems that 150 is the best number. With this many people, we can maintain stable, honest relationships.

## 1.10 Notice /θ/, /ð/, and /d/.

J = Jamie   A = Alison
J  That's a nice picture! Are they your colleagues?
A  Yes, they are. They're a great bunch. Luckily, we all get along really well.
J  When did you take that one?
A  That was taken at the Christmas party last year!
J  Looks like you had fun! What about this one? Who's that?
A  That's Lucy. She's my sister's best friend. She's a musician.
J  Does she play professionally?
A  Yes, she does. We often go to watch her.
J  Can she play any other instruments?
A  Sure! She's really talented; one of those people who can play anything!
J  Oh, what a nice shot! Who took this one?
A  My dad took it, I think. This is Dominic. We've known each other since kindergarten. He's great. The kind of person you can always depend on.
J  So, out of all these lovely people, who are you closest to?
A  Hard to say really. I love them all!

## 1.12 Notice the spellings of /k/.

A = Anna   B = Betty
A  So, who are you following on Insta these days? I want to find some new accounts to follow. Any good ones?
B  Yes, sure. I've added some really cool ones recently. Do you want to see?
A  OK, let's have a look.
B  Right, well, I like to follow accounts that I find inspiring, funny, cute, etc. For example, travel accounts. Look at this one. This couple is traveling the world together. They take amazing photographs and they really inspire me. Each photo is so creative! I mean, who doesn't want to do what they're doing?!
A  Oh, I see! Look at that picture. Wow! They sure look like they're having an amazing time. Where is that? Vietnam?
B  I think so. They certainly are worth following, I think.
A  OK, I'll add them! What else?
B  I don't know about you, but I just love anything with cute animals, so I follow a few of these accounts. Look at this one! I mean, these instantly put me in a good mood.
A  "Animal Addicts." Oh, look at the puppies! So cute!!
B  And then there's this one. These guys rescue mistreated animals. It's so moving and inspiring.
A  Ah, yeah. That one's definitely for me. I'll add it. Why would anyone ever want to hurt those animals? It's so touching to see those people with them!
B  I know. I do love this one. It's one of my favorites. Want to see some more?
A  Sure, this is fun!
B  OK, I also like following accounts that post motivational quotes. Look, this one's called "Secret to Success". It's quotes from famous people.
A  "Don't watch the clock. Do what it does. Keep going." I like that!
B  It does make perfect sense.
A  I'll follow that one, too. Thanks! I've got some great ones to follow now.

## 1.15 Notice the intonation. ↗↘

K = Kelly   R = Roberto
K  So … How did it go last night?
R  You mean the date? ↗
K  Yep. The one you met on that Player.me app, right?
R  Yes, that's the one. Well, we arranged to meet at Starbucks on 57th. You know, the cozy one, great coffee …
K  Uh-huh.
R  I got there a bit late because of the traffic and … Well, anyway, I opened the door and, to my surprise …
K  Go on … ↘
R  I spotted her immediately. Sitting right in front of me, drinking coffee. It was obvious it was her even though I had no idea what she looked like. She was just perfect, you know?
K  Hold on a sec. You mean you hadn't seen her photo?
R  No! You see, she hadn't put a picture of herself on her profile. Just an image of the character she likes playing.
K  No way! ↗
R  Yeah, but I knew straightaway she was the girl I'd been chatting to on the app! I just knew.
K  What happens next? ↘
R  Our eyes meet, we shake hands and, you know, try to break the ice, talk about the coffee, the weather, the traffic …
K  And then …
R  She gets up and leaves.
K  What do you mean "leaves"? ↘
R  She says, "Look, I don't think this is going to work out," leaves her share of the bill on the table, and walks away.
K  Just like that? ↗
R  Just like that.
K  Are you serious? ↘
R  Yep. So there you go, one more disastrous date for my collection. How about that?
K  Oh, dear. Well, don't let it get to you, Roberto. You know, you'll meet someone else.
R  Yeah, yeah … Oh well.

# Unit 2

## 2.4 Notice the silent letters.

It started out as an experiment. I wanted to see if I could leave no impact on the environment for an entire year, and I asked myself, "Was it possible I could become a happier person by reducing my impact on the environment?" And the answer I found out is a resounding "yes." So, I started by cutting out garbage, taxis, throw-away coffee cups … I eliminated tomatoes in the middle of January, A/C in the dead of August, bottled water from France, and new clothing from who knows where. I saved money, lost weight, gained energy, improved my health, spent more quality time with my family and friends, renewed my relationship with my wife, and discovered an overall sense of freedom. I learned that, yes, sometimes less is more.

## 2.7 Notice the silent h and the /ə/ in the How long questions.

1  M  Guess what! I go to the gym twice a week now! [beep]
   W  Really? How long_have you been going there?
2  M  I live near the park now, you know? [beep]
   W  Really? How long_have you been living there?
3  M  Susan's going out with Paulo. Can you believe that? [beep]
   W  Really? How long_has she been going out with him?
4  M  John's learning how to recycle glass. [beep]
   W  Really? How long_has he been learning that?
5  M  Rick plays the guitar really well. [beep]
   W  Really? How long_has he been playing it?

## 2.9 Notice the short (/) and long (//) pauses.

1  The Earth is getting hotter, / not the sun. // In fact, / a number of independent measures of solar activity / indicate that the sun has cooled by a few degrees since 1960, / over the same period that global temperatures have been increasing. // Over the last 35 years of climate change, / sun and climate have been moving in opposite directions.
2  Some people say, / "Well, we've had ice ages and warmer periods, / so climate change is natural! / It's got nothing to do with us!" // This is like saying that forest fires have happened naturally in the past, / so any recent forest fires can't be caused by humans. // It just doesn't make sense.
3  Climate researchers have been publishing papers for years / saying that climate change is happening right now. // We can see the evidence in flooding and droughts all around the world. // We need to start making changes / immediately. // Around 97% of researchers agree on this. // There is no "Planet B".

311

4 Climate change deniers say the planet has been cooling down since a peak in 1998. // However, experts have shown that in a climate being warmed by man-made carbon emissions, / it is possible to have long periods of cooler temperatures. // This does not mean that climate change isn't happening. // In fact, / globally, / the hottest 12-month period ever recorded / was from June 2009 to May 2010.

5 A large number of ancient mass extinction events have been linked to global climate change. // Because the world's climate has been changing so rapidly, / the way species typically adapt / (for example, migration) / is, / in most cases, / simply not possible. // This, / along with poaching, etc., / does not help the world's threatened species.

## ▶ 2.12

### 1 Notice /ɪ/ and /iː/.
L = Lorna  B = Beth
- L  Hi, Beth! You're looking well. Have you been on vacation?
- B  Hi! I wish. No, I haven't. Thank you, though.
- L  What have you been doing, then? I mean, you've obviously been doing something. You look great! You're really glowing!
- B  Well ... actually ... I've been trying this new dietary supplement.
- L  Ah, not another one of these "superfoods"?! They are such a load of nonsense!
- B  Yes, it is ...

### 2 Notice the letters that disappear in speech.
Z = Zach  P = Pedro
- Z  Hey, Pedro, I tried to call you, like, five times. Dude, where were you?
- P  Ah, Zach. Sorry, bro. Not my fault. It's this thing I bought ...
- Z  ... one of those green models?
- P  Yeah, but, uh, I'm taking it back to the store first thing tomorrow.
- Z  Oh yeah? How come?

### 3 Notice the /t/, /d/, and /ŋ/ endings.
B = Bruce  T = Tom
- T  Are you still working for TechStars?
- B  I quit last month.
- T  Bruce! No! You loved that place.
- B  Yeah. I worked there for over ten years. But, like, you see, I ... I just couldn't handle the stress ...
- T  I know what you mean, sure. So, uh ... Have you found a job yet?
- B  Nope.
- T  So, like, let me try a different question. Have you been looking for a job?
- B  No ... You see, I spent the whole month away from Chicago ... just meditating, relaxing, and trying to find some peace of mind, you know?

## ▶ 2.13

### 1 Notice /s/ and /z/.
L = Lorna  B = Beth
- L  Ah, not another one of these "superfoods"?! They are such a load of nonsense!
- B  Yes, it is. Moringa, have you heard of it?
- L  Mor ... what? No, I haven't. What is it?
- B  It's the leaves of the Moringa tree. They call it the "Miracle Tree". It's meant to be one of the healthiest things around.
- L  Well, it does seem to be working on you. What do you do with it?
- B  You just add it to drinks and food. It's really easy to use and I have to say, I've really noticed the benefits. I've got more energy, I'm sleeping better, and I'm not catching as many colds. It's really worth it!
- L  I can see. Let me know where you buy it. I'm definitely going to try it!

### 2 Notice the spelling of /uː/, /ʊ/, and /aʊ/.
Z = Zach  P = Pedro
- Z  Oh yeah? How come?
- P  I've been trying to call you back for about an hour, and I haven't been able to get through. This thing is useless!
- Z  No kidding! It just doesn't connect to the network?
- P  No, it just keeps dying after an hour. What a waste of money! To think I threw away the old phone! I had my old Samsung for three years, and sure, it wasn't "green", but the battery life was much better.

### 3 Notice /ŋ/ and /n/ + consonant.
B = Bruce  T = Tom
- B  No ... You see, I spent the whole month away from Chicago ... just meditating, relaxing, and trying to find some peace of mind, you know?
- T  Wow! But where exactly did you go?
- B  I went to a meditation retreat up in the mountains. I was there for about a month, you know?
- T  And ...?
- B  I'm a brand new man.
- T  No way!
- B  Yeah. Never been happier.

## ▶ 2.17 Notice the silent /r/.
Our planet has some amazing species, but too many of them face extinction. Here are some of the rarest animals on earth. Perhaps the most famous rare animal is the giant panda. In 2014, scientists found fewer than 2,000 pandas in the bamboo forests of China, and there are only 300 pandas in our zoos, too. Imagine the world without pandas!

Next, one of the rarest marine animals. The Hawaiian monk seal only lives in the ocean around the beautiful islands of Hawaii, and fewer than 1,000 of these magnificent creatures remain.

OK, next up is the adorable golden lion tamarin from the Atlantic forests of Brazil. There are only around 3,000 of them left in the wild, although at least this number is now up from just 200 in 1980. Way to go, Brazil, keep up the great work!

It's not such good news for the mountain gorilla. They are under threat from poaching, war, and loss of habitat through deforestation. These gorillas were only discovered about 120 years ago, and now there are only about 800 left in the African mountains.

Another ocean mammal in extreme danger is the North Atlantic right whale. Mostly found along the Atlantic coast of North America, they are one of the most endangered of all large whales. Despite over 70 years of protection from hunting, fewer than 400 of these extraordinary creatures are still alive.

A similar sad story is the Javanese rhino. People have been killing this beautiful animal to make medicine for hundreds of years—and now there are approximately only 60 left, living in the Ujung Kulon National Park in Java, Indonesia.

And the worst story of all. Due to loss of habitat in their native forests of the southeastern United States, scientists believe that there are very few ivory-billed woodpeckers in the world, maybe even none. How awful is that?

Come on, people! Wake up! Let's finally learn from this and try to save what is left of our rich and varied wildlife—before it's too late. It's now or never ...

## ▶ 2.19 Notice /f/, /v/, and /b/.
Are we failing to communicate? Have we forgotten what first inspired our love of nature? All the evidence shows that the single most important factor behind taking action is our childhood experience. The wellspring of our commitment comes from the emotional high we reach when in contact with nature. But how can this wonder be harnessed to change our behavior? Showing the loss of animals in faraway places may pull a few heartstrings—even attract donations. But does it really change our behavior? What if we were able to communicate to people the wonder of nature that surrounds them and promote education that leads to awareness of threatened species and the habitats they live in? In all parts of the world, we're beginning to see that public awareness does lead to change, where people can see the benefits from making their own contribution. It's not the depressing accounts of the wildlife we are losing that moves us. It's awe and wonder, enhanced by understanding, that can inspire us to take action. It's love, not loss.

## ▶ 2.20

### 1 Notice /w/ and /l/.
P = Phil  L = Laura
- P  ... threatened species. Anyway, so Claire and I went on the Internet, accessed WWF.com, and we adopted a whale.
- L  Phil, why would you want to adopt a whale?
- P  Well, we paid 50 bucks and they ...
- L  Oh, Phil! Seriously. What is the point of spending money on an animal you will never see? Life's too short. Live a little.
- P  Honestly, Laura, don't you think ...

### 2 Notice /ʌ/ and /ʊ/.
- W  ... so, anyway, guess what. I've just created this brand-new blog to try to raise public awareness and I've been getting a lot of hits ...
- M  Oh yeah? Let's have a look. Hmm ... Wow, Brenda, you've put a huge effort into this. It looks really good. Keep up the good work.
- W  Thanks a lot! Yeah, I'm really pleased with it. I know it isn't much, but I need to follow my heart. The gorillas' lives are on the line here. And you know what ...

### 3 Notice the connecting /w/.
- M1  ... and that's why, as I told you, we need to attract as many donations as we can.
- M2  Uhmm ... And how exactly are you planning to do that?
- M1  Well, I don't know. I've been thinking of going door to door.
- M2  Door to door! Wow, you are determined! Good for you. Don't give up!

### 4 Notice the connections.
- M  Honey, I have_a little surprise for you.
- W  What?
- M  Look_over there.
- W  Oh my God, don't tell me it's that new electric car you've been going_on_and_on about.
- M  Yep. Bought_it this morning. Wanna go for_a ride?
- W  Honey, what's the use_of buying that when_you know nothing's gonna change? Look_around_ you! This must be the only electric car_in the neighborhood.

### 5 Notice /ʃ/ and /s/.
- W1  ... so, since then, no more plastic bags. Ever. I've been using my own reusable bags whenever I go shopping.
- W2  Every time? Way to go, Janet! I wish I had that kind of self-discipline.

312

# Audioscript

## Review 1

### ▶ R1.2 Notice the intonation ↗ on the short questions.

OK, now put each noun and adjective together. OK? ↗ So you should have three combinations; for example, an imaginative panda, an easy-going chicken, or an outgoing whale. Right, so let's find out what this means. Ready? ↗ The first combination is how you see yourself. Your self-image—OK? ↗ The second combination is how other people see you. Yeah, that's what they think of you. And, wait for it, the third combination is the truth, it's how you really are. That's you! Surprised? ↗ Or do you agree?

### ▶ R1.3 Notice /θ/ and /ð/.

Amazing Facts!
Fact one: Are you afraid to swim in the ocean? Sharks kill 8 to 12 people a year around the world, but really they should be scared of us. Scientists estimate that humans kill 100 million sharks annually.

Fact two: In 1990, 43% of the global population lived in poverty. By 2010, only 21% were living on less than $1.25 a day. The United Nations hopes to end extreme poverty by the year 2030. Let's hope they can!

Fact three: Edison Peña is one of the 33 miners who were stuck in a Chilean mine for 69 days in 2010. Edison ran 6 miles a day when he was in the mine and one month after escaping he ran the 42 kilometer New York marathon in just 5 hours and 40 minutes.

## Unit 3

### ▶ 3.3 Notice the short (/) and long (//) pauses.

While people in Hong Kong are very familiar with western culture, / there are still unique social etiquettes that tourists should observe. // When greeting someone in Hong Kong, / a handshake is common, / but do it with a slight bow. // Kissing on the cheek and hugging is not practiced. // It is OK to gently push your way through the crowd as Hong Kong is so densely packed; // in fact, / if someone says they're sorry / while navigating the crowd, / it's considered impolite. // When giving gifts, / always give them with two hands. // Do not give clocks as the Chinese associate clocks with death. // And // gifts are never opened in front of the person that gave them. // When eating with others, / it's important to be aware of important table etiquette. // As a courtesy, / fill the tea cups of others / before pouring your own cup, / even if their cups are not empty. // When you need a refill, // keep the lid of the teapot half open, / and the waiter will get the hint. // Blowing on the soup is considered OK / to cool down the soup. // After you're done, / don't leave your chopsticks standing straight up, / as this signifies death. / Leave them flat on the table. // Tipping is customary, / a service tip of 10% is expected, // and tip the server directly, / as leaving a tip on the table is considered impolite. // Now you know a little bit more about Hong Kong. // This is Rosanna Wilcox, / informing you about Hong Kong.

### ▶ 3.7 Notice the silent final letters.

**Raul** I was studying full-time, had a part-time job to help with the student debt, I wasn't eating or sleeping properly, and my nonstop lifestyle was driving me crazy. I couldn't find that work-life balance. One day, I was studying in the middle of the night with the radio on and a classical tune came on that I used to play when I was a kid. It reminded me how much I missed playing the piano! The next morning, I sat down at my piano for the first time in years and started to play. I felt the stress just drain away from me. It's amazing how something so simple can have such a positive effect. Now, although I'm still just as busy, it doesn't really bother me as much. I always make time to sit down each day and play for ten minutes. Everything else melts away and I feel much better after. You should try it!

**Tomiko** I was getting up, drinking two cups of coffee, and grabbing an energy bar. Lunch was at my desk every day; a sandwich eaten in two minutes flat while working. I'd grab a takeout on the way home from work and in between there were more energy drinks and quick snacks. Food just didn't seem important, but I felt terrible and my energy levels were low. Things had to change! Now, I find it annoying if I don't have time to eat properly. I make sure that at least one meal a day is prepared with care. I plan what I'm going to eat, I go to the local farm shop and take time to enjoy the sights and sounds. I've made food more like a hobby. It takes more time, but I don't mind that. My health has improved and I'm hoping to start growing my own soon. I'm actually going on a beginner's gardening course this weekend.

**André** I first moved here five years ago for work. I didn't know anyone and I'd never lived alone before. Loneliness became a real problem for me. I couldn't stand coming home to an empty apartment every day. I could call my family and friends, of course, but it's not the same. I was walking home one day when this little cat started to follow me. She came right to the door and was there a couple of hours later. Eventually, I let her in and that was it! We've been best friends ever since. It's just so nice to have someone to come home to in the evening. Even though I know she can't understand me, I still talk to her. It's just nice to have the company, you know. I still find the city a bit lonely at times, but I'm OK with it.

### ▶ 3.9 Notice how the similar sounds link.

**Story 1**
R = Rachel  J = Juan
R You look a little bit depressed, Juan. What's wrong?
J Yeah, well, last Thursday I had a job interview—the third in a week.
R You poor thing!
J You see, I'd been trying to find a job as an architect for months, without success, of course, but I was really optimistic about that particular interview. Anyway, the big day finally came, and, hmm, guess what—there was a massive, massive traffic jam on the main avenue.
R Oh, no!
J Yep, but, you know, I wasn't too worried, since I'd woken up at six and left home at seven ... you know, just to be on the safe side.
R Right. What time was the interview?
J Eight thirty.
R Seems more than enough, doesn't it?
J Well, that's what I thought. At seven thirty, though, I was still stuck in exactly the same place, so I turned on the local traffic radio to see what was going on.
R And ...?
J Apparently, a bus had gone through a red light and crashed into three cars. On the day of my interview!
R Oh, no! Did you make it in time for the interview?
J Hmm ... Guess what time I got there. Eight fifty!
R You're joking! Gee! And how did it turn out?
J Surprise, surprise ... I didn't get the job I'd been dreaming of since I graduated! Darn it!
R Well, I'm sure something better will come along ... and next time be sure to rent a helicopter on the day of the interview.
J Ha, ha, very funny.

**Story 2**
S = Sandra  E = Ethan
S [singing]
E I didn't know you liked Taylor Swift.
S Oh, I'm a huge fan. I'm crazy about her.
E Really? Have you ever seen her live?
S Yep. Well, sort of.
E Uh? What do you mean?
S Well, when I heard she was coming to Rio, I bought two tickets right away. Incredibly expensive, but I didn't care. Anyway, I spent the next two months anxiously waiting for the big day—the day I'd been waiting for since I was sixteen.
E Wow!
S On the day of the show, I left work two hours early and set off for São Paulo with a friend. She had arranged to pick me up in her car.
E OK, go on ...
S Well, we'd been driving for a little while when the car started making a weird noise. Then smoke started coming out from under the hood, so both of us started to freak out.
E No wonder! That sounds a bit scary.
S Yeah, I know ... We had to pull over. People were honking like crazy, but there was nothing we could do—the car broke down and we had to wait for roadside assistance.
E So what happened in the end?
S Well, a mechanic arrived and told us we hadn't checked the oil. He fixed the car and we set off again. By the time we finally got to the stadium, she'd been singing for well over an hour. Thank goodness the security guards let us in.
E So you only caught—what—the last ten minutes of the show?
S Only the last few songs! But that was the best half hour of my life. I swear.

### ▶ 3.10

**A**
W No! No, no, no, please not my car. I only parked for a few minutes. I only went to the store.
M Don't even think about parking here. Unauthorized vehicles will be towed away at the owner's expense.

**B**
M1 Hey! You can't come in here, this is private property! Get him, Samson!
M2 Ahhhh!
M3 Trespassers will be prosecuted. If the dogs don't get you first.

**C**
M Smile! This building is under 24 hour surveillance.

**D**
W Come on, Harry. No Harry, not here. Come on Harry. Not here. Oh Harry, OK then, here.
M Attention dog guardians! Please pick up after your dog. Thank you. Attention dogs! Grrrr woof. Good dog.

**E**
M Swim at your own risk. The sharks will be delighted! By the way, no lifeguards on duty here.

313

F
M In order to maintain a relaxing environment, please refrain from cell phone use.
G
W Welcome aboard flight AA735 for Los Angeles.
M Please fasten seat belt while seated. Life vest under your seat.
H
M Speed limit ten miles per hour.
I
W Here, boy. Here, Harry. Here, Harry. Harry!
M Dogs must be on leash.

▶ **3.12** Notice the intonation in questions. ↗↘

**1**
A Excuse me ...
B Hang on a second, Julie. Yes? ↗
A Oh, hi ... uh ... Meditation 102 is about to begin.
B Yeah, I know. I'm in that group. Can't wait!
A Well, you see, we like to keep the school as quiet as possible, so ... uh ... I was wondering ... could you continue your conversation outside?
B Oh, I'm sorry. Was I speaking too loud? ↗
A I'm afraid so.
B I'm sorry. I didn't realize that. Julie, gotta go, I'll catch up with you later.

**2**
C Excuse me ... Excuse me, miss.
D Yes?
C Are you shopping with us? ↗
D Well, no, not now. Why?
C Uh ... I'm afraid you can't park here.
D What do you mean I can't park here? ↘ Says who? ↘
C Just look at the sign over there.
D Oh, come on. Be reasonable. The parking lot's nearly empty and I ... and I just need to cash a check at the bank. Can I park here for just 10 minutes? ↗
C I'm afraid not.
D But I'm starving. I can bring you a muffin on my way back, how about that? ↗
C I'm sorry, miss. Our parking area's for patrons only. There's another parking lot right across the street and ...
D Well, I want to speak to the manager ...

**3**
E How may I help you, sir? ↘
F What do you mean "how may I help you"? ↘ Can't you see I'm going for my morning run? ↗
E I'm afraid this is private property sir. You can't go beyond this point.
F Since when? ↗
E Since yesterday. Mr. Jobs just bought this whole area. You see the gate? ↗
F Well, I've been jogging here since 1999, so this is my area, too. They can't just close it off like that.
E Sir, I'm afraid I'm going to have to ask you to step back.

# Unit 4

▶ **4.3** Notice the sentence stress and weak forms.

A I can't really remember the last time I had a chance to go in the backyard and just run around.
B School's just so much pressure that every day I wake up dreading it.
C I'm afraid that our children are going to sue us for stealing their childhoods.
D I would spend six hours a night on my homework.
E You have to get into the top schools.

F You have to take tests and do interviews.
G It's gone way to the extreme.
H We're all caught up in it.
I In America, if you don't earn a lot of money, something went wrong.
J The pressure comes from the colleges, from the parents, from the government, but it has to stop.
K You have to do well now, so you can get into a good college.
L Everyone expects us to be superheroes.
M You have a fear from the parents that my kid needs to be able to get a job.
N How do you expect us to do well when you can't even make mistakes?
O You're dedicating your whole life to your grades.
P You have to be smart and you have to be involved in the arts.
Q I have soccer practice every day.
R Plus the homework on top of that.
S Produce, produce, produce ...
T It's impossible.
U I couldn't cope.

▶ **4.5 1** Notice the weak form of /ə/.

I = interviewer  J = Justin
I Right, so you're basically saying that you hate the work you do.
J Well, I'm not sure about "hate."
I But you dislike engineering?
J Yeah ... I guess. I'm good at it, though.
I Oh, yeah?
J People at work say I'm really good at what I do, and ... they must be right.
I So ... Why exactly are you looking for a career change?
J 'Cause ... 'cause that's not where my heart is. I love music. Always have, always will.
I So, how come you majored in engineering, Justin?
J Well, Dad's an engineer and I'm an only child ... Do the math.
I And you've never considered getting a degree in music, arts, or something?
J Nope. Dad wanted me to follow in his footsteps, but I shouldn't have listened to him.
I Well, you're still young, you know. Have you thought about starting over?
J Nah. I'm way too old now. I should have gone to music school years ago.
I Well, I disagree. You see ...

**2**
I = interviewer  Z = Zoe
I ... so, Zoe, you've come for some advice about your major, is that correct?
Z Uh-huh.
I Freshman?
Z Nope. I'm a sophomore.
I What seems to be the problem?
Z Well, I've been thinking of dropping out.
I Oh really? Why's that?
Z Well, basically, journalism's not my thing. I should have chosen another major.
I Right, but ... how can you be so sure that you've picked the wrong career?
Z Well, for starters, I can't stand writing and ...
I Oh ...
Z Yep. My writing really sucks. I can barely put two words together.
I I hear you, but ... um ... Did you enjoy writing at all when you were in high school? I mean, there's got to be a reason why you picked journalism.
Z Well, the truth is, I didn't want to lose touch with Kylie, Bonnie, Maria, and Tom.

I Excuse me?
Z My best friends. They all wanted to study journalism, so I ... hmmm ... I thought I'd learn how to like it eventually. Guess I was wrong ... Look, I know it was a stupid decision and I should have thought about it more carefully, but my question to you now is: Is it too late to switch majors?
I Hmm. Yes and no. You see ...

**3**
I = interviewer  G = George
I ... so what is it that you do exactly, George?
G I'm a ... Roger, get out of here. I told you to wait outside, didn't I? Just go! Bad dog.
I You were saying ...
G I'm a dog walker.
I Uh-huh.
G The money's not bad and I ... I like dogs. But I'm 41 and ... you know, my wife thinks there is no future in it.
I Did you attend university at all?
G One year. Then I dropped out. You see, I really enjoyed college, but I just hated university, I didn't like being away from my family. But now I guess I'm paying the price. Every day I wake up and ask myself: Should I have persevered a little more?
I Well, yeah ... probably. But have you considered going back?
G Hmm ... Well, the thing is ...

▶ **4.8** Notice the short (/) and long (//) pauses.

**1** One of my main goals is to get onto the property ladder as soon as possible. // Most people think I'm too young to be thinking about this kind of investment. At 22, / they think I should be going out partying and enjoying myself, / not working hard, / saving, / and putting all my money into real estate. // I'm still with my parents at the moment. // They are very supportive. // If I didn't live at home, I wouldn't be able to save anything. // My big dream / is to own lots of different apartments. // I'll buy them cheap, / do them up, and then sell them or rent them out. // If I work hard and save my money, / I'll see the benefits later. // My friends all think I'm a bit crazy, / but I'll be able to retire much earlier than them! //

**2** I've always had itchy feet. // I never want to stay in one place. // There is a whole world out there to explore! // Imagine all of those different cultures and people and food // ... I have a big map on my wall at home and I put a pin in it every time I go somewhere new. // There aren't enough pins in there at the moment. // I've been to a few places in Europe, / but that's it so far. // My main wish is to reach all seven continents. // If there were nine or ten continents, / I would still want to visit each one! // I want to go in a hot air balloon over Cappadocia, / fly in a helicopter over the Grand Canyon, / dive on the Great Barrier Reef. // I know, I know, / all of this costs a lot of money. // If I save enough this year, / I'll go backpacking around Southeast Asia. // I can't wait! // So many places, / so little time! //

**3** Earning this would mean everything to me. // It's taken me six years to get this far. // It means dedication, / perseverance. // You can't just give up. // In martial arts you have to be completely committed and dedicated to your sport. // Reaching that level is extremely difficult. // You have to go to every single class, / get beaten, / sweat, / cry. // All of this and still go to work or

314

# Audioscript

school! // If I pass this level, / I'll prove to myself that I can do anything I want. / To be honest, / if I didn't train in martial arts, // I wouldn't be the person I am now. / I feel more confident than ever before. / My ultimate aim is to become an instructor and have my own training school. //

## ▶ 4.9
1 If I had more time, I'd practice the piano more.
2 If you save money now, you'll have a good pension when you retire.
3 If we knew the answer, we'd tell you.
4 You'll be late if you don't take the bus.
5 I'll buy an apartment if I have enough money.

## ▶ 4.12 Notice the connections and /t/, /d/, and /ɪd/.
1 His parents suspected he had_a learning [beep] (disability).
2 He has trouble sleeping because he [beep] (constantly) sees numbers_in his head.
3 By the age_of three, Jacob could [beep] (easily) solve complex_equations.
4 Jacob dropped_out_of_[beep] (elementary) school.
5 At_age_eight, it was clear that his mathematical_ability was [beep] (unusually) high.
6 He joined_Purdue University and [beep] (eventually) became_a paid researcher.

## ▶ 4.13  1 (with addition in 4.14) Notice the intonation of What and Really. ↗↘
I = Iris  F = Fiona
I Hi, sorry I'm late. I missed the five o'clock bus.
F What happened to your car?
I Oh, you don't wanna know.
F What? ↗
I I drove into a tree.
F What? ↗
I Yep. A little dog ran out in front of me and I had to swerve quickly to avoid hitting it!
F Oh my goodness! Well, look, at least you didn't get hurt. It could have been worse.

### 2
J = Josh  B = Belinda
J Oh, no! Oh, no! Not again.
B What? ↘
J Seven hours of work gone to waste.
B What? ↗
J Oh, you don't wanna know.
B Know what? ↗
J PC crashed again.
B Don't tell me you had no backup. Josh, this is the third time this year! You should have known better.

### 3
G = Gina  J = Jay
G I thought this was a new car.
J It is.
G Oh ... uh ... so ...
J Worst thing I've ever bought.
G Oh, no. Really? ↗
J Yeah, this is the second time it's broken down. And don't get me started on the price I paid.
G Oh Jay, what a shame! You loved your last one like this. Well, what's done is done. You can always get rid of this one and get yourself a new model.

### 4
D = David  C = Carla  A = Anna
D God, I hate this one.
C What? ↗ No, you don't.

D What do you mean? Look at this painting. My four-year-old could have done better.
C David, shut up.
A No, go on. I'm listening.
D You know what I hate about it?
A What? ↘
D The use of colors. The whole thing's so primitive, you know? How can they call this art?
C Listen, what my friend means is that ...
A Can you excuse me for a moment? There's somebody I've got to speak to.
C David, are you out of your mind? She's the artist!
D What? ↗ Oh, no!
C What were you thinking?

# Review 2

## ▶ R2.2 Notice /w/ and /j/.
M Well, they arrived at the festival, but it had been canceled.
W Yeah. I think it had been raining.
M Yeah. It looks like it. And then they all stayed in one tent.
W Uh-huh. The wind had taken the other tent.
M Unlucky, huh? And what's this picture? They look cold.
W Yeah, right. I guess they had been expecting hot weather because they are wearing T-shirts.

# Unit 5

## ▶ 5.2 Notice /m/, /n/, and /ŋ/ endings and their spellings.
P = presenter  N = Natalie
P Hello and welcome to "Money-wise," your weekly consumer program. This week we are talking to Natalie Dupont, a social media marketing expert. Welcome, Natalie.
N Thank you.
P On this program we're talking about the phenomenon of "shopping haul" videos. Natalie, can you explain for us?
N Of course. YouTube "shopping haul" videos is a huge trend. A "haul" is a video of a vlogger unpacking and describing items they have bought.
P OK, and why do people watch these?
N For shopaholics, these videos are entertaining. It's strangely satisfying to see how people spend their money. There are millions of hauls posted on social media, and many companies have been using this user-generated content to advertise their product. However, there is now a revolution. Vloggers are moving away from these materialistic videos and posting "anti-haul" videos.
P What is an "anti-haul" video?
N Basically, they encourage viewers to buy less. In the video they post, the vlogger gives a list of products they don't plan to buy because they think the products are useless or overpriced.
P So, where did this trend for "anti-haul" videos come from?
N Well, Beauty Vlogger Kimberly Clark started doing this in 2015. In her video, which has had over 100,000 views, Clark says we should "put the brakes on consumerism" and "stop shopping". She shows the viewer 14 products they don't need and shouldn't waste their money on. Clark's fans begged her to post more videos like this. This inspired other YouTube vloggers to post similar "anti-hauls" and there are now more than 850,000 online.
P Really interesting. Why have they become so popular?

N Because they talk to hardworking, underpaid shoppers. We have too many options and not enough money! Perhaps it's this generation. Millenials and Generation Z have grown up in a financial crisis. Students are in debt, there are fewer jobs. I think these videos speak to that generation. Research shows that Millennials would much rather buy experiences than stuff.
P So, I guess the message is that you don't need most of the stuff marketed to you. Perhaps consumerism is finally going out of fashion!
N Exactly!

## ▶ 5.3 Notice /ə/ and sentence stress.
I started getting into debt when I was 18. I was at college, like you, so I took out student loans and signed up for credit cards.
I was enjoying student life! Who doesn't, right?! I would go on shopping sprees, buying clothes and music. I paid the minimum back on my credit card per month and the repayments were huge! There was 25% interest on top, so it quickly got out of control. I was overspending without even thinking about it, but what was I supposed to do? Stay home all the time? I just thought, "If I get a good job later, I'll pay it all back. No problem!"
Five years later, I graduated and I was $12,000 in debt. I had wasted a lot of money! I got my first job with a salary of about $2,000 per month, but my rent was more than 50% of that! I had to use the credit cards to keep my head above water. I managed to pay back a bit every month, but not enough. I was permanently in my overdraft. I never had any money and I kept pretending it wasn't happening. I think if I'd listened to advice at this point, I wouldn't have gotten into the mess I did.
When I turned 25, I was in more than $20,000 worth of debt. I was working hard and all the money was going to pay off the loans and credit cards. Think about that. One day, I went to the ATM and I couldn't withdraw anything. It was a wake-up call. I realized I couldn't keep living a lifestyle I couldn't afford. I had completely run out of money.
I couldn't tell my parents. They would have gone crazy! I had to change and get myself out of debt. This is how I did it: I took out one large loan to pay off all the credit cards and then started to pay off the loan. I cut up the credit cards, so I couldn't spend much. I set up a direct debit, so money automatically transferred from my account to pay off the loan every month. Every time I spent money on something nice, I "matched" it by paying the same amount off on my loan. This was one of the best tips I heard, because it made me think about how much I was spending.
If I could give you one piece of advice, I'd say, be realistic about your lifestyle. Yes, I was young, free, and single, but I couldn't afford to live the life I wanted. I set myself a goal to get out of debt by my 30th birthday and I did it! It was tough, but I did it. I haven't used a credit card for a long time, but I think I'm ready to start using one sensibly now. If I had known then what I know now, I would have been much more careful.

## ▶ 5.8 Notice the connections and /t/, /d/, and /ɪd/ endings.
You might be surprised to learn crowdfunding has been around for a very long time. But where did it all start?
An early example is the Statue of Liberty. The statue was a gift from the people of France to the United States in 1886. But after the American Committee ran out of money to pay for the site where the

315

statue would go, publisher Joseph Pulitzer started a campaign in his newspaper to raise the money they needed. In five months, over $100,000 was raised by 160,000 donors including children, street cleaners, and politicians.

Even before this, people used crowdfunding to raise money. In 1783, Mozart hoped to perform three piano concertos in Vienna. He published invitations offering copies of the composition in return for money to help put on the concert.

The basic concept of crowdfunding is still very much the same these days, but the introduction of the Internet and crowdfunding websites such as Kickstarter means that people around the world can easily connect with each other and donate to projects.

Internet crowdfunding first became popular in the art and music industry. In 1997, the rock group Marillion funded a tour through online donations from fans. They have since also funded albums this way. Their fans must really love their music! Probably the biggest crowdfunding success is Pebble Technology. Pebble raised an incredible thirty million dollars and broke the record for the fastest ever campaign to be fully funded. Supporters received a Pebble watch, one of the first smart watches on the market.

So, what is the future of crowdfunding? Critics complain that businesses now use it to market their new products to more people and it's not just used by new start-up companies. But crowdfunding is now so popular that sixteen point two billion dollars was raised in 2016. When you look at the statistics and the success stories, no matter what the critics say, it can't be bad for young entrepreneurs! Got a business idea? It could work for you!

### ▶ 5.10
1 What would you like for dinner, Rico? Tuna or chicken? Oops, we're out of tuna, Rico. Sorry.
2 Help! Somebody help! Oh my God. Not now. I'm late for work. Can anybody hear me?
3 I swear I did it, Mrs. Andrews, I swear, but Bart ate it. I tried to stop him, but I couldn't. It won't happen again, I swear.
4 [breathing]
5 OK … done that. What should I do now? Really? Well, if you say so … OK, I've closed the window, but … I don't understand … How will that help?

### ▶ 5.11 Notice the intonation. ↗↘
A = Alberto  L = Laura  E = Ernie
Mrs. A = Mrs. Andrews
T = Tony  W = woman  S = Susie  M = man
**1**
A What would you like for dinner, Rico? Tuna or chicken? ↘ Oops, we're out of tuna, Rico. Sorry. You poor baby!
**2**
L Help! Somebody help! Oh my God. Not now. I'm late for work. Can anybody hear me? ↗ Excuse me … hi … I'm stuck between the fourth and the fifth floor. Could you send someone, please? ↗ Quick!
**3**
E I swear I did it, Mrs. Andrews, I swear, but Bart ate it. I tried to stop him, but I couldn't. It won't happen again, I swear.
Mrs. A. "The dog ate my homework." Yeah, right. Pretty lame, Ernie. Pretty lame.
**4**
T [breathing]
W OK, great. Breathe in as you move your left leg, and breathe out as you move your right leg to the left. Is everybody OK? ↗ Now, feel the vital energy flowing to your arms and hands.
**5**
S OK … done that. What should I do now? ↘ Really? Well, if you say so … OK, I've closed the window, but I don't understand … How will that help? ↘
M Ma'am, I asked you to close the computer window—your browser, you know—not your living room window.
S My computer has no windows. Or doors. What are you talking about?

### ▶ 5.13 Notice the intonation ↗↘ of the echo questions.
M You know, I just can't believe you bought that stuff.
W I bought it on impulse. It was pure madness, I know.
M You bet. It can't work the way they advertised it would! Was it expensive?
W Expensive? ↗ It cost a fortune. I felt really guilty afterward, of course.
M Buyer's remorse, huh?
W Yeah, at the time it seemed like a wonderful product, but … it was such a disappointment.
M Well, what would you expect from these awful infomercials?
W I know, yeah … And I think this stuff is actually quite dangerous.
M Dangerous? ↗
W Mmm, it smelled awful. Like really strong chemicals.
M Goodness knows what it did to your skin.
W And it's not all! They go on and on in the infomercial about how "natural" it is. Well, if you like looking like an orange …!
M Oh dear. Was it really that bad?
W Yes, it was and I used it before going to Jessica's wedding, so not only did I smell weird, but I was bright orange!
M But, uh, why on earth did you want to look tanned anyway, Liz? You have gorgeous skin.
W I do? ↗ Thanks! I guess it's just so fashionable these days, I wanted to give it a go.

### ▶ 5.16 Notice /dʒ/, /tʃ/, and the consonant clusters.
**1 Choosing**
C = customer, SC = store clerk
SC Hello. Do you see anything you like?
C Oh, hi. Yeah, I like these shoes. Can I try them on?
SC What size do you take?
C Do you have a size ten in stock?
SC A ten? Uh—I'm sorry ma'am, we're sold out.
C Ah, that's such a shame! It seems impossible to find larger sizes. Can you email me when you have some in stock?
**2 Paying**
SC Next, please … Hello. Just the jeans and these two T-shirts?
C Yes … No, sorry, this dress, too.
SC OK, that looks very nice.
C Oh, it's for my girlfriend.
SC Very nice. So that's $174.70. Cash or charge?
C Uh, charge.
SC OK. Insert your card, please.
C Uh-huh.
SC Ah. I'm afraid your card has been declined. Um, do you have another card?
C Declined! I don't understand. It's a new card, and I know I'm not over my limit. There must be a problem with your card machine.

**3 Complaining**
C Hello, hello. Yes, I'd like to return this phone. I bought it here the other day and it's damaged.
SC I see. Uh … What seems to be the problem?
C Well, I bought it on … Thursday, and when I got it home, I took it out of the box and … well, you can see. The screen has a scratch on it.
SC Oh, oh yes. Well, uh, unfortunately, we can't give you a refund, but we'd be happy to exchange it for another one.
C Oh, that's great. Thank you so much.
SC Sure. Uh, I just need to see your receipt.
C Yes, of course. Uh, it's in here somewhere. Here it is.

## Unit 6

### ▶ 6.1 Notice the schwa /ə/ in the noncontent words (for, to, a, the, of).
1 Ads for a movie, showing extracts of it, are trailers.
2 Critics' opinions are reviews.
3 To pay regularly to receive something is to subscribe.
4 To really like something is to be into something.
5 All the episodes in one year of a series is a season.
6 On-screen translation of speech are subtitles.
7 Foreign movies spoken in the viewer's native language are dubbed.
8 When you are unable to stop doing something, you are addicted to it.

### ▶ 6.3 Notice the sentence stress and weak forms.
D = daughter  F = father
D Hey, did **you** have a **TV** when you were a **kid**, Dad?
F Yeah, **believe** it or **not**. **TV** has been **around pretty** much for**ever**. But it's **changed** a **lot** in **my life**time.
D **What**? **TV**'s just **TV**, isn't **it**?
F **No way!** The **first TV** I **remember** was in **black** and **white**, and it was **massive**. TVs **now**, well, you can **put** them on the **wall** and they **take** up **no** space. **When I** was a **kid**, they were like a **piece** of **furniture**.
D **Huh**?
F And the **way you** guys watch TV is **very different** from **my** gener**a**tion.
D I don't **get** it. What do you **mean**?
F Just **think**. When **I** was a **kid**, we watched TV **together** in the **evening** as a **family**.
D **Watch** TV with your **parents**? Yuck!
F **Yeah, really**, and there was **no** choosing. We watched what **Mom** and **Dad** wanted to **watch**! Now, you all just **download** or **stream** everything—sitcoms, movies, news programs—and watch **what** you want, **when** you want.
D **Live** music, soaps, yeah, **that's** true, I guess. Uh, I **mean**, I hardly **ever** watch TV in **real** time. Only big **sports** events.
F Or in the **car** on long **journeys** … You never **speak** to us! Yeah, and TV is just about **everywhere** now—on **tablets, computers, smart phones**—you name it.
D Sure …
F Hm, and even **watching** TV has changed.
D How? We still use our eyes …
F Yeah, right, but instead of **chatting** to **friends** or **family** in the same room, everybody uses their **smart phones** to chat with their "**cyber buddies**," you know, somewhere else.
D Oh, **come** on Dad! That's **social** TV! Twitter is the **best** place to talk about TV now.
F Uh-huh. But there's **one** thing I'm sure of. The word "**viewer**" will never mean the same **again**.

# Audioscript

## 6.4 Notice /æ/, /ɒ/, and /eɪ/.

**C = Clara   E = Emilia**

**C** So, have you been watching anything good recently?
**E** Yes! I'm really into *Stranger Things* at the moment. Have you seen it?
**C** No, not yet. Everyone is raving about it, but, I don't know … it just sounds … well … *strange* …
**E** Well, that's kind of the point. Oh, you've got to watch it. It's amazing!
**C** So, what's so good about it, then? What's it about?
**E** It's hard to explain. It's about this group of kids who discover lots of weird paranormal activity going on in their town.
**C** It's about kids? Isn't it really scary, though?
**E** It is pretty spooky, yeah, but that's the interesting thing about it. You know, it was rejected between 15 and 20 times by different TV companies before Netflix decided to make it. Apparently, other TV executives didn't like the fact that it was a story about children, but wasn't for kids' TV.
**C** I guess that is pretty unusual. Does it work?
**E** Totally! That's the best thing about it! The children's performances are amazing, and I got hooked on the spooky storyline immediately.
**C** I guess the industry didn't get the concept of a TV show starring kids that was actually for adults.
**E** That's it exactly. It's so unusual. And, of course, it gave Winona Ryder her big comeback. She plays a mother whose son has gone missing and she's going to do everything in her power to get him back. She's fantastic in it!
**C** Well, you've certainly sold it to me! I think I'll start watching tonight.
**E** Great … I can't wait for the third season. You'll love the pilot episode when …
**C** Stop! No spoilers!

## 6.7 Notice the pauses. //

**DJ** … and, remember, today's prize is two front row tickets for Sia's October show. Wow! This week we've been talking about moviemakers who have changed American cinema. And we have Gloria on the line. Gloria, how's it going?
**W** I'm good, thanks.
**DJ** The first question is about Ryan Coogler, // who many people consider to be one of the finest new moviemakers around.
**W** Oh my gosh, I love Ryan Coogler! I think he's the best.
**DJ** So, here's our first question … Are you ready?
**W** I guess …
**DJ** Which box office smash did Coogler direct in 2018?
**W** That's easy. *Black Panther*!
**DJ** Correct! This movie made Coogler the youngest ever Marvel moviemaker.
**W** Oh, wow! What an achievement.
**DJ** Second question … In 2013, Coogler directed a movie, which was called *Creed*. *Creed*, // which also starred Sylvester Stallone, // was a spin-off from a classic series of movies, *Rocky*. What are these movies about?
**W** Can you give me a clue?
**DJ** Well, // it's a kind of sport that involves two people and a ring.
**W** Oh, of course! I know, I know. Boxing?
**DJ** Did you say boxing?
**W** Yep.
**DJ** You're absolutely right. The movie, // which won Stallone a Golden Globe, // was highly acclaimed by critics. I loved it! … Anyway, here's our third question. Which famous person tweeted this after watching *Black Panther*: "I loved this movie and I know it will inspire people of all backgrounds to dig deep and find the courage to be heroes of their own stories."?
**W** Who said that? Oh … That's a tough one.
**DJ** OK, Gloria. Time's up.
**W** Well, I guess another director said it. Erm … Steven Spielberg?
**DJ** Good guess, but I'm afraid not. It was // Barack Obama.
**W** Wow! Imagine an ex-president saying that about your work!
**DJ** Pretty cool, huh? OK. Question 4 is actually about Steven Spielberg! Are you ready? What did …

## 6.8

1 Which fantasy prequel to *The Lord of the Rings* did director Peter Jackson shoot in New Zealand between 2011 and 2013? Was it (a) *Twilight*, (b) *The Hobbit*, or (c) *Narnia*?
The answer is (b) *The Hobbit*.
2 The video for which song by Luis Fonsi and Daddy Yankee became the most-watched video in YouTube history with over five billion views? Was it (a) Subeme La Radio, (b) Reggaeton Lento, or (c) Despacito?
Of course, it's (c) Despacito.
3 *Avengers: Infinity War* is an action movie about superheroes. The cast is like a "Who's who" of Hollywood and includes many big names. Can you name three of them?
There's a lot of choice here. The cast is full of big stars. The top-billed are Robert Downey Junior, Chris Hemsworth, Chris Evans, Mark Ruffalo, but you could also have Scarlett Johanson, Benedict Cumberbatch, and Chris Holland. The list goes on.
4 One of the biggest YouTube memes of 2013 was Harlem Shake. There were over 33 hours of Harlem Shake clips uploaded every day. What did people do in the videos? Have you seen this clip? Do they (a) play basketball, (b) sing, (c) dance?
The answer is they do a very, very strange dance.
5 British actor Tom Holland stars as which wall-climbing superhero?
British actors have starred as three famous superheroes including Batman, Superman, and Spiderman, but which one is Tom Holland? Tom Holland is Spiderman.
6 Andy Serkis, who was the gorilla in *King Kong*, had to learn to move like a chimpanzee in which famous trilogy?
Was it (a) *Star Wars*, (b) *Planet of the Apes*, or (c) *The Lord of the Rings*?
The answer is (b) *Planet of the Apes*.
7 What role does Liam Hemsworth play in the blockbuster *The Hunger Games*?
This character is a very close friend of Katniss, who is the lead character. Was he (a) Peeta Mellark, (b) Haymith Abernathy, or (c) Gale Hawthorne?
The answer is (c). He plays Gale Hawthorne.
8 Which romance movie set in Indianapolis portrays two teenagers who are suffering from cancer?
Is it (a) *The Fault in Our Sun*, (b) *The Fault in Our Moon*, (c) *The Fault in Our Stars*? [pause]
It's (c) *The Fault in Our Stars*.
9 Who wrote the script and directed the first *Star Wars* films?
An easy one to end with—it was George Lucas, of course.

## 6.9

### 1 Notice /k/.

**A** And it's just such a powerful movie, you know, like how science could destroy us eventually. I really think it could be true. I think the whole trilogy is amazing.
**B** Yeah, some of the experiments they do on animals now, it's pretty sad. But didn't they use animals for the movie, too? I mean, that's bad as well, right?
**A** No, no animals. They are all actors. The cast members who play apes have to wear this special suit when they shoot the movie. It captures all the movements of the actor and then they can add everything else with computers. It's very clever. Imagine working as an actor, wearing that special suit and acting in front of a green screen all day!
**B** No way! So the actors actually move like apes? They look so real! Man, he should get an Oscar for that role! Acting like a chimpanzee! That is real acting!

### 2 Notice /eɪ/.

**C** Bah! I've got that song in my head again!
**D** Huh, I hate it when that happens. But that is a great song!
**C** I know, there's a reason it was so popular. I saw a clip of the video on a TV show last night about the power of the Internet. It's had billions of views. It was such a cool video and the song is so catchy.
**D** Huh, really? I didn't see that. But yeah, the video was great, wasn't it? And they made a few different versions of it. A Portuguese one …
**C** Yeah, and of course the Justin Bieber version.
**D** I know! I wish I could sing in Spanish like him. They're all good, but I like the original.
**C** Of course!

### 3 Notice /ʒ/, /dʒ/, and /g/.

**E** Hey, I've got this movie from iTunes, do you wanna watch it with me?
**F** Uh … What's it about? It's not filled with explosions like that last one you got, is it?
**E** Well, probably. It's about a bunch of superheroes defending the universe, so I guess there's going to be quite a lot of explosions!
**F** Oh, come on! You know I'm not into action movies. I like something with a bit of intelligence, you know?
**E** Duh, always the same. Why can't you just relax and enjoy the fun? All the big Hollywood names star in it!
**F** Why can't we watch my choice this time? What about that one with the woman who works as a cleaner in a government lab … with the fish guy … what's it called?
**E** *The Shape of Water*?! No, I'm not watching that …

## 6.10 Notice the **sentence stress** and weak forms.

**Here** are some **tips** and **tricks** to **making** a **short video**. **Plan** your **shoot**. **What** is your video **about**? Sketch **out** your **idea**. **Think** about what your **topic** will **be** and **how** many **people** will be **in** it. **What** do you **want** the **final** video to **look like**?

**Technologies: Decide** what **media** you will be **using**: **digital camera**, **camcorder**, **webcam**, or **cell phone**. **Capture** your **clips**: **Press** the **record** button a **few seconds** before the **actual** shoot. The **professionals** always say "**Keep** it **steady**." If possible, use a **tripod**. **Take** lots of **shoots** and **still images**—they **might come in handy**. **Try** not to **cut off** the **top** of the subject's **head**.

**Lighting:** Shoot in a well-lit area. Make sure there is not a bright light like the sun behind the subject. Before your final recording, do a test shoot to check the lighting.

**Length** of shoot: Plan your script beforehand. Don't talk about one topic for too long, as this may lose the viewers' interest. Keep the video short and simple.

**Sound** and audio: It's best to use an external microphone. Always be conscious of background noise. Always do a sound check before the actual shoot.

**Copyright:** If you are shooting outside, make sure you don't capture anyone on camera without their permission. It can be difficult to use images from the Internet, so be adventurous and take your own. Always gather written permission from your subjects.

**Accessibility:** To make your video accessible to all: Prepare transcripts, use subtitles, record a voiceover if you are making a video of still images. And remember, have fun making your video.

▶ **6.11** Notice /ɪ/ and /iː/.
S = Sue  J = Joe
S  I can't get enough of Ellen. I think she's awesome.
J  So do I. I'm a huge fan. She's a terrific host.
S  Yeah, I can still remember the Sia interview a while ago.
J  Oh, yeah? Mmm ... Sia's not my thing. I like a song or two, but that's about it.
S  Really? I think she's amazing. She's written some fantastic songs. She's written a lot of songs which have been huge hits for other singers, too.
J  Like what?
S  Oh, you name it! She wrote "Titanium" ... "Diamonds" by Rihanna.
J  What? Get out of here! She wrote those?
S  Yes! Everyone knows that ... Anyway, I'll never forget that interview ...
J  Why? What happened?
S  This is how it goes ... First Ellen asks her to explain why she doesn't like showing her face.
J  Oh, I bet nobody ever asks her that!
S  Ha, ha. Yeah. But Sia is so natural and so funny. She says that she hides her face so she can go to the grocery store or use a public restroom without being recognized.
J  Like nobody would recognize her with that wig on!
S  No, silly—she only wears the wig when she's performing! Anyway, then Ellen starts saying that they've made a deal that when Sia performs on the show, she'll take her wig off so everyone can see what she looks like. And she agreed to it!
J  Really, you're kidding, right?
S  Yeah, this was in the days when nobody knew what she looked like. So all the people around me start getting really excited and ...
J  What do you mean the people around you?
S  I was actually in the audience. I got two tickets for my birthday.
J  No way! You were actually in the audience? You never told me that!

▶ **6.12** Notice the intonation. ↗↘
J  No way! ↗ You were actually in the audience? ↗ You never told me that! ↗
S  It's true! ↘ So, as I was saying .... ↘ They make this big deal over pulling the wig off ... ↘ and everyone's going crazy and then ... ↗
J  What? ↗
S  Nothing. ↘ It was all a dumb joke. ↘ She wasn't really going to reveal herself at all. ↗

J  Are you serious? ↗ You mean they were just pretending? ↗ What a disappointment! ↘
S  I know. ↘ Talk about an anti-climax! ↘ But, I guess it would spoil her image. ↘ Anyway, she performed live in the studio and I got to see that, which was amazing! ↗ She performed with the dancer, Maddie Ziegler, who's often in her videos and she hid behind this crazy long dress thing. ↘ Typical Sia. ↘
J  My goodness! ↗ Yes, Maddie Ziegler is so talented. ↘ What a show. ↗ It must have been great to see her live. I wish I could have been there. ↘
S  It was. ↘ I'm so glad I got tickets. ↘

▶ **6.17** Notice the reductions.
1  A  Wanna come on over for spaghetti tonight? I'm cooking!
   B  No way! You're making spaghetti?
   A  Well, there's always a first time.
2  C  I'm sick and tired of this SUV. Gonna buy a smaller car.
   D  Get out of here! You want to buy a smaller car?
   C  Yeah. What's wrong?
3  E  Janet's turning 18 next week. Gonna get her a puppy.
   F  What? You're going to get Janet a dog for her birthday?
   E  Uh-uh.
4  G  Love this chocolate diet! I've lost ten pounds in two weeks.
   H  No way! You've lost ten pounds in two weeks eating chocolate?
   G  Yeah. Isn't it amazing?

## Review 3

▶ **R3.3** Notice the disappearing consonants.
1  I'm dead serious. Savejohnsmith.com is my last hope.
2  There must be a problem with your card machine.
3  Although it's supposed to be for kids, I loved it!
4  They ran out of money to pay for the statue.
5  "Shopping haul" videos are a huge trend.

## Unit 7

▶ **7.4** (with addition in 7.6) Notice the intonation / emotion on right.
1  Notice stress and /ə/.
   A  God, it seems that for every five letters I type, one comes out wrong.
   B  American keyboard layout, right?
   A  Well, the salesman said some of the keys were different, but it was basically the same thing, blah, blah, blah. Yeah, right! But how was I to know? He said I would learn fast. Guess he was wrong.
2  Notice stress and /ə/.
   C  Oh, Dad, you're wearing the watch I got you. How do you like it?
   D  Well, I'd like it better if it worked properly. I missed two meetings last week. Do you have the warranty?
   C  Warranty? No, he didn't give me one.
   D  What? No warranty? Where did you get it?
   C  Well, there was a guy in the market selling this watch really cheap. He said that it worked just as well as the famous brand.
   D  In the market? So, this isn't a Rolex?
   C  Uh ... no ... Maybe not. Oh no, look, it says Polex. He told me he was there every week and

he could get me video games, too. Maybe we can ask him for a refund?
3  Notice /aʊ/.
   E  Oh, my ...!
   F  What in the name of ...
   E  Oh no ... There goes my Christmas present.
   F  But how ... how ... did it happen? You didn't ... you didn't put it up yourself, right? Right?
   E  Uh ... Well, the delivery guy told me I could mount it on the wall myself. How was I to know?
   F  But you're not a pro! You're a doctor! Doctors don't install TV sets. What were you thinking?
   E  But ... Look, he said it was easy and it would only take ten minutes!
4  Notice /e/ and /eɪ/.
   G  Paula, we're OK, right? I mean, it's just that ... Well, you haven't returned any of my calls.
   H  Sorry, didn't get your messages—yours or anybody's. My phone's dead.
   G  Dead?
   H  I bought it from this site and it came straight from the States. Turns out I can't make or receive calls. Some sort of network problem ... Which is odd, because on the site it said I'd be able to use it in any country ... Guess they were lying. But how was I to know?
   G  Can't you get a refund or something?
   H  Oh yeah—easily. They told me that lots of people had complained and so on.
5  Notice /ʌ/ and /ə/.
   I  One of these days I swear I will throw this tablet right out of the window.
   J  Oh, come on! It's not so bad!
   I  You're kidding, right? The screen sucks and the software's full of bugs. To think I could've gotten a laptop! I bought it on ... on impulse, I guess. The store manager said it had just arrived and, you know, I couldn't resist it. But how was I to know?
   J  Well, try to control yourself next time.
   I  I know ... But she said that these tablets usually sold pretty quickly, so ...
   J  You were afraid they would sell out?
   I  Bingo.

▶ **7.7**
1  Notice /ɑ/ and /uː/.
   M = mother  W = William
   M  William Bonney Junior! What is this?
   W  It's my school report, Mom.
   M  I know what it is! But you told me you'd done well this year. You wait till your father sees this.
2  Notice /g/ and /k/.
   V = Vanessa  C = Chris
   V  Hi, Chris. So good that you could come. Come in, come in.
   C  Hi, Vanessa, yeah, it's gonna be a great party. And this must be Pickles. Who's a cute little dog, then? Huh?
   V  Pickles. Pickles, no! Bad dog, bad dog.
   C  Ow! Get it off! Get it off! Vanessa! I thought you said your dog was friendly.
3  Notice the contractions and the connections.
   G = Geri  J = Josh
   G  Hi, Josh, uh, nice shirt.
   J  Geri, what is this? James Bond night?
   G  Josh, it's_a cocktail party, you_are supposed to look smart.
   J  But ... but you told me the party was_informal_ and ...
   G  No, I said "a few friends_and drinks," I didn't say "wear your beach clothes."

# Audioscript

**4** Notice /iː/ and /ɪ/.
A = Andy  Z = Zoey
A Please leave your message after the beep.
Z Andy! Where are you? I'm in the line and the movie is going to start soon. Andy, you said that you wouldn't arrive late.

## 7.9 Notice the final /k/.
P = Presenter  PB = Paul Le Bernard
P Good evening and welcome to *Tech Talk*, your weekly discussion program on what's new in tech. I'm joined in the studio this week by the editor of *Technology World* magazine, Paul Le Bernard. This week we are discussing young tech innovators. From medical breakthroughs, energy technologies, or engineering electronic devices. First, Paul, what makes someone an innovator?
PB Personally, I think innovators are persistent and inquisitive and they are easily inspired by what they see around them. Take our first example this week, Brazilian tech innovator, Neide Sellin. She's an ex-computer science teacher and she's spent most of her career inventing new technology to help improve the quality of life for people with disabilities.
P I see. We'd love to hear more. Can you tell us what her latest development is?
PB Well, do you have any idea how many Brazilian people have vision problems?
P No, I don't.
PB 6.5 million people. Do you know how many guide dogs there are in Brazil?
P Absolutely no idea.
PB There are only 100 guide dogs! The problem is that buying, training, and looking after a guide dog can cost thousands of dollars. This is impossible for many blind people.
P And this is where Neide Sellin comes in?
PB Exactly. Neide has invented a robot guide dog called Lysa. Her invention has five sensors and two engines. It can tell the user about risks and obstacles via recorded voice messages. With this device, blind users can be guided around indoor areas such as shopping malls and schools. By 2020, Neide hopes Lysa will be used outside, too.
P It sounds amazing, but I wonder if this is really a more affordable solution. Do you have any idea how much it costs?
PB Well, Lysa still costs around $3,000, but this is far cheaper than a real guide dog. At the moment, the device is available to private and public companies, such as airports and hospitals. Neide eventually hopes to improve the dog with artificial intelligence and GPS. Her greatest ambition is to offer dignity and independence to the 253 million blind and visually-impaired people around the world.
P Well, that certainly sounds very inspiring. Let's move on to our next young innovator …

## 7.11 Notice spellings of /n/, /t/, and /d/ endings.
A = Ann  B = Bruce
A Cool phone, dude.
B Thanks. Mom was like, "What's wrong with the one we gave you last year?" and I was like, "Mom, that model is so last year," so she got me this one for Christmas.
A You like it?
B Are you kidding? I love it—especially Justin.
A Justin?
B Yep—my, what do they call it—personal assistant.
A Oh, speech recognition. Sweet. Does it, uh, tell the time, check the weather, and stuff?

B Yeah, and much more. This morning I told Justin I was bored—which I was—and I thought he was going to, like, ask me to repeat the command or whatever, and, guess what, he asked if he bored me.
A Get out! No way! Man, this is, like, so cool.
B Then I asked him if he was hungry and he, uh, he was like, "I'm a cell phone, not a person." Freaking unbelievable.
A Mine has voice recognition, too, but it's not so smart, you know? It'll, like, make calls, set the alarm clock … and stuff. The other day I asked her to text someone and it took her, like, three minutes to figure out what to do.
B Her?
A Mine's not a dude—it's called Alice.

## 7.12 Notice the weak h in *he* and *him*.
A Dude, I so want to try Justin.
B Here, have fun.
A Sweet … Justin, where am I?
J I'm sorry, I don't know your name.
A And you said he was smart, right? I asked where, not who.
B He is smart, I'm telling you. Give it another shot.
A OK. Uh … Justin, will the weather get worse?
J It looks like rain tonight. Here's the forecast for the next two days …
A Wow … Pretty awesome, dude. Justin …
J Yes?
A Do you love me?
B AHAHAH—never tried to ask him that.
J I'm not ready for that kind of commitment yet.
B Isn't he amazing?
A Oh my God, I love him, I love him! Mmm … What can I ask him now … Justin, please call me an ambulance.
J OK. From now on I will call you Anne Ambulance.
A What? No way! Uh … Justin, make me a coffee.
J Ahem, I'm just a phone.
B Don't you just love him?
A But was it, like, a joke? Or did he misunderstand me?
B I think he was kidding.

## 7.14
1 I asked where I was.
2 I asked if the weather would get worse.
3 I asked him if he loved me.
4 I asked him to call me an ambulance.
5 I told him to make me a coffee.

## 7.16 Notice Mark's hesitation / repetitions and Nick's listening sounds.
M = Mark  N = Nick
M What I don't understand is how, how is it that, on the 2001 NAEP history exam, 52% of high school seniors chose Nazi Germany, Imperial Japan, or Fascist Italy as our ally. Not the Soviet Union.
N Hi, I'm Nick Gillespie with Reason TV. I'm here today with Mark Bauerlein, author of *The Dumbest Generation*. A provocative new book that says "the digital age stupefies young Americans and jeopardizes our future." In fact, there's even a, uh, second uh, subtitle, which says "don't trust anyone under thirty." Mark, what's the premise of the book?
M Digital culture … uh, means, means this to most teenagers. It doesn't open them up to the great big world … of ideas and artworks and, and, and documents and politics and foreign affairs—which is all out there on the Internet, the potential is there. Instead, it gives them what … teenagers really care about: other teenagers.

N Mmm hmm.
M Access to one another. They're not going to the Smithsonian Institution website. When Nielsen Ratings examined the most popular websites for young adults, nine out the top ten, teenagers, nine out of the top ten were for social networking.
N Mmm.
M 55% of high school students spend less than one hour a week reading and studying for class. They spend nine hours a week social networking.
N Sure.
M And this, this is what brought me into this, this work. Studies of leisure habits by, by young adults. And one thing we can say is … that … the leisure reading people do, young people do, the visits to museums that they do.
N Mmm hmm.
M The library visits that they do, those have gone down. And that's, that's just natural, because the menu of leisure options for young, for teenagers and young adults, has gotten bigger. Reading is, is, is … has a smaller portion on the menu … uh, that they have. And when you go into the average fifteen-year old's bedroom now, it's a multimedia center. Yeah, there're a few books up there on the shelf. There's the laptop, the cell phone, video game console, Blackberry, iPod, and all those diversions give them something a lot more compelling … than the story of Anthony and Cleopatra and Caesar!
N Mhm.

## 7.17 Notice the stress, pauses, and /ɔɪ/.
H = host  T = Tom  B = Barbara
H … which means, that, / yeah, the website was most probably hacked. // Speaking of the Internet, / I just got my hands on a book by a guy called Mark Bauerlein and … // well, the book's called *The Dumbest Generation* and basically it says that Internet is making young people … // stupid.
T Well, he has a point.
B Seriously, Tom?
T Yeah. I mean, / we can't deny that teens are buying fewer books and generally …
H How old are you, Tom?
T 32 … / We're not reading as much as people in their 40s or 50s, you know? // I mean, / bookstores are going out of business week after week. I find that …
B Well, it depends on what you mean by reading. // It's … / It's not that teens are reading less, / it's just that we're reading on our tablets … or e-readers, smart phones, or whatever. // For example, I'm 19 / and I've got hundreds of digital titles downloaded.
H But how many of those have you actually read?
T That's a good point.
B I don't know, but, / you see, / the point is … reading has been on the decline for …
T Barbara, / but don't you think …
B Hold on a second, let me finish. // Listen, / people have been reading less for at least 30 years, / long before the Internet ever existed. / So, / really, // we can't blame the Internet, can we?
H Well, you may agree or disagree, but he makes some valid points, / don't you think? // Young people have access to more information than we ever did, but, / honestly, how much are they actually / learning? I mean, I was talking to my son the other day and he thought Rome was a country … / a country! / And he's a pretty smart boy, you know?

B  My point exactly! / The book says teens are getting dumber ... / I totally disagree. // If anything, / people's IQs have gone up, / not down, / over the past 90 years or so.
T  Mmm ... / That may be true, but don't you think there's something wrong here? / **Rome** / — a country? / Come on! // And you know what, / I also think the, uh ... / young people are starting to avoid face-to-face contact because of the Internet ...
B  Yeah, / I couldn't agree more.
T  I mean, / most of my friends spend hours and hours locked in their rooms, / chatting on Facebook. // I mean, this can't ...

### ▶ 7.18
1
T  Yeah. I mean, we can't deny that teens are buying fewer books and generally ...
2
T  Barbara, but don't you think ...
B  Hold on a second, let me finish.
3
B  Well, it depends on what you mean by reading.
4
T  That may be true, but don't you think there's something wrong here?
5
T  Well, you may agree or disagree, but he makes some valid points.
6
T  I also think the, uh ... young people are starting to avoid face-to-face contact because of the Internet ...
B  Yeah, I couldn't agree more.
7
B  My point exactly!
8
B  The book says teens are getting dumber ... I totally disagree. If anything, people's IQs have gone up.

## Unit 8

### ▶ 8.2 Notice /ɪ/ and /iː/.
Sure, we all want to look better. Some people try makeup or even plastic surgery. Others choose Photoshop. Graphic designer and Photoshop expert James Fridman is well-known for taking people's Twitter requests for image alterations. James reads people's requests for changes to their pictures and does exactly what they ask him to do. Unfortunately for them, James does literally whatever he is asked. Most of his images are silly and fun. People ask James to remove photobombers, make them look smaller or bigger, or add something to the picture. But Fridman does not encourage people to retouch their images to meet today's often unrealistic beauty standards. He now has thousands of online followers because of the creative way he doctors the "vain" photos shared on social media.
One heart-warming example of James's work is a photo sent to him by a young woman who was suffering from an eating disorder and low self-esteem. She asked James to photoshop her to make her look beautiful. He responded by making no change to the image and telling her that nothing could make her more beautiful than she already was.

### ▶ 8.3 Notice /ð/, /θ/, and /v/.
J = Jon  E = Eliza
J  I used to love Michael Jackson. *Smooth Criminal* had the coolest video ever!
E  I know! I loved it, too. Remember that thing he did when he leaned right over. I used to try to do it and fall down ... a lot! How on earth did he do that?
J  He must have had wires attached to his jacket. It's the only explanation, surely!
E  Well ... maybe it was something to do with his shoes.
J  Yes, I suppose, he might have put magnets on them and on the floor.
E  Magnets?! To hold up the weight of a man, they must have been very strong!
J  True, but it's possible, isn't it? Or maybe he really could lean that far!
E  He was good, but not that good! He can't have been able to do that. It's impossible.
J  I bet Michael Jackson could!
E  Or, I guess his clothes were specially engineered.
J  Yeah, he may have had special pants made!

### ▶ 8.4 Notice /ʌ/, /uː/, and /ʊ/.
Fans all over the world tried to copy Michael Jackson's smooth moves. However, there was one move in particular that left everyone wondering just how he did it: that famous lean from *Smooth Criminal*. Jackson and his dancers leaned forward at an angle of 45 degrees with their feet flat on the floor and then returned to an upright position. So just how did they manage to defy gravity like that?
The truth is that Jackson had a special shoe designed. The shoe had a triangular opening in the heel which attached to a metal hook which emerged from the floor at exactly the right moment. This anchored the dancers to the floor and stopped them from falling over.
This clever shoe did the job perfectly apart from one mistake in 1996. Jackson's heel came loose from the hook during a concert and he fell flat. Luckily, the star wasn't injured, and the shoe was redesigned to make sure it didn't happen again. The shoe was sold for $600,000 after Jackson's death and is now in the Hard Rock Café in Moscow.

### ▶ 8.7 Notice /tʃ/, /ʃ/, /ʒ/, and /kt/.
What David Blaine is actually performing is an optical illusion called Balducci levitation. This method involves the illusionist positioning themselves approximately three metres away from their audience and at a 45 degree angle. The audience should be a small one so that they are always in this limited field of vision. The audience will only see the back of one foot and most of the other foot. It's also important to wear long pants which obstruct the view of the illusionist's feet. This increases the effectiveness of the trick. The performer, of course, uses various methods to misdirect and distract the audience. Then they simply stand on the toes of one foot and raise the other foot. To the audience it looks like they are really levitating.
David Copperfield had a performance area of a stage with two towers and an arch to support a huge curtain. The TV cameras and the audience could only see the statue through the arch. The curtains were closed and Copperfield distracted the audience with enthusiastic chatter. While this was happening, the stage was actually slowly rotated! When the curtains opened again, the Statue of Liberty had disappeared! In fact, it was simply concealed behind one of the towers and the audience didn't realize they had been moved. The lights on the stage were also so bright that the audience would have been partially blinded anyway!

### ▶ 8.9 Notice s = /s/ or /z/.
B = Brandon  C = Courtney
C  No way! You're kidding! You mean just like the one on *My Super Sweet 16*?
B  Yeah, but, like, a thousand times better ... Mom was like, "Sweetheart, why don't we have an ice-skating party?", and I was like, "Mom, that is so last year."
C  Yeah, totally.
B  So ... We're having a movie party.
C  Yay! Awesome!
B  There'll be a massive outdoor screen by the pool and ... Well, you'll see. It'll be, like, the most fun you've ever had ... Ever. I hope it doesn't rain.
C  Brandon, this is so exciting! What will you be wearing?
B  Dad bought me this pathetic grey suit and tie ...
C  Yuck!
B  Yeah, I know! So I told him, "Dad! Hello? This is a movie party, not a fairy tale!"
C  Duh!
B  And I wanna look just like Alden Ehrenreich.
C  Who?!
B  You know, the actor who plays Han Solo in the *Star Wars Story* movie.
C  Oh yeah, he always looks great!

### ▶ 8.10 Notice s = /s/ or /z/.
B  And I wanna look just like Alden Ehrenreich.
C  Who?!
B  You know, the actor who plays Han Solo in the *Star Wars Story* movie.
C  Oh yeah, he always looks great!
B  So Dad hired—wait for it—a fashion designer and we're going to have a new suit made.
C  Specially for you?
B  Of course.
C  That is so cool! And your hair looks awesome! Tell me, did you have it dyed?
B  Yeah. I spent, like, four hours at the salon and I got my nails done, too ... Look!
C  Oh, yeah! They look so good. So ... is everything ready?
B  No! Can you believe it? My parents are, like, so incompetent. I mean, the pool's dirty and Dad hasn't gotten it cleaned yet. Hello? Does he expect me to do it? And Mom can't cook, so we still need to have the cake made. This is all so stressful! I'm exhausted!
C  Who wouldn't be?
B  And, get ready for this, I signed all the two hundred invitations myself. It took me, like, one hour.
C  Humph! Like you had nothing better to do.

### ▶ 8.13 Notice the three-syllable words.
I love this bedroom. The double bed looks so comfortable. I like the color scheme. The dresser, mirror, and closet are the same color. It looks very fresh. The pillows and the comforter match, too. I also like the color of the walls and how it complements the color of the furniture. There are lots of cool accessories, too, and I love the light and the colorful bird hanging from the ceiling. They add a modern touch. Yes, I really like this bedroom.

### ▶ 8.14 Notice the intonation. ↗↘
B = Barry  M = Mick
B  Hey, you've gotta come and see what we've done in here.
M  Done? Hmm, you haven't done anything crazy, have you? ↗
B  No, of course not! Come and have a look.
M  Oh, wow! When did you do all this? It looks fantastic!
B  I've been doing it evenings and weekends for the last few weeks. This room really needed some attention. It's great, isn't it? ↘

320

# Audioscript

M   Well, what a sur**prise** for Tom! He'll love it, won't he? ↘
B   I hope so!

## ▶ 8.15 Notice the intonation. ↗↘

M   I can't believe it! You didn't do it all yourself, did you? ↗
B   No. I got some of the guys to come over and help me last weekend. We gave the walls a fresh coat of paint, painted some of the furniture. I had the **book**case on the wall made by a friend of mine. I remember Tom saw one like that in a maga**zine** and really liked it.
M   It's very cool. That rug wasn't there before, was it? ↘
B   No, that's new.
M   Tom's been talking about doing this for ages. You know he's going to be over the moon, don't you? ↘
B   Let's hope so! I wanted to surprise him when he got out of the **hos**pital.

## ▶ 8.17 Notice the intonation. ↗↘

B = Barry   T = Tom
B   Hey, look who's here! Welcome home!
T   Hi, Barry. Man, it's good to be back.
B   But you said you'd be discharged tomorrow, didn't you? ↗
T   Yeah … but they let me out early, thank goodness, so here I am.
B   So, how are things?
T   Good. I'm feeling a lot better and it's so good to be home. The hospital bed was just … What in the name of …?
B   Surprise!
T   Oh, wow! What have you done?!
B   You've been thinking about doing this, haven't you? ↘
T   Yes, but I wasn't expecting this? You aren't serious, are you? ↗ I don't know what to say.
B   I knew you'd love it. Just say "Thank you".
T   Thank you so much. That's the rug I saw in the department store, isn't it? ↘
B   Sure is!
T   Thank you, Barry. This is awesome!

## ▶ 8.18 Notice /ʌ/, /oʊ/, and /ɒ/.

… and we will c**o**ver that in the next c**ou**ple of days. So today, as part of our "image is everything" series, we're going to be looking at the reasons behind three different c**o**mpanies—global companies—altering their l**o**gos and how their target markets liked—or didn't like—the new versions. And tr**u**st me, s**o**me of the stories are fascinating. Our very first story involved the international …

## ▶ 8.19 Notice the **sentence stress** and **weak forms**.

So, as **most** of you probably **know**, Instagram's **for**mer **lo**go was **considered** one of the most **recognizable tech logos** of all **time**. The **retro brown** and **cream camera** with a **rainbow stripe** that re**minded** us of in**stant Polaroid cameras** was **iconic**, but **one day**, [beep – 1] for some reason, they **sadly decided** to **change** the **logo**! **Users** were not **impressed** and took to the **Internet** to **share** their **opinions**. The main com**plaint** from **original users** was that it **seemed** no **time** or **effort** had been **spent** on the **new logo**. No one really **got** it, and it didn't make **sense**. However, [beep – 2] **Instagram** was trying to at**tract new** users—you know **people** who **might've** never **visited** the site before, and **wanted** the new **logo** to reflect how the **app** had trans**formed** since its cre**ation**. The new **purple**, **orange**, and **pink** icon is more **colorful**, **sleek**, and **modern**, but was it a **good** idea? Hmm [beep – 3], I'm **not** con**vinced** it **works**.

Now, take a **look** at the **second slide** … As some of you may know, in **2011**, Starbucks celebrated its, uh, its **40th anniversary**. To **mark** the o**cca**sion, they must've **thought**: "Hey, let's **create** a **new logo** and **drop** the words 'Starbucks Coffee.'" Well, unfortunately, [beep – 4] **most** Starbucks customers were not **crazy** about the **new logo** … They preferred the **old** one and didn't quite **understand** why **Starbucks** took their **name** off. Well, **personally**, [beep – 5] I find the **new green** logo **simple** and e**le**gant. You see, **Starbucks** and its **logo** are **well-known** all over the **world**, and the **green circle** … well, the **green circle** speaks for **itself**. In **other** words, [beep – 6] the **logo doesn't** need to **tell** the **world** that it's **Starbucks Coffee**—everybody **knows that**.

## ▶ 8.20 Notice /ə/ and /ɜː/.

Now, moving on to our th**ir**d story … and the last one today … Gap re**lea**sed their new logo … yeah, this b**eau**ty … a few y**ea**rs **a**go. They must've tried to create something m**o**dern and cont**em**po**ra**ry, but, boy, were they wrong. The dark blue square of the **o**riginal logo c**er**tainly looked very tra**di**tional, didn't it? It w**a**s used for more than two de**ca**des, and most people loved it. Then the new one comes along and, guess what, everybody … hates it. In a matter of hours, there are thousands—I mean thousands—of negative comments on Facebook and Twitter. A few weeks later, Gap dis**car**ds the new logo, ret**ur**ns to the old one, and f**i**res the president. How **a**bout that? Honestly, I think they w**ere** right to go back to the old one. Mo**ra**l of the story? Well, if it ain't broke, don't fix it!

## ▶ 8.22 Notice /ʌ/, /ʊ/, and /ɔː/.

G = Guilherme   F = Fabi
G   I l**o**ve this class. It's really interesting.
F   Yeah, it's really g**oo**d, isn't it? I wish we'd had Professor Ford last year.
G   Yeah. She's awesome.
F   That Instagram logo is interesting, isn't it?
G   Honestly, I don't like the new one. I really don't.
F   Hmm … I kind of like it … It feels, I don't know, different … What about Starbucks? Which one do you like better?
G   I don't know … Both are OK, I guess, but I think I like the old one better than the new one.
F   Really? Oh, come on! It feels so … old, with the name and **all** … Well, I don't really like either of them … I'm tired of the green m**er**maid.
G   Now, maybe I'm crazy, but remember the Gap l**o**go?
F   Uh-huh.
G   I actually prefer the second one to the first.
F   You mean the one that looks like it was dr**a**wn by a child?
G   Exactly!
F   You know what? Me, too. They sh**ou**ldn't have gone back to the old one.

## Review 4

### ▶ R4.1 Notice the spellings of the repeated sounds.

1   I **a**sked, then I p**a**rked, and then the problems started.
2   We a**cc**use you of **c**ausing the a**cc**ident. No ex**c**uses!
3   Should they a**cc**elerate, a**cc**ommodate, or experiment?

# Unit 9

## ▶ 9.2

a
M   Stand back please! This is a crime scene. That's a murder.

b
M   Hello, sir, your license, please?
B   Uh … is there a problem?
M   You were driving well over the speed limit, sir. 120 in a 70 zone.
B   Oh, I'm sorry, sir. Here's my license … and …
M   That's not a fifty dollar bill in your hand, is it?
B   What? Errr …
M   You weren't thinking of trying to give that to me, were you?
B   Erm, no, of course not. I wouldn't be that stupid.
M   But stupid enough to drive over the speed limit?
B   I'm incredibly sorry, sir. It won't happen again. Bribery.

c
W   Wait a minute. Where's my wallet? It was in my back pocket! Oh no…. Theft.

d
M1   Psst, what do you want?
M2   What have you got?
M1   Everything you need, bro. Uh … I think that is drug dealing.

e
M   Shhh! Quiet. The neighbors … Burglary!

f
M   We have your husband. We want 10,000 dollars, or you won't see him again. That's a kidnapping.

g
M   OK. Nobody moves, nobody gets hurt. Put the money in the bag. Quick. Let's go. That's an armed robbery.

## ▶ 9.3 Notice /ʃ/, /θ/, and /ð/.

1   … And I mean, it's just not fair. You're simply downloading a song! **Th**is is not **th**eft! You're not a **th**ief! Why **sh**ould you go to prison? For using some**th**ing **th**at's out **th**ere for **th**e whole world to use? Just last month they arrested this 19-year-old who'd been downloading CSI episodes. **Th**at's so un**f**air! **Th**at's why I really **th**ink songs, books, and music should be completely free. Also …
2   So **th**is one's kind of hard to answer, but, uh … Gee, I don't know, maybe … armed rob**b**ery … I've lived in **th**is nei**gh**borhood for, what, two years and I've never actually seen a robber. So, yeah, I mean, I never even **th**ink about it. I feel pretty safe here, actually. By **th**e way, **th**is is really for a school project, right? I mean, you're not going to **sh**are **th**is on the Internet or anything, are you?
3   … Uh, yeah. Bur**g**lary. Our next-door neighbors went away for **th**e weekend and someone broke into **th**eir house. I was watching TV, you know, and I saw **th**e whole **th**ing. **Th**e bur**g**lar was a woman in her 40s—yeah, a woman, a blonde woman wearing a mask. I called the cops, but when **th**ey got **th**ere, **sh**e'd already left, you know? So, I wonder …
4   Yeah, and call me a pe**ss**imist, but, really, I don't see any way out. People are turning to drugs for all sorts of reasons—it's never for just one **th**ing. What has the government been doing to change **th**ings? No one knows for **s**ure. And I … well, I think drug **d**ealing is likely to get worse as the years go by. And you know what? The

new legislation next year will probably make no difference. I mean, sending drug dealers to prison isn't enough. You see ... Excuse me ...

5   ... Yeah. Well, not only me, but every mother in my neighborhood. I mean, my husband and I are doing OK: brand new car, nice house, we've just had a new pool built ... So, you know, all eyes are on us. So, uh ... I keep telling my kids to, you know, just run if someone they don't know gets too close ... Run as fast as they can, no matter who—anyone can be a potential kidnapper, you know? Or, even worse, a murderer. So, yeah, that's something that worries me. A lot. Oh, and here's something else ...

### ○ 9.7 Notice /w/ and /w/ when two vowels connect.

1   Thirty-two-year-old Shena Hardin was caught on camera driving on a sidewalk in order to go around a school bus that was dropping off children. She was taken to court and the judge sentenced her to an embarrassing punishment. She was told to stand at a busy intersection holding a sign which read, "Only an idiot would drive on a sidewalk to avoid a school bus." Just to add to her humiliation, the event was live-streamed by television crews. Hardin also had her license suspended and was ordered to pay $250 in court costs.

2   It was an ordinary morning in San Francisco's District Court, and then, without warning, someone's cell phone rang and broke the silence. Judge Robert Rather didn't like what he heard: "Whose phone is ringing? Bring it to me now!" Nobody did. "Everyone will be arrested unless I get that phone now!" Again, no one confessed at all. Judge Rather wasn't kidding: all 42 people present were charged with disturbing the peace and sent to jail. After suffering in prison for a couple of hours, they were released, of course. But the judge was permanently removed from office for abusing judicial power. In a recent interview, he said he had been under a lot of stress.

### ○ 9.10 Notice /aɪ/.

Cybercrime. This is a term we are used to hearing in the news almost every day. In fact, experts predict that by 2025 cyberattacks will have become—are you ready for this?—the world's top threat. Cybercrime covers a wide range of different offences. Cybercriminals can delete or change computer records, create fraudulent documents, and sell classified information. And there's nothing to stop them from one day saying: "I have an idea. Why don't we overheat some nuclear reactors?" With us on set this morning, we have Deniz Kaya, author, consultant, and technology guru. He'll be telling us if we should take these warnings seriously. But first, the shocking news about the tragic ...

### ○ 9.11 Notice /ə/.

H = host   D = Deniz

H   Joining us now is Deniz Kaya, senior editor of *Technology Today* and author of *Dark Times Ahead*. Deniz, thanks for being here.
D   Thanks for having me.
H   So ... is it that bad?
D   No.
H   Oh yeah?
D   It's catastrophic. And it'll get much worse.
H   Really?
D   I'm afraid so.

### ○ 9.12 Notice /j/ and /w/.

D   For starters, there's a new generation of hackers out there, and some are as young as, what, 12, 13.

H   No way!
D   Yeah, and they're only kids, you know? But at some point you have to stop and ask yourself—what's gonna happen to these kids? Will they have become big-time criminals by the time they're 20, 25?
H   Exactly.
D   Here's another problem. Malware is getting more and more intelligent.
H   Who's malware? A super villain or something?
D   No, that's not a person. Malware refers to, uh, to all sorts of viruses out there, you know? And some of them are pretty scary. Did you hear about the Facebook Messenger virus?
H   Yeah. The one with the video?
D   That's the one. By December, one out of 50 computers in New York will have been infected by that thing. Here's what it does: It sends a message, from a "friend," which says: "OMG! It's you?" and has a link to what looks like YouTube. However, when you follow the link, it downloads malware onto the computer. The same message will then be sent to more victims from your account.
H   Wow. That's awful. Do not open links to videos if you're not sure, then!
D   Bingo! But you know what really worries me? Cybercriminals will be carrying out more and more attacks wirelessly, and we won't be protected. They will have developed the ability to spread viruses across multiple devices very, very easily. They'll jump from phone to phone ... and then from phone to laptop, and then to tablet ...
H   Over wireless networks ...
D   Exactly. So you might be walking down the street and ... bang! And you know, there's actually some data suggesting that by the end of the decade, cybercriminals will have targeted 20 per cent of all the world's smart phones. And that's an optimistic estimate.
H   Wow. But is there anything we can do to protect ourselves?
D   Yep. There's all sorts of trouble you can avoid by taking a few simple precautions.

### ○ 9.13 Notice /p/, /v/, and /b/.

H   So you've told us about the dangers we'll be facing in the future. Can you offer us some advice on what we can do about it?
D   Of course! The first thing is passwords! I know it's much easier to use the same password for all your accounts, but you're putting yourself at risk. Use a unique password for everything. Each one should have at least eight characters and be a combination of letters, symbols, and numbers. Also be very aware of what you click on. It's so easy to get caught out by just clicking on a link from someone you don't know. The consequences can be dramatic. Just don't do it. If you are attacked, you might lose all of your files. To prevent this, make sure you regularly back up your files. If you are targeted, you will have already stored your information elsewhere. Another important point is to always install the latest updates. Don't ignore the messages your computer sends you. By updating, your software will be easier to use.
H   Yes, essential rules we all need to follow. Deniz, thank you very much for your input today. Coming up ...

### ○ 9.15 Notice the intonation. ↗↘

1
H = husband   W = wife   B = burglar
H   Oh, it's good to be home, isn't it? ↗
W   Sure is. ↘ I know that late flight was cheaper, ↘ but, boy, I'm exhausted! ↘

H:  Me, too. ↘ I can't wait to crawl into ...What the ...?! ↗ What's going on?! ↗ Who are you?! ↗
B   What, wait, hang on ...
W   Oh my goodness! ↗ I'm calling the police! ↗
B   No, wait ...

2
F = father   D = daughter
F   Do you have any idea what time it is? ↗ Your mother and I were worried sick ab ... Wait a second ... Are those my car keys? ↗
D   What?
F   Jennifer, what are you doing with my keys? ↗
D   Dad, uh, it's not what you're thinking.
F   Oh, that's good news. ↘ 'Cause I was starting to think my teenage daughter had stolen the family car. ↗
D   It's not what it seems. I swear. I was, uh, I was ...

3
F = flight attendant   P = passenger
F   Excuse me sir, we're about to take off. ↘ I'm gonna have to ask you to put your bag in the luggage compartment. ↘
P1  Uh, no, it's fine here, thank you. ↘
F   Sir, I'm afraid this is ...
P2  Hey, is that bag moving? ↗
P1  What? No, it's not. Of course not. ↘
P2  Yes, it is. Something's just moved in that bag. ↘
P1  Hold on, I can explain. ↘
F   Sir, I'm gonna have to ask you to ...

### ○ 9.16 Notice the sentence stress and weak forms.

1
W   The **police** will be **here** any **minute**!
B   **Wait** a **minute**. This **is not** what it **looks** like!
H   **Stay** where you **are**.
B   Just **hear** me **out! Please!** I just ... I got **kicked** out of my a**ccomm**odation and I **saw** the **house** was **empty** and ... I **haven't** taken **anything**, I **promise**.
W   **No!** We **don't** want to **hear** it! Just **keep** quiet until the **police** get here.

2
F   **Jennifer, what** are you **doing** with my **keys**?
D   **Dad,** uh, it's **not** what you're **thinking**.
F   **Oh,** that's **good news**. 'Cause I was **starting** to **think** my **teenage** daughter had **stolen** the **family car**.
D   It's **not** what it **seems**. I **swear**. I was, uh, I was **just** checking **out** your **MP3** collection.
F   **Yes,** of **course** you **were**. I **mean**, that's **just** the **kind** of music you're **into**, isn't it?
D   **No,** but, but **Dad** ... You **don't understand**.
F   **No ifs** and **buts, Jennifer.** I don't **want** to get a **phone call** from the **police.** You **stay out** of my car **unless** you're with **me.** Do you **hear me**?
D   **Yes,** Dad, but ...
F   **No!**

3
P2  **Yes, it is. Something's** just **moved** in that **bag**.
P1  **Hold on,** I can **explain**.
F   **Sir, I'm going to have to ask** you to get **off** the **plane**.
P1  **Lucy's** just **six months old,** she's not **dangerous** at **all. Look!**
P2  **Oh well,** that makes me **feel much better. Thank** you.
F   **Now sir,** please **stand up** and **come** with **me**.
P1  **OK, OK.** But **really,** she **wouldn't** hurt **anybody,** I **promise**.

## Unit 10

### ○ 10.3 Notice /j/ and /dʒ/.

C = Carlos   G = Gloria
G   Hey, what are you doing home so soon?
C   Good to see you, too! What are you doing?
G   Some silly quiz ...

# Audioscript

C Cool as a cucumber, occasionally moody, or chronically short-tempered. Let's hear your answers then. This should be interesting …
G Hey, what's that supposed to mean? I have my ups and downs, but I'm pretty stable.
C Well, yes, you do, but you're trying to work it out. How's the yoga class going by the way?
G Really well. I think it's really helping. You know, little by little, I'm learning how to relax.
C That's good. Let's have a look at the first question … Do you ever wake up feeling grumpy? Yeah, I'd have to agree with that. You definitely do!
G I know, I know, I'm grumpy in the morning, but I'm sick and tired of waking up early, Carlos! Five thirty feels like the middle of the night still!
C I guess, it's easy for me to say. I don't even dare to talk to you before 7 a.m.
G It's probably wise. I just … I need some peace and quiet in the morning, that's all.
C What about this one: Do you ever get fed up with activities and people you actually like … What do you mean "no"? You're fed up with your job!
G Well, yeah, but the question is about stuff I like. And I don't like working in retail.
C But you did when you started, right?
G Well, yeah, I did, but not anymore. "How can I help you today? That looks great on you. Have a nice day." Blah, blah, blah, blah, blah. I just … I hate doing the same things again and again …
C … and again and again. Yeah, I get it. You need variety.
G Yeah. Sooner or later, I'll need to start looking for a new job.
C Five … Do you ever swear when other drivers do something stupid? Yep, that's right. You do.
G How would you know that?
C I've been told.
G What?
C It's a small neighborhood, Gloria.
G Well, but you can't blame me, can you? I mean, you know what it's like to drive in L.A.!
C Do you ever yell at people for no serious reason? "No." You're kidding, right?
G Carlos, when did I ever yell at someone? Tell me!
C Whoa, whoa. OK, forget I said anything. You're really, really calm.

▶ **10.5** Notice the **connections**.
… and that just_about does_it for_us tonight. But before we go, here's the moment you've_all been waiting for: People's top pet peeves. Yes, we_asked_ and you voted! So, here_are the results.
At number 10, with 871 votes, people who suddenly_open the door without knocking first. Yep—we've_all done that before, haven't we?
Number 9, when people keep_interrupting you when you talk. Well, that's just rude.
Number 8, people who keep using the word "like" all the time. Yeah, that_is_annoying.
Number 7, with_a_little_over 1,000 votes, bad phone habits, like not returning texts_or phone calls.
At number 6, with 1,234 people who honk, instead_ of ringing the bell, when they come to pick_you_up— especially late_at night. Hate that, too.
Number 5, people who promise to call you and then they don't.
Number 4—oh, I hate this_one—people who_are too lazy to put their trash_in the trash can. I mean … it's right there.
Number 3, with_exactly 1,700 votes, when someone uses_a finger to pick their teeth. Well, that's just gross. Don't do_it.
The next one kind_of surprised me—I didn't_expect to see_it near the top with_as many as 1,809 votes, number 2 being the first_one to_arrive_at a party— Well, I guess it_is pretty embarrassing, isn't it?

And finally, at number 1, something I think many_of_ us hate, it's people who_are addicted to playing with their phones. What do you think? Let_us know on …

▶ **10.6** Notice /juː/ and /uː/.
C = coach  Mi = Mia  J = Jim  V = Vince  Ju = Julia
C … the last time we met. So, anyway, let's give a warm welcome to anyone who's joining our anger management group for the first time—and that's, well, everybody except Julia. So, first of all, Mia, hi. Welcome aboard.
Mi Hi.
C So, Mia, why are you here?
Mi My name's Mia and my employers have told me I have to sort my issues out. They say I'm too demanding and impatient with my staff. They are probably right. If things aren't done the way I want them or immediately … like, if I call and leave a message, and I don't hear from them in an hour, I get really mad and yell at them. You know, I really want to change, 'cause I'm afraid of losing my job.
C OK, Mia. Listen, I want to thank you for being so honest—that's the spirit! Jim, would you like to introduce yourself?
J OK, I guess.
C Go on …
J Ah, yeah, well … my girlfriend … she thinks I'm, like, too possessive. You know, I just want to know where she is and, like, what she's doing.
C OK, is that it?
J Well, I don't like it when she talks to other people––she's constantly on the phone with her friends and on Snapchat and stuff––I mean, all the time––and it makes me jealous, you know, and then she accuses me of being aggressive. So, that's why I'm here.
C I see. Interesting. Thank you, Jim. OK … Uh, next on the list is … Vince. Hi. Why don't you tell us what brought you here?
V Well, actually, I'm afraid it's people like Jim that brought me here.
C What do you mean?
V I don't mean to be arrogant, but … I'm sick and tired of hearing that kind of English. Didn't you learn anything at school?
J Excuse me? What are you talking about?
V "Like, like, like." How old are you? Like, 14?
J Wow! OK. Well, I am sorry! I apologize for upsetting your sensitive ears.
V So you should be! You know, there's just no excuse for bad grammar.
J Well, I guess we know why you're here now, don't we?
C OK, guys. I think we can talk about this reasonably.
Ju Reasonably? Do you think yelling at someone for the way they speak is reasonable?
V Hey! What's it got to do with you?
Ju Hey, didn't your mother ever teach you any manners?
C Julia! Vince! Everybody, calm down. Remember, there are ways of dealing with this … carefully, step by step. We are responsible for controlling our anger. In fact, let's use this as a good example. Let's look at some strategies to help us face these feelings and …

▶ **10.9** Notice /s/, /z/, and /ʃ/.
**1**
B = bride  G = groom
B I cannot believe that you said that. To my mother, Jose, my mother.
G Well, she just wouldn't stop talking about your ex-boyfriend, you have to admit it!

B Jose! Stop it! You should apologize for saying that or we're never going to …
G Oh, or what? I'm sick and tired of hearing how wonderful Chris is! I don't think I'm being unreasonable.

**2**
G = grandmother  Gd = granddaughter
G Oh … but … what happens if I press the wrong button by accident? I'm afraid of losing everything.
Gd Oh, don't worry, you won't. Look, there's an easy way of saving this. I promise. Just click on the file here and save here.
G Is that really all I have to do? That's easy, isn't it?
Gd Of course! I told you it was. Now you have a go.
G OK, so I just click here and then …

▶ **10.11** Notice the **sentence stress**.
Good **morning** everyone, and **welcome** to **A**ssertiveness Training. I hope you're **ready** to learn some **life-changing** lessons! What is **assertiveness**? Any **ideas**? No? OK, **assertiveness** is a way of **communicating** your **needs** and **wants** but **without hurting** other **people**.
It's **difficult** to tell the **difference** between **assertiveness** and **aggression**. **Aggression** is about **getting what** you **want** without **caring** how you **affect** others.
Now, there are many **benefits** of being **assertive**. **Assertive** people are **better managers**. They get the **job done** but **treat colleagues respectfully**. They're **good** at **negotiating** because they can **understand** the **opponent's argument** and can **reach** a **compromise** more **easily**. They are also **less stressed** because they are more **self-confident**. Sounds **good**, doesn't it?
So, how do we **become** more **assertive**? **First**, you have to **believe** in **yourself**. **Believe** that you **deserve** respect. **Next**, **identify** what you **need** and **say** that in a **clear** and **confident** way. You **shouldn't expect** others to **know what** you **want**!
**Accept** that you **cannot control** other **people**. If **someone reacts badly** to you, this is **not your fault** (but **remember** to **be respectful**). **Don't return** their **anger** and **resentment**. Stay **calm**. You can **control your own actions**. If **you** are **not offending** others, you have the **right to do** as you **wish**.
**Next**, say what **you're thinking** even if it's **difficult**. However, say it **constructively** and **with sensitivity**. You can **confront people** who **disagree** with you but **stay in control** and **be positive**.
**Accept criticism** as well as **compliments**. It's **important** to take **feedback** even when it's **negative**. If you **don't agree**, **that's fine** and **you can say so** without **being defensive**.
A very **useful tip** next. **Remember** saying **yes** to every little thing you've been **asked** to do over the **years**? Well, **stop** it. You need to **stop agreeing** to everything and **learn** to **say no** more often. **Understand** your **limits**. **Stop** to **think** about **how much** you can **manage realistically**.
**Change** your **language**. **Instead** of saying "**I could**, or **would**", say "**I will**". **Try** using more "**I**" **statements**: say "**I want**, **I feel**, **I need**" rather than "**You don't**, **you should**, **you never**", etc. This can be **very effective**.
And **finally**, something **simple**. **Listen**. **Listen** and try to **understand** the other person's **opinion**. Try **not** to **interrupt**.
So, let's **try putting** some of this **into practice**. I'd **like** to **try** some **roleplay**. Let's **get into groups** of …

## 10.13 Notice /ʃ/, /ð/, /θ/, and /f/.

Any true relationship between friends or significant others should be one between equals: you give and take equally. One person's needs aren't met over another's. Friends and partners are supposed to give you energy and lift you up when you're down, and want the best for you. But sometimes we get into relationships that drain energy from us. These are toxic relationships and they can negatively affect all aspects of our lives. On this week's *WellCast*, we're going to tell you how you can tell if you're even in a toxic relationship. And then we're going to help you extricate yourself from that unhealthy situation, pronto!

## 10.14 Notice the short (/) and long (//) pauses.

Step 1: // Diagnose the relationship. // How do you know if a friend or partner is bringing you down? // Well, / in much the same way that you know you're coming down with a cold. // Toxic relationships come with symptoms. // When you're around this person, / how do you feel? // Here are a few other questions you should ask yourself if you're thinking you might be in a toxic situation: // Does my friend put me down all the time? // Are they jealous when I spend time with others? // Do they constantly bring up parts of me that they want to change? // Do they take more than they give? // Am I only doing the things that they want to do? //

Step 2: // Recognize your role / in the relationship. // As Eleanor Roosevelt once said, / "Nobody can make you feel inferior without your consent." / All right, look, you know we got that from *Princess Diaries*, obviously. Moving on. // Listen, you have autonomy in every relationship in your life. // If a friend or partner is stealing your sunshine, / you need to figure out what you're doing to allow them to do this. // Are you being a doormat? // Are you putting this person's emotional needs ahead of your own health? //

Step 3: // Start to build boundaries for this relationship. // Does your friend invite themselves over at all hours of the night? // Are they constantly bossing you around? // Are they always borrowing money from you? // Once you know the boundary that you want to set, / stick to it! / Draw your line in the sand. //

Step 4: // Recognize that you can't change other people, / but you can stop being a doormat. // If you've determined that a friendship or relationship is toxic, / you know that you have to change the nature of that relationship. // Start by spending less time with that person / and do your best to detach yourself emotionally. // Setting boundaries will hopefully help you begin to phase this relationship out. //

Step 5: // Get a second opinion. // Especially if you're emotionally vulnerable, / the best thing you can do is surround yourself with people who love you / and who want you to be happy and healthy. // Use them as a lifeline during this time. //

Step 6: // Above all else, / look out for yourself. // Studies have shown that people with low self-esteem / are far more likely to find themselves in toxic relationships. // You will never be treated with love and respect / unless you absolutely believe that you deserve these things. // Remember: you teach people how to treat you. / So do yourself the favor of loving yourself!

## 10.16 Notice the connections that produce /w/ and /j/ sounds.

Welcome to *English for all*, the podcast for students who want to improve their English—fast! Last week, we asked you to tell us about your strengths and weaknesses, your successes and your frustrations. So, today we've chosen three messages to read on the air. The first one—where is it? Oh, here—was written by Bruna, a listener from Colombia—hi, Bruna—who says she's good at grammar, but finds it hard to express herself fluently. Listen, your English sounds fantastic and, you know, maybe you're much more fluent than you think. Anyway, here's what I think you should do: Try to focus on expressing your ideas fluently instead of speaking 100% correctly all the time. 'Cause, you see, the more you stop to think about what you're going to say next, the more you hesitate. And remember: People will still understand you if you make a few mistakes. And here's another suggestion: Have you thought about asking a friend to practice with you for a few hours a week? You probably have at least one or two friends who speak some English, right? So think about it: You can have fun and improve your English at the same time without having to, I don't know, live abroad or anything. Thanks for writing, Bruna, and good luck.

Our second message comes from South Korea. Our listener says he has trouble understanding spoken English … Yeah, that's a common problem. Byung-Sang, listen, I have two suggestions. First, listen to as much English as you can outside the classroom. For example, a good way of practicing is watching Internet videos on sites like YouTube, Dailymotion, and so on, at least every other day, for about an hour or so. Religiously. Turn the subtitles on and off sometimes, too. But be sure to choose a variety of videos—both more and less challenging, OK? And who knows, you might even learn a new expression or two! And here's the second suggestion: If you want to improve your listening, you should consider giving pronunciation a little more attention. Yeah, I'm serious. Research has shown that students with good pronunciation tend to be much better listeners. How about that?

And our final message comes from Omar—where's he from?—oh, Turkey, wow. Omar says he's not comfortable reading quickly, for, uh, for general comprehension. Omar, listen, reading too slowly is not always a good idea. For example, if you take an international exam, you'll need to be able to read fast, without a dictionary. So here's what I think you should do: Next time you approach a text, read it once quickly first. Then, if necessary, read it again, more carefully, looking for information you need. But try to avoid reading slowly all the time. And about your vocabulary question, here's something that might help: learn words together. For example, how about learning "make an effort" instead of "effort"? Or "take a course" rather than only "course"? Our brains like these kinds of associations, you know? Well, that does it for us tonight. In the next episode, we'll be talking about …

# Review 5

## R5.1 Notice /r/ and /h/.

1

R = Ron  H = Hanna

R  Hey Hanna, what are you reading?
H  Oh, hi Ron. Oh, this? It's a book Ralph lent me. He said it was really good, but I just can't get into it.
R  Huh, so, what's it about?
H  Well, uh, that's just it. Ralph said it was a really interesting detective story … but there's no crime, not much storyline, nothing really. I just can't figure it out.
R  Hmmm … Well, maybe it'll turn out better than you think. You know, keep reading!

2

L = Lenny  S = Sue

S  Lenny? Have you changed something … Your hair or something?
L  Nope, not my hair. But I'm on this diet right now. I've lost a little weight.
S  Ah! That must be it! Yeah, you look really good!
L  Oh, thanks Sue. You know, it's pretty hard to stick to it, there are so many things I can't eat, but, you know, it really lifts me up when I hear things like that. So, thank you.
S  No problem! Yeah, stick to it Lenny, don't give up!

3

J = Jackie  B = Beth

J  What is it, Beth? You look kind of miserable. You're not coming down with anything, are you?
B  Oh, I don't think so … No, it's this work. I've got so much to do and so little time. I just don't know what to do. It's really bringing me down.
J  Oh, Beth, you poor thing. Look, tell me it's none of my business, I don't want to boss you around or anything, but you really need to look out for yourself. Take a break or something, you know?
B  Yeah, Jackie, maybe you're right. But then when will I finish this work?

## R5.2 Notice the /t/, /d/, and /ɪd/ endings.

William Watts was a thief. One day he was stealing some jewels from a shop and set off the alarm. The police arrived at the shop before William had finished, so he quickly jumped out of the window and ran away. Unfortunately for William, he turned the wrong way and saw the police station in front of him. He stopped running and tried to act naturally, but he was arrested. He was taken to court and convicted of burglary. When the judge read the sentence, William started to cry.

# Songs

## 1.1

**Song line:** Please allow me to introduce myself. I am a man of wealth and taste.
**Song:** *Sympathy for the Devil,* released in 1968
**Artist:** The Rolling Stones (British)
**Lesson link:** introductions
**Notes:** This song reinforced the bad boys' image of the Rolling Stones, in contrast to the Beatles' being seen as nice boys. The song was good marketing for the band as the press reported it showing a supposed interest in Satanism. Jagger claims that the song is actually about the dark side of humankind, not a celebration of Satanism.

At any time during lesson 1.1 have sts read the song line on top of page 7 and ask: *Do you know this song?* Encourage sts to answer, then ask: *How does the person in the song introduce him or herself?* Have sts answer and make sure they notice that instead of saying his or her name, the person in the lyrics describes themselves with nonphysical characteristics. Next, have sts work in pairs to describe themselves to their partners in the same way, not only physically, but also emotionally and socially. Encourage them to take notes of what their partners say, so they can remember. Finally, have sts present their partners to the whole class in the same way.

## 1.2

**Song line:** But ooh, this time I'm telling you, I'm telling you, We are never ever ever getting back together.
**Song:** *We Are Never Ever Getting Back Together,* released in 2012
**Artist:** Taylor Swift (American)
**Lesson link:** relationships and phrasal verbs
**Notes:** Taylor says she wrote this song to one of her ex-boyfriends, but she doesn't make it clear who it is. This was the first radio single from Taylor Swift's fourth studio album, *Red*. And it was also Swift's first number 1 song on the Hot 100.

After section 1 (Vocabulary), have sts read the song line on top of page 9 and ask: *Can you find the link between the song line and the lesson?* Encourage sts to answer. At this stage, they should be able to identify the relationship link. Make sure sts can also identify the link with the phrasal verb *get (back) together* in **1**. Another possible link is the speech bubble mentioning Taylor Swift's break-up. Then, ask: *Do you know this song? Can you sing this line?* Have sts answer and sing it if they want to.

## 1.3

**Song line:** Have I made it obvious? Haven't I made it clear? Want me to spell it out for you? F-R-I-E-N-D-S.
**Song:** *Friends,* released in 2018
**Artist:** Marshmello (American), feat. Anne-Marie (British)
**Lesson link:** friends
**Notes:** The idea for the lyrics of this song was inspired by a male friend of Anne-Marie's who, according to her, actually wanted to be more than just friends with her. The singer doesn't say who it is but she said she hopes that the song won't ruin her friendship with the guy.

At any time during lesson 1.3, have sts read the song line on top of page 11 and ask: *Do you know this song?* Encourage sts to sing the song line aloud, if they want to. Next, ask: *Do you know any other songs with the word friend(s) in them?* Have sts work in pairs or trios and make a list of songs that they can remember with the word *friend(s)*. Allow sts to search the web for these songs, but only accept the ones they can sing the bit where the word is. This means that they have to know the song, not just look for the lyrics. Allow sts some time to do so, then have the pairs or trios take turns presenting one song at a time. Remind them that they cannot present a song that has already been presented by another pair or trio. The pair or trio with more songs in their list is the winner.

## 1.4

**Song line:** Near, far, wherever you are, I believe that the heart does go on.
**Song:** *My Heart Will Go On,* released in 1997
**Artist:** Celine Dion (Canadian)
**Lesson link:** emphatic forms
**Notes:** This cinema classic was composed by James Horner for the movie *Titanic*. It featured the voice of Celine Dion and it quickly became known all over the world. Horner was a composer of orchestral music for the cinema who wrote tracks for other famous movies like *Braveheart, Apollo 13,* and *Aliens*. The lyrics were written by lyricist Will Jennings, who has also written songs for Barry Manilow, Eric Clapton, B. B. King, Roy Orbison, and many others. Horner died in a plane crash in 2015 at the age of 61.

After section 3 (Grammar), have sts read the song line on page 13 and ask: *Do you recognize this song?* Encourage sts to answer and sing the song line, if they want to. Next, ask: *Why does the song line use the auxiliary **does** in an affirmative sentence?* At this stage of the lesson, sts are expected to be able to answer that it uses the auxiliary verb *does* as a way of emphasizing the main verb of the sentence. So instead of saying *I believe that the heart goes on*, the singer says *I believe that the heart **does** go on*. Encourage sts to try out some example sentences in which they could use emphatic forms with auxiliary verbs.

## 1.5

**Song line:** What do you mean? When you nod your head yes, But you wanna say no. What do you mean?
**Song:** *What Do You Mean?* released in 2015
**Artist:** Justin Bieber (Canadian)
**Lesson link:** opinions
**Notes:** Bieber said this song is about how "flip-floppy" girls are. According to the singer, girls sometimes say one thing when they actually mean something else, and this song is about this. It would appear that Bieber really does want an answer to the question that's the title of the song, as he repeats *What do you mean?* 28 times throughout the song!

Before sts arrive, write the song line from page 15 on the board with five mistakes as follows: *What you mean? Where you nod your hand yes, But you gonna say no. What you mean?* As sts arrive, tell them not to open their books yet. When all sts are in class, have them read the song line that you wrote (with mistakes) on the board and ask: *Do you know this song?* Encourage them to answer and sing the song line bit if they want to. Still with their books closed, ask sts: *Can you identify the five mistakes in the song line?* Allow sts to work in pairs for a few minutes to spot the mistakes. When they are ready have them take turns coming to the board to correct the mistakes, one at a time. Finally, allow them to open their books to page 15 and check their corrections with the song line at the bottom of the page.

## Writing 1

**Song line:** Where have you been all my life, all my life? Where have you been all my life?
**Song:** *Where Have You Been?,* released in 2011
**Artist:** Rihanna (Barbadian-American)
**Lesson link:** present perfect
**Notes:** This song, featured in Rhianna's *Talk That Talk* album, was first performed live by Rihanna at a charity fundraiser after the Grammy ceremony, on February 13, 2012. It debuted in the U. S. charts at number 65 before reaching number three.

Use the song line on page 16 to review one of the uses of the present perfect. Have sts read the song line and ask: *Why do you think the writer used the present perfect and not the simple past or another tense in the song line questions?* Allow sts to work in pairs for a minute to come up with an explanation for your

# Songs

question. When they are ready, have a volunteer explain. Make sure they understand that since the singer isn't asking about a definite time in the past, but rather about something that has happened over a period of time ("… all my life"), the present perfect is the best choice.

## 2.1

**Song line:** Heal the world, Make it a better place, For you and for me and the entire human race.
**Song:** *Heal the World*, released in 1991
**Artist:** Michael Jackson (American)
**Lesson link:** making the world a better place, sustainability
**Notes:** This song was written and produced by Michael Jackson. It was criticized at the time, because it was considered too similar to the U.S.A for Africa single *We Are the World*, which Michael Jackson co-wrote. In 2001, Michael said in an interview that this song, which was about man's inhumanity to his fellow man, was the song he was most proud of having written.

At any time during lesson 2.1, have sts read the song line on page 19 and ask: *Do you know this song?* Encourage them to answer and sing the song line if they want to. Next, ask: *Can you identify the link between the song line and the lesson?* and have sts work in pairs to scan the whole lesson and identify the link. Make sure that they connect the Going Green quiz ideas and actions we can take towards sustainability to the idea of healing the world and making it a better place for all of us.

## 2.2

**Song line:** Lately I've been, I've been losing sleep, Dreaming about the things that we could be.
**Song:** *Counting Stars*, released in 2013
**Artist:** OneRepublic (American)
**Lesson link:** present perfect continuous
**Notes:** Ryan Tedder, OneRepublic's frontman, came up with the idea for this song while working with Beyoncé. *Counting Stars* was Ryan's first ever UK number 1 single as a performer—he had previously been co-writer on other UK number 1 singles.

After section 3 (Grammar), have sts read the song line on top of page 21 and ask: *Do you recognize this song? Can you sing this bit?* Encourage sts to answer and sing the song line aloud, if they want to. Next, have them look at the second activity in the grammar box and ask: *Which question a to d best matches the song line on this page?* Encourage sts to identify that the word *lately* indicates that the question that best matches the song line is *Since when?* Make sure they understand that you cannot answer *How often? How much?* or *When?* with *lately*.

## 2.3

**Song line:** Everything is changing, And I've been here for too long. Going through the same things, I've been hurting too long.
**Song:** *Changing*, released in 2014
**Artist:** Sigma (British)
**Lesson link:** present perfect continuous
**Notes:** This song marked the second UK number 1 for the Sigma duo and Paloma Faith's debut at the top of the chart after previously getting three Top Ten hits. Sigma and Paloma Faith recorded this song with a full orchestra.

After section 3 (Grammar), have sts read the song line on top of page 23 and ask: *Do you recognize this song? Can you sing this bit?* Encourage sts to answer and sing the song line aloud, if they want to. Then, ask: *Which verb tenses can you identify in the song line?* Encourage sts to look at it again and identify the verb tenses in it. At this stage, they should be able to identify the present continuous (everything is changing), the present perfect (I've been here), and the present perfect continuous (I've been hurting).

## 2.4

**Song line:** How long has this been going on? You've been acting so shady, I've been feeling it lately.
**Song:** *How Long*, released in 2017
**Artist:** Charlie Puth (American)
**Lesson link:** present perfect continuous
**Notes:** In this song, Charlie Puth apologizes to a lover for being unfaithful. According to the singer, the honest lyrics are about something that he had actually experienced in life. The song's chorus is clearly from the betrayed girl's perspective, as she asks for details about how long it has been going on.

Before sts arrive, write the song line from page 25 on the board with three mistakes as follows: *How long have this been going on? You're been acting so shady, I've being feeling it lately.* As sts arrive, ask them not to open their books. When all sts are in class, have them read the song line that you wrote (with mistakes) on the board and ask: *Do you know this song? Can you sing it?* Encourage sts to answer and sing the song line aloud, if they want to. Next, have sts work in pairs and ask: *Can you spot the mistakes in the song line on the board?* Allow them a few minutes to spot the three mistakes in the song line that you wrote. When they are ready, have a volunteer come to the board to correct the song line. Finally, have sts open their books to page 25 to check their answers.

## 2.5

**Song line:** I got the eye of the tiger, a fighter. Dancing through the fire, 'Cause I am a champion.
**Song:** *Roar*, released in 2013
**Artist:** Katy Perry (American)
**Lesson link:** wild life
**Notes:** This song hit number 1 in 15 countries and was in the Top 10 in 38 charts all around the world. *Roar* sold 557,024 downloads on the first week of release, surpassing Perry's hit *Firework* that had previously sold 509,000, in the last week of 2010.

Before sts arrive in class, write the song line from page 27 on the board as follows, with all of the vowels removed: _ g_t th_ _y_ _f th_ t_g_r, _ f_ght_r. D_nc_ng thr__gh th_ f_r_, 'C__s_ _ _m _ ch_mp__n. As they arrive, ask them not to open their books yet. When all sts are in class, have them work in pairs to complete the song line that you wrote on the board with the missing vowels. Allow sts a few minutes to do this. When they are ready, have pairs take turns completing one or two words at a time on the board. Finally, have sts open their books to page 27 to read the song line and check their work.

## Writing 2

**Song line:** Why do I find it hard to write the next line? Oh, I want the truth to be said, I know this much is true.
**Song:** *True*, released in 1983
**Artist:** Spandau Ballet (British)
**Lesson link:** facts and opinions
**Notes:** According to Spandau Ballet's guitarist Gary Kemp, he wrote the lyrics of this song inspired by a crush he had on singer and star Clare Grogan. The musician said that, despite the fact that his feelings were not reciprocated and their relationship was only platonic, he felt this was enough to write a song about.

At any time during the Writing 2 lesson, have sts read the song line on page 28 and ask: *Why do you think the writer finds it hard to write the next line?* Elicit / explain the meaning of *writer's block*. Encourage sts to share their ideas. It may have been a case of writer's block, but, analyzing the lyrics of the song line, it may also have more to do with the writer's fear of saying the truth and hurting people. Then, ask: *Have you ever had writer's block when writing something? What did you do to overcome it?* Have sts answer and encourage them to engage in the discussion.

# Songs

## Review 1

🎵 **Song line:** I've been running through the jungle, I've been running with the wolves, To get to you, to get to you, I've been down the darkest alleys, Saw the dark side of the moon to get to you.
**Song:** *Wolves*, released in 2017
**Artist:** Selena Gomez (American) feat. Marshmello (American)
**Lesson link:** present perfect and present perfect continuous
**Notes:** This song is a collaboration between Selena Gomez and music producer and DJ Marshmello. Selena says that the DJ created a really cool tune from a rough demo Andrew Watt (a songwriter she's worked with for years) sent him. She says that besides being a very beautiful and personal song, the lyrics also have a whole story behind them.

Before the class, search the web for an audio clip of the song *Wolves*, by Selena Gomez, that contains the song line on page 31. As sts arrive in class, ask them not to open their books. When all sts are in class, explain that you are going to play the clip of a song and they have to write down what they hear. Remind sts that, since you will play the clip only twice for them to write it down, they have to be focused while listening to the song line and writing it down. Play the clip twice and then have a volunteer come to the board to write down what they got. Encourage other sts to correct him / her as necessary. Then, allow them to open their books to page 31 to check their version of the song line. Finally, ask: *What were the most difficult parts for you to understand?* and have sts share their opinions.

## 3.1

🎵 **Song line:** Concrete jungle where dreams are made of, There's nothing you can't do, Now you're in New York.
**Song:** *Empire State of Mind (Part II) Broken Down*, released in 2009
**Artist:** Alicia Keys (American)
**Lesson link:** cities / NYC
**Notes:** This song was a second version of the original track, performed by Jay-Z and featuring Alicia Keys, named *Empire State of Mind*. Keys recorded it because she wanted to see how the song would sound if it was just sung by her, showing how she personally felt about New York City.

At any stage during lesson 3.1, have sts read the song line on top of page 33 and ask: *Do you know this song? Can you sing this bit?* Encourage sts to answer and sing the song line aloud, if they want to. Next, ask: *How many more songs do you know that mention New York in their lyrics?* Have sts work in pairs to come up with a list of songs that mention New York City in their lyrics. Allow them a few minutes to do so, but remind them that the songs that they put on their list will only count to their score if they can sing the bit where New York is mentioned. This means that they must know the song and cannot just take any song from the Internet without knowing how to sing it. Finally, have the pairs take turns singing one of their songs at a time. Remind them that they cannot sing a song that has already been sung by another pair. If sts are not comfortable singing aloud, they could write their selection on the board.

## 3.2

🎵 **Song line:** For some reason I can't explain, Once you'd gone there was never, Never an honest word, And that was when I ruled the world.
**Song:** *Viva la Vida*, released in 2008
**Artist:** Coldplay (British)
**Lesson link:** past perfect
**Notes:** Chris Martin, Coldplay's frontman, told *Rolling Stone* magazine that he came up with the idea of this title (of both the song and album) after he came across the phrase on a Frida Kahlo painting. Martin explained that the Mexican painter went through a lot of problems in her life and he liked the fact that, even so, she painted a big painting saying *Viva la Vida*.

After you finish lesson 3.2, have sts read the song line on top of page 35 and ask: *Do you recognize this song? Can you sing this bit?* Encourage sts to answer and sing the song line aloud, if they want to. Next, have sts focus on the contraction *you'd* in the song line and ask: *What does this 'd stand for in this song line?* Have sts analyze the structure of the sentence and answer. At this stage, as they have just seen the past perfect in the lesson, they should be able to identify that, because of the past participle verb (gone) that comes right after the contraction 'd, in this case, the contraction can only be the past perfect auxiliary (had) contracted with the subject (you). Also, the context itself leads to the past perfect conclusion, as the lyrics talk about two different moments in the past, one (past perfect = you'd gone) which occurred before the other (past simple = there was never).

## 3.3

🎵 **Song line:** It's like a jungle, sometimes it makes me wonder how I keep from going under. A-huh-huh huh-huh.
**Song:** *The Message*, released in 1982
**Artist:** Grandmaster Flash & the Furious Five (American)
**Lesson Link:** city problems
**Notes:** This is the best-known song by hip-hop legend Grandmaster Flash & the Furious Five. This song is considered to have changed rap's tone and content forever. It was the push towards the more fearless social critics that rap so strongly represents.

Before the class, search the web for a video or audio file of the song *The Message*, by Grandmaster Flash & the Furious Five. At any time during lesson 3.3, have sts read the song line on page 37 and ask: *Have you ever heard this song?* Most sts will probably not have heard this song, so have them analyze the lyrics and ask: *By looking at the tone of the lyrics, what musical style do you think it is?* Encourage sts to discuss and share their opinions. Ask them not to use the Internet to check and do not correct them, just yet. When everybody has shared their opinions, play the video or audio file of the song that you have found before class and have sts check whether their opinions were correct.

## 3.4

🎵 **Song line:** You only get one shot, do not miss your chance to blow. This opportunity comes once in a lifetime, yo.
**Song:** *Lose Yourself*, released in 2002
**Artist:** Eminem (American)
**Lesson link:** important opportunities
**Notes:** Unlike most raps, in *Lose Yourself* there is someone playing power chords on a guitar. This song was featured in *8 Mile*'s soundtrack, Eminem's first movie, which makes some references to the singer's life. The soundtrack of the *8 Mile* movie was a very successful venture for Eminem.

As sts arrive in class, ask them not to open their books. When all sts are in class, explain that they will play *Telephone* with a song line. Organize the class in a setting in which they can play the game, and start by whispering the first sentence of the song line to the first student (they only get one shot). When this sentence gets to the end of the line, have the student who was the last to write down what he understood on the board. Next, start the game again with the second sentence, but this time inverting the order (you should now start with the student that was the last one in the first sentence). When it gets to the end, have the last student to come to the board and write down what he / she understood, as a continuation for the first part. Next, have sts open their books to page 39 and have them check the song line they were supposed to have heard. Finally, ask: *Do you know this song? Can you sing this bit?* Encourage sts to answer and sing the song line aloud, if they want to.

# Songs

### 3.5

♪ **Song line:** I don't want to go to school, I just wanna to break the rules.
**Song:** *Break The Rules*, released in 2014
**Artist:** Charli XCX (British)
**Lesson link:** breaking the rules
**Notes:** Charli XCX said that this song came when she was phasing out of her punk stage into something more pop. But she makes it clear that the song is about not worrying about anything. Later, the singer apparently regretted having recorded this song, as she told *Q* magazine that she considers *Break The Rules* a rash decision and that she hates it.

At any time during lesson 3.5, have sts read the song line at the bottom of page 41 and ask: *Do you recognize this song? Can you sing this bit?* Encourage sts to answer and sing the song line, if they want to. Next, ask: *Can you identify the link between the song line and the lesson?* Have sts scan the pages of the lesson to find the link. They should be able to find out that the link is breaking rules. Finally, ask: *Have you ever felt like the singer in these lyrics?* Encourage sts to answer and share their experiences about feeling like breaking the rules, or not feeling like going to school.

### Writing 3

♪ **Song line:** Little did I know … That you were Romeo, you were throwing pebbles, And my daddy said, "Stay away from Juliet", And I was crying on the staircase. Begging you, please, don't go.
**Song:** *Love Story*, released in 2008
**Artist:** Taylor Swift (American)
**Lesson link:** past simple / continuous
**Notes:** *Love Story* was, as most of Taylor Swift's songs, inspired by a real experience she had. She composed the song based on a relationship she was in when she was a teenager. According to the singer, her parents did not like the guy, but she did. Swift later said in an interview that the boy was indeed a creep as her parents thought, but at that time, she thought it was love.

Before the class, search the web for a video or audio file of the song *Love Story*, by Taylor Swift. As sts arrive in class, ask them not to open their books. When all sts are in class, explain that you will play a clip from a song for them to write down what they hear. Remind sts to pay attention and focus, as you will play the song clip just twice for them to write it down. When they're ready, play the video or audio file of the song line twice and have sts write down what they hear. Next, have a volunteer come to the board to write the complete song line. Allow other sts to correct the song line on the board as necessary. Then, allow sts to open their books to page 42 and have them check their song line with the one on the page. Ask sts to identify the tenses in the song line. Finally, ask: *What were the most difficult parts for you to understand?* and encourage sts to answer and share their opinions.

### 4.1

♪ **Song line:** Hey, Teacher, leave them kids alone! All in all you're just another brick in the wall.
**Song:** *Another Brick in The Wall*, released in 1979
**Artist:** Pink Floyd (British)
**Lesson link:** education
**Notes:** This classic song by Pink Floyd is a reflection of Roger Waters's views on formal education. Waters hated his grammar school teachers and understood that they were more dedicated to keeping students quiet than to teaching them. Some people think that the wall refers to the emotional barriers the singer had to build around himself when he was at school.

Before sts arrive in class, write the song line from page 45 on the board as follows, with all of the vowels removed: H_y, T__ch_r, l__v_ th_m k_ds _l_n_! _ll _n _ll y__'r_ j_st _n_th_r br_ck _n th_ w_ll. When all sts are in class, have them work in pairs to complete the song line that you wrote on the board with the vowels that are missing in it. When they are ready, have volunteers come to the board to complete two words at a time. Next, have sts open the book to page 45 and allow them to compare the song line on the page to the one they completed on the board. Finally ask: *Do you know this song? Can you sing this bit?* Encourage sts to answer and sing the song line aloud, if they want to.

### 4.2

♪ **Song line:** Baby, we don't stand a chance, It's sad but it's true, I'm way too good at goodbyes.
**Song:** *Too Good At Goodbyes*, released in 2017
**Artist:** Sam Smith (British)
**Lesson link:** too
**Notes:** According to Sam Smith, this song is about a relationship he was in during 2016. The singer explains that the song talks about him getting better and better at getting dumped, because it happened three times in that same relationship, and the last time it happened he was ready and prepared.

After section 2 (Grammar) have sts read the song line on page 47 and ask: *Do you recognize this song? Can you sing this bit?* Encourage sts to answer and sing the song line, if they want to. Next, have sts work in pairs and ask: *Can you identify the link between the song line and the lesson?* Allow them a few minutes to identify the link of the song with the lesson. When they are ready, have them share their answers. At this stage, they should be able to identify the link with the word *too*. Finally, ask: *Is there anything you consider yourself **too good at**?* and encourage sts to answer.

### 4.3

♪ **Song line:** Too young, too dumb to realize that I should have bought you flowers and held your hand.
**Song:** *When I Was Your Man*, released in 2012
**Artist:** Bruno Mars (American)
**Lesson link:** regrets / should have
**Notes:** In this ballad, Mars sings about regrets in a past relationship. The singer says he had decided not to sing another ballad, but this one came from his guts, it was "the real thing", as Mars said. The pop star says that both men and women can relate to the lyrics because we all make mistakes and sometimes realize only when it's too late.

Before sts arrive in class, write the song line from page 49 on the board with four mistakes as follows: *Two young, two dumb to realize that I should have bringed you flowers and holded your hand.* As sts arrive, ask them not to open their books. When all sts are in class, explain that you have written a song line on the board with four mistakes. Have them read the song line on the board and ask: *Do you know this song? Can you spot the mistakes?* Have sts work in pairs to spot the four mistakes and correct the song line on the board. When they are ready, allow them to open their books to page 49 and have them check their corrections.

### 4.4

♪ **Song line:** If I could turn back time, If I could find the way, I'd take back all those words that hurt you, And you'd stay.
**Song:** *If I Could Turn Back Time*, released in 1989
**Artist:** Cher (American)
**Lesson link:** second conditional
**Notes:** This song was written by Diane Warren, who has also composed songs for famous artists like Aretha Franklin, Tina Turner, Barbara Streisand, Whitney Houston, and Celine Dion. The album where this song was featured, *Heart of Stone*, was Cher's first album to sell millions of copies.

After section 2 (Grammar), have sts read the song line on page 51 and ask them: *Do you know this song? Can you sing this bit?* Encourage sts to answer and sing the song line, if they want to. Then, have sts focus on the 'd in the song line and ask *What does this 'd stand for in this song line?* Have sts answer and make sure they understand that, since these are second conditional sentences, the 'd in these cases can only stand for *would*. Remind sts that another way of identifying this is to look at the verb that follows. If the verb that follows the *'d* is in the simple form (infinitive without *to*), then *'d* means *would* and this is a second conditional sentence. But if the following verb is in the participle, then the *'d* stands for *had* and this is a past perfect sentence.

## 4.5

**Song line:** I should've known better than to cheat a friend, And waste a chance that I've been given. So I'm never gonna dance again, The way I danced with you.
**Song:** *Careless Whisper,* released in 1984
**Artist:** George Michael (British)
**Lesson link:** regrets / should have
**Notes:** This song was co-written by George Michael and his bandmate Andrew Ridgeley when they were 17 years old. The lyrics were inspired by Michael's stories from his early romantic adventures.

Before the lesson, search the web for a video or audio clip of the song *Careless Whisper*, by George Michael, which contains the section in the song line. As sts arrive in class, ask them not to open their books. When all sts are in class, explain that you're going to play a video or audio clip of a song and they have to write down what they understand from the lyrics. Explain to sts that they have to pay attention to it, as you're going to play the song line just twice for them to write it down and check. Then, play the song line twice and have sts write down what they hear. When they're ready, have a volunteer come to the board to write what he / she heard. Allow the other sts to correct the song line if necessary. Next, have sts open their books to page 53 to check the song line they wrote against the one that's in the book. Finally, ask: *What was the most difficult part for you to understand?*

## Writing 4

**Song line:** We could have had it all, Rolling in the deep, You had my heart inside of your hand, And you played it, to the beat.
**Song:** *Rolling In The Deep,* released in 2010
**Artist:** Adele (British)
**Lesson link:** could have
**Notes**: This song was the first single in Adele's second album, *21*. It was written and produced by Adele and Paul Epworth, a British producer who has worked with Bloc Party and Florence and the Machine. The singer says that the song is all about saying things in the heat of the moment.

Before students arrive in class, write the song line from page 54 on the board with five mistakes as follows: *We would had had it all, Rolling in the deep, You hand my had inside of your heart, And you played it, to the beat.* As sts arrive in class, ask them not to open their books. When all sts are in class, have them work in pairs to spot and correct the five mistakes in the song line. Next, have volunteers come to the board to correct the song line on the board. After they have done so, ask: *Do you recognize this song? Can you sing this bit?* Encourage sts to answer and sing the song line aloud, if they want to. Finally, have sts open their books to page 54 to check their work.

## Review 2

**Song line:** I should have changed that stupid lock, I should have made you leave your key.
**Song:** *I Will Survive,* released in 1978
**Artist:** Gloria Gaynor (American)
**Lesson link:** regrets / should have
**Notes:** This is a song about moving on and getting over a bad relationship. It has taken on different meanings over the years and it is now considered to be a song about female-empowerment. But according to the songwriter, Dino Fekaris, *I Will Survive* was not about personal relationships, but actually about him getting fired by Motown Records, where he used to be a staff writer.

At any point during the Review 2 lesson, have sts read the song line at the top of page 57 and ask: *Do you know this song? Can you sing this bit?* Encourage them to answer and sing the song line, if they want to. Then, ask: *Do you know what this song is about?* Have students share their opinions, and use the notes above to explain the actual inspiration for the song. Finally, ask: *What is the link between this song line and the review lesson?* Have sts work in pairs to scan the lesson for a link with the song line. Hopefully they will be able to identify that the link is regrets / *should have*.

## 5.1

**Song line:** Baby, I don't need dollar bills to have fun tonight.
**Song:** *Cheap Thrills,* released in 2016
**Artist:** Sia (Australian)
**Lesson link:** shopping / spending money
**Notes:** This song was Sia's first hit as a performer to reach the Hot 100 chart—she had previously reached number 1 as a writer for Rihanna's *Diamonds*. There's also a remix of the track featuring reggae singer Sean Paul.

As sts arrive in class, ask them not to open their books. When all sts are in class, explain that they will play *Telephone* with a song line. Organize the class in a setting in which they can play the game, and start by whispering the song line to the first student. When this sentence gets to the end of the line, have the student who was the last to write down what he / she understood on the board. Next, have the first student in the sequence write on the board what you originally told them. Then, have sts open their books to page 59 and show them that this is the song line of the lesson. Finally, ask: *Do you know this song? Can you sing this bit?* Encourage sts to answer and sing the song line, if they want to.

## 5.2

**Song line:** It's a bittersweet symphony, this life. Try to make ends meet. You're a slave to the money, then you die.
**Song:** *Bitter Sweet Symphony,* released in 1997
**Artist:** The Verve (British)
**Lesson link:** money
**Notes:** The Verve's lead singer, Richard Ashcroft, says that the song reflects his experience learning that money and happiness do not always go together. To explain the line "Try to make ends meet, you're a slave to money, then you die", Ashcroft says that his father had worked nine to five to make ends meet and died very young, when Richard was just 11 years old and his sisters even younger.

At any time during lesson 5.2, have sts read the song line on top of page 61 and ask: *Do you know this song? Can you sing this bit?* Encourage sts to answer and sing the song line, if they want to. Next, ask: *What other songs about money do you know?* Encourage sts to work in pairs to brainstorm and come up with a list of songs that they know about money. Remind them that you will only accept songs which they can actually sing the section from where money is mentioned. Allow sts a few minutes to do so, then have pairs take turns coming to the board to write one song line at a time. Explain that they cannot write one song line that has already been previously listed by another pair. Finally, when the list is complete, have the class vote for their favorite song about money.

## 5.3

**Song line:** I might be young, but I ain't stupid, Talking around in circles with your tongue.
**Song:** *Lips Are Movin,* released in 2015
**Artist:** Meghan Trainor (American)
**Lesson link:** might
**Notes:** *Lips Are Moving* is a song which appears to be about the singer breaking up with her cheating boyfriend. However, the song is really about Meghan's frustration with her record label, not a cheating boyfriend. *Lips Are Movin* was the singer's second single and, just like her first one, *All About That Bass*, this song has a retro sound and uses the same basic structure.

# Songs

Before the class, write the song line from page 63 on the board with four mistakes as follows: *I my be young, but I am stupid, Talking about in circles with your thumb*. As sts arrive, ask them not to open their books. When all sts are in class, have them work in pairs to spot and correct the four mistakes in the song line. Next, have volunteers come to the board to correct the song line on the board. Finally, have sts open their books to page 63 to check their work. As they do so, ask: *Do you recognize this song? Can you sing the song line?* Encourage sts to answer and sing the song line if they want to.

## 5.4

🎵 **Song line:** I'm advertising love for free, so you can place your ad with me.
**Song:** *Hard to Handle*, released in 1990
**Artist:** The Black Crowes (American)
**Lesson link:** advertising
**Notes:** This song was originally recorded by Otis Redding, but it became a bigger hit when the Black Crowes released their version of it. The song hit number 45 in the U.S. chart in December 1990. It's probably the Black Crowes' best known single.

Before the class, write the song line from page 65 on the board with all the vowels removed as follows: _'m _dv_rt_s_ng l_v_ f_r fr__, s_ y__ c_n pl_c_ y__r _d w_th m_. As sts arrive in class, ask them not to open their books. When all sts are in class, have them work in pairs to complete all the missing vowels from the song line. When they are ready, have the pairs take turns coming to the board to complete two words at a time in the song line. When it's completed, ask: *Is there anything you believe is not right?* Encourage sts to correct anything if necessary. Then, have them open their books to page 65 to check the song line. Finally, ask: *Do you know this song? Can you sing the song line?* Encourage sts to answer and sing the song line, if they want to.

## 5.5

🎵 **Song line:** There's a lady who's sure, All that glitters is gold, And she's buying a stairway to heaven.
**Song:** *Stairway To Heaven*, released in 1971
**Artist:** Led Zeppelin (British)
**Lesson link:** buying
**Notes:** This song is considered to be one of the most famous rock songs of all time. Robert Plant explains that the reason for its amazing success might be that people can interpret it in many different ways. He adds that, despite the fact that he wrote the lyrics himself, he often interprets the song in different ways.

Before the class, search the web for a video or audio clip of the song *Stairway To Heaven*, which features the song line. As sts arrive in class, ask them not to open their books. When all sts are in class, explain that you will play a video or audio clip of the song line of this lesson for them to write down what they hear. Remind them to focus while listening, as you will only play the song line twice. Next, play the song line clip twice and have sts write down what they understand from it. When they're ready, have a volunteer come to the board to write down the song line as he / she heard it. Encourage the other sts to correct the song line as necessary. Next, have them open their books to page 67 to check their answers and ask: *What was the most difficult part for you to understand?* Encourage sts to share their opinions.

## Writing 5

🎵 **Song line:** Come on, vogue, Let your body move to the music, Hey, hey, hey, Come on, vogue, Let your body go with the flow.
**Song:** *Vogue*, released in 1990
**Artist:** Madonna (American)
**Lesson link:** getting in shape / working out / dancing
**Notes:** This song mentions a lot of glamorous actors and actresses, like Fred Astaire, Marlon Brando, Ginger Rogers, Greta Garbo, etc. Curiously, the last surviving legendary personality from the whole list mentioned in this song was Lauren Bacall, who died after a stroke in August 2014.

Before starting Writing 5, have sts read the song line on page 68 and ask: *Do you know this song? Can you sing this bit?* Encourage sts to answer and sing the song line, if they want to. Next, ask: *Can you identify the link between the song line and the lesson?* Encourage sts to scan the lesson and answer. They should be able to identify that the link is getting in shape / dancing / working out. Next, have sts work in pairs to brainstorm and come up with a list of more songs that talk about these things (getting in shape, dancing, working out). When they're ready, have the pairs share their song lists with the whole class.

## 6.1

🎵 **Song line:** There's nothing on the TV, nothing on the radio. That means that much to me.
**Song:** *America*, released in 2006
**Artist:** Razorlight (British)
**Lesson link:** TV and radio programs
**Notes:** According to Razorlight's drummer, Andy Burrows, the idea for the drumbeat of this song came up when they were in a hotel in Ohio and they heard a Billy Joel record. Johnny Borrel, the bandleader, asked for a similar sound, so that's what inspired the drumbeat for this song.

Before the class, search the web for a video or audio clip of the song line on page 73. As sts arrive, ask them not to open their books. When all sts are in class, explain that you will play a clip of the song line and they have to write down what they hear. Tell sts that you will only play the clip twice, so they should pay attention to it. Next, play the video or audio clip twice and have sts write it down. When they are ready, have a volunteer write the song line on the board and allow sts to open their books and read the song line on top of page 73 to check. Finally, ask: *What was the most difficult part for you to understand?* and encourage sts to share their opinions.

## 6.2

🎵 **Song line:** Want you to make me feel, Like I'm the only girl in the world, Like I'm the only one that you'll ever love.
**Song:** *Only Girl (In The World)*, released in 2010
**Artist:** Rihanna (Barbadian-American)
**Lesson link:** restrictive relative clauses with *that*, *who*, etc.
**Notes:** *Only Girl (In The World)* sold 126,000 copies in its first week in the UK, but it only reached number 1 on the UK chart the following week. This song was Rihanna's fourth single to reach the top of the chart in 2010. This made Rihanna the first ever female artist to achieve four number 1 hits in the same year.

Before the class, write the song line from page 75 on the board with four mistakes as follows: *Want you two make me fill, Like I'm the only girl in the word, Like I'm the only one dead you'll ever love*. As sts arrive in class, ask them not to open their books. When all sts are in class, have them read the song line on the board and ask: *Do you know this song?* Next, have them work in pairs and explain that this song line has four mistakes that they have to correct. When sts are ready, have a volunteer come to the board to correct the mistakes in the song line. Ask: *Can you sing this bit?* Encourage sts to answer and sing the song line if they want to. Finally, have sts turn to page 75 to read the song line and check.

# Songs

## 6.3

**Song line:** When the sharpest words wanna cut me down, I'm gonna send a flood, gonna drown them out, I am brave, I am bruised, I am who I'm meant to be, This is me.
**Song:** *This Is Me,* released in 2017
**Artist:** Keala Settle (American)
**Lesson link:** movies
**Notes:** *This Is Me* is a song for people who are not accepted by society. It features in the soundtrack of the movie *The Greatest Showman* and it won the best original song award at the 2018 Golden Globes. The writers of the song, Benj Pasek and Justin Paul, had already been co-winners of the same award in 2017 for *La La Land's* "City of Stars".

At any time during lesson 6.3, have sts read the song line on page 77 and ask: *Do you know this song? Which movie was this song featured in? Have you watched it?* Encourage sts to answer and let them sing the song line if they want to. Next, have them work in pairs and explain that they have to come up with a list of as many songs from famous movies as they can remember in two minutes. Remind sts that they have to be able to sing the most famous part of the songs that they put on their lists. Finally, have the pairs share their lists with the whole class. Alternatively, once you have put together all of their suggestions into one list, you can have sts vote for the class favorite movie song.

## 6.4

**Song line:** You still look like a movie, You still sound like a song. My God, this reminds me of when we were young.
**Song:** *When We Were Young,* released in 2015
**Artist:** Adele (British)
**Lesson link:** movies
**Notes:** Adele co-wrote that song with Vancouver singer and songwriter Tobias Jesso Jr. Adele said in an interview that Tobias's grandparents were friends with Phillip Glass, regarded as one of the most influential musicians of the late 20th century. Because of that friendship, Tobias inherited Glass's old piano, which they used when they wrote *When We Were Young.*

Before sts arrive, write the song line from page 79 on the board as follows, with all the vowels removed: Y_ _ st_ll l_ _k l_k_ _ m_v_ _, Y_ _ st_ll s_ _nd l_k_ _ s_ng. My G_d, th_s r_m_nds m_ _f wh_n w_ w_r_ y_ _ng. As sts arrive in class, ask them not to open their books. When all sts are in class, have them work in pairs to complete the song line. Allow them a few minutes to do so and, when they're ready, have volunteers come to the board to complete two or three words at a time. Then, ask: *Do you know this song? Can you sing this part?* Encourage sts to answer and sing the song line if they want to. Finally, allow students to open their books to page 79 to check the actual song line.

## 6.5

**Song line:** I'm gonna swing from the chandelier, from the chandelier, I'm gonna live like tomorrow doesn't exist, like it doesn't exist.
**Song:** *Chandelier,* released in 2014
**Artist:** Sia (Australian)
**Lesson link:** Sia, the artist
**Notes:** This is an electropop song about the ups and downs of the life of a "party girl". The music video shows Maddie Ziegler from Dance Moms performing an interpretative dance routine.

As sts arrive, ask them not to open their books. When all sts are in class, explain that they will play *Telephone* with the song line of this lesson. Tell them that you'll have them come up with the song line in two parts. Organize the class so they can play the game and start by whispering the first part of the song line *I'm gonna swing from the chandelier, from the chandelier* to the first student in the sequence. When this first part gets to the last student in the sequence, have them come to the board to write down what they got. Next, do the same with the second part of the song line *I'm gonna live like tomorrow doesn't exist, like it doesn't exist* but now starting with the last student in the sequence, inverting the order. When this second part gets to the last student in the sequence, have them come to the board to complete the song line. Ask: *Can you recognize this song line?* This will of course depend on how close they got to the actual line. Finally, allow sts to open their books to page 81 to compare their version to the actual song line that's on the bottom of that page.

## Writing 6

**Song line:** I think your love would be too much, Or you'll be left in the dust, Unless I stuck by ya, You're the sunflower.
**Song:** *Sunflower,* released in 2018
**Artist:** Post Malone (American) feat. Swae Lee (American)
**Lesson link:** movies
**Notes:** This song features in the soundtrack of the animated movie *Spider-Man: Into the Spider-Verse.* The lyrics of the song have Malone and Lee talking about the same girl, Sunflower, who remains loyal by their side despite the lack of affection that both rappers show her.

At any time during writing lesson 6 have sts read the song line on page 82 and ask: *Do you know this song? Can you sing this part?* Encourage sts to answer and sing the song line if they want to. Then, ask: *Can you identify the link between the song line and the lesson?* Have sts work in pairs to scan the page and identify the link. When the pairs are ready, have them share their opinions with the rest of the class. Make sure sts realize that this song was featured in the animated movie *Spider-Man: Into the Spider-Verse* soundtrack. So the link between the song line and the lesson is movies.

## Review 3

**Song line:** Where did I go wrong? I lost a friend somewhere along in the bitterness. And I would have stayed up with you all night, Had I known how to save a life.
**Song:** *How To Save A Life,* released in 2005
**Artist:** The Fray (American)
**Lesson link:** third conditional
**Notes:** The Fray's lead singer, Isaac Slade, said in an interview that he wrote this song based on an experience he had been through when he worked at a camp for troubled youths. He explained that he was paired up with one boy, with drug and addiction problems, who was just 17 years old, but he didn't know how to help him.

Before the class, write the song line on page 85 on the board as follows with four mistakes for sts to correct: *Where did I went wrong? I loosed a friend somewhere along in the bitterness. And I will have stayed up with you all night, Had I knowed how to save a life.* As sts arrive in class, ask them not to open their books. When all sts are in class, have them look at the song line that's on the board and ask: *Do you know this song?* Encourage sts to answer. Next, have them work in pairs to find out and correct four grammatical mistakes in the song line on the board. When the pairs are ready, have volunteers come to the board to correct the song line. Finally, have sts open their books to page 85 to check their answers.

## 7.1

**Song line:** They took the credit for your second symphony. Rewritten by machine on new technology.
**Song:** *Video Killed The Radio Star,* released in 1979
**Artist:** Buggles (British)
**Lesson link:** technology
**Notes:** Trevor Horn, who started Buggles, wrote this song with Bruce Wooley, after reading a science fiction novel about a singer in a future world without sound. The song was the first video to air on MTV in 1981, and that also served as an early indicator of the network's influence in the world of music.

# Songs

At any stage during lesson 7.1, have sts read the song line that's on page 87 and ask: *Do you know this song? What's the link between the song and the lesson?* Encourage sts to answer and make sure they realize the link is technology. Next, have sts work in pairs or threes and explain that they have a few minutes to search the web and come up with a list of songs about technology that they know. Remind sts that they can search the web for the songs but they must be able to sing some of each of the songs they put in their lists, showing the class that they actually know the song. When they are ready, have them share their lists with the whole class. Check which pair or three has the most songs in their list. You can also check which song was the most popular with the class.

## 7.2

**Song line:** Well somebody told me you had a boyfriend Who looked like a girlfriend That I had in February of last year. It's not confidential, I've got potential.
**Song:** *Somebody Told Me,* released in 2004
**Artist:** The Killers (American)
**Lesson link:** tell
**Notes**: Lead singer Brandon Flowers wrote the lyrics of this song when he was around 20. According to the writer, the song deals with the difficulties faced by young men trying to get to know girls in nightclubs.

Before the class, write the song line from page 89 on the board as follows with five mistakes for sts to find and correct: *Well somebody told to me you had a boyfriend which looked like a girlfriend that I had on February of last year. Is not confidential, I'm got potential.* As sts arrive in class, ask them not to open their books. When all sts are in class, have them read the song line on the board and ask: *Do you know this song? Can you sing this bit?* Encourage sts to answer and sing the song line if they want to. Next, explain that this song line has five mistakes in it. Ask sts to work in pairs to find and correct them without looking at their books or the Internet. When the pairs are ready, have volunteers come to the board to correct the five mistakes. Let students know that the first mistake is directly linked to the lesson, and remind them that we don't use the preposition *to* after the verb *tell*. Finally, allow sts to open their books to page 89 to check the actual song line.

## 7.3

**Song line:** The world I love, The tears I drop, To be part of the wave, can't stop, Ever wonder if it's all for you?
**Song:** *Can't Stop,* released in 2002
**Artist:** Red Hot Chili Peppers (American)
**Lesson link:** wonder
**Notes:** In this song, Red Hot's lead singer, Anthony Kiedis, wrote the lyrics after the music. The words of this song are a collection of thoughts, with creative rhyming, which encourage fans to live passionately and fully, just as the American band has always done.

Before the class, search the Internet for a video or audio clip of the song *Can't Stop,* by Red Hot Chili Peppers. As sts arrive in class, ask them not to open their books. When all sts are in class, explain that you will play a video or audio clip of this lesson's song line and they have to write down what they hear. Play the clip twice and, when sts are ready, have volunteers come to the board to write down what they heard. Allow other sts to correct anything they feel like. Then, have sts open their books to page 91 to check and compare the actual song line with what they wrote on the board. Finally, ask: *What was the most difficult part for you to understand?* and encourage sts to share their opinions.

## 7.4

**Song line:** 'Cause she knew what was she was doin', When she told me how to walk this way! She told me to walk this way, talk this way.
**Song:** *Walk This Way (This Bird Has Flown),* released 1975
**Artist:** Aerosmith (American)
**Lesson link:** reported speech
**Notes:** Aerosmith's guitarist, Joe Perry created the famous guitar riff for this song and the band developed the track's melody and sequence. However, it took the singer, Steven Tyler, so long to come up with the lyrics that they actually considered dumping the track. When Tyler had finally written the lyrics and entered the studio to record the song, he realized he had left the lyrics in a taxi! He wrote new lyrics on the wall of the studio, as he didn't have any paper with him, and the band finally recorded the song that became a huge hit.

Before the class, write the song line from page 93 on the board as follows, with all of the vowels removed: *C_ _s_ sh_ kn_w wh_t w_s sh_ w_s d_ _n', Wh_n sh_ t_ld m_ h_w t_ w_lk th_s w_y! Sh_ t_ld m_ t_ w_lk th_s w_y, t_lk th_s w_y.* As sts arrive in class, ask them not to open their books. When all sts are in class, have them read the song line and explain that this is the song line from this lesson with all vowels missing. Next, have sts work in pairs to copy and complete the song line that's on the board. When they're ready, have volunteers come to the board to complete two or three words. Then, ask: *Do you know this song? Can you sing this part?* Encourage sts to answer and sing the song line if they want to. Finally, allow them to open their books to page 93 to check the actual song line.

## 7.5

**Song line:** Yeah, we're just young, dumb and broke, But we still got love to give.
**Song:** *Young, Dumb and Broke,* released in 2017
**Artist:** Khalid (American)
**Lesson link:** dumb generation
**Notes:** In this song, Khalid tries to convince people that it is OK to be young, dumb, and broke high school kids. The singer says he has been young, dumb, and broke, so he believes the whole song is about him being honest about himself.

Before the class, write the song line from page 95 on the board as follows with the words out of order: *just But young we're love still broke Yeah give got dumb to we and.* As sts arrive in class, ask them not to open their books. When all sts are in class, tell them that this is the song line from this lesson, but all scrambled up. Explain that they have to work in pairs or threes to try and unscramble the whole song line. Allow sts a few minutes to do so. When they're ready, have volunteers come to the board to write their versions of it. Then, ask: *Do you know this song?* Encourage sts to answer. Finally, allow them to open their books to page 95 to check the actual song line. You can also take the opportunity to remind sts that when we have two or more adjectives in a sentence, as we do in this song line (young, dumb, broke), the first adjective in the order should always be the one that carries the facts, not opinions, in this case *young*.

## Writing 7

**Song line:** All I wanna do is (bang, bang, bang!) And a (kkkaaa ching!) And take your money.
**Song:** *Paper Planes,* released in 2007
**Artist:** M.I.A (British)
**Lesson link:** shopping / spending money
**Notes:** This song was inspired by M.I.A.'s efforts to enter the U.S. on a visa. She is British but of Sri Lankan descent, and the whole bureaucratic process took months to complete, which M.I.A. attributed to the color of her skin and her real name, Mathangi Arulpragasam. The song uses a sample of a 1982 Clash song, *Straight To Hell.*

# Songs

As sts arrive in class, ask them not to open their books. When all sts are in class, ask for one volunteer that's good at miming and organize the other sts into teams of four. Next, explain that you will show a song line to the volunteer and he or she will have one or two minutes to think of ways of miming the song line for the teams to guess. Show the volunteer the song line from page 96 and let him or her plan ways for miming it to the others. Explain that they can mime it word by word, in chunks, etc. But they must make it clear how they're doing it when they start. Allow the game to start. The first team to guess the song line correctly wins. Finally, have sts open their books to page 96 to check the song line.

## 8.1

🎵 **Song line:** So you can keep me, Inside the pocket of your ripped jeans, Holding me closer 'til our eyes meet, You won't ever be alone.
**Song:** *Photograph*, released in 2014
**Artist:** Ed Sheeran (British)
**Lesson link:** photos
**Notes:** Ed Sheeran cowrote this song with Snow Patrol's guitarist, Johnny McDaid, in a hotel room. The singer got a tattoo saying, "6 ST", because he thought he had written this song on 6th Street in Denver, Colorado. But when he got back to the place where he wrote it, he realized that it was actually 6th Avenue, not Street. Sheeran was later sued by two songwriters, Martin Harrington and Thomas Leonard, who claimed the British singer had lifted the melody and rhythm from a song they had written.

After section 2 (Vocabulary), have sts read the song line on page 99 and ask: *Do you know this song line? Can you sing this part?* Encourage sts to answer and sing the song line if they want to. Next, ask: *What link can you find between the song line and the lesson?* Expect sts to realize that the name of the song is *Photograph* and that in the song line, the singer speaks as if he were a photograph. Next, ask: *What other songs about photographs can you remember?* Have sts work in pairs to come up with a list. Remind them that they must be able to sing a small part of the songs they put on their lists.

## 8.2

🎵 **Song line:** It must've been love, but it's over now. It must've been good, but I lost it somehow.
**Song:** *It Must Have Been Love*, released in 1990
**Artist:** Roxette (Swedish)
**Lesson link:** modal perfects / *must have been*
**Notes:** This song was written before Roxette started working on their *Joyride* album. The band recorded *It Must Have Been Love* for Julia Roberts and Richard Gere's Hollywood blockbuster, *Pretty Woman*. The soundtrack of the movie, which also featured Roy Orbison's *Pretty Woman*, was a huge success.

Before the class, write the song line from page 101 on the board as follows with four mistakes for sts to correct: *It mustn't be love, but its over now. It mustn't be good, but I tossed it somehow*. As sts arrive, ask them not to open their books. When all sts are in class, ask: *Do you recognize this song line?* Encourage sts to answer and sing the song line if they want to. Next, explain that there are four mistakes in it and ask: *Can you spot the mistakes?* Have sts work in pairs to try and find out what the mistakes are. Explain that they should not open their books or check the Internet for the lyrics. When they're ready, have volunteers come to the board to correct the song line. Finally, tell sts that this structure (*must have been*) is an example of what we call a modal perfect, and that in this lesson they will learn more about modal perfects.

## 8.3

🎵 **Song line:** Now he's getting a tattoo, yeah, he's getting ink done. He asked for a "13" but they drew a "31".
**Song:** *Pretty Fly (For A White Guy)*, released in 1998
**Artist:** The Offspring (American)
**Lesson link:** causative form
**Notes:** The Offspring guitarist, Noodle, said in an interview that the song is about a kid that wants to blend in with the "cool" gangsters, but just can't manage to do so and, instead, makes a fool of himself. The song was number one in several countries' charts.

Before starting lesson 8.3, have sts read the song line on 103 and ask: *Do you know this song?* Encourage sts to answer and sing the song line if they want to. Next, have sts work in pairs to scan the lesson pages and find the link between the song line and the lesson. Give sts a few minutes, they should be able to find a similar structure in the common mistakes box on page 103. Explain to sts that, in this lesson, they will learn about the causative form and the mistakes in the common mistakes box.

## 8.4

🎵 **Song line:** Well, I've heard there was a secret chord. That David played and it pleased the Lord. But you don't really care for music, do you?
**Song:** *Hallelujah*, released in 1994
**Artist:** Jeff Buckley (American)
**Lesson link:** tag questions
**Notes:** Jeff Buckley's most well-known work, *Hallelujah* was originally recorded by Leonard Cohen in 1984. Buckley heard the song and decided to include it in his performances in the early 90s. The song was recorded on Buckley's 1994 album, *Grace*, which was his first album.

At any stage during lesson 8.4, have sts read the song line on page 105 and ask: *Do you know this song? Can you sing this bit?* Encourage sts to answer and sing the song line if they want to. Next, ask: *Can you identify the link between the song line and the lesson?* Have sts work in pairs to scan the lesson pages and find the link. Make sure they identify the tag question at the end of the song line as the link with the lesson.

## 8.5

🎵 **Song line:** I know someday you'll have a beautiful life, I know you'll be a star, In somebody else's sky, But why can't it be mine?
**Song:** *Black*, released in 1991
**Artist:** Pearl Jam (American)
**Lesson link:** predictions
**Notes:** Pearl Jam's bandleader Eddie Vedder said in their documentary that this song is about relationships, in particular about letting go of the love of your life. The guitarist, Stone Gossard, wrote the music for this song, which he originally called *E Ballad*, The name was changed to *Black* after Vedder wrote the lyrics to the song.

Before the class, search the Internet for a video or audio clip of the song line on page 107. As sts arrive, ask them not to open their books. When all sts are in class, explain that you will play the clip of the song line from this lesson and they have to write down what they hear. Play the song line section twice and allow some time for sts to do so, then when sts are ready, have volunteers write what they heard on the board. Next, ask: *Do you recognize this song?* Encourage sts to answer and sing the song line if they want to. Then, allow sts to open their books to page 107 to check. Finally, ask: *Which were the most difficult words for you to understand?* and encourage sts to share their opinions.

# Songs

### Writing 8

🎵 **Song line:** Cause all of me loves all of you. Love your curves and all your edges, all your perfect imperfections.
**Song:** *All Of Me*, released in 2013
**Artist:** John Legend (American)
**Lesson link:** beauty
**Notes:** This was Legend's first Hot 100 number 1 single. It took the song 30 weeks to reach its peak in the chart. It was the third longest climb to the top ever. *All Of Me* also topped the charts in Australia, Canada, the Netherlands, Portugal, and Sweden. John Legend said that the first time he sang this song to his fiancée at the time, Chrissy Teigen, she cried.

Before the class, search the Internet for an instrumental version of the song *All Of Me*, by John Legend. As sts arrive in class, ask them not to open their books. When all sts are in class, play the instrumental clip of the song line and ask: *Do you recognize this song?* Encourage sts to answer and sing along if they want to. Next, explain that this is the song line from this lesson and that they have to write down the lyrics to this part of the song without looking at their books or the Internet. Allow sts some time to do so, then have volunteers share their versions of the song line on the board. Finally, have sts open their books to page 108 to check their versions against the song line.

### Review 4

🎵 **Song line:** I wonder, when I sing along with you, if everything could ever feel this real forever, if anything could ever be this good again.
**Song:** *Everlong*, released in 1997
**Artist:** Foo Fighters (American)
**Lesson Link:** could
**Notes:** Foo Fighters frontman Dave Grohl wrote this song when he was in one of the worst moments of his life. He became homeless after his divorce, and was sleeping on a friend's floor in a sleeping bag. He also couldn't access his own bank account and two of the Foo Fighter's members were on the verge of quitting the band. In the center of all these problems, Grohl wrote this song in about 45 minutes.

Before the class, write the song line from page 111 on the board with all the verbs missing. It should look like this: *I __, when I __ along with you, if everything __ ever __ this real forever, if anything __ ever __ this good again.* As sts arrive, ask them not to open their books. When all sts are in class, have them read what you wrote on the board and explain that this is the song line from this review lesson, but with all the verbs, main or auxiliary, missing. Have sts work in pairs to find the verbs that are missing to complete the song line. When they're ready, have volunteers complete the song line on the board and ask: *Do you know this song? Can you sing this bit?* Encourage sts to answer and sing the song line if they want to. Finally, allow them to open their books to page 111 to check the actual song line.

### 9.1

🎵 **Song line:** Everybody wanna steal my girl, Everybody wanna take her heart away. Couple billion in the whole wide world, Find another one 'cos she belongs to me.
**Song:** *Steal My Girl*, released in 2014
**Artist:** One Direction (British)
**Lesson link:** crime (stealing)
**Notes:** This piano ballad has One Direction complaining about guys who want to "steal" their girls. According to Julian Bunetta, the idea for the song came up completely at random. He says that they were playing a drumbeat and somebody said the main line and everybody related to it.

Before the class, write the song line from page 113 on the board as follows with nine words that have been substituted by others with a similar pronunciation to the original words, but a completely different meaning: *Everybody wanna steel my girl, Everybody wanna take heard hoard away. Cup of billion in the hole white word, Find another want 'cos she belongs two me.* As sts arrive in class, ask them not to open their books. When all sts are in class, organize them into pairs or trios and explain that they have to find and correct nine mistakes in the song line that's on the board. When they're ready, have volunteers come to the board to correct. Allow the others to change anything if they want to. Then, ask: *Do you know this song?* Encourage them to answer and sing the song line if they want to. Finally, allow sts to open their books to page 113 and check the actual song line on that page.

### 9.2

🎵 **Song line:** Sweet dreams are made of this, who am I to disagree? I travel the world and the seven seas.
**Song:** *Sweet Dreams (Are Made Of This)*, released in 1982
**Artist:** Eurythmics (British)
**Lesson link:** passive voice
**Notes:** This song was a hit in Europe in 1982, but it only became number 1 in the U.S. one year later. *Sweet Dreams* was the Eurythmics' only song to ever do that. Annie Lennox explained in her biography that the theme of the song is the search for fulfillment and happiness. It is about perseverance in going after our desires and dreams.

After section 2 (Grammar), have sts read the song line on page 115 and ask: *Do you know this song? Can you sing this line?* Encourage sts to answer and sing the song line if they want to. Next, ask: *Can you identify the link between the song line and the lesson?* Have sts work in pairs to scan pages 114 and 115 to find the link. Make sure students realize that the first sentence of the song line ("Sweet dreams are made of this") is a passive voice structure. Next, have a volunteer come to the board and ask them to rewrite that first sentence of the song line in the active voice ("This makes sweet dreams"). Remind sts who speak Spanish or Portuguese as their L1 that the structure of the passive voice in English is exactly the same as in their L1.

### 9.3

🎵 **Song line:** Breaking rocks in the hot sun. I fought the law and the law won.
**Song:** *I Fought The Law*, released in 1979
**Artist:** The Clash (British)
**Lesson link:** crimes (being convicted)
**Notes:** Originally written by Sonny Curtis in 1958, this song was first recorded in 1959 when Curtis joined the Crickets. In 1965, The Bobby Fuller Four recorded his version of Curtis's song. But it was with The Clash's version, from 1979, that *I Fought The Law* got America's attention. The idea for their version came after hearing Bobby's version. But The Clash made a more violent version of it, changing the line "I left my baby" to "I killed my baby".

Before the class, write the song line from page 117 on the board as follows, leaving the nouns and adjectives blank for sts to complete: *Breaking ____ in the ____ ____. I fought the ____ and the ____ won.* As sts arrive in class, ask them not to open their books. When all sts are in class, have them work in pairs to try and complete the song line with the missing words. You can choose whether to tell them or not that the missing words are four nouns and one adjective. Allow them some time to complete the song line, without opening their books. When they're ready, have volunteers come to the board to complete the missing words in the song line. Next, ask: *Do you recognize this song? Can you sing this line?* and encourage sts to answer and sing the song line if they want to. Then, allow sts to open their books to page 117 to check the actual song line. Finally, take the opportunity to have sts scan the pages of the lesson to find the link between the song line and the lesson (being convicted or committing a crime).

# Songs

## 9.4

**Song line:** We'll be raising our hands, shining up to the sky. 'Cause we got the fire, fire, fire, yeah we got the fire, fire, fire.
**Song:** *Burn*, released in 2013
**Artist:** Ellie Goulding (British)
**Lesson link:** future continuous
**Notes:** This song carries a very positive message, where the singer encourages us to let our fire burn and lead us to do great things. *Burn* went all the way to the top of the UK singles charts, and it was Goulding's first number 1 single.

Before the class, search the Internet for a video or audio clip of the song line that's on page 119. As sts arrive in class, ask them not to open their books. When all sts are in class, explain that you will play a clip of the song line from this lesson and they will have to write down what they hear. Play the song line video or audio clip twice and have sts write down what they hear. Allow them time to do this, then when they're ready, have a volunteer come to the board to write what they heard. Allow the other sts to suggest corrections. Then, ask: *Do you know this song?* Encourage sts to answer and encourage them to sing the song line if they want to. Then, have sts open their books and read the song line on page 119 to compare. Encourage sts to share their opinions about the most difficult words to understand. Finally, ask: *Can you identify the link between the song line and the lesson?* Encourage sts to scan the pages of the lesson to find out and make sure they realize that the first sentence of the song line is an example of the future continuous.

## 9.5

**Song line:** I don't wanna close my eyes, I don't wanna fall asleep, Cause I'd miss you, baby, And I don't wanna miss a thing.
**Song:** *I Don't Want To Miss A Thing*, released in 1998
**Artist:** Aerosmith (American)
**Lesson link:** being vigilant
**Notes:** This song was part of the soundtrack for the movie *Armagedon*, in which Liv Tyler, Steven Tyler's daughter, acted. Originally, the idea was that U2 was going to play this song for the movie. They only changed it to Aerosmith after Tyler's daughter was cast in the movie.

As sts arrive in class, ask them not to open their books. When all sts are in class, ask for a volunteer who is good at miming and organize the rest of the class into teams of three or four. As the groups get together, hand a slip of paper containing the song line to the volunteer and give them one or two minutes to come up with a miming act for it. When they're ready, have them mime the song line for the teams to guess. The first team to guess is the winner. Finally, have sts open their books to p. 121 to read the song line and ask: *Do you know this song? Can you sing this line?* Encourage sts to answer and sing the song line bit if they want to.

## Writing 9

**Song line:** Don't it always seem to go, That you don't know what you've got till it's gone; They paved paradise, And put up a parking lot.
**Song:** *Big Yellow Taxi*, released in 1970
**Artist:** Joni Mitchell (Canadian)
**Lesson link:** concern for the environment
**Notes:** Mitchell said in an interview that she wrote *Big Yellow Taxi* on her first trip to Hawaii. The singer explained that she took a taxi to the hotel and arrived there at night, so when she opened up the curtains the next day, she saw the mountains in the distance and a huge parking lot, as far as the eye could see. She said it broke her heart to see that, so she sat down and wrote the song.

At any time during Writing 9, have sts read the song line on page 122 and ask: *Do you know this song?* Encourage them to answer and sing the song line if they want to. Next, have sts look at the song line again and ask: *Can you spot a grammar mistake in this song line?* Encourage sts to discuss their answers. Make sure they identify the use of the auxiliary *don't* with the third person pronoun *it* in the first sentence of the song line. Then, have sts work in pairs to brainstorm any other songs they know with grammatical mistakes in the lyrics. Allow them a few minutes to do so and, when they're ready, have sts write the lyrics on the board. Finally, have sts work together to correct the lyrics.

## 10.1

**Song line:** You're hot then you're cold, you're yes then you're no, you're in and you're out, you're up and you're down.
**Song:** *Hot N Cold*, released in 2008
**Artist:** Katy Perry (American)
**Lesson link:** changing moods
**Notes:** This song is about problems in a relationship caused by one person constantly having mood swings and changing their mind. The video is set at a wedding, where Katy imagines the groom running away with her chasing him through various scenarios.

At any stage during lesson 10.1, have sts read the song line on page 125 and ask: *What do you think this song line is about? Can you identify the link between the song line and the lesson?* Encourage sts to scan the pages to find the link. Make sure they realize that the song line is about someone who changes their mood very easily, and this links with the vocabulary section. Finally, ask: *Do you know anyone like the person described in the song line?* and encourage sts to share their experiences.

## 10.2

**Song line:** 'Cause we were just kids when we fell in love. Not knowing what it was. I will not give you up this time.
**Song:** *Perfect*, released in 2017
**Artist:** Ed Sheeran (British)
**Lesson link:** gerunds
**Notes:** This is a love song that Ed Sheeran wrote to his then girlfriend, an old friend from school, when she was living in New York. In September 2017, he recorded a new version of the song in a duet with Beyoncé.

Before the class, write the song line from page 127 on the board as follows with five mistakes in it for sts to find and correct: *'Cause we was just kids when we felt in love. Not knowing what it were. I will not pick you up these time.* As sts arrive in class, ask them not to open their books. When all sts are in class, have them read the song line that you wrote on the board and ask: *Do you recognize this song line? Can you sing it?* Encourage sts to answer and sing the song line if they want to. Next, explain that they have to work in pairs to find and correct five mistakes in the song line. Remind them not to open their books. When sts are ready, have a volunteer correct the mistakes on the board. Allow the others to suggest corrections if they want to. Finally, have sts open their books to page 127 to check the actual song line.

## 10.3

**Song line:** I am not afraid to keep on living. I am not afraid to walk this world alone.
**Song:** *Famous Last Words*, released in 2006
**Artist:** My Chemical Romance (American)
**Lesson link:** verb + gerund / infinitive
**Notes:** This song's original title was *The Saddest Music In The World*. The song that became *Famous Last Words* came up at a moment of crisis for the band. They were doubting their ability to record another album as good as their previous one and Mikey Way, the bassist, became depressed and had to leave the band to seek treatment.

As sts arrive in class, ask them not to open their books. When all sts are in class, explain that they will play *Telephone* with the song line from this lesson. Organize students in sequence so that they can play the game. Then, whisper the whole song line from p. 129 to the first student and have them whisper it to the next student until it gets to the end of the sequence. When it does, have the last student come to the board to write down

# Songs

what he heard. Next, have them read it and ask: *Do you know this song?* Encourage sts to answer and sing the song line if they want to. Finally, allow sts to open their books to p. 129 to check the actual song line.

### 10.4

🎵 **Song line:** Oh, angel sent from up above. You know you make my world light up. When I was down, when I was hurt. You came to lift me up.
**Song:** *Hymn For The Weekend,* released in 2015
**Artist:** Coldplay (British)
**Lesson link:** phrasal verbs
**Notes:** This song features Beyoncé's vocals and, according to singer Chris Martin, the song has more of Beyoncé than originally expected. Martin wanted the *Hymn For The Weekend* to be more like a duet. The singer said he was fascinated by the American superstar's voice.

Before the class, write the song line on page 131 on the board as follows with all the verbs missing: *Oh, angel ____ from up above. You ____ you ____ my world ____ ____. When I ____ down, when I ____ hurt. You ____ to ____ me ____.* As sts arrive in class, ask them not to open their books. When all sts are in class, have them read the blanked song line on the board and explain that all the verbs are missing and that they have to work in pairs to complete it. Tell them that there are two phrasal verbs included and the short blanks are for the prepositions. When sts are ready, have volunteers come to the board to complete the song line and ask: *Do you recognize this song? Can you sing this song line?* Encourage sts to answer and sing the song line if they want to. Finally, allow them to open their books to page 131 to check the actual lyrics. Did they get it right?

### 10.5

🎵 **Song line:** I'm only human. I make mistakes. I'm only human. That's all it takes. Don't put your blame on me.
**Song:** *Human,* released in 2016
**Artist:** Rag'n'Bone Man (British)
**Lesson link:** mistakes
**Notes:** This song is an expression of human beings' vulnerability and it talks about the singer's inability to satisfy everyone's needs. *Human* was Rag'n'Bone Man's first hit single. It topped the charts in several countries, including Germany, where it stayed at the top of the charts for over three months.

Before the class, search the Internet for a video or audio clip of the song line from page 133. As sts arrive in class, ask them not to open their books. When all sts are in class, explain that you will play a video or audio clip of the song line from this lesson and that they will have to write down what they hear. Play the audio or video clip twice for sts to write what they can. When they're ready, have a volunteer come to the board to write what they heard. Allow the other sts to correct anything they believe is wrong in their classmate's version of the song line. Then, have sts open their books to page 133 to check the actual song line. Finally ask: *What were the most difficult words for you to understand?* and encourage sts to share their opinions.

### Writing 10

🎵 **Song Line:** Go, go, go, Figure it out, figure it out, but don't stop moving, Go, go, go, Figure it out, figure it out, you can do this.
**Song:** *Flames,* released in 2018
**Artist:** David Guetta (French) feat. Sia (Australian)
**Lesson Link:** giving advice, motivating someone
**Notes:** This motivational pop song was the fourth time David Guetta and Sia worked together on a track. They have also worked on the hit *Titanium,* which is one of the songs Guetta says he is most proud of. The DJ says Sia is one of his favorite artists to work with and that she has an amazing voice.

Before starting Writing 10, have sts read the song line on page 134 and ask: *Do you know this song? Can you sing this song line?* Encourage sts to answer and sing the song line if they want to. Next, ask: *What is this song line about?* and have sts answer. Make sure they realize that the song line is a motivational one. Next, have sts work in pairs and explain that they have to come up with a list of motivational / inspirational songs that they know. Remind them that they can search the Internet, but in order to put a song on their list they must be able to sing a small part of it. When the pairs are ready, have them share their lists with the whole class. Finally, have the class vote for their favorite motivational song.

### Review 5

🎵 **Song line:** Hey, Jude, don't make it bad, Take a sad song and make it better, Remember to let her into your heart, Then you can start to make it better.
**Song:** *Hey Jude,* released in 1968
**Artist:** The Beatles (British)
**Lesson link:** verb + infinitive
**Notes:** This song was originally written by Paul McCartney as *Hey Jules,* as a way of comforting John Lennon's son, Julian Lennon, because of his parents' divorce. But Julian only learned about this from Paul in 1987, when he ran into the former Beatle at the hotel they were both staying at in New York.

Before the class, search the web for the clip of an instrumental version of the song *Hey Jude,* by The Beatles. As sts arrive in class, ask them not to open their books. When all sts are in class, explain that you will play a clip of an instrumental version of the song line from this lesson and that they have to write down the lyrics for that part of the song. Play the tune twice and have students write the lyrics. When they're ready, have volunteers write the song line on the board. Play the instrumental clip again and encourage sts to sing along now that they have what they believe are the lyrics. Finally, have sts open their books to page 137 to compare their version with the actual song line.